The
McGraw-Hill Reader

Issues Across the
Disciplines

The McGraw-Hill Reader

Issues Across the Disciplines

EIGHTH EDITION

Gilbert H. Muller
The City University of New York
LaGuardia

Boston Burr Ridge, IL Dubuque, IA Madison, WI New York
San Francisco St. Louis Bangkok Bogotá Caracas Kuala Lumpur
Lisbon London Madrid Mexico City Milan Montreal New Delhi
Santiago Seoul Singapore Sydney Taipei Toronto

McGraw-Hill Higher Education

*A Division of The **McGraw-Hill** Companies*

THE MCGRAW-HILL READER: ISSUES ACROSS THE DISCIPLINES

Published by McGraw-Hill, a business unit of The McGraw-Hill Companies, Inc., 1221 Avenue of the Americas, New York, NY, 10020. Copyright © 2003, 2000, 1997, 1994, 1991, 1988, 1985, 1982 by The McGraw-Hill Companies, Inc. All rights reserved. No part of this publication may be reproduced or distributed in any form or by any means, or stored in a database or retrieval system, without the prior written consent of The McGraw-Hill Companies, Inc., including, but not limited to, in any network or other electronic storage or transmission, or broadcast for distance learning. Some ancillaries, including electronic and print components, may not be available to customers outside the United States.

This book is printed on acid-free paper.

1 2 3 4 5 6 7 8 9 0 DOC/DOC 0 9 8 7 6 5 4 3 2

ISBN 0-07-246552-2

President of McGraw-Hill Humanities/Social Sciences: *Steve Debow*
Executive editor: *Lisa Moore*
Senior developmental editor: *Carla Kay Samodulski*
Senior marketing manager: *David Patterson*
Project manager: *Jill Moline*
Production supervisor: *Susanne Riedell*
Freelance design coordinator: *Gino Cieslik*
Producer, Media technology: *Todd Vaccaro*
Supplement producer: *Nate Perry*
Photo research coordinator: *Ira C. Roberts*
Photo researcher: *Alice Lundoff*
Typeface: *10/12 Palatino*
Compositor: *GAC Indianapolis*
Printer: *R. R. Donnelley & Sons Company*

Library of Congress Cataloging-in-Publication Data

The McGraw-Hill reader: issues across the disciplines / [edited by] Gilbert H. Muller.—8th ed.
    p. cm.
    Includes index.
    ISBN 0-07-246552-2 (alk. paper)
    1. College readers. 2. Interdisciplinary approach in education—Problems, exercises, etc.
3. English language—Rhetoric—Problems, exercises, etc. 4. Academic writing—Problems, exercises, etc. I. Muller, Gilbert H., 1941-
PE1417 .M44 2003
808'.0427—dc21

                                                                                2002018799

www.mhhe.com

About the Author

GILBERT H. MULLER, who received a PhD in English and American literature from Stanford University, is currently professor of English at the LaGuardia campus of the City University of New York. He has also taught at Stanford University, Vassar College, and several universities overseas. Dr. Muller is the author of the award-winning *Nightmares and Visions: Flannery O'Connor and the Catholic Grotesque; Chester Himes; New Strangers in Paradise: The Immigrant Experience and Contemporary American Fiction;* and other critical studies. His essays and reviews have appeared in *The New York Times, The New Republic, The Nation, The Sewanee Review, The Georgia Review,* and elsewhere. He is also a noted author and editor of textbooks in English and composition, including *The Short Prose Reader* with Harvey Wiener, and, with John A. Williams, *The McGraw-Hill Introduction to Literature, Bridges: Literature across Cultures,* and *Ways In: Reading and Writing about Literature and Film.* Among Dr. Muller's awards are National Endowment for the Humanities Fellowships, a Fulbright Fellowship, and a Mellon Fellowship.

To Parisa and Darius
My favorite readers

Contents

Chapter 8 **Philosophy, Ethics, and Religion**
What Do We Believe?   426

Contents of Essays by Rhetorical Mode

NARRATION

DESCRIPTION

ILLUSTRATION

COMPARISON AND CONTRAST

ANALOGY

DEFINITION

CLASSIFICATION

PROCESS ANALYSIS

CAUSAL ANALYSIS

ARGUMENT AND PERSUASION

Contents

HUMOR, IRONY, AND SATIRE

Preface

Through seven previous editions, *The McGraw-Hill Reader* has presented the finest classic and contemporary essays, works that span various ages, cultures, and disciplines, providing students with a range of quality prose works. Eudora Welty speaks of reading as "a sweet devouring." This anthology alerts students to the vast and varied pleasures of reading and writing, while offering them opportunities to experience numerous perspectives on academic discourse.

Addressing the abiding national interest in core liberal arts programs, interdisciplinary issues, and multicultural perspectives, this eighth edition continues to offer students and instructors a full range of quality prose models important to writing courses, reading sequences, and key undergraduate disciplines. All of the selections have been chosen for their significance, vitality, and technical precision. With the high quality of its essays, its consistent humanistic emphases, and its clear organization, *The McGraw-Hill Reader* is a lively, sophisticated, and eminently flexible text for college composition and reading programs.

Organization and Proven Features

Composed of 12 chapters, *The McGraw-Hill Reader* covers the major modes of writing and most of the disciplines that college students will encounter as undergraduates. Chapter 1 presents an extensive overview of the critical thinking, reading, and writing processes. Chapter 2, new to this edition, provides extensive coverage of argument and persuasion. Chapters 3 through 11 cover core liberal arts disciplines, including education, the social sciences, business and economics, the humanities, and the sciences. Each chapter asks a key question drawn from the disciplines it represents and designed to elicit constructive class discussion and sound critical writing. These disciplinary chapters offer prose models that allow students to practice skills they will need throughout college, including analysis, criticism, argumentation, and persuasion. Chapter 12 is a concise guide to research and documentation in the electronic age.

Throughout its eight editions, instructors and students have appreciated the following features of *The McGraw-Hill Reader:*

- **A rich selection of readings:** A distinct strength of *The McGraw-Hill Reader*—perhaps the primary one for teachers who prefer to create their own approaches to composition and reading courses—is the wide range of material and the varied constituencies represented in the text. The essays in this book have been selected carefully to embrace a rich assortment of authors, to achieve balance among constituencies, to cover major historical periods, and to provide prose models and styles for class analysis, discussion, and imitation. The authors in this text—whether Plato or Maya Angelou, Jonathan Swift or Amy Tan—have high visibility as writers and thinkers of value. Some of these authors are represented by two essays. All the authors—writing from such vantage points as literature, journalism, anthropology, sociology, art history, biology, and philosophy—start from the perspective that ideas exist in the world, that we should be alert to them, and that we should be able to deal with them in our own discourse.
- **A text that works with a wide variety of levels and approaches:** Because the selections range from very simple essays to the most abstract and complex modes of prose, teachers and students will be able to use *The McGraw-Hill Reader* at virtually all levels of a program. Containing 100 complete essays, *The McGraw-Hill Reader* thus is a flexible companion for composition courses. It can be used with any of the major pedagogical perspectives common to the practice of composition today: as a writing-across-the-curricula text; as the basis for a rhetorically focused course; as a thematic reader; as a multicultural anthology, as an in-depth reader. An alternate table of contents, listing carefully selected essays in 11 rhetorical categories, also makes *The McGraw-Hill Reader* adaptable to an approach based on the rhetorical patterns. Above all, teachers can develop their own sequences of essays that will contribute not only to their students' reading and writing proficiency but also to their growing intellectual power.
- **Chapter introductions that encourage students to reflect on major issues in the discipline:** The introduction to each disciplinary chapter gives students a broad perspective on the field at hand by putting major issues and concerns in context. Each introduction ends with a previewing section that alerts students to strategies for reading, discussion, and writing.
- **Uniform apparatus that reinforces critical reading and writing:** Another major strength of *The McGraw-Hill Reader* is in the uniform apparatus that accompanies every essay. Much can be learned from any well-written essay, especially if the apparatus is systematic in design. Each selection in this text is preceded by a brief introduction that offers biographical information about the author. The questions that follow each essay are organized in a consistent format created to reinforce essential reading, writing, and oral communication skills. Arranged in three

categories—Comprehension, Rhetoric, and Writing—these questions reflect current compositional theory as they move students from audience
analysis to various modes and processes of composition. All specialized
terms used in the questions are defined for students in an extensive
Glossary of Terms at the end of the text. The integrated design of these
questions makes each essay—simple or complex, short or long, old or
new—accessible to college students who possess varied reading and
writing abilities.

- **"Connections for Critical Thinking" sections:** The essay topics listed at
  the end of each chapter help students make comparative assessments of
  various groups of essays and use Internet resources.
- **A Guide to Research and Documentation:** Chapter 12 offers guidance on
  the most current research writing processes and the documentation styles
  recommended by the Modern Language Association and the American
  Psychological Association.

Highlights of the Eighth Edition

Informed by the comments and suggestions of over 60 instructors from across
the country whose reviews and advice have shaped the eighth edition of *The
McGraw-Hill Reader*, this revision offers a number of new and significant
features.

- **Thirty-three new selections:** The new selections, on topics of current and
  enduring interest such as film, immigration, the death penalty, and work,
  will elicit provocative student writing. New readings added to this edition
  include essays by Ishmael Reed, Amy Tan, Natalie Angier, Ronald Takaki,
  Esther Dyson, Bharati Mukherjee, Stephen King, and others.
- **Expanded coverage of the critical thinking, reading, and writing process
  in Chapter 1:** In order to give instructors more options in teaching with
  this chapter, four engaging selections on reading and the writing
  process—by Mortimer Adler, Annie Dillard, Peter Elbow, and Donald
  Murray—have been added to Chapter 1. In addition, the chapter now includes a new section on reading and analyzing visual texts.
- **A new chapter on argument:** Chapter 2, Reading and Writing Effective
  Arguments, offers students guidelines for reading arguments critically
  and writing strong arguments of their own. It offers five professional readings, including classic and contemporary essays on the death penalty and
  two additional essays for analysis.
- **New classic and contemporary visuals near the beginning of each chapter:** The eighth edition provides a classic and a contemporary image near
  the beginning of each chapter. These visuals include photographs, paintings, and political cartoons. Students are engaged by visual texts, and

these provocative, high-quality images, along with the accompanying "Using a Critical Perspective" questions, will serve to interest them in the topic of the chapter and get them thinking and writing.

- **Repositioned "Classic and Contemporary" essays:** Now appearing near the beginning of each disciplinary chapter, these essay pairs—an older essayist juxtaposed with a more recent one—give students fresh perspectives on authorial influence and the essay tradition. Complemented by the classic and contemporary images, each essay pair helps promote critical thinking and provides historical perspective on an issue.
- **An emphasis on film in Chapter 9.** This chapter, retitled "Communication, Film, and Media," now contains three intriguing essays on film, a favorite subject for most students, including a classic and contemporary pair on the gangster film.

Useful Supplements

The following supplements are designed to help instructors and students derive the full benefit from *The McGraw-Hill Reader:*

- *A Guide to the McGraw-Hill Reader,* by Gilbert H. Muller and Alan Gerstle, Drexel University, offers well-considered strategies for teaching individual essays, sample rhetorical analyses, answers to questions, additional thought-provoking questions, comparative essay discussion formats, and tips for prewriting and guided writing activities. There is also a bibliography of criticism and research on the teaching of composition.
- **A comprehensive Online Learning Center.** The Web site for *The McGraw-Hill Reader* includes additional connections assignments, collaborative assignments, links to information on the authors of the reading selections, and links to further information on the great issues considered in or illustrated by the classic and contemporary essays and visuals.
- **Teaching Composition Faculty Listserv (www.mhhe.com/tcomp).** Moderated by Chris Anson at University of North Carolina, Raleigh, and offered by McGraw-Hill as a service to the composition community, this listserv brings together senior members of the college composition community with newer members—junior faculty, adjuncts, and teaching assistants—in an online newsletter and accompanying discussion group to address issues of pedagogy, in theory and in practice.

Acknowledgments

It is a pleasure to acknowledge the support, assistance, and guidance of numerous individuals who helped create *The McGraw-Hill Reader.* I want to thank the excellent McGraw-Hill family of assistants, editors, and executives who participated enthusiastically in the project from the outset and who encouraged me at every step. My editor, Lisa Moore, has been an enthusiastic supporter of *The McGraw-Hill Reader.* Marcia Muth assisted in the preparation of the chapter on research writing. Alan Gerstle helped with the text revision and preparation of the instructor's manual. Laura Barthule worked on the early stages of the revision plan and managed the initial reviews of the seventh edition. Above all, I want to thank Carla Samodulski, my development editor, a helpful friend and full partner through the revision process.

The final content and design of *The McGraw-Hill Reader,* Eighth Edition, reflects the expertise and advice offered by college instructors across the country who gave generously of their time when asked to respond to surveys submitted to them by McGraw-Hill. These include Larry Anderson, Louisiana State University, Shreveport; Kaylene D. Armstrong, Lorain County Community College; Mark Aune, Wayne State University; Kevin John Bessenbacher, San Diego State University; Gerrit W. Bleeker, Emporia State University; Jenny Brantley, University of Wisconsin—River Falls; John Campion, College of Alameda; Mary Chinery, Georgian Court College; Gina Claywell, Murray State University; Paul Colby, North Carolina State University; Peter Cortland, Quinnipiac College; Jeff E. Cravello, California State Polytechnic University; Kami Day, Johnson County Community College; Emily Dial-Driver, Rogers State University; Suzanne Dixon, Caroll Community College; Olga Dugan, Community College of Philadelphia; Charles Elwert, University of Illinois; Barbara Fanshier, Wamego High School; Hank Galmish, Green River Community College; Dan Glynn, Highland Community College; Kevin Griffith, Capital University; Christine Guillen, Long Beach City College; Stephen Hecox, New Mexico Highlands University; Lee Herrick, Fresno City College; Brenda S. Hines, Highland Community College; Timothy K. Hobert, Modesto Junior College; David E. Hoffman, Averett College; Tony J. Howard, Collin County Community College; Tammie Johnson, Lake Land College; Millard J. Kimery Jr., Howard Payne University; Robert J. Kinpoitner, Molloy College; Diane Koenig, Columbia-Greene Community College; G. Elizabeth Kom, Yeshiva College; Wallis Leslie, DeAnza College; Joe Lostracco, Austin Community College; Steven R. Luebke, University of Wisconsin—River Falls; Louise Nayer, City College of San Francisco; Dale McDaniel, Tulane University; Barbara McGrath, College of the Canyons; Sara McLaughlin, Texas Tech University; Kimberly Manner, Modesto Junior College; John L. Marsden, Indiana University of Pennsylvania; Claudia Milstead, University of Tennessee; Frederick W. Missimer, Camden County College; Clyde Moneyhun, University of Delaware; J. Morgan, University of Kentucky; Marge Morian-Boyle, Dean College; Camilla Mortensen, University of Oregon; Fred Obrecht, Los Angeles Pierce College; Catherine C. Olsen, Tomball College; C. P. Pineo, Fullerton College; Justin Pittas-Giroux, College of Charleston; Stephen Ratcliffe, Mills College; Debra Shein, Idaho State University; Maggie Sokolik, University of California, Berkeley; Michael Soto, Trinity University; Terry Spaise, University of California, Riverside; David Stowe, Michigan State University; Jeffrey H. Taylor, St. Louis Community College; Cheryl Dudasik Wiggs, East Carolina University; K. Siobhan Wright, Carroll Community College; Kenneth R. Wright, James Madison University; Joseph Zeppetello, Marist College; Da Zheng, Suffolk University.

I am pleased to acknowledge support from the Mellon Foundation, the Graduate Center of The City University of New York, and the United States Department of Education (Title III and Title IV) that enabled me to concentrate on the development of this text.

Gilbert H. Muller

The
McGraw-Hill Reader

*Issues Across the
Disciplines*

chapter *1*

Critical Thinking, Reading, and Writing

This book will help you read and write critically for college courses. Although we have entered the electronic information age, where mastery of computer skills and visual literacy seem to be essential for understanding and maintaining our lives and careers, most college work still requires an ability to understand and reflect intelligently on written texts, and subsequently, to respond in writing to them. College courses typically involve the reading of challenging texts. As a college student, you will need to approach these texts with skills that go beyond those of casual reading, that is, the type of reading you may do for leisure, for pleasure or for escapism, or simply to pass time. Even in courses where a preponderance of work is in learning forms of knowledge and new technologies, such as computers, mathematics, and science, you are sure to find a healthy amount of reading that will supplement any other work done in the classroom or laboratory.

The reading and writing skills you develop during your college years will also help you in your future profession. Think of a lawyer reviewing legal history or preparing a legal brief, a doctor reviewing current literature on medical innovations or writing an article for a professional journal, an environmental scientist reading and writing about issues regarding pollution and global warming. All these activities require the ability to think, read, and write about complex material. Learning the tools of critical reading and writing not only teaches you the "what" of an issue, but also helps you think about and respond intelligently to the relative strength of the writer's opinions, ideas, and theories. Critical thinking, reading, and writing enable you to distinguish between informed ideas and pure speculation, rational arguments and emotional ones, and organized essays and structurally deficient ones.

As you hone your critical thinking, reading, and writing skills by tackling the essays in this anthology, you should soon understand how the written word is still the primary medium with which thinkers transmit the intricacies of controversial issues involving the family, society, politics, work, gender, and class. You will encounter complex texts that require you to extract maximum meaning from them, compare your own views with those of the authors you read, and respond to what you read in an informed and coherent manner. The reading selections in this textbook have been chosen specifically to assist you in developing such skills. As you tackle these texts, you will realize that sound reading habits will permit you to understand the fine points of logic, reasoning, analysis, argumentation, and evaluation.

One way to view critical reading is through the concept of active reading. Active reading suggests that you, as a reader, have an obligation to yourself and the author to bring an alert, critical, and responsive perspective to your encounter with the written word. Active reading means learning to annotate (a strategy discussed later in this chapter), to reflect on what you read, and to develop personal responses in order to prepare yourself for writing assignments that your instructor will present to you during the term. This process—reading critically in order to write critically—is not merely an "academic" exercise. It is a skill that can enrich you as a person throughout your life and career. It will teach you to respond critically to the admonitions of politicians or to the seductions of advertisements and, if you choose, to participate intelligently in the "national conversation," which can lead to a rewarding life and responsible citizenship.

When you read an essay or any other type of text, you create meaning out of the material the author has presented. If the essay is relatively simple, clear, and concise, the experience that you construct from your reading may be very similar to what the author intended. Nevertheless, the way that you interact with even the most comprehensible texts will never be identical to the way another reader interacts.

Consider an essay that you will encounter in this anthology, Langston Hughes's "Salvation." A chapter from his autobiography, *The Big Sea* (1940), this essay tells of a childhood incident in which the young Hughes's faith was tested. The essay focuses on a church revival meeting that Hughes was taken to and the increasing pressure he sensed at the meeting to "testify" to the presence of Jesus in his life. At first the young Hughes holds out against the fervor of the congregation, but ultimately he pretends to be converted, or "saved." That night, however, he weeps and then testifies to something entirely unexpected: the loss of faith he experienced because Jesus did not "save" him in a time of need.

As your class reads this essay, individuals among you may be struck by the compressed energy of the narration and the description of the event; by the swift characterization and revealing dialogue; or by the conflict and mounting tension. Moreover, the heightened personal and spiritual conflict will force class members to consider the sad irony inherent in the title "Salvation."

Even if your class arrives at a broad consensus on the intentions of the author, individual reader responses to the text will vary. Readers who have attended revival meetings will respond differently from those who have not. Evangelical Christians will see the text from a different perspective than will Catholics, Muslims, or Jews. African-American readers (Hughes himself was black) may respond differently than white readers. Women may respond differently than men, and so on.

In this brief assessment of possible reader responses, we are trying to establish meaning from a shifting series of critical perspectives. Although we can establish a consensus of meaning over what Hughes probably intended, our own interpretation and evaluation of the text will be conditioned by our personal experiences, backgrounds, attitudes, biases, and beliefs. In other words, even as the class attempts to construct a common reading, each member of the class is also constructing a somewhat different meaning, one based on the individual's own interaction with the text.

PREPARING TO READ

This textbook contains many essays covering a variety of subjects by writers from a wealth of backgrounds and historical periods. You may be familiar with some, unfamiliar with others. All, however, have something to say and a way of saying it that others have found significant. Hence, many have stood the test of time, whether a year, a decade, or centuries. Essays are a recognized genre, or form of literature, and the finest essays have staying power. As Ezra Pound said, "Literature is news that stays news," and the best examples of the essay convey this sense of permanent value. Thus, you have an obligation to be an active and critical reader to do justice to the work that was put into these texts. Most were written with care, over extended periods of time, and by people who themselves studied the art of writing and the topics of their discourse. During your first week of class, you may wish to read some of their brief biographies to understand these authors' personal and educational backgrounds, their beliefs and credos, and some of the significant moments of their lives. You will often find that there are logical connections between the stories of their lives and the topics they have written about.

Sharpening your reading skills will be important because you may not be able to personally choose the essays from the text. You may find some topics and essays more interesting than others. But if you are prepared to read critically, you will be able to bring the same set of skills to any selection your instructor assigns. With this principle in mind, we present an overview of the active reading process, which will culminate in a case study using this process with an essay in this chapter—"The Cult of Ethnicity," by Arthur M. Schlesinger, Jr.

When you are given a reading assignment from the textbook, a good strategy in preparing to read is to locate the text as well as possible within its broader context. Read the biographical notes about the author. Focus on the title of the essay. What can you infer from the title? What is the length of the essay? Although many students delight at the thought of reading shorter texts rather than longer ones, you may find that this variable is not always the deciding one in determining how easily you "get through" the essay. Short essays can be intricate and difficult; long ones can be more transparent and simpler. A long essay on a topic in which you are interested may be more rewarding than a short essay that you find lacking in relevance. Other basic prereading activities can include noting whether there are section breaks in the essay, whether there are subheadings, whether the author has used footnotes, and if so, how extensive they are. Other preliminary questions to answer could be, What is the date of the original publication of the essay? Is the essay a fully contained work or is it an excerpt from a larger text? Are there visual or mathematical aids, such as graphs, charts, diagrams, or lists? Because authors often use typographical signals to highlight things or to help organize what they have written, you might ask, Does the author use quotation marks to "signal" certain words? Is italic type used, and if so, what is its purpose? Are other books and authors cited in the essay? Does the author use organizational tools such as Arabic or Roman numerals? Once you have answered these questions regarding mechanics, you will be prepared to deal more substantively with the essay as a unit of meaning and communication.

Preparation for reading also means understanding that you bring your own knowledge, opinions, experiences, and attitudes to the text. You are not an empty glass to be filled with the knowledge and opinions of the authors, but rather a learner who can bring to bear your own reflections on what you read even if you think your knowledge is minimal. Often we do not know just how much ability we have in thinking about a topic until we actively respond to what others confront us with in their writings. By tackling the reading assignments in the text, you will not only learn new information and confront opinions that may challenge your own, but find that reading frees up your ability to express your own opinions. For this reason, most English teachers look upon reading as a two-way process: an exchange between writer and reader.

Although the credentials and experience of a professional writer may seem impressive, they should not deter you from considering your own critical talents as you read. But first, you must find a way to harness those abilities.

CRITICAL READING

It should be evident to you by now that you are not a mere recipient of information who passively accepts what the writer conveys. Instead, you should feel comfortable about engaging the author as you might a friend in a lively conversation or argument. And just as a talk with a friend involves active listening, rebuttal, use of facts, and logic, the interaction between yourself and the author needs to be a dynamic one as well. Active reading is so important in the learning process that one of America's most popular philosophers, Mortimer Adler, wrote an article that has become a classic on this topic. It is entitled "How to Mark a Book," and is included on page 42.

Among the essential elements of your close reading are annotating, note taking, and questioning the text.

Annotating

Annotating refers to marking your text by making content notes, by using symbols such as question marks and exclamation points, and by recording personal reactions. Annotating is not, however, mere underlining or highlighting. These latter two methods often serve little purpose in helping you comprehend a text. Most likely, when you return to passages you've marked with these simple procedures, you will have forgotten why you felt they were important in the first place. If you do underline or highlight, you should be sure to link your marking with a note in the margin. Simply drawing attention to someone else's words does little in the way of expanding your own thoughts on a topic. Learning is best accomplished by restating ideas in your own words.

Note Taking

Many essays in your anthology will require more than jotting down marginal notes in order to comprehend them fully or to respond to them in depth. Just as you might take down notes during a classroom lecture, you may find it useful to take notes to supplement your annotations. You may wish, for example, to write down quotations so that you can see them together. Or you may wish to summarize the essay by outlining its key points, a reversal of the process you would use to develop your own essay, wherein you begin with an outline and expand it into paragraphs. By collapsing an essay into an outline, you have a handy reference of the author's thesis (main idea) and supporting points, and the methods used to develop them. Another function of note taking is to overcome the simple habit most of us have of thinking we will remember things without jotting them down, only to find out later we cannot recall significant information from memory. You will appreciate the benefits of taking notes when you tackle lengthy essays, which may run 15 or 20 pages in length.

Questioning the Text

Posing key questions about a text and then answering them to the best of your ability is a helpful means of understanding more cogently an essay's substance and structure. Certain basic questions are salient for nearly any text you confront, and answering them for yourself can be a powerful means of enhancing your comprehension. As you read your text, such questions help you spot the significant issues that lie within most essays, regardless of their form or length. It is a good habit to have these questions in mind as you read, and then to return to them once you've thought through your reading. They serve as guideposts along the way of your reading experience and assist you in focusing on those issues that are most important to a text. When you become comfortable with them, you will probably find that your mind automatically poses them as you read, making your comprehension of difficult texts easier.

- What is the thesis or main point of the text?
- What methods does the author use to support these points, for instance, illustration, example, citing authorities, citing studies and/or statistics, description, personal experience, or history?

- What value position, if any, does the author present? In other words, is the author either directly or indirectly presenting her or his moral framework on an issue, or is she or he summarizing or describing an issue?
- Does the author use any special terms or expressions that need to be elucidated to understand the essay? You will find that authors, when addressing innovative or revolutionary ideas within the context of their times, must use vocabulary that often needs to be defined. Take for example, the term *multiculturalism*. Exactly what does an author mean by that word?
- What is the level of discourse of the essay? Or what is the audience's level of educational attainment the author presumes?
- Who is the implied audience for the essay? Is it written for a specialized profession (such as scientists or educators); is it written for individuals with a focus on their particular role in society, for example, as parents or consumers or citizens?

The following essay, "The Cult of Ethnicity," by Arthur Schlesinger, Jr., has been annotated to demonstrate how a student might respond to it. Schlesinger's essay also will be used to explain aspects of the reading and writing process as we move through this section. (For another copy of Schlesinger's essay without annotations, see page 47).

The history of the world has been in great part the history of the mixing of peoples. Modern communication and transport accelerate mass migrations from one continent to another. Ethnic and racial diversity are more than ever a salient fact of the age.

But what happens when people of different origins, speaking different languages and professing different religions, inhabit the same locality and live under the same political sovereignty? Ethnic and racial conflict—far more than ideological conflict—is the explosive problem of our times.

This seems like the thesis. Where are his supports? Or is it the thesis?

On every side today ethnicity is breaking up nations. The Soviet Union, India, Yugoslavia, Ethiopia, are all in crisis. Ethnic tensions disturb and divide Sri Lanka, Burma, Indonesia, Iraq, Cyprus, Nigeria, Angola, Lebanon, Guyana, Trinidad—you name it. Even nations as stable and civilized as Britain and France, Belgium and Spain, face growing ethnic troubles. Is there any large multiethnic state that can be made to work?

Look these up. Demonstrates knowledge on the part of the author.

The answer to that question has been, until recently, the United States. "No other nation," Margaret Thatcher has said, "has so successfully combined people of different races and nations within a single culture." How have Americans succeeded in pulling off this almost unprecedented trick?

We have always been a multiethnic country. Hector St. John de Crevecoeur, who came from France in the 18th century, marveled at the astonishing diversity of the settlers—"a mixture of English, Scotch, Irish, French, Dutch, Germans and Swedes . . . this promiscuous breed." He propounded a famous question: "What then is the American, this new man?" And he

historical figure—who was he?

gave a famous answer: "Here individuals of all nations are melted into a new race of men." E pluribus unum.

The United States escaped the divisiveness of a multiethnic society by a brilliant solution: the creation of a brand-new national identity. The point of America was not to preserve old cultures but to *forge a new, American culture. "By an intermixture with our people," President George Washington told Vice President John Adams, immigrants will "get assimilated to our customs, measures and laws: in a word, soon become one people." This was the ideal that a century later Israel Zangwill crystallized in the title of his popular 1908 play The Melting Pot. And no institution was more potent in molding Crevecoeur's "promiscuous breed" into Washington's "one people" than the American public school.

The new American nationality was inescapably English in language, ideas, and institutions. The pot did not melt everybody, not even all the white immigrants; deeply bred racism put black Americans, yellow Americans, red Americans and brown Americans well outside the pale. Still, the infusion of other stocks, even of nonwhite stocks, and the experience of the New World reconfigured the British legacy and made the United States, as we all know, a very different country from Britain.

In the 20th century, new immigration laws altered the composition of the American people, and a cult of ethnicity erupted both among non-Anglo whites and among nonwhite minorities. This had many healthy consequences. The American culture at last began to give shamefully overdue recognition to the achievements of groups subordinated and spurned during the high noon of Anglo dominance, and it began to acknowledge the great swirling world beyond Europe. Americans acquired a more complex and invigorating sense of their world—and of themselves.

But, pressed too far, the cult of ethnicity has unhealthy consequences. It gives rise, for example, to the conception of the United States as a nation composed not of individuals making their own choices but of inviolable ethnic and racial groups. It rejects the historic American goals of assimilation and integration.

And, in an excess of zeal, well-intentioned people seek to transform our system of education from a means of creating "one people" into a means of promoting, celebrating and perpetuating separate ethnic origins and identities. The balance is shifting from unum to pluribus.

That is the issue that lies behind the hullabaloo over "multiculturalism" and "political correctness," the attack on the "Eurocentric" curriculum and the rise of the notion that history and literature should be taught not as disciplines but as therapies whose function is to raise minority self-esteem. Group separatism crystallizes the differences, magnifies tensions, intensifies hostilities. Europe—the unique source of the liberating ideas of

Marginal annotations:

is this a partly American phenomenon? *prevents racial and ethnic conflict

why?—doesn't explain

note S's use of historical process analysis

vocab.: infusion stocks zeal Eurocentric apocalyptic ferment Kleagle crucible

signals a warning—danger

is this thesis or related to thesis?

support against multiculturalism

democracy, civil liberties and human rights—is portrayed as the root of all evil, and nonEuropean cultures, their own many crimes deleted, are presented as the means of redemption.

general—where are the specific examples?

I don't want to sound apocalyptic about these developments. Education is always in ferment, and a good thing too. The situation in our universities, I am confident, will soon right itself. But the impact of separatist pressures on our public schools is more troubling. If a Kleagle of the Ku Klux Klan wanted to use the schools to disable and handicap black Americans, he would hardly come up with anything more effective than the "Afrocentric" curriculum. And if separatist tendencies go unchecked, the result can only be the fragmentation, resegregation and tribalization of American life.

Is this an exaggeration? How does he know?

I remain optimistic. My impression is that the historic forces driving toward "one people" have not lost their power. The eruption of ethnicity is, I believe, a rather superficial enthusiasm stirred by romantic ideologues on the one hand and by unscrupulous con men on the other: self-appointed spokesmen whose claim to represent their minority groups is carelessly accepted by the media. Most American-born members of minority groups, white or nonwhite, see themselves primarily as Americans rather than primarily as members of one or another ethnic group. A notable indicator today is the rate of intermarriage across ethnic lines, across religious lines, even (increasingly) across racial lines. "We Americans," said Theodore Roosevelt, "are children of the crucible."

Who are these people? He doesn't mention them specifically.

reality is stronger than "ideology"? Is this his "solution"?

The growing diversity of the American population makes the quest for unifying ideals and a common culture all the more urgent. In a world savagely rent by ethnic and racial antagonisms, the United States must continue as an example of how a highly differentiated society holds itself together.

← a sharp conclusion argument?

United States must be example. This is the thesis.

What has this annotating accomplished? It has allowed the reader/annotator to consider and think about what she has read, integrate her ideas with the ideas of the author, challenge those she may disagree with, raise issues for further study, find the seeds of ideas that may become the focus of an essay in response to the writing, review what she has read with more facility, and quickly and efficiently return to those parts of the essay she found the most salient.

The aforementioned strategies will assist you in responding intelligently in the classroom, remembering the main points of what you have read, and internalizing the critical reading skill so that it becomes automatic. However, such activities are not as challenging as the ultimate goal of most of your reading assignments, which will be to respond in formal writing to the works you've read. For this, you will need to enhance your study skills a bit further so that they will prepare you to write.

Formal writing assignments require you to demonstrate that you understood what you have read and are able to respond in an informed and intelligent manner to the material. They also require you to use appropriate form, organization, and exposition. Above all, regardless of what you want to express, you will have to communicate your ideas clearly and concisely. To this end, you will need to acquire skills that you can call on when it comes to writing at length about what you have read. To do so, you will find your ability to paraphrase, summarize, and quote directly from the original material particularly helpful.

When you move to this next phase, however, try to avoid a common practice among readers that causes them to waste time and effort put into study. Many students think they have completed a reading assignment when they read the last word of an essay. They utter a sigh of relief, look inside the refrigerator for something to eat, call up friends, or go Web browsing. However, as a critical reader, you need to spend additional time reinforcing what you have read by thinking about the author's views, considering her or his rhetorical methods, and reviewing or adding to your notes and annotations. For example, one culminating activity at this point can be to either mentally or verbally summarize what you have read. You can summarize verbally by enlisting a classmate and simply stating in your own terms the main points of your reading assignment. This oral summarizing will prevent a common problem many readers experience: the natural tendency to forget most of what they read shortly after reading.

BEYOND CONTENT: FOCUSING ON STRUCTURE

How an author presents her or his information is as important as what information the author presents. Strategies for writing may include the overall pattern of an essay—for example, is it an argument, an explanation, a definition, an evaluation, a comparison and/or contrast? While you may not think of essays in terms of genre, as you do literature (which may be presented in the form of poetry, the short story, the play, and so on), such forms can help you understand the motivation behind the writer's work and assist you as you seek out the more significant passages in a piece of writing. For example, if the essay is argumentative, you should focus on the supporting points the author has provided, determining whether they offer adequate support for the author's point of view. In an essay arguing for the return to traditional family values, for instance, the use of one anecdote to prove a point would probably not be enough to persuade most readers.

As you read an essay, you should also consider the author's *purpose* for writing. An essay about a personal experience would probably contain physical description; at the same time, the author's purpose would probably be to communicate an element in his or her life that can provide insight into personal development in general. Among the more common purposes are the following: to inform, to persuade, to disprove, to describe, to narrate, to demonstrate, to compare and contrast, to seek a solution to a problem, to explain a process, to classify, to define, to warn, and to summarize. While most essays contain a variety of purposes, one often will stand out among the others.

PARAPHRASING, SUMMARIZING, QUOTING

As you prepare to respond to the writing of others, you need to develop skills so that your own writing will reflect the hard work that went into the reading process. To this end, you can benefit from learning some shortcuts that will assist you in garnering information about what you have read. These skills include paraphrasing, summarizing, and quoting directly from another author's work.

Paraphrasing

Paraphrasing means taking what you have read and placing it in your own words. Students occasionally complain about this process, using the argument that it is a waste of time to paraphrase when the author's own words are the best way to articulate his or her ideas. However, paraphrasing serves two main purposes. The more obvious one is that it prevents you from plagiarizing, even inadvertently, what you have read. In terms of learning, however, it is particularly helpful because it requires that you digest what you have read and rewrite it. As you do so, you will develop writing patterns that over time will improve your ability to communicate. Paraphrasing forces you to truly think about what you have read and reinforces what you've read, since your mind has now been cognitively stimulated. You may find that paraphrasing often leads you to challenge the text or think more deeply about it simply because the paraphrasing process requires that you fully comprehend what you read.

It is important while paraphrasing to keep in all the essential information of the original while not using any of the author's original vocabulary or style. One rule of thumb is to never use three or more words that appeared together in the original. However, you can keep words such as articles (*a, an, the*) and conjunctions (*and, for, but,* etc.). The following are two examples of paraphrasing that demonstrate unsuccessful and successful application of the technique.

Original
But, pressed too far, the cult of ethnicity has unhealthy consequences. It gives rise, for example, to the conception of the United States as a nation composed not of individuals making their own choices but of inviolable ethnic and racial groups. It rejects the historic American goals of assimilation and integration.

Paraphrase 1
But, pressed too far, the focus on ethnicity has dangerous consequences. It suggests that the United States is a nation made up of separate ethnic and racial groups rather than individuals. It goes against the American ideals of integration and assimilation.

There are several things wrong with paraphrase 1. Rather than change key words, the writer has merely rearranged them. The sentence structure is very similar to that of the original, as is the ordering of ideas. If the student were to incorporate this paraphrase into her or his own essay, the teacher would probably consider it a form of plagiarism. It is simply too close to the original. To truly paraphrase, you must substitute vocabulary, rearrange sentence structure, change the length and order of sentences. These strategies are more evident in paraphrase 2.

Paraphrase 2

Our country is made up of both individuals and groups. The recent trend to focus on the idea that one's ethnic background should have a major influence on one's perspective as a citizen goes against the moral foundations of the United States. It is the very concept of accepting American culture as one's own that has made our country strong and relatively free from cultural conflict.

Summarizing

A summary is a short, cohesive paragraph or paragraphs that are faithful to the structure and meaning of the original essay you've read, but developed in your own words and including only the most essential elements of the original. Summaries are particularly helpful when you are planning to write lengthy assignments or assignments that require that you compare two or more sources. Because a good summary requires that you use many of the skills of active reading, it helps you to "imprint" the rhetorical features and content of what you have read in your memory, and also provides you with a means of communicating the essence of an essay to another person or group. To summarize successfully, you need to develop the ability to know what to leave out as much as what to include. As you review your source, the annotations and notes you have made previously should help immensely. Since you want to deal with only the essentials of the original, you must delete all unimportant details and redundancies. Unlike paraphrasing, however, most summaries require that you stick to the general order of ideas as they are presented in a text. They also should not be mere retellings of what you have read, but should present the relationships among the ideas in an essay. It may be helpful to think of a summary as analogous to a news story, in which the essential details of what happened are presented in an orderly chronological fashion, because readers can best understand the gist of a story that way. It is simply the way the human mind, at least the Western mind, operates. Another strategy in summarizing is to imagine that the audience you are summarizing for has not read the original. This places a strong responsibility on you to communicate the essentials of the text accurately.

The following six steps should help you in preparing a summary. After you've reviewed them, read the summary that follows and consider whether it seems to have fulfilled these suggestions.

1. Read the entire source at least twice and annotate it at least once before writing.
2. Write an opening sentence that states the author's thesis.
3. Explain the author's main supporting ideas, reviewing your notes to make sure you have included all of them. Be careful not to plagiarize, and use quotations only where appropriate:
4. Restate important concepts, key terms, principles, and so on. Do not include your opinion or judge the essay in any way.

5. Present the ideas in the order in which they originally appeared. Note that in this way summarizing is different from paraphrasing, where staying too close to the original order of words may be detrimental to the process.

6. Review your summary once it has been completed. Consider whether someone who hasn't read the original would find your summary sufficient to understand the essence of the original work. You may also wish to have classmates or friends read the essay and ask them to furnish their verbal understanding of what you've written.

Now, review the following summary of Schlesinger's essay and determine whether it adheres to these points.

Sample Summary

Schlesinger argues that the recent surge of interest in ethnic separatism that is being touted by some whom he considers self-styled spokespersons for various ethnic groups threatens the unifying principle of our country's founders and undermines the strength of our society. This principle is that the American identity that was forged by its creators would be adopted by all peoples arriving here through a process of assimilation to our culture, values, and system of government so that cultural conflict could be avoided. Although he finds some merit in the idea that recognizing the contributions of certain groups who have been kept out of the national focus, for example, "nonwhite minorities," is a positive move, he fears that this can be taken to an extreme. The result could be the development of antagonism between ethnic groups solely on the basis of overemphasizing differences rather than recognizing similarities. He further argues that efforts to fragment American culture into subgroups can have the effect of jeopardizing their own empowerment, the opposite of the movement's intention. He gives the example of "Afrocentric" schooling, which he claims would only harm students enrolled in its curriculum. Despite this new interest in the "cult of ethnicity," the author is optimistic that it is of limited effect. He claims that most Americans still strive toward unity and identify themselves as Americans first, members of ethnic or racial groups second. He buttresses this belief by explaining that intermarriage is growing across racial, religious, and ethnic lines. This striving toward unity and identification with America among groups is particularly important today since their diversity is continuously increasing.

Quoting

Sayings and adages are extremely popular. You find them quoted in everyday speech, printed in calendars, rendered in calligraphy and framed and hung in homes, and spoken by public figures. These are, in effect, direct quotes, although the authors may be anonymous. Direct quotations often have a unique power because they capture the essence of an idea accurately and briefly. Another reason is that they are stylistically powerful. You may find in an essay a sentence or group of sentences that are worded so elegantly that you feel you simply wish to savor them for yourself or plan to use them appropriately for a future writing assignment. Other times, you may wish to use direct quotations to demonstrate to a reader the effectiveness of an original essay or the authoritative voice of the author. And at still other times, it may simply be necessary to quote an author because her or his vocabulary just cannot be changed without injuring the meaning of the original. Review the following quotations taken from the Schlesinger essay, and consider how paraphrasing them would injure their rhetorical power.

Direct Quotations That Reflect the Conciseness of the Original
"The history of the world has been in great part the history of the mixing of peoples."

"On every side today ethnicity is breaking up nations."

"And if separatist tendencies go unchecked, the result can only be the fragmentation, resegregation and tribalization of American life."

Direct Quotations That Have Particular Stylistic Strength
"The pot did not melt everybody . . . "

"The balance is shifting from *unum* to *pluribus*."

Direct Quotations That Establish the Writer's Authority
"The point of America was not to preserve old cultures but to forge a new, American culture. 'By an intermixture with our people,' President George Washington told Vice President John Adams, immigrants will 'get assimilated to our customs, measures and laws: in a word, soon become one people.'"

"A notable indicator today is the rate of intermarriage across ethnic lines, across religious lines, even (increasingly) across racial lines."

Direct Quotation That Demonstrates Conceptual Power
"The eruption of ethnicity, is, I believe, a rather superficial enthusiasm stirred by romantic ideologues on the one hand and by unscrupulous con men on the other. . . . "

READING AND ANALYZING VISUAL TEXTS

In this new era of information technology, we seem to be immersed in a visual culture requiring us to contend with and think critically about the constant flow of images we encounter. From advertising to film to video to the Internet, we must respond with increasing frequency not only to written but also to visual messages—images that typically are reinforced by verbal elements. Consequently, it is important to perceive the powerful linkages that exist in today's culture between visual and verbal experience.

Frequently in courses in engineering, social science, computer science, the humanities, fine arts, and elsewhere, you have to analyze and understand visual elements that are embedded in texts. Textbooks increasingly promote visuals as frames of reference that help readers to comprehend and appreciate information. Some visual elements—charts, tables, and graphs—are integral to an understanding of verbal texts. Other visuals—comic art, drawings, photographs, paintings, advertisements—offer contexts and occasions for enjoyment and deeper understanding of the reading, writing, and thinking processes. Visual images convey messages that often are as powerful as well-composed written texts. When they appear together, image and word are like French doors, both opening to reveal a world of heightened perception and understanding.

When visual elements stand alone, as in painting and photography, they often make profound statements about human experience and frequently reflect certain persuasive purposes that are composed as skillfully as an argumentative essay. Consider, for example, the series that the great Spanish artist Francisco Goya painted, "The Disasters of War," a powerful statement of humankind's penchant for the most grotesque and violent cruelties. In the late 20th century, photographers of the Vietnam War, using a modern visual medium, similarly captured the pain and suffering of armed conflict, as in Eddie Adams's potent stills of the execution of a prisoner by the notorious chief of the Saigon national police, General Nguyen Ngoc Loan. In the framed sequence, the chief of police aims his pistol at the head of the prisoner, presses the trigger, and the viewer, in that captured instant, sees the jolt of the prisoner's head and a sudden spurt of blood. Reproduced widely in the American press in February 1968, this single image did as much as any written editorial to transform the national debate over the Vietnam War. (Both images are reprinted on pages 94–95.)

Although paintings, photographs, advertisements, and other artistic and design forms that rely heavily on visual elements often function as instruments of persuasion, it would be simplistic and simply wrong to embrace uncritically the cliché "A picture is worth a thousand words." For instance, great literary artists from Homer to the present have captured the horrors of war as vividly as artists in other media. Stephen Crane in *The Red Badge of Courage* illustrates the sordidness of America's Civil War in language as graphic as the images of the war's most noted photographer, Mathew Brady. Consider the visual impact of Crane's depiction of battlefield dead:

> The corpse was dressed in a uniform that once had been blue but was now faded to a melancholy shade of green. The eyes, staring at the youth, had changed to the dull hue to be seen on the side of a dead fish. The mouth was opened. Its red had changed to an appalling yellow. Over the grey skin of the face ran little ants. One was trundling some sort of a bundle along the upper lip.

Ultimately the best verbal and visual texts construct meaning in vivid and memorable ways. When used in combination, visual and verbal texts can mix words and images to create uniquely powerful theses and arguments.

Just as you analyze or take apart a verbal text during the process of critical reading, you also have to think critically about visual images or elements. If you encounter charts, graphs, and tables in a text, you have to understand the information these visuals present, the implications of the numbers or statistics, the emphases and highlights that are conveyed, and the way the visual element—the picture, so to speak—shapes your understanding of the material and its relationship to the text. Sometimes the material presented in such visuals is technical, requiring you to carefully analyze, let's say, a bar graph: its structure, the relationship of parts to the whole, the assertions that are advanced, and the validity of the evidence conveyed. In short, critical reading of visual material is as demanding as critical reading of the printed word. Just as you often have to reread a verbal text, you also might have to return to charts, graphs, and tables, perhaps from a fresh perspective, in order to comprehend the content of the visual text.

The following questions can guide your critical analysis of such visual texts as charts, graphs, and tables:

- What is the design or structure of the visual?
- What information do you immediately notice?
- What is the purpose of the visual?
- What thesis or point of view does the information in the visual suggest?
- What is the nature of the evidence and how can it be verified?
- What emphases and relationships do you detect among the visual details?
- How does the visual fit into the context of the verbal text surrounding it?

When responding to charts, tables, and graphs, you must develop the confidence to read such visual texts accurately and critically, taking nothing for granted and trusting your ability to sift through the evidence and the images with a critical eye in order to understand the strategies the author or graphic artist has employed to convey a specific message to the reader.

By and large, informative visuals such as tables and graphs rarely have the striking impact of the sort of graphics found in the best commercial and political advertising or in the illustrations we encounter in slick magazines or cutting-edge cartoon strips. The visual elements used by advertisers, for example, take advantage of our innate capacity to be affected by symbols—McDonald's Golden Arch, the president framed by American flags, a bottle of Coca-Cola beneath the word "America." Such visual emblems convey unspoken ideas and have enormous power to promote products, personalities, and ideas. For example, the two powerful images on pages 18–19 convey important ideas about the cultures that produced them. Visual symbols achieve even more intense effects when they are reinforced by verbal elements.

When viewing art reproductions, photographs, advertisements, and cartoons from a critical perspective, you often have to detect the explicit and implicit messages being conveyed by certain images and symbols, and the design strategies that condition your response. Because these visuals combine many different elements, you have to consider all critical details: color, light, and shadow; the number and arrangement of objects and the relationships among them; the foregrounding and backgrounding of images within the frame; the impact of typography; the impact of language if it is employed; and the inferences and values that you draw from the overall composition. Learn to treat visuals in any medium as texts that need to be "read" critically. Every visual requires its own form of annotation, in which you analyze the selection and ordering of its parts and interpret the emotional effects and significant ideas and messages it presents. Throughout this text, paired "classic and contemporary" images such as the two on pages 18–19 give you opportunities to read visual texts with a critical eye.

Classic and Contemporary Images
HOW DO WE COMMUNICATE?

Using a Critical Perspective   Carefully examine these two illustrations, which are drawn from different ages, cultures, and artistic realms. What is your overall impression of these images? What details and objects in each scene capture your attention? How does each image communicate ideas and values about the culture that has produced it? Does one appeal to you more than the other? Why or why not?

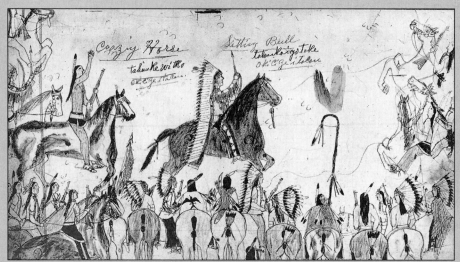

Courtesy Department of Library Services, American Museum of Natural History (Neg. No. 336471, AMNH Photo Studio).

Throughout the western plains of the United States, Indian tribes etched images of tribal life into rocks, images that scholars now know are a form of code that members of different tribes could recognize. These symbolic images, which depict battle scenes as well as spiritual events, became increasingly sophisticated in the 19th century and were often drawn on paper in ledger books by Indians in captivity, but the symbols the artists used remained consistent with the earlier images on rock. The image above is a view of chiefs Crazy Horse and Sitting Bull, probably following the Battle of Little Bighorn in 1876. It was drawn by Amos Bad Heart, a well-known ledger artist.

In the early 21st century, another powerful symbol, the famous photograph and statue of the landing of the Marines on Iwo Jima during World War II, was evoked by photographer Thomas E. Franklin in the wake of the terror attack on the World Trade Center in New York City in September 2001.

THE WRITING PROCESS

Whether you have been provided an assignment by your instructor or developed your own topic, the various tools for critical reading and analysis that you have mastered should now equip you with the foundation for what is necessary to embark on your own writing assignment. Essays are normally a three-part writing process. The three stages are termed prewriting, drafting, and revising. To illuminate the writing process, we will examine strategies employed by several student and professional writers, including one student, Jamie Taylor, as she read and responded to Schlesinger. But first we require an overview of the writing process, starting with the origins and development of a writer's ideas.

Annie Dillard, one of today's preeminent essayists, stresses the primacy of the creative imagination in the writing process in the selection on page 50. Dillard uses the central metaphor of building a house to describe the act of writing, but within her essay one can detect the three stages of the writing process: prewriting ("The line of words is a miner's pick, a woodcarver's gouge, a surgeon's probe. You wield it, and it digs a path you follow"), drafting ("You lay down the words carefully, watching all the angles"), and revising ("The part you must jettison is not only the best-written part; it is also, oddly, the part which was to have been the very point"). We will now look at each of these stages in detail.

Prewriting

Prewriting, which you have already been engaged in as you have negotiated the reading-writing connection, is the discovery, exploration, and planning stage of the composing process. It is the stage in which you discover a reason to write, select and narrow a subject, consider audience and purpose, and engage in preliminary writing activities designed to generate textual material. During the prewriting process, you are free to let ideas incubate, to let thoughts and writing strategies ripen. You are free also to get in the mood to write. Ernest Hemingway used to sharpen all his pencils as preparation for a day's writing, while the French philosopher Voltaire soaked his feet in cold water to get the creative juices flowing. Professional writers understand the importance of prewriting activities in the composing process, but college writers often undervalue or ignore them completely.

Freewriting and Brainstorming   Two methods of getting in touch with what you already know or believe are freewriting and brainstorming. Freewriting is quite simple. Merely select a predetermined amount of time, say anywhere from 5 to 15 minutes, and write down everything that you can think of regarding the subject at hand. Don't worry about punctuation or grammar. This activity is mainly to get your cognitive wheels rolling. Brainstorming is a variant of freewriting in which you jot down ideas and questions, often in numbered form. If you find freewriting and brainstorming helpful as techniques, you will probably find the length of time that suits you best. When you have finished, review what you have written. A well known composition expert, Peter Elbow, explains the value of freewriting in the selection on page 52. The freewriting that Elbow describes can help any writer generate ideas, but freewriting and brainstorming can also help writers respond to others' ideas. For example, examine the following freewriting and brainstorming exercises by a student, James Moore, which he wrote after reading an excerpt from Schlesinger's "The Cult of Ethnicity."

Freewriting Sample

This essay shows that the author really knows his history because he cites so many historical figures, places, and can quote word for word authorities that back up his argument. He makes a great argument that America's strength is in its diversity and at the same time its unity. I never thought of these two things as being able to complement one another. I always thought of them as being separate. It opens my mind to a whole new way of thinking. One thing that would have strengthened his argument, though is the fact that although he criticizes people who want to separate themselves into subgroups, he doesn't really mention them by name. He's great when it comes to advancing his own argument but he seems to be a bit too general when he comes to attacking the opposition. I would have liked it if he had mentioned by name people who are undermining America's strengths and listen in their own words.

Brainstorming Sample

1. The author says that ideological conflict isn't such a big problem, but what about the gap between rich and poor? Maybe if there were less of a gap, people wouldn't look for "false idols."
2. Schlesinger seems to be part of the white mainstream. Does this mean he is destined not to understand fully the reasons why people on the margins of society get so tempted to join "cults"?
3. He uses supporting points very well but doesn't exactly explain why "multiculturalism" and "political correctness" are happening now in our society. What is it about today that has opened the door to these ideas?
4. There are so many references to places with ethnic tensions around the world. It would be great to study one of them and see if they have any similarities to the ones that exist in the United States.
5. He seems to be writing for a very educated audience. I wonder really if he can reach the "common person" with this kind of sophisticated writing. I don't know about most of the places he mentions.
6. What's the solution? That could be the start of a topic for my paper. I don't think the author offers any.

Let's consider the benefits these processes can have. First, you can comment on the subject matter of the essay without censoring your thoughts. This prepares you for the second reading by marshalling a more coherent idea of your own perspective. Freewriting or brainstorming can be a tool that helps you understand how you can have something to contribute in the writer-reader "conversation" or helps you see a topic in a new way. For example, in the freewriting example, the student discovered for himself the idea that the strength of American society is a combination of commonality and diversity. Second, during the brainstorming process, you might come up with a potential idea for a response essay, as the student did in the example.

Now let us return to the prewriting process that Jamie Taylor followed.

Brainstorming Notes

1. Schlesinger seems to be saying that multiculturalism poses a danger because it threatens to create ethnic divisiveness rather than healthy identification.
2. This not only undermines us now, but threatens the very democratic principles upon which the United States was founded.
3. He says America must set an example for the rest of the world, which is torn with racial and ethnic strife.
4. He believes that there is a small group of individuals with a "hidden agenda" who are trying to create this divisiveness. These individuals are self-centered and have their own interests at heart, not the interests of the people they represent.
5. One flaw in the essay was that it seemed vague. He didn't mention any names or give specific examples. Only generalities.
6. He suggests the "battle" will be won by ordinary citizens; for example, he cites the many intermarriages occurring today.
7. Although he sees danger, he is optimistic because he thinks democracy is a strong institution.
8. He writes from a position of authority. He cites many historical figures and seems very well read.
9. The major problem I see in his essay is that he seems to lump everyone together in the same boat. He doesn't give enough credit to the average person to see through the hollowness of false idols. You don't need a Ph.D. to see the silliness of so many ideas floating around out there.
10. So many things to consider, how should I focus my essay??? What should be my theme??
11. Hmmm. Idea!!! Since I agree with his basic points, but find he doesn't provide specifics, and doesn't give the average person enough credit to see through the emptiness of cult rhetoric, why not use my personal observations to write a response paper in which I show just how reasonable we are in distinguishing mere rhetoric from substance?

Outlining   In addition to this brainstorming, Ms. Taylor also developed a scratch outline—yet another prewriting strategy—to guide her into the drafting stage of the composing process.

Outline

I.   Introduction: Summarize essay and thesis; provide counterthesis.
II. University life as a demonstration of "ethnic" democracies.
III. The emptiness and false promises of self-styled ethnic leaders.
IV. The rejection of "home-grown" cults.
V.   Conclusion.

Although Jamie Taylor employed brainstorming and a scratch outline to organize her thoughts prior to writing her essay, not everyone uses these prewriting activities. Some students need to go through a series of prewriting activities, while others can dive into a first draft. Nevertheless, discovering the materials and form for an essay includes a search for ideas, a willingness to discard ideas and strategies that don't work, an ability to look at old ideas in a fresh way, and a talent for moving back and forth across a range of composing activities. Rarely does that flash of insight or first draft produce the ideal flow of words resulting in a well-written and well-ordered essay.

Professional writers have their own unique approaches to the composing process. For example, Annie Dillard is a prolific keeper of journals, from which she extracts ideas for essays and books. She also jots down notes, often in rough outline form. Here are some notes she jotted down, based on journal entries and her essay "Death of a Moth."

Moth in candle:
the poet—materials of world, of bare earth at feet, sucked up, transformed,
    subsumed to spirit, to air, to light
the mystic—not through reason, but through emptiness
the martyr—virgin, sacrifice, death with meaning.

Her "moth essay," as she calls it, evolved from journal entries, doodles, and several drafts, and then fit into a much larger book that she was writing.

Drafting

Everyone approaches the entire composing process differently. There are, however, certain basic principles for the drafting stage that you must consider. These principles are discussed in the following sections.

Developing the Thesis   Every essay requires a main idea or thesis that holds all your information together. What you seek is not just any idea relevant to the bulk of your topic, but the underlying idea that best expresses your purpose in writing the essay. Your thesis is the controlling idea for the entire essay.

The thesis requires you to take a stand on your topic. It is your reason for wanting to inform or persuade an audience. The noted teacher and scholar Sheridan Baker has expressed nicely this need to take a stand or assume an angle of interpretation: "When you have something to say about *cats*, you have found your underlying idea. You have something to fight about: not just 'Cats,' but 'The cat is really man's best friend.'" Not all thesis statements involve arguments or fights. Nevertheless, you cannot have a thesis unless you have something to demonstrate or prove.

The thesis statement, which normally appears as a single sentence near the beginning of your essay, serves five important functions:

- It introduces the topic to the reader.
- It limits the topic to a single idea.

- It expresses your approach to the topic—the opinion, attitude, or outlook that creates your special angle of interpretation for the topic.
- It may provide the reader with hints about the way the essay will develop.
- It should arouse the reader's interest by revealing your originality and your honest commitment to the topic.

Here is a typical thesis statement by a student:

The automobile—America's metallic monster—takes up important public space, pollutes the environment, and makes people lazy, rude, and overweight.

In this thesis, the writer has staked out a position, limited the topic, and given the reader some idea of how the essay actually will develop.

Your thesis cannot always be captured in a single sentence. Indeed, professional writers often offer an implied or unstated thesis or articulate a thesis statement that permeates an entire paragraph. Basically, you should ask if a thesis hooks you. Do you find it provocative? Do you know where the author is coming from? Does the author offer a map for the entire essay? These are some of the issues that you should consider as you compose your own thesis sentences.

Writing Introductory Paragraphs   Your introduction should be like a door opening into the world of your essay. A good introduction entices readers into this world by arousing their curiosity about the topic and thesis with carefully chosen material and through a variety of techniques. The introduction, normally a single, short paragraph composed of a few sentences, serves several important functions:

- It introduces the topic.
- It states the writer's attitude toward the subject, normally in the form of a thesis statement.
- It offers readers a guide to the essay.
- It draws readers into the topic through a variety of techniques.

A solid introduction informs, orients, interests, and engages the audience. "Beginnings," wrote the English novelist George Eliot, "are always troublesome." Getting the introduction just right takes effort, considerable powers of invention, and often several revisions. Fortunately, there are special strategies that make effective introductions possible:

- Use a subject-clarification-thesis format. Present the essay's general subject, clarify and explain the topic briefly, and then present your attitude toward the topic in a thesis statement.
- Offer a brief story or incident that sets the stage for your topic and frames your thesis.
- Start with a shocking, controversial, or intriguing opinion.
- Begin with a comparison and/or contrast.
- Use a quotation or reference to clarify and illustrate your topic and thesis.
- Ask a question or series of questions directed toward establishing your thesis.
- Offer several relevant examples to support your thesis.

- Begin with a vivid description that supports your main idea.
- Cite a statistic or provide data.
- Correct a false assumption.

All these strategies should introduce your topic and state the thesis of the essay. They should be relatively brief and should direct the reader into the body of the essay. Finally, they should reveal your perspective and your tone or voice. In each introductory paragraph, the reader—your audience—should sense that you are prepared to address your topic in an honest and revealing manner.

Writing Body Paragraphs   The body is the middle of the essay. Usually the body consists of a series of paragraphs whose purpose is to satisfy your readers' expectations about the topic and thesis you presented in the introduction. The body of an essay gives substance, stability, and balance to your thesis. It offers facts, details, explanations, and claims supporting your main idea.

Body paragraphs reflect your ability to think critically, logically, and carefully about your topic. They are self-conscious units of expression whose indentations signal a new main point (or topic sentence) or unified and coherent unit of thought. The contour created by the series of body paragraphs that you design grows organically from the rhetorical or composing strategies that you select. As the English critic Herbert Read states in *English Prose Style*, "As thought takes shape in the mind, it takes *a* shape. . . . There is about good writing a visual actuality. It exactly reproduces what we should metaphorically call the contour of our thought. . . . The paragraph is the perception of this contour or shape." In other words, we see in the shape of an essay the shape of our thoughts. The contour created by the series of body paragraphs proceeds naturally from the material you include and the main point that you use to frame this material in each paragraph.

Effective paragraph development depends on your ability to create a unit of thought that is *unified* and *coherent,* and that presents ideas that flesh out the topic sentence or controlling idea for the paragraph, thereby informing or convincing the reader. To achieve a sense of completeness as you develop body paragraphs, be sure to have enough topic sentences and sufficient examples or evidence for each key idea. College writers often have problems writing complete essays with adequately developed body paragraphs. Remember that topic sentences are relatively general ideas. Your primary task is to make readers understand what those ideas mean or why they are important. Your secondary task is to keep readers interested in those central thoughts. The only way to accomplish these two related goals is by explaining the central ideas through various kinds of evidence or support.

Strategies for Development   Different topics and paragraphs lend themselves to different types of development. These types of rhetorical approaches are essentially special writing and reasoning strategies designed to support your critical evaluation of a topic or hypothesis. Among the major rhetorical approaches are description, narration, illustration, process analysis, comparison and contrast, causal analysis, definition, classification, and argumentation. Each strategy might very well serve as your dominant approach to a topic. On the other hand, your essay might reflect a variety of methods. Remember, however, that any blending of rhetorical strategies should not be a random sampling of approaches but should all contribute to your overall point.

Description   Good descriptive writing is often your best tool for explaining your observations about objects, people, scenes, and events. Simply, description is the creation of a picture using words. It is the translation of what the writer sees into what the writer wants the reader to imagine. Description has many applications in academic courses. For example, for a psychology course, you might need to describe the behavior of an autistic child. At an archeological dig or site, you might need to indicate accurately how a section of the excavated area looks. In a botany course, you might need to describe in detail a particular plant.

Effective description depends on several characteristics:

- It conveys ideas through images that appeal to our various senses: sight, hearing, touch, smell, and taste.
- It selects and organizes details carefully in a clearly identifiable spatial ordering—left to right, top to bottom, near to far, and so forth.
- It creates a dominant impression, a special mood or feeling.
- It is objective or subjective depending on the writer's purpose, the demands of an assignment, or the expectations of an audience.

In the following paragraph from her book *Spanish Harlem*, Patricia Cayo Sexton captures the sights, sounds, and rhythms of life in New York's East Harlem:

> Later, when the children return from school, the sidewalks and streets will jump with activity. Clusters of men, sitting on orange crates on the sidewalks, will play checkers or cards. The women will sit on the stoop, arms folded, and watch the young at play; and the young men, flexing their muscles, will look for some adventure. Vendors, ringing their bells, will hawk hot dogs, orange drinks, ice cream; and the caressing but often jarring noise of honking horns, music, children's games, and casual quarrels, whistles, singing, will go on late into the night. When you are in it you don't notice the noise, but when you stand away and listen to a taped conversation, the sound suddenly appears as a background roar. This loud stimulation of the senses may produce some of the emotionalism of the poor.

Narration   Telling stories—or narration—is a basic pattern of organizing your thoughts. You employ narration on a daily basis—to tell what happened at work, in the cafeteria, or on Saturday night. Narration is also essential to many forms of academic writing ranging from history, to sociology, to science. When planning and writing narration, keep in mind the following guidelines:

- Present the events of your narration in a logical and coherent order. Make certain that you link events through the use of appropriate transitional words.

- Select the narrative details carefully in order to suit the purpose of the essay. Narrate only those aspects of the event that serve to illustrate and support your thesis.
- Choose a point of view and perspective suitable for your topic and audience. Narrative point of view may be either first or third person. A first-person narrative is suitable for stories about yourself. A third-person narrative (*he, she, it, they*) conveys stories about others. The narrative perspective you use depends on your audience and purpose. Obviously, you would use a different perspective and tone in narrating a laboratory experiment than you would narrating a soccer match you participated in.
- Dialogue, if appropriate to your topic, may add realism and interest to your narrative.
- Limit the scope of the event you are narrating and bring it to a suitable conclusion or climax.

When narration is used for informational or expository purposes, the story makes a point, illustrates a principle, or explains something. In other words, in expository narration, the event tends to serve as evidence in support of your thesis.

Here is a sample student paragraph based on narration:

Like most little girls I thought it would be very grown up to get my hair done in a beauty parlor instead of by my mother or older sister. For more than a month I cried and badgered my family. Finally, after hearing enough of my whining, my mother gave in and made an appointment for me. At the beauty parlor, I sat with my mother and a few older women, naively waiting for my transformation into another Shirley Temple. Finally the hairdresser placed me in a chair and began to chop a mass of hair onto the floor and then subject me to a burning sensation as rollers wound my remaining hair tight. The result was a classic example of the overworked permanent. At home later that day, I tried washing and rewashing my hair to remove the tangled mess. It took a week until I would see anyone without a scarf or hat over my head and a month before I could look at someone without feeling that they were making fun of me the minute I turned my back. In a way I feel that such a fruitless journey to the hairdresser actually helped me along the road to adulthood since it was a perfect example of a disappointment that only time and patience, rather than tantrums and senseless worrying, can overcome.

Narration answers the question, What happened? It can be used to tell real or fictional stories, to relate historical events, to present personal experience, to support an analysis of events. It has broad utility in college as a critical writing skill.

Ilustration To make your paragraph or essay complete—without padding, repetition, or digression—be sure to have sufficient examples or illustrations to support key ideas. Different topics and paragraphs lend themselves to different types of examples or supporting evidence. Here are some types of illustration that will help you write well-developed paragraphs and essays:

Fact: The Supreme Court Ordered the Desegregation of Public Schools in 1964.

Statistic: A majority of schools in San Diego that were once 90 percent black are now almost 45 percent white.

Example: One example of the success of San Diego's integration effort is its magnet schools.

Personal Experience: I attended the new computer science magnet school from 1996 to 1998. . . .

Quotation: According to the *Phi Delta Kappan,* "On the first day of Los Angeles' mandatory desegregation program, 17,700 out of the total of 40,000 were not on the bus."

Process: With the magnet concept, a school first creates a special theme and emphasis for its curriculum. Then, it . . .

Comparison and Contrast: By contrast, when Los Angeles announced its forced busing plan, an estimated 15.1 percent of the white population moved out of the system into private schools.

Case Study: Jamie, an eighth-grader, had seen very few black students at the Math-Science Center prior to the implementation of San Diego's desegregation plan . . .

Illustrations develop your paragraph beyond the topic sentence. Such illustrations or examples may be short or extended. However, to make sure that your paragraphs are complete and properly developed, watch out for weak or poorly presented illustrations. For every main idea or topic sentence in a paragraph, use specific supporting evidence that sufficiently proves or amplifies your point. If you do not have the right evidence in the proper amount, your paragraph and essay will be underdeveloped, as in the following case:

> The concept of choice does seem to appeal to students. On the first day of San Diego's new plan, the only people who were absent from the programs who had volunteered were those who were sick.

This two-sentence paragraph has promise but does not follow through with the main idea adequately. The concept at the heart of the topic sentence is clearer and more complete in the revised version:

> The concept of choice does seem to appeal to San Diego's parents and students. On the first day of San Diego's new plan, the only people who were absent from the program who had volunteered were those who were sick. In contrast, on the first day of Los Angeles's mandatory desegregation program, 17,700 out of the total of 40,000 were not on the bus, according to the *Phi Delta Kappan*. Moreover, when Los Angeles announced its busing plan, an estimated 15.1 percent of the white population moved out of the district or into a private school. In San Diego, there was virtually no "white flight."

In the revision, the student chose to use contrasting evidence, highly specific in nature, to provide adequate support for the topic sentence. Other details and illustrative strategies might have been selected. In selecting illustrative material, you should always ask: Are there other examples that are more lively, specific, concrete, revealing, or interesting? It is not enough to just present examples. Illustration should be as effective as possible.

Process Analysis   When you describe how something works, how something is assembled, how something is done, or how something happens, you are explaining or analyzing a process. The complexity of your explanation will depend on how complex the process itself is, how detailed you want your explanation to be, and what you want your audience to be able to do or understand as a result of reading your explanation. Are you providing relatively simple how-to-do-it instructions for a relatively simple task, or are you attempting to explain a complicated laboratory experiment or computer program? The explanation of a process can make demands on your analytical and problem-solving abilities because you have to break down operations into component parts and actions. Process analysis always involves the systematic presentation of step-by-step or stage-by-stage procedures. You must show *how* the steps or parts in a process lead to its completion or resolution.

The explanation of processes is relevant to many college courses. Such topics as the stages of economic growth, Hobbes's view of the evolution of the state, the origins of the city, the development of the English lyric, the phenomenon of photosynthesis, and the history of abstract art could benefit from process analysis. Often process analysis can be combined with other writing strategies or even be subordinated to a more dominant writing strategy like narration, to which it bears a certain resemblance.

As with all other forms of mature and effective writing, you must assess your audience when writing process papers. You must decide whether you primarily want to inform or to give directions. When you give directions, you normally can assume that your audience wants to learn to do what you tell them about. If your primary purpose is to inform, you must assess the degree of interest of general readers and approach your subject from an objective perspective. Remember that there are natural, physical, mechanical, technical, mental, and historical types of processes. Certain topics might cut across these types, yet in each instance, your purpose is to direct the reader in how to do something or to inform the reader about the nature of the process.

Your analysis of a process can occur at paragraph level or it can control the development of an entire essay. Note how Laurence J. Peter, author of the famous book *The Peter Prescription,* uses process to structure the following paragraph:

> If you are inexperienced in relaxation techniques, begin by sitting in a comfortable chair with your feet on the floor and your hands resting easily in your lap. Close your eyes and breathe evenly, deeply, and gently. As you exhale each breath let your body become more relaxed. Starting with one hand direct your

attention to one part of your body at a time. Close your fist and tighten the muscles of your forearm. Feel the sensation of tension in your muscles. Relax your hand and let your forearm and hand become completely limp. Direct all your attention to the sensation of relaxation as you continue to let all tension leave your hand and arm. Continue this practice once or several times each day, relaxing your other hand and arm, your legs, back, abdomen, chest, neck, face, and scalp. When you have this mastered and can relax completely; turn your thoughts to scenes of natural tranquility from your past. Stay with your inner self as long as you wish, whether thinking of nothing or visualizing only the loveliest of images. Often you will become completely unaware of your surroundings. When you open your eyes you will find yourself refreshed in mind and body.

Peter establishes his relationship and his purpose with his audience in the very first sentence, and then offers step-by-step procedures that move readers toward a full understanding of the process. Remember that you are the expert when writing about a process, and that you have to think carefully about the degree of knowledge that your audience shares.

To develop a process paper, follow these guidelines:

- Select an appropriate topic.
- Decide whether your primary purpose is to direct or explain.
- Determine the knowledge gap between you and your audience.
- Explain necessary equipment or define special terms.
- Organize paragraphs in a complete sequence of steps.
- Explain each step clearly and completely.
- State results or outcomes.

Numerous subjects lend themselves to process analysis. You must decide, especially for a particular course, which topic is most appropriate and which topic you know or want to learn about the most.

Comparison and Contrast   Comparison and contrast is an analytical method organizing thought to show similarities and differences between two persons, places, things, or ideas. Comparing and contrasting comes naturally to us. If, for example, you must decide on which candidate to vote for, you might compare the party affiliations, records, and positions on issues of both candidates to find the one that best meets your expectations. Comparison and contrast serves three useful purposes in writing:

1. to evaluate the relative worth or performance of two things by comparing them point-for-point;
2. to increase understanding of two familiar things by exploring them for significant similarities and differences;
3. to explain something unfamiliar by comparing it with something familiar.

The organization of comparison-and-contrast paragraphs and essays is fairly specialized and somewhat more prescribed than other methods of writing. The following are some basic guidelines for preparing comparison-and-contrast papers.

First and foremost, limit your comparison to only two subjects (from here on we'll refer to them as A and B). If you attempt to work with more, you may find your writing becomes confused. Subjects A and B should be from the same category of things. You would do better, for example, to compare two jazz pianists than to compare a jazz pianist and Dixieland jazz as a whole. Moreover, there needs to be a *purpose* for your comparison. Unless you explain your purpose, the comparison, which might otherwise be structurally sound, will ultimately seem meaningless.

The organization of comparison-and-contrast papers generally follows two basic patterns, or methods: the *block method* and the *alternating method.* The block method presents all material on subject A and then all material on subject B. With the block method, each subtopic must be the same for both subjects. The alternating method presents all the material on each subtopic together, analyzing these subtopics in an AB, AB, AB pattern. Although there is no hard-and-fast rule, the alternating method is probably the best choice for most essays in order to avoid the standard pitfalls of the block method. Unless you are an experienced writer, using the block method can lead to an insufficiently developed paper, with some subtopics receiving more attention than others. It can also lead to a paper that seems like two separate essays, with a big chunk about subject A followed by a second disconnected chunk about subject B. Whether you are using the block or alternating method, follow through in an orderly manner, stating clearly the main thesis or reason for establishing the comparison, and providing clear transitions as you move from idea to idea.

Consider the following paragraph, written by a student, John Shin:

> The story of Noah and the Great Flood is probably the best known story of a deluge in the Mesopotamian Valley. However, there are several other accounts of a large flood in the valley. Of these, the Akkadian story of Utnapishtim, as told by Gilgamesh, is the most interesting due to its similarities to the biblical story of Noah. Utnapishtim is a king who is forewarned of the coming of a great flood. He is advised to build an ark and does so. After many days the waters recede and Utnapishtim exits the ark and is turned into a god. The stories of Noah and Utnapishtim bear a striking resemblance in several parts: a god or gods cause a flood to punish men and women; arks, of certain dimensions, are built; animals are taken on board; birds are released to find land; and the arks come to rest on mountains. These parallels are so striking that many think the two to be the same tale.

Given the design of this paragraph, we can assume that the student could develop body paragraphs that deal in detail with each of the key resemblances in the order they are mentioned: the coming of the flood, the building of the ark, the animals taken on board, the release of the birds, and the lodging of both arks on the mountaintop. By employing the alternating method, the student constructs a well-organized comparative framework for his analysis of the story of Noah and the story of Gilgamesh.

Causal Analysis   Frequently in college writing you must explain the causes or effects of some event, situation, or phenomenon. This type of investigation is termed causal analysis. When you analyze something, you divide it into its logical parts or processes for the purpose of close examination. Thus phenomena as diverse as divorce in America, the Civil War, carcinogens in asbestos, the death of Martin Luther King, Jr., or the eruption of Mount St. Helens can be analyzed in terms of their causes and effects.

Cause-and-effect relationships are part of everyday thinking and living. Why did you select the college you now attend? Why did you stop dating Freddy or Barbara, and what effect has this decision had on your life? Why did the football team lose five straight games? You need causal analysis to explain why something occurred, to predict what will occur, and to make informed choices based on your perceptions. With causal analysis, you cannot simply tell a story, summarize an event, or describe an object or phenomenon. Instead, you must explain the *why* and *what* of a topic. The analysis of causes seeks to explain why a particular condition occurred. The analysis of effects seeks to explain what the consequences or results were, are, or will be.

Causal reasoning is common to writing in many disciplines: history, economics, politics, sociology, literature, science, education, and business, to list a few. Some essays and reports focus on causes, others on effects, still others on both causes and effects. Sometimes even the simplest sort of causal reasoning based on personal experience does not admit to the complete separation of causes and effects, but depends instead on recognition that causes and effects are interdependent. For example, the following paragraph from a student's sociology paper focuses on a cause-and-effect relationship:

> My parents came to New York with the dream of saving enough money to return to Puerto Rico and buy a home with some land and fruit trees. Many Puerto Ricans, troubled by the problem of life on the island, find no relief in migration to New York City. They remain poor, stay in the barrio, are unable to cope with American society and way of life, and experience the destruction of their traditionally close family life. My parents were fortunate. After spending most of their lives working hard, they saved enough to return to the island. Today they tend their orange, lemon, banana and plantain trees in an area of Puerto Rico called "El Paraiso." It took them most of a lifetime to find their paradise—in their own backyard.

Here the writer blends personal experience with a more objective analysis of causes and effects, presenting the main cause-effect relationship in the first sentence, analyzing typical effects, providing an exception to this conventional effect, and describing the result.

There are times when you will want to focus exclusively on causes or on effects. For example, in a history course the topic might be to analyze why World War II occurred.

> It is popularly accepted that Hitler was the major cause of World War II, but the ultimate causes go much deeper than one personality. There were longstanding German grievances against reparations levied on the nation following its defeat in World War I.

Moreover, there were severe economic strains that caused resentment among the German people. Compounding these problems was the French and English reluctance to work out a sound disarmament policy and American noninvolvement in the matter. Finally, there was the European fear that Communism was a much greater danger than National Socialism. All these factors contributed to the outbreak of World War II.

Note that in his attempt to explain fully the causes of an event, the writer goes beyond *immediate* causes, that is, the most evident causes that trigger the event being analyzed. He tries to identify the *ultimate* causes, the deep-rooted reasons that completely explain the problem. In order to present a sound analysis of a problem, you need to be able to trace events logically to their underlying origins. Similarly, you have to engage in strategic thinking about immediate and ultimate effects in order to explain fully an event's results.

Writing about cause-and-effect relationships demands sound critical thinking skills with attention to logic and thorough preparation for the demands of the assignment. To write effective and logical essays of causal analysis, follow these guidelines:

- Be honest, objective, and reasonable when establishing your thesis. As a critical thinker, you have to avoid prejudices and logical fallacies, including unsupportable claims, broad generalizations and overstatements, and false relationships. (For a discussion of logical fallacies, see page 80.)
- Distinguish between causes and effects, and decide whether you plan to focus on causes, effects, or both. As a prewriting strategy, draw up a list of causes and a corresponding list of effects. You can then organize your paper around the central causes and/or effects.
- Distinguish clearly between immediate and ultimate causes and effects. Explore those causes and effects that best serve the purpose of your paper and your audience's expectations.
- Provide evidence. Do not rely on simple assertions. Statistics and testimony from reliable authorities are especially effective types of evidence to support your analysis.
- Try to establish links between causes or effects. Seek a logical sequence of related elements, a chain of causality that helps readers understand the totality of your topic.

Ultimately there are many ways to write about causes and effects, depending on whether you are looking for explanations, reasons, consequences, connections, results, or any combination of these elements.

Definition   Concepts or general ideas often require careful *definition* if readers are to make sense of them or make intelligent decisions. Could you discuss supply and demand in economic theory without knowing the concept of the invisible hand? And isn't it best to know what a political conservative actually believes in before casting your vote? Concepts form the core of any discipline, line of inquiry, or problem. Because concepts are abstract, they may mean different things to different readers. In order to make ourselves understood, we must be able to specify their meaning in a particular context.

There are three types of definition. The simple *lexical* definition, or dictionary definition, is useful when briefly identifying concrete, commonplace, or uncontroversial terms for the reader. Many places, persons, and things can be defined in this manner. The *extended* definition is an explanation that might involve a paragraph or an entire essay. It is frequently used for abstract, complex, or controversial terms. The third form of definition is the *stipulative* definition, in which you offer a special definition of a term or set limitations on your use of the term. A solid definition, whether it is lexical, extended, or stipulative, involves describing the essential nature and characteristics of a concept that distinguish it from related ideas.

Consider the following paragraph by a student, Geeta Berrera:

> The degree of loneliness that we feel can range from the mild or temporary case to a severe state which may eventually lead to depression or other psychological disorders. Being able to recognize the signs and signals of loneliness may help you to avoid it in the future. Do you find yourself unable to communicate with others? If so, you might be lonely. Do you find it difficult to put your faith in other human beings? If so, then you are setting up a situation that may be conducive to loneliness because you are preventing yourself from becoming too close to another person. Do you find yourself spending great amounts of time alone on a regular basis? Do you find that you are never invited to parties or other social events? Are you unable to love or care for another human being because you are afraid of permanent responsibilities and commitments? These are all signs and signals of either loneliness or situations that may eventually lead to loneliness. Loneliness is the feeling of sadness or grief experienced by a person at the realization that he or she lacks the companionship of other people.

Notice how the student introduces and emphasizes the central concept—loneliness—that is defined in this paragraph. She adds to the definition through a series of questions and answers—a strategy that permits her to analyze the qualities or manifestations of the concept. These symptoms serve as examples that reveal what is distinctive or representative about the condition of loneliness.

Definition can be used for several purposes. It may explain a difficult concept like phenomenology or a little-known activity like cricket. Definition can be used to identify and illustrate the special nature of a person, object, or abstract idea.

Classification   Classification is a mode of critical thinking and writing based on the division of a concept into groups and subgroups, and the examination of important elements within these groups. We have generalized ideas of classes of objects that help us organize and thereby understand the world. Many of these concepts lend themselves to classification. You think and talk frequently about types of college teachers, types of cars, types of boyfriends or girlfriends, types of movies or music. When registering for courses, you know that English is in the humanities, psychology in the social sciences, geology in the physical sciences; you select these courses on the basis of consistent classification principles, perhaps distribution requirements or the demands of your major. What you are doing is thinking about concepts within a class, sorting out and organizing information, and often evaluating possible alternatives. Classification, in short, is a basic mode of critical thought.

As a pattern of writing, classification enables you to make sense of large and potentially complex concepts. You divide a concept into groups and subgroups, and you classify elements within categories. Assume, for instance, that your politics professor asks for an analysis of the branches of the American federal government. You divide the federal government into the executive, legislative, and judicial branches, and, depending on your purpose, you subdivide even further into departments, agencies, and so forth. Then, according to some consistent principle or thesis—let's say a critical look at the erosion of the division of powers—you develop information for each category reflecting common characteristics. Essentially, if you classify in a rigorous and logical way, you sort out for analysis the parts and ideas within a scheme, progressing from general to specific in your treatment of the topic.

In developing a classification essay, you also have to determine the *system* of classification that works best for the demands of the assignment. The system you select would depend to an extent on your reader's expectations and the nature of the subject. Imagine that you have been asked to write an essay on sports by a physiology teacher, a psychology teacher, or a sociology teacher. Your system might be types of sports injuries for the physiology professor, behavior patterns of tennis players for your psychology professor, or levels of violence and aggression in team sports for your sociology professor. For a broad concept like sports, there are many possible classificatory systems depending on the purpose of your paper.

Although several classification and division strategies might be appropriate for any given concept, the following guidelines should be reviewed and applied for any classification essay:

- Think about the controlling principle for your classification. *Why* are you classifying the concept? *What* is the significance? Create a thesis statement that gives your reader a clear perspective on your classification scheme.
- Divide the subject into major categories and subdivide categories consistently. Make certain that you isolate all important categories and that these categories do not overlap excessively.
- Arrange the classification scheme in an effective, emphatic order—chronological, spatial, in order of importance, or from simple to complex.
- Present and analyze each category in a clear sequence, proceeding through the categories until the classification scheme is complete.
- Define or explain any difficult concepts within each category, providing relevant details and evidence.
- Combine classification with other appropriate writing strategies—comparison and contrast, process analysis, definition, and so forth.

Examine the following student paragraph:

To many people, fishing is finding a "fishy-looking" spot, tossing a hooked worm into the water, and hoping that a hungry fish just happens to be nearby. Anyone who has used this haphazard method can attest to the fact that failures usually outnumber successes. The problem with the "bait and wait" method is that it is very limited. The bait has less chance of encountering a fish than it would if it were presented in different areas of water. A more intelligent approach to fishing is to use the knowledge that at any given moment fish can be in three parts of a lake. Assuming that a lake has fish, anglers will find them on the surface, in the middle, or on the bottom of the lake. Fishing each of these areas involves the use of a separate technique. By fishing the surface, fishing the middle, or fishing the bottom, you greatly increase the chances of catching a fish.

This example is the student's introductory paragraph to a classification essay that blends description, process analysis, comparison and contrast, and the use of evidence to excellent effect. From the outset, however, the reader knows that this will be a classification essay.

Argumentation   Argumentation is a form of critical thinking in which you try to convince an audience to accept your position on a topic and/or persuade members of this audience to act in a certain way. In a sense, everything is an argument, for much of what you read and write, see and hear, is designed to elicit a desired response. Whether reading texts, viewing various media forms, or listening to the spoken word (especially of politicians), you know that just about anything is potentially debatable.

Argumentation in writing, however, goes beyond ordinary disagreements. With an argumentative essay, your purpose is to convince or persuade readers in a logical, reasonable, and appealing way. In other words, with formal argumentation you must distinguish mere personal opinion from opinions based on reasons derived from solid evidence. An argumentative essay has special features and even step-by-step processes that will be treated in greater detail in the next chapter. For now, it is worth noting that solid argumentative writing can combine many of the forms and purposes that have been discussed in this chapter. Your understanding of such forms and purposes of discourse as narration, illustration, analysis, and comparison and contrast and the ways these strategies can combine in powerful ways will help you compose solid argumentative essays.

Above all, with argumentation you must develop what Virginia Woolf called "some fierce attachment to an idea." Once you commit yourself to a viewpoint on a topic or issue, you will find it easy to bring an argumentative edge to your writing. Consider the following excerpt from a well-known essay by Caroline Bird that begins with the provocative title "College Is a Waste of Time and Money":

A great majority of our 9 million college students are in school not because they want to be or because they want to learn. They are there because it has become the thing to do or because college is a pleasant place to be; because it's the only way they can get parents or taxpayers to support them without working at a job they don't like; because Mother wanted them to go, or some other reason entirely irrelevant to the course of studies for which college is supposedly organized.

Clearly Bird's claim has that argumentative edge you encounter in essays designed to convince readers of a particular viewpoint or position on an issue. Do you agree or disagree with Bird's claim? How would you respond to her assertions? What evidence would you provide to support your own claim? In the next chapter, you will learn more about argumentation and the well-established practices involved in writing effective and potentially powerful appeals to reason, emotion, and ethics.

Writing End Paragraphs   If an essay does not have a strong, appropriate ending, it may leave the reader feeling confused or dissatisfied, a sense that the intention and promises built up in earlier parts of the essay have not been fulfilled. By contrast, an effective closing paragraph leaves the reader with the impression that the essay is complete and satisfying.

The techniques that follow permit you to end your essay emphatically and with grace:

- Use a full-circle pattern. Echo or repeat an opening phrase, idea, or detail that you presented in your introductory paragraph.
- State your conclusions, proofs, or theories based on the facts and supporting ideas of the essay. This strategy works especially well in papers for social science, science, and philosophy courses.
- Show the outcome or effects of the facts and ideas of the essay.
- Suggest a solution as a way to clarify your position on the problem you have discussed.
- Ask a question that sums up the main point of the essay.
- Offer an anecdote, allusion, or lighthearted point that sums up your thesis.
- Use a quotation that supports your main point or illuminates an aspect of the topic.

Other basic ways to end an essay include restating your thesis and main points, calling for action, providing a final summary evaluation, or looking at future consequences based on the essay's analysis or argument. A closing, like your introduction, should be brief. It is your one last attempt at clarity, one last chance to illuminate your topic.

Student Essay   Here is the essay that Taylor wrote in response to Schlesinger's "The Cult of Ethnicity." Consider the strategies that she used to make her composing process a success.

Jamie Taylor
Humanities 101, sec. 008
Professor Fred Segal
4 November 2001

Cultist Behavior or Doltish Behavior?

Introductory
paragraph presents
Schlesinger's main
argument, amplifies
Schlesinger's inferred
claims, and then
presents the writer's
counterargument.

In Schlesinger's "The Cult of Ethnicity," the author warns that there are forces at work within our nation that undermine our principles of democracy. These forces come in the guise of individuals and groups who claim that they know what's right for the people whom they represent. Although he doesn't mention them all specifically, one can infer he means that certain leaders from the African-American community, the Latino community, the Native American community, the Asian community, and so forth are advocating strong identification within groups to keep their identities alive since they claim Euro-centric culture has had a history of stealing and suppressing their own historic roots. But Schlesinger seems to fear that only divisiveness can result. In this regard, he does not give the individual enough credit. Rather than have a paternalistic attitude about what he fears these groups are doing, he should give more credit to the members of these groups to be able to discern which messages regarding ethnicity to accept as being benign and which to reject as being downright silly.

The first body
paragraph presents
Taylor's first point
supported with
evidence and
examples.

Take for example, the many clubs in the average college or university. Nearly every ethnic group is represented by one of these organizations. For example, my university has many groups that represent African-Americans, Latinos, Asians, Native Americans, even subgroups like the Korean Society, the Chinese Student Association, and so on. Belonging to these groups gives students a healthy place to socialize, discuss common areas of interest and concern, and assist with community outreach. For example, many of these clubs sponsor programs to give demonstrations of cultural traditions such as cooking, dance, clothing, and so on to civic and business groups. They also assist the needy in gaining access to social services, particularly for shut-ins and the elderly who may not speak English. Also, there is strength in numbers, and the fact that these clubs are popular attests to the fact that they tolerate a range of ideas so that no one "ideology" is promoted over another. Besides, if that were to happen, it is the right of the organization to vote a person out of office or membership. To say that these clubs promote divisiveness would be like saying that the Newman Society for Catholic students or Hillel House for Jewish students promotes religious intolerance.

The second point offers
a unique slant on
divisive ethnic and
racial leaders and the
ability of Americans
to reject their claims.
Again, specific
examples and evidence
buttress Taylor's
argument.

Second, self-styled leaders of various racial and ethnic groups—in their efforts to be divisive—actually help people to see through their rhetoric, or at least, to apply only that which is reasonable and reject that which is intolerable. Because of today's media, such leaders cannot "hide" their views and thus can become their own worst enemies when presenting them in front of a national audience. For example, Louis Farrakhan has not only alienated Jewish individuals owing to his open anti-Semitism, and many among the gay population for his anti-gay sentiments, but many African Americans as well, particularly women, who often condemn him for his patriarchal views regarding the family and society. A simple proof of his lack of power is the fact that he has been presenting these anti-democratic ideals for decades now, and there is little evidence that anyone is listening to them. Another example is the late Rabbi Meyer Kahane, who advocated the expulsion of all Arabs from Israel. An open opponent of democracy, he was condemned by Jewish leaders in the United States to the point where he was shunned from any discussion regarding religious issues.

Finally, one can feel confident that even within the margins of mainstream white America, cultist groups are their own worst enemy. Take for example, the various groups of survivalists (primarily white Americans), white extremists and separatists, anti-gay groups, and radical anti-abortionists. The philosophy and tactics of these organizations are condemned by the vast majority of Americans owing to their anti-democratic postures, not to mention their often violent, even murderous activities. They may capture the headlines for a while, but they will never capture the hearts of Americans so long as we stay true to the "measures and laws" that Washington spoke of in his discussion with John Adams.

The writer's third and final point encompasses a variety of "anti-democratic" groups and rejects their "postures."

In conclusion, the open democratic society we have created is just too strong a force to be weakened or undermined by "romantic ideologies" or "unscrupulous con men" as Schlesinger puts it. Mr. Schlesinger has little to worry about. Just look around your school or university cafeteria. There's no white section or Latino section or Asian section: Nowadays, it's just one big American section.

The conclusion returns to Schlesinger, while recapitulating Taylor's main points.

Revising

Revising—the rethinking and rewriting of material—takes place during every stage of the composing process. It is integral to the quest for clarity and meaning. "Writing and rewriting are a constant search for what one's saying," declares celebrated American author John Updike. Similarly, the famous essayist E. B. White admits, "I rework a lot to make it clear." If these two great prose stylists revise material in order to seek clarity for their ideas, then you also should adopt the professional attitude that you can improve what you first say or think and what you first put down on paper. In fact, one trait that distinguishes experienced from inexperienced writers is that the professional writers understand fully the need to revise.

Revision is an art. It is the only way to make your writing match the vision of what you want to accomplish. Whether at word, sentence, paragraph, or essay level, you should develop a repertoire of choices that will permit you to solve writing problems and sharpen your ideas. You might also choose to share your draft with another reader who can let you know what is or is not working and give you suggestions for improvement. To make the process of revision worthwhile, you should ask yourself the following questions during your prewriting and drafting activities (you can also give these questions to your reader):

- Is my essay long enough (or too long) to meet the demands of the assignment?
- Is my topic suitable for the assignment?
- Do I have a clear thesis statement?
- Does my writing make sense? Am I communicating with my reader instead of just with myself?.
- Have I included everything that is important to the development of my thesis or argument?
- Is there anything I should discard?
- Do I offer enough examples or evidence to support my key ideas?
- Have I ordered and developed paragraphs logically?
- Do I have a clear beginning, middle, and end?

Once you have answered these questions, you will be able to judge the extent to which you have to revise your first draft.

Proofreading   Proofreading is part of the revision process. You do not have final copy until you have carefully checked your essay for mistakes and inconsistencies. It differs from the sort of revision that moves you from an initial draft to subsequent versions of an essay in that it does not offer the opportunity to make major changes in content or organization. It does give you a last chance to correct minor errors that arise from carelessness, haste, or inaccuracy during writing, typing, or word processing.

When you proofread, do so word by word and line by line. Concentrate on spelling, punctuation, grammar, mechanics, and manuscript form. Read each sentence aloud—from the computer screen or your hard copy. If something sounds or looks wrong to you, consult a handbook, dictionary, or other reference. Then make corrections accordingly.

Here are some basic guidelines for proofreading your essay:

1. Check the title. Are words capitalized properly?
2. Check all words in the essay that should be capitalized.
3. Check the spelling of any word you are uncertain about.
4. Check the meaning of any word you think you might have misused.
5. Check to see if you have unintentionally omitted or repeated any words.
6. Check paragraph form. Have you indented each paragraph?

7. Check to make certain you have smooth, grammatically correct sentences. This is your last chance to eliminate awkward and grammatically incorrect sentences.

Responding to Editorial Comments   Even when you submit what you *think* is the final version of your essay, your teacher might not think that the essay has reached its best possible form. Teachers are experienced in detecting essays' strengths and weaknesses, pinpointing mistakes, and suggesting how material can be improved. Their comments are not attacks; they do want you to pay attention to them, to recognize and correct errors, and possibly to revise your essay once again—most likely for a higher grade. If you receive editorial comment in an objective manner and respond to it constructively, you will become a more accurate and effective writer.

When reading your essays, your instructor will use standard correction symbols that appear in English handbooks. He or she will make additional comments in the margins and compose an overall assessment of the paper at the end. Any worthwhile comment on your paper will blend supportive observations with constructive criticism. Often your instructor will offer concrete suggestions for revision. When you receive a graded paper, you typically are expected to make the necessary revisions and either add it to your portfolio or resubmit the essay.

Ultimately, refinement is integral to the entire writing process. From reading materials that you confront at the outset and respond to in various ways, you move through many composing stages to create a finished product. In *The Field of Vision,* the American novelist and critic Wright Morris refers to the important task of refinement that confronts the writer: "By raw material, I mean that comparatively crude ore that has not yet been processed by the imagination—what we refer to as *life,* or as experience, in contrast to art. By technique I mean the way the artist smelts this material down for human consumption." Your best writing is the result of this smelting process, which involves the many strategies covered in this introduction that are designed to help you acquire greater control over the art of critical reading and writing. Donald M. Murray's essay "The Maker's Eye: Revising Your Own Manuscripts," on page 56, offers one writer's summation of the stages of the revision process.

Readings for Critical Response and Writing

How to Mark a Book

Mortimer J. Adler

Mortimer Jerome Adler (1902–2001) was born in New York City and received his PhD from Columbia University in 1928. A staunch advocate for classical philosophy, Adler believed that there are unshakable truths—an idea rejected by most contemporary philosophers. For this reason, Adler has not been taken seriously by the academic establishment. He was a champion of knowledge, believing that philosophy should be a part of everyone's life and that access to the great ideas in philosophy can be of value to everyone. Many of his over 75 books attempt to edify the general reader by explaining basic philosophical concepts in everyday language. He was also chairman of the editorial board of the Encyclopedia Britannica. *To make knowledge more accessible to everyone, he also assumed editorship of the Encyclopedia Britannica's Great Books project, partly sponsored by the University of Chicago. This project, which has put 443 of the world's "classics" into a 54-volume set, graces the bookcases of many dens and studies in middle-class American homes. Despite his advancing years, Adler continued to work on many projects to promote his goal of universal education and enlightenment. "How to Mark a Book" is typical of his didactic, pragmatic approach to education.*

You know you have to read "between the lines" to get the most out of anything. 1
I want to persuade you to do something equally important in the course of your reading. I want to persuade you to "write between the lines." Unless you do, you are not likely to do the most efficient kind of reading.

I contend, quite bluntly, that marking up a book is not an act of mutilation 2
but of love.

You shouldn't mark up a book which isn't yours. Librarians (or your 3
friends) who lend you books expect you to keep them clean, and you should. If you decide that I am right about the usefulness of marking books, you will have to buy them. Most of the world's great books are available today, in reprint editions, at less than a dollar.

There are two ways in which one can own a book. The first is the property 4
right you establish by paying for it, just as you pay for clothes and furniture. But this act of purchase is only the prelude to possession. Full ownership comes only when you have made it a part of yourself, and the best way to make yourself a part of it is by writing in it. An illustration may make the point clear. You

buy a beefsteak and transfer it from the butcher's ice-box to your own. But you do not own the beefsteak in the most important sense until you consume it and get it into your bloodstream. I am arguing that books, too, must be absorbed in your bloodstream to do you any good.

Confusion about what it means to own a book leads people to a false rever- 5 ence for paper, binding, and type—a respect for the physical thing—the craft of the printer rather than the genius of the author. They forget that it is possible for a man to acquire the idea, to possess the beauty, which a great book contains, without staking his claim by pasting his bookplate inside the cover. Having a fine library doesn't prove that its owner has a mind enriched by books; it proves nothing more than that he, his father, or his wife, was rich enough to buy them.

There are three kinds of book owners. The first has all the standard sets and 6 best-sellers—unread, untouched. (This deluded individual owns woodpulp and ink, not books.) The second has a great many books—a few of them read through, most of them dipped into, but all of them as clean and shiny as the day they were bought. (This person would probably like to make books his own, but is restrained by a false respect for their physical appearance.) The third has a few books or many—every one of them dog-eared and dilapidated, shaken and loosened by continual use, marked and scribbled in from front to back. (This man owns books.)

Is it false respect, you may ask, to preserve intact and unblemished a beau- 7 tifully printed book, an elegantly bound edition? Of course not. I'd no more scribble all over the first edition of *Paradise Lost* than I'd give my baby a set of crayons and an original Rembrandt! I wouldn't mark up a painting or a statue. Its soul, so to speak, is inseparable from its body. And the beauty of a rare edition or of a richly manufactured volume is like that of a painting or a statue.

But the soul of a book *can* be separated from its body. A book is more like 8 the score of a piece of music than it is like a painting. No great musician confuses a symphony with the printed sheets of music. Arturo Toscanini reveres Brahms, but Toscanini's score of the C-minor Symphony is so thoroughly marked up that no one but the maestro himself can read it. The reason why a great conductor makes notations on his musical scores—marks them up again and again each time he returns to study them—is the reason why you should mark up your books. If your respect for magnificent binding or typography gets in the way, buy yourself a cheap edition and pay your respects to the author.

Why is marking up a book indispensable to reading it? First, it keeps you 9 awake. (And I don't mean merely conscious; I mean wide awake.) In the second place, reading, if it is active, is thinking, and thinking tends to express itself in words, spoken or written. The marked book is usually the thought-through book. Finally, writing helps you remember the thoughts you had, or the thoughts the author expressed. Let me develop these three points.

If reading is to accomplish anything more than passing time, it must be ac- 10 tive. You can't let your eyes glide across the lines of a book and come up with an understanding of what you have read. Now an ordinary piece of light fiction, like say, *Gone with the Wind*, doesn't require the most active kind of reading. The books you read for pleasure can be read in a state of relaxation, and nothing is lost. But a great book, rich in ideas and beauty, a book that raises and tries to answer great fundamental questions, demands the most active reading of which you are capable. You don't absorb the ideas of John Dewey the way you absorb the crooning of Mr. Vallee. You have to reach for them. That you cannot do while you're asleep.

If, when you've finished reading a book, the pages are filled with your 11 notes, you know that you read actively. The most famous *active* reader of great books I know is President Hutchins, of the University of Chicago. He also has the hardest schedule of business activities of any man I know. He invariably reads with a pencil, and sometimes, when he picks up a book and pencil in the evening, he finds himself, instead of making intelligent notes, drawing what he calls "caviar factories" on the margins. When that happens, he puts the book down. He knows he's too tired to read, and he's just wasting time.

But, you may ask, why is writing necessary? Well, the physical act of writ- 12 ing, with your own hand, brings words and sentences more sharply before your mind and preserves them better in your memory. To set down your reaction to important words and sentences you have read, and the questions they have raised in your mind, is to preserve those reactions and sharpen those questions.

Even if you wrote on a scratch pad, and threw the paper away when you 13 had finished writing, your grasp of the book would be surer. But you don't have to throw the paper away. The margins (top and bottom, as well as side), the end-papers, the very space between the lines, are all available. They aren't sacred. And, best of all, your marks and notes become an integral part of the book and stay there forever. You can pick up the book the following week or year, and there are all your points of agreement, disagreement, doubt, and inquiry. It's like resuming an interrupted conversation with the advantage of being able to pick up where you left off.

And that is exactly what reading a book should be: a conversation between 14 you and the author. Presumably he knows more about the subject than you do; naturally, you'll have the proper humility as you approach him. But don't let anybody tell you that a reader is supposed to be solely on the receiving end. Understanding is a two-way operation; learning doesn't consist in being an empty receptacle. The learner has to question himself and question the teacher. He even has to argue with the teacher, once he understands what the teacher is saying. And marking a book is literally an expression of your differences, or agreements of opinion, with the author.

There are all kinds of devices for marking a book intelligently and fruitfully. 15 Here's the way I do it:

1. Underlining: Of major points, of important or forceful statements.   16
2. Vertical lines at the margin: To emphasize a statement already underlined.   17
3. Star, asterisk, or other doo-dad at the margin: To be used sparingly, to em- 18 phasize the ten or twenty most important statements in the book. (You may want to fold the bottom corner of each page on which you use such marks.

It wont hurt the sturdy paper on which most modern books are printed, and you will be able to take the book off the shelf at any time and, by opening it at the folded-corner page, refresh your recollection of the book.)

4. Numbers in the margin: To indicate the sequence of points the author makes in developing a single argument.   19

5. Numbers of other pages in the margin: To indicate where else in the book the author made points relevant to the point marked; to tie up the ideas in a book, which, though they may be separated by many pages, belong together.   20

6. Circling of key words or phrases.   21

7. Writing in the margin, or at the top or bottom of the page, for the sake of: Recording questions (and perhaps answers) which a passage raised in your mind; reducing a complicated discussion to a simple statement; recording the sequence of major points right through the book. I use the end-papers at the back of the book to make a personal index of the author's points in the order of their appearance.   22

The front end-papers are, to me, the most important. Some people reserve them for a fancy bookplate. I reserve them for fancy thinking. After I have finished reading the book and making my personal index on the back endpapers, I turn to the front and try to outline the book, not page by page, or point by point (I've already done that at the back), but as an integrated structure, with a basic unity and an order of parts. This outline is, to me, the measure of my understanding of the work.   23

If you're a die-hard and anti-book-marker, you may object that the margins, the space between the lines, and the end-papers don't give you room enough. All right. How about using a scratch pad slightly smaller than the page-size of the book—so that the edges of the sheets won't protrude? Make your index, outlines, and even your notes on the pad, and then insert these sheets permanently inside the front and back covers of the book.   24

Or, you may say that this business of marking books is going to slow up your reading. It probably will. That's one of the reasons for doing it. Most of us have been taken in by the notion that speed of reading is a measure of our intelligence. There is no such thing as the right speed for intelligent reading. Some things should be read quickly and effortlessly, and some should be read slowly and even laboriously. The sign of intelligence in reading is the ability to read different things differently according to their worth. In the case of good books, the point is not to see how many of them you can get through, but rather how many can get through you—how many you can make your own. A few friends are better than a thousand acquaintances. If this be your aim, as it should be, you will not be impatient if it takes more time and effort to read a great book than it does a newspaper.   25

You may have one final objection to marking books. You can't lend them to your friends because nobody else can read them without being distracted by your notes. Furthermore, you won't want to lend them because a marked copy   26 is a kind of intellectual diary, and lending it is almost like giving your mind away.

If your friend wishes to read your *Plutarch's Lives,* "Shakespeare," or *The* 27 *Federalist Papers,* tell him gently but firmly, to buy a copy. You will lend him your car or your coat—but your books are as much a part of you as your head or your heart.

COMPREHENSION

1. Summarize what Adler means by "marking up a book."
2. In your own words, explain how you believe Adler would define the word *book.*
3. Adler mentions books throughout the essay. What particular type of book is he referring to?

RHETORIC

1. What is the tone of the essay? What can you infer from this tone about Adler's emotional relationship to books?
2. Paragraphs 16 through 22 list devices for marking a book. What is the function of enumerating them in this way? How would the tone of this section have been altered if he had summarized these devices in paragraph form?
3. The author makes reference to various intellectual and artistic figures and works in the essay. How does this help determine for whom the essay has been targeted?
4. Study the relationship between paragraph 9 and paragraphs 10, 11, and 12. What is the rhetorical format of this section? What is the method of argumentation he is employing?
5. Adler uses the analogy that "reading a book should be: a conversation between you and the author." What other analogies can you find in the essay?
6. Adler raises objections to his argument and then refutes the objections. Where does he make use of this rhetorical device? How effective is it in advancing his argument?
7. Adler calls *Gone with the Wind* "light fiction." Is this opinion or fact? Is it a mere observation or a criticism of the book?

WRITING

1. Mark up Adler's essay in the same manner he recommends that you mark up any good piece of writing. Then write an essay using process analysis to summarize the various methods you used.
2. Argue for or against the proposition that this essay has lost its relevance owing to the introduction of new forms of educational media.

3. Compare and contrast two books: one that Adler would regard as "light reading" and one that he would regard as worthy of marking up. Indicate the primary differences between these books in terms of their diction, level of discourse, insight, purpose, and scholarship.

The Cult of Ethnicity

Arthur M. Schlesinger Jr.

Arthur Meien Schlesinger Jr. (b. 1917 in Columbus, Ohio) received his AB degree from Harvard University in 1938. Schlesinger has combined careers as a writer, college professor, political activist, and President Kennedy's special assistant for Latin American affairs. Schlesinger is perhaps most responsible for the intellectual position of what is today generally known as liberalism. *He has written more than a dozen books on history and politics, among the most famous being* The Age of Jackson, *for which he won the 1946 Pulitzer Prize for history;* Robert Kennedy and His Times *(1978); and* A Thousand Days, *for which he won the 1966 Pulitzer Prize for biography. He has also edited many books on the American political process. While never earning an advanced degree as a student, he has been awarded numerous honorary degrees from universities in the United States and England. Critic Alan Brinkley wrote of Schlesinger in the* New Republic, *"He is a reminder to professional historians of the possibilities of reaching beyond their own ranks to the larger world in which they live."*

The history of the world has been in great part the history of the mixing of peoples. Modern communication and transport accelerate mass migrations from one continent to another. Ethnic and racial diversity is more than ever a salient fact of the age.

But what happens when people of different origins, speaking different languages and professing different religions, inhabit the same locality and live under the same political sovereignty? Ethnic and racial conflict—far more than ideological conflict—is the explosive problem of our times.

On every side today ethnicity is breaking up nations. The Soviet Union, India, Yugoslavia, Ethiopia, are all in crisis. Ethnic tensions disturb and divide Sri Lanka, Burma, Indonesia, Iraq, Cyprus, Nigeria, Angola, Lebanon, Guyana, Trinidad—you name it. Even nations as stable and civilized as Britain and France, Belgium and Spain, face growing ethnic troubles. Is there any large multiethnic state that can be made to work?

The answer to that question has been, until recently, the United States. "No other nation," Margaret Thatcher has said, "has so successfully combined people of different races and nations within a single culture." How have Americans succeeded in pulling off this almost unprecedented trick?

We have always been a multiethnic country. Hector St. John de Crevecoeur, 5 who came from France in the 18th century, marveled at the astonishing diversity of the settlers—a mixture of English, Scotch, Irish, French, Dutch, Germans and Swedes . . . this promiscuous breed." He propounded a famous question: "What then is the American, this new man?" And he gave a famous answer: "Here individuals of all nations are melted into a new race of men." *E pluribus unum.*

The U.S. escaped the divisiveness of a multiethnic society by a brilliant so- 6 lution: the creation of a brand-new national identity. The point of America was not to preserve old cultures but to forge a new, American culture. "By an intermixture with our people," President George Washington told Vice President John Adams, immigrants will "get assimilated to our customs, measures and laws: in a word, soon become one people." This was the ideal that a century later Israel Zangwill crystallized in the title of his popular 1908 play *The Melting Pot.* And no institution was more potent in molding Crevecoeur's "promiscuous breed" into Washington's "one people" than the American public school.

The new American nationality was inescapably English in language, ideas 7 and institutions. The pot did not melt everybody, not even all the white immigrants; deeply bred racism put black Americans, yellow Americans, red Americans and brown Americans well outside the pale. Still, the infusion of other stocks, even of nonwhite stocks, and the experience of the New World reconfigured the British legacy and made the U.S., as we all know, a very different country from Britain.

In the 20th century, new immigration laws altered the composition of the 8 American people, and a cult of ethnicity erupted both among non-Anglo whites and among nonwhite minorities. This had many healthy consequences. The American culture at last began to give shamefully overdue recognition to the achievements of groups subordinated and spurned during the high noon of Anglo dominance, and it began to acknowledge the great swirling world beyond Europe. Americans acquired a more complex and invigorating sense of their world—and of themselves.

But, pressed too far, the cult of ethnicity has unhealthy consequences. It 9 gives rise, for example, to the conception of the U.S. as a nation composed not of individuals making their own choices but of inviolable ethnic and racial groups. It rejects the historic American goals of assimilation and integration.

And, in an excess of zeal, well-intentioned people seek to transform our 10 system of education from a means of creating "one people" into a means of promoting, celebrating and perpetuating separate ethnic origins and identities. The balance is shifting from *unum* to *pluribus.*

That is the issue that lies behind the hullabaloo over "multiculturalism" 11 and "political correctness," the attack on the "Eurocentric" curriculum and the rise of the notion that history and literature should be taught not as disciplines but as therapies whose function is to raise minority self-esteem. Group separatism crystallizes the differences, magnifies tensions, intensifies hostilities. Europe—the unique source of the liberating ideas of democracy, civil liberties and human rights—is portrayed as the root of all evil, and non-European cultures, their own many crimes deleted, are presented as the means of redemption.

I don't want to sound apocalyptic about these developments. Education is   12
always in ferment, and a good thing too. The situation in our universities, I am
confident, will soon right itself. But the impact of separatist pressures in our
public schools is more troubling. If a Kleagle of the Ku Klux Klan wanted to use
the schools to disable and handicap black Americans, he could hardly come up
with anything more effective than the "Afrocentric" curriculum. And if separatist tendencies go unchecked, the result can only be the fragmentation, resegregation and tribalization of American life.

I remain optimistic. My impression is that the historic forces driving toward   13
"one people" have not lost their power. The eruption of ethnicity, is I believe, a
rather superficial enthusiasm stirred by romantic ideologues on the one hand
and by unscrupulous con men on the other: self-appointed spokesmen whose
claim to represent their minority groups is carelessly accepted by the media.
Most American-born members of minority groups, white or non-white, see
themselves primarily as Americans rather than primarily as members of one or
another ethnic group. A notable indicator today is the rate of intermarriage
across ethnic lines, across religious lines, even (increasingly) across racial lines.
"We Americans," said Theodore Roosevelt, "are children of the crucible."

The growing diversity of the American population makes the quest for uni-   14
fying ideals and a common culture all the more urgent. In a world savagely rent
by ethnic and racial antagonisms, the U.S. must continue as an example of how
a highly differentiated society holds itself together.

COMPREHENSION

1. What is a *cult?* What is the significance of the word in Schlesinger's title?
2. According to Schlesinger, what social institution has been the most significant in forging a commonality among Americans?
3. Why does Schlesinger claim that an Afrocentric curriculum would disable
   and handicap black Americans?

RHETORIC

1. This essay might be considered a problem-solution essay. What evidence is
   there in its structure to support this view?
2. In paragraph 3, the author cites many countries where internal ethnic conflict has occurred or is occurring. Why are they merely listed without being
   explained on a case-by-case basis? What does this imply about the author's
   expectations of his audience?
3. Nearly all the appeals to authority used by the author are historical figures.
   Why has he chosen to refer to thinkers hundreds of years old rather than
   present-day ones?
4. The author places terms such as *one people, multiculturalism, political correctness,*
   and *Eurocentric* in quotation marks. Why?

5. The introductory material to the essay is in the form of two paragraphs, separated by the conjunction *but*. Why didn't the author simply join these paragraphs into one?
6. Examine the rather lengthy sentence that begins paragraph 11. What formal device does the author use to keep the sentence coherent?

WRITING

1. Argue for or against the proposition that personal identification with a specific ethnic or cultural group results in alienation from society as a whole.
2. For a research project, define and describe the idea of a cult, and argue for or against the proposition that the author is using the term in an appropriate way regarding ethnicity.
3. Argue for or against the view that the United States should adopt English as its official language.

The Writing Life

Annie Dillard

Annie Dillard was born in 1945 in Pittsburgh and received her BA and MA degrees from Hollins College in Roanoke, Virginia. Her first book, Pilgrim at Tinker Creek, *won the 1975 Pulitzer Prize for general nonfiction. Other published works of nonfiction include* Teaching a Stone to Talk *(1982) and* An American Childhood *(1987). She has received awards from the National Endowment for the Arts and the Guggenheim Foundation as well as many other sources. As an essayist, poet, memoirist, and literary critic, she focuses her themes on the relationships among the self, nature, religion, and faith. Her writing is recognizable by its observations on the minutia of life and its search for meaning in such unlikely places as a stone or an insect. Dillard expanded her range of writing with the publication of her first novel,* The Living *(1992). In this excerpt from* The Writing Life *(1989), the author offers a striking analogy for the creative process.*

When you write, you lay out a line of words. The line of words is a miner's pick, a woodcarver's gouge, a surgeon's probe. You wield it, and it digs a path you follow. Soon you find yourself deep in new territory. Is it a dead end, or have you located the real subject? You will know tomorrow, or this time next year. 1

You make the path boldly and follow it fearfully. You go where the path 2 leads. At the end of the path, you find a box canyon. You hammer out reports, dispatch bulletins.

The writing has changed, in your hands, and in a twinkling, from an ex- 3
pression of your notions to an epistemological tool. The new place interests you
because it is not clear. You attend. In your humility, you lay down the words
carefully, watching all the angles. Now the earlier writing looks soft and careless. Process is nothing; erase your tracks. The path is not the work. I hope your
tracks have grown over; I hope birds ate the crumbs; I hope you will toss it all
and not look back.

The line of words is a hammer. You hammer against the walls of your 4
house. You tap the walls, lightly, everywhere. After giving many years' attention to these things, you know what to listen for. Some of the walls are bearing
walls; they have to stay, or everything will fall down. Other walls can go with
impunity; you can hear the difference. Unfortunately, it is often a bearing wall
that has to go. It cannot be helped. There is only one solution, which appalls
you, but there it is. Knock it out. Duck.

Courage utterly opposes the bold hope that this is such fine stuff the work 5
needs it, or the world. Courage, exhausted, stands on bare reality: this writing
weakens the work. You must demolish the work and start over. You can save
some of the sentences, like bricks. It will be a miracle if you can save some of the
paragraphs, no matter how excellent in themselves or hard-won. You can waste a
year worrying about it, or you can get it over with now. (Are you a woman, or a
mouse?)

The part you must jettison is not only the best-written part; it is also, oddly, 6
that part which was to have been the very point. It is the original key passage,
the passage on which the rest was to hang, and from which you yourself drew
the courage to begin. Henry James knew it well, and said it best. In his preface
to *The Spoils of Poynton,* he pities the writer, in a comical pair of sentences that
rises to a howl: "Which is the work in which he hasn't surrendered, under dire
difficulty, the best thing he meant to have kept? In which indeed, before the
dreadful *done,* doesn't he ask himself what has become of the thing all for the
sweet sake of which it was to proceed to that extremity?"

So it is that a writer writes many books. In each book, he intended several 7
urgent and vivid points, many of which he sacrificed as the book's form hardened. "The youth gets together his materials to build a bridge to the moon,"
Thoreau noted mournfully, "or perchance a palace or temple on the earth, and
at length the middle-aged man concludes to build a wood-shed with them."
The writer returns to these materials, these passionate subjects, as to unfinished
business, for they are his life's work.

COMPREHENSION

1. What is the central metaphor Dillard uses in describing the act of writing?
2. According to the author, what should a writer's attitude be toward her or
   his work?
3. Explain the meaning of the quotation taken from Thoreau.
4. Explain the meaning of the quotation taken from James.

RHETORIC

1. How does paragraph 1 prepare you for the tone and diction of what is to follow? How would you describe this tone and diction?
2. The essay is unusual in that it is written in the form of the second-person singular. To whom does *you* refer?
3. What is the intended audience of this essay: writers, would-be writers, the general public, a highly educated public? Explain by providing examples of grammar and sentence structure.
4. Paragraph 4 is distinct in its use of semicolons and short sentences. In fact, the final sentence is only one word. Assuming that good writers try to correlate the meaning of their writing with the style of their writing, how can you find a relationship between meaning and style in this paragraph?
5. What unifying image about the act of writing does the author create in paragraphs 1 and 2? Consider the number of one-syllable words in this section. How does the rhythm of these monosyllabic words complement the overriding image?
6. What is the chief purpose of this essay? Explain your view.

WRITING

1. Imitate Dillard's introductory sentence with one of your own, using the pattern, "When you _____, you _____." Follow the topic sentence with analogies that support your central image, for example, "When you ski, you launch yourself from the Earth" or "When you enter the Internet, you enter distant galaxies."
2. Describe a time in your life when you overcame tremendous obstacles to accomplish a difficult task. Explain how you achieved your goal.
3. Develop a series of interview questions in preparation for interviewing a master crafter, an artist, or a scientist. Interview your subject and write an essay employing process analysis. Explore and explain the way your subject proceeds with his or her work.

Freewriting

Peter Elbow

Peter Elbow was born in New York in 1935, and received degrees from Williams College, Exeter College, Oxford, and Brandeis University. He has taught at the University of Massachusetts at Amherst, the State University of New York at Stony Brook, the Massachusetts Institute of Technology, Franconia College, and Evergreen State College.

He is considered by some writing teachers to have revolutionized the teaching of writing through his popularization of the concept and practice called "freewriting." He is the author and/or editor of over 15 books on writing including Writing without Teachers, Writing with Power, Embracing Contraries, What Is English? *and most recently* Everyone Can Write: Essays toward a Hopeful Theory of Writing and Teaching Writing *(2000). In "Freewriting," taken from* Writing without Teachers, *Elbow explains an exercise for writing students that he helped popularize in American colleges, universities, and writing workshops.*

The most effective way I know to improve your writing is to do freewriting exercises regularly. At least three times a week. They are sometimes called "automatic writing," "babbling," or "jabbering" exercises. The idea is simply to write for ten minutes (later on, perhaps fifteen or twenty). Don't stop for anything. Go quickly without rushing. Never stop to look back, to cross something out, to wonder how to spell something, to wonder what word or thought to use, or to think about what you are doing. If you can't think of a word or a spelling, just use a squiggle or else write, "I can't think of it." Just put down something. The easiest thing is just to put down whatever is in your mind. If you get stuck it's fine to write "I can't think what to say, I can't think what to say" as many times as you want; or repeat the last word you wrote over and over again; or anything else. The only requirement is that you *never* stop. 1

What happens to a freewriting exercise is important. It must be a piece of writing which, even if someone reads it, doesn't send any ripples back to you. It is like writing something and putting it in a bottle in the sea. The teacherless class helps your writing by providing maximum feedback. Freewritings help you by providing no feedback at all. When I assign one, I invite the writer to let me read it. But also tell him to keep it if he prefers. I read it quickly and make no comments at all and I do not speak with him about it. The main thing is that a freewriting must never be evaluated in any way; in fact there must be no discussion or comment at all. 2

Here is an example of a fairly coherent exercise (sometimes they are very incoherent, which is fine): 3

> I think I'll write what's on my mind, but the only thing on my mind right now is what to write for ten minutes. I've never done this before and I'm not prepared in any way—the sky is cloudy today, how's that? now I'm afraid I won't be able to think of what to write when I get to the end of the sentence—well, here I am at the end of the sentence—here I am again, again, again, again, at least I'm still writing—Now I ask is there some reason to be happy that I'm still writing—ah yes! Here comes the question again—What am I getting out of this? What point is there in it? It's almost obscene to always ask it but I seem to question everything that way and I was gonna say something else pertaining to that but I got so busy writing down the first part that I forgot what I was leading into. This is kind of fun oh don't stop writing—cars and trucks speeding by somewhere out the window, pens clittering across people's papers. The sky is cloudy—is it symbolic that I should be mentioning it? Huh? I dunno. Maybe I should try colors, blue, red, dirty words—wait a minute—no can't do that,

orange, yellow, arm tired, green pink violet magenta lavender red brown black green—now that I can't think of any more colors—just about done—relief? maybe.

Freewriting may seem crazy but actually it makes simple sense. Think of the difference between speaking and writing. Writing has the advantage of permitting more editing. But that's its downfall too. Almost everybody interposes a massive and complicated series of editings between the time words start to be born into consciousness and when they finally come off the end of the pencil or typewriter onto the page. This is partly because schooling makes us obsessed with the "mistakes" we make in writing. Many people are constantly thinking about spelling and grammar as they try to write. I am always thinking about the awkwardness, wordiness, and general mushiness of my natural verbal product as I try to write down words.

But it's not just "mistakes" or "bad writing" we edit as we write. We also ⁴ edit unacceptable thoughts and feelings, as we do in speaking. In writing there is more time to do it so the editing is heavier: when speaking, there's someone right there waiting for a reply and he'll get bored or think we're crazy if we don't come out with *something*. Most of the time in speaking, we settle for the catch-as-catch-can way in which the words tumble out. In writing, however, there's a chance to try to get them right. But the opportunity to get them right is a terrible burden: you can work for two hours trying to get a paragraph "right" and discover it's not right at all. And then give up.

Editing, *in itself*, is not the problem. Editing is usually necessary if we want to ⁵ end up with something satisfactory. The problem is that editing goes on *at the same time* as producing. The editor is, as it were, constantly looking ever the shoulder of the producer and constantly fiddling with what he's doing while he's in the middle of trying to do it. No wonder the producer gets nervous, jumpy, inhibited, and finally can't be coherent. It's an unnecessary burden to try to think of words and also worry at the same time whether they're the right words.

The main thing about freewriting is that it is *nonediting*. It is an exercise in ⁶ bringing together the process of producing words and putting them down on the page. Practiced regularly, it undoes the ingrained habit of editing at the same time you are trying to produce. It will make writing less blocked because words will come more easily. You will use up more paper, but chew up fewer pencils.

Next time you write, notice how often you stop yourself from writing down ⁷ something you were going to write down. Or else cross it out after it's written. "Naturally," you say, "it wasn't any good." But think for a moment about the occasions when you spoke well. Seldom was it because you first got the beginning just right. Usually it was a matter of a halting or even garbled beginning, but you kept going and your speech finally became coherent and even powerful. There is a lesson here for writing: trying to get the beginning just right is a formula for failure—and probably a secret tactic to make yourself give up writing. Make some words, whatever they are, and then grab hold of that line and reel in as hard as you can. Afterwards you can throw away lousy beginnings and make new ones. This is the quickest way to get into good writing.

The habit of compulsive, premature editing doesn't just make writing hard. 8 It also makes writing dead. Your voice is damped out by all the interruptions, changes, and hesitations between the consciousness and the page. In your natural way of producing words there is a sound, a texture, a rhythm—a voice— which is the main source of power in your writing. I don't know how it works, but this voice is the force that will make a reader listen to you, the energy that drives the meanings through his thick skull. Maybe you don't *like* your voice; maybe people have made fun of it. But it's the only voice you've got. It's your only source of power. You better get back into it, no matter what you think of it. If you keep writing in it, it may change into something you like better. But if you abandon it, you'll likely never have a voice and never be heard.

Freewritings are vacuums. Gradually you will begin to carry over into your 9 regular writing some of the voice, force, and connectedness that creep into those vacuums.

COMPREHENSION

1. What is the thesis of the essay? Is it implied or stated directly in the text?
2. In paragraph 5, Elbow refers to the "producer" and the "editor." Who are they? Where are they located? How did they develop?
3. In paragraph 8, the author makes a connection between one's personal "voice" and the idea of "power." Why does Elbow focus so strongly on this connection?

RHETORIC

1. Elbow frequently uses the "imperative" (or command) sentence form in the opening paragraph. Why? What would have been the effect had he used the simple declarative form?
2. Writers often use examples to help illustrate their point. Does the example of a freewriting exercise Elbow provides in paragraph 3 help you to understand the method? Why or why not?
3. The author uses colloquial terms such as "squiggle" (paragraph 1); "crazy" and "mushiness" (paragraph 3); and "lousy" (paragraph 7). How does his use of such words affect the tone of the essay?
4. Are there any elements in Elbow's own style that suggest his essay may have started as a freewriting exercise? Consider the reasons he provides for the importance of freewriting, for example, the generating of ideas, discovering one's own voice, expressing oneself succinctly and naturally.
5. Elbow is himself a college writing teacher. Based on your assessment of the tone of the essay, whom do you think is his intended audience? Is it broad or narrow? Specialized or general? Or, could he have in mind more than one type of audience? Explain your answer.

6. Note the number of times Elbow begins his sentences with coordinating conjunctions ("but," "and," "or"). For example, in paragraph 4, he does it three times. Many writing teachers frown on this method of structuring sentences. Why does Elbow employ it?
7. Compare the essay's introduction to its conclusion. Note how the introduction is rather long, and the conclusion is quite short (two sentences in fact). How do these two elements contribute to the overall "pace" of the essay?

WRITING

1. During one week, complete three freewriting exercises. Wait one week, and then review what you have written. Explore any insights your freewriting gives you into your writer's "voice," your concerns, interests, style, and "power."
2. Write an expository paper of approximately 400 words explaining the difficulties you have when writing a homework assignment that requires submitting an essay or writing an essay-length response during an exam.
3. Write a 500-word comparison and contrast essay wherein you examine the similarities and differences of speaking and writing.

The Maker's Eye: Revising Your Own Manuscripts

Donald M. Murray

Donald M. Murray (b. 1917) has combined a career as teacher, journalist, fiction writer, poet, and author of several important textbooks on writing. He has worked as a teacher, journalist, and editor for Time *magazine. His books include* A Writer Teaches Writing, Write to Learn, Read to Write, *and more recently* Shoptalk: Learning to Write with Writers *(1991);* Crafting a Life in Essay, Story, Poem *(1996); and* The Craft of Revision *(1997). In this essay, originally published in the magazine* The Writer, *Donald Murray argues for the absolute importance of the revision process to the writer. As he presents the stages of the revision process, Murray illustrates their usefulness to any writer—whether beginner or experienced—and offers his personal views and those of other authors.*

When students complete a first draft, they consider the job of writing done— 1 and their teachers too often agree. When professional writers complete a first draft, they usually feel that they are at the start of the writing process. When a draft is completed, the job of writing can begin.

That difference in attitude is the difference between amateur and profes- 2 sional, inexperience and experience, journeyman and craftsman. Peter F. Drucker, the prolific business writer, calls his first draft "the zero draft"—after that he can start counting. Most writers share the feeling that the first draft, and all of those which follow, are opportunities to discover what they have to say and how best they can say it.

To produce a progression of drafts, each of which says more and says it 3 more clearly, the writer has to develop a special kind of reading skill. In school we are taught to decode what appears on the page as finished writing. Writers, however, face a different category of possibility and responsibility when they read their own drafts. To them the words on the page are never finished. Each can be changed and rearranged, can set off a chain reaction of confusion or clarified meaning. This is a different kind of reading, which is possibly more difficult and certainly more exciting.

Writers must learn to be their own best enemy. They must accept the criti- 4 cism of others and be suspicious of it; they must accept the praise of others and be even more suspicious of it. Writers cannot depend on others. They must detach themselves from their own pages so that they can apply both their caring and their craft to their own work.

Such detachment is not easy. Science fiction writer Ray Bradbury suppos- 5 edly puts each manuscript away for a year to the day and then rereads it as a stranger. Not many writers have the discipline or the time to do this. We must read when our judgment may be at its worst, when we are close to the euphoric moment of creation.

Then the writer, counsels novelist Nancy Hale, "should be critical of every- 6 thing that seems to him most delightful in his style. He should excise what he most admires, because he wouldn't thus admire it if he weren't . . . in a sense protecting it from criticism." John Ciardi, the poet, adds, "The last act of the writing must be to become one's own reader. It is, I suppose, a schizophrenic process, to begin passionately and to end critically, to begin hot and to end cold; and, more important, to be passion-hot and critic-cold at the same time."

Most people think that the principal problem is that writers are too proud 7 of what they have written. Actually, a greater problem for most professional writers is one shared by the majority of students. They are overly critical, think everything is dreadful, tear up page after page, never complete a draft, see the task as hopeless.

The writer must learn to read critically but constructively, to cut what is 8 bad, to reveal what is good. Eleanor Estes, the children's book author, explains: "The writer must survey his work critically, coolly, as though he were a stranger to it. He must be willing to prune, expertly and hard-heartedly. At the end of each revision, a manuscript may look . . . worked over, torn apart, pinned together, added to, deleted from, words changed and words changed back. Yet the book must maintain its original freshness and spontaneity."

Most readers underestimate the amount of rewriting it usually takes to pro- 9 duce spontaneous reading. This is a great disadvantage to the student writer, who sees only a finished product and never watches the craftsman who takes the necessary step back, studies the work carefully, returns to the task, steps back, returns, steps back, again and again. Anthony Burgess, one of the most prolific writers in the English-speaking world, admits, "I might revise a page twenty times." Roald Dahl, the popular children's writer, states, "By the time I'm nearing the end of a story, the first part will have been reread and altered and corrected at least 150 times. . . . Good writing is essentially rewriting. I am positive of this."

Rewriting isn't virtuous. It isn't something that ought to be done. It is sim- 10 ply something that most writers find they have to do to discover what they have to say and how to say it. It is a condition of the writer's life.

There are, however, a few writers who do little formal rewriting, primarily 11 because they have the capacity and experience to create and review a large number of invisible drafts in their minds before they approach the page. And some writers slowly produce finished pages, performing all the tasks of revision simultaneously, page by page, rather than draft by draft. But it is still possible to see the sequence followed by most writers most of the time in rereading their own work.

Most writers scan their drafts first, reading as quickly as possible to catch 12 the larger problems of subject and form, then move in closer and closer as they read and write, reread and rewrite.

The first thing writers look for in their drafts is *information*. They know that 13 a good piece of writing is built from specific, accurate, and interesting informa-tion. The writer must have an abundance of information from which to con-struct a readable piece of writing.

Next writers look for *meaning* in the information. The specifics must build a 14 pattern of significance. Each piece of specific information must carry the reader toward meaning.

Writers reading their own drafts are aware of *audience*. They put themselves 15 in the reader's situation and make sure that they deliver information which a reader wants to know or needs to know in a manner which is easily digested. Writers try to be sure that they anticipate and answer the questions a critical reader will ask when reading the piece of writing.

Writers make sure that the *form* is appropriate to the subject and the audi- 16 ence. Form, or genre, is the vehicle which carries meaning to the reader, but form cannot be selected until the writer has adequate information to discover its significance and an audience which needs or wants that meaning.

Once writers are sure the form is appropriate, they must then look at the 17 *structure,* the order of what they have written. Good writing is built on a solid framework of logic, argument, narrative, or motivation which runs through the entire piece of writing and holds it together. This is the time when many writers find it most effective to outline as a way of visualizing the hidden spine by which the piece of writing is supported.

The element on which writers may spend a majority of their time is *develop-* 18 *ment.* Each section of a piece of writing must be adequately developed. It must give readers enough information so that they are satisfied. How much information is enough? That's as difficult as asking how much garlic belongs in a salad. It must be done to taste, but most beginning writers underdevelop, underestimat-ing the reader's hunger for information.

As writers solve development problems, they often have to consider ques- 19
tions of *dimension*. There must be a pleasing and effective proportion among all
the parts of the piece of writing. There is a continual process of subtracting and
adding to keep the piece of writing in balance.

Finally, writers have to listen to their own voices. *Voice* is the force which 20
drives a piece of writing forward. It is an expression of the writer's authority
and concern. It is what is between the words on the page, what glues the piece
of writing together. A good piece of writing is always marked by a consistent,
individual voice.

As writers read and reread, write and rewrite, they move closer and closer 21
to the page until they are doing line-by-line editing. Writers read their own
pages with infinite care. Each sentence, each line, each clause, each phrase, each
word, each mark of punctuation, each section of white space between the type
has to contribute to the clarification of meaning.

Slowly the writer moves from word to word, looking through language to 22
see the subject. As a word is changed, cut, or added, as a construction is rearranged, all the words used before that moment and all those that follow that
moment must be considered and reconsidered.

Writers often read aloud at this stage of the editing process, muttering or 23
whispering to themselves, calling on the ear's experience with language. Does
this sound right—or that? Writers edit, shifting back and forth from eye to page
to ear to page. I find I must do this careful editing in short runs, no more than
fifteen or twenty minutes at a stretch, or I become too kind with myself. I begin
to see what I hope is on the page, not what actually is on the page.

This sounds tedious if you haven't done it, but actually it is fun. Making 24
something right is immensely satisfying, for writers begin to learn what they
are writing about by writing. Language leads them to meaning, and there is the
joy of discovery, of understanding, of making meaning clear as the writer employs the technical skills of language.

Words have double meanings, even triple and quadruple meanings. Each 25
word has its own potential for connotation and denotation. And when writers
rub one word against the other, they are often rewarded with a sudden insight,
an unexpected clarification.

The maker's eye moves back and forth from word to phrase to sentence to 26
paragraph to sentence to phrase to word. The maker's eye sees the need for variety and balance, for a firmer structure, for a more appropriate form. It peers
into the interior of the paragraph, looking for coherence, unity, and emphasis,
which make meaning clear.

I learned something about this process when my first bifocals were pre- 27
scribed. I had ordered a larger section of the reading portion of the glass because of my work, but even so, I could not contain my eyes within this new
limit of vision. And I still find myself taking off my glasses and bending my
nose towards the page, for my eyes unconsciously flick back and forth across
the page, back to another page, forward to still another, as I try to see each
evolving line in relation to every other line.

When does this process end? Most writers agree with the great Russian 28
writer Tolstoy, who said, "I scarcely ever reread my published writings, if by
chance I come across a page, it always strikes me: all this must be rewritten; this
is how I should have written it."

The maker's eye is never satisfied, for each word has the potential to ignite 29
new meaning. This article has been twice written all the way through the writing process, and it was published four years ago. Now it is to be republished in
a book. The editors make a few small suggestions, and then I read it with my
maker's eye. Now it has been re-edited, re-revised, re-read, re-re-edited, for
each piece of writing to the writer is full of potential and alternatives.

A piece of writing is never finished. It is delivered to a deadline, torn out of 30
the typewriter on demand, sent off with a sense of accomplishment and shame
and pride and frustration. If only there were a couple more days, time for just
another run at it, perhaps then . . .

COMPREHENSION

1. In paragraph 1, what does Murray mean by the phrase, "When a draft is
   completed, the job of writing can begin"? Isn't a draft a form of writing?
2. According to Murray, what are the major differences between student and
   professional writers? Why do the differences help make the "professional"
   more accomplished at his or her work?
3. What are the differences between the reading styles of novice and experienced writers? How do the differences affect their own writings?

RHETORIC

1. Compare the introduction of this essay to that of Elbow's "Freewriting."
   How do they differ in tone and structure?
2. Murray begins to classify various aspects of the writer's concern in paragraph 13. Why does he wait so long to begin this analysis? Why are certain
   key words in paragraphs 13 through 20 italicized?
3. Murray uses analogy, comparing something with another, very different
   thing, to make the writing process concrete and familiar. Identify some of
   these analogies. Why they are models of clarity?
4. Murray refers to a writer as "the maker" several times in the essay. What
   does he imply by this usage? What other professions might be included in
   this category?
5. What is the purpose of the essay? Is it to inform? To persuade? To serve as
   a model? Anything else? Explain your response.
6. Murray ends the essay with ellipses. Why?
7. Notice the sentence in paragraph 29 that has four consecutive words with
   the prefix "re-." What is the purpose and effect of this rhetorical device?

WRITING

1. Murray focuses on the process, craft, and purpose of the writer, but he does not define "writer." Write an extended definition of 350 to 400 words, explaining what he means by this occupation or profession.
2. Write an essay of 400 to 500 words explaining your own writing process. Do not be intimidated if it is not like the one described by Murray. Compare and contrast your method with that of one or more of your classmates.

CONNECTIONS FOR CRITICAL THINKING

1. Examine the "how-to" aspect of the essays by Adler, Elbow, and Murray. What general strategies do they use to develop a comprehensive process analysis of an elusive subject, for example, reading or writing? Write an essay in which you compare the tactics these writers employ to demonstrate their processes.
2. Study the tone of Schlesinger's essay, "The Cult of Ethnicity." How does he remain "civil" while arguing against a contemporary view he seems to abhor? Next, study Dillard's "The Writer's Life" and examine how she uses imagery, metaphor, and simile in addressing the inscrutable subject of creative writing. Can you make some general observations about how the stylistic elements of an essay contribute to the ability of the author to communicate difficult subjects in a manner that is appealing to the reader?
3. Synthesize the ideas in Elbow's "Freewriting" and those in Murray's "The Maker's Eye: Revising Your Own Manuscripts" so that you can write a coherent essay on writing that takes into account the transition from inspiration to craft.
4. Interview three fellow students to ascertain how they study. Compare and contrast their responses to the suggestions Adler makes in his essay.
5. Create an imaginary dialogue between Mortimer Adler and Annie Dillard in which the former lauds the joys of reading and the latter celebrates the process of writing.
6. Search a book service Web site such as "Amazon," "Barnes & Noble" or another source, and review the various readers' remarks concerning the book *The Writing Life* (from which Dillard's excerpt is taken). Write an expository essay commenting on the varied responses that readers have given the book.

 chapter **2**

Reading and Writing Effective Arguments

You encounter various forms of argumentation in everyday situations—and most assuredly in many college courses. Consequently, it is important to learn more about this mode of thinking, reading, and writing. As a common form of academic writing, argumentation seeks to explore differences of opinion and attempts to build agreement. As such, argument is not only useful in classroom situations but also in the realm of civic life and discourse, for it provides reasons for people to agree with a particular point of view or at least come to an understanding of an individual's or group's perspective on an issue. Aristotle, who wrote the first major work on argument, thought that the best and most effective argumentative writing blends rational, emotional, and ethical appeals in order to move an audience—whether one person or an entire nation—to desired action.

When you engage in *argumentation,* you offer reasons to support a position, belief, or conclusion. A typical argumentative essay presents a debatable thesis and defends it in logical fashion. Closely allied with argumentation is *persuasion,* in which the writer appeals to readers' intelligence, emotions, and beliefs in order to influence them to adopt a position or act in a certain way. Logic and persuasive appeal often combine when a writer tries to convince an audience that his or her position is valid and other perspectives, while understandable perhaps, require reconsideration.

It is important to distinguish between verbal arguments and written ones. Admittedly both spoken and written arguments have a common purpose in their attempt to convince someone to agree with a particular position, make a certain decision, or take a specific action. In both your verbal and written arguments, you will usually invoke reasons and attempt to manipulate language skillfully. However, with a verbal argument you rarely have access to the types of specific evidence needed to support your reasons, nor do you have the time or ability to martial reasons and evidence in well-organized and coherent ways. Verbal arguments, as you well know, tend to involve excessive emotion; after all, spoken arguments often erupt spontaneously and are rarely thoughtfully constructed and presented.

Unlike most verbal arguments, effective written arguments are carefully and logically planned, organized, researched, and revised. The writer analyzes the audience and anticipates objections to the assertions being made. As she or he develops the argument, the writer considers and selects various rhetorical strategies—for example, analysis, definition, or comparison and contrast—to shape the presentation. Moreover, the writer has time to choose the appropriate language and style for the argument, exploring the use of striking diction, figurative language, rhythmic sentence patterns, and various tonalities and shades of meaning during the prewriting, drafting, and revision stages. Finally, especially when composing arguments for college courses, writers must attend to logic and the techniques of valid persuasive appeal.

THE LANGUAGE OF ARGUMENT

Writers of argument often employ various modes of exposition like definition, comparison and contrast, illustration, and analysis, but they incorporate these modes of critical thinking as the means of justifying, or supporting, a logical position. The study of the special language, logic, and structure of argumentation fills volumes. For college writing, there is a core group of critical terms that you should know before you design an argumentative paper:

1. A *claim* is a statement to be justified or upheld. It is the main idea or position that you plan to present in an argument.
2. *Thesis, proposition, assertion,* and *premise* are all similar to a claim in that each is a positive statement or declaration to be supported with reasons and evidence. A *premise* should be distinguished from the other terms: It is a statement or assumption that is established before an argument is begun and is important to an understanding of logic and various errors or fallacies in reasoning.
3. *Grounds* are the reasons, support, and evidence presented to support your claim.
4. A *warrant* is a stated or unstated belief, rule, or principle that underlies an argument. A *backing* is an even larger principle that serves as the foundation for a warrant.
5. The *major proposition* is the main point of an argument, which is supported by the minor propositions.
6. The *minor propositions* are the reasons you offer in support of the major proposition.
7. *Evidence* is that part of the argument that supports the minor propositions. In argumentation, effective evidence is based either on facts, examples, statistics, and other forms of evidence or on accepted opinions. Without adequate evidence, the audience will not accept your major and minor propositions. Evidence in argument must be accurate and true.
8. A *fact* is a verifiable statement. A valid *opinion* is a judgment based on the facts and careful deductive or inductive reasoning. *Induction* is a process

of reasoning by which you develop evidence in order to reach a useful generalization. *Deduction* is a process that proceeds from the general to the particular.

9. A valid *conclusion* of an argument derives logically from the major and minor propositions. The logical conclusion is termed the *inference,* in which you arrive at a decision by reasoning from the previous evidence.

10. A *fallacy* is a line of incorrect reasoning from premises.

11. *Refutation* is the acknowledgment and handling of opposing viewpoints. You must anticipate opposing viewpoints and counter them effectively (what we term *rebuttal*) in order to convince or persuade readers.

Constructing an effective argument depends on the careful arrangement of major and minor propositions, evidence, and refutation. Like a lawyer, you build a position and subject your opponent's position to dissection in an effort to win the case.

THE TEST OF JUSTIFICATION

Whatever its components, whether a writer can construct an argument or not essentially hinges on the concept of *justification*—the recognition that a subject lends itself to legitimate difference of opinion. Justification also involves proving or demonstrating that a claim is in accordance with the reasons and evidence offered to support it.

Not all statements require justification. A statement that is a verifiable fact or a commonly accepted assumption or belief—what we term a *warrant*—generally does not need justification. To test the concept of justification, consider the following four statements.

1. President John F. Kennedy was assassinated on November 22, 1963.
2. Children shouldn't smoke.
3. Abortion is the destruction of a human life.
4. African-Americans should receive reparations for the damages caused by slavery.

Which of these statements require justification? The first statement about President Kennedy is a verifiable fact, and the second statement strikes any reasonable audience as common sense. Thus, the first two statements do not require justification and consequently could not be the subject of a useful argument, although the second statement could serve as the warrant for a more specific claim about smoking by young children. By contrast, the third statement concerning abortion makes a critical assumption that would elicit either agreement or disagreement but in either case would demand substantiation. Similarly, the fourth statement about reparations for slavery is an issue that is debatable from a variety of positions. Therefore, the third and fourth statements require justification: They are open to argumentation.

READING AND ANALYZING ARGUMENT

From the time of Aristotle to the present, numerous critical approaches to the study of argument have been devised. One of the most useful recent approaches to argument appears in *An Introduction to Reasoning* and *The Uses of Argument* by British logician and philosopher Stephen Toulmin. In his studies, Toulmin observes that any argument involves a *claim* supported by *reasons* and *evidence.* Whether writing a memo to your instructor contesting a certain grade, or a letter to the editor of your campus newspaper advocating a change in the cafeteria vendor because the food is terrible, or a petition to provide more parking space for commuting students, the argumentative method is the same. Essentially you make a general assertion—a claim—and then offer the smaller propositions or supporting reasons along with the relevant facts, examples, statistics, and expert testimony to justify all claims. And underlying the nature of claims and evidence is recognition of the importance of *warrants,* those unstated beliefs that lead from evidence to claim.

Here is the way that Toulmin presents his model:

Harry was born in Bermuda —— Harry is a British subject
　　　(Evidence)　　　　　　　　　｜　　　　(Claim)

Since a man born in
Bermuda will be a British subject
(Warrant)

In truth, Toulmin's example is basic and perhaps too simple. The claims that you deal with when reading or writing arguments typically are more complex and controversial than Toulmin's diagram suggests, and the need for extensive evidence more demanding. Nevertheless, Toulmin's model offers a useful way to understand the nature of argumentative reasoning.

Understanding Claims and Warrants

When you argue in writing, you make a specific claim, which is an assertion that you plan to prove. You present this claim or proposition as being true, and you support the claim with a series of logically related statements that are true. Think of the claim as the thesis or the main point of the argument that holds all other logically related statements together. The claim is the main idea that you set out to prove, and in a well-reasoned argument, everything makes the claim seem inevitable. Any paper that you write that fails to state a claim—your position in an argument—clearly and emphatically will leave readers shaking their heads and wondering if you actually have an argument to present.

Think of a claim as an arguable point, one that you can build a carefully reasoned paper around. Remember that by applying the test of justification, you need to exclude numerous opinions, nonarguable propositions, and statements of taste and fact that might be common in everyday situations but not legitimate subjects for papers based in sound strategies for written argument. To say "Turn down that rap music" to your roommate is the sort of command (containing perhaps an implied opinion) that doesn't in itself qualify as a claim but could get you involved in a heated conversation. To transform this command into a legitimate claim or an arguable point, you would have to state a proposition that expresses your main idea about rap music.

Suppose, for example, that after reading the essay in this anthology by Henry Louis Gates, Jr., "2 Live Crew, Decoded" (on page 508), you *are* asked to write an argumentative paper on hip-hop or rap music. In his brief but provocative essay, Gates raises significant issues about obscenity and censorship, about "mainstream" and ethnic culture, about white perceptions of black males. His claim is that we cannot address the complex, interrelated issues raised by the rap music phenomenon unless we "become literate in the vernacular traditions of African Americans. To do less is to censor through the equivalent of intellectual prior restraint—and censorship is to art what lynching is to justice." Do you readily perceive the argumentative edge in Gates's claim? Do you agree or disagree with his main point that one cannot offer an informed critique of a cultural phenomenon without knowledge of the language of that culture? And what claim would you actually make about rap music and the culture, an increasingly "crossover" youth culture, that supports it? What reasons or grounds would you produce in support of your claim?

A complex, extended argument in essay form often reveals several types of claim that the writer advances. A *claim about meaning* (What is rap music?) is a proposition that defines or interprets a subject as it establishes an arguable point. A *claim about value* (Rap music is good or bad) advances an ideally open-minded view of the subject based on a coherent framework of aesthetic or ethical values. A *claim about policy* (Music stations should be forced to regulate the most offensive forms of rap music) advances propositions concerning laws, regulations, and initiatives designed to produce specific outcomes. Finally, *claims about consequences* (Children who listen to rap musicians begin to mimic their vulgar behavior) are rooted in propositions involving various forms of cause-and-effect relationships. Constructing an argument around one or more of these types of claims is essential in gaining an audience's assent.

Many claims, of course, cannot be presented as absolute propositions— certainly not as absolute as Aristotle's major premise in his famous syllogism (see page 70) that "all human beings are mortal." Writers must seek common ground with readers and foster a degree of trust by anticipating that members of any audience will disagree with their claim, treat it with skepticism, and perhaps even respond with hostility. For this reason, it is important to qualify or clarify the nature of your claim. A *qualifier* restricts the absoluteness of a claim by using such cue words and phrases as "sometimes," "probably," "usually," and "in most cases." Qualifiers can also explain certain circumstances or conditions under which the claim might not be true. The use of qualifiers enables the writer to anticipate certain audience reactions and handle them in an effective and subtle way.

Even more important than the possible need to qualify a claim is the need to justify it in a new way: by linking the claim with reasons and evidence in such a way that the audience sees the train of thinking that leads from the data to the claim. If you look again at the model that Toulmin provides, you see that the data "Harry was born in Bermuda" does not completely support the claim "Harry is a British subject." What is required is what Toulmin calls a *warrant*, a form of justification—a general belief, principle, or rule—that links the claim and the data or support. Thus, the warrant "Since a man born in Bermuda will be a British subject" explains *why* the claim follows from the data.

Another way of understanding this admittedly challenging concept of warrant is to treat it as the process of thinking that leads writers to hold the opinions they present. Thought of from this perspective, we can see that a weak or unclear warrant will undermine an argument and render it invalid. For example, the claim "Sara graduated from an excellent high school and consequently she should do well in college" is based on the warrant or unstated (and untested) belief that all students who graduate from good high schools perform well at the college level. Obviously, this warrant is not satisfactory: To state that college success is based solely on the quality of one's high school education is to base the argument on a warrant that few readers would find acceptable. If, on the other hand, a writer claims that "Sara graduated from an excellent high school with a 3.97 cumulative average, the third highest in her class, and consequently should do well in college," we see that the warrant establishing the link between the claim and conclusion becomes more acceptable. In fact, there is a consensus, or general belief, among experts that a person's grade point average in high school is a sound predictor—perhaps sounder than SAT scores—of a person's potential for success in college.

If you disagree with a writer's assumptions, you basically are questioning the warrants underlying the argument. An effective argument should rest on an acceptable warrant and also on the *backing*—some explanation or support—for it. Remember that even if a warrant, stated or unstated, is clear, understood, and backed with support, readers might still disagree with it. For example, one could argue that Sara might have obtained her lofty GPA in high school by taking easy courses, and that consequently we cannot readily predict her success in college. Not everyone will accept even the most reasonable of warrants.

Reasoning from Evidence

Evidence is the data, or *grounds*, used to make claims or general assertions clear, concrete, and convincing. In argumentation, the presentation of evidence must be examined from the perspective of logic or sound reasoning. Central to logic is the relationship of evidence to a *generalization*, a statement or conclusion that what is applicable in one situation also applies to similar situations. You cannot think and write clearly unless you test evidence to see that it supports your claims, assumptions, or general statements. Evidence in an argumentative essay creates a common ground of understanding that you and your reader can share.

You know that one of the keenest pleasures in reading mystery fiction or viewing whodunits on television or film is the quest for evidence. The great writers of crime and mystery fiction—Edgar Allan Poe, Sir Arthur Conan

Doyle, Agatha Christie—were adept at creating a chain of clues, or evidence, leading with the inevitability of logic to the solution to the crime. Whether it is a letter lying on a desk in Poe's "The Purloined Letter" or a misplaced chair in Christie's *The Murder of Roger Ackroyd*, it is evidence that we seek in order to solve the crime.

In argumentative writing, evidence is used more to prove a point than to solve a mystery. College writers must know what constitutes evidence—examples, facts, statistics, quotations and information from authoritative sources, personal experience, careful reasoning—and how to use it to support certain claims. They must also determine if the evidence and assumptions surrounding the evidence are valid.

Here are five basic questions about evidence to consider when reading and writing argumentative essays.

1. *Is the evidence typical and representative?* Examples must fairly represent the condition or situation if your claim is to be valid. If evidence is distorted or unrepresentative, a claim will not be logical or convincing.
2. *Is the evidence relevant?* The evidence should speak directly to the claim. It should not utilize peripheral or irrelevant data.
3. *Is the evidence specific and detailed?* In reading and writing arguments, do not trust broad, catchall statements presented as "evidence." Valid evidence should involve accurate quotations, paraphrases, and presentations of data from authoritative sources.
4. *Is the evidence accurate and reliable?* A claim is only as valid as the data supporting it. Facts should come from reliable sources. (See page 77 for help with evaluating sources.) Current rather than outdated evidence should predominate in a current argument. Sources should be cited accurately for the convenience of the reader. Although personal observation and personal experience are admissible as types of evidence, such testimony rarely serves as conclusive proof for a claim.
5. *Is the evidence sufficient?* There must be enough evidence to support claims and reasons. One extended piece of evidence, no matter how carefully selected, rarely is sufficient to win an argument.

Any argumentative essay should provide a clear, logical link between the writer's claim, assertion, generalization, or conclusion and the evidence. If an argumentative essay reveals false or illogical reasoning—that is, if the step from the evidence to the generalization is wrong, confusing, or deceptive, readers will not accept the truth of the claim or the validity of the evidence.

Two Classic and Contemporary Essays

At the beginning of subsequent chapters in this textbook, you will encounter paired essays, one by a classic writer and one by a more contemporary writer, that treat a common issue or universal question. Many of these issues—on education, the family, gender and identity, human rights and the quest for values, our cultural origins—have preoccupied the best minds across generations of essayists and generated centuries of thought. In the two classic and contemporary essays at the end of this chapter, for example H. L. Mencken and Coretta Scott King take opposing viewpoints on the subject of the death penalty (page 84).

THINKING CRITICALLY ABOUT ARGUMENTS

Whether you are reading another writer's argument or starting to plan one of your own, you need to consider the purposes of the argument. When you are reading an argument, you should also look for the appeals to reason, emotion, and ethics the writer is using and decide whether or not those appeals are effective for you, the writer's audience. In your own arguments, you will need to decide the types of appeals that will carry the most weight with *your* audience.

The Purpose of Argumentation

As a college writer, your general aim is to communicate or convey messages in essay form to a literate and knowledgeable audience of teachers and scholars. When thinking about the subject for an essay, you also have to consider a more specialized *purpose*—the special nature or aim—behind your composition. You might have to report the result of an experiment in animal behavior, analyze a poem, compare and contrast Mario Puzo's novel *The Godfather* and its film adaptation, or assert the need for capital punishment. In each instance, your essay requires a key rhetorical strategy or set of strategies. These strategies reflect your purpose—your intention—in developing the essay.

An argumentative essay may serve one or more purposes:

1. To present a position, belief, or conclusion in a rational and effective way.
2. To defend a position against critics or detractors.
3. To persuade people to agree with a position or take a certain action.
4. To attack a position without necessarily presenting an alternative or opposing viewpoint.

An effective argumentative essay often combines a variety of forms and purposes. For example, an argumentative essay on legalizing marijuana might have to explain effects, analyze laws, or evaluate experiments, among a broad range of options. When you take time to consider your purpose before you even begin to write, the decisions you make will help you to think more clearly about both the design and intention of your essay.

Appeals to Reason, Emotion, and Ethics

As the definitions of special terms and the discussion of justification presented earlier in the chapter suggest, argumentation places a premium on rational discourse. In fact, the *appeal to reason* is the fundamental purpose of argumentation. However, classical rhetorical theory acknowledges that the *appeal to emotion* and the *appeal to ethics* are also important elements in the construction of argument and the effort to persuade. A mere presentation of reasons is usually not an effective argument. For your argument to be effective, you need to pay attention to the value of strategic emotional and ethical appeal.

Appeals to Reason   The *appeal to reason* or logic is the primary instrument of effective argument. The most common way of developing an argument according to the principles of sound reasoning is *deduction*, which is most readily understood as an ordering of ideas from the general to the particular. With deduction you move from a general assertion through reasons and support focused on the main assertion. Consider the following student paragraph, which uses the deductive method.

Anti-marijuana laws make people contemptuous of the legal system. This contempt is based in part on the key fact that there are too many contradictions and inconsistencies in criminal penalties for marijuana use. Laws vary radically from state to state. In Texas, you can be sentenced to life imprisonment for first-time use of marijuana. By contrast, in the District of Columbia the same "crime" would most likely result in a suspended sentence.

Deduction is a convincing way of arranging ideas and information logically. By stating the proposition or generalization first, you present the most important idea. Then, as in the paragraph above, you move to more specific ideas and details. Examined more rigorously, deductive reasoning involves a process of critical thinking known as *syllogism* in which you move from a major statement or premise, through another minor premise, to a third statement or conclusion. Aristotle's famous syllogism captures this mental process:

> Major Premise: All human beings are mortal.
> Minor Premise: Socrates is a human being.
> Conclusion: Socrates is mortal.

The soundness of any deductive argument rests on the *truth* of the premises and the *validity* of the syllogism itself. In other words, if you grant the truth of the premises, you must also grant the conclusion. The deductive method can be used effectively in many forms of expository as well as argumentative essays.

Inductive reasoning reverses the process of deduction by moving from the particular ideas to general ones. In the paragraph that follows from an essay by F. M. Esfandiary, "The Mystical West Puzzles the Practical East," the writer presents various ideas and evidence that lead to a major proposition at the end.

> Twenty-five hundred years ago, Buddha, like other Eastern philosophers before him, said: "He who sits still, wins." Asia, then immobilized in primitive torpor, had no difficulty responding. It sat still. What it won for sitting still was the perpetuation of famines and terrorizing superstitions, oppression of children, subjugation of women, emasculation of men, fratricidal wars, persecutions, mass killings. The history of Asia, like the history of all mankind, is a horrendous account of human suffering.

By presenting his supporting—and provocative—ideas first, the author is able to interest us before we reach the climactic argument at the end of the paragraph. Of course, whether we accept the Esfandiary's argument—his statement of truth—or are prepared to debate his claim depends on the strength of the reasons and evidence he offers.

Many of the argumentative essays you read and much of the argumentative writing you undertake will reflect the mental processes of deduction and induction. The novelist Robert M. Pirsig offers his version of these critical thinking strategies in his cult classic, *Zen and the Art of Motorcycle Maintenance:*

> If the cycle goes over a bump and the engine misfires, and then goes over another bump and the engine misfires, and then goes over another bump and the engine misfires, and then goes over a long smooth stretch of road and there is no misfiring, and then goes over a fourth bump and the engine misfires again, one can logically conclude that the misfiring is caused by the bumps. That is induction: reasoning from particular experiences to general truths.
>
> Deductive inferences do the reverse. They start with general knowledge and predict a specific observation. For example if, from reading the hierarchy of facts about the machine the mechanic knows the horn of the cycle is powered exclusively by electricity from the battery, then he can logically infer that if the battery is dead the horn will not work. That is deduction.

Constructing an argument through the use of logical reasoning is a powerful way to convince or persuade a particular audience about the validity of your claims.

Appeals to Emotion   In addition to developing your argument logically using the appeal to reason, you should consider the value of incorporating *appeals to emotion* into an argumentative paper. A letter home asking for more money would in all likelihood require a certain carefully modulated emotional appeal. Similarly, Martin Luther King, Jr.'s famous "I Have a Dream" speech at the 1963 March on Washington, which appears on page 309 in this textbook, is one of the finest contemporary examples of emotional appeal. King's speech ends with this invocation:

> When we let freedom ring, when we let it ring from every village and every hamlet, from every state and every city, we will be able to speed up that day when all of God's children, black men and white men, Jews and Gentiles, Protestants and Catholics, will be able to join hands and sing in the words of the old Negro spiritual, "Free at last! Free at last! Thank God almighty, we are free at last!"

King's skillful application of balanced biblical cadences, of connotative and figurative language, and a strong, almost prophetic tone demonstrates the value of carefully crafted emotional appeal in the hands of an accomplished writer of argument.

Of course, in constructing an argument you should avoid the sort of cynical manipulation of emotion that is common in the world of spoken discourse and the media in general. (For a list of unfair emotional appeals, see page 80.) But honest emotional appeal provides a human context for the rational ideas and evidence you present in an argumentative essay—ideas that might otherwise be cold and uninteresting to your audience. Assuredly if you want to persuade your audience to undertake a particular course of action, you must draw members of this audience closer to you as a person, perhaps even inspire them by your feelings about the subject or issue. In truth, you *must* establish rapport with your reader in an argumentative essay. If you fail to engage the reader's feelings, the best-constructed rational appeal could fall flat.

Appeals to Ethics   For an emotional appeal to achieve maximum effectiveness, it must not only reinforce the rational strength of your argument but also the ethical basis of your ideas. When you use *ethical appeal,* you present yourself as a well-informed, a fair-minded, and an honest person. Aristotle acknowledged the importance of *ethos,* or the character of the writer in the construction of argument, for if you create a sense that you are trustworthy, your readers or listeners will be inspired or persuaded. The "sound" or "voice" of your essay, which you convey to the reader through your choice of style and tone and which can only be perfected through the process of careful drafting and revision, will help in convincing the audience to share your opinion.

In an appeal to ethics, you try to convince the reader that you are a person of sound character—that you possess good judgment and an acceptable system of values. As a person of goodwill and good sense, you also demonstrate an ability to empathize with your audience, to understand their viewpoints and perspectives. The psychologist Carl Rogers suggests that a willingness to embrace a potentially adversarial audience, to treat this audience more like an ally in an ethical cause, is a highly effective way to establish goodwill and the credibility of your beliefs. In Rogerian argument, your willingness to understand an opposing viewpoint and actually rephrase it reflectively for mutual understanding enables you to further establish your ethical and personal qualities.

You can appreciate the powerful combination of rational, emotional, and ethical appeals in Abraham Lincoln's "Gettysburg Address," which is presented on page 91 for analysis and discussion. Following Lincoln's speech are a classic and a contemporary visual argument on the nature of war, both of which demonstrate that appeals to reason, emotion, and ethics can also be found in the visual messages that surround us.

WRITING POWERFUL ARGUMENTS

One of the most common writing assignments in college courses, especially courses in the humanities and social sciences, is the argumentative essay. Unlike narrative and descriptive essays and the major forms of expository writing—comparison and contrast, definition, classification, process, and causal analysis—the argumentative paper requires the writer to take a stand and to support a position as effectively as possible. As mentioned earlier, the rhetorical strategies underlying expository or informative writing often appear in argumentative papers. However, given the purpose of the argumentative essay, you must present your ideas as powerfully as possible in order to advance your point of view and convince your readers to accept your position or take a specific course of action. For this reason, you must construct your argumentative paper carefully and effectively. The process for writing powerful arguments that appears in this section is useful, but it is not a formula. Ultimately you can construct powerful arguments in numerous ways, but you always must consider the relationship between your ideas, your particular purpose, and your audience.

Identify an Issue

Remember that not every subject lends itself to useful or necessary argument. The notion that *"everything* is an argument" probably contains a grain of truth, but in reality some things make for more powerful arguments than others. Certain subjects—for example, stamp collecting—might appeal to you personally and powerfully, but are they worth arguing about? Consequently, your first step in writing an effective argumentative essay is to identify a subject that contains an issue—in other words, a subject that will elicit two or more differing opinions.

Clearly there are certain subjects that touch on current problems and inspire strong opinions. President Lincoln's "Gettysburg Address" dealt with a monumental issue central to the very survival of the nation; for virtually everyone in the United States at that time, the issues raised by Lincoln were debatable. Similarly, the issue of the death penalty produces two diametrically opposed viewpoints in the essays by H. L. Mencken and Coretta Scott King that are reprinted in this chapter. Social and political issues tend to be ripe subjects for debate, fostering "pro" and "con" viewpoints. (Remember that there are often more than two sides to a complex issue.) Such issues, by their very nature, often raise powerful and conflicting systems of belief that place heavy burdens on the writer to provide convincing reasons and evidence to support a claim.

Not all issues in argumentative papers have to be of national or global concern, however. Indeed, issues like capital punishment, abortion, or global warming might not be of special interest to you. Of course, if an instructor requires an argumentative essay on one of these broad "hot-button" topics, you will need to prepare to write the paper by first establishing an argumentative perspective on it—in other words, by choosing your side on the issue. Fortunately, you often have opportunities to select issues of more immediate, personal, or local concern: Should fast food franchises be permitted in the student cafeteria? Should there be a campus policy on hate language? Should sophomores be required to pass standardized tests in reading, writing, and mathematics before advancing to their junior year? Many powerfully constructed arguments can deal with issues close to home and with subjects that are of considerable personal interest. Whether dealing with an issue mandated by the instructor or selecting your own issue for an argumentative paper, ask yourself at the outset of this critical process what your position on the issue is and how it can be developed through logic and evidence.

Take a Stand and Clarify Your Claim

Once you have identified an issue that lends itself to argumentation—an issue that people might reasonably disagree about—you must take a clear stand on this issue. In other words, your claim will advance your viewpoint over all other viewpoints. The aim is not to defeat an opponent but to persuade readers—your audience—to accept your opinion. Consequently, the first step at this stage is to establish as clearly as possible what your claim is going to be. You might want to experiment with one or more of the following strategies:

- Gather information on the issue from debates on radio, television, or the Internet. Electronic resources on the World Wide Web can be helpful as you begin to research what your position on an issue is going to be. (For help with critically evaluating Web sources, see page 78 and Chapter 12.)
- Brainstorm or write informally about the issue, jotting down your immediate response to it—how it makes you feel or what you think about it. If the issue raises emotional responses, what are the causes of this response? What are your more thoughtful or intellectual responses to the issue?
- List some preliminary reasons you respond to the issue in the way you do. By listing reasons and also listing the types of evidence you will need to support those reasons, you will be able to determine at an early stage if you will have enough material for a solid argumentative paper, and what forms of research you will have to conduct.
- Jot down examples, facts, and ideas that might support your claim.
- Begin to think about possible objections to your position, and list these opposing viewpoints.

As this inventory of strategies suggests, there are numerous ways to think and write critically about your approach to an issue during the prewriting stage of your argument. Essentially, during prewriting you want to begin to articulate and pinpoint your claim, and thereby start to limit, control, and clarify the scope of your argument.

Once you have developed a preliminary approach to an issue, you should be prepared to state your claim in the form of a thesis sentence. From your reading of the information on the thesis statement in the first chapter of this textbook (page 23), you know that you must limit the scope and purpose of your thesis or claim. Too broad a claim will be hard to cover in convincing fashion in a standard argumentative paper. One useful way to limit and clarify your claim is to consider the purpose of your argument. Do you want to argue a position on a particular issue? Do you want to argue that a certain activity, belief, or situation is good or bad, harmful or beneficial, effective or ineffective? Do you want to persuade readers to undertake or avoid a particular course of action? Do you want readers to simply consider an issue in a new light? Do you want readers to endorse your interpretation or evaluation of an artistic or literary work? By sifting through the primary purposes of argument, which involve value judgments, policies, and interpretations, you will arrive at the main point of your argument—your claim.

Analyze Your Audience

All writing can be considered a process of communication, a conversation with an audience of readers. In argumentative writing, it is especially important to establish a common ground of belief with your readers if you expect them to accept your claim or undertake a certain course of action. Of course, you cannot change your ideas and approaches to an issue merely to please a particular audience. However, you do not construct an argumentative paper in order to be misunderstood, disbelieved, or rejected. Within the limits set by who you are, what you believe, and what your purpose is, you can match your argumentative style and approach to audience expectations.

To establish common ground with your audience, it is important to know them well so that you can dispose them favorably to your claim and the reasons and evidence supporting it. Your audience might be a professor, a prospective employer, an admission or financial aid officer, an editor, or a member of your family. If you determine the nature of your audience *before* you compose the first draft of your argumentative paper, you will be able to tailor style, content, and tone to a specific person or group.

Try to imagine and anticipate audience expectations by asking basic questions about your readers:

1. What are the age, gender, professional background, educational level, and political orientation of most of the members of the audience?
2. How much does the audience know about the issue? Is it an audience of experts or a general audience with only limited knowledge of the issue?
3. What does the audience expect from you in terms of the purpose behind your claim? Does the audience expect you to prove your claim and/or persuade them to accept it?
4. Will the audience be friendly, hostile, or neutral toward your argument? What political, cultural, ethical, or religious factors contribute to the audience's probable position on this issue?
5. What else do you know about the audience's opinions, attitudes, and values? How might these factors shape your approach to the argument?

Suppose, for example, that you are planning to write an argumentative essay on pollution. What common expectations would an English professor, a sociology professor, and a chemistry professor have concerning your argument? What differences in approach and content would be dictated by your decision to write for one of these instructors? Or consider these different audiences for a paper on the topic of pollution: a group of grade school children in your home town, or the Environmental Protection Agency, or the manager of a landfill operation, or a relative in Missouri whose town has been experiencing chemical pollution. In each instance, the type and nature of the audience will influence your approach to the issue and even your purpose. Remember that through *purpose* you find the proper context for your argument. Any writer who wants to communicate effectively with his or her audience will adjust the content and tone of an argument so as not to lose, confuse, or mislead the reader.

Establish Your Tone

By *tone* we mean the attitude you take toward your subject. A word that often is used interchangeably with tone is *voice*. Tone is the personal voice that a reader "hears" in your writing. This voice may vary, depending on the situation, your purpose, and the audience that you are writing for. It may be personal or impersonal and range across a spectrum of attitudes: serious or humorous, subjective or objective, straightforward or ironic, formal or casual, and so forth. You adjust your tone to match your purpose in writing.

In argumentation, an effective tone will be a true and trustworthy reflection of the writing situation. After all, you are writing an argumentative essay in order to convince and persuade, and consequently you need to sound like a reasonable, well-organized, and logical individual. When writing for college instructors, that "community of scholars," you must be especially careful to maintain a reasonable tone. You do not have to sound scholarly, legalistic, or overly technical in presenting your argument, but you do have to employ a personal voice that is appropriate to the writing occasion and audience expectations.

To achieve an appropriate tone in argumentative writing, you will often need to be forceful in presenting your ideas. Remember that you are staking out a position, perhaps on a controversial issue, and you must seem willing to defend it. Try to maintain a consistent voice of authority, but do not be overbearing: Do not move from the podium to the locker room, mixing voices in a way that will confuse or alienate your audience. A tone or voice that exceeds the limits of good taste and commonly accepted norms of argumentative style is likely to be ineffectual. A voice that is too emotional, overblown, or irrational will in all likelihood alienate the reader and erode your claim.

Your tone—your voice—is a revelation of yourself. It derives from your claims and supporting ideas, your language and sentence structure. Even if your audience is one person—typically your professor—you certainly must present yourself to that audience as convincingly as possible. When your tone is adjusted to the issue, the claim, and the supporting evidence, and also to the nature of the opposition, you stand a good chance of writing an effective argumentative essay.

Develop and Organize the Grounds for Your Claim

You establish the validity of your claim by setting out the reasons and evidence—the *grounds*—that support your main point. Whereas the claim presents your general proposition or point of view, as you develop your grounds you organize the argument into minor propositions, evidence, and refutation. By establishing the grounds for your claim, you explain the particular perspective or point of view you take on an issue. The grounds for your claim permit the reader to "see" the strength of your particular position.

There are numerous ways to state the primary reasons or grounds for holding your position. Think of these primary reasons as minor propositions underlying the basis of your claim—reasons that readers would find it difficult to rebut or reject. Three possible models for organizing claims and grounds in an essay can now be considered.

Model 1

    Introduction: Statement and clarification of claim.

    First minor proposition and evidence.

    Second minor proposition and evidence.

    Third minor proposition and evidence.

    Refutation of opposing viewpoints for minor propositions.

    Conclusion

Model 2

    Introduction: Statement and clarification of claim.

    First minor proposition and evidence; refutation.

    Second minor proposition and evidence; refutation.

    Third minor proposition and evidence; refutation.

    Conclusion.

Model 3

    Statement and clarification of claim.

    Summary of opposing viewpoints and refutation.

    First minor proposition and evidence.

    Second minor proposition and evidence.

    Third minor proposition and evidence.

    Conclusion.

In practice, arguments rarely adhere slavishly to these models. In fact, you can arrange your argument in numerous ways. However, the models can serve a useful purpose, especially in examinations that require argumentative responses to a question, for they provide a handy template for your answer. In argument, to support your claim, you will need substantial reasons, sometimes more than the three minor propositions illustrated in these models. Remember that one reason generally will not provide sufficient grounds to prove an argument. Moreover, you should keep in mind the need to distinguish between your *opinions*, which in the broadest sense are beliefs that you cannot verify logically, and reasons, which are based on logic, evidence, and direct proof.

Gather and Evaluate Your Evidence

Once you have established your claim and your reasons, you must turn your attention to developing evidence for your claim, a subject already discussed in the first chapter and also here. Collecting evidence is a bit like the strategies for successful fishing presented by the student in his classification paragraph in the first chapter (see page 36): You want to fish the top, the middle, and the bottom of your subject. Phrased somewhat differently, you want to cast a wide net as you seek evidence designed to support your claim and reasons.

At the outset, a carefully designed search of the World Wide Web can yield ample evidence. The Web will permit you to establish links to sites and listservs where you can download or print full or abstracted texts from periodicals, books, documents, and reports. Remember that searching the Web is often like navigating a minefield: Useless "facts," hoaxes, and informational marketing ploys mix with serious research, honest reporting, and critical analysis. To guard against the pitfalls involved in relying exclusively on Web surfing, you should also make a trip to the college library to augment your quest for evidence. Research librarians can help you to evaluate Web sites and direct you to the best sources—both traditional and technological—for the types of evidence you are seeking. (For more on library and Internet research, see Chapter 12.) Depending on your subject, you might consider interviewing individuals who can provide expert testimony designed to support your claim and reasons. Finally, your own personal experience and the experiences of your friends and acquaintances might provide useful evidence, although such kinds of anecdotal or firsthand support should be treated judiciously and not serve as the entire basis for your paper. You and your friends might claim that a current horror movie is great, but such personal evidence must be tempered by a willingness to consult established critics for additional support.

If you cast a wide net and fish the whole lake, you will almost always catch more than you require. Yet the very process of searching comprehensively for evidence can produce exciting unintended consequences. You might, for example, discover that certain evidence suggests a need to revise or qualify your claim. Evidence can also help you to articulate or confirm the warrants that are the foundation of your argument, for experts writing on an issue often state the assumptions, principles, or beliefs that offer connections between a claim and its grounds. The insights gained by considering other evidence might cause you to develop a new reason for your claim that you had not considered initially. You might also discover evidence that helps you to refute the ideas of your anticipated opposition. Having a wealth of evidence at your disposal is an embarrassment of riches that you can exploit skillfully.

After you have collected adequate evidence to bolster your claim and the key reasons supporting that claim, the next necessary step is to evaluate and select the best evidence available to you. Writers who carefully evaluate and select their evidence produce effective arguments. At the outset, the nature of the writing situation—an examination, a term paper, a letter to the editor—will dictate to an extent the type of evidence you need to evaluate. In most instances, however, your evidence should be *credible, comprehensive,* and *current.* Your evidence is credible when the sources of your information are reliable and the evidence itself is representative. Your evidence is comprehensive when you provide a broad range of facts, information, and data designed to cover all aspects of your argument completely. In presenting evidence comprehensively, you also make certain that there is sufficient support for each of your reasons—not too much evidence for one and too little for another, but an even balance between and among the minor propositions. Finally, always try to locate the most current evidence available to support your claim. Data and statistics often do not age well and tend to lose their accuracy. However, in some arguments older evidence can be compared with newer information: For example, a paper arguing that immigration to the United States is out of control could make skillful use of data from the 1960 Census *and* the 2000 Census.

Evidence is the heart of any argument. Without evidence, readers will not be interested in your claim and supporting reasons. Make certain that the evidence —the facts, examples, and details—you present is accurate and skillfully presented so that readers become interested in your more abstract propositions, identify with your position, and come away convinced of the validity of your argument.

Consider Your Warrants

Even as you clarify your claim and assemble your reasons and evidence, you must also consider the assumptions underlying your argument. Think of the assumption or *warrant* as the link between a claim and the supporting evidence— the underlying set of beliefs or principles governing our essential perception of the world and the human condition. Warrants answer the question of *how* the data are connected to the claim. Sometimes these warrants are stated, but often they remain unstated. In either instance, they are not necessarily self-evident or universally accepted. They are significant nevertheless, for as generalizations that are far broader than claims and evidence, warrants serve as the bedrock of an argument.

Warrants help to guarantee that a reader will accept your argument, and consequently it is important to consider them. When you are writing for a friendly or supportive audience, you can usually assume that your readers will accept the warrants supporting your claim, and therefore you might not even need to state them. For example, if you claim in a report for your biology professor that Creationism should not be taught in high school science classrooms, your argument is based on several assumptions or warrants: that the Constitution, for example, requires the separation of church and state, or that there is no scientific basis for Creationism. In fact, when making your claim about Creationism before a scientist, you also are relying on certain *backings,* which are the principles underlying the warrants themselves—for instance, the idea that a scientist is concerned with scientific objectivity rather than literal interpretations of the Bible, or that scientists deal with the empirical reality and not matters of faith. But what if you were make your claim in a letter to a local school board, several of whose members want to revise the ninth-grade earth science curriculum to emphasize Creationism and evolution equally? In this instance, you would be presenting your argument to a potentially skeptical or hostile audience, and you should expect that you will have to state your warrants clearly, bolster them with adequate support, and establish solid causal links between your warrants and your backing.

Whether you are writing an argumentative paper or reading an argumentative essay critically, you need to develop the habit of looking for and evaluating the warrants and the backing behind the argument. If the warrants are stated, it will make this task easier. If the warrants are unstated, you will have to detect and evaluate them if you are reading an argumentative essay. If you are writing an argumentative essay, you should consider whether your audience will probably understand and consent to the warrants that serve as the foundation of your paper. If you have any doubt, then you should include them.

Deal with Opposing Viewpoints

In order to make your argument effectively as possible, you need to acknowledge and deal with opposing viewpoints. Any controversial issue is going to have more than one viewpoint, and you must recognize contending claims and handle them fairly. As suggested in the section on audience analysis, you can enhance your credibility by describing these opposing viewpoints fully and accurately and with a respectful rather than hostile tone, even as you demonstrate that your position in an argument is the most reasonable and valid.

As a prewriting strategy for refutation, you might try dividing a sheet of paper or your computer screen into three columns, labeling them, from left to right, "Supporting Viewpoints," "Opposing Viewpoints," and "Refutation." Then list the main supporting points for your claim, thinking of possible opposing responses and writing them down as you go. Imagining how the opposition will respond to your supporting reasons will help you to develop refutations, or counterarguments. You can use the resulting chart as a guide to organize sections of your argumentative paper.

The listing technique for refutation forces you to acknowledge opposing viewpoints and also refute them in a systematic way. It is perfectly appropriate—and even necessary—to demonstrate the weakness or insufficiency of opposing arguments, for refutation strengthens your own position. Any complex argument that you present will not be complete unless you skillfully refute all predictable opposing viewpoints, using one of the following four techniques.

- Question the opposition's claim, asking if it is too flimsy, broad, overstated, or improperly grounded in minor propositions.
- Question the evidence. Is it insufficient, outdated, or inaccurate?
- Question the warrants and backing of an opposing argument—those assumptions and beliefs that underpin the opposition's claim.
- Concede some part of the opposition's viewpoint, a subtle but extremely attractive strategy that shows that you are a courteous and unbiased thinker and writer and that therefore constitutes an appeal to ethics.

Avoid Unfair Emotional Appeals and Errors in Reasoning

When you write and revise an argumentative essay, you need to avoid certain temptations and dangers that are unique to this form of discourse. You always have to make certain that your argumentative strategies are fair and appropriate and that you have avoided oversimplifying your argument. You also need to resist the temptation to include persuasive appeals that distort critical reasoning and to avoid errors in logical reasoning.

Emotional appeals are effective when used appropriately in argumentation, but used unfairly they can distort your logical reasoning. Such "loaded" arguments are filled with appeals to the reader's emotions, fears, and prejudices. Here are three of the most common fallacies of emotional distortion to avoid.

1. *Transfer* is the association of a proposition with a famous person. Transfer can be either positive ("In the spirit of President Franklin Delano Roosevelt, we should create a jobs program for the nation's unemployed") or negative ("President George W. Bush is the symbol of unbridled capitalism"). Another term for negative transfer is name calling. In both the positive and negative types of transfer, however, there is no logical basis for the connection.

2. *Argumentum ad hominem* ("to the man") is a strategy that discredits a person in an effort to discredit his or her argument. It attacks the person rather than the position: "Richards is a homosexual and consequently cannot understand the sanctity of heterosexual marriage." In this instance, the individual becomes a false issue.

3. *Argumentum ad populum* ("to the people") deliberately arouses an audience's emotions about certain institutions and ideas. Certain words have strong positive or negative connotations. Such words as "patriotism" and "motherhood" are *virtue* words that often prompt the creation of *glittering generalities*. Suggestive words can be used to distort meaning by illogical association and to manipulate an audience to take a stand for or against a proposition: "USC should not take the *totalitarian* step of requiring athletes to maintain a full course load." A related strategy is the *bandwagon* approach, in which the writer generalizes falsely that the crowd or majority is always right: "Everyone is voting for Erikson and you should too."

These unfair emotional appeals are often found in political speech writing, advertising, and propaganda. When you write argumentative essays, you should use persuasive appeal to reinforce rather than distort the logical presentation of your ideas, blending reasonable claims and valid emotional and ethical appeals to convince rather than trick your audience into agreeing with you.

Equally important is the need to avoid errors in reasoning in the construction of an argument. Here are some types of errors in reasoning, or *logical fallacies*, that are common in argumentative writing.

1. *Hasty generalizations.* A hasty generalization is a conclusion based on insufficient, unrepresentative, or untrue evidence: "The president of the college successfully raised 100 million dollars, so other college presidents should be able to do the same." When you indulge in hasty generalizations you jump to false conclusions. Hasty generalizations are also at the heart of stereotyping—the uncritical application of an oversimplified generalization to a group or to individual members of the group. Make certain that you have adequate and accurate evidence to support any claim or conclusion.

2. *Broad generalizations.* A broad generalization typically employs words like *all*, *never*, and *always* to state something absolutely or categorically. It is actually a form of overstatement, as in the sentence "Freud always treated sexuality as the basis of human behavior." Usually, readers can easily find exceptions to such sweeping statements, so it is best to qualify them.

3. *Oversimplification.* Oversimplification reduces alternatives. Several forms of oversimplification can be distinguished.

   a. *Either/or.* Don't assume that there are only two sides to an issue, only two possibilities, only yes or no, only right or wrong: "Either we make English a one-year requirement or college students will not be able to write well."

   b. *No choice.* Don't assume that there is only one possibility: "The United States has no other alternative than to build the Star Wars missile defense system." Parents and politicians are prone to no-other-choice propositions.

   c. *No harm or cost.* Don't assume that a potential benefit will not have significant harms, consequences, or costs: "We should sell North Korea as much wheat as it needs." No-harm generalizations or arguments may overlook dangerous implications. Always consider alternative evidence.

   d. *One solution.* Don't assume that a complicated issue has only one solution: "Embryonic stem cell should not be used for research, for using them in this way will lead to the destruction of human life." Always consider evidence for other solutions or alternative approaches to issues and problems.

4. *Begging the question.* Do not assume in your premises or in your evidence what is to be proved in the conclusion. For example, if you argue that vandalism by teenagers is unavoidable because teenagers are young and irresponsible, you are begging the question because you are not proving your premise. Another form of begging the question is to take a conclusion for granted before it is proved.

5. *False cause-and-effect relationships.* Perhaps the most common error in trying to establish causal relationships is known as the *post hoc, ergo propter hoc* fallacy ("after this, therefore because of this"). The fact that one event follows another is not proof that the first caused the second. If you maintain, for instance, that there is an increase in the crime rate every time there is a full moon, you are falsely identifying an unrelated event as a cause. Many superstitions—popular, political, and otherwise—illogically assume that one event somehow causes another.

6. *Disconnected ideas.* Termed in Latin *non sequitur* ("It does not follow"), this fault in reasoning arises when there is no logical connection between two or more ideas. Put differently, an argument's conclusion is not related to its premises: "George W. Bush makes a good president because he was a successful owner of a professional baseball team." Sometimes you think that a connection exists but you fail to state it in writing. For example, you may think that owners of baseball teams and presidents need to have strong people skills and be good judges of character. In other words, *you* may see the logical connection between your ideas about presidents and baseball

team owners, but if you don't make it explicit, readers may think there is a non sequitur.

7. *Weak or false analogies.* An *analogy* is a type of comparison that explains a subject by comparing it to the features of another essentially dissimilar subject: "Unless we learn to think critically about the niagara of information that washes over us every day, we will be lost in a flood of rumors and gossip." Analogies can be used to illustrate a point, although they should always be used carefully and with discretion. More significantly, an analogy can *never* function as evidence or logical proof of a position.

In conclusion, the hallmark of argumentation is sound critical thinking. If you present your claims, grounds, and evidence carefully, are willing to assemble the best and most objective data, treat the opposition with respect, and are flexible in responding to new ideas, you will be well on your way to constructing a solid argumentative essay. A successful argumentative paper reveals a writer who possesses an inquiring mind—one that is able to judge opinions on the basis of evidence, reason well, and back up ideas and beliefs in a convincing and valid way.

Readings for Critical Response and Writing

Classic and Contemporary Essays
How Do We Argue?

We have all been in situations where controversial issues arise. A friendly gathering may evolve into a spirited debate on abortion or cloning. Guests at a family dinner may turn their attention away from the host's expertly prepared cuisine toward a heated exchange over immigration. One issue that seems to inevitably arise when a conversation turns to issues of law and order is the death penalty or capital punishment. Arguments may range from cool statistical analysis of the value of this punishment as a "deterrent" to impassioned pleas regarding the sanctity of all human life. H. L. Mencken, in his classic essay "The Penalty of Death," provides a singular flavor to the argumentative stew by presenting the reasons for maintaining the death penalty; however, it appears evident from his style and tone that he is mocking its proponents by revealing their hypocrisy. He presents no fancy academic studies, nor does he draw on any experts or scholars. His approach is ironic. He contends in his disarming way that deterrence is merely an excuse for the exercise of the ultimate punishment; the true motive is revenge and retribution. Coretta Scott King, in her essay "The Death Penalty Is a Step Back," draws on sociology, law, psychology, morality, and logic to oppose capital punishment. Hers is a multipronged attack against the death penalty, and unlike Mencken, her tone is serious, straightforward, and unadorned. Is there *one* right way to address an issue of such seriousness? Perhaps it is not so much the style and methods one uses, but how well they are used.

The Penalty of Death

H. L. Mencken

H(enry) L(ouis) Mencken (1880–1956) was an American editor, an author, and a critic. Born in Baltimore, he served as an editor for three Baltimore newspapers: the Morning Herald, Evening Herald, *and* The Baltimore Sun. *Noted for his pungent and iconoclastic criticism, he reveled in satirizing the middle classes. He was also a student of philology and published* The American Language, *which went through several editions with added supplements. The topics for his many books ranged from studies of dramatists to the defense of women's rights. He was also a champion for a whole generation of American realist fiction writers, including Theodore Dreiser, Sherwood Anderson, Sinclair Lewis, and Eugene O'Neill. The following well-known essay reveals the hypocrisy behind the rationale many people give for supporting the death penalty and the true reason they support it.*

Of the arguments against capital punishment that issue from uplifters, two are 1 commonly heard most often, to wit:

1. That hanging a man (or frying him or gassing him) is a dreadful business, degrading to those who have to do it and revolting to those who have to witness it.
2. That it is useless, for it does not deter others from the same crime.

The first of these arguments, it seems to me, is plainly too weak to need 2 serious refutation. All it says, in brief, is that the work of the hangman is unpleasant. Granted. But suppose it is? It may be quite necessary to society for all that. There are, indeed, many other jobs that are unpleasant, and yet no one thinks of abolishing them—that of the plumber, that of the soldier, that of the garbage-man, that of the priest hearing confessions, that of the sand-hog, and so on. Moreover, what evidence is there that any actual hangman complains of his work? I have heard none. On the contrary, I have known many who delighted in their ancient art, and practised it proudly.

In the second argument of the abolitionists there is rather more force, but 3 even here, I believe, the ground under them is shaky. Their fundamental error consists in assuming that the whole aim of punishing criminals is to deter other (potential) criminals—that we hang or electrocute A simply in order to so alarm B that he will not kill C. This, I believe, is an assumption which confuses a part with the whole. Deterence, obviously, is *one* of the aims of punishment, but it is surely not the only one. On the contrary, there are at least half a dozen, and some are probably quite as important. At least one of them, practically considered, is *more* important. Commonly, it is described as revenge, but revenge is really not the word for it. I borrow a better term from the late Aristotle: *katharsis.*

Katharsis, so used, means a salubrious discharge of emotions, a healthy letting off of steam. A school-boy, disliking his teacher, deposits a tack upon the pedagogical chair; the teacher jumps and the boy laughs. This is *katharsis.* What I contend is that one of the prime objects of all judicial punishments is to afford the same grateful relief *(a)* to the immediate victims of the criminal punished, and *(b)* to the general body of moral and timorous men.

These persons, and particularly the first group, are concerned only indirectly   4
with deterring other criminals. The thing they crave primarily is the satisfaction of seeing the criminal actually before them suffer as he made them suffer. What they want is the peace of mind that goes with the feeling that accounts are squared. Until they get that satisfaction they are in a state of emotional tension, and hence unhappy. The instant they get it they are comfortable. I do not argue that this yearning is noble; I simply argue that it is almost universal among human beings. In the face of injuries that are unimportant and can be borne without damage it may yield to higher impulses; that is to say, it may yield to what is called Christian charity. But when the injury is serious, Christianity is adjourned, and even saints reach for their sidearms. It is plainly asking too much of human nature to expect it to conquer so natural an impulse. A keeps a store and has a bookkeeper, B. B steals $700, employs it in playing at dice or bingo, and is cleaned out. What is A to do? Let B go? If he does so he will be unable to sleep at night. The sense of injury, of injustice, of frustration will haunt him like pruritus. So he turns B over to the police, and they hustle B to prison. Thereafter A can sleep. More, he has pleasant dreams. He pictures B chained to the wall of a dungeon a hundred feet underground, devoured by rats and scorpions. It is so agreeable that it makes him forget his $700. He has got his *katharsis.*

This same thing precisely takes place on a larger scale when there is a crime   5
which destroys a whole community's sense of security. Every law-abiding citizen feels menaced and frustrated until the criminals have been struck down—until the communal capacity to get even with them, and more than even, has been dramatically demonstrated. Here, manifestly, the business of deterring others is no more than an afterthought. The main thing is to destroy the concrete scoundrels whose act has alarmed everyone, and thus made everyone unhappy. Until they are brought to book that unhappiness continues; when the law has been executed upon them there is a sigh of relief. In other words, there is *katharsis.*

I know of no public demand for the death penalty for ordinary crimes, even   6
for ordinary homicides. Its infliction would shock all men of normal decency of feeling. But for crimes involving the deliberate and inexcusable taking of human life, by men openly defiant of all civilized order—for such crimes it seems, to nine men out of ten, a just and proper punishment. Any lesser penalty leaves them feeling that the criminal has got the better of society—that he is free to add insult to injury by laughing. That feeling can be dissipated only by a recourse to *katharsis,* the invention of the aforesaid Aristotle. It is more effectively and economically achieved, as human nature now is, by wafting the criminal to realms of bliss.

The real objection to capital punishment doesn't lie against the actual exter-   7
mination of the condemned, but against our brutal American habit of putting it

off so long. After all, every one of us must die soon or late, and a murderer, it must be assumed, is one who makes that sad fact the cornerstone of his metaphysic. But it is one thing to die, and quite another thing to lie for long months and even years under the shadow of death. No sane man would choose such a finish. All of us, despite the Prayer Book, long for a swift and unexpected end. Unhappily, a murderer, under the irrational American system, is tortured for what, to him, must seem a whole series of eternities. For months on end he sits in prison while his lawyers carry on their idiotic buffoonery with writs, injunctions, mandamuses, and appeals. In order to get his money (or that of his friends) they have to feed him with hope. Now and then, by the imbecility of a judge or some trick of juridic science, they actually justify it. But let us say that, his money all gone, they finally throw up their hands. Their client is now ready for the rope or the chair. But he must still wait for months before it fetches him.

That wait, I believe, is horribly cruel. I have seen more than one man sitting $_8$ in the death-house, and I don't want to see any more. Worse, it is wholly useless. Why should he wait at all? Why not hang him the day after the last court dissipates his last hope? Why torture him as not even cannibals would torture their victims? The common answer is that he must have time to make his peace with God. But how long does that take? It may be accomplished, I believe, in two hours quite as comfortably as in two years. There are, indeed, no temporal limitations upon God. He could forgive a whole herd of murderers in a millionth of a second. More, it has been done.

COMPREHENSION

1. Based upon your reading of Mencken's essay, is the author for or against capital punishment? Explain.
2. Study the last three lines of the essay. Explain what they mean in your own words.
3. The author's facility with language is due partly to his impressive vocabulary. Define words such as *salubrious, timorous,* and *manifestly.*

RHETORIC

1. The author uses symbolic logic, classification, and definition as devices in paragraphs 1 through 4. Cite examples of each of these rhetorical methods. What is each one's function?
2. What is the author's purpose in using a rather droll tone in discussing a subject that usually elicits strong emotional responses?
3. In paragraph 3, the author defines *katharsis* as "a healthy letting off of steam." In the light of the author's view that carrying out the death penalty results in a societal *katharsis,* what is the implicit irony in the definition?
4. What is the author's purpose in using both the placement of a tack on a teacher's seat and the execution of a human being as examples of *katharsis?*

5. What tone does the author use in describing humankind's desire for revenge? Does he support or deride this sentiment? Explain your conclusion by citing particular clues the author provides in his writing.

6. In paragraph 4, the author states, "But when the injury is serious, Christianity is adjourned, and even saints reach for their sidearms." How does this statement relate to the theme of the essay?

WRITING

1. For a creative writing project, pretend you are a legislator. Write an essay wherein you describe a crime and what its proper particular punishment should be. Be sure to fit the punishment to the crime.

2. Argue for or against the use of the death penalty in crimes other than murder.

3. There is some evidence to suggest that the death penalty may actually *increase* the murder rate. Study this line of inquiry, and write a research paper based upon your findings that either supports or rejects the thesis.

The Death Penalty Is a Step Back

Coretta Scott King

Coretta Scott King (b. 1927) is a civil-rights activist, free-lance journalist, and, since 1980, writer and commentator for CNN. Born in Alabama, she graduated from Antioch College and the New England Conservatory of Music. She first gained international prominence as the wife of Martin Luther King, Jr., whom she married in 1953. She wrote about her experiences with the revered civil-rights leader and orator in a book entitled My Life with Martin Luther King, Jr. *(1969). The following essay states in clear, thoughtful prose her feelings about the death penalty, which she considers both racist and immoral.*

When Steven Judy was executed in Indiana [in 1981] America took another step 1
backwards towards legitimizing murder as a way of dealing with evil in our society.

Although Judy was convicted of four of the most horrible and brutal mur- 2
ders imaginable, and his case is probably the worst in recent memory for opponents of the death penalty, we still have to face the real issue squarely: Can we expect a decent society if the state is allowed to kill its own people?

In recent years, an increase of violence in America, both individual and po- 3
litical, has prompted a backlash of public opinion on capital punishment. But however much we abhor violence, legally sanctioned executions are no deterrent and are, in fact, immoral and unconstitutional.

Although I have suffered the loss of two family members by assassination, 4
I remain firmly and unequivocally opposed to the death penalty for those convicted of capital offenses.

An evil deed is not redeemed by an evil deed of retaliation. Justice is never 5
advanced in the taking of a human life.

Morality is never upheld by legalized murder. Morality apart, there are a 6
number of practical reasons which form a powerful argument against capital
punishment.

First, capital punishment makes irrevocable any possible miscarriage of jus- 7
tice. Time and again we have witnessed the specter of mistakenly convicted
people being put to death in the name of American criminal justice. To those
who say that, after all, this doesn't occur too often, I can only reply that if it happens just once, that is too often. And it has occurred many times.

Second, the death penalty reflects an unwarranted assumption that the 8
wrongdoer is beyond rehabilitation. Perhaps some individuals cannot be
rehabilitated; but who shall make that determination? Is any amount of academic training sufficient to entitle one person to judge another incapable of
rehabilitation?

Third, the death penalty is inequitable. Approximately half of the 711 per- 9
sons now on death row are black. From 1930 through 1968, 53.5% of those executed were black Americans, all too many of whom were represented by
court-appointed attorneys and convicted after hasty trials.

The argument that this may be an accurate reflection of guilt, and homicide 10
trends, instead of a racist application of laws lacks credibility in light of a recent
Florida survey which showed that persons convicted of killing whites were four
times more likely to receive a death sentence than those convicted of killing
blacks.

Proponents of capital punishment often cite a "deterrent effect" as the main 11
benefit of the death penalty. Not only is there no hard evidence that murdering
murderers will deter other potential killers, but even the "logic" of this argument defies comprehension.

Numerous studies show that the majority of homicides committed in this 12
country are the acts of the victim's relatives, friends and acquaintances in the
"heat of passion."

What this strongly suggests is that rational consideration of future conse- 13
quences are seldom a part of the killer's attitude at the time he commits a crime.

The only way to break the chain of violent reaction is to practice nonvio- 14
lence as individuals and collectively through our laws and institutions.

COMPREHENSION

1. On what grounds does King oppose capital punishment?
2. King calls the death penalty "immoral" and "unconstitutional." What does
   she mean by this?

3. Does King offer any solutions to the problem of crime and violence? What are they?

RHETORIC

1. Where in the essay does King place her thesis statement? In your own words, what is this thesis?
2. What function do paragraphs 1 to 5 have in the essay?
3. What impact do the words *practical* and *powerful* (in paragraph 6) have on the reader? Who is King's intended audience?
4. Comment on the use of language in King's essay. Is it concrete or abstract? How would you characterize her writing style?
5. Trace King's use of transitions in paragraphs 7, 8, and 9.
6. Where does the writer use refutation in her essay? How does she use it to strengthen her argument? How effective are her responses?
7. Is King's ordering of ideas inductive or deductive? Justify your answer.

WRITING

1. Write an essay for or against capital punishment, using quotes from King's essay either as support or as refutation. Provide examples and your own observations as proof.
2. If capital punishment doesn't deter crime, what will? Write an essay in which you offer detailed solutions to the problem of crime and violence. How can society take a step forward in its treatment of criminals?
3. King's essay makes a connection between the death penalty and racism. Develop this theme in an essay. Consider the roles of class, race, legal representation, and political empowerment in determining who goes to prison and who gets executed.

Classic and Contemporary: Questions for Comparison

1. Does Mencken's sarcasm and iconoclastic tone suggest he is writing for a different audience than the more austere and straightforward King? Consider that Mencken was writing at least a half-century before King. To what sorts of audiences would each of the essays appeal? Explain your view.
2. Study the language used in each of the essays. What is similar or different about the style and diction of the two pieces? Does one seem more accessible to the modern reader? Do any of Mencken's references seem "dated"? Consider such terms as *uplifters* (paragraph 1), *abolitionists* (paragraph 3), and *juridic science* (paragraph 7).
3. Both Mencken and King have had firsthand experience with gruesome events. Mencken mentions that he has observed men in the "death-house" prior to

their execution, and Coretta Scott King's husband was assassinated. Does this lend authority to their grievances? Would you be less inclined to trust an opinion from a third arguer who had never had such personal experience?

The Gettysburg Address

Abraham Lincoln

Abraham Lincoln (1809–1865) was born the son of a pioneer in 1809 in Hodgesville, Kentucky, and moved to Illinois in 1831. After brief experiences as a clerk, postmaster, and county surveyor, he studied law and was elected to the state legislature in 1834. A prominent member of the newly formed Republican party, Lincoln became president on the eve of the Civil War. In 1862, after Union victory at Antietam, Lincoln issued the Emancipation Proclamation freeing the slaves—the crowning achievement of an illustrious presidency. Although he was an outstanding orator and debater throughout his political career, "The Gettysburg Address" is one of his greatest speeches—and certainly his most famous one. It was delivered at the dedication of the Gettysburg National Cemetery in 1863. Its form and content reflect the philosophical and moral views of the time as well as the rhetorical skill of its speaker. Lincoln was assassinated by John Wilkes Booth in 1865 shortly after Robert E. Lee's surrender and the end of the Civil War.

Four score and seven years ago our fathers brought forth on this continent, a new nation, conceived in Liberty, and dedicated to the proposition that all men are created equal. 1

Now we are engaged in a great civil war, testing whether that nation, or any nation so conceived and so dedicated, can long endure. We are met on a great battlefield of that war. We have come to dedicate a portion of that field as a final resting-place for those who here gave their lives that that nation might live. It is altogether fitting and proper that we should do this. 2

But, in a larger sense, we cannot dedicate—we cannot consecrate—we cannot hallow—this ground. The brave men, living and dead, who struggled here have consecrated it, far above our poor power to add or detract. The world will little note, nor long remember, what we say here, but it can never forget what they did here. It is for us the living, rather, to be dedicated here to the unfinished work which they who fought here have thus far so nobly advanced. It is rather for us to be here dedicated to the great task remaining before us—that from these honored dead we take increased devotion to that cause for which they gave the last full measure of devotion; that we here highly resolve that these dead shall not have died in vain; this nation, under God, shall have a new birth of freedom; and that government of the people, by the people, for the people, shall not perish from the earth. 3

COMPREHENSION

1. Although this speech was supposed to be a "dedication," Lincoln states that "we cannot dedicate." What does he mean by this?
2. Lincoln uses abstract words such as "liberty," "freedom," and "nation." What does he mean specifically by each of these terms?
3. What exactly happened "four score and seven years ago" in the context of the speech? Why is this reference so significant to the purpose of Lincoln's address?

RHETORIC

1. Note the progression of imagery from that of "death" to that of "birth." How does this structure contribute the theme and coherence of the speech?
2. How do the syntax, punctuation, and choice of the "first-person plural" form of address contribute to our understanding that this message was intended to be spoken rather than written?
3. Note how Lincoln refers to the combatants as "brave" and "honored." How does he suggest their struggle was distinguished from that of "us the living"? How does this comparison and contrast create clear similarities and differences between those who fought and those who are present to carry on the work of the soldiers?
4. The American Civil War was a battle between the "North" and the "South" as were the opponents at the Battle of Gettysburg. However, Lincoln does not mention this. What is the reason behind this omission? How does it make the speech focus on more comprehensive issues?
5. Besides being president, Lincoln was by definition a politician. In what ways can we determine that this is a "political speech" as well as a dedication?
6. Speeches are intended to be heard. What are some elements—for example, vocabulary, syntax, length or brevity of the sentences, juxtaposition of sentences, and so on—that appeal to the sense of sound?
7. Does this speech appeal primarily to the intellect, the emotions, or equally between the two? What are two or three sentences that demonstrate one or both of these appeals? What was the rationale behind your selections? Does Lincoln include any ethical appeals?

WRITING

1. Research the actual historical events that occurred during the Battle of Gettysburg. Write an expository essay of 400 to 500 words in which you discuss the significance of this particular speech at this point in the American Civil War. Use a minimum of three secondary source materials.
2. Read the speech three times. Then write a paraphrase of it. Examine your paraphrase to discover what elements you recalled. Then reread the speech

and write an expository essay focusing on how the structure of the speech contributed to helping you recall the information you did remember.

3. Engage in an Internet search to find the rhetorical influences on the language and style of Abraham Lincoln. Try such search phrases as "Lincoln, rhetorical influences" and other suitable expressions. Select three authoritative "hits" and write a research paper entitled "Rhetorical Influences on Abraham Lincoln."

Classic and Contemporary Images
WHAT IS AN ARGUMENT?

Using a Critical Perspective   What images and strategies do the Spanish artist Goya and the American photographer Adams employ to construct an argument about war? What exactly is their argument? Comment on the nature and effectiveness of the details they use to illustrate their position. Which work do you find more powerful or engaging? Explain.

The Prado Museum, Spain/Art Resource

Horrified by the excesses of the Napoleonic invasion of his homeland and the Spanish war for independence, the Spanish artist Francisco de Goya (1746–1828) painted *The Third of May, 1808,* a vivid rendition of an execution during wartime.

Eddie Adams/AP/Wide World Photos

Another wartime execution, this time captured on film by Eddie Adams in an image that won the Pulitzer Prize for spot news photography in 1969, brought home to Americans the horrors and ambiguities of the war in Vietnam.

Two Argumentative Essays for Analysis

As you read the following essays, look for the elements of effective argument in each, and the ways in which other rhetorical strategies help to advance the writers' claims.

Four-Letter Words Can Hurt You

Barbara Lawrence

Barbara Lawrence was born in Hanover, New Hampshire. After receiving a BA in French literature from Connecticut College, she worked as an editor for the magazines McCall's, Redbook, Harper's Bazaar, *and the* New Yorker. *During this period she also studied at New York University, where she received an MA in philosophy. Currently a professor of humanities at the State University of New York's College of Old Westbury, Lawrence has published criticism, poetry, and fiction in* Choice, Commonweal, Columbia Poetry, The New York Times, *and* The New Yorker. *"Four-Letter Words Can Hurt You" first appeared in* The New York Times *in 1973 and was later published in* Redbook. *In arguing against the "earthy, gut-honest" language often preferred by her students, the author provides a thoughtful, scholarly definition of the term* obscenity *itself.*

Why should any words be called obscene? Don't they all describe natural hu- 1 man functions? Am I trying to tell them, my students demand, that the "strong, earthy, gut-honest"—or, if they are fans of Norman Mailer, the "rich, liberating, existential"—language they use to describe sexual activity isn't preferable to "phony-sounding, middle-class words like 'intercourse' and 'copulate'?" "Cop You Late!" they say with fancy inflections and gagging grimaces. "Now, what is *that* supposed to mean?"

Well, what is it supposed to mean? And why indeed should one group of 2 words describing human functions and human organs be acceptable in ordinary conversation and another, describing presumably the same organs and functions, be tabooed—so much so, in fact, that some of these words still cannot appear in print in many parts of the English-speaking world?

The argument that these taboos exist only because of "sexual hangups" 3 (middle-class, middle-age, feminist), or even that they are a result of class oppression (the contempt of the Norman conquerors for the language of their Anglo-Saxon serfs), ignores a much more likely explanation, it seems to me, and that is the sources and functions of the words themselves.

The best known of the tabooed sexual words, for example, comes from the 4 German *ficken* meaning "to strike"; combined, according to Partridge's etymological dictionary *Origins*, with the Latin sexual verb *futuere;* associated in turn with the Latin *fustis,* "a staff or cudgel"; the Celtic *buc,* "a point, hence to pierce"; the Irish *bot,* "the male member"; the Latin *battuere,* "to beat"; the Gaelic *batair,* "a cudgeller'"; the Early Irish *bualaim,* "I strike"; and so forth. It is one of what etymologists sometimes called "the sadistic group of words for the man's part in copulation."

The brutality of this word, then, and its equivalents ("screw," "bang," etc.) is not an illusion of the middle class or a crotchet of Women's Liberation. In their origins and imagery these words carry undeniably painful, if not sadistic, implications, the object of which is almost always female. Consider, for example, what a "screw" actually does to the wood it penetrates; what a painful, even mutilating, activity this kind of analogy suggests. "Screw" is particularly interesting in this context, since the noun, according to Partridge, comes from words meaning "groove," "nut," "ditch," "breeding sow," "scrofula" and "swelling," while the verb, besides its explicit imagery, has antecedent associations to "write on," "scratch," "scarify," and so forth—a revealing fusion of a mechanical or painful action with an obviously denigrated object.

Not all obscene words, of course, are as implicitly sadistic or denigrating to women as these, but all that I know seem to serve a similar purpose: to reduce the human organism (especially the female organism) and human functions (especially sexual and procreative) to their least organic, most mechanical dimension; to substitute a trivializing or deforming resemblance for the complex human reality of what is being described.

Tabooed male descriptives, when they are not openly denigrating to women, often serve to divorce a male organ or function from any significant interaction with the female. Take the word *"testes,"* for example, suggesting "witnesses" (from the Latin *testis*) to the sexual and procreative strengths of the male organ; and the obscene counterpart of this word, which suggests little more than a mechanical shape. Or compare almost any of the "rich," "liberating" sexual verbs, so fashionable today among male writers, with that much-derived Latin word "copulate" ("to bind or join together") or even that Anglo-Saxon phrase (which seems to have had no trouble surviving the Norman Conquest) "make love."

How arrogantly self-involved the tabooed words seem in comparison to either of the other terms, and how contemptuous of the female partner. Understandably so, of course, if she is only a "skirt," a "broad," a "chick," a "pussycat" or a "piece." If she is, in other words no more than her skirt, or what her skirt conceals; no more than a breeder, or the broadest part of her; no more than a piece of a human being or a "piece of tail."

The most severely tabooed of all the female descriptives, incidentally, are those like a "piece of tail," which suggests (either explicitly or through antecedents) that there is no significant difference between the female channel through which we are all conceived and born and the anal outlet common to both sexes—a distinction that pornographers have always enjoyed obscuring.

This effort to deny women their biological identity, their individuality, their humanness, is such an important aspect of obscene language that one can only marvel at how seldom, in an era preoccupied with definitions of obscenity, this fact is brought to our attention. One problem, of course, is that many of the people in the best position to do this (critics, teachers, writers) are so reluctant today to admit that they are angered or shocked by obscenity. Bored, maybe, unimpressed, aesthetically displeased, but—no matter how brutal or denigrating the material—never angered, never shocked.

And yet how eloquently angered, how piously shocked many of these same 11 people become if denigrating language is used about any minority group other than women; if the obscenities are racial or ethnic, that is, rather than sexual. Words like "coon," "kike," "spic," "wop," after all, deform identity, deny individuality and humanness in almost exactly the same way that sexual vulgarisms and obscenities do.

No one that I know, least of all my students, would fail to question the val- 12 ues of a society whose literature and entertainment rested heavily on racial or ethnic pejoratives. Are the values of a society whose literature and entertainment rest as heavily as ours on sexual pejoratives any less questionable?

COMPREHENSION

1. Lawrence considers several reasons why certain "four-letter words" should be obscene. What are these reasons? What do they all have in common?
2. Lawrence offers reasons why she considers words obscene and provides examples of these reasons. From her argument, what do you infer would be her definition of "obscene"?
3. In paragraph 8, Lawrence claims that obscene words are "arrogantly self-involved." What does she mean by this?
4. What is the essay's thesis?

RHETORIC

1. Lawrence introduces her topic with a series of questions. What is the purpose of this strategy? How does it help organize the argument that follows?
2. In paragraph 5, Lawrence claims that the analogies between the literal meaning of certain words and their obscene uses make them unacceptable. What is it about such analogies that makes the terms offensive?
3. The topic of this essay may obscure some of the rhetorical flourishes in Lawrence's writing. Study the length, punctuation, and complexity of paragraph 6. How do these components reflect on Lawrence's mastery of English prose? Does the structure of this paragraph make it forceful and effective or confusing and overbearing?
4. What tone does Lawrence use when she discusses the attitude toward obscenity of certain "critics, teachers, writers"? What vocabulary choices does she use to convey this tone?

5. In paragraph 4, Lawrence uses evidence from etymological sources to support her thesis. How does this evidence strengthen her thesis that some words are authentically "obscene"? How does her knowledge of word origins and history contribute to her authority on the subject?
6. Lawrence discusses her students in the introduction and conclusion. Why does she consider it particularly important to communicate an understanding of obscenity to this group? Why doesn't she refer to this group in the body of her essay?
7. Define the following words: *existential* (paragraph 1), *etymological* (paragraph 4), *explicit, antecedent, scarify* (paragraph 5). What words were unfamiliar to you when you first read the essay? How much clearer is the essay assuming you've looked them up in the dictionary?

WRITING

1. For a research project, trace the etymology of a particular "obscene" word, and write a 350- to 400-word expository essay on it entitled "History of an Obscene Word."
2. Can words Lawrence considers obscene have legitimate uses in public discourse? Write an argumentative essay of approximately 400 words arguing for or against this proposition.
3. In paragraph 10, Lawrence claims we are "in an era preoccupied with definitions of obscenity." Research current legal issues involving the use of obscenity and how they apply to the media such as television, films, the Internet, and popular music. Write a report on some of the major issues involving obscenity that are currently confronting lawmakers.

Get a Knife, Get a Dog, but Get Rid of Guns

Molly Ivins

Molly Ivins (Mary Tyler Ivins) (b. 1944) received a BA from Smith College, a Master's in journalism from Columbia University, and studied for a year at the Institute of Political Science in Paris. She has worked as an editor for the Texas Observer *and is the former Rocky Mountain bureau chief for* The New York Times. *She has also worked for the* Houston Chronicle, *the* Minneapolis Star-Tribune, *and the* Dallas Times Herald. *Her freelance work has appeared in* Esquire, Atlantic, The Nation, Harper's, *the* Progressive, Mother Jones, TV Guide, *and numerous other publications. Her books include* Molly Ivins Can't Say That, Can She? *(1992),* Nothin' but Good Times Ahead *(1994),* You Got to Dance with Them What Brung You: Politics in the Clinton Years *(1999), and* Shrub: The Short but Happy Political Life of George W. Bush *(2000) which she coauthored with Lou Dubose. In the following column, Ivins uses her wry humor and common sense to persuade and entertain her wide readership by pointing out what she sees as the conceptual weaknesses in arguments offered by those who use the Second Amendment to support gun ownership.*

Guns. Everywhere guns.   1

Let me start this discussion by pointing out that I am not antigun. I'm pro- 2 knife. Consider the merits of the knife.

In the first place, you have to catch up with someone in order to stab him. 3 A general substitution of knives for guns would promote physical fitness. We'd turn into a whole nation of great runners. Plus, knives don't ricochet. And people are seldom killed while cleaning their knives.

As a civil libertarian, I, of course, support the Second Amendment. And I 4 believe it means exactly what it says:

A well-regulated militia being necessary to the security of a free state, the right of 5 *the people to keep and bear arms shall not be infringed.* Fourteen-year-old boys are not part of a well-regulated militia. Members of wacky religious cults are not part of a well-regulated militia. Permitting unregulated citizens to have guns is destroying the security of this free state.

I am intrigued by the arguments of those who claim to follow the judicial 6 doctrine of original intent. How do they know it was the dearest wish of Thomas Jefferson's heart that teenage drug dealers should cruise the cities of this nation perforating their fellow citizens with assault rifles? Channeling?

There is more hooey spread about the Second Amendment. It says quite 7 clearly that guns are for those who form part of a well-regulated militia, that is, the armed forces, including the National Guard. Their reasons for keeping them away from everyone else get clearer by the day.

The comparison most often used is that of the automobile, another lethal 8 object that is regularly used to wreak great carnage. Obviously, this society is full of people who haven't enough common sense to use an automobile properly. But we haven't outlawed cars yet.

We do, however, license them and their owners, restrict their use to pre- 9 sumably sane and sober adults, and keep track of who sells them to whom. At a minimum, we should do the same with guns.

In truth, there is no rational argument for guns in this society. This is no 10 longer a frontier nation in which people hunt their own food. It is a crowded, overwhelmingly urban country in which letting people have access to guns is a continuing disaster. Those who want guns—whether for target shooting, hunting, or potting rattlesnakes (get a hoe)—should be subject to the same restrictions placed on gun owners in England, a nation in which liberty has survived nicely without an armed populace.

The argument that "guns don't kill people" is patent nonsense. Anyone 11 who has ever worked in a cop shop knows how many family arguments end in murder because there was a gun in the house. Did the gun kill someone? No.

But if there had been no gun, no one would have died. At least not without a good foot race first. Guns do kill. Unlike cars, that is all they do.

Michael Crichton makes an interesting argument about technology in his 12 thriller *Jurassic Park*. He points out that power without discipline is making this society into a wreckage. By the time someone who studies the martial arts becomes a master—literally able to kill with bare hands—that person has also undergone years of training and discipline. But any fool can pick up a gun and kill with it.

"A well-regulated militia" surely implies both long training and long disci- 13 pline. That is the least, the very least, that should be required of those who are permitted to have guns, because a gun is literally the power to kill. For years I used to enjoy taunting my gun-nut friends about their psychosexual hang-ups—always in a spirit of good cheer, you understand. But letting the noisy minority in the NRA force us to allow this carnage to continue is just plain insane.

I do think gun nuts have a power hang-up. I don't know what is missing in 14 their psyches that they need to feel they have the power to kill. But no sane society would allow this to continue.

Ban the damn things. Ban them all.   15

You want protection? Get a dog.

COMPREHENSION

1. Ivins claims to support the Second Amendment, and quotes it *verbatim*. What is the source of the original Second Amendment? When was it written? Why is it a federal law?
2. Ivins also claims to be a civil libertarian. What is the definition of one? What do civil libertarians believe?
3. Ivins refers to "the judicial doctrine of original intent." What is this doctrine? Why has it been of particular concern in contemporary politics?

RHETORIC

1. Ivins is noted for a breezy style that often presents serious issues in down-to-earth terms. For example, in paragraph 15, she states, "Ban the damn things" and in paragraph 12, she states, "Any damn fool can pick up a gun." Where does Ivins use other colloquial phrases such as these? What is their effect on the relationship between writer and reader?
2. Ivins uses irony—in which she means something other than what she says—for comic effect to advance her argument. For example, in paragraph 2, she states, "I'm pro-knife." And in paragraph 3, she offers justification for her stance by saying it would "promote physical fitness." What is her intent in using these remarks?
3. "Sarcasm" is defined as "a taunting, sneering, cutting, or caustic remark; generally ironical." Ivins employs sarcasm to dispute the arguments of anti-

gun-control advocates. For example, she says in paragraph 6, "How do they know it was the dearest wish of Thomas Jefferson's heart that teenage drug dealers should cruise the cities . . . " What function does her sarcasm serve in advancing her argument and discounting the arguments of her opponents? What other examples of sarcasm can you find in the essay? What function do they serve?

4. Ivins repeats part of the Second Amendment in paragraph 13. Why does she focus on it as an important aspect of her argument?

5. In paragraph 13, Ivins refers to her "gun-nut friends." If they are gun nuts and she is opposed to guns, why does she consider them friends? Also, why does the fact that she has "gun nuts" as friends help bolster her authority on the subject?

6. How does the concluding paragraph reinforce the writer's argument? What is the rhetorical effect of beginning and ending the essay with one-sentence paragraphs? How are they both examples of her conversational style?

7. Define the following words: *carnage* (paragraph 8), *martial* (paragraph 12), *psychosexual* (paragraph 13), and *psyches* (paragraph 14).

WRITING

1. Write an essay of approximately 400 words in which you argue for or against the idea that Ivins's tone strengthens her thesis.

2. Write an essay of approximately 400 words in which you argue for the absolute necessity of owning a cell phone or for the need to ban them entirely. Use irony and sarcasm in the spirit of Ivins's style.

3. After researching the topic of concealed weapons, write a 750- to 1,000-word essay in which you argue for or against the proposition that concealed weapons among the common citizenry reduces violence.

CONNECTIONS FOR CRITICAL THINKING

1. Study the prose of Mencken's "The Penalty of Death" (written over 50 years ago) and Lincoln's "Gettysburg Address" (written nearly 150 years ago). Discuss how you can discern the "classical" influence on their writing, for example, tone, vocabulary, assumptions, and references. Also discuss the differences between the two writing styles in light of the fact that they were written for different generations.

2. Both Mencken and Ivins employ plenty of irony and sarcasm. What methods do both of these authors have in common to assure they communicate their derisive sensibility to their intended readership?

3. Review the various strategies and methods the authors in this chapter use to buttress their arguments. Make a list of these methods and create a "glossary" of argumentative techniques.

4. All of the authors in this chapter argue about a subject with which they've had firsthand experience. Mencken observed condemned prisoners. King endured the assassination, of her husband and, as an African American, is acutely aware of the disparity in the imposition of the death penalty between Caucasian and African American convicts. Lincoln was obviously deeply embroiled in the American Civil War. Lawrence reflects on obscenity from the perspective of a teacher who witnesses her students unabashedly use "profanity." And Ivins, a Texan, lives in a state with liberal "gun carry" laws and refers to having worked in a "cop shop." Write an essay about a subject you feel you have the ability to argue well because of personal experience.

5. Search the Web for critical essays on the life of H. L. Mencken. Collect enough information so that you can intelligently write an explanatory essay on his views toward society and how he came to be a champion of unpopular causes.

6. Argue for or against the proposition that stand-up comedians and rock singers have the right to use any language they think effective so long as it conveys their intended message.

7. Write an essay in which you compare the differences between verbal argument as it might occur in conversation and written argument as it is traditionally structured in editorials, essays, and speeches.

 chapter *3*

Education
How, What, and Why Do We Learn?

In "Learning to Read and Write," a chapter from his autobiography, Frederick Douglass offers a spirited affirmation of the rights we all should have to pursue an education. For Douglass, who began his life in slavery, knowledge began not only with experience but also with the need to articulate that experience through literacy. The ability to read and write should be the possession of all human beings, and Douglass was willing to risk punishment—even death—to gain that ability. Today, all over the globe, as ethnic and political conflicts arise, men and women are faced with the same challenge of expressing themselves. For even with a tool like the Internet, if one does not have the tools to express oneself or if the expression of thought is suppressed, the vehicle for conveying ideas, no matter how powerful, is rendered useless.

Perhaps the struggle for an education always involves a certain amount of effort and risk, but the struggle also conveys excitement and the deep, abiding satisfaction that derives from achieving knowledge of oneself and of the world. Time and again in the essays included in this chapter, we discover that there is always a price to be paid for acquiring knowledge, developing intellectual skills, and attaining wisdom. However, numerous task forces and national commissions tell us that students today are not willing to pay this price and that, as a consequence, we have become academically mediocre. Is it true that we no longer delight in educating ourselves through reading, as Richard Rodriguez recounts in "The Lonely Good Company of Books"? Is it true that we take libraries for granted—we expect them to be available but never visit them? A democratic society requires an educated citizenry, people who refuse to commit intellectual suicide or self-neglect. The writers in this chapter, who take many pathways to understanding, remind us that we cannot afford to be passive or compliant when our right to an education is challenged.

Today we are in an era of dynamic change in attitudes toward education. Such issues as sex education, multiculturalism, racism, sexism, and immigration suggest the liveliness of the educational debate on campus. Any debate over contemporary education touches on the themes of politics, economics, religion, or the social agenda, forcing us to recognize that configurations of power are at the heart of virtually all educational issues in society today.

In an upcoming chapter, Francis Fukuyama will demonstrate how so many of our ideas about recent immigrants are stereotyped and prejudiced, bearing no relationship to the truth. It is easy to understand how such views can arise if we are merely passive vessels for others' uninformed opinions rather than active learners who seek true knowledge. If we judge the tenor of the essayists in this section, we discover that many of them are subversives, waging war against both ignorance *and* received dogma. These writers treat education as the key to upset the status quo and effect change. Operating from diverse backgrounds, they challenge many assumptions about our educational system and invite us to think critically about its purpose.

Previewing the Chapter

As you read the essays in this chapter and respond to them in discussion and writing, consider the following questions:

- What is the main educational issue that the author deals with?
- What tone does the author establish in treating the subject? Does the author take a positive or a negative value position to the topic?
- Does the author define *education?* If so, how? If not, does the author suggest what he or she means by it?
- What is the impact of society at large on the way the role of education is perceived?
- What forms of evidence do the authors use to support their views on education?
- How do the rhetorical features of the essays that focus on personal experience differ from those of the essays that examine education from a more global perspective?
- What have you learned about the value of education from reading these selections?
- Which essays persuaded you the most? The least? Why?

Classic and Contemporary Images
DOES EDUCATION CHANGE OVER TIME?

Using a Critical Perspective   Consider these two photographs of students in science laboratories, the first from the 19th century and the second from the present. What is the setting of each laboratory like? Who are the people? What does each photographer frame and leave out of the scene? Which educational setting seems more conducive to scientific or educational inquiry? Why?

Oberlin College Archives, Oberlin, Ohio

Founded in 1833, Oberlin College in Ohio was the first U.S. college to grant undergraduate degrees to women. The photograph reprinted here shows both male and female students in a zoology lab at Oberlin sometime during the 1890s.

Tom Stewart/Corbis/Stock Market

At the beginning of the 21st century, most colleges and universities in the United States are coeducational, and it is no longer unusual to see both male and female students in a laboratory setting, as shown in the contemporary photo of a food science lab at the University of Maine.

Classic and Contemporary Essays
WHAT IS THE VALUE OF EDUCATION?

A famous dictum proclaims that "the pen is mightier than the sword." In Frederick Douglass's narrative and the excerpt from the work of Richard Rodriguez, we get two portraits that demonstrate the truth of the adage. Douglass's efforts at becoming fully literate freed him from what would have been a life of slavery. No weapon could have done that for him. It is obvious that Douglass learned his lesson well, for his prose is stately, clear, direct, and precise. His story speaks of a determined youth and man who had a powerful motivation in learning to read and write. Would he have done so without this motivation? Perhaps, because he seems like a very self-directed individual, as is evident from the anecdotes he relates. Rodriguez, too, has a strong motivation to master, even to excel at, reading and writing. Writing nearly 150 years after Douglass, and at a time when he needn't fear slavery looming over him, Rodriguez nevertheless perceived that by emulating his teachers, who promoted book reading, his own reading would make him a better person. He, like Douglass, sensed that there was something about acquiring knowledge and about expanding one's view of the world by learning how others viewed it that would provide him with a certain amount of independence. As you read the following two essays, you may wish to consider whether the quiet, modest tone each author seems to project may have something to do with the subject matter. For reading, although active and mind-opening, is still a private and "lonely" activity.

Learning to Read and Write

Frederick Douglass

Frederick Douglass (1817–1895) was an American abolitionist, orator, and journal-
ist. Born of the union between a slave and a white man, Douglass later escaped to Mass-
achusetts. An impassioned antislavery speech brought him recognition as a powerful
orator; thereafter he was much in demand for speaking engagements. He described his
experience as a black man in America in Narrative of the Life of Frederick Douglass *(1845). After managing to buy his freedom, Douglass founded the* North Star, *a*
newspaper he published for the next 17 years. In the following excerpt from his stirring
autobiography, Douglass recounts the tremendous obstacles he overcame in his efforts
to become literate.

I lived in Master Hugh's family about seven years. During this time, I suc- 1
ceeded in learning to read and write. In accomplishing this, I was compelled to
resort to various stratagems. I had no regular teacher. My mistress, who had
kindly commenced to instruct me, had, in compliance with the advice and direction of her husband, not only ceased to instruct, but had set her face against
my being instructed by any one else. It is due, however, to my mistress to say of
her, that she did not adopt this course of treatment immediately. She at first
lacked the depravity indispensable to shutting me up in mental darkness. It was
at least necessary for her to have some training in the exercise of irresponsible
power, to make her equal to the task of treating me as though I were a brute.

My mistress was, as I have said, a kind and tender-hearted woman; and in 2
the simplicity of her soul she commenced, when I first went to live with her, to
treat me as she supposed one human being ought to treat another. In entering
upon the duties of a slaveholder, she did not seem to perceive that I sustained to
her the relation of a mere chattel, and that for her to treat me as a human being
was not only wrong, but dangerously so. Slavery proved as injurious to her as it
did to me. When I went there, she was a pious, warm, and tender-hearted
woman. There was no sorrow or suffering for which she had not a tear. She had
bread for the hungry, clothes for the naked, and comfort for every mourner that
came within her reach. Slavery soon proved its ability to divest her of these heavenly qualities. Under its influence, the tender heart became stone, and the lamb-
like disposition gave way to one of tiger-like fierceness. The first step in her
downward course was in her ceasing to instruct me. She now commenced to
practise her husband's precepts. She finally became. even more violent in her opposition than her husband himself. She was not satisfied with simply doing as
well as he had commanded; she seemed anxious to do better. Nothing seemed to
make her more angry than to see me with a newspaper. She seemed to think that
here lay the danger. I have had her rush at me with a face made all up of fury,

and snatch from me a newspaper, in a manner that fully revealed her apprehension. She was an apt woman; and a little experience soon demonstrated, to her satisfaction, that education and slavery were incompatible with each other.

From this time I was most narrowly watched. If I was in a separate room 3 any considerable length of time, I was sure to be suspected of having a book, and was at once called to give an account of myself. All this, however, was too late. The first step had been taken. Mistress, in teaching me the alphabet, had given me the *inch,* and no precaution could prevent me from taking the *ell.*

The plan which I adopted, and the one by which I was most successful, was 4 that of making friends of all the little white boys whom I met in the street. As many of these as I could, I converted into teachers. With their kindly aid, obtained at different times and in different places, I finally succeeded in learning to read. When I was sent on errands, I always took my book with me, and by doing one part of my errand quickly, I found time to get a lesson before my return. I used also to carry bread with me, enough of which was always in the house, and to which I was always welcome; for I was much better off in this regard than many of the poor white children in our neighborhood. This bread I used to bestow upon the hungry little urchins, who, in return, would give me that more valuable bread of knowledge. I am strongly tempted to give the names of two or three of those little boys, a testimonial of the gratitude and affection I bear them; but prudence forbids—not that it would injure me, but it might embarrass them; for it is almost an unpardonable offence to teach slaves to read in this Christian country. It is enough to say of the dear little fellows, that they lived on Philpot Street, very near Durgin and Bailey's shipyard. I used to talk this matter of slavery over with them. I would sometimes say to them, I wished I could be as free as they would be when they got to be men. "You will be free as soon as you are twenty-one, *but I am a slave for life!* Have not I as good a right to be free as you have?" These words used to trouble them; they would express for me the liveliest sympathy, and console me with the hope that something would occur by which I might be free.

I was now about twelve years old, and the thought of being a *slave for life* 5 began to bear heavily upon my heart. Just about this time, I got hold of a book entitled "The Colombian Orator." Every opportunity I got, I used to read this book. Among much of other interesting matter, I found in it a dialogue between a master and his slave. The slave was represented as having run away from his master three times. The dialogue represented the conversation which took place between them, when the slave was retaken the third time. In this dialogue, the whole argument in behalf of slavery was brought forward by the master, all of which was disposed of by the slave. The slave was made to say some very smart as well as impressive things in reply to his master—things which had the desired though unexpected effect; for the conversation resulted in the voluntary emancipation of the slave on the part of the master.

In the same book, I met with one of Sheridan's mighty speeches on and in 6 behalf of Catholic emancipation. These were choice documents to me. I read them over and over again with unabated interest. They gave tongue to interesting thoughts of my own soul, which had frequently flashed through my mind, and died away for want of utterance. The moral which I gained from the dialogue was the power of truth over the conscience of even a slaveholder. What I got from Sheridan was a bold denunciation of slavery, and a powerful vindication of human rights. The reading of these documents enabled me to utter my thoughts, and to meet the arguments brought forward to sustain slavery; but while they relieved me of one difficulty, they brought on another even more painful than the one of which I was relieved. The more I read, the more I was led to abhor and detest my enslavers. I could regard them in no other light than a band of successful robbers, who had left their homes, and gone to Africa, and stolen us from our homes, and in a strange land reduced us to slavery. I loathed them as being the meanest as well as the most wicked of men. As I read and contemplated the subject, behold! that very discontentment which Master Hugh had predicted would follow my learning to read had already come, to torment and sting my soul to unutterable anguish. As I writhed under it, I would at times feel that learning to read had been a curse rather than a blessing. It had given me a view of my wretched condition, without the remedy. It opened my eyes to the horrible pit, but to no ladder upon which to get out. In moments of agony, I envied my fellow-slaves for their stupidity. I have often wished myself a beast. I preferred the condition of the meanest reptile to my own. Any thing, no matter what, to get rid of thinking! It was this everlasting thinking of my condition that tormented me. There was no getting rid of it. It was pressed upon me by every object within sight or hearing, animate or inanimate. The silver trump of freedom had roused my soul to eternal wakefulness. Freedom now appeared, to disappear no more forever. It was heard in every sound, and seen in every thing. It was ever present to torment me with a sense of my wretched condition. I saw nothing without seeing it, I heard nothing without hearing it, and felt nothing without feeling it. It looked from every star, it smiled in every calm, breathed in every wind, and moved in every storm.

I often found myself regretting my own existence, and wishing myself 7 dead; and but for the hope of being free, I have no doubt but that I should have killed myself, or done something for which I should have been killed. While in this state of mind, I was eager to hear anyone speak of slavery. I was a ready listener. Every little while, I could hear something about the abolitionists. It was some time before I found what the word meant. It was always used in such connections as to make it an interesting word to me. If a slave ran away and succeeded in getting clear, or if a slave killed his master, set fire to a barn, or did any thing very wrong in the mind of a slaveholder, it was spoken of as the fruit of *abolition*. Hearing the word in this connection very often, I set about learning what it meant. The dictionary afforded me little or no help. I found it was "the act of abolishing;" but then I did not know what was to be abolished. Here I was perplexed. I did not dare to ask any one about its meaning, for I was satisfied that it was something they wanted me to know very little about. After a patient waiting, I got one of our city papers, containing an account of the number of petitions from the north, praying for the abolition of slavery in the District of

Columbia, and of the slave trade between the States. From this time I understood the words *abolition* and *abolitionist,* and always drew near when that word
was spoken, expecting to hear something of importance to myself and fellow-
slaves. The light broke in upon me by degrees. I went one day down on the
wharf of Mr. Waters; and seeing two Irishmen unloading a scow of stone, I
went, unasked, and helped them. When we had finished, one of them came to
me and asked me if I were a slave. I told him I was. He asked, "Are ye a slave
for life?" I told him that I was. The good Irishman seemed to be deeply affected
by the statement. He said to the other that it was a pity so fine a little fellow as
myself should be a slave for life. He said it was a shame to hold me. They both
advised me to run away to the north; that I should find friends there, and that I
should be free. I pretended not to be interested in what they said, and treated
them as if I did not understand them; for I feared they might be treacherous.
White men have been known to encourage slaves to escape, and then, to get the
reward, catch them and return them to their masters. I was afraid that these seemingly good men might use me so; but I nevertheless remembered their advice,
and from that time I resolved to run away. I looked forward to a time at which
it would be safe for me to escape. I was too young to think of doing so immediately; besides, I wished to learn how to write, as I might have occasion to write
my own pass. I consoled myself with the hope that I should one day find a good
chance. Meanwhile, I would learn to write.

The idea as to how I might learn to write was suggested to me by being in 8
Durgin and Bailey's ship-yard, and frequently seeing the ship carpenters, after
hewing, and getting a piece of timber ready for use, write on the timber the
name of that part of the ship for which it was intended. When a piece of timber
was intended for the larboard side, it would be marked thus—"L." When a
piece was for the starboard side, it would be marked thus—"S." A piece for the
larboard side forward, would be marked thus—"L. F." When a piece was for
starboard side forward would be marked thus—"S. F." For larboard aft, it
would be marked thus—"L. A." For starboard aft, it would be marked thus—
"S. A." I soon learned the names of these letters, and for what they were intended when placed upon a piece of timber in the ship-yard. I immediately
commenced copying them, and in a short time was able to make the four letters
named. After that, when I met with any boy who I knew could write, I would
tell him I could write as well as he. The next word would be, "I don't believe
you. Let me see you try it." I would then make the letters which I had been so
fortunate as to learn, and ask him to beat that. In this way I got a good many
lessons in writing, which it is quite possible I should never have gotten in any
other way. During this time, my copy-book was the board fence, brick wall, and
pavement; my pen and ink was a lump of chalk. With these, I learned mainly how
to write. I then commenced and continued copying the Italics in Webster's
Spelling Book, until I could make them all without looking on the book. By this
time, my little Master Thomas had gone to school, and learned how to write,
and had written over a number of copy-books. These had been brought home,
and shown to some of our near neighbors, and then laid aside. My mistress

used to go to class meeting at the Wilk Street meetinghouse every Monday afternoon, and leave me to take care of the house. When left thus, I used to spend the time in writing in the spaces left in Master Thomas's copy-book, copying what he had written. I continued to do this until I could write a hand very similar to that of Master Thomas. Thus, after a long, tedious effort for years, I finally succeeded in learning how to write.

COMPREHENSION

1. What strategies does Douglass use to continue his education after his mistress's abandonment?
2. Why did the author's mistress find his reading newspapers particularly threatening?
3. Why does Douglass call learning to read "a curse rather than a blessing"?

RHETORIC

1. What is the thesis of Douglass's narration? How well is it supported and developed by the body paragraphs? Explain.
2. The first couple of sentences in the story, though simple, are very powerful. How do they serve to set up the mood of the piece and the reader's expectations?
3. Cite examples of Douglass's use of metaphors, and discuss why they work in those paragraphs.
4. How would you describe Douglass's writing style and level of language? Does it reveal anything about the writer's character? Justify your response.
5. Explain the way in which the author uses comparison and contrast.
6. What is Douglass's definition of *abolition,* and how does Douglass help the reader define it? How does this method contribute to the reader's understanding of the learning process?

WRITING

1. What does Douglass mean when he writes that "education and slavery were incompatible with each other"? Write an essay in which you consider the relationship between the two.
2. Both Douglass and his mistress were in inferior positions to Master Hugh. Write an essay in which you compare and contrast their positions in society at the time.
3. Illiteracy is still a major problem in the United States. Write an account of what your day-to-day life would be like if you couldn't write or read. What impact would this deficiency have on your life? Use concrete examples to illustrate your narrative.

The Lonely, Good Company
of Books

Richard Rodriguez

Richard Rodriguez was born in 1944 in San Francisco and received degrees from Stanford University and Columbia University. He also did graduate study at the University of California, Berkeley, and at the Warburg Institute, London. Rodriguez became a nationally known writer with the publication of his autobiography, Hunger of Memory: The Education of Richard Rodriguez *(1982). In it, he describes the struggles of growing up biculturally—feeling alienated from his Spanish-speaking parents yet not wholly comfortable in the dominant culture of the United States. He opposes bilingualism and affirmative action as they are now practiced in the United States, and his stance has caused much controversy in educational and intellectual circles. Rodriguez continues to write about social issues such as acculturation, education, and language. In the following essay, Rodriguez records his childhood passion for reading.*

From an early age I knew that my mother and father could read and write both   1
Spanish and English. I had observed my father making his way through what, I
now suppose, must have been income tax forms. On other occasions I waited ap-
prehensively while my mother read onion-paper letters air-mailed from Mexico
with news of a relative's illness or death. For both my parents, however, reading
was something done out of necessity and as quickly as possible. Never did I see
either of them read an entire book. Nor did I see them read for pleasure. Their
reading consisted of work manuals, prayer books, newspapers, recipes. . . .

In our house each school year would begin with my mother's careful in-   2
struction: "Don't write in your books so we can sell them at the end of the year."
The remark was echoed in public by my teachers, but only in part: "Boys and
girls, don't write in your books. You must learn to treat them with great care
and respect."

OPEN THE DOORS OF YOUR MIND WITH BOOKS, read the red and white poster   3
over the nun's desk in early September. It soon was apparent to me that reading
was the classroom's central activity. Each course had its own book. And the information gathered from a book was unquestioned. READ TO LEARN, the sign on
the wall advised in December. I privately wondered: What was the connection
between reading and learning? Did one learn something only by reading it?
Was an idea only an idea if it could be written down? In June, CONSIDER BOOKS
YOUR BEST FRIENDS. Friends? Reading was, at best, only a chore. I needed to look
up whole paragraphs of words in a dictionary. Lines of type were dizzying, the
eye having to move slowly across the page, then down, and across. . . . The sentences of the first books I read were coolly impersonal. Toned hard. What most

bothered me, however, was the isolation reading required. To console myself for the loneliness I'd feel when I read, I tried reading in a very soft voice. Until: "Who is doing all that talking to his neighbor?" Shortly after, remedial reading classes were arranged for me with a very old nun.

At the end of each school day, for nearly six months, I would meet with her in the tiny room that served as the school's library but was actually only a store-room for used textbooks and a vast collection of *National Geographics.* Every-thing about our sessions pleased me: the smallness of the room; the noise of the janitor's broom hitting the edge of the long hallway outside the door; the green of the sun, lighting the wall; and the old woman's face blurred white with a beard. Most of the time we took turns. I began with my elementary text. Sen-tences of astonishing simplicity seemed to me lifeless and drab: "The boys ran from the rain. . . . She wanted to sing. . . . The kite rose in the blue." Then the old nun would read from her favorite books, usually biographies of early American presidents. Playfully she ran through complex sentences, calling the words alive with her voice, making it seem that the author somehow was speaking directly to me. I smiled just to listen to her. I sat there and sensed for the very first time some possibility of fellowship between a reader and a writer, a communication, never *intimate* like that I heard spoken words at home convey, but one nonethe-less *personal.*

One day the nun concluded a session by asking me why I was so reluctant to read by myself. I tried to explain; said something about the way written words made me feel all alone—almost, I wanted to add but didn't, as when I spoke to myself in a room just emptied of furniture. She studied my face as I spoke; she seemed to be watching more than listening. In an uneventful voice she replied that I had nothing to fear. Didn't I realize that reading would open up whole new worlds? A book could open doors for me. It could introduce me to people and show me places I never imagined existed. She gestured toward the bookshelves. (Bare-breasted African women danced, and the shiny hubcaps of automobiles on the back covers of the *Geographic* gleamed in my mind.) I lis-tened with respect. But her words were not very influential. I was thinking then of another consequence of literacy, one I was too shy to admit but nonetheless trusted. Books were going to make me "educated." *That* confidence enabled me, several months later, to overcome my fear of the silence.

In fourth grade I embarked upon a grandiose reading program. "Give me the names of important books," I would say to startled teachers. They soon found out that I had in mind "adult books." I ignored their suggestion of any-thing I suspected was written for children. (Not until I was in college, as a re-sult, did I read *Huckleberry Finn* or *Alice's Adventures in Wonderland.*) Instead, I read *The Scarlet Letter* and Franklin's *Autobiography.* And whatever I read I read for extra credit. Each time I finished a book, I reported the achievement to a teacher and basked in the praise my effort earned. Despite my best efforts, how-ever, there seemed to be more and more books I needed to read. At the library I would literally tremble as I came upon whole shelves of books I hadn't read. So I read and I read and I read: *Great Expectations;* all the short stories of Kipling;

The Babe Ruth Story; the entire first volume of the *Encyclopedia Britannica* (A-ANSTEY); the *Iliad; Moby Dick; Gone with the Wind; The Good Earth; Ramona; Forever Amber; The Lives of the Saints; Crime and Punishment; The Pearl.* . . . Librarians who initially frowned when I checked out the maximum ten books at a time started saving books they thought I might like. Teachers would say to the rest of the class, "I only wish the rest of you took reading as seriously as Richard obviously does."

But at home I would hear my mother wondering, "What do you see in your 7
books?" (Was reading a hobby like her knitting? Was so much reading even healthy for a boy? Was it the sign of "brains"? Or was it just a convenient excuse for not helping around the house on Saturday mornings?) Always, "What do you see . . . ?"

What *did* I see in my books? I had the idea that they were crucial for my aca- 8
demic success, though I couldn't have said exactly how or why. In the sixth grade I simply concluded that what gave a book its value was some major idea or theme it contained. If that core essence could be mined and memorized, I would become learned like my teachers. I decided to record in a notebook the themes of the books that I read. After reading *Robinson Crusoe*, I wrote that its theme was "the value of learning to live by oneself." When I completed *Wuthering Heights,* I noted the danger of "letting emotions get out of control." Rereading these brief moralistic appraisals usually left me disheartened. I couldn't believe that they were really the source of reading's value. But for many years, they constituted the only means I had of describing to myself the educational value of books.

In spite of my earnestness, I found reading a pleasurable activity. I came to 9
enjoy the lonely, good company of books. Early on weekday mornings, I'd read in my bed. I'd feel a mysterious comfort then, reading in the dawn quiet—the blue-gray silence interrupted by the occasional churning of the refrigerator motor a few rooms away or the more distant sounds of a city bus beginning its run. On weekends I'd go to the public library to read, surrounded by old men and women. Or, if the weather was fine, I would take my books to the park and read in the shade of a tree. Neighbors would leave for vacation and I would water their lawns. I would sit through the twilight on the front porches or in backyards, reading to the cool, whirling sounds of the sprinklers.

I also had favorite writers. But often those writers I enjoyed most I was least 10
able to value. When I read William Saroyan's *The Human Comedy,* I was immediately pleased by the narrator's warmth and the charm of his story. But as quickly I became suspicious. A book so enjoyable to read couldn't be very "important." Another summer I determined to read all the novels of Dickens. Reading his fat novels, I loved the feeling I got—after the first hundred pages—of being at home in a fictional world where I knew the names of the characters and cared about was going to happen to them. And it bothered me that I was forced away at the conclusion, when the fiction closed tight, like a fortune-teller's fist—the futures of all the major characters neatly resolved. I never knew how to take such feelings seriously, however. Nor did I suspect that these experiences could be part of a novel's meaning. Still, there were pleasures to sustain me after I'd finish my books. Carrying a volume back to the library, I would

be pleased by its weight. I'd run my fingers along the edge of the pages and marvel at the breadth of my achievement. Around my room, growing stacks of paperback books reinforced my assurance.

I entered high school having read hundreds of books. My habit of reading made me a confident speaker and writer of English. Reading also enabled me to sense something of the shape, the major concerns, of Western thought. (I was able to say something about Dante and Descartes and Engels and James Baldwin in my high school term papers.) In these various ways, books brought me academic success as I hoped that they would. But I was not a good reader. Merely bookish, I lacked a point of view when I read. Rather, I read in order to acquire a point of view. I vacuumed books for epigrams, scraps of information, ideas, themes—anything to fill the hollow within me and make me feel educated. When one of my teachers suggested to his drowsy tenth-grade English class that a person could not have a "complicated idea" until he had read at least two thousand books, I heard the remark without detecting either its irony or its very complicated truth. I merely determined to compile a list of all the books I had ever read. Harsh with myself, I included only once a title I might have read several times. (How, after all, could one read a book more than once?) And I included only those books over a hundred pages in length. (Could anything shorter be a book?)

There was yet another high school list I compiled. One day I came across a newspaper article about the retirement of an English professor at a nearby state college. The article was accompanied by a list of the "hundred most important books of Western Civilization." "More than anything else in my life," the professor told the reporter with finality, "these books have made me all that I am." That was the kind of remark I couldn't ignore. I clipped out the list and kept it for the several months it took me to read all of the titles. Most books, of course, I barely understood. While reading Plato's *Republic,* for instance, I needed to keep looking at the book jacket comments to remind myself what the text was about. Nevertheless, with the special patience and superstition of a scholarship boy, I looked at every word of the text. And by the time I reached the last word, relieved, I convinced myself that I had read *The Republic.* In a ceremony of great pride, I solemnly crossed Plato off my list.

COMPREHENSION

1. What was Rodriguez's parents' attitude toward reading? Did it influence his attitude? Cite examples from the essay that support your opinion.
2. What does Rodriguez mean by "the fellowship between a reader and a writer"? Why does he differentiate between "intimate" and "personal" forms of communication?
3. Rodriguez hoped that reading would fill "the hollow" inside him. What was the cause of his emptiness? Did he succeed in filling the void? Why did he find reading a lonely experience? Did reading fulfill any of his expectations?

RHETORIC

1. What is the thesis of Rodriguez's essay? Is it stated or implied? Explain.
2. How does the author's use of narrative advance his views on reading and education?
3. What is the writer's tone? How effective is it in conveying his point of view?
4. Rodriguez uses uppercase letters when referring to signs advocating reading. Why does he use this device? How does it support his point of view?
5. The essay ends with an ironic anecdote. Why did Rodriguez choose to conclude this way? Does it satisfactorily illustrate the writer's attitude?
6. What words or phrases imply that there is an ethnic component in Rodriguez's conflict? Is the subtlety effective? Justify your response.

WRITING

1. Rodriguez's parents had a pragmatic attitude toward reading. What was the attitude in your home as you were growing up? Did your parents encourage your interest in reading? Did they read themselves? What is the first book you remember reading by yourself? Write an essay in which you describe your reading history.
2. Rodriguez believed reading would make him "educated." Do you agree or disagree? Is reading vitally important to a person's education? How do you define *education?* Can it be acquired only through reading, or are there other contributing factors? Write an argumentative essay on this topic.
3. Is reading still a significant source of information and entertainment, or has it been usurped by television? Is it important (or necessary) to be a reader today?

Classic and Contemporary: Questions for Comparison

1. Both Rodriguez and Douglass were motivated to educate themselves in a society inimical to this achievement. Compare and contrast their struggles and attitudes in their quests for knowledge.
2. Pretend you are Richard Rodriguez, and write a letter to Douglass addressing the issues of minorities and education in present-day America. What would Rodriguez say about the progress of minorities in our society?
3. Although Rodriguez and Douglass treat a similar theme, they communicate their messages differently. Which narration do you consider more powerful, and why?
4. Rodriguez explores the theme of isolation in his story. Is there any evidence that this feeling was shared by Douglass in his efforts to learn how to read? Use proof from both narratives to support your view.

5. Slavery was an obvious obstacle to Douglass's attempt to educate himself. What impeded Rodriguez's progress? Were similar forces at work? Cite examples from Rodriguez's narrative to prove your point.

Graduation

Maya Angelou

Maya Angelou *(b. 1928) is an American poet, playwright, television writer, actress, and singer. Her autobiographical books, notably* I Know Why the Caged Bird Sings *(1970), from which the following selection is taken, provide rich accounts of the black female experience. Fluent in six languages and active in artistic, educational, and political affairs, Angelou often presents autobiographical material against the backdrop of larger cultural concerns. In this vivid reminiscence of her 1940 graduation from grade school in Stamps, Arkansas, she provides insights into a community of young scholars who gain inspiration and wisdom from their experience during commencement ceremonies.*

The children in Stamps trembled visibly with anticipation. Some adults were 1 excited too, but to be certain the whole young population had come down with graduation epidemic. Large classes were graduating from both the grammar school and the high school. Even those who were years removed from their own day of glorious release were anxious to help with preparations as a kind of dry run. The junior students who were moving into the vacating classes' chairs were tradition-bound to show their talents for leadership and management. They strutted through the school and around the campus exerting pressure on the lower grades. Their authority was so new that occasionally if they pressed a little too hard it had to be overlooked. After all, next term was coming, and it never hurt a sixth grader to have a play sister in the eighth grade, or a tenth-year student to be able to call a twelfth grader Bubba. So all was endured in a spirit of shared understanding. But the graduating classes themselves were the nobility. Like travelers with exotic destinations on their minds, the graduates were remarkably forgetful. They came to school without their books, or tablets or even pencils. Volunteers fell over themselves to secure replacements for the missing equipment. When accepted, the willing workers might or might not be thanked, and it was of no importance to the pregraduation rites. Even teachers were respectful of the now quiet and aging seniors, and tended to speak to them, if not as equals, as beings only slightly lower than themselves. After tests were returned and grades given, the student body, which acted like an extended family, knew who did well, who excelled, and what piteous ones had failed.

Unlike the white high school, Lafayette County Training School distin- 2 guished itself by having neither lawn, nor hedges, nor tennis court, nor climbing ivy. Its two buildings (main classrooms, the grade school and home economics) were set on a dirt hill with no fence to limit either its boundaries or those of bordering farms. There was a large expanse to the left of the school which was used alternately as a baseball diamond or a basketball court. Rusty hoops on the swaying poles represented the permanent recreational equipment, although bats and balls could be borrowed from the P.E. teacher if the borrower was qualified and if the diamond wasn't occupied.

Over this rocky area relieved by a few shady tall persimmon trees the grad- ³ uating class walked. The girls often held hands and no longer bothered to speak to the lower students. There was a sadness about them, as if this old world was not their home and they were bound for higher ground. The boys, on the other hand, had become more friendly, more outgoing. A decided change from the closed attitude they projected while studying for finals. Now, they seemed not ready to give up the old school, the familiar paths and classrooms. Only a small percentage would be continuing on to college—one of the South's A & M (agricultural and mechanical) schools, which trained Negro youths to be carpenters, farmers, handymen, masons, maids, cooks and baby nurses. Their future rode heavily on their shoulders, and blinded them to the collective joy that had pervaded the lives of the boys and girls in the grammar school graduating class.

Parents who could afford it had ordered new shoes and ready-made clothes ⁴ for themselves from Sears and Roebuck or Montgomery Ward. They also engaged the best seamstresses to make the floating graduation dresses and to cut down secondhand pants which would be pressed to a military slickness for the important event.

Oh, it was important, all right. Whitefolks would attend the ceremony, and ⁵ two or three would speak of God and home, and the Southern way of life, and Mrs. Parsons, the principal's wife, would play the graduation march while the lower-grade graduates paraded down the aisles and took their seats below the platform. The high school seniors would wait in empty classrooms to make their dramatic entrance.

In the Store I was the person of the moment. The birthday girl. The center. ⁶ Bailey had graduated the year before, although to do so he had had to forfeit all pleasures to make up for his time lost in Baton Rouge.

My class was wearing butter-yellow piqué dresses, and Momma launched ⁷ out on mine. She smocked the yoke into tiny crisscrossing puckers, then shirred the rest of the bodice. Her dark fingers ducked in and out of the lemony cloth as she embroidered raised daisies around the hem. Before she considered herself finished she had added a crocheted cuff on the puff sleeves, and a pointy crocheted collar.

I was going to be lovely. A walking model of all the various styles of fine ⁸ hand sewing and it didn't worry me that I was only twelve years old and merely graduating from the eighth grade. Besides, many teachers in Arkansas Negro schools had only that diploma and were licensed to impart wisdom.

The days had become longer and more noticeable. The faded beige of for- ⁹ mer times had been replaced with strong and sure colors. I began to see my classmates' clothes, their skin tones, and the dust that waved off pussy willows. Clouds that lazed across the sky were objects of great concern to me. Their shiftier shapes might have held a message that in my new happiness and with a little bit of time I'd soon decipher. During that period I looked at the arch of heaven so religiously my neck kept a steady ache. I had taken to smiling more often, and my jaws hurt from the unaccustomed activity. Between the two physical sore spots, I suppose I could have been uncomfortable, but that was not the case. As a member of the winning team (the graduating class of 1940) I had outdistanced unpleasant sensations by miles. I was headed for the freedom of open fields.

Youth and social approval allied themselves with me and we trammeled 10 memories of slights and insults. The wind of our swift passage remodeled my features. Lost tears were pounded to mud and then to dust. Years of withdrawal were brushed aside and left behind, as hanging ropes of parasitic moss.

My work alone had awarded me a top place and I was going to be one of 11 the first called in the graduating ceremonies. On the classroom blackboard, as well as on the bulletin board in the auditorium, there were blue stars and white stars and red stars. No absences, no tardiness, and my academic work was among the best of the year. I could say the preamble to the Constitution even faster than Bailey. We timed ourselves often: "We the people of the United States in order to form a more perfect union. . . . " I had memorized the Presidents of the United States from Washington to Roosevelt in chronological as well as alphabetical order.

My hair pleased me too. Gradually the black mass had lengthened and 12 thickened, so that it kept at last to its braided pattern, and I didn't have to yank my scalp off when I tried to comb it.

Louise and I had rehearsed the exercises until we tired out ourselves. Henry 13 Reed was class valedictorian. He was a small, very black boy with hooded eyes, a long, broad nose and an oddly shaped head. I had admired him for years because each term he and I vied for the best grades in our class. Most often he bested me, but instead of being disappointed, I was pleased that we shared top places between us. Like many Southern black children, he lived with his grandmother, who was as strict as Momma and as kind as she knew how to be. He was courteous, respectful and softspoken to elders, but on the playground he chose to play the roughest games. I admired him. Anyone, I reckoned, sufficiently afraid or sufficiently dull could be polite. But to be able to operate at a top level with both adults and children was admirable.

His valedictory speech was entitled "To Be or Not to Be." The rigid tenth- 14 grade teacher had helped him write it. He'd been working on the dramatic stresses for months.

The weeks until graduation were filled with heady activities. A group of 15 small children were to be presented in a play about buttercups and daisies and bunny rabbits. They could be heard throughout the building practicing their hops and their little songs that sounded like silver bells. The older girls (nongraduates, of course) were assigned the task of making refreshments for the night's festivities. A tangy scent of ginger, cinnamon, nutmeg and chocolate wafted around the home economics building as the budding cooks made samples for themselves and their teachers.

In every corner of the workshop, axes and saws split fresh timber as the   16 woodshop boys made sets and stage scenery. Only the graduates were left out of the general bustle. We were free to sit in the library at the back of the building or look in quite detachedly, naturally, on the measures being taken for our event.

Even the minister preached on graduation the Sunday before. His subject   17 was, "Let your light so shine that men will see your good works and praise your Father, Who is in Heaven." Although the sermon was purported to be addressed to us, he used the occasion to speak to backsliders, gamblers and general ne'er-do-wells. But since he had called our names at the beginning of the service we were mollified.

Among Negroes the tradition was to give presents to children going only   18 from one grade to another. How much more important this was when the person was graduating at the top of the class. Uncle Willie and Momma had sent away for a Mickey Mouse watch like Bailey's. Louise gave me four embroidered handkerchiefs. (I gave her three crocheted doilies.) Mrs. Sneed, the minister's wife, made me an underskirt to wear for graduation, and nearly every customer gave me a nickel or maybe even a dime with the instruction "Keep on moving to higher ground," or some such encouragement.

Amazingly the great day finally dawned and I was out of bed before I knew   19 it. I threw open the back door to see it more clearly, but Momma said, "Sister, come away from that door and put your robe on."

I hoped the memory of that morning would never leave me. Sunlight was   20 itself still young, and the day had none of the insistence maturity would bring it in a few hours. In my robe and barefoot in the backyard, under cover of going to see about my new beans, I gave myself up to the gentle warmth and thanked God that no matter what evil I had done in my life He had allowed me to live to see this day. Somewhere in my fatalism I had expected to die, accidentally, and never have the chance to walk up the stairs in the auditorium and gracefully receive my hard-earned diploma. Out of God's merciful bosom I had won reprieve.

Bailey came out in his robe and gave me a box wrapped in Christmas paper.   21 He said he had saved his money for months to pay for it. It felt like a , box of chocolates, but I knew Bailey wouldn't save money to buy candy when we had all we could want under our noses.

He was as proud of the gift as I. It was a soft-leather-bound copy of a col-   22 lection of poems by Edgar Allan Poe, or, as Bailey and I called him, "Eap." I turned to "Annabel Lee" and we walked up and down the garden rows, the cool dirt between our toes, reciting the beautifully sad lines.

Momma made a Sunday breakfast although it was only Friday. After we   23 finished the blessing, I opened my eyes to find the watch on my plate. It was a dream of a day. Everything went smoothly and to my credit. I didn't have to be reminded or scolded for anything. Near evening I was too jittery to attend to chores, so Bailey volunteered to do all before his bath.

Days before, we had made a sign for the Store, and as we turned out the 24 lights Momma hung the cardboard over the doorknob. It read clearly: CLOSED. GRADUATION.

My dress fitted perfectly and everyone said that I looked like a sun-beam in 25 it. On the hill, going toward the school, Bailey walked behind with Uncle Willie, who muttered, "Go on, Ju." He wanted to walk ahead with us because it embarrassed him to have to walk so slowly. Bailey said he'd let the ladies walk together, and the men would bring up the rear. We all laughed, nicely.

Little children dashed by out of the dark like fireflies. Their crepe-paper 26 dresses and butterfly wings were not made for running and we heard more than one rip, dryly, and the regretful "uh uh" that followed.

The school blazed without gaiety. The windows seemed cold and un- 27 friendly from the lower hill. A sense of ill-fated timing crept over me, and if Momma hadn't reached for my hand I would have drifted back to Bailey and Uncle Willie, and possibly beyond. She made a few slow jokes about my feet getting cold, and tugged me along to the now-strange building.

Around the front steps, assurance came back. There were my fellow 28 "greats," the graduating class. Hair brushed back, legs oiled, new dresses and pressed pleats, fresh pocket handkerchiefs and little handbags, all homesewn. Oh, we were up to snuff, all right. I joined my comrades and didn't even see my family go in to find seats in the crowded auditorium.

The school band struck up a march and all classes filed in as had been re- 29 hearsed. We stood in front of our seats, as assigned, and on a signal from the choir director, we sat. No sooner had this been accomplished than the band started to play the national anthem. We rose again and sang the song, after which we recited the pledge of allegiance. We remained standing for a brief minute before the choir director and the principal signaled to us, rather desperately I thought, to take our seats. The command was so unusual that our carefully rehearsed and smooth-running machine was thrown off. For a full minute we fumbled for our chairs and bumped into each other awkwardly. Habits change or solidify under pressure, so in our state of nervous tension we had been ready to follow our usual assembly pattern: the American national anthem, then the pledge of allegiance, then the song every Black person I knew called the Negro National Anthem. All done in the same key, with the same passion and most often standing on the same foot.

Finding my seat at last, I was overcome with a presentiment of worse things 30 to come. Something unrehearsed, unplanned, was going to happen, and we were going to be made to look bad. I distinctly remember being explicit in the choice of pronoun. It was "we," the graduating class, the unit, that concerned me then.

The principal welcomed "parents and friends" and asked the Baptist min- 31 ister to lead us in prayer. His invocation was brief and punchy, and for a second I thought we were getting back on the high road to right action. When the principal came back to the dais, however, his voice had changed. Sounds always affected me profoundly and the principal's voice was one of my favorites. During assembly it melted and lowered weakly into the audience. It had not been in my plan to listen to him, but my curiosity was piqued and I straightened up to give him my attention.

He was talking about Booker T. Washington, our "late great leader," who 32 said we can be as close as the fingers on the hand, etc. . . . Then he said a few vague things about friendship and the friendship of kindly people to those less fortunate than themselves. With that his voice nearly faded, thin, away. Like a river diminishing to a stream and then to a trickle. But he cleared his throat and said, "Our speaker tonight, who is also our friend, came from Texarkana to deliver the commencement address, but due to the irregularity of the train schedule, he's going to, as they say, 'speak and run.'" He said that we understood and wanted the man to know that we were most grateful for the time he was able to give us and then something about how we were willing always to adjust to another's program, and without more ado—"I give you Mr. Edward Donleavy."

Not one but two white men came through the door offstage. The shorter 33 one walked to the speaker's platform, and the tall one moved over to the center seat and sat down. But that was our principal's seat, and already occupied. The dislodged gentleman bounced around for a long breath or two before the Baptist minister gave him his chair, then with more dignity than the situation deserved, the minister walked off the stage.

Donleavy looked at the audience once (on reflection, I'm sure that he 34 wanted only to reassure himself that we were really there), adjusted his glasses and began to read from a sheaf of papers.

He was glad "to be here and to see the work going on just as it was in the 35 other schools."

At the first "Amen" from the audience I willed the offender to immediate 36 death by choking on the word. But Amens and Yes, sir's began to fall around the room like rain through a ragged umbrella.

He told us of the wonderful changes we children in Stamps had in store. 37 The Central School (naturally, the white school was Central) had already been granted improvements that would be in use in the fall. A well-known artist was coming from Little Rock to teach art to them. They were going to have the newest microscopes and chemistry equipment for their laboratory. Mr. Donleavy didn't leave us long in the dark over who made these improvements available to Central High. Nor were we to be ignored in the general betterment scheme he had in mind.

He said that he had pointed out to people at a very high level that one of the 38 first-line football tacklers at Arkansas Agricultural and Mechanical College had graduated from good old Lafayette County Training School. Here fewer Amens were heard. Those few that did break through lay dully in the air with the heaviness of habit.

He went on to praise us. He went on to say how he had bragged that "one 39 of the best basketball players at Fisk sank his first ball right here at Lafayette County Training School."

The white kids were going to have a chance to become Galileos and 40 Madame Curies and Edisons and Gauguins, and our boys (the girls weren't even in on it) would try to be Jesse Owenses and Joe Louises.

Owens and the Brown Bomber were great heroes in our world, but what 41
school official in the white-goddom of Little Rock had the right to decide that
those two men must be our only heroes? Who decided that for Henry Reed to
become a scientist he had to work like George Washington Carver, as a boot-
black, to buy a lousy microscope? Bailey was obviously always going to be too
small to be an athlete, so which concrete angel glued to what country seat had
decided that if my brother wanted to become a lawyer he had to first pay
penance for his skin by picking cotton and hoeing corn and studying correspondence books at night for twenty years?

The man's dead words fell like bricks around the auditorium and too many 42
settled in my belly. Constrained by hard-learned manners I couldn't look behind me, but to my left and right the proud graduating class of 1940 had
dropped their heads. Every girl in my row had found something new to do with
her handkerchief. Some folded the tiny squares into love knots, some into trian-
gles, but most were wadding them, then pressing them flat on their yellow laps.

On the dais, the ancient tragedy was being replayed. Professor Parsons sat, 43
a sculptor's reject, rigid. His large, heavy body seemed devoid of will or willingness, and his eyes said he was no longer with us. The other teachers examined the flag (which was draped stage right) or their notes, or the windows
which opened on our now-famous playing diamond.

Graduation, the hush-hush magic time of frills and gifts and congratula- 44
tions and diplomas, was finished for me before my name was called. The accomplishment was nothing. The meticulous maps, drawn in three colors of ink,
learning, and spelling decasyllabic words, memorizing the whole of *The Rape of
Lucrece*—it was for nothing. Donleavy had exposed us.

We were maids and farmers, handymen and washerwomen, and anything 45
higher that we aspired to was farcical and presumptuous.

Then I wished that Gabriel Prosser and Nat Turner had killed all whitefolks 46
in their beds and that Abraham Lincoln had been assassinated before the signing
of the Emancipation Proclamation, and that Harriet Tubman had been killed by
that blow on her head and Christopher Columbus had drowned in the *Santa
Maria*.

It was awful to be Negro and have no control over my life. It was brutal to 47
be young and already trained to sit quietly and listen to charges brought against
my color with no chance of defense. We should all be dead. I thought I should
like to see us all dead, one on top of the other. A pyramid of flesh with the
whitefolks on the bottom, as the broad base, then the Indians with their silly
tomahawks and tepees and wigwams and treaties, the Negroes with their mops
and recipes and cotton sacks and spirituals sticking out of their mouths. The
Dutch children should all stumble in their wooden shoes and break their necks.
The French should choke to death on the Louisiana Purchase (1803) while silk-
worms ate all the Chinese with their stupid pigtails. As a species, we were an
abomination. All of us.

Donleavy was running for election, and assured our parents that if he won 48
we could count on having the only colored paved playing field in that part of
Arkansas. Also—he never looked up to acknowledge the grunts of acceptance—

also, we were bound to get some new equipment for the home economics building and the workshop.

He finished, and since there was no need to give any more than the most 49 perfunctory thank-you's, he nodded to the men on the stage, and the tall white man who was never introduced joined him at the door. They left with the attitude that now they were off to something really important. (The graduation ceremonies at Lafayette County Training School had been a mere preliminary.)

The ugliness they left was palpable. An uninvited guest who wouldn't 50 leave. The choir was summoned and sang a modern arrangement of "Onward, Christian Soldiers," with new words pertaining to graduates seeking their place in the world. But it didn't work. Elouise, the daughter of the Baptist minister, recited "Invictus," and I could have cried at the impertinence of "I am the master of my fate, I am the captain of my soul."

My name had lost its ring of familiarity and I had to be nudged to go and 51 receive my diploma. All my preparations had fled. I neither marched up to the stage like a conquering Amazon, nor did I look in the audience for Bailey's nod of approval. Marguerite Johnson, I heard the name again, my honors were read, there were noises in the audience of appreciation, and I took my place on the stage as rehearsed.

I thought about colors I hated: ecru, puce, lavender, beige and black. 52

There was shuffling and rustling around me, then Henry Reed was giving 53 his valedictory address, "To Be or Not to Be." Hadn't he heard the whitefolks? We couldn't *be* so the question was a waste of time. Henry's voice came clear and strong. I feared to look at him. Hadn't he got the message? There was no "nobler in the mind" for Negroes because the world didn't think we had minds, and they let us know it. "Outrageous fortune"? Now, that was a joke. When the ceremony was over I had to tell Henry Reed some things. That is, if I still cared. Not "rub," Henry, "erase." "Ah, there's the erase." Us.

Henry had been a good student in elocution. His voice rose on tides of 54 promise and fell on waves of warnings. The English teacher had helped him to create a sermon winging through Hamlet's soliloquy. To be a man, a doer, a builder, a leader, or to be a tool, an unfunny joke, a crusher of funky toadstools, I marveled that Henry could go through the speech as if we had a choice.

I had been listening and silently rebutting each sentence with my eyes 55 closed; then there was a hush, which in an audience warns that something unplanned is happening. I looked up and saw Henry Reed, the conservative, the proper, the A student, turn his back to the audience and turn to us (the proud graduating class of 1940) and sing, nearly speaking,

> Lift ev'ry voice and sing
> Till earth and heaven ring
> Ring with the harmonies of Liberty. . . .

It was the poem written by James Weldon Johnson. It was the music composed by J. Rosamond Johnson. It was the Negro national anthem. Out of habit we were singing it.

Our mothers and fathers stood in the dark hall and joined the hymn of en- 56
couragement. A kindergarten teacher led the small children onto the stage and
the buttercups and daisies and bunny rabbits marked time and tried to follow:

Stony the road we trod
Bitter the chastening rod
Felt in the days when hope, unborn, had died.
Yet with a steady beat
Have not our weary feet
Come to the place for which our father sighed?

Every child I knew had learned that song with his ABC's and along with 57
"Jesus Loves Me This I Know." But I personally had never heard it before.
Never heard the words, despite the thousands of times I had sung them. Never
thought they had anything to do with me.

On the other hand, the words of Patrick Henry had made such an impression 58
on me that I had been able to stretch myself tall and trembling and say, "I know
not what course others may take, but as for me, give me liberty or give me death."

And now I heard, really for the first time: 59

We have come over away that with tears has been watered,
We have come, treading our path through the blood of the slaughtered.

While echoes of the song shivered in the air, Henry Reed bowed his head, 60
said "Thank you," and returned to his place in the line. The tears that slipped
down many faces were not wiped away in shame.

We were on top again. As always, again. We survived. The depths had been 61
icy and dark, but now a bright sun spoke to our souls. I was no longer simply a
member of the proud graduating class of 1940; I was a proud member of the
wonderful beautiful Negro race.

COMPREHENSION

1. Is Angelou a neutral observer or subjective participant in the events of this
   narrative? How can you tell?
2. How is the author's "presentiment of worse things to come" actually borne
   out? What is the "ancient tragedy" alluded to? How, specifically, does education relate to this allusion?
3. What do you learn about Marguerite—the young Maya Angelou—from
   this essay? What are her moods, emotions, thoughts, and attitudes? In what
   way is she "bound for higher ground"?

RHETORIC

1. Angelou is a highly impressionistic stylist in this essay. Provide examples of
   details that create vivid descriptive impressions. How do these details control the shifting moods of the selection?

2. Explain Angelou's allusions to *The Rape of Lucrece,* Gabriel Prosser and Nat Turner, Harriet Tubman, and "Invictus." How are these allusions and others related to the thesis? State that thesis in your own words.

3. What is the purpose of the relatively long five-paragraph introduction? What contrasts and latent ironies do you detect?

4. Cite examples of the author's ability to blend description, narration, and exposition. At what points is the expository mode the strongest? What is Angelou's purpose?

5. Why are the descriptions of Henry Reed and Donleavy juxtaposed?

6. Which paragraphs constitute the conclusion? How does Angelou achieve the transition from the body to the end?

WRITING

1. To what extent does American education still try to "track" students? What are the implications of such tracking? Discuss this issue in an essay; be certain to provide appropriate evidence.

2. Reconstruct your own graduation from grade school or high school.

3. Analyze and evaluate the many strategies that Angelou employs to honor and celebrate black culture and black wisdom in this essay.

By Any Other Name

Santha Rama Rau

Santha Rama Rau (b. 1923) is an Indian novelist and essayist who, throughout her career, has interpreted the Eastern experience for Western audiences. She is a gifted travel writer and memoirist. Her principal works include Home to India *(1944),* Remember the House *(1955), and* Gifts of Passage *(1961). This narrative essay sensitively portrays the conflict in cultures perceived by the author in her early childhood.*

At the Anglo-Indian day school in Zorinabad to which my sister and I were sent when she was eight and I was five and a half, they changed our names. On the first day of school, a hot, windless morning of a north Indian September, we stood in the headmistress's study and she said, "Now you're the *new* girls. What are your names?"

My sister answered for us. "I am Premila, and she"—nodding in my direction—"is Santha."

The headmistress had been in India, I suppose, fifteen years or so, but she still smiled her helpless inability to cope with Indian names. Her rimless half-glasses glittered, and the precarious bun on top of her head trembled as she shook her head. "Oh, my dears, those are much too hard for me. Suppose we give you pretty English names. Wouldn't that be more jolly? Let's see, now—Pamela for you, I think." She shrugged in a baffled way at my sister. "That's as close as I can get. And for *you*," she said to me, "how about Cynthia? Isn't that nice?"

My sister was always less easily intimidated than I was, and while she kept a stubborn silence, I said, "Thank you," in a very tiny voice. 4

We had been sent to that school because my father, among his responsibili- 5 ties as an officer of the civil service, had a tour of duty to perform in the villages around that steamy little provincial town, where he had his headquarters at that time. He used to make his shorter inspection tours on horseback, and a week before, in the stale heat of a typically postmonsoon day, we had waved good-by to him and a little procession—an assistant, a secretary, two bearers, and the man to look after the bedding rolls and luggage. They rode away through our large garden, still bright green from the rains, and we turned back into the twilight of the house and the sound of fans whispering in every room.

Up to then, my mother had refused to send Premila to school in the British- 6 run establishments of that time, because, she used to say, "you can bury a dog's tail for seven years and it still comes out curly, and you can take a Britisher away from his home for a lifetime, and he still remains insular." The examinations and degrees from entirely Indian schools were not, in those days, considered valid. In my case, the question had never come up, and probably never would have come up if Mother's extraordinary good health had not broken down. For the first time in my life, she was not able to continue the lessons she had been giving us every morning. So our Hindi books were put away, the stories of the Lord Krishna as a little boy were left in midair, and we were sent to the Anglo-Indian school.

That first day at school is still, when I think of it, a remarkable one. At that 7 age, if one's name is changed, one develops a curious form of dual personality. I remember having a certain detached and disbelieving concern in the actions of "Cynthia," but certainly no responsibility. Accordingly, I followed the thin, erect back of the headmistress down the veranda to my classroom feeling, at most, a passing interest in what was going to happen to me in this strange, new atmosphere of School.

The building was Indian in design, with wide verandas opening onto a cen- 8 tral courtyard, but Indian verandas are usually whitewashed, with stone floors. These, in the tradition of British schools, were painted dark brown and had matting on the floors. It gave a feeling of extra intensity to the heat.

I suppose there were about a dozen Indian children in the school—which 9 contained perhaps forty children in all—and four of them were in my class. They were all sitting at the back of the room, and I went to join them. I sat next to a small, solemn girl who didn't smile at me. She had long, glossy-black braids and wore a cotton dress, but she still kept on her Indian jewelry—gold chain around her neck, thin gold bracelets, and tiny ruby studs in her ears. Like most Indian children, she had a rim of black kohl around her eyes. The cotton dress should have looked strange, but all I could think of was that I should ask my mother if I couldn't wear a dress to school, too, instead of my Indian clothes.

I can't remember too much about the proceedings in class that day, except 10 for the beginning. The teacher pointed to me and asked me to stand up. "Now, dear, tell the class your name."

I said nothing.   11

"Come along," she said, frowning slightly. "What's your name, dear?"   12

"I don't know," I said, finally.   13

The English children in the front of the class—there were about eight or ten 14 of them—giggled and twisted around in their chairs to look at me. I sat down quickly and opened my eyes very wide, hoping in that way to dry them off. The little girl with the braids put out her hand and very lightly touched my arm. She still didn't smile.

Most of that morning I was rather bored. I looked briefly at the children's 15 drawings pinned to the wall, and then concentrated on a lizard clinging to the ledge of the high, barred window behind the teacher's head. Occasionally it would shoot out its long yellow tongue for a fly, and then it would rest, with its eyes closed and its belly palpitating, as though it were swallowing several times quickly. The lessons were mostly concerned with reading and writing and simple numbers—things that my mother had already taught me—and I paid very little attention. The teacher wrote on the easel blackboard words like "bat" and "cat," which seemed babyish to me; only "apple" was new and incomprehensible.

When it was time for the lunch recess, I followed the girl with braids out 16 onto the veranda. There the children from the other classes were assembled. I saw Premila at once and ran over to her, as she had charge of our lunchbox. The children were all opening packages and sitting down to eat sandwiches. Premila and I were the only ones who had Indian food—thin wheat chapatties, some vegetable curry, and a bottle of buttermilk. Premila thrust half of it into my hand and whispered fiercely that I should go and sit with my class, because that was what the others seemed to be doing.

The enormous black eyes of the little Indian girl from my class looked at my 17 food longingly, so I offered her some. But she only shook her head and plowed her way solemnly through her sandwiches.

I was very sleepy after lunch, because at home we always took a siesta. It 18 was usually a pleasant time of day, with the bedroom darkened against the harsh afternoon sun, the drifting off into sleep with the sound of Mother's voice reading a story in one's mind, and, finally, the shrill, fussy voice of the ayah waking one for tea.

At school, we rested for a short time on low, folding cots on the veranda, 19 and then we were expected to play games. During the hot part of the afternoon we played indoors, and after the shadows had begun to lengthen and the slight breeze of the evening had come up we moved outside to the wide courtyard.

I had never really grasped the system of competitive games. At home, 20 whenever we played tag or guessing games, I was always allowed to "win"—

"because," Mother used to tell Premila, "she is the youngest, and we have to allow for that." I had often heard her say it, and it seemed quite reasonable to me, but the result was that I had no clear idea of what "winning" meant.

When we played twos-and-threes that afternoon at school, in accordance 21 with my training, I let one of the small English boys catch me, but was naturally rather puzzled when the other children did not return the courtesy. I ran about for what seemed like hours without ever catching anyone, until it was time for school to close. Much later I learned that my attitude was called "not being a good sport," and I stopped allowing myself to be caught, but it was not for years that I really learned the spirit of the thing.

When I saw our car come up to the school gate, I broke away from my class- 22 mates and rushed toward it yelling, "Ayah Ayah!" It seemed like an eternity since I had seen her that morning—a wizened, affectionate figure in her white cotton sari, giving me dozens of urgent and useless instructions on how to be a good girl at school. Premila followed more sedately, and she told me on the way home never to do that again in front of the other children.

When we got home we went straight to Mother's high, white room to have 23 tea with her, and I immediately climbed onto the bed and bounced gently up and down on the springs. Mother asked how we had liked our first day in school. I was so pleased to be home and to have left that peculiar Cynthia behind that I had nothing whatever to say about school, except to ask what "apple" meant. But Premila told Mother about the classes, and added that in her class they had weekly tests to see if they learned their lessons well.

I asked, "What's a test?" 24

Premila said, "You're too small to have them. You won't have them in your 25 class for donkey's years." She had learned the expression that day and was using it for the first time. We all laughed enormously at her wit. She also told Mother, in an aside, that we should take sandwiches to school the next day. Not, she said, that *she* minded. But they would be simpler for me to handle.

That whole lovely evening I didn't think about school at all. I sprinted bare- 26 foot across the lawns with my favorite playmate, the cook's son, to the stream at the end of the garden. We quarreled in our usual way, waded in the tepid water under the lime trees, and waited for the night to bring out the smell of the jasmine. I listened with fascination to his stories of ghosts and demons, until I was too frightened to cross the garden alone in the semidarkness. The ayah found me, shouted at the cook's son, scolded me, hurried me into supper—it was an entirely usual, wonderful evening.

It was a week later, the day of Premila's first test, that our lives changed 27 rather abruptly. I was sitting at the back of my class, in my usual inattentive way, only half listening to the teacher. I had started a rather guarded friendship with the girl with the braids, whose name turned out to be Nalini (Nancy, in school). The three other Indian children were already fast friends. Even at that age it was apparent to all of us that friendship with the English or Anglo-Indian children was out of the question. Occasionally, during the class, my new friend and I would draw pictures and show them to each other secretly.

The door opened sharply and Premila marched in. At first, the teacher 28
smiled at her in a kindly and encouraging way and said, "Now, you're little
Cynthia's sister?"

Premila didn't even look at her. She stood with her feet planted firmly apart 29
and her shoulders rigid, and addressed herself directly to me. "Get up," she
said. "We're going home."

I didn't know what had happened, but I was aware that it was a crisis of 30
some sort. I rose obediently and started to walk toward my sister.

"Bring your pencils and your notebook," she said. 31

I went back for them, and together we left the room. The teacher started to 32
say something just as Premila closed the door, but we didn't wait to hear what
it was.

In complete silence we left the school grounds and started to walk home. 33
Then I asked Premila what the matter was. All she would say was "We're going
home for good."

It was a very tiring walk for a child of five and a half, and I dragged along 34
behind Premila with my pencils growing sticky in my hand. I can still remember looking at the dusty hedges, and the tangles of thorns in the ditches by the
side of the road, smelling the faint fragrance from the eucalyptus trees and wondering whether we would ever reach home. Occasionally a horse-drawn tonga
passed us, and the women, in their pink or green silks, stared at Premila and me
trudging along on the side of the road. A few coolies and a line of women carrying baskets of vegetables on their heads smiled at us. But it was nearing the
hottest time of day, and the road was almost deserted. I walked more and more
slowly, and shouted to Premila, from time to time, "Wait for me!" with increasing peevishness. She spoke to me only once, and that was to tell me to carry my
notebook on my head, because of the sun.

When we got to our house the ayah was just taking a tray of lunch into 35
Mother's room. She immediately started a long, worried questioning about
what are you children doing back here at this hour of the day.

Mother looked very startled and very concerned, and asked Premila what 36
had happened.

Premila said, "We had our test today, and she made me and the other Indians 37
sit at the back of the room, with a desk between each one."

Mother said, "Why was that, darling?" 38

"She said it was because Indians cheat," Premila added. "So I don't think 39
we should go back to that school."

Mother looked very distant, and was silent a long time. At last she said, "Of 40
course not, darling." She sounded displeased.

We all shared the curry she was having for lunch, and afterward I was sent 41
off to the beautifully familiar bedroom for my siesta. I could hear Mother and
Premila talking through the open door.

Mother said, "Do you suppose she understood all that?" 42
Premila said, "I shouldn't think so. She's a baby." 43
Mother said, "Well, I hope it won't bother her." 44

Of course, they were both wrong. I understood it perfectly, and I remember ₄₅ it all very clearly. But I put it happily away, because it had all happened to a girl called Cynthia, and I never was really particularly interested in her.

COMPREHENSION

1. What does the title of this essay mean? State the thesis that emerges from it.
2. Cite five examples the author gives to demonstrate that her attendance at the Anglo-Indian day school was an alien experience for her. How is the author's experience similar to Angelou's in "Graduation"?
3. According to the author's inferences, what was the effect of British rule on Indian society? How does the headmistress embody this impact? Compare and contrast Rau's perception of colonialism and that of Orwell in "Shooting an Elephant" (see Chapter 6).

RHETORIC

1. Define these Indian words, preferably from the contexts in which they are used: *kohl* (paragraph 9); *chapatties* (paragraph 16); *ayah* (paragraph 18); *sari* (paragraph 22); and *tonga* (paragraph 34).
2. Explain the author's use of sensory language in paragraphs 1, 3, 5, 8, 9, 15, 26, and 34.
3. What is the theme of this narrative essay? How does the author state it?
4. Identify the tone and mood of the essay.
5. What is the utility and value of the author's use of dialogue in the essay?
6. How do various causal patterns inform the narrative?

WRITING

1. Although dealing specifically with a colonial situation, the author also illuminates the universal experience of being made to feel different, strange, or alien. Why is this ironic for the author? Why does it remain so vivid in her memory? Do we become more or less conscious of this phenomenon at a later age? Write a narrative essay centering on a time when you were made to feel strange or foreign in an educational situation.
2. Write an essay of 400 to 500 words arguing for or against the proposition that colleges should offer a required course that teaches students about the different cultural backgrounds of their student populations, or that such training should be optional.
3. Describe a time in your life when you witnessed a form of cultural prejudice, whether it was in school, in your neighborhood, or in your place of employment. Discuss your feelings about what you saw, whether you took action in response to it, and your reasons for either intervening or not.

Sex Ed

Anna Quindlen

Anna Quindlen (b. 1953), a journalist and editor, began her writing career as a re-
porter for the New York Post *and later moved on to* The New York Times, *where she*
was a syndicated columnist. A graduate of Barnard College, Quindlen has written a
number of books, including Living Out Loud *(1986),* Object Lessons *(1991),* One
True Thing *(1994), and* Black and Blue: A Novel *(1998). Quindlen received the*
Pulitzer Prize for Commentary in 1992. She is currently a columnist for Newsweek
magazine. In this essay, Quindlen focuses on the problem of teenage pregnancy and
suggests children be given more than textbook information to help them cope with their
sexuality.

Several years ago I spent the day at a family planning clinic in one of New York 1
City's poorest neighborhoods. I sat around a Formica table with a half-dozen
sixteen-year-old girls and listened with some amazement as they showed off
their knowledge of human sexuality.

They knew how long sperm lived inside the body, how many women out of 2
a hundred using a diaphragm were statistically likely to get pregnant and the
medical term for the mouth of the cervix. One girl pointed out all the parts of
the female reproductive system on a placard; another recited the stages of the
ovulation cycle from day one to twenty-eight. There was just one problem with
this performance: although the results of their laboratory tests would not be
available for fifteen more minutes, every last one of them was pregnant.

I always think of that day when someone suggests that sex education at 3
school is a big part of the answer to the problem of teenage pregnancy. I happen
to be a proponent of such programs; I think human sexuality is a subject for dispassionate study, like civics and ethics and dozens of other topics that have a
moral component. I'd like my sons to know as much as possible about how
someone gets pregnant, how pregnancy can be avoided, and what it means
when avoidance techniques have failed.

I remember adolescence about as vividly as I remember anything, however, 4
and I am not in the least convinced that that information alone will significantly
alter the rate of teenage pregnancy. It seemed to me that day in the clinic, and on
days I spent at schools and on street corners, that teenage pregnancy has a lot
more to do with what it means to be a teenager than with how someone gets
pregnant. When I was in high school, at the tail end of the sixties, there was a
straightforward line on sex among my friends. Boys could have it; girls could-
n't. A girl who was not a virgin pretended she was. A girl who was sleeping
with her boyfriend, no matter how long-playing the relationship, pretended she
was not.

It is the nature of adolescence that there is no past and no future, only the $_5$ present, burning as fierce, bright, and merciless as a bare light bulb. Girls had sex with boys because nothing seemed to matter except right now, not pregnancy, not parental disapprobation, nothing but those minutes, this dance, that face, those words. Most of them knew that pregnancy could result, but they assured themselves that they would be the lucky ones who would not get caught. Naturally, some of them were wrong, and in my experience they did one of three things: they went to Puerto Rico for a mysterious weekend trip; visited an aunt in some faraway state for three months and came back with empty eyes and a vague reputation, or got married, quickly, in Empire-waist dresses.

What seems to have changed most since then is that there is little philo- $_6$ sophical counterpoint, hypocritical or not, to the raging hormones of adolescence, and that so many of the once-hidden pregnancies are hidden no more.

Not long after the day at the family planning clinic, I went to a public high $_7$ school in the suburbs. In the girl's room was this graffito: Jennifer Is a Virgin. I asked the kids about it and they said it was shorthand for geek, nerd, weirdo, somebody who was so incredibly out of it that they were in high school and still hadn't had sex. If you were a virgin, they told me, you just lied about it so that no one would think you were that immature. The girls in the family planning clinic told me much the same thing—that everyone did it, that the boys wanted it, that not doing it made them seem out of it. The only difference, really, was that the girls in the clinic were poor and would have their babies, and the girls in the high school were well-to-do and would have abortions. Pleasure didn't seem to have very much to do with sex for either group. After she learned she was pregnant, one of the girls at the clinic said, without a trace of irony, that she hoped childbirth didn't hurt as much as sex had. Birth control was easily disposed of in both cases. The pill, the youngsters said, could give you a stroke; the IUD could make you sterile. A diaphragm was disgusting.

One girl told me the funniest thing her boyfriend—a real original thinker— $_8$ had told her: they couldn't use condoms because it was like taking a shower with a raincoat on. She was a smart girl and pretty, and I wanted to tell her that it sounded as if she was sleeping with a jerk who didn't deserve her. But that is the kind of basic fact of life that must be taught not in the classroom, not by a stranger, but at home by the family. It is this that, finally, I will try to teach my sons about sex, after I've explained fertile periods and birth control and all the other mechanics that are important to understand but never really go to the heart of the matter: I believe I will say that when you sleep with someone you take off a lot more than your clothes.

COMPREHENSION

1. Does Quindlen approve of sex education? Explain.
2. How does the writer characterize the attitude of adolescents regarding sex and pregnancy?
3. What advice or information about sex will the writer give her sons? Why?

RHETORIC

1. Why did Quindlen choose "Sex Ed" as a title? What is its significance in relation to the thesis?
2. What is Quindlen's thesis? Where is it contained in the essay? Is it directly stated or implied?
3. Is Quindlen's writing an argumentative essay? Support your position with citations from the text.
4. What point is the writer making through use of accumulated details in paragraph 2?
5. What does Quindlen mean by the term "moral component" in paragraph 3? Where else in the essay does she allude to it? How does the author employ definition in this essay?
6. What does Quindlen mean by her final statement that "when you sleep with someone you take off a lot more than your clothes"? How does this ending serve to underscore the thesis of the essay?

WRITING

1. Write a letter to a teenage son or daughter in which you discuss sexuality and pregnancy.
2. Write a paper analyzing the most common forms of birth control available and listing the advantages and disadvantages of each.
3. In an essay, consider possible solutions to the problem of teenage pregnancy. What role do you think sex education has in ameliorating the problem? Use support from the Quindlen essay if applicable.

Unplugged: The Myth of Computers in the Classroom

David Gelernter

David Gelernter is a professor of computer science at Yale University. He is a leading figure in the field of human cognition and a seminal thinker in the field known as parallel computing. Gelernter, who was injured by a package sent by the Unabomber in 1993, is the author of Mirror Worlds *(1991),* The Muse in the Machine *(1994),* 1939: The Lost World of the Fair *(1995), and* Machine Beauty *(1998). In the following essay, published in* The New Republic *in 1994, Gelernter offers a cogent analysis of the limits of technology in the classroom.*

Over the last decade an estimated $2 billion has been spent on more than 2 million computers for America's classrooms. That's not surprising. We constantly hear from Washington that the schools are in trouble and that computers are a godsend. Within the education establishment, in poor as well as rich schools, the machines are awaited with nearly religious awe. An inner-city principal bragged to a teacher friend of mine recently that his school "has a computer in every classroom . . . despite being in a bad neighborhood!"

Computers should be in the schools. They have the potential to accomplish great things. With the right software, they could help make science tangible or teach neglected topics like art and music. They help students form a concrete idea of society by displaying onscreen a version of the city in which they live— a picture that tracks real life moment by moment.

In practice, however, computers make our worst educational nightmares come true. While we bemoan the decline of literacy, computers discount words in favor of pictures and pictures in favor of video. While we fret about the decreasing cogency of public debate, computers dismiss linear argument and promote fast, shallow romps across the information landscape. While we worry about basic skills, we allow into the classroom software that will do a student's arithmetic or correct his spelling.

Take multimedia. The idea of multimedia is to combine text, sound and pictures in a single package that you browse on screen. You don't just *read* Shakespeare; you watch actors performing, listen to songs, view Elizabethan buildings. What's wrong with that? By offering children candy-coated books, multimedia is guaranteed to sour them on unsweetened reading. It makes the printed page look even more boring than it used to look. Sure, books will be available in the classroom, too—but they'll have all the appeal of a dusty piano to a teen who has a Walkman handy.

So what if the little nippers don't read? If they're watching Olivier instead, what do they lose? The text, the written word along with all of its attendant pleasures. Besides, a book is more portable than a computer, has a higher-resolution display, can be written on and dog-eared and is comparatively dirt cheap.

Hypermedia, multimedia's comrade in the struggle for a brave new classroom, is just as troubling. It's a way of presenting documents on screen without imposing a linear start-to-finish order. Disembodied paragraphs are linked by theme; after reading one about the First World War, for example, you might be able to choose another about the technology of battleships, or the life of Woodrow Wilson, or hemlines in the '20s. This is another cute idea that is good in minor ways and terrible in major ones. Teaching children to understand the orderly unfolding of a plot or a logical argument is a crucial part of education. Authors don't merely agglomerate paragraphs; they work hard to make the narrative read a certain way, prove a particular point. To turn a book or a document into hypertext is to invite readers to ignore exactly what counts—the story.

The real problem, again, is the accentuation of already bad habits. Dynamiting documents into disjointed paragraphs is one more expression of the sorry fact that sustained argument is not our style. If you're a newspaper or magazine editor and your readership is dwindling, what's the solution? Shorter pieces. If you're a politician and you want to get elected, what do you need? Tasty sound bites. Logical presentation be damned.   8

Another software species, "allow me" programs, is not much better. These programs correct spelling and, by applying canned grammatical and stylistic rules, fix prose. In terms of promoting basic skills, though, they have all the virtues of a pocket calculator.   9

In Kentucky, as *The Wall Street Journal* recently reported, students in grades K-3 are mixed together regardless of age in a relaxed environment. It works great, the *Journal* says. Yes, scores on computation tests have dropped 10 percent at one school, but not to worry: "Drilling addition and subtraction in an age of calculators is a waste of time," the principal reassures us. Meanwhile, a Japanese educator informs University of Wisconsin mathematician Richard Akey that in his country, "calculators are not used in elementary or junior high school because the primary emphasis is on helping students develop their mental abilities." No wonder Japanese kids blow the pants off American kids in math. Do we really think "drilling addition and subtraction in an age of calculators is a waste of time"? If we do, then "drilling reading in an age of multimedia is a waste of time" can't be far behind.   10

Prose-correcting programs are also a little ghoulish, like asking a computer for tips on improving your personality. On the other hand, I ran this article through a spell-checker, so how can I ban the use of such programs in schools? Because to misspell is human; to have no idea of correct spelling is to be semiliterate.

There's no denying that computers have the potential to perform inspiring   11 feats in the classroom. If we are ever to see that potential realized, however, we ought to agree on three conditions. First, there should be a completely new crop of children's software. Most of today's offerings show no imagination. There are hundreds of similar reading and geography and arithmetic programs, but almost nothing on electricity or physics or architecture. Also, they abuse the technical capacities of new media to glitz up old forms instead of creating new ones. Why not build a time-travel program that gives kids a feel for how history is structured by zooming you backward? A spectrum program that lets users twirl a frequency knob to see what happens?

Second, computers should be used only during recess or relaxation periods.   12 Treat them as fillips, not as surrogate teachers. When I was in school in the '60s, we all loved educational films. When we saw a movie in class, everybody won: teachers didn't have to teach, and pupils didn't have to learn. I suspect that classroom computers are popular today for the same reasons.

Most important, educators should learn what parents and most teachers al-   13 ready know: you cannot teach a child anything unless you look him in the face. We should not forget what computers are. Like books—better in some ways, worse in others—they are devices that help children mobilize their own resources and learn for themselves. The computer's potential to do good is modestly greater than a book's in some areas. Its potential to do harm is vastly greater, across the board.

COMPREHENSION

1. State the author's main thesis in one sentence.
2. In the final paragraph, Gelernter defines what he believes to be the most important shortcoming of the computer as a teaching tool. Explain the reason why this weakness is so significant.
3. In your own words, explain the author's dislike of hypermedia as a pedagogic tool (as expressed in paragraph 6) and why the orderly arrangement of paragraphs in a book is superior to this newer technological capability.

RHETORIC

1. The introductory paragraph goes from a general fact to a specific quotation. What is the effect of this method of paragraph patterning?
2. Much of the author's argument hinges on providing evidence that one medium is superior to another. Explain terms such as *linear argument* (paragraph 3), *agglomerate paragraphs* (paragraph 6), and *allow me programs* (paragraph 8). How do these terms help Gelernter prove his point?
3. The essay has a three-part structure, each section divided by space. How would you characterize the purpose of each section? How does the author use transitions to move from one section to the next?
4. The author states that the overuse of computers in the classroom can hinder the development of clear thinking and reasoned argument. How clearly written is *his* essay? How reasoned is his argument? Gather evidence for your answer by reviewing the essay and determining whether each sentence seems to flow logically from the next and whether each paragraph seems to move reasonably to the next.
5. The author uses metaphors, similes, and other rhetorical devices. Explain the effectiveness of expressions such as "have all the appeal of a dusty piano to a teen who has a Walkman handy" (paragraph 4), "dynamiting documents" (paragraph 7), and "software species" (paragraph 8). Locate other unconventional descriptions.
6. Who is the intended audience for this essay? Educators?, Parents?, Students?, Politicians? What evidence can you show to back up your view?
7. What rhetorical device is the author using in his title? What is the implicit meaning of the title?

WRITING

1. Select one of the teaching capabilities of modern computers—multimedia, hypertext, or spell- and grammar-check programs. Argue for the benefits of one of these features.
2. Visit the writing or reading computer lab in your school. As an objective observer, study the interaction of student and computer. Write a descriptive essay focusing on the demeanor and behavior of the student and

the atmosphere of the classroom. If you wish, compare it to a traditional classroom.

3. Copy a paragraph from the essay, and enter it into a word-processing program that has a grammar-check function. Record any comments that the program makes in response to its evaluation of the writing. Do the computer's responses to the author's sentence structure make sense?

When Bright Girls Decide That Math Is "a Waste of Time"

Susan Jacoby

Susan Jacoby (b. 1945) has worked as an educator and as a reporter for The Washington Post. *As a freelance journalist in the former Soviet Union (from 1969 to 1971), she produced two books about her experiences. Jacoby now contributes to* The Nation *and* McCall's; *her books include* The Possible She *(1979), a collection of autobiographical essays,* Wild Justice: The Evolution of Revenge *(1983), and* Half-Jew: A Daughter's Search for Her Buried Past *(2000). In this essay from* The New York Times, *Jacoby examines the reasons why girls are often deficient in math and science.*

Susannah, a 16-year-old who has always been an A student in every subject from algebra to English, recently informed her parents that she intended to drop physics and calculus in her senior year of high school and replace them with a drama seminar and a work-study program. She expects a major in art or history in college, she explained, and "any more science or math will just be a waste of my time."

Her parents were neither concerned by nor opposed to her decision. "Fine, dear," they said. Their daughter is, after all, an outstanding student. What does it matter if, at age 16, she has taken a step that may limit her understanding of both machines and the natural world for the rest of her life?

This kind of decision, in which girls turn away from studies that would give them a sure footing in the world of science and technology, is a self-inflicted female disability that is, regrettably, almost as common today as it was when I was in high school. If Susannah had announced that she had decided to stop taking English in her senior year, her mother and father would have been horrified. I also think they would have been a good deal less sanguine about her decision if she were a boy.

In saying that scientific and mathematical ignorance is a self-inflicted female wound, I do not, obviously, mean that cultural expectations play no role in the process. But the world does not conspire to deprive modern women of access to science as it did in the 1930s, when Rosalyn S. Yalow, the Nobel Prize–winning physicist, graduated from Hunter College and was advised to go to work as a secretary because no graduate school would admit her to its physics department. The current generation of adolescent girls—and their parents, bred on old expectations about women's interests—are active conspirators in limiting their own intellectual development.

It is true that the proportion of young women in science-related graduate 5 and professional schools, most notably medical schools, has increased significantly in the past decade. It is also true that so few women were studying advanced science and mathematics before the early 1970s that the percentage increase in female enrollment does not yet translate into large numbers of women actually working in science.

The real problem is that so many girls eliminate themselves from any serious 6 possibility of studying science as a result of decisions made during the vulnerable period of midadolescence, when they are most likely to be influenced—on both conscious and subconscious levels—by the traditional belief that math and science are "masculine" subjects.

During the teen-age years the well-documented phenomenon of "math 7 anxiety" strikes girls who never had any problem handling numbers during earlier schooling. Some men, too, experience this syndrome—a form of panic, akin to a phobia, at any task involving numbers—but women constitute the overwhelming majority of sufferers. The onset of acute math anxiety during the teen-age years is, as Stalin was fond of saying, "not by accident."

In adolescence girls begin to fear that they will be unattractive to boys if 8 they are typed as "brains." Science and math epitomize unfeminine braininess in a way that, say, foreign languages do not. High-school girls who pursue an advanced interest in science and math (unless they are students at special institutions like the Bronx High School of Science where everyone is a brain) usually find that they are greatly outnumbered by boys in their classes. They are, therefore, intruding on male turf at a time when their sexual confidence, as well as that of the boys, is most fragile.

A 1981 assessment of female achievement in mathematics, based on re- 9 search conducted under a National Institute for Education grant, found significant differences in the mathematical achievements of 9th and 12th graders. At age 13 girls were equal to or slightly better than boys in tests involving algebra, problem solving and spatial ability; four years later the boys had outstripped the girls.

It is not mysterious that some very bright high-school girls suddenly decide 10 that math is "too hard" and "a waste of time." In my experience, self-sabotage of mathematical and scientific ability is often a conscious process. I remember deliberately pretending to be puzzled by geometry problems in my sophomore year in high school. A male teacher called me in after class and. said, in a baffled tone, "I don't see how you can be having so much trouble when you got straight A's last year in my algebra class."

The decision to avoid advanced biology, chemistry, physics and calculus in 11 high school automatically restricts academic and professional choices that ought to be wide open to anyone beginning college. At all coeducational universities women are overwhelmingly concentrated in the fine arts, social sciences and traditionally female departments like education. Courses leading to degrees in science- and technology-related fields are filled mainly by men.

In my generation, the practical consequences of mathematical and scientific 12 illiteracy are visible in the large number of special programs to help professional women overcome the anxiety they feel when they are promoted into jobs that require them to handle statistics.

The consequences of this syndrome should not, however, be viewed in nar- 13 rowly professional terms. Competence in science and math does not mean one is going to become a scientist or mathematician any more than competence in writing English means one is going to become a professional writer. Scientific and mathematical illiteracy—which has been cited in several recent critiques by panels studying American education from kindergarten through college—produces an incalculably impoverished vision of human experience.

Scientific illiteracy is not, of course, the exclusive province of women. In 14 certain intellectual circles it has become fashionable to proclaim a willed, aggressive ignorance about science and technology. Some female writers specialize in ominous, uninformed diatribes against genetic research as a plot to remove control of childbearing from women, while some well-known men of letters proudly announce that they understand absolutely nothing about computers, or, for that matter, about electricity. This lack of understanding is nothing in which women or men ought to take pride.

Failure to comprehend either computers or chromosomes leads to a terrible 15 sense of helplessness, because the profound impact of science on everyday life is evident even to those who insist they don't, won't, can't understand why the changes are taking place. At this stage of history women are more prone to such feelings of helplessness than men because the culture judges their ignorance less harshly and because women themselves acquiesce in that indulgence.

Since there is ample evidence of such feelings in adolescence, it is up to par- 16 ents to see that their daughters do not accede to the old stereotypes about "masculine" and "feminine" knowledge. Unless we want our daughters to share our intellectual handicaps, we had better tell them no, they can't stop taking mathematics and science at the ripe old age of 16.

COMPREHENSION

1. What reasons does Jacoby give for girls' deficiency in math and science?
2. Why does she call it a "self-inflicted disability"?
3. What are the consequences of being math- and science-illiterate?

RHETORIC

1. Explain the main idea of Jacoby's essay in your own words.
2. Does the writer use abstract or concrete language in her essay? Cite examples to support your response.

3. What technique does Jacoby use in paragraphs 1 and 2? How does it aid in setting up her argument?
4. What rhetorical strategies does the writer use in her essay?
5. How does the use of dialogue aid in developing paragraph 10? What effect does the general use of dialogue have on the writer's point?
6. How is Jacoby's conclusion consistent in tone with the rest of the essay? Does it supply a sense of unity? Why, or why not?

WRITING

1. Write an essay describing a school-related phobia you once had, or continue to have (for example, in math, writing, physical education, biology). Explain where you think that fear came from, how it affected your performance in school, and what you did (or are doing) to cope with the problem.
2. Write an argumentation essay proposing that math and science phobia is not "self-inflicted," but caused primarily by the continued presence of sexism in society.
3. Write an essay about the need for math and science literacy in today's world. Use support from Jacoby's essay.

Why America's Universities Are Better Than Its Schools

E. D. Hirsch Jr.

E. D. Hirsch Jr. (b. 1928) was born in Memphis, Tennessee. He received his BA from Cornell University and his MA and PhD from Yale University. While his early literary work was directed at analyzing romantic poetry, he soon turned to more global issues of literary interpretation and of culture and knowledge, particularly as they pertained to the society at large. Two of his books, Cultural Literacy: What Every American Needs to Know *(1987) and* Dictionary of Cultural Literacy: What Every American Needs to Know—*cowritten with Joseph Kett and James Trefil—(1988; revised edition, 1993), raised a national debate over the "dumbing down" of America and warned that Americans were in danger of losing their ability to deal with the important historical, political, and social issues of the day if this trend continued. Hailed by some as bringing to light a dangerous threat to democracy, while condemned by others as being too elitist, Hirsch nevertheless has been quite influential in making educators reconsider the required curriculum in our schools. Besides his scholarly work for adults, he has also written a number of "Core Knowledge" books in conjunction with his founding the Cultural Literacy Foundation. Geared for parents and teachers of various age groups, this series provides Hirsch's thoughts on what students need to know at various developmental periods in their lives. In the following essay, he presents an encapsulated view of the dangers he sees in trying to teach "methods" without a healthy helping of "content" to preuniversity students.*

The influence of the intellectual orthodoxy that controls our public schooling 1 and its reformers may partly be gauged by contrasting our K-12 system with an education domain *not* controlled by the educationist point of view—our public colleges and universities. There is wide agreement in the international community that the United States has created the best public universities and the worst public schools in the developed world.

What causes this startling contrast in quality between American schools 2 and American universities? It is not inevitable that a nation must fail to achieve educational excellence in both spheres. In fact, it is *easier* to create a good K-12 system than a good university system, the evidence being that many nations have created better elementary schools than ours but few or none have created better universities.

Perhaps American culture is friendly to first-rate universities (I don't mean 3 to imply that all of them are first rate or that their faculties are uniformly admirable) because of our tradition of free speech and our consequent toleration, even encouragement, of dissent. Open discussion and iconoclasm create the sort of atmosphere in which intellectual excellence can flourish. Over a portal of the University of Virginia's Cabell Hall are Jefferson's words about the kind of university he wished to create: "This institution will be based on the illimitable freedom of the human mind. For here we are not afraid to follow truth wherever it may lead, nor to tolerate any error so long as reason is left free to combat it." That concept is a universe away from the intolerant, conformist atmosphere of the educational community.

But there is another difference, in addition to their openness and competi- 4 tiveness, that distinguishes our universities from our schools, and I think it may be the most critical difference of all. Our colleges and universities, and the scholars who control their destinies, place great value on depth, breadth and accuracy of knowledge, as well as on independence of thought. But depth, breadth, and accuracy of knowledge are the very things that our K-12 system tends to disparage as belonging to the "banking theory of schooling." Knowledge is considered less desirable than more "practical" all-purpose goals such as "higher order skills," "self-esteem," "metacognitive skills," and "critical-thinking skills." "Mere facts" are conceived to be indissolubly connected to "rote learning," which may be the most disparaging phrase in the educationists' glossary.

It is unclear how long our best universities can maintain their excellence 5 when the students who enter them and who will subsequently staff them are ill prepared. Since 1965, for example, there has been a 75 percent decline in the absolute number of students who score above 650 in verbal and math college-entrance tests, proving that the decline of our best students is not owing simply to the inclusion of a greater number of minority students. Helping to maintain quality against this tide of ill-preparedness has been an influx of well-educated foreigners to our research universities. Many of these postgraduate students stay in the United States, but many do not. The Japanese high-technology industry, for example, has strong intellectual roots in American universities, with more than 13,000 Japanese students in the United States (compared with about 700 American students in Japan).

Despite this influx of intellectual capital from abroad, which parallels the influx of financial capital, we cannot permanently maintain a K-12 intellectual deficit any more than we can permanently maintain a negative trade balance. All of our most-difficult-to-enter universities must now maintain remedial centers for writing and mathematics, and in some cases for reading. It is disconcerting to see these centers pop up everywhere. No doubt many of the students who use them are foreign students or affirmative action students, but their clientele is definitely not limited entirely to minority and disadvantaged students. It is an inherently unstable situation and must lead to a decline of standards at all American universities, and probably has already done so. 6

If an emphasis on knowledge and dissent has led to high quality in a remarkable number of our universities, while an emphasis on process and conformity has led to low quality in most of our schools, common sense suggests that giving knowledge and dissent an energetic trial may carry practical benefits. The very existence of this quality gap is presumptive evidence that the slogans dominating our K-12 system and the efforts to reform it are defective and do not deserve the benefit of the doubt. The controlling theories and the people who propound them have, with the best of intentions, served the nation ill. It is not mainly our schools that need "restructuring," but the ideas of those who would restructure them. 7

COMPREHENSION

1. What does the author mean by "intellectual orthodoxy"? What relevance does it have to the theme of his essay?
2. According to the author, what are priority subjects for America's K-12 system? Why are these subjects considered important?
3. What does Hirsch mean by stating that our schools have "an emphasis on process"?

RHETORIC

1. Is the title of the essay a fact or an opinion? Explain your answer.
2. What is the rhetorical function of employing a question as the topic sentence in paragraph 2? What forms of evidence does Hirsch use to answer this question? Are his answers convincing or not? Explain your view.
3. In paragraph 4, Hirsch lists four subjects that are purportedly taught in school. Define each of them. What is implied by Hirsch's placing each of these subjects in quotation marks?

4. In paragraph 5, Hirsch cites statistics regarding declining scores on college-entrance tests. Does this help prove his thesis? Explain your view.
5. In Hirsch's conclusion, he refers to "controlling theories and the people who propound them," yet fails to mention any person or theory specifically. Is this absence an issue of rhetorical style or a weakness of argument? Consider the overall structure, length, and form of the essay.
6. In paragraph 7, Hirsch uses the term *low quality* in referring to our schools. What does the author mean by it? Is this a clear or an ambiguous term as applied to education? Explain your view.
7. Locate changes in focus in the essay. Where does one begin and the other end? What transitional expressions does the author use to signal these sections?

WRITING

1. Write a 250-word summary of Hirsch's essay, being sure to include his main arguments and supports. Use paraphrase where appropriate.
2. Write a 500-word expository essay exploring how you would improve schooling on the high school or secondary level.
3. Hirsch states that the things that universities support as important to education are "depth, breadth and accuracy of knowledge" and "independence of thought." Argue for or against the proposition that these two domains can be taught simultaneously.

The Good News Is: These Are Not the Best Years of Your Life

Gloria Steinem

Gloria Steinem (b. 1934) was born in Toledo, Ohio. After college, she won a fellowship to study in India, but on her return to America focused her attention on helping found the modern women's liberation movement, becoming active as a writer, an editor, a speaker, and a political activist. She gained national recognition when she founded Ms. *magazine in 1971. Some of her many essays are collected in* Outrageous Acts and Everyday Rebellions *(1983). In the following essay, first published in* Ms. *in 1979, Steinem asserts that women, unlike men, grow "more radical with age."*

If you had asked me a decade or more ago, I certainly would have said the cam- 1
pus was the first place to look for the feminist or any other revolution. I also
would have assumed that student-age women, like student-age men, were much
more likely to be activist and open to change than their parents. After all, campus
revolts have a long and well-publicized tradition, from the students of medieval

France, whose "heresy" was suggesting that the university be separate from the church, through the anticolonial student riots of British India; from students who led the cultural revolution of the People's Republic of China, to campus demonstrations against the Shah of Iran. Even in this country, with far less tradition of student activism, the populist movement to end the war in Vietnam was symbolized by campus protests and mistrust of anyone over thirty.

It has taken me many years of traveling as a feminist speaker and organizer 2 to understand that I was wrong about women; at least, about women acting on their own behalf. In activism, as in so many other things, I had been educated to assume that men's cultural pattern was the natural or the only one. If student years were the peak time of rebellion and openness to change for men, then the same must be true for women. In fact, a decade of listening to every kind of women's group—from brown-bag lunchtime lectures organized by office workers to all-night rap sessions at campus women's centers; from housewives' self-help groups to campus rallies—has convinced me that the reverse is more often true. Women may be the one group that grows more radical with age. Though some students are big exceptions to this rule, women in general don't begin to challenge the politics of our own lives until later.

Looking back, I realize that this pattern has been true for my life, too. My col- 3 lege years were full of uncertainties and the personal conservatism that comes from trying to win approval and fit into the proper grown-up and womanly role whether that means finding a well-to-do man to be supported by or a male radical to support. Nonetheless, I went right on assuming that brave exploring youth and cowardly conservative old age were the norms for everybody, and that I must be just an isolated and guilty accident. Though every generalization based on female culture has many exceptions, and should never be used as a crutch or excuse, I think we might be less hard on ourselves and each other as students, feel better about our potential for change as we grow older—and educate reporters who announce feminism's demise because its red-hot center is not on campus—if we figured out that for most of us as women, the traditional college period is an unrealistic and cautious time. Consider a few of the reasons.

As students, women are probably treated with more equality than we ever 4 will be again. For one thing, we're consumers. The school is only too glad to get the tuitions we pay, or that our families or government grants pay on our behalf. With population rates declining because of women's increased power over childbearing, that money is even more vital to a school's existence. Yet more than most consumers, we're too transient to have much power as a group. If our families are paying our tuition, we may have even less power.

As young women, whether students or not, we're still in the stage most val- 5 ued by male-dominant cultures: We have our full potential as workers, wives, sex partners, and childbearers.

That means we haven't yet experienced the life events that are most radi- 6 calizing for women: entering the paid-labor force and discovering how women are treated there; marrying and finding out that it is not yet an equal partnership; having children and discovering who is responsible for them and who is not; and aging, still a greater penalty for women than for men.

Furthermore, new ambitions nourished by the rebirth of feminism may ⁊ make young women feel and behave a little like a classical immigrant group. We are determined to prove ourselves, to achieve academic excellence, and to prepare for interesting and successful careers. More noses are kept to more grindstones in an effort to demonstrate newfound abilities, and perhaps to allay suspicions that women still have to have more and better credentials than men. This doesn't leave much time for activism. Indeed, we may not yet know that it is necessary.

In addition, the very progress into previously all-male careers that may be ₈ revolutionary for women is seen as conservative and conformist by outside critics. Assuming male radicalism to be the measure of change, they interpret any concern with careers as evidence of "campus conservatism." In fact, "dropping out" may be a departure for men, but "dropping in" is a new thing for women. Progress lies in the direction we have not been.

Like most groups of the newly arrived or awakened, our faith in education ₉ and paper degrees also has yet to be shaken. For instance, the percentage of women enrolled in colleges and universities has been increasing at the same time that the percentage of men has been decreasing. Among students entering college in 1978, women *outnumbered* men for the first time. This hope of excelling at the existing game is probably reinforced by the greater cultural pressure on females to be "good girls" and observe somebody else's rules.

Though we may know intellectually that we need to have new games with ₁₀ new rules, we probably haven't quite absorbed such facts as the high unemployment rate among female Ph.D.s; the lower average salary among women college graduates of all races than among counterpart males who graduated from high school or less; the middle-management ceiling against which even those eagerly hired new business-school graduates seem to bump their heads after five or ten years; and the barrier-breaking women in nontraditional fields who become the first fired when recession hits. Sadly enough, we may have to personally experience some of these reality checks before we accept the idea that lawsuits, activism, and group pressure will have to accompany our individual excellence and crisp new degrees.

Then there is the female guilt trip, student edition. If we're not sailing along ₁₁ as planned, it must be *our* fault. If our mothers didn't "do anything" with their educations, it must have been *their* fault. If we can't study as hard as we think we must (because women still have to be better prepared than men), and have a substantial personal and sexual life at the same time (because women are supposed to care more about relationships than men do), then we feel inadequate, as if each of us were individually at fault for a problem that is actually culture-wide.

I've yet to be on a campus where most women weren't worrying about ₁₂ some aspect of combining marriage, children, and a career. I've yet to find one where many men were worrying about the same thing. Yet women will go right on suffering from the double-role problem and terminal guilt until men are encouraged, pressured, or otherwise forced, individually and collectively, to integrate themselves into the "women's work" of raising children and homemaking. Until then, and until there are changed job patterns to allow equal parenthood, children will go right on growing up with the belief that only women can be loving and nurturing, and only men can be intellectual or active outside the home. Each half of the world will go on limiting the full range of its human talent.

Finally, there is the intimate political training that hits women in the teens and early twenties: the countless ways we are still brainwashed into assuming that women are dependent on men for our basic identities, both in our work and our personal lives, much more than vice versa. After all, if we're going to enter a marriage system that's still legally designed for a person and a half, submit to an economy in which women still average about fifty-nine cents on the dollar earned by men, and work mainly as support staff and assistants, or co-directors and vice-presidents at best, then we have to be convinced that we are not whole people on our own.   13

In order to make sure that we will see ourselves as half-people, and thus be addicted to getting our identity from serving others, society tries hard to convert us as young women into "man junkies"; that is, into people who are addicted to regular shots of male-approval and presence, both professionally and personally. We need a man standing next to us, actually and figuratively, whether it's at work, on Saturday night, or throughout life. (If only men realized how little it matters *which* man is standing there, they would understand that this addiction depersonalizes them, too.) Given the danger to a male-dominant system if young women stop internalizing this political message of derived identity, it's no wonder that those who try to kick the addiction—and, worse yet, to help other women do the same—are likely to be regarded as odd or dangerous by everyone from parents to peers.   14

With all that pressure combined with little experience, it's no wonder that younger women are often less able to support each other. Even young women who espouse feminist goals as individuals may refrain from identifying themselves as "feminist": it's okay to want equal pay for yourself (just one small reform) but it's not okay to want equal pay for women as a group (an economic revolution). Some retreat into individualized career obsessions as a way of avoiding this dangerous discovery of shared experience with women as a group. Others retreat into the safe middle ground of "I'm not a feminist but. . . ." Still others become politically active, but only on issues that are taken seriously by their male counterparts.   15

The same lesson about the personal conservatism of younger women is taught by the history of feminism. If I hadn't been conned into believing the masculine stereotype of youth as the "natural" time for freedom and rebellion, a time of "sowing wild oats" that actually is made possible by the assurance of power and security later on, I could have figured out the female pattern of activism by looking at women's movements of the past.   16

In this country, for instance, the nineteenth-century wave of feminism was started by older women who had been through the radicalizing experience of getting married and becoming the legal chattel of their husbands (or the equally   17 radicalizing experience of *not* getting married and being treated as spinsters). Most of them had also worked in the antislavery movement and learned from the political parallels between race and sex. In other countries, that wave was also led by women who were past the point of maximum pressure toward marriageability and conservatism.

Looking at the first decade of this second wave, it's clear that the early fem- 18 inist activist and consciousness-raising groups of the 1960s were organized by women who had experienced the civil rights movement, or homemakers who had discovered that raising kids and cooking didn't occupy all their talents. While most campuses of the late sixties were still circulating the names of illegal abortionists privately (after all, abortion could damage our marriage value), slightly older women were holding press conferences and speak-outs about the reality of abortions (including their own, even though that often meant confessing to an illegal act) and demanding reform or repeal of antichoice laws. Though rape had been a quiet epidemic on campus for generations, younger women victims were still understandably fearful of speaking up, and campuses encouraged silence in order to retain their reputation for safety with tuition-paying parents. It took many off-campus speak-outs, demonstrations against laws of evidence and police procedures, and testimonies in state legislatures before most student groups began to make demands on campus and local cops for greater rape protection. In fact, "date rape"—the common campus phenomenon of a young woman being raped by someone she knows, perhaps even by several students in a fraternity house—is just now being exposed. Marital rape, a more difficult legal issue, was taken up several years ago. As for battered women and the attendant exposé of husbands and lovers as more statistically dangerous than unknown muggers in the street, that issue still seems to be thought of as a largely noncampus concern, yet at many of the colleges and universities where I've spoken, there has been at least one case within current student memory of a young woman beaten or murdered by a jealous lover.

This cultural pattern of youthful conservatism makes the growing number 19 of older women going back to school very important. They are life examples and pragmatic activists who radicalize women young enough to be their daughters. Now that the median female undergraduate age in this country is twenty-seven because so many older women have returned, the campus is becoming a major place for cross-generational connections.

None of this should denigrate the courageous efforts of young women, es- 20 pecially women on campus, and the many changes they've pioneered. On the contrary, they should be seen as even more remarkable for surviving the conservative pressures, recognizing societal problems they haven't yet fully experienced, and organizing successfully in the midst of a transient student population. Every women's history course, rape hot line, or campus newspaper that is finally covering *all* the news; every feminist professor whose job has been created or tenure saved by student pressure, or male administrator whose consciousness has been permanently changed; every counselor who's stopped guiding women one way and men another; every lawsuit that's been fueled by student energies against unequal athletic funds or graduate school requirements:

all those accomplishments are even more impressive when seen against the backdrop of the female pattern of activism.

Finally, it would help to remember that a feminist revolution rarely resembles a masculine-style one—just as a young woman's most radical act toward her mother (that is, connecting as women in order to help each other get some power) doesn't look much like a young man's most radical act toward his father (that is, breaking the father-son connection in order to separate identities or take over existing power). 21

It's those father-son conflicts at a generational, national level that have often provided the conventional definition of revolution; yet they've gone on for centuries without basically changing the role of the female half of the world. They have also failed to reduce the level of violence in society, since both fathers and sons have included some degree of aggressiveness and superiority to women in their definition of masculinity, thus preserving the anthropological model of dominance. 22

Furthermore, what current leaders and theoreticians define as revolution is usually little more than taking over the army and the radio stations. Women have much more in mind than that. We have to uproot the sexual caste system that is the most pervasive power structure in society, and that means transforming the patriarchal values of those who run the institutions, whether they are politically the "right" or the "left," the fathers or the sons. This cultural part of the change goes very deep, and is often seen as too intimate, and perhaps too threatening, to be considered as either serious or possible. Only conflicts among men are "serious." Only a takeover of existing institutions is "possible." 23

That's why the definition of "political," on campus as elsewhere, tends to be limited to who's running for president, who's demonstrating against corporate investments in South Africa, or which is the "moral" side of some conventional revolution, preferably one that is thousands of miles away. 24

As important as such activities are, they are also the most comfortable ones when we're young. They provide a sense of virtue without much disruption in the power structure of our daily lives. Even when the most consistent energies on campus are actually concentrated around feminist issues, they may be treated as apolitical and invisible. Asked "What's happening on campus?" a student may reply, "The antinuke movement," even though that resulted in one demonstration of two hours, while student antirape squads have been patrolling the campus every night for two years and women's studies have begun to transform the very textbooks we read. 25

No wonder reporters and sociologists looking for revolution on campus often miss the depth of feminist change and activity that is really there. Women students themselves may dismiss it as not political and not serious. Certainly, it rarely comes in the masculine sixties style of bombing buildings or burning draft cards. In fact, it goes much deeper than protesting a temporary symptom—say, the draft—and challenges the right of one group to dominate another, which is the disease itself. 26

Young women have a big task of resisting pressures and challenging definitions. Their increasing success is a miracle of foresight and courage that should 27 make us all proud. But they should know that they, too, may grow more radical with age.

One day, an army of gray-haired women may quietly take over the earth.   28

COMPREHENSION

1. What is the thesis of the essay? Is it implied or expressed? If the latter, where?
2. In paragraph 21, Steinem uses the term *radical act*. What does it mean? What importance does it have to the overall theme of the essay?
3. Steinem claims she was "wrong about women." What was she wrong about? How did her newfound "enlightenment" have an impact on her views of women and change in general, and the theme of the essay in particular?

RHETORIC

1. Does the tone of the essay discriminate against males? Cite specific references to defend your view.
2. The title implies that this essay is being written for a particular audience. What audience is being addressed? What word or words support this contention?
3. The author uses a number of abstract terms in the service of her argument. Among these are *revolution, natural, activism, culture,* and *political.* How is each term specifically used by Steinem to advance her thesis?
4. Many of the authors in this text employ a host of statistics to support their views. Yet Steinem—in this relatively long essay—uses only one. Does this have an impact on the authority of her stance as a writer? Explain your view.
5. Steinem seems to employ a style that presents her argument incrementally, in other words, by adding new evidence to her thesis as she writes. Track paragraphs 2 through 13 and explain how Steinem builds her argument through her use of topic sentences and transitional phrases.
6. How would you describe the author's style: academic, conversational, educated, urbane, sophisticated, down-to-earth, personal, intimate, or a combination of these? Explain your view.
7. Does Steinem's conclusion provide closure to the essay? What effect is the author trying to achieve by concluding with a one-sentence paragraph?

WRITING

1. Argue for or against the view that this 20-year-old essay is largely irrelevant in today's society.
2. Steinem suggests that one day "an army of gray-haired women may quietly take over the earth." Should any group take over the earth? In an essay of 750 to 1,000 words, argue for or against the idea that Steinem—in the end—is merely advocating for that very "patriarchal" concept, domination.

3. For a research project, write a 1,000- to 1,500-word comparison-and-contrast paper in which you explore the ideas behind feminism and post-feminism, especially on today's college campus.

America Skips School

Benjamin R. Barber

Benjamin R. Barber (b. 1939) received his master of arts degree and his PhD from Harvard University. He is the author of numerous books on democracy, community, and politics, including Strong Democracy *(1984),* The Conquest of Politics *(1988),* The Struggle for Democracy *(1988), and* A Place for Us *(1998). He has also contributed articles to such periodicals as* Harper's, The New York Times, *and* The Atlantic Monthly. *He is currently a professor at Rutgers University and director of the Walt Whitman Center for the Culture and Politics of Democracy. In the following essay, which originally appeared in* Harper's *magazine (November 1993), he suggests that rather than reflect upon the work done in schools to assess our shortcomings as a society, we would more profitably hold up the mirror to ourselves.*

On September 8, the day most of the nation's children were scheduled to return 1 to school, the Department of Education Statistics issued a report, commissioned by Congress, on adult literacy and numeracy in the United States. The results? More than 90 million adult Americans lacked simple literacy. Fewer than 20 percent of those surveyed could compare two metaphors in a poem; not 4 percent could calculate the cost of carpeting at a given price for a room of a given size, using a calculator. As the DOE report was being issued, as if to echo its findings, two of the nation's largest school systems had delayed their openings: in New York, to remove asbestos from aging buildings; in Chicago, because of a battle over the budget.

Inspired by the report and the delays, pundits once again began chanting 2 the familiar litany of the education crisis. We've heard it all many times before: 130,000 children bring guns along with their pencils and books to school each morning; juvenile arrests for murder increased by 85 percent from 1987 to 1991; more than 3,000 youngsters will drop out today and every day for the rest of the school year, until about 600,000 are lost by June—in many urban schools, perhaps half the enrollment. A lot of the dropouts will end up in prison, which is a surer bet for young black males than college: one in four will pass through the correctional system, and at least two out of three of those will be dropouts.

In quiet counterpoint to those staggering facts is another set of statistics: 3 teachers make less than accountants, architects, doctors, lawyers, engineers, judges, health professionals, auditors, and surveyors. They can earn higher salaries teaching in Berlin, Tokyo, Ottawa, or Amsterdam than in New York or Chicago. American children are in school only about 180 days a year, as against 240 days or more for children in Europe or Japan. The richest school districts (school financing is local, not federal) spend twice as much per student as poorer ones do. The poorer ones seem almost beyond help: children with vene-real disease or AIDS (2.5 million adolescents annually contract a sexually trans-mitted disease), gangs in the schoolyard, drugs in the classroom, children doing babies instead of homework, playground firefights featuring Uzis and Glocks.

Clearly, the social contract that obliges adults to pay taxes so that children 4 can be educated is in imminent danger of collapse. Yet for all the astonishing statistics, more astonishing still is that no one seems to be listening. The educa-tion crisis is kind of like violence on television: the worse it gets the more inert we become, and the more of it we require to rekindle our attention. We've had a "crisis" every dozen years or so at least since the launch of *Sputnik,* in 1957, when American schools were accused of falling behind the world standard in science education. Just ten years ago, the National Commission on Excellence in Education warned that America's pedagogical inattention was putting America "at risk." What the commission called "a rising tide of mediocrity" was imper-iling "our very future as a Nation and a people." What was happening to edu-cation was an "act of war."

Since then, countless reports have been issued decrying the condition of our 5 educational system, the DOE report being only the most recent. They have come from every side, Republican as well as Democrat, from the private sector as well as the public. Yet for all the talk, little happens. At times, the schools look more like they are being dismantled than rebuilt. How can this be? If Americans over a broad political spectrum regard education as vital, why has nothing been done?

I have spent thirty years as a scholar examining the nature of democracy, 6 and even more as a citizen optimistically celebrating its possibilities, but today I am increasingly persuaded that the reason for the country's inaction is that Americans do not really care about education—the country has grown comfort-able with the game of "let's pretend we care."

As America's educational system crumbles, the pundits, instead of looking 7 for solutions, search busily for scapegoats. Some assail the teachers—those "Profscam" pedagogues trained in the licentious Sixties who, as aging hippies, are supposedly still subverting the schools—or producing a dire illiteracy. Oth-ers turn on the kids themselves, so that at the same moment as we are transfer-ring our responsibilities to the shoulders of the next generation, we are blaming them for our own generation's most conspicuous failures. Allan Bloom was typ-ical of the many recent critics who have condemned the young as vapid, lazy, selfish, complacent, self-seeking, materialistic, smallminded, apathetic, greedy, and, of course, illiterate. E. D. Hirsch in his *Cultural Literacy* and Diane Ravitch and Chester E. Finn Jr. in their *What Do Our Seventeen-Year-Olds Know?* have lambasted the schools, the teachers, and the children for betraying the adult generation from which they were to inherit, the critics seemed confident, a pre-cious cultural legacy.

How this captious literature reeks of hypocrisy! How sanctimonious all the   8
hand-wringing over still another "education crisis" seems. Are we ourselves really so literate? Are our kids stupid or smart for ignoring what we preach and
copying what we practice? The young, with their keen noses for hypocrisy, are
in fact adept readers—but not of books. They are society-smart rather than
school-smart, and what they read so acutely are the social signals emanating
from the world in which they will have to make a living. Their teachers in that
world, the nation's true pedagogues, are television, advertising, movies, politics, and the celebrity domains they define. We prattle about deficient schools
and the gullible youngsters they turn out, so vulnerable to the siren song of
drugs, but think nothing of letting the advertisers into the classroom to fashion
what an *Advertising Age* essay calls "brand and product loyalties through class-
room-centered, peer-powered lifestyle patterning."

Our kids spend 900 hours a year in school (the ones who go to school) and   9
from 1,200 to 1,800 hours a year in front of the television set. From which are
they likely to learn more? Critics such as Hirsch and Ravitch want to find out
what our seventeen-year-olds know, but it's really pretty simple: they know
exactly what our forty-seven-year-olds know and teach them by example—
on television, in the boardroom, around Washington, on Madison Avenue, in
Hollywood. The very first lesson smart kids learn is that it is much more
important to heed what society teaches implicitly by its deeds and reward structures than what school teaches explicitly in its lesson plans and civic sermons.
Here is a test for adults that may help reveal what the kids see when they look
at our world.

REAL-WORLD CULTURAL LITERACY

1. According to television, having fun in America means
   a) going blond
   b) drinking Pepsi
   c) playing Nintendo
   d) wearing Air Jordans
   e) reading Mark Twain
2. A good way to prepare for a high-income career and to acquire status in our
   society is to
   a) win a slam-dunk contest
   b) take over a company and sell off its assets
   c) start a successful rock band
   d) earn a professional degree
   e) become a kindergarten teacher
3. Book publishers are financially rewarded today for publishing
   a) mega-cookbooks
   b) mega-cat books
   c) megabooks by Michael Crichton
   d) megabooks by John Grisham
   e) mini-books by Voltaire

4. A major California bank that advertised "no previous credit history required" in inviting Berkeley students to apply for Visa cards nonetheless turned down one group of applicants because
   a) their parents had poor credit histories
   b) they had never held jobs
   c) they had outstanding student loans
   d) they were "humanities majors"
5. Colleges and universities are financially rewarded today for
   a) supporting bowl-quality football teams
   b) forging research relationships with large corporations
   c) sustaining professional programs in law and business
   d) stroking wealthy alumni
   e) fostering outstanding philosophy departments
6. Familiarity with *Henry IV, Part II* is likely to be of vital importance in
   a) planning a corporate takeover
   b) evaluating budget cuts in the Department of Education
   c) initiating a medical-malpractice lawsuit
   d) writing an impressive job résumé
   e) taking a test on what our seventeen-year-olds know
7. To help the young learn that "history is a living thing," Scholastic, Inc., a publisher of school magazines and paperbacks, recently distributed to 40,000 junior and senior high-school classrooms
   a) a complimentary video of the award-winning series *The Civil War*
   b) free copies of Plato's *Dialogues*
   c) an abridgment of Alexis de Tocqueville's *Democracy in America*
   d) a wall-size Periodic Table of the Elements
   e) gratis copies of Billy Joel's hit single "We Didn't Start the Fire" (which recounts history via a vaguely chronological list of warbled celebrity names)

My sample of forty-seven-year-olds scored very well on the test. Not sur- 10 prisingly, so did their seventeen-year-old children. (For each question, either the last entry is correct or all responses are correct *except* the last one.) The results of the test reveal again the deep hypocrisy that runs through our lamentations about education. The illiteracy of the young turns out to be our own reflected back to us with embarrassing force. We honor ambition, we reward greed, we celebrate materialism, we worship acquisitiveness, we cherish success, and we commercialize the classroom—and then we bark at the young about the gentle arts of the spirit. We recommend history to the kids but rarely consult it ourselves. We make a fuss about ethics but are satisfied to see it taught as an "add-on," as in "ethics in medicine" or "ethics in business"—as if Sunday morning in church could compensate for uninterrupted sinning from Monday to Saturday.

The children are onto this game. They know that if we really valued school- 11 ing, we'd pay teachers what we pay stockbrokers; if we valued books, we'd spend a little something on the libraries so that adults could read, too; if we valued citizenship, we'd give national service and civic education more than pilot status; if we valued children, we wouldn't let them be abused, manipulated, impoverished, and killed in their beds by gang-war cross fire and stray bullets. Schools can and should lead, but when they confront a society that in every instance tells a story exactly opposite to the one they are supposed to be teaching, their job becomes impossible. When the society undoes each workday what the school tries to do each school day, schooling can't make much of a difference.

Inner-city children are not the only ones who are learning the wrong 12 lessons. TV sends the same messages to everyone, and the success of Donald Trump, Pete Rose, Henry Kravis, or George Steinbrenner makes them potent role models, whatever their values. Teen dropouts are not blind; teen drug sellers are not deaf; teen college students who avoid the humanities in favor of pre-business or pre-law are not stupid. Being apt pupils of reality, they learn their lessons well. If they see a man with a rubber arm and an empty head who can throw a ball at 95 miles per hour pulling down millions of dollars a year while a dedicated primary-school teacher is getting crumbs, they will avoid careers in teaching even if they can't make the major leagues. If they observe their government spending up to $35,000 a year to keep a young black behind bars but a fraction of that to keep him in school, they will write off school (and probably write off blacks as well).

Our children's illiteracy is merely our own, which they assume with com- 13 mendable prowess. They know what we have taught them all too well: there is nothing in Homer or Virginia Woolf, in Shakespeare or Toni Morrison, that will advantage them in climbing to the top of the American heap. Academic credentials may still count, but schooling in and of itself is for losers. Bookworms. Nerds. Inner-city rappers and fraternity-house wise guys are in full agreement about that. The point is to start pulling down the big bucks. Some kids just go into business earlier than others. Dropping out is the national pastime, if by dropping out we mean giving up the precious things of the mind and the spirit in which America shows so little interest and for which it offers so little payback. While the professors argue about whether to teach the ancient history of a putatively white Athens or the ancient history of a putatively black Egypt, the kids are watching televised political campaigns driven by mindless image-mongering and inflammatory polemics that ignore history altogether. Why, then, are we so surprised when our students dismiss the debate over the origins of civilization, whether Eurocentric or Afrocentric, and concentrate on cash-and-carry careers? Isn't the choice a tribute not to their ignorance but to their adaptive intelligence? Although we can hardly be proud of ourselves for what we are teaching them, we should at least be proud of them for how well they've learned our lessons.

Not all Americans have stopped caring about the schools, however. In the fi- 14 nal irony of the educational endgame, cynical entrepreneurs like Chris Whittle are insinuating television into the classroom itself, bribing impoverished school boards by offering free TV sets on which they can show advertising for children—sold to sponsors at premium rates. Whittle, the mergers and acquisitions mogul of education, is trying to get rich off the poverty of public schools and the fears of parents. Can he really believe advertising in the schools enhances education? Or is he helping to corrupt public schools in ways that will make parents even more anxious to use vouchers for private schools—which might one day be run by Whittle's latest entrepreneurial venture, the Edison Project.

According to Lifetime Learning Systems, an educational-software company, 15 "kids spend 40 percent of each day . . . where traditional advertising can't reach them." Not to worry, says Lifetime Learning in an *Advertising Age* promo: "Now, you can enter the classroom through custom-made learning materials created with your specific marketing objectives in mind. Communicate with young spenders directly and, through them, their teachers and families as well." If we redefine young learners as "young spenders," are the young really to be blamed for acting like mindless consumers? Can they become young spenders and still become young critical thinkers, let alone informed citizens? If we are willing to give TV cartoons the government's imprimatur as "educational television" (as we did a few years ago, until the FCC changed its mind), can we blame kids for educating themselves on television trash?

Everyone can agree that we should educate our children to be something 16 more than young spenders molded by "lifestyle patterning." But what should the goals of the classroom be? In recent years it has been fashionable to define the educational crisis in terms of global competition and minimal competence, as if schools were no more than vocational institutions. Although it has talked sensibly about education, the Clinton Administration has leaned toward this approach, under the tutelage of Secretary of Labor Robert Reich.

The classroom, however, should not be merely a trade school. The funda- 17 mental task of education in a democracy is what Tocqueville once called the apprenticeship of liberty: learning to be free. I wonder whether Americans still believe liberty has to be learned and that its skills are worth learning. Or have they been deluded by two centuries of rhetoric into thinking that freedom is "natural" and can be taken for granted?

The claim that all men are born free, upon which America was founded, is 18 at best a promising fiction. In real life, as every parent knows, children are born fragile, born needy, born ignorant, born unformed, born weak, born foolish, born dependent—born in chains. We acquire our freedom over time, if at all. Embedded in families, clans, communities, and nations, we must learn to be free. We may be natural consumers and born narcissists, but citizens have to be made. Liberal-arts education actually means education in the arts of liberty; the "servile arts" were the trades learned by unfree men in the Middle Ages, the vocational education of their day. Perhaps this is why Thomas Jefferson preferred to memorialize his founding of the University of Virginia on his tombstone rather than his two terms as president; it is certainly why he viewed his Bill for the More General Diffusion of Knowledge in Virginia as a centerpiece of his career (although it failed passage as legislation—times were perhaps not so different). John Adams, too, boasted regularly about Massachusetts's high literacy rates and publicly funded education.

Jefferson and Adams both understood that the Bill of Rights offered little   19
protection in a nation without informed citizens. Once educated, however,
a people was safe from even the subtlest tyrannies. Jefferson's democratic
proclivities rested on his conviction that education could turn a people into a
safe refuge—indeed "the only safe depository" for the ultimate powers of society. "Cherish therefore the spirit of our people," he wrote to Edward Carrington
in 1787, "and keep alive their attention. Do not be severe upon their errors, but
reclaim them by enlightening them. If once they become inattentive to public affairs, you and I and Congress and Assemblies, judges and governors, shall all
become wolves."

The logic of democracy begins with public education, proceeds to informed   20
citizenship, and comes to fruition in the securing of rights and liberties. We
have been nominally democratic for so long that we presume it is our natural
condition rather than the product of persistent effort and tenacious responsibility. We have decoupled rights from civic responsibilities and severed citizenship
from education on the false assumption that citizens just happen. We have forgotten that the "public" in public schools means not just paid for by the public
but procreative of the very idea of a public. Public schools are how a public—a
citizenry—is forged and how young, selfish individuals turn into conscientious,
community-minded citizens.

Among the several literacies that have attracted the anxious attention of   21
commentators, civic literacy has been the least visible. Yet this is the fundamental literacy by which we live in a civil society. It encompasses the competence to
participate in democratic communities, the ability to think critically and act
with deliberation in a pluralistic world, and the empathy to identify sufficiently
with others to live with them despite conflicts of interest and differences in
character. At the most elementary level, what our children suffer from most,
whether they're hurling racial epithets from fraternity porches or shooting one
another down in schoolyards, is the absence of civility. Security guards and
metal detectors are poor surrogates for civility, and they make our schools look
increasingly like prisons (though they may be less safe than prisons). Jefferson
thought schools would produce free men: we prove him right by putting
dropouts in jail.

Civility is a work of the imagination, for it is through the imagination that   22
we render others sufficiently like ourselves for them to become subjects of tolerance and respect, if not always affection. Democracy is anything but a "natural" form of association. It is an extraordinary and rare contrivance of
cultivated imagination. Give the uneducated the right to participate in making
collective decisions, and what results is not democracy but, at best, mob rule:
the government of private prejudice once known as the tyranny of opinion. For
Jefferson, the difference between the democratic temperance he admired in
agrarian America and the rule of the rabble he condemned when viewing the
social unrest of Europe's teeming cities was quite simply education. Madison
had hoped to "filter" out popular passion through the device of representation.
Jefferson saw in education a filter that could be installed within each individual,
giving to each the capacity to rule prudently. Education creates a ruling aristocracy

constrained by temperance and wisdom; when that education is public and universal, it is an aristocracy to which all can belong. At its best, the American dream of a free and equal society governed by judicious citizens has been this dream of an aristocracy of everyone.

To dream this dream of freedom is easy, but to secure it is difficult as well as 23 expensive. Notwithstanding their lamentations, Americans do not appear ready to pay the price. There is no magic bullet for education. But I no longer can accept that the problem lies in the lack of consensus about remedies—in a dearth of solutions. There is no shortage of debate over how to repair our educational infrastructure. National standards or more local control? Vouchers or better public schools? More parental involvement or more teacher autonomy? A greater federal presence (only 5 or 6 percent of the nation's education budget is federally funded) or fairer local school taxes? More multicultural diversity or more emphasis on what Americans share in common? These are honest disputes. But I am convinced that the problem is simpler and more fundamental. Twenty years ago, writer and activist Frances Moore Lappé captured the essence of the world food crisis when she argued that starvation was caused not by a scarcity of food but by a global scarcity in democracy. The education crisis has the same genealogy. It stems from a dearth of democracy: an absence of democratic will and a consequent refusal to take our children, our schools, and our future seriously.

Most educators, even while they quarrel among themselves, will agree that 24 a genuine commitment to any one of a number of different solutions could help enormously. Most agree that although money can't by itself solve problems, without money few problems can be solved. Money also can't win wars or put men in space, but it is the crucial facilitator. It is also how America has traditionally announced, We are serious about this!

If we were serious, we would raise teachers' salaries to levels that would at- 25 tract the best young professionals in our society: starting lawyers get from $70,000 to $80,000—why don't starting kindergarten teachers get the same? Is their role in vouchsafing our future less significant? And although there is evidence suggesting that an increase in general educational expenditures doesn't translate automatically into better schools, there is also evidence that an increase aimed specifically at instructional services does. Can we really take in earnest the chattering devotion to excellence of a country wedded in practice to mediocrity, a nation so ready to relegate teachers—conservators of our common future—to the professional backwaters?

If we were serious, we would upgrade physical facilities so that every 26 school met the minimum standards of our better suburban institutions. Good buildings do not equal good education, but can any education at all take place in leaky, broken-down habitats of the kind described by Jonathan Kozol in his *Savage Inequalities?* If money is not a critical factor, why are our most successful suburban school districts funded at nearly twice the level of our inner-city schools? Being even at the starting line cannot guarantee that the runners will win or even finish the race, but not being even pretty much assures failure. We would rectify the balance not by penalizing wealthier communities but by bringing poorer communities up to standard, perhaps, by finding other sources of funding for our schools besides property taxes.

If we were serious, we'd extend the school year by a month or two so that 27 learning could take place throughout the year. We'd reduce class size (which means more teachers) and nurture more cooperative learning so that kids could become actively responsible for their own education and that of their class-mates. Perhaps most important, we'd raise standards and make teachers and students responsible for them. There are two ways to breed success: to lower standards so that everybody "passes" in a way that loses all meaning in the real world; and to raise standards and then meet them, so that school success trans-lates into success beyond the classroom. From Confucian China to Imperial England, great nations have built their success in the world upon an education of excellence. The challenge in a democracy is to find a way to maintain excel-lence while extending educational opportunity to everyone.

Finally, if we were serious, parents, teachers, and students would be the real 28 players while administrators, politicians, and experts would be secondary, at best advisers whose chief skill ought to be knowing when and how to facilitate the work of teachers and then get out of the way. If the Democrats can clean up federal government bureaucracy (the Gore plan), perhaps we can do the same for educational bureaucracy. In New York up to half of the city's teachers oc-cupy jobs outside the classroom. No other enterprise is run that way: Half the soldiers at company headquarters? Half the cops at stationhouse desks? Half the working force in the assistant manager's office? Once the teachers are back in the classroom, they will need to be given more autonomy, more professional responsibility for the success or failure of their students. And parents will have to be drawn in not just because they have rights or because they are politically potent but because they have responsibilities and their children are unlikely to learn without parental engagement. How to define the parental role in the class-room would become serious business for educators.

Some Americans will say this is unrealistic. Times are tough, money's short, 29 and the public is fed up with almost all of its public institutions: the schools are just one more frustrating disappointment. With all the goodwill in the world, it is still hard to know how schools can cure the ills that stem from the failure of so many other institutions. Saying we want education to come first won't put it first.

America, however, has historically been able to accomplish what it sets its 30 mind to. When we wish it and will it, what we wish and will has happened. Our successes are willed; our failures seem to happen when will is absent. There are, of course, those who benefit from the bankruptcy of public education and the failure of democracy. But their blame is no greater than our own: in a world where doing nothing has such dire consequences, complacency has become a greater sin than malevolence.

In wartime, whenever we have known why we were fighting and believed 31 in the cause, we have prevailed. Because we believe in profits, we are consum-mate salespersons and efficacious entrepreneurs. Because we love sports, ours are the dream teams. Why can't a Chicago junior high school be as good as the

Chicago Bulls? Because we cherish individuality and mobility, we have created a magnificent (if costly) care culture and the world's largest automotive consumer market. Even as our lower schools are among the worst in the Western world, our graduate institutions are among the very best—because professional training in medicine, law, and technology is vital to our ambitions and because corporate America backs up state and federal priorities in this crucial domain. Look at the things we do well and observe how very well we do them: those are the things that as a nation we have willed.

Then observe what we do badly and ask yourself, Is it because the challenge is too great? Or is it because, finally, we aren't really serious? Would we will an end to the carnage and do whatever it took—more cops, state militias, federal marshals, the Marines?—if the dying children were white and middle class? Or is it a disdain for the young—white, brown, and black—that inures us to the pain? Why are we so sensitive to the retirees whose future (however foreshortened) we are quick to guarantee—don't worry, no reduced cost-of-living allowances, no taxes on social security except for the well-off—and so callous to the young? Have you noticed how health care is on every politician's agenda and education on no one's? 32

To me, the conclusion is inescapable: we are not serious. We have given up on the public schools because we have given up on the kids And we have given up on the kids because we have given up on the future—perhaps because it looks too multicolored or too dim or too hard. "Liberty," said Jean-Jacques Rousseau, "is a food easy to eat but hard to digest." America is suffering from a bad case of indigestion. Finally, in giving up on the future, we have given up on democracy. Certainly there will be no liberty, no equality, no social justice without democracy, and there will be no democracy without citizens and the schools that forge civic identity and democratic responsibility. If I am wrong (I'd like to be), my error will be easy to discern, for before the year is out we will put education first on the nation's agenda. We will put it ahead of the deficit, for if the future is finished before it starts, the deficit doesn't matter. Ahead of defense, for without democracy, what liberties will be left to defend? Ahead of all the other public issues and public goods, for without public education there can be no public and hence no truly public issues or public goods to advance. When the polemics are spent and we are through hyperventilating about the crisis in education, there is only one question worth asking: are we serious? If we are, we can begin by honoring that old folk homily and put our money where for much too long our common American mouth has been. Our kids, for once, might even be grateful. 33

COMPREHENSION

1. What is the author's thesis? Where is it succinctly stated?
2. Define the following words that are employed in the course of the essay: *pundit, litany, pedagogue, captious, prattle,* and *procreative.*

3. What does Barber mean when he states that the youth today demonstrate "adaptive intelligence"?

RHETORIC

1. What rhetorical strength does providing the multiple-choice test for the reader have over simply commenting on it?
2. In paragraphs 1 through 3, Barber introduces his topic with a compendium of statistics on the woeful state of American literacy. Why does he begin this way, and why does he refrain from this rhetorical strategy for the rest of the essay?
3. In the second part of the essay, Barber launches a preemptive attack on his would-be adversaries, that is, those who would attribute our educational problems to factors other than those that the author presents. What is the purpose of this strategy? Is it effective? What tone does the author use in challenging these critics?
4. Note the effective use of language and syntax in the following sentence: "When the society undoes each workday what the school tried to do each school day, schooling can't make much of a difference." Find three other sentences that have this sort of rhetorical power, and explain why they work well in communicating the author's views. Consider such elements as repetition and rhythm.
5. The essay is divided into five sections, indicated by extra space between the parts. Examine the last and first paragraphs of each section, and explain how the author uses transitions to keep his argument on track.
6. Describe the implied audience for this essay. Consider the fact that Barber has included many historical and literary references.
7. Paragraphs 25 through 27 begin with the same phrase, "If we were serious." First, what rhetorical effect does this repetition have? Second, who is the "we" alluded to in these paragraphs?

WRITING

1. In an essay of 500 to 750 words, argue for or against the proposition that the school system should conform to our society's values, not the other way around.
2. Interview a lawyer, an executive, or an entrepreneur to find out why that person was motivated to enter his or her chosen profession. Write an expository essay exploring your subject's choices.
3. Barber harps on the idea that we do not treat our teachers well. In an essay of 500 to 1,000 words, argue for or against the proposition that teachers should receive the same salaries as lawyers.

CONNECTIONS FOR CRITICAL THINKING

1. Select 5 to 10 magazine ads and explore their implicit messages regarding the values each attempts to display. Use these as examples to demonstrate Barber's contention in his essay "America Skips School" that the values taught in real life contradict those taught in school.
2. Compare and contrast the rhetoric of the personal essay as it is represented in Santha Rama Rau's "By Any Other Name" or Angelou's "Graduation" with the rhetoric of such expository and argumentative essays as Barber's "America Skips School" or Hirsch's "Why America's Universities Are Better Than Its Schools."
3. Analyze an event in your education when you had a disagreement with a teacher or administrator. Explain and explore whether the differences in viewpoint were based on emotional perspective, intellectual perspective, or both.
4. Select the essay in this chapter you find most pertinent to your life as a student. Explain why you have selected the essay, and explore your intellectual and emotional responses to it.
5. Does your college seem to support Steinem's views regarding the educational lives of women? Explain why or why not.
6. Argue for or against the proposition that the primary function of colleges and universities is to prepare students for the world of work. Use at least two essays from this chapter to support your view.
7. Argue for or against the view that the publicized sexual activities of politicians and other celebrities makes the decision whether or not to keep sex education out of the schools entirely moot.
8. It is 2203. Write an essay in which you explore the physical, technological, and communicative dimensions of a typical college classroom. Your essay should not only describe this environment but also explain why the classroom has the characteristics you have chosen.
9. Open up a computer chat room and discuss the psychological and emotional implications of having children witness the grand jury testimony of President Clinton during Kenneth Starr's investigation.
10. Write an essay that classifies at least three educational issues that the authors in this chapter examine. Establish a clear thesis to unify the categories that you establish.
11. Analyze the patterns and techniques used by Gelernter, Jacoby, and Steinam to advance their claims about education today.
12. Search the Web for *sex education* AND *France* (or another country of your choice). Write a 500-word essay describing the policies of your chosen country toward the topic.
13. Look up your college's or university's mission statement on its home Web page. Is the statement relevant? Is it truthful? Explain why or why not. Use personal observation and experience to support your view.

14. Argue for or against the proposition that despite Gelernter's warnings about the purported shortcomings of computers in the classroom, in the future one will be about to acquire a bachelor of arts degree completely via computer and the Internet.

chapter *4*

Family Roles and Gender Roles
How Do We Become Who We Are?

Every culture has its own ideas about identity, how it is formed, and where it comes from. What is the influence of family on the creation of identity, of environment, of gender and, as we have seen in Chapter 3, of education? Although it is challenging to reconcile these various cross-cultural ideas, the writers in this chapter attempt to make sense of identity from the perspectives of family and gender, and they invite readers to liberate themselves from the tyranny of stereotyping.

Families nourish us during childhood, and the values our families seek to maintain usually affect our identities in powerful ways, whether we adopt them wholly, modify them, or reject them outright. Writers have always been aware of the importance of the family in human development and behavior, and have written about it from various perspectives, using narration, sociological and psychological analysis, and cultural criticism, among other approaches. Tolstoy wrote that "Happy families are all alike; every unhappy family is unhappy in its own way." But we shall discover that Tolstoy had a limited view of family life and its values—probably circumscribed by the mores of the time he lived in. Some of our finest essayists and observers of social life today demonstrate in this chapter that what constitutes the definition of a family is up for grabs as we begin the new millennium.

The family is one of the few institutions that we find in every society throughout the world, at least every thriving society. Anthropologists, sociologists, and psychologists tell us that family patterns are exceedingly diverse even in the same societies. In the past and even more so today, children grow up in many ways: in nuclear and in nontraditional households; in single-parent and in dual-parent arrangements; in extended families and in the new blended family; and in patriarchal and matriarchal, heterosexual and homosexual, monogamous and polygamous situations. And the dynamics of family life assume added dimension as we move across cultures, studying European families, African-American families, Hispanic families, Asian families, and so forth. Even within these groups, we find variables that affect family life and values, such as economic class, social class, and educational levels. For example, Fuyukama shows the many varieties of Hispanic families currently living in the United States.

Unlike in previous periods in our history, Americans today seem to be groping for a definition of what constitutes the happy family. With the influences of the media and of peer pressure on children, the rise in the number of latchkey children, and the fact that there is a growing diversity of cultures in America owing to the new wave of immigration, the family appears to be less of a traditional haven than it was even a generation ago. This chapter contains vivid accounts of the long-standing bonds within the family that have been treasured for their capacity to build values of love and sharing. It also contains essays that demonstrate how family life is filled with emotional complexities and conflicts that the child must negotiate as she or he finds meaning and attempts to construct an identity. Each writer, whether writing narration, exposition, or argumentation, shows how significant the family is for the development of our values, personalities, and lifestyles.

As much as our identities are shaped by powerful institutional forces like the family, what we are might be even more powerfully determined by the forces of sexuality and gender. Freud asserted that human behavior is rooted in sexuality, that gender (rather than family or school or any social institution) is destiny. It is clear that notions of what it means to be a man or woman have an impact on the construction of our identities.

The identity issues discussed in this chapter might prove to be controversial, but they will encourage you to confront your own sense of identity. These essays are like a mirror in which you can see and evaluate what you really are.

Previewing the Chapter

As you read the essays in this chapter and respond to them in discussion and writing, consider the following questions:

- What form of rhetoric is the author using: narration, exposition, argumentation? Why is this form appropriate for the author's purpose?
- What perspective does the writer take on the subject of identity formation? Is the writer optimistic, pessimistic, or something else?
- What are the cultural, social, and economic issues addressed in the essay?
- How do you regard the authority of the author? Does she or he seem to be speaking from experience and knowledge? In essays that explain or argue, does the evidence appear substantial or questionable? Explain.
- What stylistic devices does the author employ to recreate a memory, explain a function, or argue a stance regarding an issue of identity?
- Which essays appear alike in purpose and method, and why?
- What have you learned or discovered about your own identity from reading these essays?
- Do you prefer one rhetorical form over another, for example, personal narration over argumentation? If so, why?

Classic and Contemporary Images

How Do We Respond to Social Events?

Using a Critical Perspective   What was your first impression of Brueghel's *Rustic Wedding* and Vanessa Vick's *Bride and Groom?* What details do you see? What senses do the artist and the photographer draw on to convey the atmosphere of the wedding? What does each want to say about the institution of marriage? How do you know?

Museum of Fine Art, Ghent, Belgium/The Bridgeman Art Library.

The Flemish artist Pieter Bruegel the Elder (1525–1569), was one of the greatest painters of the 16th century and was renowned for his exuberant depictions of peasant life. His son Pieter Brueghel the Younger (1564–1638) copied many of his father's works and also painted religious subjects. He was responsible for *Rustic Wedding*, shown here.

Vanessa Vick/Photo Researchers

Contemporary weddings are frequently captured by photographers, who typically take numerous pictures of the bride and groom, along with their families and members of their wedding parties.

Classic and Contemporary Essays
How Much Do Families Matter?

E. B. White and Barbara Kingsolver represent two generations, each raised with different values regarding the function, structure, and role of the family. Both authors are master stylists, but each reflects a style of writing, an intellectual universe, and an external world that views the healthy family differently. White writes in clear, concise, elegiac prose. It marches on in a quiet, evenly patterned rhythm. Perhaps it is a metaphor of his view of life in general and family life in particular. Tradition is to be treasured; continuity is to be celebrated. He attends to the details of a nature outing and suggests that the sights, sounds, and smells that imbue the events he and his son experience are the same as those he experienced years before with his own father. For White, it seems, pleasure is derived from connectivity and permanence.

Kingsolver is passionate about her own perspective on what constitutes a healthy family structure, but it is a family transformed, reconfigured, and rearranged by contemporary events and values. Kingsolver's notion of family is various while White's view is archetypal. Kingsolver seems to believe that change in families creates security, particularly if one is moving from a dysfunctional environment to a more coherent one. Is White conservative in his views? Is Kingsolver a liberal? Perhaps a better way to get a sense of their differences is to inquire whether our amorphous contemporary world requires us to be more flexible and critical. And of course, one must consider that Kingsolver adds a woman's voice to the conversation about family, a voice that was not as frequently heard by the members of White's generation.

Once More to the Lake

E. B. White

Elwyn Brooks White (1899–1985), perhaps the finest American essayist of the twentieth century, was at his most distinctive in his treatments of people and nature. A recipient of the National Medal for Literature, and associated for years with The New Yorker, *White is the author of* One Man's Meat *(1942),* Here Is New York *(1949), and* The Second Tree from the Corner *(1954), among numerous other works. He was also one of the most talented writers of literature for children, the author of* Stuart Little *(1945),* Charlotte's Web *(1952), and* The Trumpet of the Swan *(1970). In this essay, White combines narration and description to make a poignant and vivid statement about past and present, youth and age, life and death.*

One summer, along about 1904, my father rented a camp on a lake in Maine and took us all there for the month of August. We all got ringworm from some kittens and had to rub Pond's Extract on our arms and legs night and morning, and my father rolled over in a canoe with all his clothes on; but outside of that the vacation was a success and from then on none of us ever thought there was any place in the world like that lake in Maine. We returned summer after summer—always on August 1st for one month. I have since become a salt-water man, but sometimes in summer there are days when the restlessness of the tides and the fearful cold of the sea water and the incessant wind which blows across the afternoon and into the evening make me wish for the placidity of a lake in the woods. A few weeks ago this feeling got so strong I bought myself a couple of bass hooks and a spinner and returned to the lake where we used to go, for a week's fishing and to revisit old haunts.

I took along my son, who had never had any fresh water up his nose and who had seen lily pads only from train windows. On the journey over to the lake I began to wonder what it would be like. I wondered how time would have marred this unique, this holy spot—the coves and streams, the hills that the sun set behind, the camps and the paths behind the camps. I was sure the tarred road would have found it out and I wondered in what other ways it would be desolated. It is strange how much you can remember about places like that once you allow your mind to return into the grooves which lead back. You remember one thing, and that suddenly reminds you of another thing. I guess I remembered clearest of all the early mornings, when the lake was cool and motionless, remembered how the bedroom smelled of the lumber it was made of and of the wet woods whose scent entered through the screen. The partitions in the camp were thin and did not extend clear to the top of the rooms, and as I was always the first up I would dress softly so as not to wake the others, and sneak out into the sweet outdoors and start out in the canoe, keeping close along the shore in the long shadows of the pines. I remembered being very careful never to rub my paddle against the gunwale for fear of disturbing the stillness of the cathedral.

The lake had never been what you would call a wild lake. There were cot- 3
tages sprinkled around the shores, and it was in farming country although the shores of the lake were quite heavily wooded. Some of the cottages were owned by nearby farmers, and you would live at the shore and eat your meals at the farmhouse. That's what our family did. But although it wasn't wild, it was a fairly large and undisturbed lake and there were places in it which, to a child at least, seemed infinitely remote and primeval.

I was right about the tar: it led to within half a mile of the shore. But when 4
I got back there, with my boy, and we settled into a camp near a farmhouse and into the kind of summertime I had known, I could tell that it was going to be pretty much the same as it had been before—I knew it, lying in bed the first morning, smelling the bedroom, and hearing the boy sneak quietly out and go off along the shore in a boat. I began to sustain the illusion that he was I, and therefore, by simple transposition, that I was my father. This sensation persisted, kept cropping up all the time we were there. It was not an entirely new feeling, but in this setting it grew much stronger. I seemed to be living a dual existence. I would be in the middle of some simple act, I would be picking up a bait box or laying down a table fork, or I would be saying something, and suddenly it would be not I but my father who was saying the words or making the gesture. It gave me a creepy sensation.

We went fishing the first morning. I felt the same damp moss covering the 5
worms in the bait can, and saw the dragonfly alight on the tip of my rod as it hovered a few inches from the surface of the water. It was the arrival of this fly that convinced me beyond any doubt that everything was as it always had been, that the years were a mirage and there had been no years. The small waves were the same, chucking the rowboat under the chin as we fished at anchor, and the boat was the same boat, the same color green and the ribs broken in the same place, and under the floor-boards the same fresh-water leavings and débris—the dead hellgrammite, the wisps of moss, the rusty discarded fishhook, the dried blood from yesterday's catch. We stared silently at the tips of our rods, at the dragonflies that came and went. I lowered the tip of mine into the water, tentatively, pensively dislodging the fly, which darted two feet away, poised, darted two feet back, and came to rest again a little farther up the rod. There had been no years between the ducking of this dragonfly and the other one—the one that was part of memory. I looked at the boy, who was silently watching his fly, and it was my hands that held his rod, my eyes watching. I felt dizzy and didn't know which rod I was at the end of.

We caught two bass, hauling them in briskly as though they were mackerel, 6
pulling them over the side of the boat in a businesslike manner without any landing net, and stunning them with a blow on the back of the head. When we got back for a swim before lunch, the lake was exactly where we had left it, the same number of inches from the dock, and there was only the merest suggestion of a breeze. This seemed an utterly enchanted sea, this lake you could leave

to its own devices for a few hours and come back to, and find that it had not stirred, this constant and trustworthy body of water. In the shallows, the dark, water-soaked sticks and twigs, smooth and old, were undulating in clusters on the bottom against the clean ribbed sand, and the track of the mussel was plain. A school of minnows swam by, each minnow with its small individual shadow, doubling the attendance, so clear and sharp in the sunlight. Some of the other campers were in swimming, along the shore, one of them with a cake of soap, and the water felt thin and clear and unsubstantial. Over the years there had been this person with the cake of soap, this cultist, and here he was. There had been no years.

Up to the farmhouse to dinner through the teeming, dusty field, the road 7 under our sneakers was only a two-track road. The middle track was missing, the one with the marks of the hooves and the splotches of dried, flaky manure. There had always been three tracks to choose from in choosing which track to walk in; now the choice was narrowed down to two. For a moment I missed terribly the middle alternative. But the way led past the tennis court, and something about the way it lay there in the sun reassured me; the tape had loosened along the backline, the alleys were green with plaintains and other weeds, and the net (installed in June and removed in September) sagged in the dry noon, and the whole place steamed with midday heat and hunger and emptiness. There was a choice of pie for dessert, and one was blueberry and one was apple, and the waitresses were the same country girls, there having been no passage of time, only the illusion of it as in a dropped curtain—the waitresses were still fifteen; their hair had been washed, that was the only difference—they had been to the movies and seen the pretty girls with the clean hair.

Summertime, oh summertime, pattern of life indelible, the fade-proof lake, 8 the woods unshatterable, the pasture with the sweetfern and the juniper forever and ever, summer without end; this was the background, and the life along the shore was the design, the cottagers with their innocent and tranquil design, their tiny docks with the flagpole and the American flag floating against the white clouds in the blue sky, the little paths over the roots of the trees leading from camp to camp and the paths leading back to the outhouses and the can of lime for sprinkling, and at the souvenir counters at the store the miniature birch-bark canoes and the post cards that showed things looking a little better than they looked. This was the American family at play, escaping the city heat, wondering whether the newcomers in the camp at the head of the cove were "common" or "nice," wondering whether it was true that the people who drove up for Sunday dinner at the farmhouse were turned away because there wasn't enough chicken.

It seemed to me, as I kept remembering all this, that those times and those 9 summers had been infinitely precious and worth saving. There had been jollity and peace and goodness. The arriving (at the beginning of August) had been so big a business in itself, at the railway station the farm wagon drawn up, the first smell of the pine-laden air, the first glimpse of the smiling farmer, and the great importance of the trunks and your father's enormous authority in such matters, and the feel of the wagon under you for the long ten-mile haul, and at the top of the last long hill catching the first view of the lake after eleven months of not seeing this cherished body of water. The shouts and cries of the other campers when they saw you, and the trunks to be unpacked, to give up their rich burden. (Arriving was less exciting nowadays, when you sneaked up in your car and parked it under a tree near the camp and took out the bags and in five minutes it was all over, no fuss, no loud wonderful fuss about trunks.)

Peace and goodness and jollity. The only thing that was wrong now, really, ₁₀ was the sound of the place, an unfamiliar nervous sound of the outboard motors. This was the note that jarred, the one thing that would sometimes break the illusion and set the years moving. In those other summertimes all motors were inboard; and when they were at a little distance, the noise they made was a sedative, an ingredient of summer sleep. They were one-cylinder and two-cylinder engines, and some were make-and-break and some were jump-spark, but they all made a sleepy sound across the lake. The one-lungers throbbed and fluttered, and the twin-cylinder ones purred and purred, and that was a quiet sound too. But now the campers all had outboards. In the daytime, in the hot mornings, these motors made a petulant, irritable sound; at night, in the still evening when the afterglow lit the water, they whined about one's ears like mosquitoes. My boy loved our rented outboard, and his great desire was to achieve singlehanded mastery over it, and authority, and he soon learned the trick of choking it a little (but not too much), and the adjustment of the needle valve. Watching him I would remember the things you could do with the old one-cylinder engine with the heavy flywheel, how you could have it eating out of your hand if you got really close to it spiritually. Motor boats in those days didn't have clutches, and you would make a landing by shutting off the motor at the proper time and coasting in with a dead rudder. But there was a way of reversing them, if you learned the trick, by cutting the switch and putting it on again exactly on the final dying revolution of the flywheel, so that it would kick back against compression and begin reversing. Approaching a dock in a strong following breeze, it was difficult to slow up sufficiently by the ordinary coasting method, and if a boy felt he had complete mastery over his motor, he was tempted to keep it running beyond its time and then reverse it a few feet from the dock. It took a cool nerve, because if you threw the switch a twentieth of a second too soon you would catch the flywheel when it still had speed enough to go up past center, and the boat would leap ahead, charging bull-fashion at the dock.

We had a good week at the camp. The bass were biting well and the sun ₁₁ shone endlessly, day after day. We would be tired at night and lie down in the accumulated heat of the little bedrooms after the long hot day and the breeze would stir almost imperceptibly outside and the smell of the swamp drift in through the rusty screens. Sleep would come easily and in the morning the red squirrel would be on the roof, tapping out his gay routine. I kept remembering everything, lying in bed in the mornings—the small steamboat that had a long rounded stern like the lip of a Ubangi, and how quietly she ran on the moonlight sails, when the older boys played their mandolins and the girls sang and we ate doughnuts dipped in sugar, and how sweet the music was on the water in the shining night, and what it had felt like to think about girls then. After breakfast we would go up to the store and the things were in the same place—minnows in a bottle, the plugs and spinners disarranged and pawed over by the youngsters from the boys' camp, the fig newtons and the Beeman's gum. Outside, the road was tarred and cars stood in front of the store. Inside, all was just as it had always been, except there was more Coca-Cola and not so much Moxie and root beer and birch beer and sarsaparilla. We would walk out with a bottle of pop apiece and sometimes the pop would backfire up our noses and hurt. We explored the streams, quietly, where the turtles slid off the sunny logs and dug their way into the soft bottom, and we lay on the town wharf and fed worms to the tame bass. Everywhere we went I had trouble making out which was I, the one walking at my side, the one walking in my pants.

One afternoon while we were there at that lake a thunderstorm came up. It 12 was like the revival of an old melodrama that I had seen long ago with childish awe. The second-act climax of the drama of the electrical disturbance over a lake in America had not changed in any important respect. This was the big scene, still the big scene. The whole thing was so familiar, the first feeling of oppression and heat and a general air around camp of not wanting to go very far away. In midafternoon (it was all the same) a curious darkening of the sky, and a lull in everything that had made life tick; and then the way the boats suddenly swung the other way at their moorings with the coming of a breeze out of the new quarter, and the premonitory rumble. Then the kettle drum, then the snare, then the bass drum and cymbals, then crackling light against the dark, and the gods grinning and licking their chops in the hills. Afterward the calm, the rain steadily rustling in the calm lake, the return of light and hope and spirits, and the campers running out in joy and relief to go swimming in the rain, their bright cries perpetuating the deathless joke about how they were getting simply drenched, and the children screaming with delight at the new sensation of bathing in the rain, and the joke about getting drenched linking the generations in a strong indestructible chain. And the comedian who waded in carrying an umbrella.

When the others went swimming my son said he was going in too. He 13 pulled his dripping trunks from the line where they had hung all through the shower, and wrung them out. Languidly, and with no thought of going in, I watched him, his hard little body, skinny and bare, saw him wince slightly as he pulled up around his vitals the small, soggy, icy garment. As he buckled the swollen belt suddenly my groin felt the chill of death.

COMPREHENSION

1. At what point in the essay do you begin to sense White's main purpose? What is his purpose? What type of reader might his purpose appeal to?

2. What motivates White to return to the lake in Maine? Explain the "simple transposition" that he mentions in paragraph 4. List the illustrations that he gives of this phenomenon. What change does he detect in the lake?
3. Explain the significance of White's last sentence. Where are there foreshadowings of this statement?

RHETORIC

1. Describe the author's use of figurative language in paragraphs 2, 10, and 12.
2. Identify those words and phrases that White invokes to establish the sense of mystery about the lake. Why are these words and their connotations important to the nature of the illusion that he describes?
3. Explain the organization of the essay in terms of the following paragraph units: 1 to 4; 5 to 7; 8 to 10; and 11 to 13. Explain the function of paragraphs 8 and 12.
4. There are many vivid and unusual descriptive details in this essay—for example, the dragonfly in paragraph 5 and the two-track road in paragraph 7. How does White create symbolic overtones for these descriptive details and others? Why is the lake itself a complex symbol? Explain with reference to paragraph 6.
5. Describe the persona that White creates for himself in the essay. How does this persona function?
6. What is the relation between the introductory and concluding paragraphs, specifically in terms of irony of statement?

WRITING

1. Explore in an essay the theme of nostalgia in "Once More to the Lake." What are the beauties and the dangers of nostalgia? Can the past ever be recaptured or relived? Justify your answer.
2. White consistently compares an outing with his father to one with his son. How does this structure help to emphasize the continuity of generations? Explain in an analytical and comparative essay of 500 to 750 words.
3. Referring to revisiting a site on the lake that he had visited years before with his father, White remarks in paragraph 4, "I could tell that it was going to be pretty much the same as it had been before." How does this observation reflect the general sentiment White has about the role and function of the family? Respond to the question in an analytical essay.

Stone Soup

Barbara Kingsolver

Barbara Kingsolver (b. 1955) was born in Annapolis, Maryland, grew up in rural Kentucky, and was educated at DePauw University and the University of Arizona. Her fiction includes The Bean Trees *(1988);* Homeland *(1990);* Animal Dreams *(1991), for which she won a PEN fiction prize and an Edward Abbey Ecofiction Award;* Pigs in Heaven *(1993), which won a Los Angeles Times Book Award for Fiction; and* The Poisonwood Bible *(1998). She has also worked as a biologist, is active in the field of human rights, and plays keyboard with an amateur rock and roll band. The following essay, first published in the January 1995 issue of* Parenting, *eschews the idea of the nuclear family as being the standard by which the healthy family should be judged.*

In the catalog of family values, where do we rank an occasion like this? A curly-haired boy who wanted to run before he walked, age seven now, a soccer player scoring a winning goal. He turns to the bleachers with his fists in the air and a smile wide as a gap-toothed galaxy. His own cheering section of grown-ups and kids all leap to their feet and hug each other, delirious with love for this boy. He's Andy, my best friend's son. The cheering section includes his mother and her friends, his brother, his father and stepmother, a stepbrother and stepsister, and a grandparent. Lucky is the child with this many relatives on hand to hail a proud accomplishment. I'm there too, witnessing a family fortune. But in spite of myself, defensive words take shape in my head. I am thinking: I dare *anybody* to call this a broken home.

Families change, and remain the same. Why are our names for home so slow to catch up to the truth of where we live?

When I was a child, I had two parents who loved me without cease. One of them attended every excuse for attention I ever contrived, and the other made it to the ones with higher production values, like piano recitals and appendicitis. So I was a lucky child too. I played with a set of paper dolls called "The Family of Dolls," four in number, who came with the factory-assigned names of Dad, Mom, Sis, and Junior. I think you know what they looked like, at least before I loved them to death and their heads fell off.

Now I've replaced the dolls with a life. I knit my days around my daughter's survival and happiness, and am proud to say her head is still on. But we aren't the Family of Dolls. Maybe you're not, either. And if not, even though you are statistically no oddity, it's probably been suggested to you in a hundred ways that yours isn't exactly a real family, but an impostor family, a harbinger of cultural ruin, a slapdash substitute—something like counterfeit money. Here at the tail end of our century, most of us are up to our ears in the noisy business of trying to support and love a thing called family. But there's a current in the air with ferocious moral force that finds its way even into political campaigns, claiming there is only one right way to do it, the Way It Has Always Been.

In the face of a thriving, particolored world, this narrow view is so pickled and ₅ absurd I'm astonished that it gets airplay. And I'm astonished that it still stings.

Every parent has endured the arrogance of a child-unfriendly grump sitting ₆ in judgment, explaining what those kids of ours really need (for example, "a good licking"). If we're polite, we move our crew to another bench in the park. If we're forthright (as I am in my mind, only, for the rest of the day), we fix them with a sweet imperious stare and say, "Come back and let's talk about it after you've changed a thousand diapers."

But it's harder somehow to shrug off the Family-of-Dolls Family Values ₇ crew when they judge (from their safe distance) that divorced people, blended families, gay families, and single parents are failures. That our children are at risk, and the whole arrangement is messy and embarrassing. A marriage that ends is not called "finished," it's called *failed*. The children of this family may have been born to a happy union, but now they are called *the children of divorce*.

I had no idea how thoroughly these assumptions overlaid my culture until ₈ I went through divorce myself. I wrote to a friend: "This might be worse than being widowed. Overnight I've suffered the same losses—companionship, financial and practical support, my identity as a wife and partner, the future I'd taken for granted. I am lonely, grieving, and hard-pressed to take care of my household alone. But instead of bringing casseroles, people are acting like I had a fit and broke up the family china."

Once upon a time I held these beliefs about divorce: that everyone who does ₉ it could have chosen not to do it. That it's a lazy way out of marital problems. That it selfishly puts personal happiness ahead of family integrity. Now I tremble for my ignorance. It's easy, in fortunate times, to forget about the ambush that could leave your head reeling: serious mental or physical illness, death in the family, abandonment, financial calamity, humiliation, violence, despair.

I started out like any child, intent on being the Family of Dolls. I set upon ₁₀ young womanhood believing in most of the doctrines of my generation: I wore my skirts four inches above the knee. I had that Barbie with her zebra-striped swimsuit and a figure unlike anything found in nature. And I understood the Prince Charming Theory of Marriage, a quest for Mr. Right that ends smack dab where you find him. I did not completely understand that another whole story *begins* there, and no fairy tale prepared me for the combination of bad luck and persistent hope that would interrupt my dream and lead me to other arrangements. Like a cancer diagnosis, a dying marriage is a thing to fight, to deny, and finally, when there's no choice left, to dig in and survive. Casseroles would help. Likewise, I imagine it must be a painful reckoning in adolescence (or later on) to realize one's own true love will never look like the soft-focus fragrance ads because Prince Charming (surprise!) is a princess. Or vice versa. Or has skin the color your parents didn't want you messing with, except in the Crayola box.

It's awfully easy to hold in contempt the straw broken home, and that ₁₁ mythical category of persons who toss away nuclear family for the sheer fun of it. Even the legal terms we use have a suggestion of caprice. I resent the phrase "irreconcilable differences," which suggests a stubborn refusal to accept a spouse's little quirks. This is specious. Every happily married couple I know has loads of irreconcilable differences. Negotiating where to set the thermostat is not the point. A nonfunctioning marriage is a slow asphyxiation. It is waking up despised each morning, listening to the pulse of your own loneliness before the radio begins to blare its raucous gospel that you're nothing if you aren't loved. It is sharing your airless house with the threat of suicide or other kinds of violence, while the ghost that whispers, "Leave here and destroy your children," has passed over every door and nailed it shut. Disassembling a marriage in these circumstances is as much *fun* as amputating your own gangrenous leg. You do it, if you can, to save a life—or two, or more.

I know of no one who really went looking to hoe the harder row, especially 12 the daunting one of single parenthood. Yet it seems to be the most American of customs to blame the burdened for their destiny. We'd like so desperately to believe in freedom and justice for all, we can hardly name that rogue bad luck, even when he's a close enough snake to bite us. In the wake of my divorce, some friends (even a few close ones) chose to vanish, rather than linger within striking distance of misfortune.

But most stuck around, bless their hearts, and if I'm any the wiser for my 13 trials, it's from having learned the worth of steadfast friendship. And also, what not to say. The least helpful question is: "Did you want the divorce, or didn't you?" Did I want to keep that gangrenous leg, or not? How to explain, in a culture that venerates choice: two terrifying options are much worse than none at all. Give me any day the quick hand of cruel fate that will leave me scarred but blameless. As it was, I kept thinking of that wicked third-grade joke in which some boy comes up behind you and grabs your ear, starts in with a prolonged tug, and asks, "Do you want this ear any longer?"

Still, the friend who holds your hand and says the wrong thing is made of 14 dearer stuff than the one who stays away. And generally, through all of it, you live. My favorite fictional character, Kate Vaiden (in the novel by Reynolds Price), advises: "Strength just comes in one brand—you stand up at sunrise and meet what they send you and keep your hair combed."

Once you've weathered the straits, you get to cross the tricky juncture from 15 casualty to survivor. If you're on your feet at the end of a year or two, and have begun putting together a happy new existence, those friends who were kind enough to feel sorry for you when you needed it must now accept you back to the ranks of the living. If you're truly blessed, they will dance at your second wedding. Everybody else, for heavens sake, should stop throwing stones.

Arguing about whether nontraditional families deserve pity or tolerance is 16 a little like the medieval debate about left-handedness as a mark of the devil. Divorce, remarriage, single parenthood, gay parents, and blended families simply are. They're facts of our time. Some of the reasons listed by sociologists for these family reconstructions are: the idea of marriage as a romantic partnership rather than a pragmatic one; a shift in women's expectations, from servility to self-respect and independence; and longevity (prior to antibiotics no marriage was expected to last many decades—in Colonial days the average couple lived to be married less than twelve years). Add to all this, our growing sense of entitlement to happiness and safety from abuse. Most would agree these are all good things. Yet their result—a culture in which serial monogamy and the consequent reshaping of families are the norm—gets diagnosed as "failing."

For many of us, once we have put ourselves Humpty-Dumpty–wise back   17
together again, the main problem with our reorganized family is that other people think we have a problem. My daughter tells me the only time she's uncomfortable about being the child of divorced parents is when her friends say they feel sorry for her. It's a bizarre sympathy, given that half the kids in her school and nation are in the same boat, pursuing childish happiness with the same energy as their married-parent peers. When anyone asks how she feels about it, she spontaneously lists the benefits: our house is in the country and we have a dog, but she can go to her dad's neighborhood for the urban thrills of a pool and sidewalks for roller-skating. What's more, she has three sets of grandparents!

Why is it surprising that a child would revel in a widened family and the   18
right to feel at home in more than one house? Isn't it the opposite that should worry us—a child with no home at all, or too few resources to feel safe? The child at risk is the one whose parents are too immature themselves to guide wisely; too diminished by poverty to nurture; too far from opportunity to offer hope. The number of children in the U.S. living in poverty at this moment is almost unfathomably large: twenty percent. There are families among us that need help all right, and by no means are they new on the landscape. The rate at which teenage girls had babies in 1957 (ninety-six per thousand) was twice what it is now. That remarkable statistic is ignored by the religious right—probably because the teen birth rate was cut in half mainly by legalized abortion. In fact, the policy gatekeepers who coined the phrase "family values" have steadfastly ignored the desperation of too-small families, and since 1979 have steadily reduced the amount of financial support available to a single parent. But, this camp's most outspoken attacks seem aimed at the notion of families getting too complex, with add-ons and extras such as a gay parent's partner, or a remarried mother's new husband and his children.

To judge a family's value by its tidy symmetry is to purchase a book for its   19
cover. There's no moral authority there. The famous family comprised by Dad, Mom, Sis, and Junior living as an isolated economic unit is not built on historical bedrock. In *The Way We Never Were*, Stephanie Coontz writes, "Whenever people propose that we go back to the traditional family, I always suggest that they pick a ballpark date for the family they have in mind." Colonial families were tidily disciplined, but their members (meaning everyone but infants) labored incessantly and died young. Then the Victorian family adopted a new division of labor, in which women's role was domestic and children were allowed time for study and play, but this was an upper-class construct supported by myriad slaves. Coontz writes, "For every nineteenth-century middle-class family that protected its wife and child within the family circle, there was an Irish or German girl scrubbing floors . . . A Welsh boy mining coal to keep the homebaked goodies warm, a black girl doing the family laundry, a black mother and child

picking cotton to be made into clothes for the family, and a Jewish or an Italian daughter in a sweatshop making 'ladies' dresses or artificial flowers for the family to purchase."

The abolition of slavery brought slightly more democratic arrangements, in 20 which extended families were harnessed together in cottage industries; at the turn of the century came a steep rise in child labor in mines and sweat-shops. Twenty percent of American children lived in orphanages at the time; their parents were not necessarily dead, but couldn't afford to keep them.

During the Depression and up to the end of World War II, many millions of 21 U.S. households were more multigenerational than nuclear. Women my grandmother's age were likely to live with a fluid assortment of elderly relatives, in-laws, siblings, and children. In many cases they spent virtually every waking hour working in the company of other women—a companionable scenario in which it would be easier, I imagine, to tolerate an estranged or difficult spouse. I'm reluctant to idealize a life of so much hard work and so little spousal intimacy, but its advantage may have been resilience. A family so large and varied would not easily be brought down by a single blow: it could absorb a death, long-illness, an abandonment here or there, and any number of irreconcilable differences.

The Family of Dolls came along midcentury as a great American experi- 22 ment. A booming economy required a mobile labor force and demanded that women surrender jobs to returning soldiers. Families came to be defined by a single breadwinner. They struck out for single-family homes at an earlier age than ever before, and in unprecedented numbers they raised children in suburban isolation. The nuclear family was launched to sink or swim.

More than a few sank. Social historians corroborate that the suburban fam- 23 ily of the postwar economic boom, which we have recently selected as our definition of "traditional," was no panacea. Twenty-five percent of Americans were poor in the mid-1950s, and as yet there were no food stamps. Sixty percent of the elderly lived on less than $1,000 a year, and most had no medical insurance. In the sequestered suburbs, alcoholism and sexual abuse of children were far more widespread than anyone imagined.

Expectations soared, and the economy sagged. It's hard to depend on one 24 other adult for everything, come what may. In the last three decades, that amorphous, adaptable structure we call "family" has been reshaped once more by economic tides. Compared with fifties families, mothers are far more likely now to be employed. We are statistically more likely to divorce, and to live in blended families or other extranuclear arrangements. We are also more likely to plan and space our children, and to rate our marriages as "happy." We are less likely to suffer abuse without recourse, or to stare out at our lives through a glaze of prescription tranquilizers. Our aged parents are less likely to be destitute, and we're half as likely to have a teenage daughter turn up a mother herself. All in all, I would say that if "intact" in modern family-values jargon means living quietly desperate in the bell jar, then hip-hip-hooray for "broken." A neat family model constructed to service the Baby Boom economy seems to be returning gradually to a grand, lumpy shape that human families apparently have tended toward since they first took root in the Olduvai Gorge. We're social animals, deeply fond of companionship, and children love best to run in packs. If there is a *normal* for humans, at all, I expect it looks like two or three Families of Dolls, connected variously by kinship and passion, shuffled like cards and strewn over several shoeboxes.

The sooner we can let go the fairy tale of families functioning perfectly in   25 isolation, the better we might embrace the relief of community. Even the admirable parents who've stayed married through thick and thin are very likely, at present, to incorporate other adults into their families—household help and baby-sitters if they can afford them or neighbors and grandparents if they can't. For single parents, this support is the rock-bottom definition of family. And most parents who have split apart, however painfully, still manage to maintain family continuity for their children, creating in many cases a boisterous phenomenon that Constance Ahrons in her book *The Good Divorce* calls the "binuclear family." Call it what you will—when ex-spouses beat swords into plowshares and jump up and down at a soccer game together, it makes for happy kids.

Cinderella, look, who needs her? All those evil stepsisters? That story al-   26 ways seemed like too much cotton-picking fuss over clothes. A childhood tale that fascinated me more was the one called "Stone Soup," and the gist of it is this: Once upon a time, a pair of beleaguered soldiers straggled home to a village empty-handed, in a land ruined by war. They were famished, but the villagers had so little they shouted evil words and slammed their doors. So the soldiers dragged out a big kettle, filled it with water, and put it on a fire to boil. They rolled a clean round stone into the pot, while the villagers peered through their curtains in amazement.

"What kind of soup is that?" they hooted.   27

"Stone soup," the soldiers replied. "Everybody can have some when it's   28 done."

"Well, thanks," one matron grumbled, coming out with a shriveled carrot.   29 "But it'd be better if you threw this in."

And so on, of course, a vegetable at a time, until the whole suspicious vil-   30 lage managed to feed itself grandly.

Any family is a big empty pot, save for what gets thrown in. Each stew   31 turns out different. Generosity, a resolve to turn bad luck into good, and respect for variety—these things will nourish a nation of children. Name-calling and suspicion will not. My soup contains a rock or two of hard times, and maybe yours does too. I expect it's a heck of a bouillabaisse.

COMPREHENSION

1. What is the essay's thesis?
2. According to Kingsolver, why is our society so apt to condemn divorce?
3. What is the author's view of family symmetry (paragraph 19)?

RHETORIC

1. What rhetorical function does the opening anecdote serve in introducing the essay's subject matter?
2. What is the author's purpose in capitalizing, italicizing, and placing quotation marks around certain phrases, for example, "Way It Has Always Been" (paragraph 4); *failed* and *children of divorce* (paragraph 7); "family values" (paragraph 18)?
3. What is the author's purpose in creating a gap between paragraphs 15 and 16? What is the focus of the author's argument after this break?
4. Compare the introductory paragraph with the concluding one. How do they differ? How are they similar? How do they help set the boundaries of the essay?
5. This essay contains personal observation, personal experience, historical data, and anecdote. How would you describe the author's overall method to a person who has not read the essay?
6. Unlike the titles of most essays, the title "Stone Soup" gives no hint at the essay's content. What is the rhetorical purpose in keeping the meaning of the title a mystery until the very end?
7. In paragraph 2, the author asks the question, "Why are our names for home so slow to catch up to the truth of where we live?" Does the author suggest an answer to this question either implicitly or explicitly during the course of the essay? If so, where?

WRITING

1. Write an essay of approximately 500 words exploring some negative outcomes that could occur in the type of family the author celebrates.
2. Interview two individuals at least 25 years apart in age. Compare and contrast their views on divorce.
3. Describe the dynamics of a blended family with which you are familiar. It may be your own or a friend's.

Classic and Contemporary: Questions for Comparison

1. Compare and contrast the tone of each writer. How does tone affect purpose? How does it affect mood? Select at least three passages from White and three from Kingsolver that demonstrate how their tones differ. Do they offer any hints as to the "voice" or personality of the writers? Why or why not?
2. What contemporary issues does Kingsolver address that White either ignores or is unaware of? Consider that White was born 58 years before Kingsolver, so his world was quite a different one. Are there other variables that

might help us distinguish their concerns and outlooks? For example, gender, class, environment?

3. What central values does each author have regarding the family? How are they similar? How do they differ? How do their values reflect their times?

An American Childhood

Annie Dillard

Annie Dillard (b. 1945 in Pittsburgh) received her BA and MA degrees from Hollins College. Her first book, Pilgrim at Tinker Creek *(1975), won the Pulitzer Prize for general nonfiction. Her other published works of nonfiction include* Teaching a Stone to Talk *(1982) and* An American Childhood *(1987). Dillard expanded her range of writing with the publication of her first novel,* The Living *(1992). She has received awards from the National Endowment for the Arts and the Guggenheim Foundation as well as many other sources. As an essayist, poet, memoirist, and literary critic, she focuses her themes on the relationships among the self, nature, religion, and faith. Her writing is recognizable by its observations of the minutiae of life and its search for meaning in unlikely places, such as a stone or an insect. In this passage from* An American Childhood, *the author gives us a portrait of her mother by focusing on her small idiosyncrasies of speech, gesture, and attitude.*

One Sunday afternoon Mother wandered through our kitchen, where Father   1
was making a sandwich and listening to the ball game. The Pirates were playing the New York Giants at Forbes Field. In those days, the Giants had a utility infielder named Wayne Terwilliger. Just as Mother passed through, the radio announcer cried—with undue drama—"Terwilliger bunts one!"

"Terwilliger bunts one?" Mother cried back, stopped short. She turned. "Is   2
that English?"

"The player's name is Terwilliger," Father said. "He bunted."   3

"That's marvelous," Mother said. "'Terwilliger bunts one.' No wonder you   4
listen to baseball. 'Terwilliger bunts one.'"

For the next seven or eight years, Mother made this surprising string of syl-   5
lables her own. Testing a microphone, she repeated, "Terwilliger bunts one";
testing a pen or a typewriter, she wrote it. If, as happened surprisingly often in
the course of various improvised gags, she pretended to whisper something
else in my ear, she actually whispered, "Terwilliger bunts one." Whenever
someone used a French phrase, or a Latin one, she answered solemnly, "Terwilliger bunts one." If Mother had had, like Andrew Carnegie, the opportunity
to cook up a motto for a coat of arms, hers would have read simply and
tellingly, "Terwilliger bunts one." (Carnegie's was "Death to Privilege.")

She served us with other words and phrases. On a Florida trip, she repeated 6 tremulously, "That . . . is a royal poinciana." I don't remember the tree; I remember the thrill in her voice. She pronounced it carefully, and spelled it. She also liked to say "portulaca."

The drama of the words "Tamiami Trail" stirred her, we learned on the 7 same Florida trip. People built Tampa on one coast, and they built Miami on another. Then—the height of visionary ambition and folly—they piled a slow, tremendous road through the terrible Everglades to connect them. To build the road, men stood sunk in muck to their armpits. They fought off cottonmouth moccasins and six-foot alligators. They slept in boats, wet. They blasted muck with dynamite, cut jungle with machetes; they laid logs, dragged drilling machines, hauled dredges, heaped limestone. The road took fourteen years to build up by the shovelful, a Panama Canal in reverse, and cost hundreds of lives from tropical, mosquito-carried diseases. Then, capping it all, some genius thought of the word Tamiami: they called the road from Tampa to Miami, this very road under our spinning wheels, the Tamiami Trail. Some called it Alligator Alley. Anyone could drive over this road without a thought.

Hearing this, moved, I thought all the suffering of road building was worth 8 it (it wasn't my suffering), now that we had this new thing to hang these new words on—Alligator Alley for those who liked things cute, and, for connoisseurs like Mother, for lovers of the human drama in all its boldness and terror, the Tamiami Trail.

Back home, Mother cut clips from reels of talk, as it were, and played them 9 back at leisure. She noticed that many Pittsburghers confuse "leave" and "let." One kind relative brightened our morning by mentioning why she'd brought her son to visit: "He wanted to come with me, so I left him." Mother filled in Amy and me on locutions we missed. "I can't do it on Friday," her pretty sister told a crowded dinner party, "because Friday's the day I lay in the stores."

(All unconsciously, though, we ourselves used some pure Pittsburghisms. 10 We said "tele pole," pronounced "telly pole," for that splintery sidewalk post I loved to climb. We said "slippy"—the sidewalks are "slippy." We said, "That's all the farther I could go." And we said, as Pittsburghers do say, "This glass needs washed," or "The dog needs walked"—a usage our father eschewed; he knew it was not standard English, nor even comprehensible English, but he never let on.)

"Spell 'poinsettia,'" Mother would throw out at me, smiling with pleasure. 11 "Spell 'sherbet.'" The idea was not to make us whizzes, but, quite the contrary, to remind us—and I, especially, needed reminding—that we didn't know it all just yet.

"There's a deer standing in the front hall," she told me one quiet evening in 12 the country.

"Really?" 13

"No. I just wanted to tell you something once without your saying, 'I know.'" 14

Supermarkets in the middle 1950s began luring, or bothering, customers by 15 giving out Top Value Stamps or Green Stamps. When, shopping with Mother, we got to the head of the checkout line, the checker, always a young man, asked, "Save stamps?"

"No," Mother replied genially, week after week, "I build model airplanes." I 16 believe she originated this line. It took me years to determine where the joke lay.

Anyone who met her verbal challenges she adored. She had surgery on one 17 of her eyes. On the operating table, just before she conked out, she appealed feelingly to the surgeon, saying, as she had been planning to say for weeks, "Will I be able to play the piano?" "Not on me," the surgeon said. "You won't pull that old one on me."

It was, indeed, an old one. The surgeon was supposed to answer, "Yes, my 18 dear, brave woman, you will be able to play the piano after this operation," to which Mother intended to reply, "Oh, good, I've always wanted to play the piano." This pat scenario bored her; she loved having it interrupted. It must have galled her that usually her acquaintances were so predictably unalert; it must have galled her that, for the length of her life, she could surprise everyone so continually, so easily, when she had been the same all along. At any rate, she loved anyone who, as she put it, saw it coming, and called her on it.

She regarded the instructions on bureaucratic forms as straight lines. "Do 19 you advocate the overthrow of the United States government by force or violence?" After some thought she wrote, "Force." She regarded children, even babies, as straight men. When Molly learned to crawl, Mother delighted in buying her gowns with drawstrings at the bottom, like Swee'pea's, because, as she explained energetically, you could easily step on the drawstring without the baby's noticing, so that she crawled and crawled and crawled and never got anywhere except into a small ball at the gown's top.

When we children were young, she mothered us tenderly and dependably; 20 as we got older, she resumed her career of anarchism. She collared us into her gags. If she answered the phone on a wrong number, she told the caller, "Just a minute," and dragged the receiver to Amy or me, saying, "Here, take this, your name is Cecile," or, worse, just, "It's for you." You had to think on your feet. But did you want to perform well as Cecile, or did you want to take pity on the wretched caller?

During a family trip to the Highland Park Zoo, Mother and I were alone for a 21 minute. She approached a young couple holding hands on a bench by the seals, and addressed the young man in dripping tones: "Where have you been? Still got those baby-blue eyes; always did slay me. And this"—a swift nod at the dumbstruck young woman, who had removed her hand from the man's—"must be the one you were telling me about. She's not so bad, really, as you used to make out. But listen, you know how I miss you, you know where to reach me, same old place. And there's Ann over there—see how she's grown? See the blue eyes?"

And off she sashayed, taking me firmly by the hand, and leading us around 22 briskly past the monkey house and away. She cocked an ear back, and both of us heard the desperate man begin, in a high-pitched wail, "I swear, I never saw her before in my life . . ."

On a long, sloping beach by the ocean, she lay stretched out sunning with 23
Father and friends, until the conversation gradually grew tedious, when without forethought she gave a little push with her heel and rolled away. People
were stunned. She rolled deadpan and apparently effortlessly, arms and legs extended and tidy, down the beach to the distant water's edge, where she lay at
ease just as she had been, but half in the surf, and well out of earshot.

She dearly loved to fluster people by throwing out a game's rules at a 24
whim—when she was getting bored, losing in a dull sort of way, and when
everybody else was taking it too seriously. If you turned your back, she moved
the checkers around on the board. When you got them all straightened out, she
denied she'd touched them; the next time you turned your back, she lined them
up on the rug or hid them under your chair. In a betting rummy game called
Michigan, she routinely played out of turn, or called out a card she didn't hold,
or counted backward, simply to amuse herself by causing an uproar and watching the rest of us do double-takes and have fits. (Much later, when serious suit-
ors came to call, Mother subjected them to this fast card game as a trial by
ordeal; she used it as an intelligence test and a measure of spirit. If the poor man
could stay a round without breaking down or running out, he got to marry one
of us, if he still wanted to.)

She excelled at bridge, playing fast and boldly, but when the stakes were 25
low and the hands dull, she bid slams for the devilment of it, or raised her opponents' suit to bug them, or showed her hand, or tossed her cards in a handful
behind her back in a characteristic swift motion accompanied by a vibrantly innocent look. It drove our stolid father crazy. The hand was over before it began,
and the guests were appalled. How do you score it, who deals now, what do
you do with a crazy person who is having so much fun? Or they were down
seven, and the guests were appalled. "Pam!" "Dammit, Pam!" He groaned.
What ails such people? What on earth possesses them? He rubbed his face.

She was an unstoppable force; she never let go. When we moved across 26
town, she persuaded the U.S. Post Office to let her keep her old address—forever—because she'd had stationery printed. I don't know how she did it. Every
new post office worker, over decades, needed to learn that although the Doaks'
mail is addressed to here, it is delivered to there.

Mother's energy and intelligence suited her for a greater role in a larger 27
arena—mayor of New York, say—than the one she had. She followed American
politics closely; she had been known to vote for Democrats. She saw how things
should be run, but she had nothing to run but our household. Even there, small
minds bugged her; she was smarter than the people who designed the things
she had to use all day for the length of her life.

"Look," she said. "Whoever designed this corkscrew never used one. Why 28
would anyone sell it without trying it out?" So she invented a better one. She
showed me a drawing of it. The spirit of American enterprise never faded in
Mother. If capitalizing and tooling up had been as interesting as theorizing and
thinking up, she would have fired up a new factory every week, and chaired
several hundred corporations.

"It grieves me," she would say, "it grieves my heart," that the company that 29
made one superior product packaged it poorly, or took the wrong tack in its
advertising. She knew, as she held the thing mournfully in her two hands, that
she'd never find another. She was right. We children wholly sympathized, and
so did Father; what could she do, what could anyone do, about it? She was
Samson in chains. She paced.

She didn't like the taste of stamps so she didn't lick stamps; she licked the 30
corner of the envelope instead. She glued sandpaper to the sides of kitchen
drawers, and under kitchen cabinets, so she always had a handy place to strike
a match. She designed, and hounded workmen to build against all norms, dou-
bly wide kitchen counters and elevated bathroom sinks. To splint a finger, she
stuck it in a lightweight cigar tube. Conversely, to protect a pack of cigarettes,
she carried it in a Band-Aid box. She drew plans for an over-the-finger tooth-
brush for babies, an oven rack that slid up and down, and—the family
favorite—Lendalarm. Lendalarm was a beeper you attached to books (or tools)
you loaned friends. After ten days, the beeper sounded. Only the rightful owner
could silence it.

She repeatedly reminded us of P. T. Barnum's dictum: You could sell any- 31
thing to anybody if you marketed it right. The adman who thought of making
Americans believe they needed underarm deodorant was a visionary. So, too,
was the hero who made a success of a new product, Ivory soap. The executives
were horrified, Mother told me, that a cake of this stuff floated. Soap wasn't
supposed to float. Anyone would be able to tell it was mostly whipped-up air.
Then some inspired adman made a leap: Advertise that it floats. Flaunt it. The
rest is history.

She respected the rare few who broke through to new ways. "Look," she'd 32
say, "here's an intelligent apron." She called upon us to admire intelligent control knobs and intelligent pan handles, intelligent andirons and picture frames
and knife sharpeners. She questioned everything, every pair of scissors, every
knitting needle, gardening glove, tape dispenser. Hers was a restless mental
vigor that just about ignited the dumb household objects with its force.

Torpid conformity was a kind of sin; it was stupidity itself, the mighty 33
stream against which Mother would never cease to struggle. If you held no minority opinions, or if you failed to risk total ostracism for them daily, the world
would be a better place without you.

Always I heard Mother's emotional voice asking Amy and me the same few 34
questions: "Is that your own idea? Or somebody else's?" "*Giant* is a good
movie," I pronounced to the family at dinner. "Oh, really?" Mother warmed to
these occasions. She all but rolled up her sleeves. She knew I hadn't seen it. "Is
that your considered opinion?"

She herself held many unpopular, even fantastic, positions. She was 35
scathingly sarcastic about the McCarthy hearings while they took place, right
on our living-room television; she frantically opposed Father's wait-and-see
calm. "We don't know enough about it," he said. "I do," she said. "I know all I
need to know."

She asserted, against all opposition, that people who lived in trailer parks ₃₆ were not bad but simply poor, and had as much right to settle on beautiful land, such as rural Ligonier, Pennsylvania, as did the oldest of families in the finest of hidden houses. Therefore, the people who owned trailer parks, and sought zoning changes to permit trailer parks, needed our help. Her profound belief that the country-club pool sweeper was a person, and that the department-store saleslady, the bus driver, telephone operator, and house-painter were people, and even in groups the steelworkers who carried pickets and the Christmas shoppers who clogged intersections were people—this was a conviction common enough in democratic Pittsburgh, but not altogether common among our friends' parents, or even, perhaps, among our parents' friends.

Opposition emboldened Mother, and she would take on anybody on any is- ₃₇ sue—the chairman of the board, at a cocktail party, on the current strike; she would fly at him in a flurry of passion, as a songbird selflessly attacks a big hawk.

"Eisenhower's going to win," I announced after school. She lowered her ₃₈ magazine and looked me in the eyes: "How do you know?" I was doomed. It was fatal to say, "Everyone says so." We all knew well what happened. "Do you consult this Everyone before you make your decisions? What if Everyone decided to round up all the Jews?" Mother knew there was no danger of cowing me. She simply tried to keep us all awake. And in fact it was always clear to Amy and me, and to Molly when she grew old enough to listen, that if our classmates came to cruelty, just as much as if the neighborhood or the nation came to madness, we were expected to take, and would be each separately capable of taking, a stand.

COMPREHENSION

1. The writer creates a picture of her mother's personality through a number of anecdotes and explanations. How would you sum up the mother's personality?
2. The mother appears to have a special appreciation for words and language. To what purpose does she apply this appreciation? What effect does it have on her family and acquaintances?
3. What values does the mother hold? What behaviors and attitudes does she abhor and discourage?

RHETORIC

1. In paragraph 7, the author explains that the highway from Tampa to Miami is referred to either as "Tamiami Trail" or "Alligator Alley." What is the connotation of each of these terms? Why does the mother prefer to call it "Tamiami Trail"?
2. The author herself seems to have inherited a special fascination for language. Study her use of dashes and semicolons in paragraphs 26 and 27. How do they help contribute to an energetic use of writing?

3. What are the functions of the spaces between paragraphs 19 and 20; 22 and 23; and 32 and 33? How do these divisions contribute to the structure of the essay as a whole?
4. How does the author use her writing talents to create paragraph 8 out of one long sentence? What other examples can you provide of long sentences in the essay? How do they contribute to the overall style of the writing?
5. What is the overall emotional "tone" of the writer toward her subject— admiring, loving, cautionary? What adjectives does the writer use in describing her mother that provides the reader with clues to the tone?
6. The author quotes her mother directly on several occasions. Can we assume that the author is quoting precisely, given that the essay was written years after the incidents described? Does it matter?
7. The final paragraph not only provides closure to the essay, but transmits a lesson the mother wants her family to learn. How do the style and structure of this paragraph contribute to the ultimate message of the essay? In other words, how does the form help convey the meaning?

WRITING

1. Write a descriptive essay about someone you know, using at least five anecdotes from that person's life, so that by the end of the essay, we have a mental picture of your subject's personality, values, and attitudes.
2. Argue for or against the proposition that an effective parent should have— at least—a touch of unconventionality.
3. Describe an incident in your life when the unexpected taught you an important lesson.

Family Values

Richard Rodriguez

Richard Rodriguez (b. 1944) received degrees from Stanford University and Columbia University. He also did graduate study at the University of California, Berkeley, and at the Warburg Institute, London. He is a writer and editor for Pacifica News Service *and a contributing editor and writer for many major American magazines and journals including* Harper's *and the* Los Angeles Times. *His books include* Hunger of Memory: The Education of Richard Rodriguez (1982) *and* Days of Obligation: An Argument with My Mexican Father (1992). *Both books have been profoundly influential in the public discussion on race, bilingualism, affirmative action, and biculturalism. He has also made many appearances as a commentator on the* News Hour with Jim Lehrer. *In the following essay, originally published in the Sunday "Opinion" section of the* Los Angeles Times *in 1992, he addresses the concept of "family values" and focuses on the controversial thesis that homosexuality—rather than being a threat to family values—is actually a buttress against their dissolution.*

I am sitting alone in my car, in front of my parents' house—a middle-aged man 1 with a boy's secret to tell. What words will I use to tell them? I hate the word *gay*, find its little affirming sparkle more pathetic than assertive. I am happier with the less polite *queer*. But to my parents I would say *homosexual*, avoiding the Mexican slang *joto* (I had always heard it said in our house with hints of condescension), though *joto* is less mocking than the sissy-boy *maricon*.

The buzz on everyone's lips now: Family values. The other night on TV, the 2 vice president of the United States, his arm around his wife, smiled into the camera and described homosexuality as "mostly a choice." But how would he know? Homosexuality never felt like a choice to me.

A few minutes ago Rush Limbaugh, the radio guy with a voice that reminds 3 me, for some reason, of a butcher's arms, was banging his console and booming a near-reasonable polemic about family values. Limbaugh was not very clear about which values exactly he considers to be family values. A divorced man who lives alone in New York?

My parents live on a gray, treeless street in San Francisco not far from the 4 ocean. Probably more than half of the neighborhood is immigrant. India lives next door to Greece, who lives next door to Russia. I wonder what the Chinese lady next door to my parents makes of the politicians' phrase *family values*.

What immigrants know, what my parents certainly know, is that when you 5 come to this country, you risk losing your children. The assurance of family—continuity, inevitability—is precisely what America encourages its children to overturn. *Become your own man.* We who are native to this country know this too, of course, though we are likely to deny it. Only a society so guilty about its betrayal of family would tolerate the pieties of politicians regarding family values.

On the same summer day that Republicans were swarming in Houston 6 (buzzing about family values), a friend of mine who escaped family values awhile back and who now wears earrings resembling intrauterine devices, was complaining to me over coffee about the Chinese. The Chinese will never take over San Francisco, my friend said, because the Chinese do not want to take over San Francisco. The Chinese do not even see San Francisco! All they care about is their damn families. All they care about is double-parking smack in front of the restaurant on Clement Street and pulling granny out of the car—and damn anyone who happens to be in the car behind them or the next or the next.

Politicians would be horrified by such an American opinion, of course. But 7 then, what do politicians, Republicans or Democrats, really know of our family life? Or what are they willing to admit? Even in that area where they could reasonably be expected to have something to say—regarding the relationship of family life to our economic system—the politicians say nothing. Republicans celebrate American economic freedom, but Republicans don't seem to connect that economic freedom to the social breakdown they find appalling. Democrats, on the other hand, if more tolerant of the drift from familial tradition, are suspicious of the very capitalism that creates social freedom.

How you become free in America: Consider the immigrant. He gets a job. 8 Soon he is earning more money than his father ever made (his father's authority is thereby subtly undermined). The immigrant begins living a life his father never knew. The immigrant moves from one job to another, changes houses. His economic choices determine his home address—not the other way around. The immigrant is on his way to becoming his own man.

When I was broke a few years ago and trying to finish a book, I lived with 9 my parents. What a thing to do! A major theme of America is leaving home. We trust the child who forsakes family connections to make it on his own. We call that the making of a man.

Let's talk about this man stuff for a minute. America's ethos is anti-domestic. 10 We may be intrigued by blood that runs through wealth—the Kennedys or the Rockefellers—but they seem European to us. Which is to say, they are movies. They are Corleones. Our real pledge of allegiance: We say in America that nothing about your family—your class, your race, your pedigree—should be as important as what you yourself achieve. We end up in 1992 introducing ourselves by first names.

What authority can Papa have in a country that formed its identity in an act 11 of Oedipal rebellion against a mad British king? Papa is a joke in America, a stock sitcom figure—Archie Bunker or Homer Simpson. But my Mexican father went to work every morning, and he stood in a white smock, making false teeth, oblivious of the shelves of grinning false teeth mocking his devotion.

The nuns in grammar school—my wonderful Irish nuns—used to push 12 Mark Twain on me. I distrusted Huck Finn, he seemed like a gringo kid I would steer clear of in the schoolyard. (He was too confident.) I realize now, of course, that Huck is the closest we have to a national hero. We trust the story of a boy who has no home and is restless for the river. (Huck's Pap is drunk.) Americans are more forgiving of Huck's wildness than of the sweetness of the Chinese boy who walks to school with his mama or grandma. (There is no worse thing in America than to be a mama's boy, nothing better than to be a real boy—all boy—like Huck, who eludes Aunt Sally, and is eager for the world of men.)

There's a bent old woman coming up the street. She glances nervously as 13 she passes my car. What would you tell us, old lady, of family values in America?

America is an immigrant country, we say. Motherhood—parenthood—is 14 less our point than adoption. If I had to assign gender to America, I would note the consensus of the rest of the world. When America is burned in effigy, a male is burned. Americans themselves speak of Uncle Sam.

Like the Goddess of Liberty, Uncle Sam has no children of his own. He 15 steals children to make men of them, mocks all reticence, all modesty, all memory. Uncle Sam is a hectoring Yankee, a skinflint uncle, gaunt, uncouth, unloved. He is the American Savonarola—hater of moonshine, destroyer of stills, burner of cocaine. Sam has no patience with mamas' boys.

You betray Uncle Sam by favoring private over public life, by seeking to ex- 16 empt yourself, by cheating on your income taxes, by avoiding jury duty, by trying to keep your boy on the farm.

Mothers are traditionally the guardians of the family against America— 17
though even Mom may side with America against queers and deserters, at least
when the Old Man is around. Premature gray hair. Arthritis in her shoulders.
Bowlegged with time, red hands. In their fiercely flowered housedresses, mothers are always smarter than fathers in America. But in reality they are betrayed
by their children who leave. In a thousand ways. They end up alone.

We kind of like the daughter who was a tomboy. Remember her? It was al- 18
ways easier to be a tomboy in America than a sissy. Americans admired Annie
Oakley more than they admired Liberace (who, nevertheless, always remembered his mother). But today we do not admire Annie Oakley when we see
Mom becoming Annie Oakley.

The American household now needs two incomes, everyone says. Meaning: 19
Mom is *forced* to leave home out of economic necessity. But lots of us know lots
of moms who are sick and tired of being mom, or only mom. It's like the nuns
getting fed up, teaching kids for all those years and having those kids grow up
telling stories of how awful Catholic school was! Not every woman in America
wants her life's work to be forgiveness. Today there are moms who don't want
their husbands' names. And the most disturbing possibility: What happens
when Mom doesn't want to be Mom at all? Refuses pregnancy?

Mom is only becoming an American like the rest of us. Certainly, people all 20
over the world are going to describe the influence of feminism on women (all
over the world) as their "Americanization." And rightly so.

Nothing of this, of course, will the politician's wife tell you. The politician's 21
wife is careful to follow her husband's sentimental reassurances that nothing
has changed about America except perhaps for the sinister influence of de-
viants. Like myself.

I contain within myself an anomaly at least as interesting as the Republican 22
Party's version of family values. I am a homosexual Catholic, a communicant in
a tradition that rejects even as it upholds me.

I do not count myself among those Christians who proclaim themselves 23
protectors of family values. They regard me as no less an enemy of the family
than the "radical feminists." But the joke about families that all homosexuals
know is that we are the ones who stick around and make families possible. Call
on us. I can think of 20 or 30 examples. A gay son or daughter is the only one
who is "free" (married brothers and sisters are too busy). And, indeed, because
we have admitted the inadmissible about ourselves (that we are queer)—we are
adepts at imagination—we can even imagine those who refuse to imagine us.
We can imagine Mom's loneliness, for example. If Mom needs to be taken to
church or to the doctor or ferried between Christmas dinners, depend on the
gay son or lesbian daughter.

I won't deny that the so-called gay liberation movement, along with femi- 24
nism, undermined the heterosexual household, if that's what politicians mean
when they say family values. Against churchly reminders that sex was for pro-
creation, the gay bar as much as the birth-control pill taught Americans not to
fear sexual pleasure. In the past two decades—and, not coincidentally, parallel
to the feminist movement—the gay liberation movement moved a generation of
Americans toward the idea of a childless adulthood. If the women's movement

was ultimately more concerned about getting out of the house and into the workplace, the gay movement was in its way more subversive to puritan America because it stressed the importance of play.

Several months ago, the society editor of the morning paper in San Francisco ²⁵ suggested (on a list of "must haves") that every society dame must have at least one gay male friend. A ballet companion. A lunch date. The remark was glib and incorrect enough to beg complaints from homosexual readers, but there was a truth about it as well. Homosexual men have provided women with an alternate model of masculinity. And the truth: The Old Man, God bless him, is a bore. Thus are we seen as preserving marriages? Even Republican marriages?

For myself, homosexuality is a deep brotherhood but does not involve do- ²⁶ mestic life. Which is why, my married sisters will tell you, I can afford the time to be a writer. And why are so many homosexuals such wonderful teachers and priests and favorite aunts, if not because we are freed from the house? On the other hand, I know lots of homosexual couples (male and female) who model their lives on the traditional heterosexual version of domesticity and marriage. Republican politicians mock the notion of a homosexual marriage, but ironically such marriages honor the heterosexual marriage by imitating it.

"The only loving couples I know," a friend of mine recently remarked, "are ²⁷ all gay couples."

This woman was not saying that she does not love her children or that she ²⁸ is planning a divorce. But she was saying something about the sadness of American domestic life: the fact that there is so little joy in family intimacy. Which is perhaps why gossip (public intrusion into the private) has become a national industry. All day long, in forlorn houses, the television lights up a freakish parade of husbands and mothers-in-law and children upon the stage of Sally or Oprah or Phil. They tell on each other. The audience ooohhhs. Then a psychiatrist-shaman appears at the end to dispense prescriptions—the importance of family members granting one another more "space."

The question I desperately need to ask you is whether we Americans have ²⁹ ever truly valued the family. We are famous, or our immigrant ancestors were famous, for the willingness to leave home. And it is ironic that a crusade under the banner of family values has been taken up by those who would otherwise pass themselves off as patriots. For they seem not to understand America, nor do I think they love the freedoms America grants. Do they understand why, in a country that prizes individuality and is suspicious of authority, children are disinclined to submit to their parents? You cannot celebrate American values in the public realm without expecting them to touch our private lives. As Barbara Bush remarked recently, family values are also neighborhood values. It may be harmless enough for Barbara Bush to recall a sweeter America—Midland, Texas, in the 1950s. But the question left begging is why we chose to leave Midland, Texas. Americans like to say that we can't go home again. The truth is that we don't want to go home again, don't want to be known, recognized. Don't want to respond in the same old ways. (And you know you will if you go back there.)

Little 10-year-old girls know that there are reasons for getting away from the ³⁰ family. They learn to keep their secrets—under lock and key—addressed to Dear

Diary. Growing up queer, you learn to keep secrets as well. In no place are those secrets more firmly held than within the family house. You learn to live in closets. I know a Chinese man who arrived in America about 10 years ago. He got a job and made some money. And during that time he came to confront his homosexuality. And then his family arrived. I do not yet know the end of this story.

The genius of America is that it permits children to leave home, it permits 31 us to become different from our parents. But the sadness, the loneliness of America, is clear too.

Listen to the way Americans talk about immigrants. If, on the one hand, 32 there is impatience when today's immigrants do not seem to give up their family, there is also a fascination with this reluctance. In Los Angeles, Hispanics are considered people of family. Hispanic women are hired to be at the center of the American family—to babysit and diaper, to cook and to clean and to ease the dying. Hispanic attachment to family is seen by many Americans, I think, as the reason why Hispanics don't get ahead. But if Asians privately annoy us for being so family oriented, they are also stereotypically celebrated as the new "whiz kids" in school. Don't Asians go to college, after all, to honor their parents?

More important still is the technological and economic ascendancy of Asia, 33 particularly Japan, on the American imagination. Americans are starting to wonder whether perhaps the family values of Asia put the United States at a disadvantage. The old platitude had it that ours is a vibrant, robust society for being a society of individuals. Now we look to Asia and see team effort paying off.

In this time of national homesickness, of nostalgia, for how we imagine 34 America used to be, there are obvious dangers. We are going to start blaming each other for the loss. Since we are inclined, as Americans, to think of ourselves individually, we are disinclined to think of ourselves as creating one another or influencing one another.

But it is not the politician or any political debate about family values that 35 has brought me here on a gray morning to my parents' house. It is some payment I owe to my youth and to my parents' youth. I imagine us sitting in the living room, amid my mother's sentimental doilies and the family photographs, trying to take the measure of the people we have turned out to be in America.

A San Francisco poet, when he was in the hospital and dying, called a priest 36 to his bedside. The old poet wanted to make his peace with Mother Church. He wanted baptism. The priest asked why. "Because the Catholic Church has to accept me," said the poet. "Because I am a sinner."

Isn't willy-nilly inclusiveness the point, the only possible point to be derived 37 from the concept of family? Curiously, both President Bush and Vice President Quayle got in trouble with their constituents recently for expressing a real family value. Both men said that they would try to dissuade a daughter or granddaughter from having an abortion. But, finally, they said they would support her decision, continue to love her, never abandon her.

There are families that do not accept. There are children who are forced to 38 leave home because of abortions or homosexuality. There are family secrets that Papa never hears. Which is to say there are families that never learn the point of families.

But there she is at the window. My mother has seen me and she waves me 39
in. Her face asks: Why am I sitting outside? (Have they, after all, known my secret for years and kept it, out of embarrassment, not knowing what to say?)
Families accept, often by silence. My father opens the door to welcome me in.

COMPREHENSION

1. The title of this essay is "Family Values." What does Rodriguez mean by
   family values? According to the author, do Americans respect family values
   as they claim? Why or why not?
2. According to the author, do immigrants newly arrived to the United States
   possess a traditional allegiance to family values? Explain your answer.
3. In the conclusion, the author reflects—regarding his own homosexuality—
   that "Families accept, often in silence." Is this an aspect of traditional family values? Why or why not?
4. Why does Rodriguez think that gay men and women are often the primary
   upholders of family values within their own families?
5. What is the thesis of the essay? Is it implicit or explicit? Explain.

RHETORIC

1. Although much of this essay is expositional, Rodriguez begins and ends his
   essay with an event, that is, visiting his family to announce his homosexuality. Why has he shaped his essay in this way? What is problematic about
   his own relationship to the "gay" community? Why does Rodriguez feel
   uncomfortable with the term "gay" to denote homosexual?
2. Rodriguez employs considerable irony in his essay. For example, in paragraph 15, he notes that two icons of American democracy, the Statue of Liberty and "Uncle Sam," are childless. Select two other ironic statements the
   author makes in order to point out the contradiction between the "idea" of
   family values in America and the actual state of family values.
3. In paragraph 20, Rodriguez uses the term *Americanization*. What does he
   mean by this term? How is it central to his thesis?
4. Does Rodriguez suggest that much of what is said in public regarding
   "family values" in America is hypocritical? If so, what group or groups
   does he focus on? How does he support his argument?
5. Explain the meaning of the following stylistic flourishes: "the word *gay* . . .
   [is a] little affirming sparkle more pathetic than assertive" (paragraph 1);
   "America's ethos is anti-domestic" (paragraph 10); "Oedipal rebellion"
   (paragraph 11); "American Savonarola" (paragraph 15); "psychiatrist-
   shaman" (paragraph 28); "national homesickness" (paragraph 34); and
   "willy-nilly inclusiveness" (paragraph 37).
6. In paragraph 10, Rodriguez states that the Kennedys and Rockefellers "are
   movies." What does he mean?

7. Describe the emotional tone of this essay, considering that it is written by a man who is openly gay and understands that he is considered suspect and outside the mainstream of the American "value" system. Is it angry, thoughtful, defiant, sympathetic? Select three or four passages that led you to your conclusion regarding tone.

WRITING

1. In an essay of 400 to 500 words, argue for or against the proposition that choosing to follow a tradition of "family values" is entirely the choice of the individual. Be sure to use at least three supporting points to advance your argument.
2. Interview a member of your grandparents' generation; a member of your parents' generation; and a member of your own generation regarding their views on family values. Write an essay summarizing the similarities and differences among the three views.
3. Interview a counselor at your college or university. Ask the counselor to explain the various issues surrounding family conflict he or she comes across in the course of his or her job. Write an essay exploring your interview findings. Be sure to obtain permission from your interviewee and follow appropriate guidelines for protecting his or her anonymity.
4. For a creative writing project, imagine yourself 25 years from today. Write a letter of 350 to 400 words to an old classmate, describing your family life.

Parenting as an Industry

Amitai Etzioni

Amitai Etzioni (b. 1929) is a noted sociologist and social policy advisor and a leader of the Communitarian movement to improve society. He graduated from Hebrew University in Jerusalem and received a PhD in sociology from the University of California at Berkeley. In addition, he has received numerous honorary doctorates. Among his many elected offices is president of the American Sociological Association from 1994 to 1995. He has taught at the University of Cologne, Columbia, George Washington University, and Harvard. He is the author of numerous books, including The Moral Dimension *(1988);* A Responsive Society *(1991);* The Spirit of Community *(1993), from which the following work is excerpted; and* The New Golden Rule: Community and Morality in a Democratic Society *(1997). In this essay he discusses what he perceives to be the woeful state of parenting in America.*

Consider for a moment parenting as an industry. As farming declined, most fa- 1
thers left to work away from home. Over the past twenty years millions of
American mothers have sharply curtailed their work in the "parenting industry" by moving to work outside the home. By 1991 two-thirds (66.7 percent) of
all mothers with children under eighteen were in the labor force and more than
half (55.4 percent) of women with children under the age of three. At the same
time a much smaller number of child care personnel moved into the parenting
industry.[1]

If this were any other business, say, shoemaking, and more than half of the 2
labor force had been lost and replaced with fewer, less-qualified hands and still
we asked the shoemakers to produce the same number of shoes of the same
quality (with basically no changes in technology), we would be considered
crazy. But this is what happened to parenting. As first men and then women left
to work outside the home, they were replaced by some child care services, a relatively small increase in baby-sitters and nannies, and some additional service
by grandparents—leaving parenting woefully shorthanded. The millions of
latchkey children, who are left alone for long stretches of time, are but the most
visible result of the parenting deficit.

Is this the "fault" of the women's movement, feminism, or mothers per se? 3
Obviously not. All women did was demand for themselves what men had long
possessed, working outside the home not only for their own personal satisfaction, but because of what they often perceived as the economic necessity. Whatever the cause, the result is an empty nest. Only it isn't the small fry who grew
up and took off: it is the parents who flew the coop. Those who did not leave altogether increased their investment of time, energy, involvement, and commitment outside the home.

Although parenting is the responsibility of both parents—and may well be 4
discharged most effectively in two-parent families immersed in a community
context of kin and neighbors—*most important is the scope of commitment.* Single
parents may do better than two-career absentee parents. Children require attention, as Robert Beliah and the other authors of *The Good Society* declared. Kids
also require a commitment of time, energy, and, above all, of self.

The prevalent situation is well captured by a public service commercial in 5
which a mother calls her child and reassures him that she has left money for
him next to the phone. "Honey, have some dinner," she mutters as the child
takes the twenty-dollar bill she left behind, rolls it up, and snorts cocaine. One
might add that the father didn't even call.

The fact is that parenting cannot be carried out over the phone, however 6
well meaning and loving the calls may be. It requires physical presence. The notion of "quality time" (not to mention "quality phone calls") is a lame excuse for
parental absence; it presupposes that bonding and education can take place in

---

[1]Two-thirds of mothers with children under eighteen are in the labor force: *Current Population Survey,* Bureau of Labor Statistics, unpublished tabulations, 1991. [This and subsequent notes in the selection are the author's.]

brief time bursts, on the run. *Quality time occurs within quantity time.* As you spend time with one's children—fishing, gardening, camping, or "just" eating a meal—there are unpredictable moments when an opening occurs and education takes hold. As family expert Barbara Dafoe Whitehead puts it: "Maybe there is indeed such a thing as a one-minute manager, but there is no such thing as a one-minute parent."[2]

Is the answer to the parenting deficit building more child care centers? After all, other societies have delegated the upbringing of their children, from black nannies in the antebellum South to Greek slaves in ancient Rome. True enough. But in these historical situations the person who attended to the children was an adjunct to the parents rather than a replacement for them and an accessory reserved mostly for upper-class families with leisure. A caregiver remained with the family throughout the children's formative years and often beyond; she was, to varying degrees, integrated into the family. The caregiver, in turn, reflected, at least in part, the family's values and educational posture. Some children may have been isolated from their parents, but as a rule there was a warm, committed figure dedicated to them, one who bonded and stayed with them. 7

Today most child care centers are woefully understaffed with poorly paid and underqualified personnel. Child care workers are in the lowest tenth of all wage earners (with an average salary of $5.35 per hour in 1988), well below janitors.[3] They frequently receive no health insurance or other benefits, which makes child care an even less attractive job. As Edward Zigler, a professor of child development at Yale, put it: "We pay these people less than we do zoo keepers—and then we expect them to do wonders."[4] The personnel come and go, at a rate of 41 percent per year at an average day care center. 8

Bonding between children and caregivers under these circumstances is very difficult to achieve. Moreover, children suffer a loss every time their surrogate parents leave. It would be far from inaccurate to call the worst of these facilities "kennels for kids." Sure, there are exceptions. There are a few fine, high-quality child care centers, but they are as rare and almost as expensive as the nannies that some truly affluent households can command. These exceptions should not distract us from the basically dismal picture: substandard care and all-too-frequent warehousing of children, with overworked parents trying frantically to make up the deficit in their free time. 9

---

[2]Barbara Dafoe Whitehead says there's no such thing as a one-minute parent: Barbara Whitehead, "The New Politics in Action—Fortifying the Family," presentation at the conference "Left and Right: The Emergence of a New Politics in the 1990s?" sponsored by the Heritage Foundation and the Progressive Foundation, October 30, 1991, Washington, D.C. (see transcript, 25).
[3]Child care workers in the lowest tenth percentile for income: Richard T. Gill, Nathan Glazer, Stephen A. Thernstrom, *Our Changing Population* (Englewood Cliffs, NJ: Prentice-Hall, 1992), 278. Child care workers' average salary: *Who Cares? Child Care and the Quality of Care in America* (Oakland, CA: Child Care Employee Project, 1989), 49.
[4]Zigler says child care workers are treated like zoo keepers: Kenneth Labich, "Can Your Career Hurt Your Kids?" *Fortune*, May 20, 1991, 49.

Government or social supervision of the numerous small institutions   10
and home facilities in which child care takes place to ensure proper sanitation
and care, even to screen out child abusers, is difficult and is often completely
neglected or only nominally carried out. We should not be surprised to encounter
abuses such as the case of the child care home in which fifty-four children were
left in the care of a sixteen-year-old and were found strapped into child car seats
for the entire day.[5]

Certainly many low-income couples and single parents have little or no   11
choice except to use the minimum that such centers provide. All we can offer
here is to urge that before parents put their children in such institutions, they
should check them out as extensively as possible (including surprise visits in
the middle of the day). Moreover, we should all support these parents' quest for
additional support from corporations and government if they cannot themselves spend more on child care.

Particularly effective are cooperative arrangements that require each parent   12
to contribute some time—four hours a week—to serve at his or her child's center. Not only do such arrangements reduce the center's costs, they also allow
parents to see firsthand what actually goes on, ensuring some measure of *built-
in accountability.* It provides for continuity—while staff come and go, parents
stay. (Even if they divorce, they may still participate in their child care center.)
And as parents get to know other parents of children in the same stage of development, they form social bonds, which can be drawn upon to work together
to make these centers more responsive to children's needs.

Above all, age matters. Infants under two years old are particularly vulner-   13
able to separation anxiety. Several bodies of data strongly indicate that infants
who are institutionalized at a young age will not mature into well-adjusted
adults.[6] As Edward Zigler puts it: "We are cannibalizing children. Children are

---

[5]Children strapped into car seats all day: ibid., 49.
[6]Several bodies of data showing that institutionalized children become maladjusted adults: N. Bay-
dar and Jeanne Brooks-Gunn, "Effects of Maternal Employment and Child Care Arrangements on
Preschoolers' Cognitive and Behavioral Outcomes: Evidence from the Children of the National Longitudinal Survey of Youth," *Developmental Psychology* 27 (November 1991): 932–46; J. Belsky and
Michael J. Rovine, "Nonmaternal Care in the First Year of Life and the Security of Infant-Parent
Attachment," *Child Development* 59 (February 1988): 157–67; T. B. Brazelton, "Issues for Working Par-
ents," *American Journal of Orthopsychiatry* 56 (1986): 14–25; J. Belsky and D. Eggebeen, "Early and Ex-
tensive Maternal Employment in Young Children's Socioemotional Development: Children of the
National Longitudinal Survey of Youth," *Journal of Marriage and Family* 53 (November 1991):
1083–1110; B. E. Vaughn, K. E. Deane, and E. Waters, "The Impact of Out-of-Home Care on Child-
Mother Attachment Quality: Another Look at Some Enduring Questions," 1–2, in I. Bretherton and
E. Water, eds., *Growing Points of Attachment Theory and Research Monographs for the Society for Research
in Child Development* 50 (1985): 1–2, serial no. 209.
   Some studies have found that the effects of child care are not different from parental care. For
example, see K. A. Clarke-Stewart and G. G. Fein, "Early Childhood Programs," 917–99, in P. H.
Mussen, ed., *Handbook of Child Psychology,* Vol. 2 (New York: Wiley, 1983). And a few studies show
that child care rather than parental care is more effective for the intellectual development of poor
children. For example, see Jay Belsky, "Two Waves of Day Care Research: Development Effects
and Conditions of Quality," 1–34, in R. C. Ainslie, ed., *The Child and the Day Care Setting: Qualitative
Variations and Development* (New York: Praeger, 1984).

dying in the system, never mind achieving optimum development."[7] A study of third-graders by two University of Texas researchers compared children who returned home after school to their mothers with children who remained in day care centers:

> children who stayed at the day care centers after school were having problems. They received more negative peer nominations, and their negative nominations outweighed their positive nominations. In addition, the day care third-graders made lower academic grades on their report card and scored lower on standardized tests. There was some evidence of poor conduct grades.[8]

Unless the parents are absent or abusive, infants are better off at home. Older children, between two and four, may be able to handle some measure of institutionalization in child care centers, but their personalities often seem too unformed to be able to cope well with a nine-to-five separation from a parent. 14

As a person who grew up in Israel, I am sometimes asked whether it is true that kibbutzim succeed in bringing up toddlers in child care centers. I need to note first that unlike the personnel in most American child care centers, the people who care for children in kibbutzim are some of the most dedicated members of the work force because these communities consider child care to be a very high priority. As a result, child care positions are highly sought after and there is little turnover, which allows for essential bonding to take place. In addition, both parents are intimately involved in bringing up their children, and they frequently visit the child care centers, which are placed very close to where they live and work. Even so, Israeli kibbutzim are rapidly dismantling their collective child care centers and returning children to live with their families—because both the families and the community established that even a limited disassociation of children from their parents at a tender age is unacceptable. 15

There is no sense looking back and beating our breasts over how we got ourselves into the present situation. But we must acknowledge that as a matter of social policy (as distinct from some individual situations) we have made a mistake in assuming that strangers can be entrusted with the effective personality formation of infants and toddlers. Over the last twenty-five years we have seen the future, and it is not a wholesome one. With poor and ineffective community child care, and with ever more harried parents, it will not suffice to tell their graduates to "just say no" and expect them to resist all temptations, to forgo illegal drugs and alcohol, and to postpone sexual activity. If we fervently wish them to grow up in a civilized society, and if we seek to live in one, let's face facts: it will not happen unless we dedicate more of ourselves to our children and their care and education. . . . 16

[7]Zigler says we are cannibalizing children: Kenneth Labich, "Can Your Career Hurt Your Kids?" *Fortune*, May 20, 1991, 38.
[8]University of Texas study: Deborah Lowe Vandell and Mary Anne Corasaniti, "The Relationship between Third-Graders' After-School Care and Social, Academic, and Emotional Functioning," *Child Development* 59 (August 1988): 874.

Nobody likes to admit it, but between 1960 and 1990 American society   17
allowed children to be devalued, while the golden call of "making it" was put on
a high pedestal. Recently, college freshmen listed "being well off financially" as
more important than "raising a family." (In 1990 the figures were 74 percent versus
70 percent, respectively, and in 1991 they were 74 percent versus 68 percent.)[9] . . .

Some blame this development on the women's rights movement, others on   18
the elevation of materialism and greed to new historical heights. These and
other factors may have all combined to devalue children. However, women are
obviously entitled to all the same rights men are, including the pursuit of greed.

But few people who advocated equal rights for women favored a society in   19
which sexual equality would mean a society in which all adults would act like
men, who in the past were relatively inattentive to children. The new gender-
equalized world was supposed to be a combination of all that was sound and
ennobling in the traditional roles of women and men. Women were to be free to
work any place they wanted, and men would be free to show emotion, care, and
domestic commitment. For children this was not supposed to mean, as it too often has, that they would be bereft of dedicated parenting. Now that we have
seen the result of decades of widespread neglect of children, the time has come
for both parents to revalue children and for the community to support and recognize their efforts. . . .

We return then to the value we as a community put on having and bringing   20
up children. In a society that places more value on Armani suits, winter skiing,
and summer houses than on education, parents are under pressure to earn more,
whatever their income. They feel that it is important to work over-time and to
dedicate themselves to enhancing their incomes and advancing their careers. We
must recognize now, after two decades of celebrating greed and in the face of a
generation of neglected children, the importance of educating one's children.

COMPREHENSION

1. Does Etzioni consider parenting a true industry, or is he using the term as a
   metaphor? Explain.
2. What does the author mean by "quality time occurs within quantity time"?
3. What sort of community does Etzioni suggest America has become? Does
   he state this explicitly or suggest it through examples? Explain.

RHETORIC

1. Etzioni states that if we applied the same criteria to any other business as
   we do to child care, we would be "considered crazy" and calls child care
   centers "kennels for kids." Why does he judge the current child care situation so severely?

---

[9]Poll on college freshmen's views on being well off, raising a family: American Enterprise Institute,
1990.

2. What purpose do the citations to studies and surveys serve in advancing Etzioni's argument? Do they contribute significantly to advancing his thesis? Why or why not?

3. What audience does the author seem to be addressing? What is the implied educational level of the readership to which the essay is geared?

4. Is the author's concluding paragraph based on fact or opinion? Is his depiction of American society a caricature, or is it based on reality? Or is it both?

5. The author addresses the plight of poorer parents in paragraphs 11 and 12. How does his tone regarding their dilemma differ from the one he uses when he criticizes more affluent members of society?

6. The author has chosen to address all aspects of the "parenting industry" in a relatively short essay. Does the author sacrifice depth of understanding for breadth of inclusiveness, or does he do a good job of presenting all major facets of the problem? Explain your view.

7. In paragraph 15, Etzioni veers somewhat from his objective analysis by citing personal experience. Does this added dimension aid his argument? Why or why not?

WRITING

1. Argue for or against the proposition that by not including a comprehensive child care plan, the author is not contributing to solving the crisis he addresses.

2. Write a 250- to 300-word summary of the essay. Follow the suggestions for summary writing discussed in Chapter 1.

3. Enlist three child care workers and have them read the article. Ask them to respond to Etizioni's complaints; then write a response essay, using their views as its focus.

4. Research the child care policy of the United States and that of another modern technological country. Compare and contrast the two.

Immigrants and Family Values

Francis Fukuyama

Francis Fukuyama (b. 1952) received his BA in classics from Cornell University in 1974 and his PhD in Soviet foreign policy from Harvard University in 1981. He was resident consultant at the RAND Corporation, a research organization, and deputy director for the State Department's policy planning staff before becoming the Omar L. and Nancy Hirst Professor of Public Policy at the Institute of Public Policy at George Mason University in 1996. He has written numerous articles and reports about social

and foreign policy and has authored three books: The End of History and the Last
Man *(1992);* Trust: The Social Virtues and the Creation of Prosperity *(1995); and*
The End of Order *(1997). In the following essay, first published in the May 1993 issue
of* Commentary, *Fukuyama attempts to set the record straight regarding the influence
of recent immigrants to the United States. He demonstrates through statistics and
analysis that many of our assumptions about immigration and demographic are faulty
and uninformed.*

I

At the Republican convention in Houston last August, Patrick J. Buchanan   1
announced the coming of a block-by-block war to "take back our culture."
Buchanan is right that a cultural war is upon us, and that this fight will be a central American preoccupation now that the Cold War is over. What he understands less well, however, is that the vast majority of the non-European
immigrants who have come into this country in the past couple of decades are
not the enemy. Indeed, many of them are potentially on his side.

Conservatives have for long been sharply divided on the question of immi-   2
gration. Many employers and proponents of free-market economics, like Julian
Simon or the editorial page of *The Wall Street Journal,* are strongly pro-immigration; they argue for open borders because immigrants are a source of cheap labor and ultimately create more wealth than they consume. Buchanan and other
traditional right-wing Republicans, by contrast, represent an older nativist position. They dispute the economic benefits of immigration, but more importantly look upon immigrants as bearers of foreign and less desirable cultural
values. It is this group of conservatives who forced the inclusion of a plank in
the Republican platform last August calling for the creation of "structures" to
maintain the integrity of America's southern border.

Indeed, hostility to immigration has made for peculiar bedfellows. The Clin-   3
ton administration's difficulties in finding an attorney general who had not at
some point hired an illegal-immigrant baby-sitter is testimony to the objective
dependence of liberal Yuppies on immigration to maintain their lifestyles, and
they by and large would support *The Wall Street Journal's* open-borders position.

On the other hand, several parts of the liberal coalition—blacks and envi-   4
ronmentalists—have been increasingly vocal in recent years in opposition to
further immigration, particularly from Latin America. The Black Leadership
Forum, headed by Coretta Scott King and Congressman Walter Fauntroy, has
lobbied to maintain sanctions against employers hiring illegal immigrant labor
on the ground that this takes away jobs from blacks and "legal" browns. Jack
Miles, a former *Los Angeles Times* book-review editor with impeccable liberal
credentials, has in a recent article in the *Atlantic* lined up with the Federation for
American Immigration Reform (FAIR) in calling for a rethinking of open borders, while liberal activist groups like the Southern California Interfaith Task
Force on Central America have supported Senator Orrin Hatch's legislation

strengthening employer sanctions. Environmental groups like the Sierra Club, for their part, oppose immigration because it necessitates economic growth, use of natural resources, and therefore environmental degradation.

But if much of the liberal opposition to immigration has focused on eco- 5 nomic issues, the conservative opposition has concentrated on the deeper cultural question; and here the arguments made by the right are very confused. The symptoms of cultural decay are all around us, but the last people in the world we should be blaming are recent immigrants.

II

The most articulate and reasoned recent conservative attack on immigration 6 came last summer in an article in *National Review* by Peter Brimelow. Brimelow, a senior editor at *Forbes* and himself a naturalized American of British and Canadian background, argues that immigration worked in the past in America only because earlier waves of nativist backlash succeeded in limiting it to a level that could be successfully assimilated into the dominant Anglo-Saxon American culture. Brimelow criticizes pro-immigration free-marketeers like Julian Simon for ignoring the issue of the skill levels of the immigrant labor force, and their likely impact on blacks and others at the bottom end of the economic ladder. But his basic complaint is a cultural one. Attacking *The Wall Street Journal*'s Paul Gigot for remarking that a million Zulus would probably work harder than a million Englishmen today, Brimelow notes:

> This comment reveals an utter innocence about the reality of ethnic and cultural differences, let alone little things like tradition and history—in short, the greater part of the conservative vision. Even in its own purblind terms, it is totally false. All the empirical evidence is that immigrants from developed countries assimilate better than those from underdeveloped countries. It is developed countries that teach the skills required for success in the United States. . . . It should not be necessary to explain that the legacy of [the Zulu kings] Shaka and Cetewayo—overthrown just over a century ago—is not that of Alfred the Great, let alone Elizabeth II or any civilized society.

Elsewhere, Brimelow suggests that culture is a key determinant of eco- 7 nomic performance, and that people from certain cultures are therefore likely to do less well economically than others. He implies, furthermore, that some immigrants are more prone to random street crime because of their "impulsiveness and present-orientation," while others are responsible for organized crime which is, by his account, ethnically based. Finally, Brimelow argues that the arrival of diverse non-European cultures fosters the present atmosphere of multiculturalism, and is, to boot, bad for the electoral prospects of the Republican party.

A similar line of thought runs through Buchanan's writings and speeches, 8 and leads to a similar anti-immigrant posture. Buchanan has explicitly attacked the notion that democracy represents a particularly positive form of government, and hence would deny that belief in universal democratic principles ought to be at the core of the American national identity.[1] But if one subtracts democracy from American nationality, what is left? Apparently, though Buchanan is somewhat less explicit on this point, a concept of America as a Christian, ethnically European nation with certain core cultural values that are threatened by those coming from other cultures and civilizations.

There is an easy, Civics 101–type answer to the Brimelow-Buchanan argu-   9
ment. In contrast to other West European democracies, or Japan, the American national identity has never been directly linked to ethnicity or religion. Nationality has been based instead on universal concepts like freedom and equality that are in theory open to all people. Our Constitution forbids the establishment of religion, and the legal system has traditionally held ethnicity at arm's length. To be an American has meant to be committed to a certain set of ideas, and not to be descended from an original tribe of Ur-Americans. Those elements of a common American culture visible today—belief in the Constitution and the individualist-egalitarian principles underlying it, plus modern American pop and consumer culture—are universally accessible and appealing, making the United States, in Ben Wattenberg's phrase, the first "universal nation."

This argument is correct as far as it goes, but there is a serious counterargu-   10
ment that reaches to the core of last year's debate over "family values." It runs as follows:

America began living up to its universalist principles only in the last half of   11
this century. For most of the period from its revolutionary founding to its rise as a great, modern, industrial power, the nation's elites conceived of the country not just as a democracy based on universal principles, but also as a Christian, Anglo-Saxon nation.

American democracy—the counterargument continues—is, of course, em-   12
bodied in the laws and institutions of the country, and will be imbibed by anyone who learns to play by its rules. But virtually every serious theorist of American democracy has noted that its success depended heavily on the presence of certain predemocratic values or cultural characteristics that were neither officially sanctioned nor embodied in law. If the Declaration of Independence and the Constitution were the basis of America's *gesellschaft* (society), Christian Anglo-Saxon culture constituted its *gemeinschaft* (community).

Indeed—the counterargument goes on—the civic institutions that Toc-   13
queville observed in the 1830s, whose strength and vitality he saw as a critical manifestation of the Americans' "art of association," were more often than not of a religious (i.e., Christian) nature, devoted to temperance, moral education of the young, or the abolition of slavery. There is nothing in the Constitution which states that parents should make large sacrifices for their children, that workers

---

[1]See, for example, his article "America First—and Second, and Third," the *National Interest*, Spring 1990.

should rise early in the morning and labor long hours in order to get ahead, that people should emulate rather than undermine their neighbors' success, that they should be innovative, entrepreneurial, or open to technological change. Yet Americans, formed by a Christian culture, possessed these traits in abundance for much of their history, and the country's economic prosperity and social cohesion arguably rested on them.

It is this sort of consideration that underlay the family-values controversy 14 during last year's election. Basic to this line of thought is that, all other things being equal, children are better off when raised in stable, two-parent, heterosexual families. Such family structures and the web of moral obligations they entail are the foundation of educational achievement, economic success, good citizenship, personal character, and a host of other social virtues.

The issue of family values was badly mishandled by the Republicans and 15 deliberately misconstrued by the press and the Democrats (often not distinguishable), such that mere mention of the phrase provoked derisive charges of narrow-minded gay-bashing and hostility to single mothers. Yet while many Americans did not sign on to last year's family-values theme, few would deny that the family and community are in deep crisis today. The breakdown of the black family in inner-city neighborhoods around America in the past couple of generations shows in particularly stark form the societal consequences of a loss of certain cultural values. And what has happened among blacks is only an extreme extension of a process that has been proceeding apace among whites as well.

The issue, then, is not whether the questions of culture and cultural values 16 are important, or whether it is legitimate to raise them, but whether immigration really threatens those values. For while the values one might deem central either to economic success or to social cohesion may have arisen out of a Christian, Anglo-Saxon culture, it is clear that they are not bound to that particular social group: some groups, like Jews and Asians, might come to possess those values in abundance, while Wasps themselves might lose them and decay. The question thus becomes: which ethnic groups in today's America are threatening, and which groups are promoting, these core cultural values?

III

The notion that non-European immigrants are a threat to family values and 17 other core American cultural characteristics is, in a way, quite puzzling. After all, the breakdown of traditional family structures, from extended to nuclear, has long been understood to be a disease of advanced industrial countries and not of nations just emerging from their agricultural pasts.

Some conservatives tend to see the Third World as a vast, global underclass, 18 teeming with the same social pathologies as Compton in Los Angeles or Bedford-Stuyvesant in Brooklyn. But the sad fact is that the decay of basic social relationships evident in American inner cities, stretching to the most intimate moral bonds linking parents and children, may well be something with few precedents in human history. Economic conditions in most Third World countries simply would not permit a social group suffering so total a collapse of family structure to survive: with absent fathers and no source of income, or mothers addicted to drugs, children would not live to adulthood.

But it would also seem a priori likely that Third World immigrants should 19 have stronger family values than white, middle-class, suburban Americans, while their work ethic and willingness to defer to traditional sources of authority should be greater as well. Few of the factors that have led to family breakdown in the American middle class over the past couple of generations—rapidly changing economic conditions, with their attendant social disruptions; the rise of feminism and the refusal of women to play traditional social roles; or the legitimization of alternative lifestyles and consequent proliferation of rights and entitlements on a retail level—apply in Third World situations. Immigrants coming from traditional developing societies are likely to be poorer, less educated, and in possession of fewer skills than those from Europe, but they are also likely to have stronger family structures and moral inhibitions. Moreover, despite the greater ease of moving to America today than in the last century, immigrants are likely to be a self-selecting group with a much greater than average degree of energy, ambition, toughness, and adaptability.

These intuitions are largely borne out by the available empirical data, par- 20 ticularly if one disaggregates the different parts of the immigrant community.

The strength of traditional family values is most evident among immigrants 21 from East and South Asia, where mutually supportive family structures have long been credited as the basis for their economic success. According to Census Bureau statistics, 78 percent of Asian and Pacific Islander households in the United States were family households, as opposed to 70 percent for white Americans. The size of these family households is likely to be larger: 74 percent consist of three or more persons, compared to 57 percent for white families. While Asians are equally likely to be married as whites, they are only half as likely to be divorced.[2] Though dropping off substantially in the second and third generations, concern for elderly parents is high in Chinese, Japanese, and Vietnamese households; for many, the thought of sticking a mother or father out of sight and out of mind in a nursing home continues to be anathema. More importantly, most of the major Asian immigrant groups are intent on rapid assimilation into the American mainstream, and have not been particularly vocal in pressing for particularistic cultural entitlements.

While most white Americans are ready to recognize and celebrate the social 22 strengths of Asians, the real fears of cultural invasion surround Latinos. Despite their fast growth, Asians still constitute less than 3 percent of the U.S. population, while the number of Hispanics increased from 14.6 to over 22 million between 1980 and 1990, or 9 percent of the population. But here as well, the

---

[2]Census Bureau Press Release CB92-89, "Profile of Asians and Pacific Islanders."

evidence suggests that most Latin American immigrants may be a source of strength with regard to family values, and not a liability.

Latinos today constitute an extremely diverse group. It is certainly the case 23 that a segment of the Latino community has experienced many of the same social problems as blacks. This is particularly true of the first large Latino community in the United States: Puerto Ricans who came to the mainland in the early postwar period and settled predominantly in New York and other cities of the Northeast. Forty percent of Puerto Rican families are headed by women, compared to 16 percent for the non-Hispanic population; only 57 percent of Puerto Rican households consist of families, while their rate of out-of-wedlock births is almost double the rate for non-Hispanics. In New York, Puerto Ricans have reexported social pathologies like crack-cocaine use to Puerto Rico over the past generation.

Other Latino groups have also brought social problems with them: the 24 Mariel boat lift from Cuba, during which Castro emptied his country's jails and insane asylums, had a measurable impact on crime in the United States. Many war-hardened immigrants from El Salvador and other unstable Central American countries have contributed to crime in the United States, and Chicano gangs in Los Angeles and other Southwestern cities have achieved their own notoriety beside the black Bloods and Crips. Half of those arrested in the Los Angeles riot last year were Latinos.

Such facts are highly visible and contribute to the impression among white 25 Americans that Latinos as a whole have joined inner-city blacks to form one vast, threatening underclass. But there are very significant differences among Latino groups. Latinos of Cuban and Mexican origin, for example, who together constitute 65 percent of the Hispanic community, have a 50 percent lower rate of female-headed households than do Puerto Ricans—18.9 and 19.6 percent versus 38.9 percent. While the rate of Puerto Rican out-of-wed-lock births approaches that of blacks (53.0 vs. 63.1 percent of live births), the rates for Cuban- and Mexican-origin Latinos are much lower, 16.1 and 28.9 percent, respectively, though they are still above the white rate of 13.9 percent.[3]

When looked at in the aggregate, Latino family structure stands somewhere 26 between that of whites and blacks. For example, the rates of female-headed families with no husband present as a proportion of total families is 13.5 percent for whites, 46.4 percent for blacks, and 24.4 percent for Hispanics. If we adjust these figures for income level, however, Hispanics turn out to be much closer to the white norm.

Poverty is hard on families regardless of race; part of the reason for the 27 higher percentage of Latino female-headed households is simply that there are more poor Latino families. If we compare families below the poverty level, the Hispanic rate of female-headed families is very close to that of whites (45.7 vs. 43.6 percent), while the comparable rate for blacks is much higher than either (78.3 percent). Considering the substantially higher rate of family breakdown

[3]Data taken from Linda Chavez, *Out of the Barrio* (New York: Basic Books, 1991), p. 103.

within the sizable Puerto Rican community, this suggests that the rate of single-parent families for Cuban- and Mexican-origin Latinos is actually lower than that for whites at a comparable income level.

Moreover, Latinos as a group are somewhat more likely to be members of families than either whites or blacks.[4] Another study indicates that Mexican Americans have better family demographics than do whites, with higher birth-weight babies even among low-income mothers due to taboos on smoking, drinking, and drug use during pregnancy. Many Latinos remain devout Catholics, and the rate of church attendance is higher in the Mexican community than for the United States as a whole as well. But even if one does not believe that the United States is a "Christian country," the fact that so many immigrants are from Catholic Latin America should make them far easier to assimilate than, say, Muslims in Europe.

These statistics are broadly in accord with the observations of anyone who has lived in Los Angeles, San Diego, or any other community in the American Southwest. Virtually every early-morning commuter in Los Angeles knows the streetcorners on which Chicano day-laborers gather at 7:00 A.M., looking for work as gardeners, busboys, or on construction sites. Many of them are illegal immigrants with families back in Mexico to whom they send their earnings. While they are poor and unskilled, they have a work ethic and devotion to family comparable to those of the South and East European immigrants who came to the United States at the turn of the century. It is much less common to see African Americans doing this sort of thing.

Those who fear Third World immigration as a threat to Anglo-American cultural values do not seem to have noticed what the real sources of cultural breakdown have been. To some extent, they can be traced to broad socioeconomic factors over which none of us has control: the fluid, socially disruptive nature of capitalism; technological change; economic pressures of the contemporary workplace and urban life; and so on. But the ideological assault on traditional family values—the sexual revolution; feminism and the delegitimization of the male-dominated household; the celebration of alternative lifestyles; attempts ruthlessly to secularize all aspects of American public life; the acceptance of no-fault divorce and the consequent rise of single-parent households—was not the creation of recently arrived Chicano agricultural workers or Haitian boat people, much less of Chinese or Korean immigrants. They originated right in the heart of America's well-established white, Anglo-Saxon community. The "Hollywood elite" that created the now celebrated Murphy Brown, much like the establishment "media elite" that Republicans enjoy attacking, does not represent either the values or the interests of most recent Third-World immigrants.

---

[4]Figures taken from *Poverty in the United States: 1991*, Bureau of the Census, Series P-60, no. 181, pp. 7–9; the percentage of people in families for whites, black, and Hispanics is 84.5, 84.8, and 89.0, respectively (pp. 2–3).

In short, though the old, traditional culture continues to exist in the United   31
States, it is overlaid today with an elite culture that espouses very different values. The real danger is not that these elites will become corrupted by the habits
and practices of Third World immigrants, but rather that the immigrants will
become corrupted by them. And that is in fact what tends to happen.

While the first generation of immigrants to the United States tends to be   32
deferential to established authority and preoccupied with the economic problems of "making it," their children and grandchildren become aware of their
own entitlements and rights, more politicized, and able to exploit the political
system to defend and expand those entitlements. While the first generation is
willing to work quietly at minimum- or subminimum-wage jobs, the second
and third generations have higher expectations as to what their labor is worth.
The extension of welfare and other social benefits to noncitizens through a series of court decisions has had the perverse effect of hastening the spread of
welfare dependency. Part of the reason that Puerto Ricans do less well than
other Latino groups may be that they were never really immigrants at all, but
U.S. citizens, and therefore eligible for social benefits at a very early stage.

As Julian Simon has shown, neither the absolute nor the relative levels of   33
immigration over the past decade have been inordinately high by historical
standards. What is different and very troubling about immigration in the present period is that the ideology that existed at the turn of the century and promoted assimilation into the dominant Anglo-Saxon culture has been replaced
by a multicultural one that legitimates and even promotes continuing cultural
differentness.

The intellectual and social origins of multiculturalism are complex, but one   34
thing is clear: it is both a Western and an American invention. The American
founding was based on certain Enlightenment notions of the universality of human equality and freedom, but such ideas have been under attack within the
Western tradition itself for much of the past two centuries. The second half of
the late Allan Bloom's *The Closing of the American Mind* (the part that most buy-
ers of the book skipped over) chronicles the way in which the relativist ideas of
Nietzsche and Heidegger were transported to American shores at midcentury.
Combined with an easygoing American egalitarianism, they led not just to a belief in the need for cultural tolerance, but to a positive assertion of the equal moral
validity of all cultures. Today the writings of Michel Foucault, a French epigone
of Nietzsche, have become the highbrow source of academic multiculturalism.

France may have produced Foucault, but France has not implemented a   35
multicultural educational curriculum to anything like the degree the United
States has. The origins of multiculturalism here must therefore be traced to the
specific circumstances of American social life. Contrary to the arguments of multiculturalism's promoters, it was not a necessary adjustment to the reality of our
pluralistic society. The New York City public-school system in the year 1910 was
as diverse as it is today, and yet it never occurred to anyone to celebrate and preserve the native cultures of the city's Italians, Greeks, Poles, Jews, or Chinese.

The shift in attitudes toward cultural diversity can be traced to the after- 36
math of the civil rights movement, when it became clear that integration was
not working for blacks. The failure to assimilate was interpreted as an indictment of the old, traditional mainstream Anglo-Saxon culture: "Wasp" took on a
pejorative connotation, and African Americans began to take pride in the sepa-
rateness of their own traditions. Ironically, the experience of African Americans
became the model for subsequent immigrant groups like Latinos who could
have integrated themselves into mainstream society as easily as the Italians or
Poles before them.

It is true that Hispanic organizations now constitute part of the multicul- 37
turalist coalition and have been very vocal in pushing for bilingual/bicultural
education. There is increasing evidence, however, that rank-and-file immigrants
are much more traditionally assimilationist than some of their more vocal leaders. For example, most Chinese and Russian immigrant parents in New York
City deliberately avoid sending their children to the bilingual-education classes
offered to them by the public-school system, believing that a cold plunge into
English will be a much more effective means of learning to function in American
society.

Hispanics generally show more support for bilingual education, but even 38
here a revealing recent study indicates that an overwhelming number of Hispanic parents see bilingualism primarily as a means of learning English, and not
of preserving Hispanic culture.[5] This same study indicates that most Hispanics
identify strongly with the United States, and show a relatively low level of
Spanish maintenance in the home. By contrast, multiculturalism is more
strongly supported by many other groups—blacks, feminists, gays, Native
Americans, etc.—whose ancestors have been in the country from the start.

Brimelow's *National Review* piece suggests that even if immigrants are not 39
responsible for our anti-assimilationist multiculturalism, we need not pour oil
on burning waters by letting in more immigrants from non-Western cultures.
But this argument can be reversed: even if the rate of new immigration fell to
zero tomorrow, and the most recent five million immigrants were sent home,
we would still have an enormous problem in this country with the breakdown
of a core culture and the infatuation of the school system with trendy multiculturalist educational policies.

The real fight, the central fight, then, should not be over keeping newcom- 40
ers out: this will be a waste of time and energy. The real fight ought to be over
the question of assimilation itself: whether we believe that there is enough to
our Western, rational, egalitarian, democratic civilization to force those coming
to the country to absorb its language and rules, or whether we carry respect for
other cultures to the point that Americans no longer have a common voice with
which to speak to one another.

[5]See Rodolfo O. de la Garza, Louis DeSipio, et al., *Latino Voices: Mexican, Puerto Rican, and Cuban Perspectives on American Politics* (Boulder: Westview Press, 1992).

Apart from the humble habits of work and family values, opponents of im- 41
migration ought to consider culture at the high end of the scale. As anyone who
has walked around an elite American university recently would know, immigration from Asia is transforming the nature of American education. For a country that has long prided itself on technological superiority, and whose economic
future rests in large part on a continuing technical edge, a depressingly small
number of white Americans from long-established families choose to go into engineering and science programs in preference to business and, above all, law
school. (This is particularly true of the most dynamic and vocal part of the white
population, upwardly mobile middle-class women.) The one bright spot in an
otherwise uniform horizon of decline in educational test scores has been in
math, where large numbers of new Asian test-takers have bumped up the numbers.[6] In Silicon Valley alone, there are some twelve thousand engineers of Chinese descent, while Chinese account for two out of every five engineering and
science graduates in the University of California system.

Indeed, if one were to opt for "designer immigration" that would open the 42
gates to peoples with the best cultural values, it is not at all clear that certain European countries would end up on top.

In the past decade, England's per-capita GNP has fallen behind Italy's, and 43
threatens to displace Portugal and Greece at the bottom of the European Community heap by the end of the decade. Only a fifth of English young people receive any form of higher education, and despite Margaret Thatcher's best
efforts, little progress has been made over the past generation in breaking down
the stifling social rigidities of the British class system. The English working class
is among the least well-educated, most state- and welfare-dependent, and im-
mobile of any in the developed world. While the British intelligentsia and upper classes continue to intimidate middle-class Americans, they can do so only
on the basis of snobbery and inherited but rapidly dwindling intellectual capital. Paul Gigot may or may not be right that a million Zulus would work harder
than a million English, but a million Taiwanese certainly would, and would
bring with them much stronger family structures and entrepreneurship to boot.

IV

This is not to say that immigration will not be the source of major economic and 44
social problems for the United States in the future. There are at least three areas
of particular concern.

The first has to do with the effects of immigration on income distribution, 45
particularly at the low end of the scale. The growing inequality of American income distribution over the past decade is not, as the Democrats asserted during
the election campaign, the result of Reagan-Bush tax policies or the failure of

---

[6]This same group of Asians appears also to have lowered verbal scores, though this is something
that will presumably be corrected over time.

"trickle-down" economics. Rather, it proceeds from the globalization of the American economy: low-skill labor increasingly has to compete with low-skill labor in Malaysia, Brazil, Mexico, and elsewhere. But it has also had to compete with low-skill immigrant labor coming into the country from the Third World, which explains why Hispanics themselves tend to oppose further Hispanic immigration. The country as a whole may be better off economically as a result of this immigration, but those against whom immigrants directly compete have been hurt, just as they will be hurt by the North American Free Trade Agreement (NAFTA), the General Agreement on Tariffs and Trade (GATT), and other trade-liberalizing measures that are good for the country as a whole. In a city like Los Angeles, Hispanics with their stronger social ties have displaced blacks out of a variety of menial jobs, adding to the woes of an already troubled black community.

The second problem area has to do with the regional concentration of recent 46 Hispanic immigration. As everyone knows, the twenty-five million Hispanics in the United States are not evenly distributed throughout the country, but are concentrated in the Southwest portion of it, where the problems normally accompanying the assimilation of immigrant communities tend to be magnified. The L.A. public-school system is currently in a state of breakdown, as it tries to educate burgeoning numbers of recent immigrants on a recession-starved budget.

The third problem concerns bilingualism and the elite Hispanic groups 47 which promote and exist off of it. As noted earlier, the rank-and-file of the Hispanic community seems reasonably committed to assimilation; the same cannot be said for its leadership. Bilingualism, which initially began as a well-intentioned if misguided bridge toward learning English, has become in the eyes of many of its proponents a means of keeping alive a separate Spanish language and culture. Numerous studies have indicated that students in bilingual programs learn English less well than those without access to them, and that their enrollments are swelled by a large number of Hispanics who can already speak English perfectly well. In cities with large Hispanic populations like New York and Los Angeles, the bilingual bureaucracy has become something of a monster, rigidly tracking students despite the wishes of parents and students. *The New York Times* recently reported the case of a Hispanic-surnamed child, born in the United States and speaking only English, who was forced by New York City officials to enroll in an English as a second language class. Bilingualism is but one symptom of a much broader crisis in American public education, and admittedly makes the problems of assimilation much greater.

These problems can be tackled with specific changes in public policy. But 48 the central issue raised by the immigration question is indeed a cultural one, and as such less susceptible of policy manipulation. The problem here is not the foreign culture that immigrants bring with them from the Third World, but the contemporary elite culture of Americans—Americans like Kevin Costner, who believes that America began going downhill when the white man set foot here, or another American, Ice T, whose family has probably been in the country longer than Costner's and who believes that women are bitches and that the chief enemy of his generation is the police. In the upcoming block-by-block cultural war, the enemy will not speak Spanish or have a brown skin. In Pogo's words, "He is us."

COMPREHENSION

1. What does the author mean in paragraph 1 by a "cultural war"?
2. Fukuyama focuses quite a bit of attention on the differing views of the liberal versus conservative perspective regarding immigration. What are some of the differences between the two? What are some of their similarities?
3. How do the tenets of American democracy make America different from other nations regarding the emphasis it places on ethnicity?
4. In paragraph 42, what does the author mean by "designer immigration"?
5. What is the thesis of the essay?

RHETORIC

1. The author begins his essay with the description of an event. What rhetorical purpose does this serve?
2. The author has divided his essay into four sections. Why? Summarize the topic of each section.
3. The author cites numerous studies and quotes a variety of politicians and editorialists. Does this enhance Fukuyama's authority on the subject? Could he have made the same argument without referring to them?
4. Who is the implied audience for this essay? What does the author assume about the knowledge base and educational background of this audience?
5. Study the author's use of conjunctions as a means of connecting paragraphs, for example, "On the other hand" in paragraph 4, "But" in paragraph 5, "Elsewhere" in paragraph 7, and any others you encounter. How do these words help to lend coherence and structure to the essay?
6. The author quotes directly a rather lengthy passage by Brimelow. Using the criteria for selecting quotations for inclusion into one's own writing as discussed in Chapter 1, explain why Fukuyama has inserted this quote in his essay.
7. Compare the rhetorical methods of Fukuyama with those of the individuals he cites or quotes. How do they differ?

WRITING

1. Select one of the new immigrant groups the author mentions in his essay. Research the group's family life, demographics, and value system. Write a report examining these factors.
2. Write an analysis of the essay, focusing on the means by which Fukuyama challenges assumptions regarding the effect of immigrants on family and cultural values.

3. Argue for or against the proposition that those who rail against the new immigrants are merely practicing a form of disguised ethnic prejudice.
4. Write an essay in which you show three specific examples from mainstream American popular culture that challenge traditional family values. Be sure to explain each value and how it is being challenged.

The Female Body

Margaret Atwood

Margaret Atwood (b. 1939) is a Canadian poet, novelist, short story writer, and critic whose work explores the role of personal consciousness in a troubled world. Her second collection of poems, The Circle Game *(1966), brought her recognition; she is also well known for her novels, including* Surfacing *(1973),* Life before Man *(1979),* The Handmaid's Tale *(1986),* Cat's Eye *(1988),* Alias Grace *(1996), and* The Blind Assassin *(2000). Atwood is interested in the complexities of language, and her subjects are wide-ranging, from the personal to the global. In the following essay from* Good Bones *(1992), Atwood uses a lively, unconventional style to address a serious theme.*

> *. . . entirely devoted to the subject of "The Female Body." Knowing how well you have written on this topic . . . this capacious topic . . .*
> —Letter from the *Michigan Quarterly Review*

1.   I agree, it's a hot topic. But only one? Look around, there's a wide range. Take my own, for instance.
I get up in the morning. My topic feels like hell. I sprinkle it with water, brush parts of it, rub it with towels, powder it, add lubricant. I dump in the fuel and away goes my topic, my topical topic, my controversial topic, my capacious topic, my limping topic, my nearsighted topic, my topic with back problems, my badly behaved topic, my vulgar topic, my outrageous topic, my aging topic, my topic that is out of the question and anyway still can't spell, in its oversized coat and worn winter boots, scuttling along the sidewalk as if it were flesh and blood, hunting for what's out there, an avocado, an alderman, an adjective, hungry as ever.

2.   The basic Female Body comes with the following accessories: garter belt, panti-girdle, crinoline, camisole, bustle, brassiere, stomacher, chemise, virgin zone, spike heels, nose ring, veil, kid gloves, fishnet stockings, fichu, bandeau, Merry Widow, weepers, chokers, barrettes, bangles, beads, lorgnette, feather boa, basic black, compact, Lycra stretch one-piece with modesty panel, designer peignoir, flannel nightie, lace teddy, bed, head.
3.   The Female Body is made of transparent plastic and lights up when you plug it in. You press a button to illuminate the different systems. The circulatory

system is red, for the heart and arteries, purple for the veins; the respiratory system is blue; the lymphatic system is yellow; the digestive system is green, with liver and kidneys in aqua. The nerves are done in orange and the brain is pink. The skeleton, as you might expect, is white.

The reproductive system is optional, and can be removed. It comes with or 4 without a miniature embryo. Parental judgment can thereby be exercised. We do not wish to frighten or offend.

4.   He said, I wont have one of those things in the house. It gives a young 5 girl a false notion of beauty, not to mention anatomy. If a real woman was built like that she'd fall on her face.

She said, If we don't let her have one like all the other girls she'll feel sin- 6 gled out. It'll become an issue. She'll long for one and she'll long to turn into one. Repression breeds sublimation. You know that.

He said, It's not just the pointy plastic tits, it's the wardrobes. The 7 wardrobes and that stupid male doll, what's his name, the one with the underwear glued on.

She said, Better to get it over with when she's young. He said, All right, but 8 don't let me see it.

She came whizzing down the stairs, thrown like a dart. She was stark 9 naked. Her hair had been chopped off, her head was turned back to front, she was missing some toes and she'd been tattooed all over her body with purple ink in a scrollwork design. She hit the potted azalea, trembled there for a moment like a botched angel, and fell.

He said, I guess we're safe. 10

5.   The Female Body has many uses. It's been used as a door knocker, a 11 bottle opener, as a clock with a ticking belly, as something to hold up lampshades, as a nutcracker, just squeeze the brass legs together and out comes your nut. It bears torches, lifts victorious wreaths, grows copper wings and raises aloft a ring of neon stars; whole buildings rest on its marble heads.

It sells cars, beer, shaving lotion, cigarettes, hard liquor; it sells diet plans 12 and diamonds, and desire in tiny crystal bottles. Is this the face that launched a thousand products? You bet it is, but don't get any funny big ideas, honey, that smile is a dime a dozen.

It does not merely sell, it is sold. Money flows into this country or that 13 country, flies in, practically crawls in, suitful after suitful, lured by all those hairless pre-teen legs. Listen, you want to reduce the national debt, don't you? Aren't you patriotic? That's the spirit. That's my girl.

She's a natural resource, a renewable one luckily, because those things wear 14 out so quickly. They don't make 'em like they used to. Shoddy goods.

6.   One and one equals another one. Pleasure in the female is not a re- 15 quirement. Pair-bonding is stronger in geese. We're not talking about love, we're talking about biology. That's how we all got here, daughter.

Snails do it differently. They're hermaphrodites, and work in threes. 16

7. Each Female Body contains a female brain. Handy. Makes things work. 17
Stick pins in it and you get amazing results. Old popular songs. Short circuits.
Bad dreams.

Anyway: each of these brains has two halves. They're joined together by a 18
thick cord; neural pathways flow from one to the other, sparkles of electric information washing to and fro. Like light on waves. Like a conversation. How
does a woman know? She listens. She listens in.

The male brain, now, that's a different matter. Only a thin connection. Space 19
over here, time over there, music and arithmetic in their own sealed compart-
ments. The right brain doesn't know what the left brain is doing. Good for aiming though, for hitting the target when you pull the trigger. What's the target?
Who's the target? Who cares? What matters is hitting it. That's the male brain
for you. Objective.

This is why men are so sad, why they feel so cut off, why they think of 20
themselves as orphans cast adrift, footloose and stringless in the deep void.
What void? she asks. What are you talking about? The void of the universe, he
says, and she says Oh and looks out the window and tries to get a handle on it,
but it's no use, there's too much going on, too many rustlings in the leaves, too
many voices, so she says, Would you like a cheese sandwich, a piece of cake, a
cup of tea? And he grinds his teeth because she doesn't understand, and wan-
ders off, not just alone but Alone, lost in the dark, lost in the skull, searching for
the other half, the twin who could complete him.

Then it comes to him: he's lost the Female Body! Look, it shines in the 21
gloom, far ahead, a vision of wholeness, ripeness, like a giant melon, like an apple, like a metaphor for "breast" in a bad sex novel; it shines like a balloon, like
a foggy noon, a watery moon, shimmering in its egg of light.

Catch it. Put it in a pumpkin, in a high tower, in a compound, in a chamber, 22
in a house, in a room. Quick, stick a leash on it, a lock, a chain, some pain, settle
it down, so it can never get away from you again.

COMPREHENSION

1. Why do you think this essay was written? Justify your response.
2. List the different ways in which Atwood views the female body.
3. What distinction does Atwood make between male and female brains?

RHETORIC

1. What is the tone of Atwood's essay? Supply concrete evidence from her
   writing.
2. Does the essay contain a thesis? Is it stated or implied?
3. Define the following words in section 2: *fichu, bandeau, Merry Widow, weepers.* Why do the words *bed* and *head* also appear in this list?
4. How does Atwood's use of details and metaphors strengthen her points in
   the essay? Cite specific examples.

5. What is the object being described in section 4? How does its inclusion help underscore Atwood's point?
6. Why did Atwood choose this particular way to organize her essay? What does it tell the reader about her attitude toward the subject?
7. Is the tone of the final paragraph similar to that of the rest of the essay? Provide evidence from the writing and explain.

WRITING

1. Using a style similar to Atwood's, write a brief essay in which you describe the female brain, the male brain, or the male body.
2. In an argumentative essay, consider the role played by sex-specific toys in reinforcing sexual stereotyping in children. Use Atwood's essay as well as your personal experience as support.
3. Analyze the ways in which sex and the female body have been used in sales and advertising.

Being a Man

Paul Theroux

Paul Theroux (b. 1941) has explored the effects of colonialism on Americans and Europeans—effects that he experienced firsthand as a teacher in Malawi, Uganda, and Singapore—in books such as Saint Jack *(1973) and* The Consul's File *(1977). Theroux's other fictional works include* The Mosquito Coast *(1982),* O-Zone *(1986), and* Chicago Loop *(1990). In addition, he has written a number of travel books, among them* The Great Railway Bazaar *(1975) and* The Odd Patagonian Express *(1979). In the following essay from* Sunrise with Seamonsters *(1985), Theroux explores the meaning of masculinity and its relation to writing.*

There is a pathetic sentence in the chapter "Fetishism" in Dr. Norman 1
Cameron's book *Personality Development and Psychopathology.* It goes, "Fetishists are nearly always men; and their commonest fetish is a woman's shoe." I cannot read that sentence without thinking that it is just one more awful thing about being a man—and perhaps it is an important thing to know about us.

I have always disliked being a man. The whole idea of manhood in Amer- 2
ica is pitiful, in my opinion. This version of masculinity is a little like having to wear an ill-fitting coat for one's entire life (by contrast, I imagine femininity to be an oppressive sense of nakedness). Even the expression "Be a man!" strikes me as insulting and abusive. It means: Be stupid, be unfeeling, obedient, soldierly, and stop thinking. Man means "manly"—how can one think about men

without considering the terrible ambition of manliness? And yet it is part of every man's life. It is a hideous and crippling lie; it not only insists on difference and connives at superiority, it is also by its very nature destructive—emotionally damaging and socially harmful.

The youth who is subverted, as most are, into believing in the masculine ₃ ideal is effectively separated from women and he spends the rest of his life finding women a riddle and a nuisance. Of course, there is a female version of this male affliction. It begins with mothers encouraging little girls to say (to other adults) "Do you like my new dress?" In a sense, little girls are traditionally urged to please adults with a kind of coquettishness, while boys are enjoined to behave like monkeys towards each other. The nine-year-old coquette proceeds to become womanish in a subtle power game in which she learns to be sexually indispensable, socially decorative, and always alert to a man's sense of inadequacy.

Femininity—being ladylike—implies needing a man as witness and seducer; ₄ but masculinity celebrates the exclusive company of men. That is why it is so grotesque; and that is also why there is no manliness without inadequacy— because it denies men the natural friendship of women.

It is very hard to imagine any concept of manliness that does not belittle ₅ women, and it begins very early. At an age when I wanted to meet girls—let's say the treacherous years of thirteen to sixteen—I was told to take up a sport, get more fresh air, join the Boy Scouts, and I was urged not to read so much. It was the 1950s and if you asked too many questions about sex you were sent to camp—boy's camp, of course: the nightmare. Nothing is more unnatural or prisonlike than a boy's camp, but if it were not for them we would have no Elks' Lodges, no pool rooms, no boxing matches, no Marines.

And perhaps no sports as we know them. Everyone is aware of how few in ₆ number are the athletes who behave like gentlemen. Just as high school basketball teaches you how to be a poor loser, the manly attitude towards sports seems to be little more than a recipe for creating bad marriages, social misfits, moral degenerates, sadists, latent rapists, and just plain louts. I regard high school sports as a drug far worse than marijuana, and it is the reason that the average tennis champion, say, is a pathetic oaf.

Any objective study would find the quest for manliness essentially right- ₇ wing, puritanical, cowardly, neurotic, and fueled largely by a fear of women. It is also certainly philistine. There is no book-hater like a Little League coach. But indeed all the creative arts are obnoxious to the manly ideal, because at their best the arts are pursued by uncompetitive and essentially solitary people. It makes it very hard for a creative youngster, for any boy who expresses the desire to be alone seems to be saying that there is something wrong with him.

It ought to be clear by now that I have something of an objection to the ₈ way we turn boys into men. It does not surprise me that when the President of the United States has his customary weekend off he dresses like a cowboy—it is both a measure of his insecurity and his willingness to please. In many ways, American culture does little more for a man than prepare him for modeling clothes in the L. L. Bean catalogue. I take this as a personal insult because for many years I found it impossible to admit to myself that I wanted to be a writer. It was my guilty secret, because being a writer was incompatible with being a man.

There are people who might deny this, but that is because the American 9 writer, typically, has been so at pains to prove his manliness that we have come to see literariness and manliness as mind qualities. But first there was a fear that writing was not a manly profession—indeed, not a profession at all. (The paradox in American letters is that it has always been easier for a woman to write and for a man to be published.) Growing up, I had thought of sports as wasteful and humiliating, and the idea of manliness was a bore. My wanting to become a writer was not a flight from that oppressive role-playing, but I quickly saw that it was at odds with it. Everything in stereotyped manliness goes against the life of the mind. The Hemingway personality is too tedious to go into here, and in any case his exertions are well known, but certainly it was not until this aberrant behavior was examined by feminists in the 1960s that any male writer dared question the pugnacity in Hemingway's fiction. All the bullfighting and arm wrestling and elephant shooting diminished Hemingway as a writer, but it is consistent with a prevailing attitude in American writing: one cannot be a male writer without first proving that one is a man.

It is normal in America for a man to be dismissive or even somewhat apolo- 10 getic about being a writer. Various factors make it easier. There is a heartiness about journalism that makes it acceptable—journalism is the manliest form of American writing and, therefore, the profession the most independent-minded women seek (yes, it is an illusion, but that is my point). Fiction-writing is equated with a kind of dispirited failure and is only manly when it produces wealth—money is masculinity. So is drinking. Being a drunkard is another assertion, if misplaced, of manliness. The American male writer is traditionally proud of his heavy drinking. But we are also a very literal-minded people. A man proves his manhood in America in old-fashioned ways. He kills lions, like Hemingway; or he hunts ducks, like Nathaniel West, or he makes pronouncements like, "A man should carry enough knife to defend himself with," as James Jones once said to a *Life* interviewer. Or he says he can drink you under the table. But even tiny drunken William Faulkner loved to mount a horse and go fox hunting, and Jack Kerouac roistered up and down Manhattan in a lumberjack shirt (and spent every night of *The Subterraneans* with his mother in Queens). And we are familiar with the lengths to which Norman Mailer is prepared, in his endearing way, to prove that he is just as much a monster as the next man.

When the novelist John Irving was revealed as a wrestler, people took him 11 to be a very serious writer, and even a bubble reputation like Eric *(Love Story)* Segal's was enhanced by the news that he ran the marathon in a respectable time. How surprised we would be if Joyce Carol Oates were revealed as a sumo wrestler or Joan Didion active in pumping iron. "Lives in New York City with her three children" is the typical woman writer's biographical note, for just as the male writer must prove he has achieved a sort of muscular manhood, the woman writer—or rather her publicist—must prove her motherhood.

There would be no point in saying any of this if it were not generally accepted 12
that to be a man is somehow—even now in feminist-influenced America—a
privilege. It is on the contrary an unmerciful and punishing burden. Being a
man is bad enough; being manly is appalling (in this sense, women's lib has
done much more for men than for women). It is the sinister silliness of men's
fashions and a clubby attitude in the arts. It is the subversion of good students.
It is the so-called Dress Code of the Ritz-Carlton Hotel in Boston, and it is the
institutionalized cheating in college sports. It is the most primitive insecurity.

And this is also why men often object to feminism, but are afraid to explain 13
why: of course women have a justified grievance, but most men believe—and
with reason—that their lives are just as bad.

COMPREHENSION

1. What does Theroux hate about being a man?
2. What does the writer mean by "the terrible ambition of manliness"?
3. According to Theroux, why are writing and manliness at odds?

RHETORIC

1. What is Theroux's thesis? Where is it stated?
2. Explain Theroux's choice for an introductory paragraph. How does it help
   set up the reader for what follows? What was the writer's intention?
3. Does the writer's example in paragraph 5 help validate the paragraph's
   topic sentence? Why or why not?
4. Explain the reference to the L. L. Bean catalogue in paragraph 8. What connection is Theroux making between it and the American concept of masculinity?
5. Trace the sequence of ideas through the paragraphs in the essay. Do they
   follow a coherent pattern? How does the conclusion help unify the ideas
   presented?
6. What argumentative strategies does Theroux employ in this essay?

WRITING

1. Write a definition essay on *manliness,* considering both the denotative and
   the connotative meanings of the word. Use support from Theroux's work.
   Theroux states that being a man is "an unmerciful and punishing burden."
   Write an argumentative essay in which you agree or disagree with this
   assessment.
2. Write an essay in which you pretend to be a member of the opposite sex for
   a day. Describe how your conditions, behaviors, and perceptions might be
   different. Consider how others would respond to you.

Why Men Don't Last: Self-Destruction as a Way of Life

Natalie Angier

Natalie Angier (b. 1958) grew up in New York City and graduated from Barnard College in 1978. She has worked as a magazine staff writer for Discover *and* Time *and became a reporter for* The New York Times *in 1990. Her work as a* Times *science correspondent led to a Pulitzer Prize in 1991. She is also a recipient of the Lewis Thomas Award and was one of only seven journalists to receive four stars in the* Forbes Media Guide *that rated 500 reporters. She has also published in the* Atlantic, Parade, Washington Monthly, *and* Reader's Digest. *Her books in include* The Beauty of the Beastly: New Views on the Nature of Life *(1995) and* Women: An Intimate Geography *(1999). In the following essay, first published in* The New York Times *(in 1999), Angier examines the biological, social, and psychological differences between men and women in order to explain the reason why there is a marked difference in life expectancy between the genders.*

My father had great habits. Long before ficus trees met weight machines, he 1 was a dogged exerciser. He did pushups and isometrics. He climbed rocks. He went for long, vigorous walks. He ate sparingly and avoided sweets and grease. He took such good care of his teeth that they looked fake.

My father had terrible habits. He was chronically angry. He threw things 2 around the house and broke them. He didn't drink often, but when he did, he turned more violent than usual. He didn't go to doctors, even when we begged him to. He let a big, ugly mole on his back grow bigger and bigger, and so he died of malignant melanoma, a curable cancer, at 51.

My father was a real man—so good and so bad. He was also Everyman.   3

Men by some measures take better care of themselves than women do and 4 are in better health. They are less likely to be fat, for example; they exercise more, and suffer from fewer chronic diseases like diabetes, osteoporosis and arthritis.

By standard measures, men have less than half the rate of depression seen 5 in women. When men do feel depressed, they tend to seek distraction in an activity, which, many psychologists say, can be a more effective technique for dispelling the mood than is a depressed woman's tendency to turn inward and ruminate. In the United States and many other industrialized nations, women are about three times more likely than men to express suicidal thoughts or to attempt to kill themselves.

And yet . . . men don't last. They die off in greater numbers than women do 6 at every stage of life, and thus their average life span is seven years shorter.

Women may attempt suicide relatively more often, but in the United States, four times more men than women die from the act each year.

Men are also far more likely than women to die behind the wheel or to kill others as a result of their driving. From 1977 to 1995, three and a half times more male drivers than female drivers were involved in fatal car crashes. Death by homicide also favors men; among those under 30, the male-to-female ratio is 8 to 1. 7

Yes, men can be impressive in their tendency to self-destruct, explosively or gradually. They are at least twice as likely as women to be alcoholics and three times more likely to be drug addicts. They have an eightfold greater chance than women do of ending up in prison. Boys are much more likely than girls to be thrown out of school for a conduct or antisocial personality disorder, or to drop out on their own surly initiative. Men gamble themselves into a devastating economic and emotional pit two to three times more often than women do. 8

"Between boys' suicide rates, dropout rates and homicide rates, and men's self-destructive behaviors generally, we have a real crisis in America," said William S. Pollack, a psychologist at Harvard Medical School and co-director of the Center for Men at McLean Hospital in Belmont, Mass. "Until recently, the crisis has gone unheralded." 9

It is one thing to herald a presumed crisis, though, and to cite a ream of gloomy statistics. It is quite another to understand the crisis, or to figure out where it comes from or what to do about it. As those who study the various forms of men's self-destructive behaviors realize, there is not a single, glib, overarching explanation for the sex-specific patterns they see. 10

A crude evolutionary hypothesis would have it that men are natural risk-takers, given to showy displays of bravado, aggression and daring all for the sake of attracting a harem of mates. By this premise, most of men's self-destructive, violent tendencies are a manifestation of their need to take big chances for the sake of passing their genes into the river of tomorrow. 11

Some of the data on men's bad habits fit the risk-taker model. For example, those who study compulsive gambling have observed that men and women tend to display very different methods and preferences for throwing away big sums of money. 12

"Men get enamored of the action in gambling," said Linda Chamberlain, a psychologist at Regis University in Denver who specializes in treating gambling disorders. "They describe an overwhelming rush of feelings and excitement associated with the process of gambling. They like the feeling of being a player, and taking on a struggle with the house to show that they can overcome the odds and beat the system. They tend to prefer the table games, where they can feel powerful and omnipotent while everybody watches them." 13

Dr. Chamberlain noted that many male gamblers engage in other risk-taking behaviors, like auto racing or hang gliding. By contrast, she said, "Women tend to use gambling more as a sedative, to numb themselves and escape from daily responsibilities, or feelings of depression or alienation. Women tend to prefer the solitary forms of gambling, the slot machines or video poker, where there isn't as much social scrutiny." 14

Yet the risk-taking theory does not account for why men outnumber 15 women in the consumption of licit and illicit anodynes. Alcohol, heroin and marijuana can be at least as numbing and sedating as repetitively pulling the arm of a slot machine. And some studies have found that men use drugs and alcohol for the same reasons that women often overeat: as an attempt to self-medicate when they are feeling anxious or in despair.

"We can speculate all we want, but we really don't know why men drink 16 more than women," said Enoch Gordis, the head of the National Institute on Alcohol Abuse and Alcoholism. Nor does men's comparatively higher rate of suicide appear linked to the risk-taking profile. To the contrary, Paul Duberstein, as assistant professor of psychiatry and oncology at the University of Rochester School of Medicine, has found that people who complete a suicidal act are often low in a personality trait referred to as "openness to experience," tending to be rigid and inflexible in their behaviors. By comparison, those who express suicidal thoughts tend to score relatively high on the openness-to-experience scale.

Given that men commit suicide more often that women, and women talk 17 about it more, his research suggests that, in a sense, women are the greater risk-takers and novelty seekers, while the men are likelier to feel trapped and helpless in the face of changing circumstances.

Silvia Cara Canetto, an associate professor of psychology at Colorado State 18 University in Fort Collins, has extensively studied the role of gender in suicidal behaviors. Dr. Canetto has found that cultural narratives may determine why women attempt suicide more often while men kill themselves more often. She proposes that in Western countries, to talk about suicide or to survive a suicidal act is often considered "feminine," hysterical, irrational, and weak. To actually die by one's own hand may be viewed as "masculine," decisive, strong. Even the language conveys the polarized, weak-strong imagery: a "failed" suicide attempt as opposed to a "successful" one.

"There is indirect evidence that there is negative stigma toward men who 19 survive suicide," Dr. Canetto said. "Men don't want to 'fail,' even though failing in this case means surviving. If the "suicidal script" that identifies completing the acts as "rational, courageous and masculine" can be "undermined and torn to pieces," she said, we might have a new approach to prevention.

Dr. Pollak of the Center for Men also blames many of men's self-destructive 20 ways on the persistent image of the dispassionate, resilient, action-oriented male—the Marlboro Man who never even gasps for breath. For all the talk of the sensitive "new man," he argues, men have yet to catch up with women in expanding their range of acceptable emotions and behaviors. Men in our culture, Dr. Pollack says, are pretty much limited to a menu of three strong feelings: rage, triumph, lust. "Anything else and you risk being seen as a sissy," he said.

In a number of books, most recently, "Real Boys: Rescuing Our Sons from 21 the Myths of Boyhood," he proposes that boys "lose their voice, a whole half of their emotional selves," beginning at age 4 or 5. "Their vulnerable, sad feelings and sense of need are suppressed or shamed out of them," he said—by their peers, parents, the great wide televised fist in their face.

He added: "If you keep hammering it into a kid that he has to look tough 22 and stop being a crybaby and a mama's boy, the boy will start creating a mask of bravado."

That boys and young men continue to feel confused over the proper har- 23 monics of modern masculinity was revealed in a study that Dr. Pollack conducted of 200 eighth-grade boys. Through questionnaires, he determined their scores on two scales, one measuring their "egalitarianism"—the degree to which they think men and women are equal, that men should change a baby's diapers, that mothers should work and the like—and the other gauging their "traditionalism" as determined by their responses to conventional notions, like the premise that men must "stand on their own two feet" and must "always be willing to have sex if someone asks."

On average, the boys scored high on both scales. "They are split on what it 24 means to be a man," said Dr. Pollack.

The cult of masculinity can beckon like a siren song in baritone. Dr. Franklin 25 L. Nelson, a clinical psychologist at the Fairbanks Community Mental Health Center in Alaska, sees many men who get into trouble by adhering to sentimental notions of manhood. "A lot of men come up here hoping to get away from a wimpy world and live like pioneers by old-fashioned masculine principles of individualism, strength and ruggedness," he said. They learn that nothing is simple; even Alaska is part of a wider, interdependent world and they really do need friends, warmth and electricity.

"Right now, it's 35 degrees below zero outside," he said during a January 26 interview. "If you're not prepared, it doesn't take long at that temperature to freeze to death."

COMPREHENSION

1. What does the second sentence in the essay mean? What comment is the author suggesting about modern life by including it?
2. Angier makes a number of comparisons between the lifestyles of men and women. Does the author suggest one overriding principle regarding why "men don't last," or is it really a compilation of many factors? Explain.
3. Does Angier suggest that ideas of "masculinity" are hereditary or environmental or both? Explain by using examples from the text.
4. Angier begins her essay with a personal anecdote about her father. She claims that he was "Everyman." Does he appear to you to have acted like the "typical male"?

RHETORIC

1. Angier often mixes facts with theory. For example, in paragraph 11, she refers to a hypothesis that "men are natural risk-takers," while in other sections, she provides hard data about men's mortality rates. Does this combination make her argument more robust or does it make it less convincing?

2. Describe Angier's tone. Is she sympathetic that men die younger, or does she seem to castigate them? Select three examples from her essay that support your view.

3. Writers will often mention opposing viewpoints to buttress their own arguments. Angier doesn't. Does this strengthen or weaken her main premise? Explain.

4. Angier is noted for her lively prose style. Examine the following phrases and discuss their meaning and why they add "color" to her writing: "the great wide televised fist in their face" (paragraph 21); "the proper harmonics of modern masculinity" (paragraph 23); and "beckon like a siren song in baritone" (paragraph 25).

5. Compare and contrast the introduction and conclusion of the essay. How do they differ in imagery and tone? How does the subject matter of the conclusion help Angier achieve "closure" in her argument?

6. Angier often employs the "vocabulary of masculinity" in her argument. For example, she states, "My father was a real man" (paragraph 3); other masculine terms include "action-oriented" and "Marlboro man" (paragraph 20) and "away from a wimpy world" (paragraph 25). How does the use of this vocabulary contribute to her portrayal of the "masculine image"?

7. In paragraphs 5 through 14, Angier lists a number of statistics and behaviors that she attributes to male self-destructiveness. Is there a rationale behind the order in which she lists them, or does it seem more like a compendium of facts? Regardless of your answer, what is the rhetorical effect?

WRITING

1. Write an essay of 400 to 500 words in the form of a "process analysis" with the title "How Men Can Live Longer." Be sure to provide examples and illustrations to support your report.

2. Write a narrative essay in which you describe an event in which you took or witnessed an unnecessary risk. Reflect on why the risk was taken and what its consequences were—whether positive or negative.

3. For a research paper of 750 to 1,000 words, compare and contrast the "masculine traits" of American males with those of males from a different country or culture. Include at least four secondary sources.

Sex, Lies and Conversation:

Why Is It So Hard for Men and Women to Talk to Each Other?

Deborah Tannen

*Deborah Tannen (b. 1945 in Brooklyn, New York) holds a PhD in linguistics from the
University of California at Berkeley. Tannen published numerous specialized articles
and books on language and linguistics before becoming nationally known as a best-
selling author. She publishes regularly in such magazines as* Vogue *and* New York,
and her book That's Not What I Meant: How Conversational Style Makes or
Breaks Your Relations with Others *(1986) drew national attention to her work on interpersonal communication. Her other popular books on communication include* You
Just Don't Understand: Women and Men in Conversation *(1990),* Talking from
9 to 5: How Women's and Men's Conversational Styles Affect Who Gets Heard,
Who Gets Credit, and What Gets Done at Work *(1994), and* I Only Say This Because I Love You: How the Way We Talk Can Make or Break Family Relationships Throughout Our Lives *(2001). The following essay was published in the*
Washington Post *in 1990.*

I was addressing a small gathering in a suburban Virginia living room—a   1
women's group that had invited men to join them. Throughout the evening, one
man had been particularly talkative, frequently offering ideas and anecdotes,
while his wife sat silently beside him on the couch. Toward the end of the
evening, I commented that women frequently complain that their husbands
don't talk to them. This man quickly concurred. He gestured toward his wife
and said, "She's the talker in our family." The room burst into laughter; the man
looked puzzled and hurt. "It's true," he explained. "When I come home from
work I have nothing to say. If she didn't keep the conversation going, we'd
spend the whole evening in silence."

This episode crystallizes the irony that although American men tend to talk   2
more than women in public situations, they often talk less at home. And this
pattern is wreaking havoc with marriage.

The pattern was observed by political scientist Andrew Hacker in the late   3
'70s. Sociologist Catherine Kohler Riessman reports in her new book *Divorce
Talk* that most of the women she interviewed—but only a few of the men—gave
lack of communication as the reason for their divorces. Given the current divorce rate of nearly 50 percent, that amounts to millions of cases in the United
States every year—a virtual epidemic of failed conversation.

In my own research, complaints from women about their husbands most   4
often focused not on tangible inequities such as having given up the chance for
a career to accompany a husband to his, or doing far more than their share of

daily life-support work like cleaning, cooking, social arrangements and errands. Instead, they focused on communication: "He doesn't listen to me," "He doesn't talk to me." I found, as Hacker observed years before, that most wives want their husbands to be, first and foremost, conversational partners, but few husbands share this expectation of their wives.

In short, the image that best represents the current crisis is the stereotypical 5 cartoon scene of a man sitting at the breakfast table with a newspaper held up in front of his face, while a woman glares at the back of it, wanting to talk.

Linguistic Battle of the Sexes

How can women and men have such different impressions of communication 6 in marriage? Why the widespread imbalance in their interests and expectations?

In the April [1990] issue of *American Psychologist*, Stanford University's 7 Eleanor Maccoby reports the results of her own and others' research showing that children's development is most influenced by the social structure of peer interactions. Boys and girls tend to play with children of their own gender, and their sex-separate groups have different organizational structures and interactive norms.

I believe these systematic differences in childhood socialization make talk 8 between women and men like cross-cultural communication, heir to all the attraction and pitfalls of that enticing but difficult enterprise. My research on men's and women's conversations uncovered patterns similar to those described for children's groups.

For women, as for girls, intimacy is the fabric of relationships, and talk is 9 the thread from which it is woven. Little girls create and maintain friendships by exchanging secrets; similarly, women regard conversation as the cornerstone of friendship. So a woman expects her husband to be a new and improved version of a best friend. What is important is not the individual subjects that are discussed but the sense of closeness, of a life shared, that emerges when people tell their thoughts, feelings, and impressions.

Bonds between boys can be as intense as girls', but they are based less on 10 talking, more on doing things together. Since they don't assume talk is the cement that binds a relationship, men don't know what kind of talk women want, and they don't miss it when it isn't there.

Boys' groups are larger, more inclusive, and more hierarchical, so boys must 11 struggle to avoid the subordinate position in the group. This may play a role in women's complaints that men don't listen to them. Some men really don't like to listen, because being the listener makes them feel one-down, like a child listening to adults or an employee to a boss.

But often when women tell men, "You aren't listening," and the men 12 protest, "I am," the men are right. The impression of not listening results from misalignments in the mechanics of conversation. The misalignment begins as soon as a man and a woman take physical positions. This became clear when I studied videotapes made by psychologist Bruce Dorval of children and adults talking to their same-sex best friends. I found that at every age, the girls and women faced each other directly, their eyes anchored on each other's faces. At every age, the boys and men sat at angles to each other and looked elsewhere in the room, periodically glancing at each other. They were obviously attuned to each other, often mirroring each other's movements. But the tendency of men to face away can give women the impression they aren't listening even when they are. A young woman in college was frustrated: Whenever she told her boyfriend she wanted to talk to him, he would lie down on the floor, close his eyes, and put his arm over his face. This signaled to her, "He's taking a nap." But he insisted he was listening extra hard. Normally, he looks around the room, so he is easily distracted. Lying down and covering his eyes helped him concentrate on what she was saying.

Analogous to the physical alignment that women and men take in conver- 13 sation is their topical alignment. The girls in my study tended to talk at length about one topic, but the boys tended to jump from topic to topic. The second-grade girls exchanged stories about people they knew. The second-grade boys teased, told jokes, noticed things in the room and talked about finding games to play. The sixth-grade girls talked about problems with a mutual friend. The sixth-grade boys talked about 55 different topics, none of which extended over more than a few turns.

Listening to Body Language

Switching topics is another habit that gives women the impression men aren't 14 listening, especially if they switch to a topic about themselves. But the evidence of the 10th-grade boys in my study indicates otherwise. The 10th-grade boys sprawled across their chairs with bodies parallel and eyes straight ahead, rarely looking at each other. They looked as if they were riding in a car, staring out the windshield. But they were talking about their feelings. One boy was upset because a girl had told him he had a drinking problem, and the other was feeling alienated from all his friends.

Now, when a girl told a friend about a problem, the friend responded by 15 asking probing questions and expressing agreement and understanding. But the boys dismissed each other's problems. Todd assured Richard that his drinking was "no big problem" because "sometimes you're funny when you're off your butt." And when Todd said he felt left out, Richard responded, "Why should you? You know more people than me."

Women perceived such responses as belittling and unsupportive. But the 16 boys seemed satisfied with them. Whereas women reassure each other by implying, "You shouldn't feel bad because I've had similar experiences," men do so by implying, "You shouldn't feel bad because your problems aren't so bad."

There are even simpler reasons for women's impression that men don't lis- 17 ten. Linguist Lynette Hirschman found that women make more listener-noise, such as "mhm," "uhuh," and "yeah," to show "I'm with you." Men, she found, more often give silent attention. Women who expect a stream of listener-noise interpret silent attention as no attention at all.

Women's conversational habits are as frustrating to men as men's are to 18
women. Men who expect silent attention interpret a stream of listener-noise as
overreaction or impatience. Also, when women talk to each other in a close,
comfortable setting, they often overlap, finish each other's sentences and anticipate what the other is about to say. This practice, which I call "participatory
listenership," is often perceived by men as interruption, intrusion and lack of
attention.

A parallel difference caused a man to complain about his wife, "She just 19
wants to talk about her own point of view. If I show her another view, she gets
mad at me." When most women talk to each other, they assume a conversa-
tionalist's job is to express agreement and support. But many men see their conversational duty as pointing out the other side of an argument. This is heard as
disloyalty by women, and refusal to offer the requisite support. It is not that
women don't want to see other points of view, but that they prefer them
phrased as suggestions and inquiries rather than as direct challenges.

In his book *Fighting for Life,* Walter Ong points out that men use "agonistic" 20
or warlike, oppositional formats to do almost anything; thus discussion becomes debate, and conversation a competitive sport. In contrast, women see
conversation as a ritual means of establishing rapport. If Jane tells a problem
and June says she has a similar one, they walk away feeling closer to each other.
But this attempt at establishing rapport can backfire when used with men. Men
take too literally women's ritual "troubles talk," just as women mistake men's
ritual challenges for real attack.

The Sounds of Silence

These differences begin to clarify why women and men have such different ex- 21
pectations about communication in marriage. For women, talk creates intimacy.
Marriage is an orgy of closeness: you can tell your feelings and thoughts, and
still be loved. Their greatest fear is being pushed away. But men live in a hierarchical world, where talk maintains independence and status. They are on
guard to protect themselves from being put down and pushed around.

This explains the paradox of the talkative man who said of his silent wife, 22
"She's the talker." In the public setting of a guest lecture, he felt challenged to
show his intelligence and display his understanding of the lecture. But at home,
where he has nothing to prove and no one to defend against, he is free to remain
silent. For his wife, being home means she is free from the worry that something
she says might offend someone, or spark disagreement, or appear to be showing off; at home she is free to talk.

The communication problems that endanger marriage can't be fixed by me- 23
chanical engineering. They require a new conceptual framework about the role
of talk in human relationships. Many of the psychological explanations that have
become second nature may not be helpful, because they tend to blame either
women (for not being assertive enough) or men (for not being in touch with their
feelings). A sociolinguistic approach by which male-female conversation is seen

as cross-cultural communication allows us to understand the problem and forge solutions without blaming either party.

Once the problem is understood, improvement comes naturally, as it did to 24 the young woman and her boyfriend who seemed to go to sleep when she wanted to talk. Previously, she had accused him of not listening, and he had refused to change his behavior, since that would be admitting fault. But then she learned about and explained to him the differences in women's and men's habitual ways of aligning themselves in conversation. The next time she told him she wanted to talk, he began, as usual, by lying down and covering his eyes. When the familiar negative reaction bubbled up, she reassured herself that he really was listening. But then he sat up and looked at her. Thrilled she asked why. He said, "You like me to look at you when we talk, so I'll try to do it." Once he saw their differences as cross-cultural rather than right and wrong, he independently altered his behavior.

Women who feel abandoned and deprived when their husbands won't lis 25 ten to or report daily news may be happy to discover their husbands trying to adapt once they understand the place of small talk in women's relationships. But if their husbands don't adapt, the women may still be comforted that for men, this is not a failure of intimacy. Accepting the difference, the wives may look to their friends or family for that kind of talk. And husbands who can't provide it shouldn't feel their wives have made unreasonable demands. Some couples will still decide to divorce, but at least their decisions will be based on realistic expectations.

In these times of resurgent ethnic conflicts, the world desperately needs 26 cross-cultural understanding. Like charity, successful cross-cultural communication should begin at home.

COMPREHENSION

1. What is the thesis of this essay? Where does the author most clearly articulate it?
2. To advance her argument, the author cites political scientists and sociologists, while she, herself, is a linguist. What exactly is the nature of these three professions? What do professionals in the first two fields do? Why does the author use their observations in developing her argument?
3. Why does the author employ a question in her title? What other device does she employ in her title to capture the reader's attention? (*Hint:* It is a reference to the title of a movie.)

RHETORIC

1. The author begins her essay with an anecdote. Is this an effective way of opening this particular essay? Why or why not?

2. Besides anecdotes, the author uses statistics, social science research, appeals to authority, and definition in advancing her argument. Find at least one example of each device. Explain the effectiveness or lack thereof.
3. Where and how does the author imply that she is an authority on the subject? How does this contribute to or detract from her ability to win the reader's confidence?
4. The author divides her essay into four sections: one untitled and three with headings. How does each section relate to the others structurally and thematically?
5. The author dramatically states that "Given the current divorce rate of nearly 50 percent" the United States has a "virtual epidemic of failed conversation." Is this fact or opinion? Does it serve to heighten or weaken the import of her thesis?
6. Concerning the lack of proper communication between men and women, the author states, "Once the problem is understood, improvement comes naturally." Is this statement substantiated or backed up with evidence? Explain.
7. Explain the analogy the author employs in the final paragraph. Is it a good or poor analogy? Explain.

WRITING

1. Another linguist has written an essay entitled "The Communication Panacea," which argues that much of what is blamed on lack of communication actually has economic and political causes. Argue for or against this proposition in the light of the ideas advanced in Tannen s essay.
2. Using some of the observational methods described in the essay, conduct your own ethnographic research by observing a couple communicating. Write a report discussing your findings.
3. The author states, "Once the problem is understood, improvement comes naturally." Argue for or against this proposition.

CONNECTIONS FOR CRITICAL THINKING

1. Both Annie Dillard's "An American Childhood" and E. B. White's "Once More to the Lake" explore the experience of childhood from a different perspective. Do they share a common voice or mood? What is distinctive about each essay? Which essay do you prefer? Why? Consider the style and emotional impact of the writing.

2. Both Barbara Kingsolver's "Stone Soup" and Francis Fukuyama's "Immigrants and Family Values" attempt to alter stereotypes commonly held about contemporary families. What type of family does each author address? How do the authors differ in their rhetorical strategies and their use of supporting points to buttress their arguments? Who is the implied audience for each of the essays? How did you reach your conclusion?

3. In his essay "Parenting as an Industry," Amitai Etzioni describes the gross shortcomings of current child care practice with regard to its clients. Using Dillard's "An American Childhood," discuss how the communal nature of childhood experience could not be achieved in the typical "industrial" setting of contemporary child care.

4. Argue for or against the idea that proposals for the relatively new types of family constellations as described by Kingsolver in "Stone Soup" are presented in an overly romanticized way.

5. Argue for or against the idea that descriptions of the relatively new types of family relationships described by Kingsolver in "Stone Soup" and/or in Rodriguez's "Family Values" are presented in a biased, romanticized manner.

6. Argue for or against the view that changes in society and its norms, specifically, increased geographical mobility, an evolving workplace, ideas about economic class, and individual liberties, and sexual preference, have resulted in new forms of identity. Use examples from the work of Atwood, Etzioni, Theroux, and Rodriguez.

7. Select the two more substantially argued essays in this chapter, Etzioni's "Parenting as an Industry" and Fukuyama's "Immigrants and Family Values." Compare and contrast their methods of argumentation.

8. Theroux criticizes many of the traits associated with manhood. Analyze his critique and argue for or against the proposition that if men were to abandon many of the behaviors and attitudes he describes, they would "last" longer, thus solving the issue of men's lower life expectancy as discussed in Angier's "Why Men Don't Last."

9. Establish your own definition of what it means to be a male or a female. Refer to the essays of Ephron, Atwood, Theroux, Rodriguez, and Tannen.

10. Search the Web for *family values* AND *Patrick Buchanan* or any of the other individuals cited in Fukuyama's "Immigrants and Family Values." Write an extended analysis of the views of that particular individual regarding the topic of family values.

11. Join several newsgroups that focus on immigration issues. Compare and contrast the ideological focus of the conversations among members.

12. Create your own home page, and develop an interface that includes a selected quote regarding the family taken from one of your essays. Create a link to the home page with a response page where fellow students can make comments regarding the quotation. At the end of the semester, write a report and summary of the responses you receive. You may ask students to include their country of origin or their ethnicity to help you find possible connections between these factors and the responses.

 chapter **5**

History, Culture, and Civilization

Are We Citizens of the World?

At the start of a new century, the paroxysms caused by conflicts among peoples, nations, ethnic groups, and cultures continue to shake continents. The United States might have emerged from the cold war as the dominant super power, but numerous local and global threats remain. We seem to be at a crossroads in history, culture, and civilization, but does the future hold great promise or equally great danger?

The future assuredly holds significant peril as well as promise. History tells us that while there has never been complete absence of barbarism and nonrational behavior in human affairs, there have been societies, cultures, and nations committed to harmonious, or civil, conduct within various social realms. While it is clear that we have not attained an ideal state of cultural or world development, at the same time, we have advanced beyond the point in primitive civilization where someone chipped at a stone in order to make a better tool.

As we consider the course of contemporary civilization, we must contend with our own personal histories and cultures as well as with the interplay of contradictory global forces. We have become increasingly concerned with finding a purpose beyond the parameters of our very limiting personal and nationalistic identities, something that the Czech writer and statesman Václav Havel calls the "divine revolution." Indeed, we have entered an era of renewed ethnic strife, where a preoccupation with cultural difference seems stronger than the desire for universal civilization. The writers assembled here grapple with these contradictions; they move from the United States to Mexico to Canada to Europe to the Mideast as they search for those constituents of history and culture that might hasten the advent of a civilized world.

The idea of civilization suggests a pluralistic ethos whereby people of diverse histories and backgrounds can maintain cultural identities but also coexist with other cultural representatives in a spirit of tolerance and mutual respect. The wars, upheavals, and catastrophes of the twentieth century were spawned by a narrow consciousness. Hopefully, as we enter a new century, all of us can advance the goal of a universal civilization based on the best that we have been able to create for humankind.

Previewing the Chapter

As you read the essays in this chapter and respond to them in discussion and writing, consider the following questions:

- How does the author define *culture, history,* or *civilization?* Is this definition stated or implied? Is the definition broad or narrow? Explain.
- Is the writer hopeful or pessimistic about the state of culture and history?
- What values does the author seem to think are necessary to advance the idea of history and culture?
- Do you find the author's tone to be objective or subjective? What is the author's purpose? Does the author have a personal motive in addressing the topic in the way he or she does?
- Which areas of knowledge—for example, history, philosophy, political science—does the author bring to bear on the subject?
- Do you agree or disagree with the author's view of the contemporary state of civilization?
- What cultural problems and historical conflicts are raised by the author in his or her treatment of the subject?
- Does the author have a narrow or broad focus on the relationship of history and culture to the larger society?
- Which authors altered your perspective on a topic, and why?
- Based on your reading of these essays, how would you define *civilization?* Are you hopeful about the current state of civilization?

Classic and Contemporary Images

HOW DO WE BECOME AMERICANS?

Using a Critical Perspective   Compare the scene of 19th-century immigrants arriving at New York City's Ellis Island with the March 1999 X-ray photo taken by Mexican authorities of human forms and cargo in a truck. What mood is conveyed by each representation? Does each photograph have a thesis or argument? Explain. Which photo do you find more engaging and provocative, and why?

Photo by Alice Austen/Culver Pictures

From the time of the first European settlers, the North American continent has experienced wave after wave of immigration from every part of the world. One period of heavy immigration occurred in the late 19th and early 20th centuries, when millions of people from eastern and southern Europe entered the United States through Ellis Island in New York City, as shown in the classic photograph.

Reforma Archivo/AP/Wide World Photos

More recently, immigrants continue to come from all over the world, often entering the country illegally. The X-ray photo shows a wide shot and a close-up image of people being smuggled across Mexico's border with Guatemala.

Classic and Contemporary Essays
ARE WE HEADING TOWARD A WORLD CULTURE?

Both of these essays address the issues of prejudice and national identification. As you read them, consider not only the differing styles and methods of discourse of their authors (to be expected of essays written over 200 years apart) but also their themes and import. In addition, consider that Reed is writing from the perspective of a racial (and to his mind) cultural minority and may therefore be particularly aware of those who would claim America's values, beliefs, doctrines, and cultural influences are homogeneous. Additionally, it may be ironic to note that Reed is writing within the context of a modern democratic state, while in 1762, the publication year of Goldsmith's essay, the United States did not even *exist*. Goldsmith's tone and style are immediately identifiable as being from another era. However, you should not confuse the formality of his rhetoric with the casual and intimate relationship to his reader. He addresses the reader quite directly, and the inspiration for his essay comes, he claims, from an informal conversation at a local tavern or coffeehouse. So, while his writing may appear abstruse, recall that Shakespeare wrote for an audience that had little formal education but understood his work with ease. Contemporary readers, on the other hand, often have trouble deciphering him because temporal distance often makes phrasing, vocabulary, and specific references obscure. Goldsmith uses no statistics, no historical record, no ideological analysis in his testimony. Rather, he assumes the tone of the "gentleman observer," a common form of address in his era. He may sound formal, but his tone is friendly. He disputes his colleagues' views that the English character represents the height of human development, but disarms his opponents through civility and deference. Reed is a contemporary African American writer of both fiction and nonfiction. From the perspective of a creative artist and keen observer of the modern intellectual and political scene, he combines personal experience and the historical record to demonstrate that much of "Western Civilization" draws its roots from a multiplicity of sources, not just European. Ironically, Reed, whose style is more colloquial than that of his distinguished predecessor, presents his argument using more of the traditional modes of support, for example, cultural analysis, appeals to authority, and historical evidence. Reed, however, unlike the courteous Goldsmith, is more forthright and direct in his disagreements. Can this be attributed to the reserved style of the English character versus the more direct discourse of the modern American? Or are we examining the reflections of two different personalities with different agendas?

National Prejudices

Oliver Goldsmith

Oliver Goldsmith (1730–1774), the son of an Anglican curate, was an Anglo-Irish es-
sayist, poet, novelist, dramatist, and journalist. His reputation as an enduring figure in
English literature is based on his novel, The Vicar of Wakefield *(1766); his play,* She
Stoops to Conquer *(1773); his major poem,* The Deserted Village *(1770); and the es-*
says and satiric letters collected in The Bee *(1759) and* The Citizen of the World
(1762). In this essay from the latter, Goldsmith argues quietly for a new type of citizen,
one who can transcend the xenophobia governing national behavior.

As I am one of that sauntering tribe of mortals, who spend the greatest part of ₁
their time in taverns, coffee houses, and other places of public resort, I have
thereby an opportunity of observing an infinite variety of characters, which, to
a person of a contemplative turn, is a much higher entertainment than a view of
all the curiosities of art or nature. In one of these, my late rambles, I accidentally
fell into the company of half a dozen gentlemen, who were engaged in a warm
dispute about some political affair; the decision of which, as they were equally
divided in their sentiments, they thought proper to refer to me, which naturally
drew me in for a share of the conversation.

Amongst a multiplicity of other topics, we took occasion to talk of the dif- ₂
ferent characters of the several nations of Europe; when one of the gentlemen,
cocking his hat, and assuming such an air of importance as if he had possessed
all the merit of the English nation in his own person, declared that the Dutch
were a parcel of avaricious wretches; the French a set of flattering sycophants;
that the Germans were drunken sots, and beastly gluttons; and the Spaniards
proud, haughty, and surly tyrants; but that in bravery, generosity, clemency, and
in every other virtue, the English excelled all the rest of the world.

This very learned and judicious remark was received with a general smile of ₃
approbation by all the company—all, I mean, but your humble servant; who, endeavoring to keep my gravity as well as I could, and reclining my head upon my
arm, continued for some time in a posture of affected thoughtfulness, as if I had
been musing on something else, and did not seem to attend to the subject of conversation; hoping by these means to avoid the disagreeable necessity of explaining myself, and thereby depriving the gentleman of his imaginary happiness.

But my pseudo-patriot had no mind to let me escape so easily. Not satisfied ₄
that his opinion should pass without contradiction, he was determined to have
it ratified by the suffrage of every one in the company; for which purpose addressing himself to me with an air of inexpressible confidence, he asked me if I
was not of the same way of thinking. As I am never forward in giving my opinion, especially when I have reason to believe that it will not be agreeable; so,

when I am obliged to give it, I always hold it for a maxim to speak my real sentiments. I therefore told him that, for my own part, I should not have ventured to talk in such. a peremptory strain, unless I had made the tour of Europe, and examined the manners of these several nations with great care and accuracy: that, perhaps, a more impartial judge would not scruple to affirm that the Dutch were more frugal and industrious, the French more temperate and polite, the Germans more hardy and patient of labour and fatigue, and the Spaniards more staid and sedate, than the English; who, though undoubtedly brave and generous, were at the same time rash, headstrong, and impetuous; too apt to be elated with prosperity, and to despond in adversity.

I could easily perceive that all the company began to regard me with a jealous eye before I had finished my answer, which I had no sooner done, than the patriotic gentleman observed, with a contemptuous sneer, that he was greatly surprised how some people could have the conscience to live in a country which they did not love, and to enjoy the protection of a government, to which in their hearts they were inveterate enemies. Finding that by this modest declaration of my sentiments I had forfeited the good opinion of my companions, and given them occasion to call my political principles in question, and well knowing that it was in vain to argue with men who were so very full of themselves, I threw down my reckoning and retired to my own lodgings, reflecting on the absurd and ridiculous nature of national prejudice and prepossession. 5

Among all the famous sayings of antiquity, there is none that does greater honour to the author, or affords greater pleasure to the reader (at least if he be a person of a generous and benevolent heart), than that of the philosopher, who, being asked what "countryman he was," replied, that he was, "a citizen of the world."—How few are there to be found in modern times who can say the same, or whose conduct is consistent with such a profession!—We are now become so much Englishmen, Frenchmen, Dutchmen, Spaniards or Germans, that we are no longer citizens of the world; so much the natives of one particular spot, or members of one petty society, that we no longer consider ourselves as the general inhabitants of the globe, or members of that grand society which comprehends the whole human kind. 6

Did these prejudices prevail only among the meanest and lowest of the people, perhaps they might be excused, as they have few, if any, opportunities of correcting them by reading, travelling, or conversing with foreigners; but the misfortune is, that they infect the minds, and influence the conduct, even of our gentlemen; of those, I mean, who have every title to this appellation but an exemption from prejudice, which however, in my opinion, ought to be regarded as the characteristical mark of a gentleman; for let a man's birth be ever so high, his station ever so exalted, or his fortune ever so large, yet if he is not free from national and other prejudices, I should make bold to tell him, that he had a low and vulgar mind, and had no just claim to the character of a gentleman. And in fact, you will always find that those are most apt to boast of national merit, who have little or no merit of their own to depend on; than which, to be sure, nothing is more natural: the slender vine twists around the sturdy oak, for no other reason in the world but because it has not strength sufficient to support itself. 7

Should it be alleged in defense of national prejudice, that it is the natural 8 and necessary growth of love to our country, and that therefore the former cannot be destroyed without hurting the latter, I answer, that this is a gross fallacy and delusion. That it is the growth of love to our country, I will allow; but that it is the natural and necessary growth of it, I absolutely deny. Superstition and enthusiasm too are the growth of religion; but who ever took it in his head to affirm that they are the necessary growth of this noble principle? They are, if you will, the bastard sprouts of this heavenly plant, but not its natural and genuine branches, and may safely enough be lopped off, without doing any harm to the parent stock; nay, perhaps, till once they are lopped off, this goodly tree can never flourish in perfect health and vigour.

Is it not very possible that I may love my own country, without hating the 9 natives of other countries? that I may exert the most heroic bravery, the most undaunted resolution, in defending its laws and liberty, without despising all the rest of the world as cowards and poltroons? Most certainly it is; and if it were not—But why need I suppose what is absolutely impossible?—But if it were not, I must own, I should prefer the title of the ancient philosopher, viz. a citizen of the world, to that of an Englishman, a Frenchman, a European, or to any other appellation whatever.

COMPREHENSION

1. Why does Goldsmith maintain that he is "a citizen of the world"? According to the author, could such an individual also be a patriot? Explain.
2. What connection does Goldsmith make between national prejudices and the conduct of gentlemen? Why does he allude to the manners of gentlemen?
3. Compare and contrast Goldsmith's observations with those of Schlesinger in "The Cult of Ethnicity."

RHETORIC

1. Locate in the essay examples of the familiar style in writing. What is the relationship between this style and the tone and substance of the essay?
2. Explain the metaphors at the end of paragraphs 7 and 8.
3. What is the relevance of the introductory narrative, with its description of characters, to the author's declaration of thesis? Where does the author state his proposition concerning national prejudices?
4. Analyze the function of classification and contrast in paragraphs 2 to 5. How does the entire essay serve as a pattern of definition?
5. Examine the pattern of reasoning involved in the author's presentation of his argument in the essay, notably in paragraphs 6 to 8. What appeals to emotion and to reason does he make?
6. Assess the rhetorical effectiveness of Goldsmith's concluding paragraph.

WRITING

1. Why has it been difficult to eliminate the problem that Goldsmith posed in 1762? Are we better able today to function as citizens of the world? In what ways? What role does the United Nations play in this issue? What factors contribute to a new world citizenry? Explore these questions in an essay.
2. Write an argumentative essay on the desirability of world government or on the need to be a citizen of the world.
3. Write a paper on contemporary national prejudices—from the viewpoint of an ingenious foreigner.

America: The Multinational Society

Ishmael Reed

Ishmael Reed (b. 1938), an American novelist, poet, and essayist, is the founder and editor (along with Al Young) of Quilt *magazine, begun in 1981. In his writing, Reed uses a combination of standard English, black dialect, and slang to satirize American society. He believes that African Americans must move away from identification with Europe in order to rediscover their African qualities. Reed's books include* Flight to Canada *(1976),* The Terrible Twos *(1982),* The Terrible Threes *(1989), and* Japanese by Spring *(1993). In addition, he has written volumes of verse, including* Secretary to the Spirits *(1975), and has published collections of his essays, including* Airing Dirty Laundry *(1993). In the following essay from* Writin' Is Fightin' *(1990), Reed seeks to debunk the myth of the European ideal and argues for a universal definition of culture.*

At the annual Lower East Side Jewish Festival yesterday, a Chinese woman ate a pizza slice in front of Ty Thuan Duc's Vietnamese grocery store. Beside her a Spanish-speaking family patronized a cart with two signs: "Italian Ices" and "Kosher by Rabbi Alper." And after the pastrami ran out, everybody ate knishes.
—The New York Times, *June 23, 1983*

On the day before Memorial Day, 1983, a poet called me to describe a city he 1
had just visited. He said that one section included mosques, built by the Islamic people who dwelled there. Attending his reading, he said, were large numbers of Hispanic people, forty thousand of whom lived in the same city. He was not talking about a fabled city located in some mysterious region of the world. The city he'd visited was Detroit.

A few months before, as I was leaving Houston, Texas, I heard it announced 2
on the radio that Texas's largest minority was Mexican American, and though a foundation recently issued a report critical of bilingual education, the taped voice used to guide the passengers on the air trams connecting terminals in Dallas

Airport is in both Spanish and English. If the trend continues, a day will come when it will be difficult to travel through some sections of the country without hearing commands in both English and Spanish; after all, for some western states, Spanish was the first written language and the Spanish style lives on in the western way of life.

Shortly after my Texas trip, I sat in an auditorium located on the campus of ₃ the University of Wisconsin at Milwaukee as a Yale professor—whose original work on the influence of African cultures upon those of the Americas has led to his ostracism from some monocultural intellectual circles—walked up and down the aisle, like an old-time southern evangelist, dancing and drumming the top of the lectern, illustrating his points before some serious Afro-American intellectuals and artists who cheered and applauded his performance and his mastery of information. The professor was "white." After his lecture, he joined a group of Milwaukeeans in a conversation. All of the participants spoke Yoruban, though only the professor had ever traveled to Africa.

One of the artists told me that his paintings, which included African and ₄ Afro-American mythological symbols and imagery, were hanging in the local McDonald's restaurant. The next day I went to McDonald's and snapped pictures of smiling youngsters eating hamburgers below paintings that could grace the walls of any of the country's leading museums. The manager of the local McDonald's said, "I don't know what you boys are doing, but I like it," as he commissioned the local painters to exhibit in his restaurant.

Such blurring of cultural styles occurs in everyday life in the United States to ₅ a greater extent than anyone can imagine and is probably more prevalent than the sensational conflict between people of different backgrounds that is played up and often encouraged by the media. The result is what the Yale professor, Robert Thompson, referred to as a cultural bouillabaisse, yet members of the nation's present educational and cultural Elect still cling to the notion that the United States belongs to some vaguely defined entity they refer to as "Western civilization," by which they mean, presumably, a civilization created by the people of Europe, as if Europe can be viewed in monolithic terms. Is Beethoven's Ninth Symphony, which includes Turkish marches, a part of Western civilization, or the late nineteenth- and twentieth-century French paintings, whose creators were influenced by Japanese art? And what of the cubists, through whom the influence of African art changed modern painting, or the surrealists, who were so impressed with the art of the Pacific Northwest Indians that, in their map of North America, Alaska dwarfs the lower forty-eight in size?

Are the Russians, who are often criticized for their adoption of "Western" ₆ ways by Tsarist dissidents in exile, members of Western civilization? And what of the millions of Europeans who have black African and Asian ancestry, black Africans having occupied several countries for hundreds of years? Are these "Europeans" members of Western civilization, or the Hungarians, who originated across the Urals in a place called Greater Hungary, or the Irish, who came from the Iberian Peninsula?

Even the notion that North America is part of Western civilization because ₇ our "system of government" is derived from Europe is being challenged by

Native American historians who say that the founding fathers, Benjamin Franklin especially, were actually influenced by the system of government that had been adopted by the Iroquois hundreds of years prior to the arrival of large numbers of Europeans.

Western civilization, then, becomes another confusing category like Third 8 World, or Judeo-Christian culture, as man attempts to impose his small-screen view of political and cultural reality upon a complex world. Our most publicized novelist recently said that Western civilization was the greatest achievement of mankind, an attitude that flourishes on the street level as scribbles in public restrooms: "White Power," "Niggers and Spics Suck," or "Hitler was a prophet," the latter being the most telling, for wasn't Adolph Hitler the archetypal monoculturalist who, in his pigheaded arrogance, believed that one way and one blood was so pure that it had to be protected from alien strains at all costs? Where did such an attitude, which has caused so much misery and depression in our national life, which has tainted even our noblest achievements, begin? An attitude that caused the incarceration of Japanese-American citizens during World War II, the persecution of Chicanos and Chinese Americans, the near-extermination of the Indians, and the murder and lynchings of thousands of Afro-Americans.

Virtuous, hardworking, pious, even though they occasionally would wan- 9 der off after some fancy clothes, or rendezvous in the woods with the town prostitute, the Puritans are idealized in our schoolbooks as "a hardy band" of no-nonsense patriarchs whose discipline razed the forest and brought order to the New World (a term that annoys Native American historians). Industrious, responsible, it was their "Yankee ingenuity" and practicality that created the work ethic. They were simple folk who produced a number of good poets, and they set the tone for the American writing style, of lean and spare lines, long before Hemingway. They worshiped in churches whose colors blended in with the New England snow, churches with simple structures and ornate lecterns.

The Puritans were a daring lot, but they had a mean streak. They hated the 10 theater and banned Christmas. They punished people in a cruel and inhuman manner. They killed children who disobeyed their parents. When they came in contact with those whom they considered heathens or aliens, they behaved in such a bizarre and irrational manner that this chapter in the American history comes down to us as a late-movie horror film. They exterminated the Indians, who taught them how to survive in a world unknown to them, and their encounter with the calypso culture of Barbados resulted in what the tourist guide in Salem's Witches' House refers to as the Witchcraft Hysteria.

The Puritan legacy of hard work and meticulous accounting led to the es- 11 tablishment of a great industrial society; it is no wonder that the American industrial revolution began in Lowell, Massachusetts, but there was the other side, the strange and paranoid attitudes toward those different from the Elect.

The cultural attitudes of that early Elect continue to be voiced in everyday 12 life in the United States: the president of a distinguished university, writing a letter to the *Times*, belittling the study of African civilizations; the television network that promoted its show on the Vatican art with the boast that this art represented "the finest achievements of the human spirit." A modern up-tempo state of complex rhythms that depends upon contacts with an international community can no longer behave as if it dwelled in a "Zion Wilderness" surrounded by beasts and pagans.

When I heard a schoolteacher warn the other night about the invasion of 13 the American educational system by foreign curriculums, I wanted to yell at the television set, "Lady, they're already here." It has already begun because the world is here. The world has been arriving at these shores for at least ten thousand years from Europe, Africa, and Asia. In the late nineteenth and early twentieth centuries, large numbers of Europeans arrived, adding their cultures to those of the European, African, and Asian settlers who were already here, and recently millions have been entering the country from South America and the Caribbean, making Yale Professor Bob Thompson's bouillabaisse richer and thicker.

One of our most visionary politicians said that he envisioned a time when 14 the United States could become the brain of the world, by which he meant the repository of all of the latest advanced information systems. I thought of that remark when an enterprising poet friend of mine called to say that he had just sold a poem to a computer magazine and that the editors were delighted to get it because they didn't carry fiction or poetry. Is that the kind of world we desire? A humdrum homogeneous world of all brains but no heart, no fiction, no poetry; a world of robots with human attendants bereft of imagination, of culture? Or does North America deserve a more exciting destiny? To become a place where the cultures of the world crisscross. This is possible because the United States is unique in the world: The world is here.

COMPREHENSION

1. Why does Reed believe that the notion of Western or European civilization is fallacious?
2. According to Reed, what are the origins of our monoculturalist view?
3. What are the dangers of such a narrow view? What historical examples does Reed allude to?

RHETORIC

1. How do paragraphs 1 to 4 help set the stage for Reed's discourse? Does this section contain Reed's thesis?
2. Does the computer analogy in Reed's conclusion work? Do his rhetorical questions underscore the thesis?
3. Comment on the author's extensive use of details and examples. How do they serve to support his point? Which examples are especially illuminating? Why?

4. What kind of humor does Reed use in his essay? Does its use contribute to the force of his essay? Why, or why not?
5. Is Reed's reasoning inductive or deductive? Justify your answer.
6. How does Reed employ definitions to structure his essay?

WRITING

1. Write an essay arguing that a multinational society is often riddled with complex problems. What are some of the drawbacks or disadvantages of such a society? What causes these conflicts? Explore these issues in your writing.
2. How does America's insistence that it is a European country affect its dealings with other nations? How does it influence the way it treats its own citizens? Explore these questions in a causal-analysis essay, using support from Reed.
3. Write an essay in which you consider how a multinational United States affects you on a day-to-day basis. How does it enrich your life or the life of the country? Use specific examples and details to support your opinion.

Classic and Contemporary: Questions for Comparison

1. How do the respective tones of Goldsmith's and Reed's essays differ? What clues are contained in the texts that make this difference evident? Use examples from both.
2. In his essay, Goldsmith argues against nationalism and professes to be a citizen of the world. Compare Goldsmith's view with Reed's argument that to be an "American" means to accept the variety of influences that have converged into a "multinational society." How do these arguments differ? How are they similar?
3. Discuss both Goldsmith's and Reed's essays in terms of formality of voice. Does one author speak with more authority than the other? Or are they equally authoritative, but employing the stylistic modes of their times? Use examples from both essays.

The Myth of the Latin Woman: I Just Met a Girl Named Maria

Judith Ortiz Cofer

Judith Ortiz Cofer (b. 1952 in Puerto Rico) immigrated to the United States in 1956. Once a bilingual teacher in Florida public schools, Cofer has written two books of poetry; several plays; a novel, The Line of the Sun *(1989); an award-winning collection of essays and poems,* Silent Dancing: A Partial Remembrance of a Puerto Rican Childhood *(1990); and a collection of short stories,* An Island Like You: Stories of the Barrio *(1995). She is a professor of English and creative writing at the University of Georgia. In the following essay, she offers both personal insight and philosophical reflection on the theme of ethnic stereotyping.*

On a bus trip to London from Oxford University where I was earning some 1 graduate credits one summer, a young man, obviously fresh from a pub, spotted me and as if struck by inspiration went down on his knees in the aisle. With both hands over his heart he broke into an Irish tenor's rendition of "Maria" from *West Side Story*. My politely amused fellow passengers gave his lovely voice the round of gentle applause it deserved. Though I was not quite as amused, I managed my version of an English smile: no show of teeth, no extreme contortions of the facial muscles—I was at this time of my life practicing reserve and cool. Oh, that British control, how I coveted it. But "Maria" had followed me to London, reminding me of a prime fact of my life: you can leave the island, master the English language, and travel as far as you can, but if you are a Latina, especially one like me who so obviously belongs to Rita Moreno's gene pool, the island travels with you.

This is sometimes a very good thing. it may win you that extra minute of 2 someone's attention. But with some people, the same things can make *you* an island—not a tropical paradise but an Alcatraz, a place nobody wants to visit. As a Puerto Rican girl living in the United States and wanting like most children to "belong," I resented the stereotype that my Hispanic appearance called forth from many people I met.

Growing up in a large urban center in New Jersey during the 1960s, I suf- 3 fered from what I think of as "cultural schizophrenia." Our life was designed by my parents as a microcosm of their *casas* on the island. We spoke in Spanish, ate Puerto Rican food bought at the *bodega*, and practiced strict Catholicism at a church that allotted us a one-hour slot each week for mass, performed in Spanish by a Chinese priest trained as a missionary for Latin America.

As a girl. I was kept under strict surveillance by my parents, since my virtue 4 and modesty were, by their cultural equation, the same as their honor. As a teenager I was lectured constantly on how to behave as a proper *senorita*. But it was a conflicting message I received, since the Puerto Rican mothers also encouraged their daughters to look and act like women and to dress in clothes our Anglo friends and their mothers found too "mature" and flashy. The difference was, and is, cultural; yet I often felt humiliated when I appeared at an American friend's party wearing a dress more suitable to a semiformal than to a playroom birthday celebration. At Puerto Rican festivities, neither the music nor the colors we wore could be too loud.

I remember Career Day in our high school, when teachers told us to come 5 dressed as if for a job interview. It quickly became obvious that to the Puerto Rican girls "dressing up" meant wearing their mother's ornate jewelry and clothing, more appropriate (by mainstream standards) for the company Christmas party than as daily office attire. That morning I had agonized in front of my closet, trying to figure out what a "career girl" would wear. I knew how to dress for school (at the Catholic school I attended, we all wore uniforms), I knew how to dress for Sunday mass, and I knew what dresses to wear for parties at my relatives' homes. Though I do not recall the precise details of my Career Day outfit, it must have been a composite of these choices. But I remember a comment my friend (an Italian American) made in later years that coalesced my impressions of that day. She said that at the business school she was attending, the Puerto Rican girls always stood out for wearing "everything at once." She meant, of course, too much jewelry, too many accessories. On that day at school we were simply made the negative models by the nuns, who were themselves not credible fashion experts to any of us. But it was painfully obvious to me that to the others, in their tailored skirts and silk blouses, we must have seemed "hopeless" and "vulgar." Though I now know that most adolescents feel out of step much of the time, I also know that for the Puerto Rican girls of my generation that sense was intensified. The way our teachers and classmates looked at us that day in school was just a taste of the cultural clash that awaited us in the real world, where prospective employers and men on the street would often misinterpret our tight skirts and jingling bracelets as a "come-on."

Mixed cultural signals have perpetuated certain stereotypes—for example, 6 that of the Hispanic woman as the "hot tamale" or sexual firebrand. It is a one-dimensional view that the media have found easy to promote. In their special vocabulary, advertisers have designated "sizzling" and "smoldering" as the adjectives of choice for describing not only the foods but also the women of Latin America. From conversations in my house I recall hearing about the harassment that Puerto Rican women endured in factories where the "boss-men" talked to them as if sexual innuendo was all they understood, and worse, often gave them the choice of submitting to their advances or being fired.

It is custom, however, not chromosomes, that leads us to choose scarlet over 7 pale pink. As young girls it was our mothers who influenced our decisions about clothes and colors—mothers who had grown up on a tropical island where the natural environment was a riot of primary colors, where showing your skin was one way to keep cool as well as to look sexy. Most important of all, on the island, women perhaps felt freer to dress and move more provocatively since, in most cases, they were protected by the traditions, mores, and laws of a Spanish/ Catholic system of morality and machismo whose main rule was: *You may look at my sister, but if you touch her I will kill you.* The extended family and church structure could provide a young woman with a circle of safety in her small pueblo on the island; if a man "wronged" a girl, everyone would close in to save her family honor.

My mother has told me about dressing in her best party clothes on Saturday 8 nights and going to the town's plaza to promenade with her girlfriends in front of the boys they liked. The males were thus given an opportunity to admire the women and to express their admiration in the form of *piropos:* erotically charged street poems they composed on the spot. (I have myself been subjected to a few *piropos* while visiting the island, and they can be outrageous, although custom dictates that they must never cross into obscenity.) This ritual, as I understand it, also entails a show of studied indifference on the woman's part; if she is "decent," she must not acknowledge the man's impassioned words. So I do understand how things can be lost in translation. When a Puerto Rican girl dressed in her idea of what is attractive meets a man from the mainstream culture who has been trained to react to certain types of clothing as a sexual signal, a clash is likely to take place. I remember the boy who took me to my first formal dance leaning over to plant a sloppy, overeager kiss painfully on my mouth; when I didn't respond with sufficient passion, he remarked resentfully: "I thought you Latin girls were supposed to mature early," as if I were expected to *ripen* like a fruit or vegetable, not just grow into womanhood like other girls.

It is surprising to my professional friends that even today some people, in- 9 cluding those who should know better, still put others "in their place." It happened to me most recently during a stay at a classy metropolitan hotel favored by young professional couples for weddings. Late one evening after the theater, as I walked toward my room with a colleague (a woman with whom I was coordinating an arts program), a middle-aged man in a tuxedo, with a young girl in satin and lace on his arm, stepped directly into our path. With his champagne glass extended toward me, he exclaimed "Evita!"

Our way blocked, my companion and I listened as the man half-recited, 10 half-bellowed "Don't Cry for Me, Argentina." When he finished, the young girl said: "How about a round of applause for my daddy?" We complied, hoping this would bring the silly spectacle to a close. I was becoming aware that our little group was attracting the attention of the other guests. "Daddy" must have perceived this too, and he once more barred the way as we tried to walk past him. He began to shout-sing a ditty to the tune of "La Bamba"—except the lyrics were about a girl named Maria whose exploits rhymed with her name and gonorrhea. The girl kept saying "Oh, Daddy" and looking at me with pleading eyes. She wanted me to laugh along with the others. My companion and I stood silently waiting for the man to end his offensive song. When he finished, I looked not at him but at his daughter. I advised her calmly never to ask her father what he had done in the army. Then I walked between them and to my room. My friend complimented me on my cool handling of the situation, but I confessed that I had really wanted to push the jerk into the swimming pool. This same man—probably a corporate executive, well-educated, even worldly by most standards—would not have been likely to regale an Anglo woman with a dirty song in public. He might have checked his impulse by assuming that she could be somebody's wife or mother, or at least *somebody* who might take offense. But, to him, I was just an Evita or a Maria: merely a character in his cartoon-populated universe.

Another facet of the myth of the Latin woman in the United States is the menial, the domestic—Maria the housemaid or countergirl. It's true that work as domestics, as waitresses, and in factories is all that's available to women with little English and few skills. But the myth of the Hispanic menial—the funny maid, mispronouncing words and cooking up a spicy storm in a shiny California kitchen—has been perpetuated by the media in the same way that "Mammy" from *Gone with the Wind* became America's idea of the black woman for generations. Since I do not wear my diplomas around my neck for all to see, I have on occasion been sent to that "kitchen" where some think I obviously belong.   11

One incident has stayed with me, though I recognize it as a minor offense. My first public poetry reading took place in Miami, at a restaurant where a luncheon was being held before the event. I was nervous and excited as I walked in with notebook in hand. An older woman motioned me to her table, and thinking (foolish me) that she wanted me to autograph a copy of my newly published slender volume of verse, I went over. She ordered a cup of coffee from me, assuming that I was the waitress. (Easy enough to mistake my poems for menus, I suppose.) I know it wasn't an intentional act of cruelty. Yet of all the good things that happened later, I remember that scene most clearly, because it reminded me of what I had to overcome before anyone would take me seriously. In retrospect I understand that my anger gave my reading fire. In fact, I have almost always taken any doubt in my abilities as a challenge, the result most often being the satisfaction of winning a convert, of seeing the cold, appraising eyes warm to my words, the body language change, the smile that indicates I have opened some avenue for communication. So that day as I read, I looked directly at that woman. Her lowered eyes told me she was embarrassed at her faux pas, and when I willed her to look up at me, she graciously allowed me to punish her with my full attention. We shook hands at the end of the reading and I never saw her again. She has probably forgotten the entire incident, but maybe not.   12

Yet I am one of the lucky ones. There are thousands of Latinas without the privilege of an education or the entrees into society that I have. For them life is a constant struggle against the misconceptions perpetuated by the myth of the Latina. My goal is to try to replace the old stereotypes with a much more interesting set of realities. Every time I give a reading, I hope the stories I tell, the dreams and fears I examine in my work, can achieve some universal truth that will get my audience past the particulars of my skin color, my accent, or my clothes.   13

I once wrote a poem in which I called all Latinas "God's brown daughters." This poem is really a prayer of sorts, offered upward, but also, through the human-to-human channel of art, outward. It is a prayer for communication and   14 for respect. In it, Latin women pray "in Spanish to an Anglo God/with a Jewish heritage," and they are "fervently hoping/that if not omnipotent,/ at least He be bilingual."

COMPREHENSION

1. What is the theme of the essay?
2. What does Cofer mean by the expression "cultural schizophrenia"?
3. Define the following words: *coveted* (paragraph 1), *Anglo* (paragraph 4), *coalesced* (paragraph 5), *machismo* (paragraph 7), and *entrees* (paragraph 13).

RHETORIC

1. Cofer uses many anecdotes in her discussion of stereotyping. How does this affect the tone of the essay?
2. What is the implied audience for this essay? What aspects of the writing led you to your conclusion?
3. This essay is written in the first person, which tends to reveal a lot about the writer's personality. What adjectives come to mind when you think of the writer's singular voice?
4. Although this essay has a sociological theme, Cofer demonstrates that she has a poet's sensitivity toward language. What in the following sentence from paragraph 7 demonstrates this poetic style: "It is custom, however, not chromosomes, that leads us to choose scarlet over pale pink"? Select two other sentences from the essay that demonstrate Cofer's stylistic talent, and explain why they, too, are poetic.
5. In paragraph 8, Cofer demonstrates differing cultural perceptions between Hispanic and Anglo behavior. How is the paragraph structured so that this difference is demonstrated dramatically?
6. Cofer uses quotation marks to emphasize the connotation of certain words. Explain the significance of the following words: *"mature"* (paragraph 4); *"hopeless"* (paragraph 5); *"hot tamale"* (paragraph 6); *"wronged"* (paragraph 7); and *"decent"* (paragraph 8).

WRITING

1. In an essay of 400 to 500 words, argue for or against the proposition that stereotyping is excusable because it often is based on learned assumptions about which an individual cannot be expected to have knowledge.
2. Write a problem-solution essay of approximately 500 words in which you (a) discuss the reasons behind cultural stereotyping and (b) provide suggestions on how to overcome stereotyped thinking.
3. Select an ethnic, racial, or cultural group, and explain how group members undergo stereotyping through their depiction in the media.

The Way to Rainy Mountain

N. Scott Momaday

Navarre Scott Momaday (b. 1934), Pulitzer Prize–winning poet, critic, and acade-mician, is the author of House Made of Dawn *(1968),* The Way to Rainy Mountain *(1969),* The Names *(1976), and other works. "I am an American Indian (Kiowa), and am vitally interested in American Indian art, history and culture," Momaday has writ-ten. In this essay, he elevates personal experience to the realm of poetry and tribal myth.*

A single knoll rises out of the plain in Oklahoma, north and west of the Wichita   1
Range. For my people, the Kiowas, it is an old landmark, and they gave it the
name Rainy Mountain. The hardest weather in the world is there. Winter brings
blizzards, hot tornadic winds arise in the spring, and in summer the prairie is
an anvil's edge. The grass turns brittle and brown, and it cracks beneath your
feet. There are green belts along the rivers and creeks, linear groves of hickory
and pecan, willow and witch hazel. At a distance in July or August the steaming foliage seems almost to writhe in fire. Great green and yellow grasshoppers
are everywhere in the tall grass, popping up like corn to sting the flesh, and tor-
toises crawl about on the red earth, going nowhere in the plenty of time. Loneliness is an aspect of the land. All things in the plain are isolate; there is no
confusion of objects in the eye, but *one* hill or *one* tree or *one* man. To look upon
that landscape in the early morning, with the sun at your back, is to lose the
sense of proportion. Your imagination comes to life, and this, you think, is
where Creation was begun.

I returned to Rainy Mountain in July. My grandmother had died in the   2
spring, and I wanted to be at her grave. She had lived to be very old and at last
infirm. Her only living daughter was with her when she died, and I was told
that in death her face was that of a child.

I like to think of her as a child. When she was born, the Kiowas were living   3
the last great moment of their history. For more than a hundred years they had
controlled the open range from the Smoky Hill River to the Red, from the head-
waters of the Canadian to the fork of the Arkansas and Cimarron. In alliance
with the Comanches, they had ruled the whole of the southern Plains. War was
their sacred business, and they were among the finest horsemen the world has
ever known. But warfare for the Kiowas was preeminently a matter of disposition rather than of survival, and they never understood the grim, unrelenting
advance of the U.S. Cavalry. When at last, divided and ill-provisioned, they
were driven onto the Staked Plains in the cold rains of autumn, they fell into
panic. In Palo Duro Canyon they abandoned their crucial stores to pillage and
had nothing then but their lives. In order to save themselves, they surrendered
to the soldiers at Fort Sill and were imprisoned in the old stone corral that now

stands as a military museum. My grandmother was spared the humiliation of those high gray walls by eight or ten years, but she must have known from birth the affliction of defeat, the dark brooding of old warriors.

Her name was Aho, and she belonged to the last culture to evolve in North 4 America. Her forebears came down from the high country in western Montana nearly three centuries ago. They were a mountain people, a mysterious tribe of hunters whose language has never been positively classified in any major group. In the late seventeenth century they began a long migration to the south and east. It was a journey toward the dawn, and it led to a golden age. Along the way the Kiowas were befriended by the Crows, who gave them the culture and religion of the Plains. They acquired horses, and their ancient nomadic spirit was suddenly free of the ground. They acquired Tai-me, the sacred Sun Dance doll, from that moment the object and symbol of their worship, and so shared in the divinity of the sun. Not least, they acquired the sense of destiny, therefore courage and pride. When they entered upon the southern Plains they had been transformed. No longer were they slaves to the simple necessity of survival; they were a lordly and dangerous society of fighters and thieves, hunters and priests of the sun. According to their origin myth, they entered the world through a hollow log. From one point of view, their migration was the fruit of an old prophecy, for indeed they emerged from a sunless world.

Although my grandmother lived out her long life in the shadow of Rainy 5 Mountain, the immense landscape of the continental interior lay like memory in her blood. She could tell of the Crows, whom she had never seen, and of the Black Hills, where she had never been. I wanted to see in reality what she had seen more perfectly in the mind's eye, and traveled fifteen hundred miles to begin my pilgrimage.

Yellowstone, it seemed to me, was the top of the world, a region of deep 6 lakes and dark timber, canyons and waterfalls. But, beautiful as it is, one might have the sense of confinement there. The skyline in all directions is close at hand, the high wall of the woods and deep cleavages of shade. There is a perfect freedom in the mountains, but it belongs to the eagle and the elk, the badger and the bear. The Kiowas reckoned their stature by the distance they could see, and they were bent and blind in the wilderness.

Descending eastward, the highland meadows are a stairway to the plain. In 7 July the inland slope of the Rockies is luxuriant with flax and buckwheat, stonecrop and larkspur. The earth unfolds and the limit of the land recedes. Clusters of trees, and animals grazing far in the distance, cause the vision to reach away and wonder to build upon the mind. The sun follows a longer course in the day, and the sky is immense beyond all comparison. The great billowing clouds that sail upon it are shadows that move upon the grain like water, dividing light. Farther down, in the land of the Crows and Blackfeet, the plain is yellow. Sweet clover takes hold of the hills and bends upon itself to cover and seal the soil. There the Kiowas paused on their way; they had come to the place where they must change their lives. The sun is at home on the plains. Precisely there does it have the certain character of a god. When the

Kiowas came to the land of the Crows, they could see the dark lees of the hills at dawn across the Bighorn River, the profusion of light on the grain shelves, the oldest deity ranging after the solstices. Not yet would they veer southward to the caldron of the land that lay below; they must wean their blood from the northern winter and hold the mountains a while longer in their view. They bore Tai-me in procession to the east.

A dark mist lay over the Black Hills, and the land was like iron. At the top 8
of a ridge I caught sight of Devil's Tower upthrust against the gray sky as if in the birth of time the core of the earth had broken through its crust and the motion of the world was begun. There are things in nature that engender an awful quiet in the heart of man; Devil's Tower is one of them. Two centuries ago, because they could not do otherwise, the Kiowas made a legend at the base of the rock. My grandmother said:

> Eight children were there at play, seven sisters and their brother. Suddenly the boy was struck dumb; he trembled and began to run upon his hands and feet. His fingers became claws, and his body was covered with fur. Directly there was a bear where the boy had been. The sisters were terrified; they ran, and the bear after them. They came to the stump of a great tree, and the tree spoke to them. It bade them climb upon it, and as they did so it began to rise into the air. The bear came to kill them, but they were just beyond its reach. It reared against the tree and scored the bark all around with its claws. The seven sisters were borne into the sky, and they became the stars of the Big Dipper.

From that moment, and so long as the legend lives, the Kiowas have kinsmen in 9
the night sky. Whatever they were in the mountains, they could be no more. However tenuous their well-being, however much they had suffered and would suffer again, they had found a way out of the wilderness.

My grandmother had a reverence for the sun, a holy regard that now is all 10
but gone out of mankind. There was a wariness in her, and an ancient awe. She was a Christian in her later years, but she had come a long way about, and she never forgot her birthright. As a child she had been to the Sun Dances; she had taken part in those annual rites, and by them she had learned the restoration of her people in the presence of Tai-me. She was about seven when the last Kiowa Sun Dance was held in 1887 on the Washita River above Rainy Mountain Creek. The buffalo were gone. In order to consummate the ancient sacrifice—to impale the head of a buffalo bull upon the medicine tree—a delegation of old men journeyed into Texas, there to beg and barter for an animal from the Goodnight herd. She was ten when the Kiowas came together for the last time as a living Sun Dance culture. They could find no buffalo; they had to hang an old hide from the sacred tree. Before the dance could begin, a company of soldiers rode out from Fort Sill under orders to disperse the tribe. Forbidden without cause the essential act of their faith, having seen the wild herds slaughtered and left to rot upon the ground, the Kiowas backed away forever from the medicine tree. That was July 20, 1890, at the great bend of the Washita. My grandmother was there. Without bitterness, and for as long as she lived, she bore a vision of deicide.

Now that I can have her only in memory, I see my grandmother in the sev- 11
eral postures that were peculiar to her: standing at the wood stove on a winter
morning and turning meat in a great iron skillet; sitting at the south window,
bent above her beadwork, and afterwards, when her vision failed, looking
down for a long time into the fold of her hands; going out upon a cane, very
slowly as she did when the weight of age came upon her; praying. I remember
her most often at prayer. She made long, rambling prayers out of suffering and
hope, having seen many things. I was never sure that I had the right to hear, so
exclusive were they of all mere custom and company. The last time I saw her
she prayed standing by the side of her bed at night, naked to the waist, the light
of a kerosene lamp moving upon her dark skin. Her long, black hair, always
drawn and braided in the day, lay upon her shoulders and against her breasts
like a shawl. I do not speak Kiowa, and I never understood her prayers, but
there was something inherently sad in the sound, some merest hesitation upon
the syllables of sorrow. She began in a high and descending pitch, exhausting
her breath to silence; then again and again—and always the same intensity of
effort, of something that is, and is not, like urgency in the human voice. Transported so in the dancing light among the shadows of her room, she seemed beyond the reach of time. But that was illusion; I think I knew then that I should
not see her again.

Houses are like sentinels in the plain, old keepers of the weather watch. 12
There, in a very little while, wood takes on the appearance of great age. All colors wear soon away in the wind and rain, and then the wood is burned gray
and the grain appears and the nails turn red with rust. The windowpanes are
black and opaque; you imagine there is nothing within, and indeed there are
many ghosts, bones given up to the land. They stand here and there against the
sky, and you approach them for a longer time than you expect. They belong in
the distance; it is their domain.

Once there was a lot of sound in my grandmother's house, a lot of coming 13
and going, feasting and talk. The summers there were full of excitement and reunion. The Kiowas are a summer people; they abide the cold and keep to themselves, but when the season turns and the land becomes warm and vital they
cannot hold still; an old love of going returns upon them. The aged visitors who
came to my grandmother's house when I was a child were made of lean and
leather, and they bore themselves upright. They wore great black hats and
bright ample shirts that shook in the wind. They rubbed fat upon their hair and
wound their braids with strips of colored cloth. Some of them painted their,
faces and carried the scars of old and cherished enmities. They were an old
council of warlords, come to remind and be reminded of who they were. Their
wives and daughters served them well. The women might indulge themselves;
gossip was at once the mark and compensation of their servitude. They made
loud and elaborate talk among themselves, full of jest and gesture, fright and
false alarm. They went abroad in fringed and flowered shawls, bright beadwork
and German silver. They were at home in the kitchen, and they prepared meals
that were banquets.

There were frequent prayer meetings, and great nocturnal feasts. When I 14
was a child I played with my cousins outside, where the lamplight fell upon the
ground and the singing of the old people rose up around us and carried away
into the darkness. There were a lot of good things to eat, a lot of laughter and
surprise. And afterwards, when the quiet returned, I lay down with my grandmother and could hear the frogs away by the river and feel the motion of the air.

Now there is funeral silence in the rooms, the endless wake of some final 15
word. The walls have closed in upon my grandmother's house. When I returned to it in mourning, I saw for the first time in my life how small it was. It
was late at night, and there was a white moon, nearly full. I sat for a long time
on the stone steps by the kitchen door. From there I could see out across the
land; I could see the long row of trees by the creek, the low light upon the
rolling plains, and the stars of the Big Dipper. Once I looked at the moon and
caught sight of a strange thing. A cricket had perched upon the handrail, only a
few inches away from me. My line of vision was such that the creature filled the
moon like a fossil. It had gone there, I thought, to live and die, for there, of all
places, was its small definition made whole and eternal. A warm wind rose up
and purled like the longing within me.

The next morning I awoke at dawn and went out on the dirt road to Rainy 16
Mountain. It was already hot, and the grasshoppers began to fill the air. Still, it
was early in the morning, and the birds sang out of the shadows. The long yellow grass on the mountain shone in the bright light, and a scissortail hied above
the land. There, where it ought to be, at the end of a long and legendary way,
was my grandmother's grave. Here and there on the dark stones were ancestral
names. Looking back once, I saw the mountain and came away.

COMPREHENSION

1. What is the significance of Momaday's title? How does the title help explain
   the author's purpose?
2. Why does Momaday return to his grandmother's house and journey to her
   grave?
3. List the various myths and legends the author mentions in the essay. What
   subjects do they treat? How are these subjects interrelated?

RHETORIC

1. Locate and explain instances of sensory, metaphorical, and symbolic language in the essay. Why are these modes of language consistent with the
   subject and theme elaborated by Momaday?
2. How does Momaday's use of abstract language affect the concrete vocabulary in the essay?
3. What is the method of development in the first paragraph? How does the
   introduction serve as a vehicle for the central meanings in the essay?

4. Consider the relationship of narration to description in the organization of the essay. What forms of narrative serve to unify the selection? Are the narrative patterns strictly linear, or do they shift for other purposes? Explain. In what sense is Momaday's descriptive technique cinematic?
5. How do the land, the Kiowas, and Momaday's grandmother serve as reinforcing frames of the essay?
6. Describe in detail the creation of mood in this essay. Explain specifically the mood at the conclusion.

WRITING

1. Momaday implies that myth is central to his life and the life of the Kiowas. What *is* myth? Do you think that myth is as strong in general American culture as it is in Kiowa culture? In what ways does it operate? How can myth sustain the individual, community, and nation? Write an analytical essay on this subject.
2. Write about a person and place that, taken together, inspire a special reverence in you.
3. In an essay, explore the ways in which environment molds personality in "The Way to Rainy Mountain" and in "The Solace of Open Spaces" by Gretel Ehrlich (see pp. 643–649)

Salvation

Langston Hughes

James Langston Hughes (1902–1967), poet, playwright, fiction writer, biographer, and essayist, was for more than 50 years one of the most productive and significant modern American authors. In The Weary Blues *(1926),* Simple Speaks His Mind *(1950),* The Ways of White Folks *(1940),* Selected Poems *(1959), and dozens of other books, he strove, in his own words, "to explain the Negro condition in America." This essay, from his 1940 autobiography,* The Big Sea, *reflects the sharp, humorous, often bitter sweet insights contained in Hughes's examination of human behavior.*

I was saved from sin when I was going on thirteen. But not really saved. It happened like this. There was a big revival at my Auntie Reed's church. Every night for weeks there had been much preaching, singing, praying, and shouting, and some very hardened sinners had been brought to Christ, and the membership of the church had grown by leaps and bounds. Then just before the revival   1 ended, they held a special meeting for children, "to bring the young lambs to the fold." My aunt spoke of it for days ahead. That night I was escorted to the front row and placed on the mourners' bench with all the other young sinners, who had not yet been brought to Jesus.

My aunt told me that when you were saved you saw a light, and something ₂ happened to you inside! And Jesus came into your life! And God was with you from then on! She said you could see and hear and feel Jesus in your soul. I believed her. I had heard a great many old people say the same thing and it seemed to me they ought to know. So I sat there calmly in the hot, crowded church, waiting for Jesus to come to me.

The preacher preached a wonderful rhythmical sermon, all moans and ₃ shouts and lonely cries and dire pictures of hell, and then he sang a song about the ninety and nine safe in the fold, but one little lamb was left out in the cold. Then he said: "Won't you come? Won't you come to Jesus? Young lambs, won't you come?" And he held out his arms to all us young sinners there on the mourners' bench. And the little girls cried. And some of them jumped up and went to Jesus right away. But most of us just sat there.

A great many old people came and knelt around us and prayed, old women ₄ with jet-black faces and braided hair, old men with work-gnarled hands. And the church sang a song about the lower lights are burning, some poor sinners to be saved. And the whole building rocked with prayer and song.

Still I kept waiting to *see* Jesus.   ₅

Finally all the young people had gone to the altar and were saved, but one ₆ boy and me. He was a rounder's son named Westley. Westley and I were surrounded by sisters and deacons praying. It was very hot in the church, and getting late now. Finally Westley said to me in a whisper: "God damn! I'm tired o' sitting here. Let's get up and be saved." So he got up and was saved.

Then I was left all alone on the mourners' bench. My aunt came and knelt ₇ at my knees and cried, while prayers and song swirled all around me in the little church. The whole congregation prayed for me alone, in a mighty wail of moans and voices. And I kept waiting serenely for Jesus, waiting, waiting—but he didn't come. I wanted to see him, but nothing happened to me. Nothing! I wanted something to happen to me, but nothing happened.

I heard the songs and the minister saying: "Why don't you come? My dear ₈ child, why don't you come to Jesus? Jesus is waiting for you. He wants you. Why don't you come? Sister Reed, what is this child's name?"

"Langston," my aunt sobbed.   ₉

"Langston, why don't you come? Why don't you come and be saved? Oh, ₁₀ Lamb of God! Why don't you come?"

Now it was really getting late. I began to be ashamed of myself, holding ₁₁ everything up so long. I began to wonder what God thought about Westley, who certainly hadn't seen Jesus either, but who was now sitting proudly on the platform, swinging his knickerbockered legs and grinning down at me, surrounded by deacons and old women on their knees praying. God had not struck Westley dead for taking his name in vain or for lying in the temple. So I decided that maybe to save further trouble, I'd better lie, too, and say that Jesus had come, and get up and be saved.

So I got up.   12

Suddenly the whole room broke into a sea of shouting, as they saw me rise.   13
Waves of rejoicing swept the place. Women leaped in the air. My aunt threw her arms around me. The minister took me by the hand and led me to the platform.

When things quieted down, in a hushed silence, punctuated by a few ecsta-   14
tic "Amens," all the new young lambs were blessed in the name of God. Then joyous singing filled the room.

That night, for the last time in my life but one—for I was a big boy twelve   15
years old—I cried. I cried, in bed alone, and couldn't stop. I buried my head under the quilts, but my aunt heard me. She woke up and told my uncle I was crying because the Holy Ghost had come into my life, and because I had seen Jesus. But I was really crying because I couldn't bear to tell her that I had lied, that I had deceived everybody in the church, that I hadn't seen Jesus, and that now I didn't believe there was a Jesus any more, since he didn't come to help me.

COMPREHENSION

1. What does the title tell you about the subject of this essay? How would you state, in your own words, the thesis that emerges from the title and the essay?
2. How does Hughes recount the revival meeting he attended? What is the dominant impression?
3. Explain Hughes's shifting attitude toward salvation in this essay. Why is he disappointed in the religious answers provided by his church? What does he say about salvation in the last paragraph?

RHETORIC

1. Key words and phrases in this essay relate to the religious experience. Locate five of these words and expressions, and explain their connotations.
2. Identify the level of language in the essay. How does Hughes employ language effectively?
3. Where is the thesis statement in the essay? Consider the following: the use of dialogue, the use of phrases familiar to you (idioms), and the sentence structure. Cite examples of these elements.
4. How much time elapses, and why is this important to the effect? How does the author achieve narrative coherence?
5. Locate details and examples in the essay that are especially vivid and interesting. Compare your list with what others have listed. What are the similarities? The differences?
6. What is the tone of the essay? What is the relationship between tone and point of view?

WRITING

1. Describe a time in your life when you suppressed your feelings before adults because you thought they would misunderstand.
2. Recount an event in your life during which you surrendered to group pressures.
3. Write a narrative account of the most intense religious experience in your life.
4. Narrate an episode in which you played a trick on people simply to win their approval or satisfy their expectations.

The Woman Warrior

Maxine Hong Kingston

Maxine Hong Kingston (b. 1940) has written three books on the Chinese-American experience that have established her as a major contemporary prose stylist. The Woman Warrior *(1976) and* China Men *(1980) are brilliant explorations of personal and ethnic consciousness. Her third work, a novel, is entitled* Tripmaster Monkey *(1989). The following selection, from her first book, is filled with the mysteries, family tales, and legends that she uses to create the tapestry of her complex cultural identity.*

My American life has been such a disappointment.   1

"I got straight A's, Mama."   2

"Let me tell you a true story about a girl who saved her village."   3

I could not figure out what was my village. And it was important that I do   4
something big and fine, or else my parents would sell me when we made our
way back to China. In China there were solutions for what to do with little girls
who ate up food and threw tantrums. You cant eat straight A's.

When one of my parents or the emigrant villagers said, "Feeding girls is   5
feeding cowbirds," I would thrash on the floor and scream so hard I couldn't
talk. I couldn't stop.

"What's the matter with her?"   6

"I don't know. Bad, I guess. You know how girls are. 'There's no profit in   7
raising girls. Better to raise geese than girls.'"

"I would hit her if she were mine. But then there's no use wasting all   8
that discipline on a girl. 'When you raise girls, you're raising children for
strangers.'"

"Stop that crying!" my mother would yell. "I'm going to hit you if you   9
don't stop. Bad girl! Stop!" I'm going to remember never to hit or to scold my
children for crying, I thought, because then they will only cry more.

"I'm not a bad girl," I would scream. "I'm not a bad girl. I'm not a bad girl." 10
I might as well have said, "I'm not a girl."

"When you were little, all you had to say was 'I'm not a bad girl,' and you 11
could make yourself cry," my mother says, talking-story about my childhood.

I minded that the emigrant villagers shook their heads at my sister and me. 12
"One girl—and another girl," they said, and made our parents ashamed to take
us out together. The good part about my brothers being born was that people
stopped saying, "All girls," but I learned new grievances. "Did you roll an egg
on *my* face like that when I was born?" "Did you have a full-month party for
me?" "Did you turn on all the lights?" "Did you send *my* picture to Grandmother?" "Why not? Because I'm a girl? Is that why not?" "Why didn't you
teach me English?" "You like having me beaten up at school, don't you?"

"She is very mean, isn't she?" the emigrant villagers would say. 13

"Come, children. Hurry. Hurry. Who wants to go out with Great-Uncle?" 14
On Saturday mornings, my great-uncle, the ex-river pirate, did the shopping.
"Get your coats, whoever's coming."

"I'm coming. I'm coming. Wait for me." 15

When he heard girls' voices, he turned on us and roared, "No girls!" and 16
left my sisters and me hanging our coats back up, not looking at one another.
The boys came back with candy and new toys. When they walked trough Chinatown, the people must have said, "A boy—and another boy—and another
boy!" At my great-uncle's funeral I secretly tested out feeling glad that he was
dead—the six-foot bearish masculinity of him.

I went away to college—Berkeley in the sixties—and I studied, and I 17
marched to change the world, but I did not turn into a boy. I would have liked
to bring myself back as a boy for my parents to welcome with chickens and
pigs. That was for my brother, who returned alive from Vietnam.

If I went to Vietnam, I would not come back; females desert families. It was 18
said, "There is an outward tendency in females," which meant that I was getting straight A's for the good of my future husband's family, not my own. I did
not plan ever to have a husband. I would show my mother and father and the
nosey emigrant villagers that girls have no outward tendency. I stopped getting
straight A's.

And all the time I was having to turn myself American-feminine, or no 19
dates.

There is a Chinese word for the female *I*—which is "slave." Break the 20
women with their own tongues!

I refused to cook. When I had to wash dishes, I would crack one or two. 21
"Bad girl," my mother yelled, and sometimes that made me gloat rather than
cry. Isn't a bad girl almost a boy?

"What do you want to be when you grow up, little girl?" 22

"A lumberjack in Oregon." 23

Even now, unless I'm happy, I burn the food when I cook. I do not feed peo- 24
ple. I let the dirty dishes rot. I eat at other people's tables but won't invite them
to mine, where the dishes are rotting.

If I could not-eat, perhaps I could make myself a warrior like the   25
swordswoman who drives me. I will—I must—rise and plow the fields as soon
as the baby comes out.

Once I get outside the house, what bird might call me; on what horse could   26
I ride away? Marriage and childbirth strengthen the swordswoman, who is not
a maid like Joan of Arc. Do the women's work; then do more work, which will
become ours too. No husband of mine will say, "I could have been a drummer,
but I had to think about the wife and kids. You know how it is." Nobody supports me at the expense of his own adventure. Then I get bitter: no one supports
me; I am not loved enough to be supported. That I am not a burden has to compensate for the sad envy when I look at women loved enough to be supported.
Even now China wraps double binds around my feet.

When urban renewal tore down my parents' laundry and paved over our   27
slum for a parking lot, I only made up gun and knife fantasies and did nothing
useful.

From the fairy tales, I've learned exactly who the enemy are. I easily recog-   28
nize them—business-suited in their modern American executive guise, each
boss two feet taller than I am and impossible to meet eye to eye.

I once worked at an art supply house that sold paints to artists. "Order   29
more of that nigger yellow, willya?" the boss told me. "Bright, isn't it? Nigger
yellow."

"I don't like that word," I had to say in my bad, smallperson's voice that   30
makes no impact. The boss never deigned to answer.

I also worked at a land developer's association. The building industry was   31
planning a banquet for contractors, real estate dealers, and real estate editors.
"Did you know the restaurant you chose for the banquet is being picketed by
CORE and the NAACP?" I squeaked.

"Of course I know." The boss laughed. "That's why I chose it."   32

"I refuse to type these invitations," I whispered, voice unreliable.   33

He leaned back in his leather chair, his bossy stomach opulent. He picked   34
up his calendar and slowly circled a date. "You will be paid up to here," he said.
"We'll mail you the check."

If I took the sword, which my hate must surely have forged out of the air,   35
and gutted him, I would put color and wrinkles into his shirt.

It's not just the stupid racists that I have to do something about, but the   36
tyrants who for whatever reason can deny my family food and work. My job is
my own only land.

To avenge my family, I'd have to storm across China to take back our farm   37
from the Communists; I'd have to rage across the United States to take back the
laundry in New York and the one in California. Nobody in history has conquered and united both North America and Asia. A descendant of eighty pole
fighters, I ought to be able to set out confidently, march straight down our
street, get going right now. There's work to do, ground to cover. Surely, the
eighty pole fighters, though unseen, would follow me and lead me and protect
me, as is the wont of ancestors.

Or it may well be that they're resting happily in China, their spirits dis- 38
persed among the real Chinese, and not nudging me at all with their poles: I
mustn't feel bad that I haven't done as well as the swordswoman did; after all,
no bird called me, no wise old people tutored me. I have no magic beads, or water gourd sight, no rabbit that will jump in the fire when I'm hungry. I dislike
armies.

I've looked for the bird. I've seen clouds make pointed angel wings that 39
stream past the sunset, but they shred into clouds. Once at a beach after a long
hike I saw a seagull, tiny as an insect. But when I jumped up to tell what miracle I saw, before I could get the words out I understood that the bird was insect-
size because it was far away. My brain had momentarily lost its depth
perception. I was that eager to find an unusual bird.

The news from China has been confusing. It also had something to do with 40
birds. I was nine years old when the letters made my parents, who are rocks,
cry. My father screamed in his sleep. My mother wept and crumpled up the letters. She set fire to them page by page in the ashtray, but new letters came almost every day. The only letters they opened without fear were the ones with
red borders, the holiday letters that mustn't carry bad news. The other letters
said that my uncles were made to kneel on broken glass during their trials and
had confessed to being land-owners. They were all executed, and the aunt
whose thumbs were twisted off drowned herself. Other aunts, mothers-in-law,
and cousins disappeared; some suddenly began writing to us again from com-
munes or from Hong Kong. They kept asking for money. The ones in com-
munes got four ounces of fat and one cup of oil a week, they said, and had to
work from 4 A.M. to 9 P.M. They had to learn to do dances waving red kerchiefs;
they had to sing nonsense syllables. The Communists gave axes to the old ladies
and said, "Go and kill yourself. You're useless." If we overseas Chinese would
just send money to the Communist bank, our relatives said, they might get a
percentage of it for themselves. The aunts in Hong Kong said to send money
quickly; their children were begging on the sidewalks and mean people put dirt
in their bowls.

When I dream that I am wire without flesh, there is a letter on blue airmail 41
paper that floats above the night ocean between here and China. It must arrive
safely or else my grandmother and I will lose each other.

My parents felt bad whether or not they sent money. Sometimes they got 42
angry at their brothers and sisters for asking. And they would not simply ask
but have to talk-story too. The revolutionaries had taken Fourth Aunt and Uncle's
store, house, and lands. They attacked the house and killed the grandfather and
oldest daughter. The grandmother escaped with the loose cash and did not return to help. Fourth Aunt picked up her sons, one under each arm, and hid in
the pig house, where they slept that night in cotton clothes. The next day she
found her husband, who had also miraculously escaped. The two of them collected twigs and yams to sell while their children begged. Each morning they
tied the faggots on each other's back. Nobody bought from them. They ate the
yams and some of the children's rice. Finally Fourth Aunt saw what was wrong.

"We have to shout 'Fuel for sale' and 'Yams for sale,'" she said, "We can't just walk unobtrusively up and down the street." "You're right," said my uncle, but he was shy and walked in back of her. "Shout," my aunt ordered, but he could not. "They think we're carrying these sticks home for our own fire," she said. "Shout." They walked about miserably, silently, until sundown, neither of them able to advertise themselves. Fourth Aunt, an orphan since the age of ten, mean as my mother, threw her bundle down at his feet and scolded Fourth Uncle, "Starving to death, his wife and children starving to death, and he's too damned shy to raise his voice." She left him standing by himself and afraid to return empty-handed to her. He sat under a tree to think, when he spotted a pair of nesting doves. Dumping his bag of yams, he climbed up and caught the birds. That was when the Communists trapped him, in the tree. They criticized him for selfishly taking food for his own family and killed him, leaving his body in the tree as an example. They took the birds to a commune kitchen to be shared.

It is confusing that my family was not the poor to be championed. They [43] were executed like the barons in the stories, when they were not barons. It is confusing that birds tricked us.

What fighting and killing I have seen have not been glorious but slum [44] grubby. I fought the most during junior high school and always cried. Fights are confusing as to who has won. The corpses I've seen had been rolled and dumped, sad little dirty bodies covered with a police khaki blanket. My mother locked her children in the house so we couldn't look at dead slum people. But at news of a body, I would find a way to get out; I had to learn about dying if I wanted to become a swordswoman. Once there was an Asian man stabbed next door, a word on cloth pinned to his corpse. When the police came around asking questions, my father said, "No read Japanese. Japanese words. Me Chinese."

I've also looked for old people who could be my gurus. A medium with red [45] hair told me that a girl who died in a far country follows me wherever I go. This spirit can help me if I acknowledge her, she said. Between the head line and heart line in my right palm, she said, I have the mystic cross. I could become a medium myself. I don't want to be a medium. I don't want to be a crank taking "offerings" in a wicker plate from the frightened audience, who, one after another, asked the spirits how to raise rent money, how to cure their coughs and skin diseases, how to find a job. And martial arts are for unsure little boys kicking away under fluorescent lights.

I live now where there are Chinese and Japanese, but no emigrants from my [46] own village looking at me as if I had failed them. Living among one's own emigrant villagers can give a good Chinese far from China glory and a place. "That old busboy is really a swordsman," we whisper when he goes by, "He's a swordsman who's killed fifty. He has a tong ax in his closet." But I am useless, one more girl who couldn't be sold. When I visit the family now, I wrap my American successes around me like a private shawl; I *am* worthy of eating the food. From afar I can believe my family loves me fundamentally. They only say,

"When fishing for treasures in the flood, be careful not to pull in girls;" because that is what one says about daughters. But I watched such words come out of my own mother's and father's mouths; I looked at their ink drawing of poor people snagging their neighbor's flotage with long flood hooks and pushing the girl babies on down the river. And I had to get out of hating range. I read in an anthropology book that Chinese say, "Girls are necessary too"; I have never heard the Chinese I know make this concession. Perhaps it was a saying in another village. I refuse to shy my way anymore through our Chinatown, which tasks me with the old sayings and the stories.

The swordswoman and I are not so dissimilar. May my people understand 47 the resemblance soon so that I can return to them. What we have in common are the words at our backs. The ideographs for *revenge* are "report at crime" and "report to five families." The reporting is the vengeance—not the beheading, not the gutting, but the words. And I have so many words—"chink" words and "gook" words too—that they do not fit on my skin.

COMPREHENSION

1. What is the historical context of this personal narrative? What assumptions does the author make about her audience?
2. Summarize the "autobiography" that Kingston presents of herself in this selection. What are her family and its individual members like?
3. Explain the author's American life. How does she relate to Chinese culture and to American culture? What is her major problem? How would she overcome it?

RHETORIC

1. What connotations does Kingston explore for the words *girls* and *female* ? What connotations does she bring to the word *swordswoman?*
2. Locate five Chinese expressions or sayings in this selection. What is their effect on the tone of the essay?
3. The author's introductory paragraph consists of a single sentence. Is this strategy effective? Why?
4. Analyze the author's presentation of chronology. List the scenes into which the action is divided. Where are there stories within stories? Why does Kingston present such a complex tapestry of chronology and events? How, finally, does the author use narration to advance expository or explanatory ends?
5. Why is characterization important to the development of Kingston's thesis? How does the author create vivid characters? Cite specific examples and techniques.
6. Which paragraphs constitute the conclusion? How do these paragraphs reflect some of the major motifs of the essay?

WRITING

1. In *China Men*, Kingston speaks of "trying to unravel the mysteries" of her family. What mysteries does she explore here? Look up the word *mystery* in your dictionary. What mysteries concerning your family or your origins would you like to explore? Write an essay on this topic.
2. Write an autobiographical or narrative essay tracing a particular problem that you had to face while growing up in your family.
3. Narrate an event that happened to one of your relatives or ancestors in the old country, the nation of your family's origin.

The Arab World

Edward T. Hall

Edward T. Hall (b. 1914 in Missouri) earned a master's degree at the University of Arkansas and a PhD in anthropology at Columbia University. He was a professor of anthropology at the Illinois Institute of Technology and at Northwestern University. Hall is also the author of many books on anthropology and culture, among the most famous of which are The Silent Language *(1959),* The Hidden Dimension *(1966),* The Dance of Life *(1983),* Hidden Differences: Doing Business with the Japanese *(1987), and* Understanding Cultural Differences: Germans, French and Americans *(1990). In this selection from* The Hidden Dimension, *Hall demonstrates how such basic concepts as public and private space are perceived far differently depending upon one's culture of origin.*

In spite of over two thousand years of contact, Westerners and Arabs still do not 1
understand each other. Proxemic research reveals some insights into this difficulty. Americans in the Middle East are immediately struck by two conflicting sensations. In public they are compressed and overwhelmed by smells, crowding, and high noise levels; in Arab homes Americans are apt to rattle around, feeling exposed and often somewhat inadequate because of too much space! (The Arab houses and apartments of the middle and upper classes which Americans stationed abroad commonly occupy are much larger than the dwellings such Americans usually inhabit.) Both the high sensory stimulation which is experienced in public places and the basic insecurity which comes from being in a dwelling that is too large provide Americans with an introduction to the sensory world of the Arab.

Behavior in Public

Pushing and shoving in public places is characteristic of Middle Eastern culture. 2
Yet it is not entirely what Americans think it is (being pushy and rude) but

stems from a different set of assumptions concerning not only the relations between people but how one experiences the body as well. Paradoxically, Arabs
consider northern Europeans and Americans pushy, too. This was very puzzling to me when I started investigating these two views. How could Americans
who stand aside and avoid touching be considered pushy? I used to ask Arabs
to explain this paradox. None of my subjects was able to tell me specifically
what particulars of American behavior were responsible, yet they all agreed
that the impression was widespread among Arabs. After repeated unsuccessful
attempts to gain insight into the cognitive world of the Arab on this particular
point, I filed it away as a question that only time would answer. When the answer came, it was because of a seemingly inconsequential annoyance.

While waiting for a friend in a Washington, D.C., hotel lobby and wanting   3
to be both visible and alone, I had seated myself in a solitary chair outside the
normal stream of traffic. In such a setting most Americans follow a rule, which
is all the more binding because we seldom think about it, that can be stated as
follows: as soon as a person stops or is seated in a public place, there balloons
around him a small sphere of privacy which is considered inviolate. The size of
the sphere varies with the degree of crowding, the age, sex, and the importance
of the person, as well as the general surroundings. Anyone who enters this zone
and stays there is intruding. In fact, a stranger who intrudes, even for a specific
purpose, acknowledges the fact that he has intruded by beginning his request
with "Pardon me, but can you tell me . . . ?"

To continue, as I waited in the deserted lobby, a stranger walked up to   4
where I was sitting and stood close enough so that not only could I easily touch
him but I could even hear him breathing. In addition, the dark mass of his body
filled the peripheral field of vision on my left side. If the lobby had been
crowded with people, I would have understood his behavior, but in an empty
lobby his presence made me exceedingly uncomfortable. Feeling annoyed by
this intrusion, I moved my body in such a way as to communicate annoyance.
Strangely enough, instead of moving away, my actions seemed only to encourage him, because he moved even closer. In spite of the temptation to escape the
annoyance, I put aside thoughts of abandoning my post, thinking, "To hell with
it. Why should I move? I was here first and I'm not going to let this fellow drive
me out even if he is a boor." Fortunately, a group of people soon arrived whom
my tormentor immediately joined. Their mannerisms explained his behavior,
for I knew from both speech and gestures that they were Arabs. I had not been
able to make this crucial identification by looking at my subject when he was
alone because he wasn't talking and he was wearing American clothes.

In describing the scene later to an Arab colleague, two contrasting patterns   5
emerged. My concept and my feelings about my own circle of privacy in a
"public" place immediately struck my Arab friend as strange and puzzling. He
said, "After all, it's a public place, isn't it?" Pursuing this line of inquiry, I found
that in Arab thought I had no rights whatsoever by virtue of occupying a given
spot; neither my place nor my body was inviolate! For the Arab, there is no such
thing as an intrusion in public. Public means public. With this insight, a great
range of Arab behavior that had been puzzling, annoying, and sometimes even

frightening began to make sense. I learned, for example, that if *A* is standing on a street corner and *B* wants his spot, *B* is within his rights if he does what he can to make *A* uncomfortable enough to move. In Beirut only the hardy sit in the last row in a movie theater, because there are usually standees who want seats and who push and shove and make such a nuisance that most people give up and leave. Seen in this light, the Arab who "intruded" on my space in the hotel lobby had apparently selected it for the very reason I had: it was a good place to watch two doors and the elevator. My show of annoyance, instead of driving him away, had only encouraged him. He thought he was about to get me to move.

Another silent source of friction between Americans and Arabs is in an area   6
that Americans treat very informally—the manners and rights of the road. In general, in the United States we tend to defer to the vehicle that is bigger, more powerful, faster, and heavily laden. While a pedestrian walking along a road may feel annoyed he will not think it unusual to step aside for a fast-moving automobile. He knows that because he is moving he does not have the right to the space around him that he has when he is standing still (as I was in the hotel lobby). It appears that the reverse is true with the Arabs who apparently *take on rights to space as they move.* For someone else to move into a space an Arab is also moving into is a violation of his rights. It is infuriating to an Arab to have someone else cut in front of him on the highway. It is the American's cavalier treatment of moving space that makes the Arab call him aggressive and pushy.

Concepts of Privacy

The experience described above and many others suggested to me that Arabs   7
might actually have a wholly contrasting set of assumptions concerning the body and the rights associated with it. Certainly the Arab tendency to shove and push each other in public and to feel and pinch women in public conveyances would not be tolerated by Westerners. It appeared to me that they must not have any concept of a private zone outside the body. This proved to be precisely the case.

In the Western world, the person is synonymous with an individual inside   8
a skin. And in northern Europe generally, the skin and even the clothes may be inviolate. You need permission to touch either if you are a stranger. This rule applies in some parts of France, where the mere touching of another person during an argument used to be legally defined as assault. For the Arab the location of the person in relation to the body is quite different. The person exists somewhere down inside the body. The ego is not completely hidden, however, because it can be reached very easily with an insult. It is protected from touch but not from words. The dissociation of the body and the ego may explain why the public amputation of a thief's hand is tolerated as standard punishment in Saudi Arabia. It also sheds light on why an Arab employer living in a modern apartment can provide his servant with a room that is a boxlike cubicle approximately 5 by 10 by 4 feet in size that is not only hung from the ceiling to conserve floor space but has an opening so that the servant can be spied on.

As one might suspect, deep orientations toward the self such as the one just 9 described are also reflected in the language. This was brought to my attention one afternoon when an Arab colleague who is the author of an Arab English dictionary arrived in my office and threw himself into a chair in a state of obvious exhaustion. When I asked him what had been going on, he said: "I have spent the entire afternoon trying to find the Arab equivalent of the English word 'rape.' There is no such word in Arabic. All my sources, both written and spoken, can come up with no more than an approximation, such as 'He took her against her will.' There is nothing in Arabic approaching your meaning as it is expressed in that one word."

Differing concepts of the placement of the ego in relation to the body are not 10 easily grasped. Once an idea like this is accepted, however, it is possible to understand many other facets of Arab life that would otherwise be difficult to explain. One of these is the high population density of Arab cities like Cairo, Beirut, and Damascus. According to the animal studies described in the earlier chapters [of *The Hidden Dimension*], the Arabs should be living in a perpetual behavioral sink. While it is probable that Arabs are suffering from population pressures, it is also just as possible that continued pressure from the desert has resulted in a cultural adaptation to high density which takes the form described above. Tucking the ego down inside the body shell not only would permit higher population densities but would explain why it is that Arab communications are stepped up as much as they are when compared to northern European communication patterns. Not only is the sheer noise level much higher, but the piercing look of the eyes, the touch of the hands, and the mutual bathing in the warm moist breath during conversation represent stepped up sensory inputs to a level which many Europeans find unbearably intense.

The Arab dream is for lots of space in the home, which unfortunately many 11 Arabs cannot afford. Yet when he has space, it is very different from what one finds in most American homes. Arab spaces inside their upper middle-class homes are tremendous by our standards. They avoid partitions because Arabs *do not like to be alone*. The form of the home is such as to hold the family together inside a single protective shell, because Arabs are deeply involved with each other. Their personalities are intermingled and take nourishment from each other like the roots and soil. If one is not with people and actively involved in some way, one is deprived of life. An old Arab saying reflects this value: "Paradise without people should not be entered because it is Hell." Therefore, Arabs in the United States often feel socially and sensorially deprived and long to be back where there is human warmth and contact.

Since there is no physical privacy as we know it in the Arab family, not even 12 a word for privacy, one could expect that the Arabs might use some other means to be alone. Their way to be alone is to stop talking. Like the English, an Arab who shuts himself off in this way is not indicating that anything is wrong or that he is withdrawing, only that he wants to be alone with his own thoughts or does not want to be intruded upon. One subject said that her father would come and go for days at a time without saying a word, and no one in the family thought anything of it. Yet for this very reason, an Arab exchange student visiting a Kansas farm failed to pick up the cue that his American hosts were mad at him when they gave him the "silent treatment." He only discovered something was wrong when they took him to town and tried forcibly to put him on a bus to Washington, D.C., the headquarters of the exchange program responsible for his presence in the U.S.

Arab Personal Distances

Like everyone else in the world, Arabs are unable to formulate specific rules for their informal behavior patterns. In fact, they often deny that there are any rules, and they are made anxious by suggestions that such is the case. Therefore, in order to determine how the Arab sets distances, I investigated the use of each sense separately. Gradually, definite and distinctive behavioral patterns began to emerge.   13

Olfaction occupies a prominent place in the Arab life. Not only is it one of the distance-setting mechanisms, but it is a vital part of a complex system of behavior. Arabs consistently breathe on people when they talk. However, this habit is more than a matter of different manners. To the Arab good smells are pleasing and a way of being involved with each other. To smell one's friend is not only nice but desirable, for to deny him your breath is to act ashamed. Americans, on the other hand, trained as they are not to breathe in people's faces, automatically communicate shame in trying to be polite. Who would expect that when our highest diplomats are putting on their best manners they are also communicating shame? Yet this is what occurs constantly, because diplomacy is not only "eyeball to eyeball" but breath to breath.   14

By stressing olfaction, Arabs do not try to eliminate all the body's odors, only to enhance them and use them in building human relationships. Nor are they self-conscious about telling others when they don't like the way they smell. A man leaving his house in the morning may be told by his uncle, "Habib, your stomach is sour and your breath doesn't smell too good. Better not talk too close to people today." Smell is even considered in the choice of a mate. When couples are being matched for marriage, the man's go-between will sometimes ask to smell the girl, who may be turned down if she doesn't "smell nice." Arabs recognize that smell and disposition may be linked.   15

In a word, the olfactory boundary performs two roles in Arab life. It enfolds those who want to relate and separates those who don't. The Arab finds it essential to stay inside the olfactory zone as a means of keeping tab on changes in emotion. What is more, he may feel crowded as soon as he smells something unpleasant. While not much is known about "olfactory crowding," this may prove to be as significant as any other variable in the crowding complex because it is tied directly to the body chemistry and hence to the state of health and emotions. . . . It is not surprising, therefore, that the olfactory boundary constitutes for the Arabs an informal distance-setting mechanism in contrast to the visual mechanisms of the Westerner.   16

Facing and Not Facing

One of my earliest discoveries in the field of intercultural communication was 17 that the position of the bodies of people in conversation varies with the culture. Even so, it used to puzzle me that a special Arab friend seemed unable to walk and talk at the same time. After years in the United States, he could not bring himself to stroll along, facing forward while talking. Our progress would be arrested while he edged ahead, cutting slightly in front of me and turning sideways so we could see each other. Once in this position, he would stop. His behavior was explained when I learned that for the Arabs to view the other person peripherally is regarded as impolite, and to sit or stand back-to-back is considered very rude. You must be involved when interacting with Arabs who are friends.

One mistaken American notion is that Arabs conduct all conversations at 18 close distances. This is not the case at all. On social occasions, they may sit on opposite sides of the room and talk across the room to each other. They are, however, apt to take offense when Americans use what are to them ambiguous distances, such as the four- to seven-foot social-consultative distance. They frequently complain that Americans are cold or aloof or "don't care." This was what an elderly Arab diplomat in an American hospital thought when the American nurses used "professional" distance. He had the feeling that he was being ignored, that they might not take good care of him. Another Arab subject remarked, referring to American behavior, "What's the matter? Do I smell bad? Or are they afraid of me?"

Arabs who interact with Americans report experiencing a certain flatness 19 traceable in part to a very different use of the eyes in private and in public as well as between friends and strangers. Even though it is rude for a guest to walk around the Arab home eyeing things, Arabs look at each other in ways which seem hostile or challenging to the American. One Arab informant said that he was in constant hot water with Americans because of the way he looked at them without the slightest intention of offending. In fact, he had on several occasions barely avoided fights with American men who apparently thought their masculinity was being challenged because of the way he was looking at them. As noted earlier, Arabs look each other in the eye when talking with an intensity that makes most Americans highly uncomfortable.

Involvement

As the reader must gather by now, Arabs are involved with each other on many 20 different levels simultaneously. Privacy in a public place is foreign to them. Business transactions in the bazaar, for example, are not just between buyer and seller, but are participated in by everyone. Anyone who is standing around may join in. If a grownup sees a boy breaking a window, he must stop him even if he doesn't know him. Involvement and participation are expressed in other ways as well. If two men are fighting, the crowd must intervene. On the political level, *to fail to intervene* when trouble is brewing is to take sides, which is what our State Department always seems to be doing. Given the fact that few people in the world today are even remotely aware of the cultural mold that forms their thoughts, it is normal for Arabs to view *our* behavior as though it stemmed from *their* own hidden set of assumptions.

Feelings about Enclosed Spaces

In the course of my interviews with Arabs the term "tomb" kept cropping up 21 in conjunction with enclosed space. In a word, Arabs don't mind being crowded by people but hate to be hemmed in by walls. They show a much greater overt sensitivity to architectural crowding than we do. Enclosed space must meet at least three requirements that I know of if it is to satisfy the Arabs: there must be plenty of unobstructed space in which to move around (possibly as much as a thousand square feet); very high ceilings—so high in fact that they do not normally impinge on the visual field; and, in addition, there must be an unobstructed view. It was spaces such as these in which the Americans referred to earlier felt so uncomfortable. One sees the Arab's need for a view expressed in many ways, even negatively, for to cut off a neighbor's view is one of the most effective ways of spiting him. In Beirut one can see what is known locally as the "spite house." It is nothing more than a thick, four-story wall, built at the end of a long fight between neighbors, on a narrow strip of land for the express purpose of denying a view of the Mediterranean to any house built on the land behind. According to one of my informants, there is also a house on a small plot of land between Beirut and Damascus which is completely surrounded by a neighbor's wall built high enough to cut off the view from all windows!

Boundaries

Proxemic patterns tell us other things about Arab culture. For example, the 22 whole concept of the boundary as an abstraction is almost impossible to pin down. In one sense, there are no boundaries. "Edges" of towns, yes, but permanent boundaries out in the country (hidden lines), no. In the course of my work with Arab subjects I had a difficult time translating our concept of a boundary into terms which could be equated with theirs. In order to clarify the distinctions between the two very different definitions, I thought it might be helpful to pinpoint acts which constituted trespass. To date, I have been unable to discover anything even remotely resembling our own legal concept of trespass.

Arab behavior in regard to their own real estate is apparently an extension 23 of, and therefore consistent with, their approach to the body. My subjects simply failed to respond whenever trespass was mentioned. They didn't seem to understand what I meant by this term. This may be explained by the fact that they organize relationships with each other according to closed social systems rather than spatially. For thousands of years Moslems, Marinites, Druses, and

Jews have lived in their own villages, each with strong kin affiliations. Their hierarchy of loyalties is: first to one's self, then to kinsman, townsman, or tribesman, co-religionist and/or countryman. Anyone not in these categories is a stranger. Strangers and enemies are very closely linked, if not synonymous, in Arab thought. Trespass in this context is a matter of who you are, rather than a piece of land or a space with a boundary that can be denied to anyone and everyone, friend and foe alike.

In summary, proxemic patterns differ. By examining them it is possible to 24 reveal hidden cultural frames that determine the structure of a given people's perceptual world. Perceiving the world differently leads to differential definitions of what constitutes crowded living, different interpersonal relations, and a different approach to both local and international politics.

COMPREHENSION

1. This excerpt is from Hall's book entitled *The Hidden Dimension*. What is the hidden dimension, according to the author?
2. In paragraph 10, Hall explains that "differing concepts of the placement of the ego in relation to the body are not easily grasped." What does he mean by this statement? How is it relevant to the theme of his essay?
3. The title of this essay is "The Arab World." What does the term *world* mean within the context of the writing?
4. Define the following words: *proxemic* (paragraph 1), *paradox* (paragraph 2), *inviolate* (paragraph 3), *defer* (paragraph 6), *olfaction* (paragraph 14), and *peripherally* (paragraph 17).

RHETORIC

1. Anthropology is often thought of as an intellectual pursuit. How would you characterize Hall's voice, considering his style of language and method of analysis?
2. How does Hall develop his comparison and contrast of the American versus the Arab perception of manners and driving?
3. People often favor their own perspective of life over a foreign perspective. Is Hall's comparison value-free, or does he seem to prefer one cultural system to another? Explain by making reference to his tone.
4. Who is the implied audience for this essay? Explain your view.
5. Hall makes use of personal anecdote in explaining his theme. What other forms of support does he offer the reader? Cite at least two others and provide an example of each.
6. Writers often have various purposes for writing, for example, to entertain, to inform, to effect change, to advise, or to persuade. What is Hall's purpose or purposes in writing this essay? Explain your view.

WRITING

1. In an essay of 500 to 750 words, argue for or against the proposition that some cultures are better than others.
2. Write an expository essay in which you explain the use and interpretation of personal space by observing students in social situations at your college or university.
3. Write a personal anecdote about a time in your life in which cultural perception caused a conflict between yourself and another person.

"This Is the End of the World": The Black Death

Barbara Tuchman

Barbara Tuchman (1912–1989) was born in New York City and graduated from Radcliffe College. A self-taught historian, she worked as a writer for The Nation *magazine and during World War II served as an editor at the U.S. Office of War Information. Her book* The Guns of August *(1960), a narrative history of the outbreak of World War I, won the Pulitzer Prize. She won it again for her book* Stilwell and the American Experience in China: 1911–45 *(1971). Her other books included such best-sellers as* A Distant Mirror: The Calamitous 14th Century *(1978) and* The First Salute *(1989). In her later years, she was a lecturer at Harvard University and at the U.S. Naval War College. In this selection, excerpted from* A Distant Mirror, *Tuchman explains in her vivid narrative style the effects of the bubonic plague on Western Europe.*

In October 1347, two months after the fall of Calais, Genoese trading ships put   1
into the harbor of Messina in Sicily with dead and dying men at the oars. The ships had come from the Black Sea port of Caffa (now Feodosiya) in the Crimea, where the Genoese maintained a trading post. The diseased sailors showed strange black swellings about the size of an egg or an apple in the armpits and groin. The swellings oozed blood and pus and were followed by spreading boils and black blotches on the skin from internal bleeding. The sick suffered severe pain and died quickly within five days of the first symptoms. As the disease spread, other symptoms of continuous fever and spitting of blood appeared instead of the swellings or buboes. These victims coughed and sweated heavily and died even more quickly, within three days or less, sometimes in 24 hours. In both types everything that issued from the body—breath, sweat, blood from the buboes and lungs, bloody urine, and blood-blackened excrement—smelled foul. Depression and despair accompanied the physical symptoms, and before the end "death is seen seated on the face."

The disease was bubonic plague, present in two forms: one that infected the ₂ bloodstream, causing the buboes and internal bleeding, and was spread by contact; and a second, more virulent pneumonic type that infected the lungs and was spread by respiratory infection. The presence of both at once caused the high mortality and speed of contagion. So lethal was the disease that cases were known of persons going to bed well and dying before they woke, of doctors catching the illness at a bedside and dying before the patient. So rapidly did it spread from one to another that to a French physician, Simon de Covino, it seemed as if one sick person "could infect the whole world." The malignity of the pestilence appeared more terrible because its victims knew no prevention and no remedy.

The physical suffering of the disease and its aspect of evil mystery were ex- ₃ pressed in a strange Welsh lament which saw "death coming into our midst like black smoke, a plague which cuts off the young, a rootless phantom which has no mercy for fair countenance. Woe is me of the shilling in the armpit! It is seething, terrible . . . a head that gives pain and causes a loud cry . . . a painful angry knob . . . Great is its seething like a burning cinder . . . a grievous thing of ashy color." Its eruption is ugly like the "seeds of black peas, broken fragments of brittle sea-coal . . . the early ornaments of black death, cinders of the peelings of the cockle weed, a mixed multitude, a black plague like halfpence, like berries. . . ."

Rumors of a terrible plague supposedly arising in China and spreading ₄ through Tartary (Central Asia) to India and Persia, Mesopotamia, Syria, Egypt, and all of Asia Minor had reached Europe in 1346. They told of a death toll so devastating that all of India was said to be depopulated, whole territories covered by dead bodies, other areas with no one left alive. As added up by Pope Clement VI at Avignon, the total of reported dead reached 23,840,000. In the absence of a concept of contagion, no serious alarm was felt in Europe until the trading ships brought their black burden of pestilence into Messina while other infected ships from the Levant carried it to Genoa and Venice.

By January 1348 it penetrated France via Marseille, and North Africa via Tu- ₅ nis. Shipborne along coasts and navigable rivers, it spread westward from Marseille through the ports of Languedoc to Spain and northward up the Rhône to Avignon, where it arrived in March. It reached Narbonne, Montpellier, Carcassonne, and Toulouse between February and May, and at the same time in Italy spread to Rome and Florence and their hinterlands. Between June and August it reached Bordeaux, Lyon, and Paris, spread to Burgundy and Normandy, and crossed the Channel from Normandy into southern England. From Italy during the same summer it crossed the Alps into Switzerland and reached eastward to Hungary.

In a given area the plague accomplished its kill within four to six months ₆ and then faded, except in the larger cities, where, rooting into the close-quartered population, it abated during the winter, only to reappear in spring and rage for another six months.

In 1349 it resumed in Paris, spread to Picardy, Flanders, and the Low Coun- ₇ tries, and from England to Scotland and Ireland as well as to Norway, where a ghost ship with a cargo of wool and a dead crew drifted offshore until it ran aground near Bergen. From there the plague passed into Sweden, Denmark, Prussia, Iceland, and as far as Greenland. Leaving a strange pocket of immunity in Bohemia, and Russia unattacked until 1351, it had passed from most of Europe by mid-1350. Although the mortality rate was erratic, ranging from one fifth in some places to nine tenths or almost total elimination in others, the overall estimate of modern demographers has settled—for the area extending from India to Iceland—around the same figure expressed in Froissart's casual words: "a third of the world died." His estimate, the common one at the time, was not an inspired guess but a borrowing of St. John's figure for mortality from plague in Revelation, the favorite guide to human affairs of the Middle Ages.

A third of Europe would have meant about 20 million deaths. No one   8
knows in truth how many died. Contemporary reports were an awed impression, not an accurate count. In crowded Avignon, it was said, 400 died daily; 7,000 houses emptied by death were shut up; a single graveyard received 11,000 corpses in six weeks; half the city's inhabitants reportedly died, including 9 cardinals or one third of the total, and 70 lesser prelates. Watching the endlessly passing death carts, chroniclers let normal exaggeration take wings and put the Avignon death toll at 62,000 and even at 120,000, although the city's total population was probably less than 50,000.

When graveyards filled up, bodies at Avignon were thrown into the Rhône   9
until mass burial pits were dug for dumping the corpses. In London in such pits corpses piled up in layers until they overflowed. Everywhere reports speak of the sick dying too fast for the living to bury. Corpses were dragged out of

Burial of the plague victims. From Annales de Gilles de Muisit.
Bibliotheque Royale, Brussels/The Bridgeman Art Library

homes and left in front of doorways. Morning light revealed new piles of bodies. In Florence the dead were gathered up by the Compagnia della Misericordia—founded in 1244 to care for the sick—whose members wore red robes and hoods masking the face except for the eyes. When their efforts failed, the dead lay putrid in the streets for days at a time. When no coffins were to be had, the bodies were laid on boards, two or three at once, to be carried to graveyards or common pits. Families dumped their own relatives into the pits, or buried them so hastily and thinly "that dogs dragged them forth and devoured their bodies."

Amid accumulating death and fear of contagion, people died without last rites and were buried without prayers, a prospect that terrified the last hours of the stricken. A bishop in England gave permission to laymen to make confession to each other as was done by the Apostles, "or if no man is present then even to a woman," and if no priest could be found to administer extreme unction, "then faith must suffice." Clement VI found it necessary to grant remissions of sin to all who died of the plague because so many were unattended by priests. "And no bells tolled," wrote a chronicler of Siena, "and nobody wept no matter what his loss because almost everyone expected death. . . . And people said and believed, 'This is the end of the world.'" 10

In Paris, where the plague lasted through 1349, the reported death rate was 800 a day, in Pisa 500, in Vienna 500 to 600. The total dead in Paris numbered 50,000 or half the population. Florence, weakened by the famine of 1347, lost three to four fifths of its citizens, Venice two thirds, Hamburg and Bremen, though smaller in size, about the same proportion. Cities, as centers of transportation, were more likely to be affected than villages, although once a village was infected, its death rate was equally high. At Givry, a prosperous village in Burgundy of 1,200 to 1,500 people, the parish register records 615 deaths in the space of fourteen weeks, compared to an average of thirty deaths a year in the previous decade. In three villages of Cambridgeshire, manorial records show a death rate of 47 percent, 57 percent, and in one case 70 percent. When the last survivors, too few to carry on, moved away, a deserted village sank back into the wilderness and disappeared from the map altogether, leaving only a grass-covered ghostly outline to show where mortals once had lived. 11

In enclosed places such as monasteries and prisons, the infection of one person usually meant that of all, as happened in the Franciscan convents of Carcassonne and Marseille, where every inmate without exception died. Of the 140 Dominicans at Montpellier only seven survived. Petrarch's brother Gherardo, member of a Carthusian monastery, buried the prior and 34 fellow monks one by one, sometimes three a day, until he was left alone with his dog and fled to look for a place that would take him in. Watching every comrade die, men in such places could not but wonder whether the strange peril that filled the air had not been sent to exterminate the human race. In Kilkenny, Ireland, Brother John Clyn of the Friars Minor, another monk left alone among dead men, kept a record of what had happened lest "things which should be remembered perish with time and vanish from the memory of those who come after us." Sensing "the whole world, as it were, placed within the grasp of the Evil One," and 12 waiting for death to visit him too, he wrote, "I leave parchment to continue this work, if perchance any man survive and any of the race of Adam escape this pestilence and carry on the work which I have begun." Brother John, as noted by another hand, died of the pestilence, but he foiled oblivion.

The largest cities of Europe, with populations of about 100,000, were Paris   13
and Florence, Venice and Genoa. At the next level, more than 50,000 were Ghent and Bruges in Flanders, Milan, Bologna, Rome, Naples, and Palermo, and Cologne. London hovered below 50,000, the only city in England except York with more than 10,000. At the level of 20,000 to 50,000 were Bordeaux, Toulouse, Montpellier, Marseille, and Lyon in France, Barcelona, Seville, and Toledo in Spain, Siena, Pisa, and other secondary cities in Italy, and the Hanseatic trading cities of the Empire. The plague raged through them all, killing anywhere from one third to two thirds of their inhabitants. Italy, with a total population of 10 to 11 million, probably suffered the heaviest toll. Following the Florentine bankruptcies, the crop failures and workers' riots of 1346–47, the revolt of Cola di Rienzi that plunged Rome into anarchy, the plague came as the peak of successive calamities. As if the world were indeed in the grasp of the Evil One, its first appearance on the European mainland in January 1348 coincided with a fearsome earthquake that carved a path of wreckage from Naples up to Venice. Houses collapsed, church towers toppled, villages were crushed, and the destruction reached as far as Germany and Greece. Emotional response, dulled by horrors, underwent a kind of atrophy epitomized by the chronicler who wrote, "And in these days was burying without sorrowe and wedding without friendschippe."

In Siena, where more than half the inhabitants died of the plague, work was   14
abandoned on the great cathedral, planned to be the largest in the world, and never resumed, owing to loss of workers and master masons and "the melancholy and grief" of the survivors. The cathedral's truncated transept still stands in permanent witness to the sweep of death's scythe. Angolo di Tura, a chronicler of Siena, recorded the fear of contagion that froze every other instinct. "Father abandoned child, wife husband, one brother another," he wrote, "for this plague seemed to strike through the breath and sight. And so they died. And no one could be found to bury the dead for money or friendship. . . . And I, Angolo di Tura, called the Fat, buried my five children with my own hands, and so did many others likewise."

There were many to echo his account of inhumanity and few to balance it,   15
for the plague was not the kind of calamity that inspired mutual help. Its loathsomeness and deadliness did not herd people together in mutual distress, but only prompted their desire to escape each other. "Magistrates and notaries refused to come and make the wills of the dying," reported a Franciscan friar of Piazza in Sicily; what was worse, "even the priests did not come to hear their confessions." A clerk of the Archbishop of Canterbury reported the same of English priests who "turned away from the care of their benefices from fear of death." Cases of parents deserting children and children their parents were reported across Europe from Scotland to Russia. The calamity chilled the hearts of men, wrote Boccaccio in his famous account of the plague in Florence that

serves as introduction to the *Decameron.* "One man shunned another . . . kins-
folk held aloof, brother was forsaken by brother, oftentimes husband by wife;
nay, what is more, and scarcely to be believed, fathers and mothers were found
to abandon their own children to their fate, untended, unvisited as if they had
been strangers." Exaggeration and literary pessimism were common in the 14th
century, but the Pope's physician, Guy de Chauliac, was a sober, careful observer who reported the same phenomenon: "A father did not visit his son, nor
the son his father. Charity was dead."

Yet not entirely. In Paris, according to the chronicler Jean de Venette, the [16]
nuns of the Hôtel Dieu or municipal hospital, "having no fear of death, tended
the sick with all sweetness and humility." New nuns repeatedly took the places
of those who died, until the majority "many times renewed by death now rest
in peace with Christ as we may piously believe."

When the plague entered northern France in July 1348, it settled first in [17]
Normandy and, checked by winter, gave Picardy a deceptive interim until the
next summer. Either in mourning or warning, black flags were flown from
church towers of the worst-stricken villages of Normandy. "And in that time,"
wrote a monk of the abbey of Fourcarment, "the mortality was so great among
the people of Normandy that those of Picardy mocked them." The same un-
neighborly reaction was reported of the Scots, separated by a winter's immunity from the English. Delighted to hear of the disease that was scourging the
"southrons," they gathered forces for an invasion, "laughing at their enemies."
Before they could move, the savage mortality fell upon them too, scattering
some in death and the rest in panic to spread the infection as they fled.

In Picardy in the summer of 1349 the pestilence penetrated the castle of [18]
Coucy to kill Enguerrand's mother, Catherine, and her new husband. Whether
her nine-year-old son escaped by chance or was perhaps living elsewhere with
one of his guardians is unrecorded. In nearby Amiens, tannery workers, responding quickly to losses in the labor force, combined to bargain for higher
wages. In another place villagers were seen dancing to drums and trumpets,
and on being asked the reason, answered that, seeing their neighbors die day by
day while their village remained immune, they believed they could keep the
plague from entering "by the jollity that is in us. That is why we dance." Further
north in Tournai on the border of Flanders, Gilles li Muisis, Abbot of St. Martin's, kept one of the epidemic's most vivid accounts. The passing bells rang all
day and all night, he recorded, because sextons were anxious to obtain their fees
while they could. Filled with the sound of mourning, the city became oppressed
by fear, so that the authorities forbade the tolling of bells and the wearing of
black and restricted funeral services to two mourners. The silencing of funeral
bells and of criers' announcements of deaths was ordained by most cities. Siena
imposed a fine on the wearing of mourning clothes by all except widows.

Flight was the chief recourse of those who could afford it or arrange it. The [19]
rich fled to their country places like Boccaccio's young patricians of Florence,
who settled in a pastoral palace "removed on every side from the roads" with "wells
of cool water and vaults of rare wines." The urban poor died in their burrows, "and

only the stench of their bodies informed neighbors of their death." That the poor were more heavily afflicted than the rich was clearly remarked at the time, in the north as in the south. A Scottish chronicler, John of Fordun, stated flatly that the pest "attacked especially the meaner sort and common people—seldom the magnates." Simon de Covino of Montpellier made the same observation. He ascribed it to the misery and want and hard lives that made the poor more susceptible, which was half the truth. Close contact and lack of sanitation was the unrecognized other half. It was noticed too that the young died in greater proportion than the old. Simon de Covino compared the disappearance of youth to the withering of flowers in the fields.

In the countryside peasants dropped dead on the roads, in the fields, in their houses. Survivors in growing helplessness fell into apathy, leaving ripe wheat uncut and livestock untended. Oxen and asses, sheep and goats, pigs and chickens ran wild and they too, according to local reports, succumbed to the pest. English sheep, bearers of the precious wool, died throughout the country. The chronicler Henry Knighton, canon of Leicester Abbey, reported 5,000 dead in one field alone, "their bodies so corrupted by the plague that neither beast nor bird would touch them," and spreading an appalling stench. In the Austrian Alps wolves came down to prey upon sheep and then, "as if alarmed by some invisible warning, turned and fled back into the wilderness." In remote Dalmatia bolder wolves descended upon a plague-stricken city and attacked human survivors. For want of herdsmen, cattle strayed from place to place and died in hedgerows and ditches. Dogs and cats fell like the rest.

The dearth of labor held a fearful prospect because the 14th century lived 21 close to the annual harvest both for food and for next year's seed. "So few servants and laborers were left," wrote Knighton, "that no one knew where to turn for help." The sense of a vanishing future created a kind of dementia of despair. A Bavarian chronicler of Neuberg on the Danube recorded that "Men and women . . . wandered around as if mad" and let their cattle stray "because no one had any inclination to concern themselves about the future." Fields went uncultivated, spring seed unsown. Second growth with nature's awful energy crept back over cleared land, dikes crumbled, salt water reinvaded and soured the lowlands. With so few hands remaining to restore the work of centuries, people felt, in Walsingham's words, that "the world could never again regain its former prosperity."

Though the death rate was higher among the anonymous poor, the known 22 and the great died too. King Alfonso XI of Castile was the only reigning monarch killed by the pest, but his neighbor King Pedro of Aragon lost his wife, Queen Leonora, his daughter Marie, and a niece in the space of six months. John Cantacuzene, Emperor of Byzantium, lost his son. In France the lame Queen Jeanne and her daughter-in-law Bonne de Luxemburg, wife of the Dauphin, both died in 1349 in the same phase that took the life of Enguerrand's mother. Jeanne, Queen of Navarre, daughter of Louis X, was another victim. Edward III's second daughter, Joanna, who was on her way to marry Pedro, the heir of Castile, died in Bordeaux. Women appear to have been more vulnerable than men, perhaps because, being more housebound, they were more exposed to fleas. Boccaccio's mistress Fiammetta, illegitimate daughter of the King of Naples, died, as did Laura, the beloved—whether real or fictional—of Petrarch. Reaching out to us in the future, Petrarch cried, "Oh happy posterity who will not experience such abysmal woe and will look upon our testimony as a fable."

In Florence Giovanni Villani, the great historian of his time, died at 68 in the midst of an unfinished sentence: "... *e dure questo pistolenza fino a* ... (in the midst of this pestilence there came to an end ....)." Siena's master painters, the brothers Ambrogio and Pietro Lorenzetti, whose names never appear after 1348, presumably perished in the plague, as did Andrea Pisano, architect and sculptor of Florence. William of Ockham and the English mystic Richard Rolle of Hampole both disappear from mention after 1349. Francisco Datini, merchant of Prato, lost both his parents and two siblings. Curious sweeps of mortality afflicted certain bodies of merchants in London. All eight wardens of the Company of Cutters, all six wardens of the Hatters, and four wardens of the Goldsmiths died before July 1350. Sir John Pulteney, master draper and four times Mayor of London, was a victim, likewise Sir John Montgomery, Governor of Calais.

Among the clergy and doctors the mortality was naturally high because of the nature of their professions. Out of 24 physicians in Venice, 20 were said to have lost their lives in the plague, although according to another account, some were believed to have fled or to have shut themselves up in their houses. At Montpellier, site of the leading medieval medical school, the physician Simon de Covino reported that, despite the great number of doctors, "hardly one of them escaped." In Avignon, Guy de Chauliac confessed that he performed his medical visits only because he dared not stay away for fear of infamy, but "I was in continual fear." He claimed to have contracted the disease but to have cured himself by his own treatment; if so, he was one of the few who recovered.

Clerical mortality varied with rank. Although the one-third toll of cardinals reflects the same proportion as the whole, this was probably due to their concentration in Avignon. In England, in strange and almost sinister procession, the Archbishop of Canterbury, John Stratford, died in August 1348, his appointed successor died in May 1349, and the next appointee three months later, all three within a year. Despite such weird vagaries, prelates in general managed to sustain a higher survival rate than the lesser clergy. Among bishops the deaths have been estimated at about one in twenty. The loss of priests, even if many avoided their fearful duty of attending the dying, was about the same as among the population as a whole.

Government officials, whose loss contributed to the general chaos, found, on the whole, no special shelter. In Siena four of the nine members of the governing oligarchy died, in France one third of the royal notaries, in Bristol 15 out of the 52 members of the Town Council or almost one third. Tax-collecting obviously suffered, with the result that Philip VI was unable to collect more than a fraction of the subsidy granted him by the Estates in the winter of 1347–48.

Lawlessness and debauchery accompanied the plague as they had during 27 the great plague of Athens of 430 B.C., when according to Thucydides, men grew bold in the indulgence of pleasure: "For seeing how the rich died in a moment and those who had nothing immediately inherited their property, they reflected that life and riches were alike transitory and they resolved to enjoy themselves while they could." Human behavior is timeless. When St. John had his vision of plague in Revelation, he knew from some experience or race memory that those who survived "repented not of the work of their hands. . . . Neither repented they of their murders, nor of their sorceries, nor of their fornication, nor of their thefts."

COMPREHENSION

1. The title of this essay suggests a religious theme. Why did intellectuals and religious leaders associate the bubonic plague with biblical prophecy?
2. Does this essay have a thesis or does it merely record in detail a period in European history? If it does have a thesis, is it implied or expressed directly? Explain your answer.
3. Does Tuchman suggest that Europe was "fated" to endure the tragic consequences of the plague owing to a higher power, or does she attribute the disaster to a confluence of history and chance? Explain your answer.

RHETORIC

1. Tuchman begins her essay by describing in detail the physical symptoms of the plague. What strategy lies behind this rhetorical decision?
2. Tuchman has a reputation as a historian whose goal was to bring "history to life." What methods does she use to realize this goal? Is she successful? Why or why not? What does the illustration on page 278 contribute?
3. Contemporary authors and filmmakers often select morbid themes for their sensational value and/or for financial gain. For example, there is a plethora of "true-crime" stories, "re-creations" of natural disasters, and profiles of aberrant and murderous personalities such as Jeffrey Dahmer, Ted Bundy, and the "Hillside Strangler." Is this Tuchman's purpose? Explain why or why not?
4. Note the particular parts of speech Tuchman uses to begin paragraphs 5 through 7, 9, 11, 12, 14, 16 through 18, 20, 22, and 23. All begin with either conjunctions or prepositions. How do these grammatical devices help maintain the flow of Tuchman's narrative?
5. Tuchman makes references to a vast number of historical figures and specific locations in 14th century Europe. What is her assumption about the educational level of her intended audience? About the specialization of her

readership? Is it necessary to know something about the people and places she cites to appreciate the essay? Or, is Tuchman writing a book of general interest, with the implicit supposition that different readers will extract their own level of appreciation from her narrative? Explain.

6. Tuchman uses direct quotations from the observers and chroniclers of the times. Examine the use of such sources in paragraphs 11, 13, 15, 16, 17, 18, 20, and 23, among others. How does Tuchman weave their observations into her own narrative so that the essay maintains unity and coherence? How does her use of these citations affect the strength of her writing?

WRITING

1. For a research project, study the literary theory commonly known as the "reader-response" school. Apply its principles, particularly those that claim reading is a negotiation between the experience and knowledge of the reader and the text, and write a 400 to 500 word essay exploring your personal response to the essay. Consult with your instructor for propitious ways to fulfill the assignment

2. For a creative writing project, take on the persona of a chronicler of the 14th century, and write a 500- to 600-word narrative reflecting your own eyewitness account of the effect of the plague in your community.

3. For a research project, study Barbara Tuchman's philosophy regarding how history should be reported. Apply your research to examining the techniques used in this particular essay.

Strangers from a Distant Shore

Ronald Takaki

Ronald Takaki (b. 1939) was born in Honolulu, Hawaii. He earned his BA from the college of Wooster in 1961 and his MA and PhD from the University of California, Berkeley, where he is currently a professor of ethnic studies. He also taught American history at the College of San Mateo from 1965 to 1967. Takaki feels that American history is still viewed from a predominantly white perspective and is devoted to more accurately representing all Americans in our society. He has written a number of books: A Pro-Slavery Crusade: The Agitation to Reopen the African Slave Trade *(1971),* Strangers from a Distant Shore: A History of Asian Americans *(1989),* Hiroshima: Why America Dropped the Bomb *(1996),* Iron Cages: Race and Culture in 19th Century America *(1999), and* Double Victory: A Multicultural

History of America in World War II (2000). He is a frequent lecturer and a frequent contributor to history journals as well as other publications. In the following essay, he reflects on the internment of Japanese citizens during World War II and describes his attempts to establish a connection with his Japanese relatives.

To confront the current problems of racism, Asian Americans know they must   1
remember the past and break its silence. This need was felt deeply by Japanese
Americans during the hearings before the commission reviewing the issue of
redress and reparations for Japanese Americans interned during World War II.
Memories of the internment nightmare have haunted the older generation like
ghosts. But the former prisoners have been unable to exorcise them by speaking
out and ventilating their anger.

> When we were children,
> you spoke Japanese
> in lowered voices
> between yourselves.
> Once you uttered secrets
> which we should not know,
> were not to be heard by us.
> When you spoke
> of some dark secret
> you would admonish us,
> "Don't tell it to anyone else."
> It was a suffocated vow of silence.[1]

"Stigmatized," the ex-internees have been carrying the "burden of shame"   2
for over forty painful years. "They felt like a rape victim," explained Congressman Norman Mineta, a former internee of the Heart Mountain internment
camp. "They were accused of being disloyal. They were the victims but they
were on trial and they did not want to talk about it." But Sansei, or third-gener-
ation Japanese Americans, want their elders to tell their story. Warren Furutani,
for example, told the commissioners that young people like himself had been
asking their parents to tell them about the concentration camps and to join them
in pilgrimages to the internment camp at Manzanar. "Why? Why!" their parents
would reply defensively. "Why would you want to know about it? It's not important, we don't need to talk about it." But, Furutani continued, they need to
tell the world what happened during those years of infamy.[2]

---

[1]Richard Oyama, poem published in *Transfer 38* (San Francisco, 1979), p. 43, reprinted in Elaine Kim, *Asian American Literature: An Introduction to the Writings and Their Social Context* (Philadelphia, 1982), pp. 308–309.
[2]Congressman Robert Matsui, speech in the House of Representatives on bill 442 for redress and reparations, September 17, 1987, *Congressional Record* (Washington, 1987), p. 7584; Congressman Norman Mineta, interview with author, March 26, 1988; Warren Furutani, testimony, reprinted in *Amerasia*, vol. 8, no. 2 (1981), p. 104.

Suddenly, during the commission hearings, scores of Issei and Nisei came ³
forward and told their stories. "For over thirty-five years I have been the stereotype Japanese American," Alice Tanabe Nehira told the commission. "I've kept
quiet, hoping in due time we will be justly compensated and recognized for our
years of patient effort. By my passive attitude, I can reflect on my past years to
conclude that it doesn't pay to remain silent." The act of speaking out has enabled the Japanese-American community to unburden itself of years of anger
and anguish. Sometimes their testimonies before the commission were long and
the chair urged them to conclude. But they insisted the time was theirs. "Mr.
Commissioner," protested poet Janice Mirikitani,

> So when you tell me my time is
> up I tell you this.
> Pride has kept my lips
> pinned by nails,
> my rage coffined.
> But I exhume my past
> to claim this time.³

The former internees finally had spoken, and their voices compelled the ⁴
nation to redress the injustice of internment. In August 1988, Congress passed a
bill giving an apology and a payment of $20,000 to each of the survivors of the
internment camps. When President Ronald Reagan signed the bill into law, he
admitted that the United States had committed "a grave wrong," for during
World War II, Japanese Americans had remained "utterly loyal" to this country.
"Indeed, scores of Japanese Americans volunteered for our Armed Forces—
many stepping forward in the internment camps themselves. The 442nd Regi-
mental Combat Team, made up entirely of Japanese Americans, served with
immense distinction to defend this nation, their nation. Yet, back at home, the
soldiers' families were being denied the very freedom for which so many of the
soldiers themselves were laying down their lives." Then the president recalled
an incident that happened forty-three years ago. At a ceremony to award the
Distinguished Service Cross to Kazuo Masuda, who had been killed in action
and whose family had been interned, a young actor paid tribute to the slain
Nisei soldier. "The name of that young actor," remarked the president, who had
been having trouble saying the Japanese names, "—I hope I pronounce this
right—was Ronald Reagan." The time had come, the president acknowledged,
to end "a sad chapter in American history."⁴

Asian Americans have begun to claim their time not only before the com- ⁵
mission on redress and reparations but elsewhere as well, in the novels of Maxine
Hong Kingston and Milton Murayama, the plays of Frank Chin and Philip

---

³Alice Tanabe Nehira, testimony, reprinted in *Amerasia,* vol. 8, no. 2 (1981), p. 93; Janice Mirikitani,
"Breaking Silences," reprinted ibid., p. 109.
⁴Text of Reagan's Remarks:" reprinted in *Pacific Citizen,* August 19–26, 1988, p. 5; *San Francisco
Chronicle,* August 5 and 11, 1988.

Gotanda, the scholarly writings of Sucheng Chan and Elaine Kim, the films of Steve Okazaki and Wa Wang, and the music of Hiroshima and Fred Houn. Others, too, have been breaking silences. Seventy-five-year-old Tomo Shoji, for example, had led a private life, but in 1981 she enrolled in an acting course because she wanted to try something frivolous and to take her mind off her husband's illness. In the beginning, Tomo was hesitant, awkward on the stage. "Be yourself," her teacher urged. Then suddenly she felt something surge through her, springing from deep within, and she began to tell funny and also sad stories about her life. Now Tomo tours the West Coast, a wonderful wordsmith giving one-woman shows to packed audiences of young Asian Americans. "Have we really told our children all we have gone through?" she asks. Telling one of her stories, Tomo recounts: "My parents came from Japan and I was born in a lumber camp. One day, at school, my class was going on a day trip to a show, and I was pulled aside and told I would have to stay behind. All the white kids went." Tomo shares stories about her husband: "When I first met him, I thought, 'wow. Oh, he was so macho! And he wanted his wife to be a good, submissive wife. But then he married me." Theirs had been at times a stormy marriage. "Culturally we were different because he was Issei and I was American, and we used to argue a lot. Well, one day in 1942 right after World War II had started he came home and told me we had to go to an internment camp. 'I'm not going to one because I'm an American citizen,' I said to him. 'You have to go to camp, but not me.' Well, you know what, that was one time my husband was right!" Tomo remembers the camp: "We were housed in barracks, and we had no privacy. My husband and I had to share a room with another couple. So we hanged a blanket in the middle of the room as a partition. But you could hear everything from the other side. Well, one night, while we were in bed, my husband and I got into an argument, and I dumped him out of the bed. The other couple thought we were making violent love." As she stands on the stage and talks stories excitedly, Tomo cannot be contained: "We got such good, fantastic stories to tell. All our stories are different."[5]

Today, young Asian Americans want to listen to these stories—to shatter [6] images of themselves and their ancestors as "strangers" and to understand who they are as Asian Americans. "What don't you know?" their elders ask. Their question seems to have a peculiar frame: it points to the blank areas of collective memory. And the young people reply that they want "to figure out how the invisible world the emigrants built around [their] childhoods fit in solid America." They want to know more about their "no name" Asian ancestors. They want to decipher the signs of the Asian presence here and there across the landscape of America—railroad tracks over high mountains, fields of cane virtually carpeting entire islands, and verdant agricultural lands.

---

[5]Tomo Shoji, "Born Too Soon . . . It's Never Too Late: Growing Up Nisei in Early Washington," presentations at the University of California, Berkeley, September 19, 1987, and the Ohana Cultural Center, Oakland, California, March 4, 1988.

Deserts to farmlands
Japanese-American
Page in history.[6]

They want to know what is their history and "what is the movies." They   7
want to trace the origins of terms applied to them. "Why are we called 'Oriental'?" they question, resenting the appellation that has identified Asians as exotic, mysterious, strange, and foreign. "The word 'orient' simply means 'east.'
So why are Europeans 'West' and why are Asians 'East'? Why did empire-
minded Englishmen in the sixteenth century determine that Asia was 'east' of
London? Who decided what names would be given to the different regions and
peoples of the world? Why does 'American' usually mean 'white'?" Weary of
Eurocentric history, young Asian Americans want their Asian ancestral lives in
America chronicled, "given the name of a place." They have earned the right to
belong to specific places like Washington, California, Hawaii, Puunene,
Promontory Point, North Adams, Manzanar, Doyers Street. "And today, after
125 years of our life here," one of them insists, "I do not want just a home that
time allowed me to have." Seeking to lay claim to America, they realize they can
no longer be indifferent to what happened in history no longer embarrassed by
the hardships and humiliations experienced by their grandparents and parents.

My heart, once bent and cracked, once
ashamed of your China ways.
Ma, hear me now, tell me your story
again and again.[7]

As they listen to the stories and become members of a "community of mem- 8
ory," they are recovering roots deep within this country and the homelands of
their ancestors. Sometimes the journey leads them to discover rich and interesting things about themselves. Alfred Wong, for example, had been told repeatedly for years by his father, "Remember your Chinese name. Remember your
village in Toisha. Remember you are Chinese. Remember all this and you will
have a home." One reason why it was so important for the Chinese immigrants
to remember was that they never felt sure of their status in America. "Unlike
German and Scottish immigrants, the Chinese immigrants never felt comfortable here," Wong explained. "So they had a special need to know there was a
place, a home for them somewhere."[8]

---

[6]Kingston, Maxine Hong, *The Woman Warrior,* p. 6; poem in Kazuo Ito, *Issei: A History of Japanese Immigrants in North America* (Seattle, 1973), p. 493.
[7]Kingston, *The Woman Warrior,* p. 6; Robert Kwan, "Asian v. Oriental: A difference that Counts," *Pacific Citizen,* April 25, 1980; Sir James Augustus Henry Murry (ed.), *The Oxford English Dictionary* (Oxford, 1933), vol. 7, p. 200; Aminur Rahim, "Is Oriental an Occident?" in *The Asiandian,* vol. 5, no. 1, April 1983, p. 20; Shawn Wong, *Homebase* (New York, 1979), p. 111; Nellie Wong, "From a Heart of Rice Straw," in Nellie Wong, *Dreams in Harrison Railroad Park* (Berkeley, 1977), p. 41.
[8]Robert Bellah et al., *Habits of the Heart: Individualism and Commitment in American Life* (Berkeley, 1985), p. 153; Alfred Wong, interviewed by Carol Takaki, April 6 and 13, 1988.

But Wong had a particular reason to remember. His father had married by   9
mutual agreement two women on the same day in China and had come to
America as a merchant in the 1920s. Later he brought over one of his wives. But
she had to enter as a "paper wife," for he had given the immigration authorities
the name of the wife he had left behind. Born here in 1938, Wong grew up
knowing about his father's other wife and the other half of the family in China;
his parents constantly talked about them and regularly sent money home to
Quangdong. For years the "family plan" had been for him to see China someday. In 1984 he traveled to his father's homeland, and there in the family
home—the very house his father had left decades earlier—Alfred Wong was
welcomed by his *Chunk Gwok Ma* ("China Mama"). "You look just like I had
imagined you would look," she remarked. On the walls of the house, he saw
hundreds of photographs—of himself as well as sisters, nieces, nephews, and
his own daughter—that had been placed there over the years. He suddenly realized how much he had always belonged there, and had a warm connectedness. "It's like you were told there was this box and there was a beautiful
diamond in it," Wong said. "But for years and years you couldn't open the box.
Then finally you got a chance to open the box and it was as wonderful as you
had imagined it would be."[9]

Mine is a different yet similar story. My father, Toshio Takaki, died in 1945,   10
when I was only five years old; my mother married Koon Keu Young about a
year later, and I grew up knowing very little about my father. Many years later,
in 1968, after my parents had moved to Los Angeles, my mother passed away
and I had to clear out her room after the funeral. In one of her dresser drawers,
I found an old photograph of my father as a teenager: it was his immigration
photograph. I noticed some Japanese writing on the back. Later a friend translated: "This is Toshio Takaki, registered as an emigrant in Mifune, Kumamoto
Prefecture, 1918." I wondered how young Toshio managed to come to the
United States. Why did he go to Hawaii? Did he go alone? What dreams burned
within the young boy? But a huge silence stood before me, and I could only
speculate that he must have come alone and entered as a student, since the 1908
Gentlemen's Agreement had prohibited the immigration of Japanese laborers.
In Hawaii, he met and married my mother, Catherine Okawa, a Nisei. I had no
Takaki relatives in Hawaii, I thought.

Ten years later, while on a sabbatical in Hawaii, I was "talking story" with   11
my uncle Richard Okawa. I was telling him about the book I was then writing—*Iron Cages,* a study of race and culture in America. Suddenly his eyes lit
up as he exclaimed: "Hey, why you no go write a book about us, huh? About
the Japanese in Hawaii. After all, your grandparents came here as plantation
workers and your mother and all your aunts and uncles were born on the plantation." Smiling, I replied: "Why not?" I went on to write a history of the plantation laborers. The book was published in 1983, and I was featured on
television news and educational programs in Hawaii. One of the programs was

[9]Ibid.

aired in January 1985; a plantation laborer on the Puunene Plantation, Maui, was watching the discussion on television when he exclaimed to his wife: "Hey, that's my cousin, Ronald!" "No joke with me," she said, and he replied: "No, for real, for real."

A few months later, in July, I happened to visit Maui to give a lecture on the plantation experience. While standing in the auditorium shortly before my presentation, I noticed two Japanese men approaching me. One of them draped a red carnation lei around my shoulders and smiled: "You remember me, don't you?" I had never seen this man before and was confused. Then he said again. "You remember me?" After he asked for the third time, he pulled a family photograph from a plastic shopping bag. I saw among the people in the picture my father as a young man, and burst out excitedly: "Oh, you're a Takaki!" He replied: "I'm your cousin, Minoru. I saw you on television last January and when I found out you were going to come here I wanted to see you again. You were five years old when I last saw you. I was in the army on my way to Japan and I came by your house in Palolo Valley. But I guess you don't remember. I've been wondering what happened to you for forty years." Our families had lost contact with each other because of the war, the isolation of the plantation located on another island, my father's death, and my mother's remarriage. Minoru introduced me to his brother Susumu and his son, Leighton, who works on the Puunene Plantation and represents the fourth generation of Takaki plantation workers. Afterward they took me to the Puunene Plantation, showing me McGerrow Camp, where my branch of the Takaki family had lived, and filling me with stories about the old days. "You also have two cousins, Jeanette and Lillian in Honolulu," Minoru said, "and a big Takaki family in Japan."

A year later I visited my Takaki family in Japan. On the day I arrived, my cousin Nobuo showed me a box of old photographs that had been kept for decades in an upstairs closet. "We don't know who this baby is," he said, pointing to a picture of a baby boy. "That's me!" I exclaimed in disbelief. The box contained many photographs of my father, mother, sister. and me. My father had been sending pictures to the family in Kumamoto. I felt a part of me had been there all along and I had in a sense come home. Nobuo's wife Keiko told me that I was *Kumamoto kenjin*—"one of the people of Kumamoto." During my visit, I was taken to the farm where my father was born. We drove up a narrow winding road past waterfalls and streams, tea farms, and rice paddies, to a village nestled high in the mountains. The scene reminded me of old Zen paintings of Japanese landscapes and evoked memories of my mother telling me the story of Momotaro. Toshino Watanabe, an old woman in her eighties, gave me a family portrait that her sister had sent in 1915, there they were in fading sepia—my uncle Teizo, grandfather Santaro, aunt Yukino, cousin Tsutako, uncle Nobuyoshi, and father Toshio, just fourteen years old—in McGerrow Camp on the Puunene Plantation.

The stories of Alfred Wong and myself branch from the late history of Asian Americans and America itself—from William Hooper and Aaron Palmer, westward expansion, the economic development of California and Hawaii, the

Chinese Exclusion Act, the Gentlemen's Agreement. The history of America is essentially the story of immigrants, and many of them, coming from a "different shore" than their European brethren, had sailed east to this new world. After she had traveled across the vast Pacific Ocean and settled here, a woman captured the vision of the immigrants from Asia in haiku's seventeen syllables:

> All the dreams of youth
> Shipped in emigration boats
> To reach this far shore.[10]

In America, Asian immigrants and their offspring have been actors in history— 15
the first Chinese working on the plantations of Hawaii and in the gold fields of California, the early Japanese immigrants transforming the brown San Joaquin Valley into verdant farmlands, the Korean immigrants struggling to free their homeland from Japanese colonialism, the Filipino farm workers and busboys seeking the America in their hearts, the Asian-Indian immigrants picking fruit and erecting Sikh temples in the West, the American-born Asians like Jean Park and Jade Snow Wong and Monica Sone trying to find an identity for themselves as Asian Americans, the second-wave Asian immigrants bringing their skills and creating new communities as well as revitalizing old communities with culture and enterprise, and the refugees from the war-torn countries of Southeast Asia trying to put their shattered lives together and becoming our newest Asian Americans. Their dreams and hopes unfurled here before the wind, all of them— from the first Chinese miners sailing through the Golden Gate to the last Vietnamese boat people flying into Los Angeles International Airport—have been making history in America. And they have been telling us about it all along.

COMPREHENSION

1. Why does Takaki think it important for younger Asian Americans to know about their culture?
2. Why were the adults reluctant to talk about their experiences in the internment camps?
3. What does the writer mean when he says, "Asian Americans have begun to claim their time"?

RHETORIC

1. Takaki uses poetry and dialogue in his essay. How do these devices help to advance his point of view?
2. What is the main idea of the essay? Where in the writing does it appear?

---

[10]Poem by Shigeko, in Kazuo Ito, *Issei,* p. 40.

3. What use does Takaki make of historical facts and details? Cite some examples of these in the essay, and discuss what effect they have on the theme?
4. How does Takaki organize his essay? Trace his ideas through the first five paragraphs. What transitions does he use to shift focus? What is the reasoning behind this strategy?
5. Much of the information Takaki provides comes from individuals. What makes this a powerful technique? Cite examples from the essay to support your response.
6. Examine the conclusion. Why does Takaki crowd so much information into it? How does it work to reinforce Takaki's thesis?

WRITING

1. Photographs play an important role in Takaki's essay as reminders of the past. Find an old family photograph (preferably one taken before your birth), and describe it in detail, including the people in it, their relation to you, the setting, the year it was taken, and its significance to you and your family. Use details and sensory images.
2. Write a research paper about one of the major historical events mentioned in Takaki's essay (the internment of Asian Americans during WWII or the building of railroads across the United States.)

The American Way of Death

Jessica Mitford

Jessica Mitford (1917–1996) was born in England and grew up with her brother and five sisters. She moved to the United States in 1939 and became a naturalized citizen in 1944. Her book The American Way of Death *(1963), a critical examination of the American funeral industry, became a best-seller. Other books included* The Trial of Doctor Spock *(1969),* Kind and Usual Punishment: The Prison Business *(1973),* A Fine Old Conflict *(1977), an account of her experiences as a member of the U.S. Communist Party, and* The American Way of Birth *(1992). In the following essay, Mitford explains in ironic and painstaking terms the processes of embalming and restoring a cadaver, using meticulous detail to support her thesis.*

Embalming is indeed a most extraordinary procedure, and one must wonder at the docility of Americans who each year pay hundreds of millions of dollars for its perpetuation, blissfully ignorant of what it is all about, what is done, how it is done. Not one in ten thousand has any idea of what actually takes place. Books on the subject are extremely hard to come by. They are not to be found in most libraries or bookshops.

In an era when huge television audiences watch surgical operations in the 2 comfort of their living rooms, when, thanks to the animated cartoon, the geography of the digestive system has become familiar territory even to the nursery school set, in a land where the satisfaction of curiosity about almost all matters is a national pastime, the secrecy surrounding embalming can, surely, hardly be attributed to the inherent gruesomeness of the subject. Custom in this regard has within this century suffered a complete reversal. In the early days of American embalming, when it was performed in the home of the deceased, it was almost mandatory for some relative to stay by the embalmer's side and witness the procedure. Today, family members who might wish to be in attendance would certainly be dissuaded by the funeral director. All others, except apprentices, are excluded by law from the preparation room.

A close look at what does actually take place may explain in large measure 3 the undertaker's intractable reticence concerning a procedure that has become his major *raison d'être*. Is it possible he fears that public information about embalming might lead patrons to wonder if they really want this service? If the funeral men are loath to discuss the subject outside the trade, the reader may, understandably, be equally loath to go on reading at this point. For those who have the stomach for it, let us part the formaldehyde curtain. . . .

The body is first laid out in the undertaker's morgue—or rather, Mr. Jones 4 is reposing in the preparation room—to be readied to bid the world farewell.

The preparation room in any of the better funeral establishments has the 5 tiled and sterile look of a surgery, and indeed the embalmer-restorative artist who does his chores there is beginning to adopt the term "dermasurgeon" (appropriately corrupted by some mortician-writers as "demisurgeon") to describe his calling. His equipment, consisting of scalpels, scissors, augers, forceps, clamps, needles, pumps, tubes, bowls and basins, is crudely imitative of the surgeon's as is his technique, acquired in a nine- or twelve-month post-high-school course in an embalming school. He is supplied by an advanced chemical industry with a bewildering array of fluids, sprays, pastes, oils, powders, creams, to fix or soften tissue, shrink or distend it as needed, dry it here, restore the moisture there. There are cosmetics, waxes and paints to fill and cover features, even plaster of Paris to replace entire limbs. There are ingenious aids to prop and stabilize the cadaver: a Vari-Pose Head Rest, the Edwards Arm and Hand Positioner, the Repose Block (to support the shoulders during the embalming), and the Throop Foot Positioner, which resembles an old-fashioned stocks.

Mr. John H. Eckels, president of the Eckels College of Mortuary Science, 6 thus describes the first part of the embalming procedure: "In the hands of a skilled practitioner, this work may be done in a comparatively short time and without mutilating the body other than by slight incision—so slight that it scarcely would cause serious inconvenience if made upon a living person. It is necessary to remove all the blood, and doing this not only helps in the disinfecting, but removes the principal cause of disfigurements due to discoloration."

Another textbook discusses the all-important time element: "The earlier ⁊ this is done, the better, for every hour that elapses between death and embalming will add to the problems and complications encountered. . . ." Just how soon should one get going on the embalming? The author tells us, "On the basis of such scanty information made available to this profession through its rudimentary and haphazard system of technical research, we must conclude that the best results are to be obtained if the subject is embalmed before life is completely extinct—that is, before cellular death has occurred. In the average case, this would mean within an hour after somatic death." For those who feel that there is something a little rudimentary, not to say haphazard, about this advice, a comforting thought is offered by another writer. Speaking of fears entertained in early days of premature burial, he points out, "One of the effects of embalming by chemical injection, however, has been to dispel fears of live burial." How true; once the blood is removed, chances of live burial are indeed remote.

To return to Mr. Jones, the blood is drained out through the veins and re- ₈ placed by embalming fluid pumped in through the arteries. As noted in *The Principles and Practices of Embalming,* "every operator has a favorite injection and drainage point—a fact which becomes a handicap only if he fails or refuses to forsake his favorites when conditions demand it." Typical favorites are the carotid artery, femoral artery, jugular vein, subclavian vein. There are various choices of embalming fluid. If Flextone is used, it will produce a "mild, flexible rigidity. The skin retains a velvety softness, the tissues are rubbery and pliable. Ideal for women and children." It may be blended with B. and G. Products Company's Lyf-Lyk tint, which is guaranteed to reproduce "nature's own skin texture . . . the velvety appearance of living tissue." Suntone comes in three separate tints: Suntan; Special Cosmetic Tint, a pink shade "especially indicated for young female subjects"; and Regular Cosmetic Tint, moderately pink.

About three to six gallons of a dyed and perfumed solution of formalde- ₉ hyde, glycerin, borax, phenol, alcohol and water is soon circulating through Mr. Jones, whose mouth has been sewn together with a "needle directed upward between the upper lip and gum and brought out through the left nostril," with the corners raised slightly "for a more pleasant expression." If he should be bucktoothed, his teeth are cleaned with Bon Ami and coated with colorless nail polish. His eyes, meanwhile, are closed with flesh-tinted eye caps and eye cement.

The next step is to have at Mr. Jones with a thing called a trocar. This is a ₁₀ long, hollow needle attached to a tube. It is jabbed into the abdomen, poked around the entrails and chest cavity, the contents of which are pumped out and replaced with "cavity fluid." This is done, and the hole in the abdomen sewed up, Mr. Jones's face is heavily creamed (to protect the skin from burns which may be caused by leakage of the chemicals), and he is covered with a sheet and left unmolested for a while. But not for long—there is more, much more, in store for him. He has been embalmed, but not yet restored, and the best time to start restorative work is eight to ten hours after embalming, when the tissues have become firm and dry.

The object of all this attention to the corpse, it must be remembered, is to   11
make it presentable for viewing in an attitude of healthy repose. "Our customs
require the presentation of our dead in the semblance of normality . . . unmarred
by the ravages of illness, disease or mutilation," says Mr. J. Sheridan Mayer in
his *Restorative Art.* This is rather a large order since few people die in the full
bloom of health, unravaged by illness and unmarked by some disfigurement.
The funeral industry is equal to the challenge: "In some cases the gruesome appearance of a mutilated or disease-ridden subject may be quite discouraging.
The task of restoration may seem impossible and shake the confidence of the
embalmer. This is the time for intestinal fortitude and determination. Once the
formative work is begun and affected tissues are cleaned or removed, all doubts
of success vanish. It is surprising and gratifying to discover the results which
may be obtained."

The embalmer, having allowed an appropriate interval to elapse, returns to   12
the attack, but now he brings into play' the skill and equipment of sculptor and
cosmetician. Is a hand missing? Casting one in plaster of Paris is a simple matter.
"For replacement purposes, only a cast of the back of the hand is necessary; this
is within the ability of the average operator and is quite adequate." If a lip or
two, a nose or an ear should be missing, the embalmer has at hand a variety of
restorative waxes with which to model replacements. Pores and skin texture are
simulated by stippling with a little brush, and over this cosmetics are laid on.
Head off? Decapitation cases are rather routinely handled. Ragged edges are
trimmed, and head joined to torso with a series of splints, wires and sutures. It is
a good idea to have a little something at the neck—a scarf or high collar—when
time for viewing comes. Swollen mouth? Cut out tissue as needed from inside
the lips. If too much is removed, the surface contour can easily be restored by
padding with cotton. Swollen necks and cheeks are reduced by removing tissue
through vertical incisions made down each side of the neck. "When the deceased
is casketed, the pillow will hide the suture incisions . . . as an extra precaution
against leakage, the suture may be painted with liquid sealer."

The opposite condition is more likely to be present itself—that of emacia-   13
tion. His hypodermic syringe now loaded with massage cream, the embalmer
seeks out and fills the hollowed and sunken areas by injection. In this procedure
the backs of the hands and fingers and the under-chin area should not be
neglected.

Positioning the lips is a problem that recurrently challenges the ingenuity of   14
the embalmer. Closed too tightly, they tend to give a stern, even disapproving
expression. Ideally, embalmers feel, the lips should give the impression of being
ever so slightly parted, the upper lip protruding slightly for a more youthful appearance. This takes some engineering, however, as the lips tend to drift apart.
Lip drift can sometimes be remedied by pushing one or two straight pins
through the inner margin of the lower lip and then inserting them between the
two front upper teeth. If Mr. Jones happens to have no teeth, the pins can just as
easily be anchored in his Armstrong Face Former and Denture Replacer. Another method to maintain lip closure is to dislocate the lower jaw, which is then

held in its new position by a wire run through holes which have been drilled through the upper jaws at the midline. As the French are fond of saying, *il faut souffrir pour être belle.**

If Mr. Jones has died of jaundice, the embalming fluid will very likely turn 15 him green. Does this deter the embalmer? Not if he has intestinal fortitude. Masking pastes and cosmetics are heavily laid on, burial garments and casket interiors are color-correlated with particular care, and Jones is displayed beneath rose-colored lights. Friends will say, "How *well* he looks." Death by carbon monoxide, on the other hand, can be rather a good thing from the embalmer's viewpoint: "One advantage is the fact that this type of discoloration is an exaggerated form of a natural pink coloration." This is nice because the healthy glow is already present and needs but little attention.

The patching and filling completed, Mr. Jones is now shaved, washed and 16 dressed. Cream-based cosmetic, available in pink, flesh, suntan, brunette and blonde, is applied to his hands and face, his hair is shampooed and combed (and, in the case of Mrs. Jones, set), his hands manicured. For the horny-handed son of toil special care must be taken; cream should be applied to remove ingrained grime, and the nails cleaned. "If he were not in the habit of having them manicured in life, trimming and shaping is advised for better appearance— never questioned by kin."

Jones is now ready for casketing (this is the present participle of the verb "to 17 casket"). In this operation his right shoulder should be depressed slightly "to turn the body a bit to the right and soften the appearance of lying flat on the back." Positioning the hands is a matter of importance, and special rubber positioning blocks may be used. The hands should be cupped slightly for a more lifelike, relaxed appearance. Proper placement of the body requires a delicate sense of balance. It should lie as high as possible in the casket, yet not so high that the lid, when lowered, will hit the nose. On the other hand, we are cautioned, placing the body too low "creates the impression that the body is in a box."

Jones is next wheeled into the appointed slumber room where a few last 18 touches may be added—his favorite pipe placed in his hand or, if he was a great reader, a book propped into position. (In the case of little Master Jones a Teddy bear may be clutched.) Here he will hold open house for a few days, visiting hours 10 A.M. to 9 P.M.

COMPREHENSION

1. What is Mitford's value judgment regarding the work of the contemporary American embalmer? By extension, what is her view of the American public that seeks out his or her services? Explain.

---

*ED'S. NOTE—It is necessary to suffer in order to be beautiful.

2. In paragraph 2, Mitford tells us that at one time a family member was present during the embalming procedure. Nowadays, however, embalmers would probably oppose nearly anyone who might wish to witness their craft. Why do you suppose this practice has changed? What does it suggest about changes in American culture?
3. Why does Mitford refer to the "generic" corpse as "Mr. Jones"?
4. Does this essay contain a thesis, or is it simply an example of "process analysis"? Explain your answer.

RHETORIC

1. At what point does the introduction to the essay end and its body paragraphs begin? How does Mitford signal this transition? How can this transition be considered as a metaphor for the embalming process?
2. Embalmers, embalming, and embalming products are referred to in a number of ways. For example, a practitioner is referred to as "dermasurgeon" or "demisurgeon" (paragraph 5). Embalming is referred to as "Mortuary Science" (paragraph 6). Products include such items as "Flextone," "Lyf-Lyk tint," "Suntan," and "Regular Cosmetic Tint." What is the irony behind the names and functions of these nomenclatures? What does the inclusion of these terms suggest about Mitford's attitude toward the embalming process?
3. Why does Mitford quote various "experts" in the field of embalming? What attitude does she seem to have toward these experts?
4. Mitford employs considerable irony in her essay. What is ironic about her explanation of the effects of two types of death (through "jaundice" and "carbon monoxide") in paragraph 15?
5. Mitford uses extensive detail to convey her attitude about the "American Way of Death." How does she convey her attitude through her tone, without directly stating it?
6. What is the ironic purpose for using a French expression at the conclusion of paragraph 14?
7. Define the following terms employed by the author: *perpetuation* (paragraph 1), *dissuaded* (paragraph 2), *pliable* (paragraph 8), *unravaged* (paragraph 11), and *stippling* (paragraph 12).
8. In paragraph 17, Mitford describes several methods embalmers use to position the body in the casket. What are these methods, and why does Mitford present them as ironic?

WRITING

1. Write an explanation of a process you personally find disgusting or delightful that seems to reflect the "American Way of Life." Make your attitude clear by your choice of words.

2. In the role of a loved one of someone recently deceased, write a letter to Mitford defending your decision to have the deceased embalmed for public viewing.

3. Interview a fellow student who is from another culture about funeral practices and attitudes toward dying in his or her country. Compare them to those you have observed in America.

Connections for Critical Thinking

1. Cofer writes about Latino culture and Kingston about Chinese-American culture in their respective essays. What connections do they make between their subjects and cultural alienation? How do they present their ideas? How are their tones similar? How are they different?

2. Write an essay exploring the role of parents and relatives in the essays by Cofer, Momaday, Hughes, and Kingston. Compare the impact these individuals had on the writers. How strong is the presence of family in these essays?

3. Consider the current position of women in culture. Refer to any three essays in this chapter to support your main observations.

4. How does one's experience of being an outsider or stranger to a culture affect one's understanding of that culture? Use essays from this chapter to support your key points.

5. Write an essay exploring the shape of contemporary American culture as it is reflected in the essays in this chapter. Cite specific support from at least five of the selections you have read.

6. How does a nation maintain a strong sense of self and still remain open to outside influences? Is a national identity crucial to a nation's survival? Use the opinions of representative authors in this chapter to address the question.

7. Is there such a thing as ethnic character, something that distinguishes Native Americans from African Americans, or Latinos from Asian immigrants? What factors contribute to identification with culture and with nation?

8. Argue for or against the proposition that Americans are ignorant of both the contributions and values of "non-Western" cultures in our country. Refer specifically to Reed and Takaki.

9. Design a chat room with five class members and discuss the differences in perspectives between people in the Middle Ages and their response to the "Black Death" (referring specifically to Tuchman) with the attitude of Americans toward the AIDS epidemic or the anthrax scare.

10. Search the Web for information on Judith Ortiz Cofer and Maxine Hong Kingston. Download appropriate material, and then write a brief research paper on their perceptions of ethnicity and the American experience.

 chapter **6**

Government, Politics, and Social Justice
How Do We Decide What Is Fair?

Recent studies indicate that American students have an extremely weak understanding of government and politics. In fact, one-third of all high school juniors cannot identify the main purpose of the Declaration of Independence or say in which century it was signed. This document is one of the selections in this chapter. If we are ignorant of such a basic instrument in the making of our history and society, what can that say about our concepts of citizenship? Do we now see ourselves purely in terms of economic units, that is, our ability or potential to make money, or as consumers, the roles we play in spending it? Other notable essays on government, politics, and social justice in this chapter will help us understand our cultural legacies, and what has traditionally been thought of as the impetus in developing America as a country.

Major writers can bring politics and issues of social justice to life, enabling us to develop a sense of the various processes that have influenced the development of cultures over time. By studying the course of history and politics, we develop causal notions of how events are interrelated and how traditions have evolved. The study of history and politics can be an antidote to the continuous "present tense" of the media, which often have the power to make us believe we live from moment to moment, discouraging reflection on serious issues, such as why we live the way we do and how we came to be the people we are. Essays, speeches, documents, biographies, narratives, and many other literary forms capture events and illuminate the past while holding up a mirror to the present. Our political story can be brought to life out of the plain but painfully eloquent artifacts of oral culture. On the other hand, Thomas Jefferson employs classical rhetorical structures—notably argumentation—in outlining democratic vistas in the Declaration of Independence.

Even the briefest reflection will remind us of how important political processes and institutions are. Put simply, a knowledge of government and politics, and of our quest for social justice, validates our memory, a remembrance of how important the past is to our current existence. When, for example, Martin Luther King Jr. approaches the subject of oppression from a theological perspective, we are reminded of how important the concept of freedom is to our heritage and the various ways it can be addressed. Indeed, had we been more familiar with chapters in human history, we might have avoided some of the commensurate responses to the crises in our own era. The essays in this chapter help remind us—as the philosopher Santayana warned—"Those who forget the lessons of history are doomed to repeat them."

Only through a knowledge of government and politics can we make informed choices. Through a study of government and politics, we learn about challenges and opportunities, conflicts and their resolutions, and the use and abuse of power across time in numerous cultures and civilizations. It is through the study of historical processes and political institutions that we seek to define ourselves and to learn how we have evolved.

Previewing the Chapter

As you read the selections in this chapter and respond to them in discussion and writing, consider the following questions:

- What specific events does the author concentrate on? What is the time frame?
- What larger historical and political issues concern the author?
- From what perspective does the author treat the subject, from that of participant, observer, commentator, or some other perspective?
- What is the author's purpose in treating events and personalities: to explain, to instruct, to amuse, to criticize, or to celebrate?
- What does the author learn about history and politics from his or her inquiry into events?
- What sorts of conflicts—historical, political, economic, social, religious—emerge in the essay?
- Are there any correspondences among the essays? What analogies do the authors themselves draw?
- What is the relationship of people and personalities to the events under consideration?
- Which biases and ideological positions do you detect in the authors' works?
- How has your understanding of history and politics been challenged by the essays in this chapter?

Classic and Contemporary Images
IS THERE TOO MUCH MONEY IN POLITICS?

Using a Critical Perspective   As these two cartoons suggest, from the 1800s to the present day, American artists have considered politicians to be fair game for satire. What graphic elements in each representation are highlighted? How do these elements help us focus on the "message" the cartoonist wishes to convey? What are the advantages and disadvantages of using cartoon art to convey a statement about politics and political life? Do you agree or disagree with the cartoonists' message, and why?

THE "BRAINS"

THAT ACHIEVED THE TAMMANY VICTORY AT THE ROCHESTER DEMOCRATIC CONVENTION.

Library of Congress

Corruption in politics has been a perennial subject for cartoonists. In his day, the classic political cartoonist Thomas Nast (1840–1902) lampooned New York City's infamous William M. ("Boss") Tweed (1823–1878) and his Tammany Hall cronies unmercifully, as shown in the cartoon above.

In June 2000, Ann Telnaes, winner of the 2001 Pulitzer Prize for political cartoons, offered her view of the influence of "soft money" (unlimited contributions to political parties) on both the Democratic and Republican parties.

Classic and Contemporary Essays
WHAT IS THE AMERICAN DREAM?

Both Thomas Jefferson and Martin Luther King, Jr., are now safely placed within the pantheon of American historical figures. The following two writing samples help indicate why. Both are concerned with perhaps the most significant issue that concerns contemporary humankind: freedom. Jefferson creates a doctrine that is powerful owing to his use of concise and powerful language, which he employs both to enumerate British offenses as well as to call upon his fellow Americans to revolt if need be. While his list of grievances may seem unquestionably correct to the contemporary mind, one must consider that Jefferson was a product of the Enlightenment, when philosophers had finally turned their attention to the primacy of individual rights after millennia of living under monarchic rule. King also provides us with the powerful theme of freedom in his famous speech; while his reflections address the peculiarly American racial divide, his style contains many biblical references and his rhetoric is that of the sermon. The reader should consider why these two documents, regardless of their historical context, seem to be milestones in our nation's history.

The Declaration of Independence
In Congress, July 4, 1776

Thomas Jefferson

Thomas Jefferson (1743–1826) was governor of Virginia during the American Revolution, America's first secretary of state, and the third president of the United States. He had a varied and monumental career as politician, public servant, scientist, architect, educator (he founded the University of Virginia), and man of letters. Jefferson attended the Continental Congress in 1775, where he wrote the rough draft of the Declaration of Independence and revised it. Other hands made contributions to the document that was signed on July 4, 1776, but the wording, style, structure, and spirit of the final version are distinctly Jefferson's. Like Thomas Paine, Benjamin Franklin, James Madison, and other major figures of the Revolutionary era, Jefferson was notable for his use of prose as an instrument for social and political change. In the Declaration of Independence, we see the direct, precise, logical, and persuasive statement of revolutionary principles that makes the document one of the best known and best written texts in world history. Jefferson died in his home at Monticello on July 4, fifty years to the day from the signing of the Declaration of Independence.

When in the Course of human events it becomes necessary for one people to dissolve the political bands which have connected them with another, and to assume among the powers of the earth, the separate and equal station to which the Laws of Nature and of Nature's God entitle them, a decent respect to the opinions of mankind requires that they should declare the causes which impel them to the separation. 1

We hold these truths to be self-evident, that all men are created equal, that they are endowed by their Creator with certain unalienable Rights, that among these are Life, Liberty and the pursuit of Happiness.—That to secure these rights, Governments are instituted among Men, deriving their just powers from the consent of the governed.—That whenever any Form of Government becomes destructive of these ends, it is the Right of the People to alter or to abolish it, and to institute new Government, laying its foundation on such principles and organizing its powers in such form, as to them shall seem most likely to effect their Safety and Happiness. Prudence, indeed, will dictate that Governments long established should not be changed for light and transient causes; and accordingly all experience hath shewn that mankind are more disposed to suffer, while evils are sufferable, than to right themselves by abolishing the forms to which they are accustomed. But when a long train of abuses and usurpations, pursuing invariably the same Object evinces a design to reduce them under absolute Despotism, it is their right, it is their duty, to throw off such Government, and to provide new Guards for their future security.—Such 2 has been the patient sufferance of these Colonies; and such is now the necessity which constrains them to alter their former Systems of Government. The history of the present King of Great Britain is a history of repeated injuries and usurpations, all having in direct object the establishment of an absolute Tyranny over these States. To prove this, let Facts be submitted to a candid world.

He has refused his Assent to Laws, the most wholesome and necessary for 3 the public good.

He has forbidden his Governors to pass Laws of immediate and pressing 4 importance, unless suspended in their operation till his Assent should be obtained; and when so suspended, he has utterly neglected to attend to them.

He has refused to pass other Laws for the accommodation of large districts 5 of people, unless those people would relinquish the right of Representation in the Legislature, a right inestimable to them and formidable to tyrants only.

He has called together legislative bodies at places unusual, uncomfortable, 6 and distant from the depository of their public Records, for the sole purpose of fatiguing them into compliance with his measures.

He has dissolved Representative Houses repeatedly, for opposing with 7 manly firmness his invasions on the rights of the people.

He has refused for a long time, after such dissolutions, to cause others to be 8 elected; whereby the Legislative powers, incapable of Annihilation, have returned to the People at large for their exercise; the State remaining in the mean time exposed to all the dangers of invasion from without, and convulsions within.

He has endeavoured to prevent the population of these States; for that pur- 9 pose obstructing the Laws for Naturalization of Foreigners; refusing to pass others to encourage their migrations hither, and raising the conditions of new Appropriations of Lands.

He has obstructed the Administration of Justice, by refusing his Assent to 10 Laws for establishing Judiciary powers.

He has made Judges dependent on his Will alone, for the tenure of their of- 11 fices, and the amount and payment of their salaries.

He has erected a multitude of New Offices, and sent hither swarms of Offi- 12 cers to harass our people, and eat out their substance.

He has kept among us, in times of peace, Standing Armies without the Con- 13 sent of our legislatures.

He has affected to render the Military independent of and superior to the 14 Civil power.

He has combined with others to subject us to a jurisdiction foreign to our 15 constitution, and unacknowledged by our laws; giving his Assent to their Acts of pretended Legislation:

For quartering large bodies of armed troops among us:

For protecting them, by a mock Trial, from punishment for any Murders which they should commit on the Inhabitants of these States:

For cutting off our Trade with all parts of the world:

For imposing Taxes on us without our Consent:

For depriving us in many cases, of the benefits of Trial by jury:

For transporting us beyond Seas to be tried for pretended offences:

For abolishing the free System of English Laws in a neighboring Province, establishing therein an Arbitrary government, and enlarging its Boundaries so as to render it at once an example and fit instrument for introducing the same absolute rule into these Colonies:

For taking away our Charters, abolishing our most valuable Laws and altering fundamentally the Forms of our Governments:

For suspending our own Legislatures, and declaring themselves invested with power to legislate for us in all cases whatsoever.

He has abdicated Government here, by declaring us out of his Protection 16 and waging War against us.

He has plundered our seas, ravaged our Coasts, burnt our towns, and de- 17 stroyed the lives of our people.

He is at this time transporting large Armies of foreign Mercenaries to com- 18 plete the works of death, desolation and tyranny, already begun with circumstances of Cruelty & Perfidy scarcely paralleled in the most barbarous ages, and totally unworthy the Head of a civilized nation.

He has constrained our fellow Citizens taken Captive on the high Seas to 19 bear Arms against their Country, to become the executioners of their friends and Brethren, or to fall themselves by their Hands.

He has excited domestic insurrections amongst us, and has endeavoured to 20 bring on the inhabitants of our frontiers, the merciless Indian Savages, whose known rule of warfare, is an undistinguished destruction of all ages, sexes and conditions.

In every stage of these Oppressions We have Petitioned for Redress in the 21 most humble terms: Our repeated Petitions have been answered only by repeated injury. A Prince, whose character is thus marked by every act which may define a Tyrant, is unfit to be the ruler of a free people.

Nor have We been wanting in attentions to our British brethren. We have 22 warned them from time to time of attempts by their legislature to extend an unwarrantable jurisdiction over us. We have reminded them of the circumstances of our emigration and settlement here. We have appealed to their native justice and magnanimity, and we have conjured them by the ties of our common kindred to disavow these usurpations, which would inevitably interrupt our connections and correspondence. They too have been deaf to the voice of justice and of consanguinity. We must, therefore, acquiesce in the necessity, which denounces our Separation, and hold them, as we hold the rest of mankind, Enemies in War, in Peace Friends.

We, therefore, the Representatives of the United States of America, in General 23 Congress, Assembled, appealing to the Supreme Judge of the world for the rectitude of our intentions, do, in the Name, and by Authority of the good People of these Colonies, solemnly publish and declare, That these United Colonies are, and of Right ought to be Free and Independent States; that they are Absolved from all Allegiance to the British Crown, and that all political connection between them and the State of Great Britain, is and ought to be totally dissolved; and that as Free and Independent States, they have full Power to levy War, conclude Peace, contract Alliances, establish Commerce, and to do all other Acts and Things which Independent States may of right do. And for the support of this Declaration, with a firm reliance on the protection of divine Providence, we mutually pledge to each other our Lives, our Fortunes and our sacred Honor.

COMPREHENSION

1. Explain Jefferson's main and subordinate purposes in this document.
2. What is Jefferson's key assertion, or argument? Mention several reasons that he gives to support his argument.
3. Summarize Jefferson's definition of human nature and government.

RHETORIC

1. There are many striking words and phrases in the Declaration of Independence, notably in the beginning. Locate three such examples, and explain their connotative power and effectiveness.
2. Jefferson and his colleagues had to draft a document designed for several audiences. What audiences did they have in mind? How do their language and style reflect their awareness of multiple audiences?
3. The Declaration of Independence is a classic model of syllogistic reasoning and deductive argument (see the Glossary). What is its major premise, and where is this premise stated? The minor premise? The conclusion?
4. What sort of inductive evidence does Jefferson offer?
5. Why is the middle portion, or body, of the Declaration of Independence considerably longer than the introduction or conclusion? What holds the body together?
6. Explain the function and effect of parallel structure in this document.

WRITING

1. Do you believe that "all men are created equal"? Justify your answer.
2. Discuss the relevance of the Declaration of Independence to politics today.
3. Explain why the Declaration of Independence is a model of effective prose.
4. Write your own declaration of independence—from family, employer, required courses, or the like. Develop this declaration as an op-ed piece for a newspaper.

I Have a Dream

Martin Luther King, Jr.

Martin Luther King, Jr. (1929–1968) was born in Atlanta, Georgia, and learned degrees from Morehouse College, Crozer Theological Seminary, Boston University, and Chicago Theological Seminary. As Baptist clergyman, civil rights leader, founder and president of the Southern Christian Leadership Conference, and, in 1964, Nobel Peace Prize winner, King was a celebrated advocate of nonviolent resistance to achieve equality and racial integration in the world. King was a gifted orator and a highly persuasive writer. His books include Stride Toward Freedom *(1958);* Letter from Birmingham City Jail *(1963);* Strength to Love *(1963);* Why We Can't Wait *(1964); and* Where Do We Go from Here: Chaos or Community? *(1967), a book published shortly before Reverend King was assassinated on April 4, 1968, in Memphis, Tennessee. This selection, a milestone of American oratory, was the keynote address at the March on Washington, August 28, 1963.*

I am happy to join with you today in what will go down in history as the greatest demonstration for freedom in the history of our nation. 1

Fivescore years ago, a great American, in whose symbolic shadow we stand 2 today, signed the Emancipation Proclamation. This momentous decree came as a great beacon light of hope to millions of Negro slaves who had been seared in the flames of withering injustice. It came as a joyous daybreak to end the long night of their captivity.

But one hundred years later, the Negro still is not free; one hundred years 3 later, the life of the Negro is still sadly crippled by the manacles of segregation and the chains of discrimination; one hundred years later, the Negro lives on a lonely island of poverty in the midst of a vast ocean of material prosperity; one hundred years later, the Negro is still languishing in the corners of American society and finds himself in exile in his own land.

So we've come here today to dramatize a shameful condition. In a sense 4 we've come to our nation's capital to cash a check. When the architects of our republic wrote the magnificent words of the Constitution and the Declaration of Independence, they were signing a promissory note to which every American was to fall heir. This note was the promise that all men, yes, black men as well as white men, would be guaranteed the unalienable rights of life, liberty, and the pursuit of happiness.

It is obvious today that America has defaulted on this promissory note in so 5 far as her citizens of color are concerned. Instead of honoring this sacred obligation, America has given the Negro people a bad check; a check which has come back marked "insufficient funds." We refuse to believe that there are insufficient funds in the great vaults of opportunity of this nation. And so we've come to

cash this check, a check that will give us upon demand the riches of freedom
and the security of justice.

We have also come to this hallowed spot to remind America of the fierce ur- 6
gency of now. This is no time to engage in the luxury of cooling off or to take the
tranquilizing drug of gradualism. Now is the time to make real the promises of
democracy; now is the time to rise from the dark and desolate valley of segregation to the sunlit path of racial justice; now is the time to lift our nation from
the quicksands of racial injustice to the solid rock of brotherhood; now is the
time to make justice a reality for all God's children. It would be fatal for the nation to overlook the urgency of the moment. This sweltering summer of the
Negro's legitimate discontent will not pass until there is an invigorating autumn of freedom and equality.

Nineteen sixty-three is not an end, but a beginning. And those who hope 7
that the Negro needed to blow off steam and will now be content, will have a
rude awakening if the nation returns to business as usual.

There will be neither rest nor tranquility in America until the Negro is 8
granted his citizenship rights. The whirlwinds of revolt will continue to shake
the foundations of our nation until the bright day of justice emerges.

But there is something that I must say to my people who stand on the warm 9
threshold which leads into the palace of justice. In the process of gaining our
rightful place we must not be guilty of wrongful deeds.

Let us not seek to satisfy our thirst for freedom by drinking from the cup of 10
bitterness and hatred. We must forever conduct our struggle on the high plane
of dignity and discipline. We must not allow our creative protest to degenerate
into physical violence. Again and again we must rise to the majestic heights of
meeting physical force with soul force.

The marvelous new militancy which has engulfed the Negro community 11
must not lead us to a distrust of all white people, for many of our white brothers, as evidenced by their presence here today, have come to realize that their
destiny is tied up with our destiny and they have come to realize that their freedom is inextricably bound to our freedom. This offense we share mounted to
storm the battlements of injustice must be carried forth by a biracial army. We
cannot walk alone.

And as we walk, we must make the pledge that we shall always march 12
ahead. We cannot turn back. There are those who are asking the devotees of
civil rights, "When will you be satisfied?" We can never be satisfied as long as
the Negro is the victim of the unspeakable horrors of police brutality.

We can never be satisfied as long as our bodies, heavy with fatigue of travel, 13
cannot gain lodging in the motels of the highways and the hotels of the cities.
We cannot be satisfied as long as the Negro's basic mobility is from a smaller
ghetto to a larger one.

We can never be satisfied as long as our children are stripped of their self- 14
hood and robbed of their dignity by signs stating "for whites only." We cannot
be satisfied as long as a Negro in Mississippi cannot vote and a Negro in New
York believes he has nothing for which to vote. No, we are not satisfied, and we

will not be satisfied until justice rolls down like waters and righteousness like a mighty stream.

I am not unmindful that some of you have come here out of excessive trials 15 and tribulation. Some of you have come fresh from narrow jail cells. Some of you have come from areas where your quest for freedom left you battered by the storms of persecution and staggered by the winds of police brutality. You have been the veterans of creative suffering. Continue to work with the faith that unearned suffering is redemptive.

Go back to Mississippi; go back to Alabama; go back to South Carolina; go 16 back to Georgia; go back to Louisiana; go back to the slums and ghettos of the northern cities, knowing that somehow this situation can, and will be changed. Let us not wallow in the valley of despair.

So I say to you, my friends, that even though we must face the difficulties of 17 today and tomorrow, I still have a dream. It is a dream deeply rooted in the American dream that one day this nation will rise up and live out the true meaning of its creed—we hold these truths to be self-evident, that all men are created equal.

I have a dream that one day on the red hills of Georgia, sons of former 18 slaves and sons of former slave-owners will be able to sit down together at the table of brotherhood.

I have a dream that one day, even the state of Mississippi, a state sweltering 19 with the heat of injustice, sweltering with the heat of oppression, will be transformed into an oasis of freedom and justice.

I have a dream my four little children will one day live in a nation where 20 they will not be judged by the color of their skin but by the content of their character. I have a dream today!

I have a dream that one day, down in Alabama, with its vicious racists, with 21 its governor having his lips dripping with the words of interposition and nullification, that one day, right there in Alabama, little black boys and black girls will be able to join hands with little white boys and white girls as sisters and brothers. I have a dream today!

I have a dream that one day every valley shall be exalted, every hill and 22 mountain shall be made low, the rough places shall be made plain, and the crooked places shall be made straight and the glory of the Lord will be revealed and all flesh shall see it together.

This is our hope. This is the faith that I go back to the South with. 23

With this faith we will be able to hear out of the mountain of despair a stone 24 of hope. With this faith we will be able to transform the jangling discords of our nation into a beautiful symphony of brotherhood.

With this faith we will be able to work together, to pray together, to strug- 25 gle together, to go to jail together, to stand up for freedom together, knowing that we will be free one day. This will be the day when all of God's children will be able to sing with new meaning—"my country 'tis of thee; sweet land of liberty; of thee I sing; land where my fathers died, land of the pilgrims' pride; from every mountain side, let freedom ring"—and if America is to be a great nation, this must become true.

So let freedom ring from the prodigious hilltops of New Hampshire.   26
Let freedom ring from the mighty mountains of New York.   27
Let freedom ring from the heightening Alleghenies of Pennsylvania.   28
Let freedom ring from the snow-capped Rockies of Colorado.   29
Let freedom ring from the curvaceous slopes of California.   30
But not only that.   31
Let freedom ring from Stone Mountain of Georgia.   32
Let freedom ring from Lookout Mountain of Tennessee.   33

Let freedom ring from every hill and molehill of Mississippi, from every   34
mountainside, let freedom ring.

And when we allow freedom to ring, when we let it ring from every village
and hamlet, from every state and city, we will be able to speed up that day
when all of God's children—black men and white men, Jews and Gentiles,   35
Catholics and Protestants—will be able to join hands and to sing in the words of
the old Negro spiritual, "Free at last, free at last; thank God Almighty, we are
free at last."

COMPREHENSION

1. What is the main purpose behind this speech? Where does King state this
    purpose most clearly?
2. Why does King make use of "fivescore years ago" (paragraph 2)? How is
    this more appropriate than simply saying, "a hundred years ago"?
3. Who is King's audience? Where does he acknowledge the special historic
    circumstances influencing his speech?

RHETORIC

1. From what sources does King adapt phrases to give his work allusive richness?
2. What do the terms *interposition* and *nullification* (paragraph 21) mean? What
    is their historical significance?
3. Why does King make use of repetition? Does this technique work well in
    print? Explain.
4. What is the purpose of the extended metaphor in paragraphs 4 and 5?
    Which point in paragraph 3 does it refer to?
5. In which paragraphs does King address the problems of African Americans?
6. Why is this selection entitled "I Have a Dream"? How do dreams serve as a
    motif for this speech?

WRITING

1. "I Have a Dream" is considered by many people to be among the greatest
    speeches delivered by an American. Do you think that it deserves to be?
    Explain in an essay.

2. Write a comparative essay analyzing King's assessment of black Americans' condition in 1963 and their condition today. What do you think King would say if he knew of contemporary conditions?
3. Write your own "I Have a Dream" essay, basing it on your vision of America or of a special people.
4. Prepare a newspaper editorial advocating a solution to one aspect of racial, ethnic, or sexual injustice.

Classic and Contemporary: Questions for Comparison

1. Compare the Declaration of Independence with King's speech in terms of the level of language, style, and content. Are they equally powerful and resonant? Cite specific passages from the essays to illustrate your responses.
2. Rewrite the Declaration of Independence in modern English as you believe Dr. King might, reflecting his concerns about the African American and other minorities in this country. Include a list of grievances similar to the one concerning British rule.
3. Write a research paper about the lives and times of King and Jefferson. Compare and contrast any significant events or pertinent biographical data in their backgrounds.

Shooting an Elephant

George Orwell

George Orwell (1903–1950) was the pseudonym of Eric Blair, an English novelist, essayist, and journalist. Orwell served with the Indian Imperial Police from 1922 to 1927 in Burma, fought in the Spanish Civil War, and acquired from his experiences a disdain of totalitarian and imperialistic systems. This attitude is reflected in his satiric fable, Animal Farm *(1945), and in his bleak futuristic novel,* 1984 *(1949). In this essay, Orwell invokes personal experience to expose the contradictions inherent in British imperialism.*

In Moulmein, in Lower Burma, I was hated by large numbers of people—the 1 only time in my life that I have been important enough for this to happen to me. I was subdivisional police officer of the town, and in an aimless, petty kind of way anti-European feeling was very bitter. No one had the guts to raise a riot, but if a European woman went through the bazaars alone somebody would probably spit betel juice over her dress. As a police officer I was an obvious target and was baited whenever it seemed safe to do so. When a nimble Burman tripped me up on the football field and the referee (another Burman) looked the other way, the crowd yelled with hideous laughter. This happened more than once. In the end the sneering yellow faces of young men that met me everywhere, the insults hooted after me when I was at a safe distance, got badly on my nerves. The young Buddhist priests were the worst of all. There were several thousands of them in the town and none of them seemed to have anything to do except stand on street corners and jeer at Europeans.

All this was perplexing and upsetting. For at that time I had already made   2 up my mind that imperialism was an evil thing and the sooner I chucked up my job and got out of it the better. Theoretically—and secretly, of course—I was all for the Burmese and all against their oppressors, the British. As for the job I was doing, I hated it more bitterly than I can perhaps make clear. In a job like that you see the dirty work of Empire at close quarters. The wretched prisoners huddling in the stinking cages of the lock-ups, the grey, cowed faces of the long-term convicts, the scarred buttocks of the men who had been flogged with bamboo—all these oppressed me with an intolerable sense of guilt. But I could get nothing into perspective. I was young and ill-educated and I had had to think out my problems in the utter silence that is imposed on every Englishman in the East. I did not even know that the British Empire is dying, still less did I know that it is a great deal better than the younger empires that are going to supplant it. All I knew was that I was stuck between my hatred of the empire I served and my rage against the evil-spirited little beasts who tried to make my job impossible. With one part of my mind I thought of the British Raj as an unbreakable tyranny, as something clamped down, *in saecula saeculorum,* upon the will of prostrate peoples; with another part I thought that the greatest joy in the world would be to drive a bayonet into a Buddhist priest's guts. Feelings like these are the normal by-products of imperialism; ask any Anglo-Indian official, if you can catch him off duty.

One day something happened which in a roundabout way was enlighten-   3 ing. It was a tiny incident in itself, but it gave me a better glimpse than I had had before of the real nature of imperialism—the real motives for which despotic governments act. Early one morning the sub-inspector at a police station the other end of the town rang me up on the Phone and said that an elephant was ravaging the bazaar. Would I please come and do something about it? I did not know what I could do, but I wanted to see what was happening and I got on to a pony and started out. I took my rifle, an old .44 Winchester and much too small to kill an elephant, but I thought the noise might be useful *in terrorem.* Various Burmans stopped me on the way and told me about the elephant's doings. It was not, of course, a wild elephant, but a tame one which had gone "must." It had been chained up as tame elephants always are when their attack of "must" is due, but on the previous night it had broken its chain and escaped. Its mahout, the only person who could manage it when it was in that state, had set out in pursuit, but he had taken the wrong direction and was now twelve hours' journey away, and in the morning the elephant had suddenly reappeared in the town. The Burmese population had no weapons and were quite helpless against it. It had already destroyed somebody's bamboo hut, killed a cow and raided some fruit-stalls and devoured the stock; also it had met the municipal rubbish van, and, when the driver jumped out and took to his heels, had turned the van over and inflicted violence upon it.

The Burmese sub-inspector and some Indian constables were waiting for 4 me in the quarter where the elephant had been seen. It was a very poor quarter, a labyrinth of squalid bamboo huts, thatched with palm-leaf, winding all over a steep hillside. I remember that it was a cloudy stuffy morning at the beginning of the rains. We began questioning the people as to where the elephant had gone, and, as usual, failed to get any definite information. That is invariably the case in the East; a story always sounds clear enough at a distance, but the nearer you get to the scene of events the vaguer it becomes. Some of the people said that the elephant had gone in one direction, some said that he had gone in another, some professed not even to have heard of any elephant. I had almost made up my mind that the whole story was a pack of lies, when we heard yells a little distance away. There was a loud, scandalized cry of "Go away, child! Go away this instant!" and an old woman with a switch in her hand came round the corner of a hut, violently shooing away a crowd of naked children. Some more women followed, clicking their tongues and exclaiming; evidently there was something there that the children ought not to have seen. I rounded the hut and saw a man's dead body sprawling in the mud. He was an Indian, a black Dravidian coolie, almost naked, and he could not have been dead many minutes. The people said that the elephant had come suddenly upon him round the corner of the hut, caught him with its trunk, put its foot on his back and ground him into the earth. This was the rainy season and the ground was soft, and his face had scored a trench a foot deep and a couple of yards long. He was lying on his belly with arms crucified and head sharply twisted to one side. His face was coated with mud, the eyes wide open, the teeth bared and grinning with an expression of unendurable agony. (Never tell me, by the way, that the dead look peaceful. Most of the corpses I have seen looked devilish.) The friction of the great beast's foot had stripped the skin from his back as neatly as one skins a rabbit. As soon as I saw the dead man I sent an orderly to a friend's house nearby to borrow an elephant rifle. I had already sent back the pony, not wanting it to go mad with fright and throw me if it smelled the elephant.

The orderly came back in a few minutes with a rifle and five cartridges, and 5 meanwhile some Burmans had arrived and told us that the elephant was in the paddy fields below, only a few hundred yards away. As I started forward practically the whole population of the quarter flocked out of their houses and followed me. They had seen the rifle and were all shouting excitedly that I was going to shoot the elephant. They had not shown much interest in the elephant when he was merely ravaging their homes, but it was different now that he was going to be shot. It was a bit of fun to them, as it would be to an English crowd; besides, they wanted the meat. It made me vaguely uneasy. I had no intention of shooting the elephant—I had merely sent for the rifle to defend myself if necessary—and it is always unnerving to have a crowd following you. I marched down the hill, looking, and feeling, a fool, with the rifle over my shoulder and an ever-growing army of people jostling at my heels. At the bottom, when you got away from the huts, there was a metalled road and beyond that a miry waste of paddy fields a thousand yards across, not yet ploughed but soggy from the first rains and dotted with coarse grass. The elephant was standing eighty yards from the road, his left side towards us. He took not the slightest notice of the crowd's approach. He was tearing up bunches of grass, beating them against his knees to clean them and stuffing them into his mouth.

I had halted on the road. As soon as I saw the elephant I knew with perfect   6
certainty that I ought not to shoot him. It is a serious matter to shoot a working elephant—it is comparable to destroying a huge and costly piece of machinery—and obviously one ought not to do it if it can possibly be avoided. And at a distance, peacefully eating, the elephant looked no more dangerous than a cow. I thought then and I think now that his attack of "must" was already passing off; in which case he would merely wander harmlessly about until the mahout came back and caught him. Moreover, I did not in the least want to shoot him. I decided that I would watch him for a little while to make sure that he did not turn savage again, and then go home.

But at that moment I glanced round at the crowd that had followed me. It was   7
an immense crowd, two thousand at the least and growing every minute. It blocked the road for a long distance on either side. I looked at the sea of yellow faces above the garish clothes—faces all happy and excited over this bit of fun, all certain that the elephant was going to be shot. They were watching me as they would watch a conjuror about to perform a trick. They did not like me, but with the magical rifle in my hands I was momentarily worth watching. And suddenly I realised that I should have to shoot the elephant after all. The people expected it of me and I had got to do it; I could feel their two thousand wills pressing me forward, irresistibly. And it was at this moment, as I stood there with the rifle in my hands, that I first grasped the hollowness, the futility of the white man's dominion in the East. Here was I, the white man with his gun, standing in front of the unarmed native crowd—seemingly the leading actor of the piece, but in reality I was only an absurd puppet pushed to and fro by the will of those yellow faces behind. I perceived in this moment that when the white man turns tyrant it is his own freedom that he destroys. He becomes a sort of hollow, posing dummy, the conventionalised figure of a sahib. For it is the condition of his rule that he shall spend his life in trying to impress the "natives" and so in every crisis he has got to do what the "natives" expect of him. He wears a mask, and his face grows to fit it. I had got to shoot the elephant. I had committed myself to doing it when I sent for the rifle. A sahib has got to act like a sahib; he has got to appear resolute, to know his own mind and do definite things. To come all that way, rifle in hand, with two thousand people marching at my heels, and then to trail feebly away, having done nothing—no, that was impossible. The crowd would laugh at me. And my whole life, every white man's life in the East, was one long struggle not to be laughed at.

But I did not want to shoot the elephant. I watched him beating his bunch of grass against his knees, with that preoccupied grandmotherly air that elephants have. It seemed to me that it would be murder to shoot him. At that age I was not squeamish about killing animals, but I had never shot an elephant and never wanted to. (Somehow it always seems worse to kill a large animal.) Besides, there was the beast's owner to be considered. Alive, the elephant was worth at least a hundred pounds; dead, he would only be worth the value of his tusks—five pounds, possibly. But I had got to act quickly. I turned to some experienced-looking Burmans who had been there when we arrived, and asked them how the elephant had been behaving. They all said the same thing: he took no notice of you if you left him alone, but he might charge if you went too close to him. 8

It was perfectly clear to me what I ought to do. I ought to walk up to within, say, twenty-five yards of the elephant and test his behaviour. If he charged I could shoot, if he took no notice of me it would be safe to leave him until the mahout came back. But also I knew that I was going to do no such thing. I was a poor shot with a rifle and the ground was soft mud into which one would sink at every step. If the elephant charged and I missed him, I should have about as much chance as a toad under a steam-roller. But even then I was not thinking particularly of my own skin, only the watchful yellow faces behind. For at that moment, with the crowd watching me, I was not afraid in the ordinary sense, as I would have been if I had been alone. A white man mustn't be frightened in front of "natives"; and so, in general, he isn't frightened. The sole thought in my mind was that if anything went wrong those two thousand Burmans would see me pursued, caught, trampled on and reduced to a grinning corpse like that Indian up the hill. And if that happened it was quite probable that some of them would laugh. That would never do. There was only one alternative. I shoved the cartridges into the magazine and lay down on the road to get a better aim. 9

The crowd grew very still, and a deep, low, happy sigh, as of people who see the theatre curtain go up at last, breathed from innumerable throats. They were going to have their bit of fun after all. The rifle was a beautiful German thing with cross-hair sights. I did not then know that in shooting an elephant one should shoot to cut an imaginary bar running from ear-hole to ear-hole. I ought therefore, as the elephant was sideways on, to have aimed straight at his ear-hole; actually I aimed several inches in front of this, thinking the brain would be further forward. 10

When I pulled the trigger I did not hear the bang or feel the kick—one never does when a shot goes home—but I heard the devilish roar of glee that went up from the crowd. In that instant, in too short a time, one would have thought, even for the bullet to get there, a mysterious, terrible change had come over the elephant. He neither stirred nor fell, but every line of his body had altered. He looked suddenly stricken, shrunken, immensely old, as though the frightful impact of the bullet had paralysed him without knocking him down. At last, after what seemed a long time—it might have been five seconds, I dare say—he sagged flabbily to his knees. His mouth slobbered. An enormous senility seemed to have settled upon him. One could have imagined him thousands 11

of years old. I fired again into the same spot. At the second shot he did not collapse but climbed with desperate slowness to his feet and stood weakly upright,
with legs sagging and head drooping. I fired a third time. That was the shot that
did for him. You could see the agony of it jolt his whole body and knock the last
remnant of strength from his legs. But in falling he seemed for a moment to rise,
for as his hind legs collapsed beneath him he seemed to tower upwards like a
huge rock toppling, his trunk reaching skyward like a tree. He trumpeted, for
the first and only time. And then down he came, his belly towards me, with a
crash that seemed to shake the ground even where I lay.

I got up. The Burmans were already racing past me across the mud. It was 12
obvious that the elephant would never rise again, but he was not dead. He was
breathing very rhythmically with long rattling gasps, his great mound of a side
painfully rising and falling. His mouth was wide open—I could see far down
into caverns of pale pink throat. I waited a long time for him to die, but his
breathing did not weaken. Finally I fired my two remaining shots into the spot
where I thought his heart must be. The thick blood welled out of him like red
velvet, but still he did not die. His body did not even jerk when the shots hit
him, the tortured breathing continued without a pause. He was dying, very
slowly and in great agony, but in some world remote from me where not even a
bullet could damage him further. I felt that I had got to put an end to that dreadful noise. It seemed dreadful to see the great beast lying there, powerless to
move and yet powerless to die, and not even to be able to finish him. I sent back
for my small rifle and poured shot after shot into his heart and down his throat.
They seemed to make no impression. The tortured gasps continued as steadily
as the ticking of a clock.

In the end I could not stand it any longer and went away. I heard later that 13
it took him half an hour to die. Burmans were arriving with dahs and baskets
even before I left, and I was told they had stripped his body almost to the bones
by the afternoon.

Afterwards, of course, there were endless discussions about the shooting of 14
the elephant. The owner was furious, but he was only an Indian and could do
nothing. Besides, legally I had done the right thing, for a mad elephant has to be
killed, like a mad dog, if its owner fails to control it. Among the Europeans
opinion was divided. The older men said I was right, the younger men said it
was a damn shame to shoot an elephant for killing a coolie, because an elephant
was worth more than any damn Coringhee coolie. And afterwards I was very
glad that the coolie had been killed; it put me legally in the right and it gave me
a sufficient pretext for shooting the elephant. I often wondered whether any of
the others grasped that I had done it solely to avoid looking a fool.

COMPREHENSION

1. State in your own words the thesis of this essay.
2. How does the shooting of the elephant give Orwell a better understanding of "the real nature of imperialism—the real motives for which despotic governments act" (paragraph 3)? Why does Orwell kill the elephant? What is his attitude toward the Burmese people?
3. Why does Orwell concentrate on the prolonged death of the elephant? What effect does it have?

RHETORIC

1. How would you describe the level of language in the essay? Point to specific words, sentences, and phrases to support your answer.
2. Define *supplant* (paragraph 2), *labyrinth* (paragraph 4), *jostling* (paragraph 5), *conjuror* (paragraph 7), and *senility* (paragraph 11).
3. What is the function of the first two paragraphs? Where is the thesis stated in the essay?
4. Analyze Orwell's use of dramatic techniques to develop the narrative. Examine consecutive paragraphs in the essay to determine the author's presentation of action from different perspectives. What other essays in this chapter strike you as dramatic, and why?
5. Select and analyze some of the details in the essay that are designed to impress the reader's senses and emotions. Why does Orwell rely so heavily on the presentation and accumulation of detail in the essay?
6. How is the entire essay structured by irony of situation and paradox? How do these devices relate to the ethical issues raised by Orwell?

WRITING

1. In this essay, written in 1936, Orwell declares: "I did not even know that the British Empire is dying, still less did I know that it is a great deal better than the younger empires that are going to supplant it" (paragraph 2). In what ways is Orwell's statement prophetic?
2. Write a narrative essay about an episode in your life that brought you into conflict with social or political forces.
3. For a research project, consult library sources, and then write a report, employing proper documentation, on the importance of Orwell as an essayist.

Cyberspace: If You Don't Love It, Leave It

Esther Dyson

Esther Dyson (b. 1951) was born in Zurich, Switzerland, grew up in Princeton, New Jersey, and received a BA in economics from Harvard University. She is the daughter of Freeman Dyson, a physicist prominent in arms control. She is the editor and publisher of the widely respected computer newsletter Release 1.0, *which is circulated to many computer industry leaders. She is also chairperson of the Electronic Frontier Foundation and on the board of the Santa Fe Institute, the Global Business Network, and the Institute for East/West Studies. She served as a reporter for* Forbes *magazine for four years. The following essay appeared in* The New York Times Magazine *in July 1995. In it, Dyson defends the free-market approach to cyberspace content, arguing that regulation of the Internet is simply impossible and counterproductive.*

Something in the American psyche loves new frontiers. We hanker after wide-open spaces; we like to explore; we like to make rules instead of follow them. But in this age of political correctness and other intrusions on our national cult of independence, it's hard to find a place where you can go and be yourself without worrying about the neighbors. 1

There is such a place: cyberspace. Lost in the furor over porn on the Net is the exhilarating sense of freedom that this new frontier once promised—and still does in some quarters. Formerly a playground for computer nerds and techies, cyberspace now embraces every conceivable constituency: schoolchildren, flirtatious singles, Hungarian-Americans, accountants—along with pederasts and porn fans. Can they all get along? Or will our fear of kids surfing for cyberporn behind their bedroom doors provoke a crackdown? 2

The first order of business is to grasp what cyberspace *is*. It might help to leave behind metaphors of highways and frontiers and to think instead of real estate. Real estate, remember, is an intellectual, legal, artificial environment constructed *on top of* land. Real estate recognizes the difference between parkland and shopping mall, between red-light zone and school district, between church, state and drugstore. 3

In the same way, you could think of cyberspace as a giant and unbounded world of virtual real estate. Some property is privately owned and rented out; other property is common land; some places are suitable for children, and others are best avoided by all but the kinkiest citizens. Unfortunately, it's those places that are now capturing the popular imagination: places that offer bomb-making instructions, pornography, advice on how to procure stolen credit cards. They make cyberspace sound like a nasty place. Good citizens jump to a conclusion: Better regulate it. 4

The most recent manifestation of this impulse is the Exon-Coats Amendment, a well-meaning but misguided bill drafted by Senators Jim Exon, Democrat of Nebraska, and Daniel R. Coats, Republican of Indiana, to make cyberspace "safer" for children. Part of the telecommunications reform bill passed by the Senate and awaiting consideration by the House, the amendment would outlaw making "indecent communication" available to anyone under 18.[1] Then there's the Amateur Action bulletin board case, in which the owners of a porn service in Milpitas, Calif., were convicted in a Tennessee court of violating "community standards" after a local postal inspector requested that the material be transmitted to him. 5

Regardless of how many laws or lawsuits are launched, regulation won't work. 6

Aside from being unconstitutional, using censorship to counter indecency and other troubling "speech" fundamentally misinterprets the nature of cyberspace. Cyberspace isn't a frontier where wicked people can grab unsuspecting children, nor is it a giant television system that can beam offensive messages at unwilling viewers. In this kind of real estate, users have to *choose* where they visit, what they see, what they do. It's optional, and it's much easier to bypass a place on the Net than it is to avoid walking past an unsavory block of stores on the way to your local 7-11. 7

Put plainly, cyberspace is a voluntary destination—in reality, many destinations. You don't just get "onto the net"; you have to go someplace in particular. That means that people can choose where to go and what to see. Yes, community standards should be enforced, but those standards should be set by cyberspace communities themselves, not by the courts or by politicians in Washington. What we need isn't Government control over all these electronic communities: We need self-rule. 8

What makes cyberspace so alluring is precisely the way in which it's *different* from shopping malls, television, highways and other terrestrial jurisdictions. But let's define the territory: 9

First, there are private E-mail conversations, akin to the conversations you have over the telephone or voice mail. These are private and consensual and require no regulation at all. 10

Second, there are information and entertainment services, where people can download anything from legal texts and lists of "great new restaurants" to game software or dirty pictures. These places are like bookstores, malls and movie houses—places where you go to buy something. The customer needs to request an item or sign up for a subscription; stuff (especially pornography) is not sent out to people who don't ask for it. Some of these services are free or included as part of a broader service like Compuserve or America Online; others charge and may bill their customers directly. 11

---

[1]The Communications Decency Act (CDA) was passed by Congress, but the Supreme Court ruled that it was unconstitutional in 1996.

Third, there are "real" communities—groups of people who communicate   12
among themselves. In real-estate terms, they're like bars or restaurants or bath-
houses. Each active participant contributes to a general conversation, generally
through posted messages. Other participants may simply listen or watch. Some
are supervised by a moderator; others are more like bulletin boards—anyone is
free to post anything. Many of these services started out unmoderated but are
now imposing rules to keep out unwanted advertising, extraneous discussions
or increasingly rude participants. Without a moderator, the decibel level often
gets too high.

Ultimately, it's the rules that determine the success of such places. Some of   13
the rules are determined by the supplier of content; some of the rules concern
prices and membership fees. The rules may be simple: "Only high-quality content about oil-industry liability and pollution legislation: $120 an hour." Or:
"This forum is unmoderated, and restricted to information about copyright issues. People who insist on posting advertising or unrelated material will be
asked to desist (and may eventually be barred)." Or: "Only children 8 to 12, on
school-related topics and only clean words. The moderator will decide what's
acceptable."

Cyberspace communities evolve just the way terrestrial communities do: 14
people with like-minded interests band together. Every cyberspace community
has its own character. Overall, the communities on Compuserve tend to be more
techy or professional; those on America Online, affluent young singles; Prodigy,
family oriented. Then there are independents like Echo, a hip, downtown New
York service, or Women's Wire, targeted to women who want to avoid the male
culture prevalent elsewhere on the Net. There's SurfWatch, a new program allowing access only to locations deemed suitable for children. On the Internet itself, there are lots of passionate noncommercial discussion groups on topics
ranging from Hungarian politics (Hungary-Online) to copyright law.

And yes, there are also porn-oriented services, where people share dirty   15
pictures and communicate with one another about all kinds of practices, often
anonymously. Whether these services encourage the fantasies they depict is
subject to debate—the same debate that has raged about pornography in other
media. But the point is that no one is forcing this stuff on anybody.

What's unique about cyberspace is that it liberates us from the tyranny of   16
government, where everyone lives by the rule of the majority. In a democracy,
minority groups and minority preferences tend to get squeezed out, whether
they are minorities of race and culture or minorities of individual taste. Cyberspace allows communities of any size and kind to flourish; in cyberspace, communities are chosen by the users, not forced on them by accidents of geography.
This freedom gives the rules that preside in cyberspace a moral authority that
rules in terrestrial environments don't have. Most people are stuck in the country of their birth, but if you don't like the rules of a cyberspace community, you
can just sign off. Love it or leave it. Likewise, if parents don't like the rules of a
given cyberspace community, they can restrict their children's access to it.

What's likely to happen in cyberspace is the formation of new communities,   17
free of the constraints that cause conflict on earth. Instead of a global village,

which is a nice dream but impossible to manage, we'll have invented another world of self-contained communities that cater to their own members' inclinations without interfering with anyone else's. The possibility of a real market-style evolution of governance is at hand. In cyberspace, we'll be able to test and evolve rules governing what needs to be governed—intellectual property, content and access control, rules about privacy and free speech. Some communities will allow anyone in; others will restrict access to members who qualify on one basis or another. Those communities that prove self-sustaining will prosper (and perhaps grow and split into subsets with ever-more-particular interests and identities). Those that can't survive—either because people lose interest or get scared off—will simply wither away.

In the near future, explorers in cyberspace will need to get better at defining 18 and identifying their communities. They will need to put in place—and accept—their own local governments, just as the owners of expensive real estate often prefer to have their own security guards rather than call in the police. But they will rarely need help from any terrestrial government.

Of course, terrestrial governments may not agree. What to do, for instance, 19 about pornography? The answer is labeling—not banning—questionable material. In order to avoid censorship and lower the political temperature, it makes sense for cyberspace participants themselves to agree on a scheme for questionable items, so that people or automatic filters can avoid them. In other words, posting pornography in "alt.sex, bestiality" would be O.K.; it's easy enough for software manufacturers to build an automatic filter that would prevent you—or your child—from ever seeing that item on a menu. (It's as if all the items were wrapped with labels on the wrapper.) Someone who posted the same material under the title "Kid-Fun" could be sued for mislabeling.

Without a lot of fanfare, private enterprises and local groups are already 20 producing a variety of labeling and ranking services, along with kid-oriented sites like Kidlink, EdWeb and Kids' Space. People differ in their tastes and values and can find services or reviewers on the Net that suit them in the same way they select books and magazines. Or they can wander freely if they prefer, making up their own itinerary.

In the end, our society needs to grow up. Growing up means understand- 21 ing that there are no perfect answers, no all-purpose solutions, no government-sanctioned safe havens. We haven't created a perfect society on earth and we won't have one in cyberspace either. But at least we can have individual choice—and individual responsibility.

COMPREHENSION

1. The title of the essay is a variation of a phrase popularized in the 1960s. What is the original expression and what was its significance? What is its relevance to this essay?
2. What is Dyson's thesis? Is it stated explicitly? If so, where in the essay does it occur? If it is merely suggested, how is it suggested and where?

3. There are many forms of new media that are not considered communities. Why does Dyson refer to cyberspace as a community?
4. According to Dyson, what distinguishes cyberspace from physical space?
5. What does Dyson mean when she states that cyberspace needs "self-rule" (paragraph 8)?

RHETORIC

1. How does Dyson use her introduction to foreshadow her main concerns about censorship in cyberspace?
2. How does Dyson use metaphor in paragraphs 11 through 13 to help us understand the structure of cyberspace? Why is metaphor a particularly good literary device to use when explaining a new concept?
3. Key to Dyson's views on cyberspace is that it is a "voluntary destination" (paragraph 8). What evidence does Dyson present that it is voluntary? What argument can be made that it is not always "voluntary"?
4. Who is the implied audience for this essay? What level of education does one need to have and how sophisticated about the world of cyberspace does one need to be in order to comprehend and process the author's views? Explain your answer.
5. Dyson refers to laws, rules, and regulations as strategies that various interest groups may use to determine access to content in cyberspace. How does Dyson distinguish these three related tactics? What significance does differentiating these methods have in the author's presentation of her argument?
6. Dyson concludes her essay with an analogy between human society and cyberspace culture. Why has she saved this final support for last? How does it extend her argument rather than merely restate it?

WRITING

1. In a comparison and contrast essay of approximately 500 words, select three "cyberspace communities" and describe each one's character (refer to Dyson's reference to cyberspace character in paragraph 14).
2. In paragraph 18, Dyson refers to the "global village," a term coined by the media critic Marshall McLuhan. For a 1,000–1,500-word research project, study McLuhan's views on the nature of the "global village" and compare and contrast them to Dyson's views of the nature of cyberspace.
3. Dyson argues that technology can create filters, labeling and ranking services to prevent children from viewing inappropriate material. In an essay of 500 words, argue for or against the proposition that there can be a non-technological solution to this issue, for example, instilling values in children or developing a society that does not create a mystique about "taboo" subject matter.

The Circle of Governments

Niccolò Machiavelli

Niccolò Machiavelli (1469–1527), Italian patriot, statesman, and writer, is one of the seminal figures in the history of Western political thought. His inquiries into the nature of the state, the amoral quality of political life, and the primacy of power are distinctly modernist in outlook. He began his studies of political and historical issues after being forced to retire from Florentine politics in 1512. Exiled outside the city, Machiavelli wrote The Prince *(1513),* The Discourses *(1519),* The Art of War *(1519–1520), and* The Florentine History *(1525). The following selection from* The Discourses *(conceived by the author as commentaries on the first 10 books of Livy's* History of Rome) *analyzes the varieties of government and their political implications in history.*

Having proposed to myself to treat of the kind of government established at 1 Rome, and of the events that led to its perfection, I must at the beginning observe that some of the writers on politics distinguished three kinds of government, vis. the monarchical, the aristocratic, and the democratic; and maintain that the legislators of a people must choose from these three the one that seems to them most suitable. Other authors, wiser according to the opinion of many, count six kinds of governments, three of which are very bad, and three good in themselves, but so liable to be corrupted that they become absolutely bad. The three good ones are those which we have just named; the three bad ones result from the degradation of the other three, and each of them resembles its corresponding original, so that the transition from the one to the other is very easy. Thus monarchy becomes tyranny; aristocracy degenerates into oligarchy; and the popular government lapses readily into licentiousness. So that a legislator who gives to a state which he founds either of these three forms of government, constitutes it but for a brief time; for no precautions can prevent either one of the three that are reputed good from degenerating into its opposite kind; so great are in these the attractions and resemblances between the good and the evil.

Chance has given birth to these different kinds of governments amongst 2 men; for at the beginning of the world the inhabitants were few in number and lived for a time dispersed, like beasts. As the human race increased, the necessity for uniting themselves for defence made itself felt; the better to attain this object they chose the strongest and most courageous from amongst themselves and placed him at their head promising to obey him. Thence they began to know the good and the honest, and to distinguish them from the bad and vicious; for seeing a man injure his benefactor aroused at once two sentiments in every heart, hatred against the ingrate and love for the benefactor. They blamed the first, and on the contrary honoured those the more who showed themselves grateful, for each felt that he in turn might be subject to a like wrong; and to prevent similar evils, they set to work to make laws, and to institute punishments for those who contravened them. Such was the origin of justice. This caused them, when they had afterwards to choose a prince, neither to look to the strongest nor bravest, but to the wisest and most just. But when they began to make sovereignty hereditary and non-elective, the children quickly degenerated from their fathers; and, so far from trying to equal their virtues, they considered that a prince had nothing else to do than to excel all the rest in luxury, indulgence, and every other variety of pleasure. The prince consequently soon drew upon himself the general hatred. An object of hatred, he naturally felt fear; fear in turn dictated to him precautions and wrongs, and thus tyranny quickly developed itself. Such were the beginning and causes of disorders, conspiracies, and plots against the sovereigns, set on foot, not by the feeble and timid, but by those citizens who, surpassing the others in grandeur of soul, in wealth, and in courage, could not submit to the outrages and excesses of their princes.

Under such powerful leaders the masses armed themselves against the 3 tyrant, and after having rid themselves of him, submitted to these chiefs as their liberators. These, abhorring the very name of prince, constituted themselves a new government; and at first bearing in mind the past tyranny, they governed in strict accordance with the laws which they had established themselves; preferring public interests to their own, and to administer and protect with greatest care both public and private affairs. The children succeeded their fathers, and ignorant of the changes of fortune, having never experienced its reverses, and indisposed to remain content with this civil equality, they in turn gave themselves up to cupidity, ambition, libertinage, and violence, and soon caused the aristocratic government to degenerate into an oligarchic tyranny, regardless of all civil rights. They soon, however, experienced the same fate as the first tyrant; the people, disgusted with their government, placed themselves at the command of whoever was willing to attack them, and this disposition soon produced an avenger, who was sufficiently well seconded to destroy them. The memory of the prince and the wrongs committed by him being still fresh in their minds, and having overthrown the oligarchy, the people were not willing to return to the government of a prince. A popular government was therefore resolved upon, and it was so organized that the authority would not again fall into the hands of a prince or a small number of nobles. And as all governments are at first looked up to with some degree of reverence, the popular state also maintained itself for a time, but which was never of long duration, and lasted generally only about as long as the generation that had established it; for it soon ran into that kind of licence which inflicts injury upon public as well as private interests. Each individual only consulted his own passions, and a thousand acts of injustice were daily committed, so that, constrained by necessity, or directed by the counsels of some good man, or for the purpose of escaping from this anarchy, they returned anew to the government of a prince, and from this they generally lapsed again into anarchy, step-by-step, in the same manner and from the same causes as we have indicated.

Such is the circle which all republics are destined to run through. Seldom, 4
however, do they come back to the original form of government, which results
from the fact that their duration is not sufficiently long to be able to undergo
these repeated changes and preserve their existence. But it may well happen
that a republic lacking strength and good counsel in its difficulties becomes subject after a while to some neighbouring state, that is better organized than itself;
and if such is not the case, then they will be apt to revolve indefinitely in the circle of revolutions. I say, then, that all kinds of government are defective; those
three which we have qualified as good because they are too short-lived, and the
three bad ones because of their inherent viciousness. Thus sagacious legislators,
knowing the vices of each of these systems of government by themselves, have
chosen one that should partake of all of them, judging that to be the most stable
and solid. In fact, when there is combined under the same constitution a prince,
a nobility, and the power of the people, then these three powers will watch and
keep each other reciprocally in check.

COMPREHENSION

1. Where in the essay does Machiavelli state his thesis? What is his thesis?
2. Explain in your own words the three types of government Machiavelli describes, their origins, and their pitfalls.
3. Ultimately, who determines what system of government a country will
   have—the governed or the legislators? Explain your view.

RHETORIC

1. In paragraph 1, Machiavelli states the motivation for writing his essay. How
   does he create a transition from explaining this motivation to addressing his
   subject directly?
2. Machiavelli explains the three forms of government in a particular order.
   What is the unifying rhetoric behind the order in which he describes them?
   How does it relate to the theme of the essay?
3. Both paragraphs 2 and 3 describe the process by which governments are
   formed. What methods does the author use to create coherent paragraphs
   in providing a step-by-step description of these formations?
4. Would you consider this essay descriptive, narrative, expository, or a combination of two or more of these methods? Explain your answer.
5. Define *oligarchy, benefactor, licentiousness, cupidity, libertinage,* and *sagacious.*
   What does the use of these words in the essay suggest about the author and
   his intended audience?
6. From what vantage point does the author appear to view his subject matter:
   participant, reporter, critic, or teacher? Explain your view.

WRITING

1. Argue for or against the proposition that the United States has an ideal form of government, according to Machiavelli's view of what a government should be.
2. Argue for or against *one* of the forms of government that Machiavelli describes in his essay.
3. Using the terms *monarchy, oligarchy,* and *democracy,* describe the various governing bodies of your school, their functions, and where they fit into Machiavelli's taxonomy.

Grant and Lee:
A Study in Contrasts

Bruce Catton

Bruce Catton (1899–1978) was born in Petosky, Michigan. After serving in the Navy during World War I, he attended Oberlin College but left in his junior year to pursue a career in journalism. From 1942 to 1952, Catton served in the government, first on the War Production Board and later in the departments of Commerce and the Interior. He left government to devote himself to literary work as a columnist for The Nation *and a historian of the Civil War. His many works include* A Stillness at Appomattox *(1953), which won the 1954 Pulitzer Prize;* Mr. Lincoln's Army *(1951);* The Centennial History of the Civil War *(1961–1965); and* Prefaces to History *(1970). In the following selection, Catton presents vivid portraits of two well-known but little understood figures from American history.*

When Ulysses S. Grant and Robert E. Lee met in the parlor of a modest house at   1
Appomattox Court House, Virginia, on April 9, 1865, to work out the terms for the surrender of Lee's Army of Northern Virginia, a great chapter in American life came to a close, and a great new chapter began.

These men were bringing the Civil War to its virtual finish. To be sure, other   2
armies had yet to surrender, and for a few days the fugitive Confederate government would struggle desperately and vainly, trying to find some way to go on living now that its chief support was gone. But in effect it was all over when Grant and Lee signed the papers. And the little room where they wrote out the terms was the scene of one of the poignant, dramatic contrasts in American history.

They were two strong men, these oddly different generals, and they repre-   3
sented the strengths of two conflicting currents that, through them, had come into final collision.

Back of Robert E. Lee was the notion that the old aristocratic concept might 4
somehow survive and be dominant in American life.

Lee was tidewater Virginia, and in his background were family, culture, and 5
tradition . . . the age of chivalry transplanted to a New World which was making its own legends and its own myths. He embodied a way of life that had
come down through the age of knighthood and the English country squire.
America was a land that was beginning all over again, dedicated to nothing
much more complicated than the rather hazy belief that all men had equal
rights and should have an equal chance in the world. In such a land Lee stood
for the feeling that it was somehow of advantage to human society to have a
pronounced inequality in the social structure. There should be a leisure class,
backed by ownership of land; in turn, society itself should be keyed to the land
as the chief source of wealth and influence. It would bring forth (according to
this ideal) a class of men with a strong sense of obligation to the community;
men who lived not to gain advantage for themselves, but to meet the solemn
obligations which had been laid on them by the very fact that they were privi-
leged. From them the country would get its leadership; to them it could look for
the higher values—of thought, of conduct, of personal deportment—to give it
strength and virtue.

Lee embodied the noblest elements of this aristocratic ideal. Through him, 6
the landed nobility justified itself. For four years, the Southern states had fought
a desperate war to uphold the ideals for which Lee stood. In the end, it almost
seemed as if the Confederacy fought for Lee; as if he himself was the Confederacy
. . . the best thing that the way of life for which the Confederacy stood could ever
have to offer. He had passed into legend before Appomattox. Thousands of tired,
underfed, poorly clothed Confederate soldiers, long since past the simple enthusiasm of the early days of the struggle, somehow considered Lee the symbol of
everything for which they had been willing to die. But they could not quite put
this feeling into words. If the Lost Cause, sanctified by so much heroism and so
many deaths, had a living justification, its justification was General Lee.

Grant, the son of a tanner on the Western frontier, was everything Lee was 7
not. He had come up the hard way and embodied nothing in particular except
the eternal toughness and sinewy fiber of the men who grew up beyond the
mountains. He was one of a body of men who owed reverence and obeisance to
no one, who were self-reliant to a fault, who cared hardly anything for the past
but who had a sharp eye for the future.

These frontier men were the precise opposites of the tidewater aristocrats. 8
Back of them, in the great surge that had taken people over the Alleghenies and
into the opening Western country, there was a deep, implicit dissatisfaction with
a past that had settled into grooves. They stood for democracy, not from any reasoned conclusion about the proper ordering of human society, but simply because
they had grown up in the middle of democracy and knew how it worked. Their
society might have privileges, but they would be privileges each man had won
for himself. Forms and patterns meant nothing. No man was born to anything,
except perhaps to a chance to show how far he could rise. Life was competition.

Yet along with this feeling had come a deep sense of belonging to a national 9
community. The Westerner who developed a farm, opened a shop, or set up in
business as a trader, could hope to prosper only as his own community pros-
pered—and his community ran from the Atlantic to the Pacific and from
Canada down to Mexico. If the land was settled, with towns and highways and
accessible markets, he could better himself. He saw his fate in terms of the
nation's own destiny. As its horizons expanded, so did his. He had, in other
words, an acute dollars-and-cents stake in the continued growth and development of his country.

And that, perhaps, is where the contrast between Grant and Lee becomes most 10
striking. The Virginia aristocrat, inevitably, saw himself in relation to his own
region. He lived in a static society which could endure almost anything except
change. Instinctively, his first loyalty would go to the locality in which that society
existed. He would fight to the limit of endurance to defend it, because in defending it he was defending everything that gave his own life its deepest meaning.

The Westerner, on the other hand, would fight with an equal tenacity for the 11
broader concept of society. He fought so because everything he lived by was
tied to growth, expansion, and a constantly widening horizon. What he lived by
would survive or fall with the nation itself. He could not possibly stand by un-
moved in the face of an attempt to destroy the Union. He would combat it with
everything he had, because he could only see it as an effort to cut the ground
out from under his feet.

So Grant and Lee were in complete contrast, representing two diametrically 12
opposed elements in American life. Grant was the modern man emerging; beyond him, ready to come on the stage, was the great age of steel and machinery,
of crowded cities and a restless burgeoning vitality. Lee might have ridden
down from the old age of chivalry, lance in hand, silken banner fluttering over
his head. Each man was the perfect champion of his cause, drawing both his
strengths and his weaknesses from the people he led.

Yet it was not all contrast, after all. Different as they were—in background, 13
in personality, in underlying aspiration—these two great soldiers had much in
common. Under everything else, they were marvelous fighters. Furthermore,
their fighting qualities were really very much alike.

Each man had, to begin with, the great virtue of utter tenacity and fidelity. 14
Grant fought his way down the Mississippi Valley in spite of acute personal dis-
couragement and profound military handicaps. Lee hung on in the trenches at
Petersburg after hope itself had died. In each man there was an indomitable
quality . . . the born fighter's refusal to give up as long as he can still remain on
his feet and lift his two fists.

Daring and resourcefulness they had, too; the ability to think faster and 15
move faster than the enemy. These were the qualities which gave Lee the dazzling campaigns of Second Manassas and Chancellorsville and won Vicksburg
for Grant.

Lastly, and perhaps greatest of all, there was the ability, at the end, to turn 16
quickly from war to peace once the fighting was over. Out of the way these two

men behaved at Appomattox came the possibility of a peace of reconciliation. It was a possibility not wholly realized, in the years to come, but which did, in the end, help the two sections to become one nation again . . . after a war whose bitterness might have seemed to make such a reunion wholly impossible. No part of either man's life became him more than the part he played in their brief meeting in the McLean house at Appomattox. Their behavior there put all succeeding generations of Americans in their debt. Two great Americans, Grant and Lee—very different, yet under everything very much alike. Their encounter at Appomattox was one of the great moments of American history.

COMPREHENSION

1. What is the central purpose of Catton's study? Cite evidence to support your view. Who is his audience?
2. What is the primary appeal to readers of describing history through the study of individuals rather than through the recording of events? How does Catton's essay reflect this appeal?
3. According to Catton, what special qualities did Grant and Lee share, and what qualities set them apart?

RHETORIC

1. What role does the opening paragraph have in setting the tone for the essay? Is the tone typical of what you would expect of an essay describing military generals? Explain your view. How does the conclusion echo the introductory paragraph?
2. Note that the sentence, "Two great Americans, Grant and Lee—very different, yet under everything very much alike" (paragraph 16), has no verb. What does this indicate about Catton's style? What other sentences contain atypical syntax? What is their contribution to the unique quality of the writing?
3. Although this essay is about a historical era, there is a notable lack of specific facts—dates, statistics, and events. What has Catton focused on instead?
4. What is the function of the one-sentence paragraph 3?
5. Paragraphs 9, 10, 12, and 13 begin with coordinating conjunctions. How do these transitional words give the paragraphs their special coherence? How would more typical introductory expressions, such as *in addition, furthermore*, or *moreover*, have altered this coherence?
6. What strategy does Catton use in comparing and contrasting the two generals? Study paragraphs 5 through 16. Which are devoted to describing each man separately, and which include aspects of each man? What is the overall development of the comparisons?

WRITING

1. Does Lee's vision of society exist in the United States today? If not, why not? If so, where do you find this vision? Write a brief essay on this topic.
2. Select two well-known individuals in the same profession—for example, politics, entertainment, or sports. Make a list for each, enumerating the different aspects of their character, behavior, beliefs, and background. Using this as an outline, devise an essay comparing and contrasting the two.
3. Apply, in a comparative essay, Catton's observation about "two diametrically opposed elements in American life" to the current national scene.

American Dreamer

Bharati Mukherjee

Bharati Mukherjee (b. 1940) was born in Calcutta, India, and learned to read and write by the age of three. In 1947, she moved to Britain with her family. After receiving her BA from the University of Calcutta and her MA in English and Ancient Indian Culture from the University of Boroda, she came to the United States, where she received an MFA in Creative Writing and a PhD in English and Comparative Literature at the University of Iowa. Mukherjee is the author of Jasmine *(1989) and* The Middleman and Other Stories, *which won the 1988 National Book Critic's Circle Award for Fiction. Her more recent work includes the novels* The Holder of the World *(1993) and* Leave It to Me *(1997). She is currently professor at the University of California, Berkeley. Mukherjee is often interested in and writing about issues of cultural identity. In the following essay, which first appeared in the magazine* Mother Jones *in 1997, she examines why "hyphenated Americans" always seem to be members of nonwhite groups.*

The United States exists as a sovereign nation. "America," in contrast, exists as a myth of democracy and equal opportunity to live by, or as an ideal goal to reach. 1

I am a naturalized U.S. citizen, which means that, unlike native-born citizens, I had to prove to the U.S. government that I merited citizenship. What I didn't have to disclose was that I desired "America," which to me is the stage for the drama of self-transformation. 2

I was born in Calcutta and first came to the United States—to Iowa City, to be precise—on a summer evening in 1961. I flew into a small airport surrounded by cornfields and pastures, ready to carry out the two commands my father had written out for me the night before I left Calcutta: Spend two years studying creative writing at the Iowa Writers' Workshop, then come back home and marry the bridegroom he selected for me from our caste and class. 3

In traditional Hindu families like ours, men provided and women were 4
provided for. My father was a patriarch and I a pliant daughter. The neighborhood I'd grown up in was homogeneously Hindu, Bengali-speaking, and middle-class. I didn't expect myself to ever disobey or disappoint my father by
setting my own goals and taking charge of my future.

When I landed in Iowa 35 years ago, I found myself in a society in which al- 5
most everyone was Christian, white, and moderately well-off. In the women's
dormitory I lived in my first year, apart from six international graduate students
(all of us were from Asia and considered "exotic"), the only non-Christian was
Jewish, and the only nonwhite an African-American from Georgia. I didn't anticipate then, that over the next 35 years, the Iowa population would become so
diverse that it would have 6,931 children from non-English-speaking homes
registered as students in its schools, nor that Iowans would be in the grip of a
cultural crisis in which resentment against immigrants, particularly refugees
from Vietnam, Sudan, and Bosnia, as well as unskilled Spanish-speaking workers, would become politicized enough to cause the Immigration and Naturalization Service to open an "enforcement" office in Cedar Rapids in October for
the tracking and deporting of undocumented aliens.

In Calcutta in the '50s, I heard no talk of "identity crisis"—communal or in- 6
dividual. The concept itself—a person not knowing who he or she is—was
unimaginable in our hierarchical, classification-obsessed society. One's identity
was fixed, derived from religion, caste, patrimony, and mother tongue. A Hindu
Indian's last name announced his or her forefathers' caste and place of origin. A
Mukherjee could *only* be a Brahmin from Bengal. Hindu tradition forbade in-
tercaste, interlanguage, interethnic marriages. Bengali tradition even discouraged emigration: To remove oneself from Bengal was to dilute true culture.

Until the age of 8, I lived in a house crowded with 40 or 50 relatives. My 7
identity was viscerally connected with ancestral soil and genealogy. I was who
I was because I was Dr. Sudhir Lal Mukherjee's daughter, because I was a
Hindu Brahmin, because I was Bengali-speaking, and because my *desh*—the
Bengali word for homeland—was an East Bengal village called Faridpur.

The University of Iowa classroom was my first experience of coeducation. And 8
after not too long, I fell in love with a fellow student named Clark Blaise, an
American of Canadian origin, and impulsively married him during a lunch
break in a lawyer's office above a coffee shop.

That act cut me off forever from the rules and ways of upper-middle-class 9
life in Bengal, and hurled me into a New World life of scary improvisations and
heady explorations. Until my lunch-break wedding, I had seen myself as an
Indian foreign student who intended to return to India to live. The five-minute
ceremony in the lawyer's office suddenly changed me into a transient with conflicting loyalties to two very different cultures.

The first 10 years into marriage, years spent mostly in my husband's native 10
Canada, I thought of myself as an expatriate Bengali permanently stranded in
North America because of destiny or desire. My first novel, *The Tiger's Daughter,*

embodies the loneliness I felt but could not acknowledge, even to myself, as I negotiated the no man's land between the country of my past and the continent of my present. Shaped by memory, textured with nostalgia for a class and culture I had abandoned, this novel quite naturally became an expression of the expatriate consciousness.

It took me a decade of painful introspection to put nostalgia in perspective 11 and to make the transition from expatriate to immigrant. After a 14-year stay in Canada, I forced my husband and our two sons to relocate to the United States. But the transition from foreign student to U.S. citizen, from detached onlooker to committed immigrant, has not been easy.

The years in Canada were particularly harsh. Canada is a country that offi- 12 cially, and proudly, resists cultural fusion. For all its rhetoric about a cultural "mosaic," Canada refuses to renovate its national self-image to include its changing complexion. It is a New World country with Old World concepts of a fixed, exclusivist national identity. Canadian official rhetoric designated me as one of the "visible minority" who, even though I spoke the Canadian languages of English and French, was straining "the absorptive capacity" of Canada. Canadians of color were routinely treated as "not real" Canadians. One example: In 1985 a terrorist bomb, planted in an Air-India jet on Canadian soil, blew up after leaving Montreal, killing 329 passengers, most of whom were Canadians of Indian origin. The prime minister of Canada at the time, Brian Mulroney, phoned the prime minister of India to offer Canada's condolences for India's loss.

Those years of race-related harassments in Canada politicized me and 13 deepened my love of the ideals embedded in the American Bill of Rights. I don't forget that the architects of the Constitution and the Bill of Rights were white males and slaveholders. But through their declaration, they provided us with the enthusiasm for human rights, and the initial framework from which other empowerments could be conceived and enfranchised communities expanded.

I am a naturalized U.S. citizen and I take my American citizenship very seri- 14 ously. I am not an economic refugee, nor am I a seeker of political asylum. I am a voluntary immigrant. I became a citizen by choice, not by simple accident of birth.

Yet these days, questions such as who is an American and what is American 15 culture are being posed with belligerence, and being answered with violence. Scapegoating of immigrants has once again become the politicians' easy remedy for all that ails the nation. Hate speeches fill auditoriums for demagogues willing to profit from stirring up racial animosity. An April [1996] Gallup poll indicated that half of Americans would like to bar almost all legal immigration for the next five years.

The United States, like every sovereign nation, has a right to formulate its 16 immigration policies. But in this decade of continual, large-scale diasporas, it is imperative that we come to some agreement about who "we" are, and what our goals are for the nation, now that our community includes people of many races, ethnicities, languages, and religions.

The debate about American culture and American identity has to date been 17 monopolized largely by Eurocentrists and ethnocentrists whose rhetoric has been flamboyantly divisive, pitting a phantom "us" against a demonized "them."

All countries view themselves by their ideals. Indians idealize the cultural con- 18 tinuum, the inherent value system of India, and are properly incensed when foreigners see nothing but poverty, intolerance, strife, and injustice. Americans see themselves as the embodiments of liberty, openness, and individualism, even as the world judges them for drugs, crime, violence, bigotry, militarism, and homelessness. I was in Singapore in 1994 when the American teenager Michael Fay was sentenced to caning for having spraypainted some cars. While I saw Fay's actions as those of an individual, and his sentence as too harsh, the overwhelming local sentiment was that vandalism was an "American" crime, and that flogging Fay would deter Singapore youths from becoming "Americanized."

Conversely, in 1994, in Tavares, Florida, the Lake County School Board an- 19 nounced its policy (since overturned) requiring middle school teachers to instruct their students that American culture, by which the board meant European-American culture, is inherently "superior to other foreign or historic cultures." The policy's misguided implication was that culture in the United States has not been affected by the American Indian, African-American, Latin-American, and Asian-American segments of the population. The sinister implication was that our national identity is so fragile that it can absorb diverse and immigrant cultures only by recontextualizing them as deficient.

Our nation is unique in human history in that the founding idea of "America" 20 was in opposition to the tenet that a nation is a collection of like-looking, like-speaking, like-worshipping people. The primary criterion for nationhood in Europe is homogeneity of culture, race, and religion—which has contributed to blood-soaked balkanization in the former Yugoslavia and the former Soviet Union.

America's pioneering European ancestors gave up the easy homogeneity of 21 their native countries for a new version of Utopia. Now, in the 1990s, we have the exciting chance to follow that tradition and assist in the making of a new American culture that differs from both the enforced assimilation of a "melting pot" and the Canadian model of a multicultural "mosaic."

The multicultural mosaic implies a contiguity of fixed, self-sufficient, ut- 22 terly distinct cultures. Multiculturalism, as it has been practiced in the United States in the past 10 years, implies the existence of a central culture, ringed by peripheral cultures. The fallout of official multiculturalism is the establishment of one culture as the norm and the rest as aberrations. At the same time, the multiculturalist emphasis on race- and ethnicity-based group identity leads to a lack of respect for individual differences within each group, and to vilification of those individuals who place the good of the nation above the interests of their particular racial or ethnic communities.

We must be alert to the dangers of an "us" vs. "them" mentality. In Califor- 23 nia, this mentality is manifesting itself as increased violence between minority, ethnic communities. The attack on Korean American merchants in South Central Los Angeles in the wake of the Rodney King beating trial is only one recent example of the tragic side effects of this mentality. On the national level, the politicization of ethnic identities has encouraged the scapegoating of legal immigrants, who are blamed for economic and social problems brought about by flawed domestic and foreign policies.

We need to discourage the retention of cultural memory if the aim of that   24
retention is cultural balkanization. We must think of American culture and nationhood as a constantly reforming, transmogrifying "we."

In this age of diasporas, one's biological identity may not be one's only   25
identity. Erosions and accretions come with the act of emigration. The experience of cutting myself off from a biological homeland and settling in an adopted homeland that is not always welcoming to its dark-complexioned citizens has tested me as a person, and made me the writer I am today.

I choose to describe myself on my own terms, as an American, rather than as an   26
Asian-American. Why is it that hyphenation is imposed only on nonwhite Americans? Rejecting hyphenation is my refusal to categorize the cultural landscape into a center and its peripheries; it is to demand that the American nation deliver the promises of its dream and its Constitution to all its citizens equally.

My rejection of hyphenation has been misrepresented as race treachery by   27
some India-born academics on U.S. campuses who have appointed themselves guardians of the "purity" of ethnic cultures. Many of them, though they reside permanently in the United States and participate in its economy, consistently denounce American ideals and institutions. They direct their rage at me because, by becoming a U.S. citizen and exercising my voting rights, I have invested in the present and not the past; because I have committed myself to help shape the future of my adopted homeland; and because I celebrate racial and cultural mongrelization.

What excites me is that as a nation we have not only the chance to retain   28
those values we treasure from our original cultures but also the chance to acknowledge that the outer forms of those values are likely to change. Among Indian immigrants, I see a great deal of guilt about the inability to hang on to what they commonly term "pure culture." Parents express rage or despair at their U.S.-born children's forgetting of, or indifference to, some aspects of Indian culture. Of those parents I would ask: What is it we have lost if our children are acculturating into the culture in which we are living? Is it so terrible that our children are discovering or are inventing homelands for themselves?

Some first-generation Indo-Americans, embittered by racism and by unof-   29
ficial "glass ceilings," construct a phantom identity, more-Indian-than-Indians-in-India, as a defense against marginalization. I ask: Why don't you get actively involved in fighting discrimination? Make your voice heard. Choose the forum most appropriate for you. If you are a citizen, let your vote count. Reinvest your energy and resources into revitalizing your city's disadvantaged residents and neighborhoods. Know your constitutional rights, and when they are violated, use the agencies of redress the Constitution makes available to you. Expect change, and when it comes, deal with it!

As a writer, my literary agenda begins by acknowledging that America has 30 transformed me. It does not end until I show that I (along with the hundreds of thousands of immigrants like me) am minute by minute transforming America. The transformation is a two-way process: It affects both the individual and the national-cultural identity.

Others who write stories of migration often talk of arrival at a new place 31 as a loss, the loss of communal memory and the erosion of an original culture. I want to talk of arrival as a gain.

COMPREHENSION

1. What is the significance of the title? In what way is Mukherjee a "dreamer?" In what way does the United States inspire "dreaming?"
2. In paragraph 6, Mukherjee states that in India, she had a strong sense of identity. Why was it difficult for her to feel at ease with her "American identity"?
3. A country is a geographical area with national boundaries as well as a concept and an ideal. Does Mukherjee focus on these aspects of the United States and Canada equally, or does she emphasize one more than the other? Explain.

RHETORIC

1. The essay is divided into four parts. Why has the author contrived this structure? What is the focus of each? How does each section function rhetorically in relation to the other three?
2. Mukherjee introduces her essay with her own explanations of the terms "America" and "the United States." What is her purpose, considering that this is an autobiographical essay?
3. Mukherjee explores her transition from "expatriate" to "immigrant" to "U.S. citizen" in paragraphs 10 and 11. Explain the significance of each term in general and each term's particular role in the author's cultural metamorphosis.
4. Mukherjee rejects and condemns the belligerence toward and scapegoating of immigrants. How would you characterize the effect of these attacks on Mukherjee, an immigrant herself? Note, in particular, her statements in paragraphs 13 and 26.
5. How does Mukherjee employ irony in paragraph 12 to demonstrate the double standard imposed on individuals who do not fit the stereotypical mold of what it means to be a "citizen?"
6. In paragraph 14, the author states, "I take my American citizenship very seriously." Is the tone of the essay serious? Explain your view.
7. As you define the following words, identify the intended audience for this essay: *exclusivist* (paragraph 12), *demagogues* (paragraph 15), *diasporas* (paragraph 16), *ethnocentrists* and *demonized* (paragraph 17), and *balkanization* (paragraph 24).

WRITING

1. In a personal essay of 400 to 500 words, write about a time in your life when your allegiance, honesty, or integrity were unfairly questioned. Be sure to use specifics such as the circumstances of who, what, when, where, and why. Also describe how you felt at the time and the emotional outcome.
2. In an essay of 400 to 500 words, argue for or against the proposition that a course on cultural diversity should be taught at your college or university. Consider whether other ways of approaching the subject would be more profitable, or whether the subject needs to be addressed at all.
3. Write an essay based on personal experience or observation, explaining whether Mukherjee is correct in stating that "hyphenation is imposed only on nonwhite Americans" (paragraph 26). A variation on this theme might be an exploration why "hyphenated" terms used to describe certain white American groups have a different tone and purpose than terms used for nonwhites.
4. In her conclusion, Mukherjee criticizes "guardians of the 'purity' of ethnic cultures." Is there such a thing as a "pure" ethnic culture? Write an essay of 500 words, arguing your viewpoint.

The World House

Martin Luther King, Jr.

Martin Luther King, Jr. (1929–1968) was born in Atlanta, Georgia, and earned degrees from Morehouse College, Crozer Theological Seminary, Boston University, and Chicago Theological Seminary. As a Baptist clergyman, civil rights leader, founder and president of the Southern Christian Leadership Council, and, in 1964, Nobel Peace Prize winner, King was a celebrated advocate of nonviolent resistance to achieve equality and racial integration in the world. King was a gifted orator and a highly persuasive writer. His books include Letter from Birmingham City Jail *(1963);* Why We Can't Wait *(1964);* Stride Toward Freedom *(1958),* Strength to Love *(1963), and* Where Do We Go from Here: Chaos or Community? *(1967), a book published shortly before Reverend King was assassinated on April 4, 1968, in Memphis, Tennessee. In "The World House," a section from his last book, King uses analogy to promote his long-standing vision of a peaceful and united world civilization.*

Some years ago a famous novelist died. Among his papers was found a list of   1
suggested plots for future stories, the most prominently underscored being this one: "A widely separated family inherits a house in which they have to live together." This is the great new problem of mankind. We have inherited a large house, a great "world house" in which we have to live together—black and

white, Easterner and Westerner, Gentile and Jew, Catholic and Protestant, Moslem and Hindu—a family unduly separated in ideas, culture and interest, who, because we can never again live apart, must learn somehow to live with each other in peace.

However deeply American Negroes are caught in the struggle to be at last 2 at home in our homeland of the United States, we cannot ignore the larger world house in which we are also dwellers. Equality with whites will not solve the problem of either whites or Negroes if it means equality in a world society stricken by poverty and in a universe doomed to extinction by war.

All inhabitants of the globe are now neighbors. This worldwide neighbor- 3 hood has been brought into being largely as a result of the modern scientific and technological revolutions. The world of today is vastly different from the world of just one hundred years ago. A century ago Thomas Edison had not yet invented the incandescent lamp to bring light to many dark places of the earth. The Wright brothers had not yet invented that fascinating mechanical bird that would spread its gigantic wings across the skies and soon dwarf distance and place time in the service of man. Einstein had not yet challenged an axiom and the theory of relativity had not yet been posited.

Human beings, searching a century ago as now for better understanding, 4 had no television, no radios, no telephones and no motion pictures through which to communicate. Medical science had not yet discovered the wonder drugs to end many dread plagues and diseases. One hundred years ago military men had not yet developed the terrifying weapons of warfare that we know today—not the bomber, an airborne fortress raining down death; nor napalm, that burner of all things and flesh in its path. A century ago there were no skyscraping buildings to kiss the stars and no gargantuan bridges to span the waters. Science had not yet peered into the unfathomable ranges of interstellar space, nor had it penetrated oceanic depths. All these new inventions, these new ideas, these sometimes fascinating and sometimes frightening developments came later. Most of them have come within the past sixty years, sometimes with agonizing slowness, more characteristically with bewildering speed, but always with enormous significance for our future.

The years ahead will see a continuation of the same dramatic develop- 5 ments. Physical science will carve new highways through the stratosphere. In a few years astronauts and cosmonauts will probably walk comfortably across the uncertain pathways of the moon. In two or three years it will be possible, because of the new supersonic jets, to fly from New York to London in two and one-half hours. In the years ahead medical science will greatly prolong the lives of men by finding a cure for cancer and deadly heart ailments. Automation and cybernation will make it possible for working people to have undreamed-of amounts of leisure time. All this is a dazzling picture of the furniture, the workshop, the spacious rooms, the new decorations and the architectural pattern of the large world house in which we are living.

Along with the scientific and technological revolution, we have also wit- 6 nessed a world-wide freedom revolution over the last few decades. The present upsurge of the Negro people of the United States grows out of a deep and passionate determination to make freedom and equality a reality "here" and "now." In one sense the civil rights movement in the United States is a special American phenomenon which must be understood in the light of American history and dealt with in terms of the American situation. But on another and more important level, what is happening in the United States today is a significant part of a world development.

We live in a day, said the philosopher Alfred North Whitehead, "when civ- 7 ilization is shifting its basic outlook; a major turning point in history where the presuppositions on which society is structured are being analyzed, sharply challenged, and profoundly changed." What we are seeing now is a freedom explosion, the realization of "an idea whose time has come," to use Victor Hugo's phrase. The deep rumbling of discontent that we hear today is the thunder of disinherited masses, rising from dungeons of oppression to the bright hills of freedom. In one majestic chorus the rising masses are singing, in the words of our freedom song, "Ain't gonna let nobody turn us around." All over the world like a fever, freedom is spreading in the widest liberation movement in history. The great masses of people are determined to end the exploitation of their races and lands. They are awake and moving toward their goal like a tidal wave. You can hear them rumbling in every village street, on the docks, in the houses, among the students, in the churches and at political meetings. For several centuries the direction of history flowed from the nations and societies of Western Europe out into the rest of the world in "conquests" of various sorts. That period, the era of colonialism, is at an end. East is moving West. The earth is being redistributed. Yes, we are "shifting our basic outlooks."

These developments should not surprise any student of history. Oppressed 8 people cannot remain oppressed forever. The yearning for freedom eventually manifests itself. The Bible tells the thrilling story of how Moses stood in Pharaoh's court centuries ago and cried, "Let my people go." This was an opening chapter in a continuing story. The present struggle in the United States is a later chapter in the same story. Something within has reminded the Negro of his birthright of freedom, and something without has reminded him that it can be gained. Consciously or unconsciously, he has been caught up by the spirit of the times, and with his black brothers of Africa and his brown and yellow brothers in Asia, South America and the Caribbean, the United States Negro is moving with a sense of great urgency toward the promised land of racial justice.

Nothing could be more tragic than for men to live in these revolutionary 9 times and fail to achieve the new attitudes and the new mental outlooks that the new situation demands. In Washington Irving's familiar story of Rip Van Winkle, the one thing that we usually remember is that Rip slept twenty years. There is another important point, however, that is almost always overlooked. It was the sign on the inn in the little town on the Hudson from which Rip departed and scaled the mountain for his long sleep. When he went up, the sign had a picture of King George III of England. When he came down, twenty years later, the sign had a picture of George Washington. As he looked at the picture of the first President of the United States, Rip was confused, flustered and lost. He knew not who Washington was. The most striking thing about this story is not that Rip slept twenty years, but that he slept through a revolution that would alter the course of human history.

One of the great liabilities of history is that all too many people fail to re- 10 main awake through great periods of social change. Every society has its protectors of the status quo and its fraternities of the indifferent who are notorious for sleeping through revolutions. But today our very survival depends on our ability to stay awake, to adjust to new ideas, to remain vigilant and to face the challenge of change. The large house in which we live demands that we transform this worldwide neighborhood into a worldwide brotherhood. Together we must learn to live as brothers or together we will be forced to perish as fools.

We must work passionately and indefatigably to bridge the gulf between 11 our scientific progress and our moral progress. One of the great problems of mankind is that we suffer from a poverty of the spirit which stands in glaring contrast to our scientific and technological abundance. The richer we have become materially, the poorer we have become morally and spiritually.

Every man lives in two realms, the internal and the external. The internal is 12 that realm of spiritual ends expressed in art, literature, morals and religion. The external is that complex of devices, techniques, mechanisms and instrumentalities by means of which we live. Our problem today is that we have allowed the internal to become lost in the external. We have allowed the means by which we live to outdistance the ends for which we live. So much of modern life can be summarized in that suggestive phrase of Thoreau: "Improved means to an unimproved end." This is the serious predicament, the deep and haunting problem, confronting modern man. Enlarged material powers spell enlarged peril if there is not proportionate growth of the soul. When the external of man's nature subjugates the internal, dark storm clouds begin to form.

Western civilization is particularly vulnerable at this moment, for our ma- 13 terial abundance has brought us neither peace of mind nor serenity of spirit. An Asian writer has portrayed our dilemma in candid terms:

> You call your thousand material devices "labor-saving machinery," yet you are forever "busy." With the multiplying of your machinery you grow increasingly fatigued, anxious, nervous, dissatisfied. Whatever you have, you want more; and wherever you are you want to go somewhere else . . . your devices are neither time-saving nor soul-saving machinery. They are so many sharp spurs which urge you on to invent more machinery and to do more business.[1]

This tells us something about our civilization that cannot be cast aside as a prej- 14 udiced charge by an Eastern thinker who is jealous of Western prosperity. We cannot escape the indictment.

This does not mean that we must turn back the clock of scientific progress. 15 No one can overlook the wonders that science has wrought for our lives. The

[1]Abraham Mitrie Rihbany, *Wise Men from the East and from the West,* Houghton-Mifflin, 1922.

automobile will not abdicate in favor of the horse and buggy, or the train in favor of the stagecoach, or the tractor in favor of the hand plow, or the scientific
method in favor of ignorance and superstition. But our moral and spiritual
"lag" must be redeemed. When scientific power outruns moral power, we end
up with guided missiles and misguided men. When we foolishly minimize the
internal of our lives and maximize the external, we sign the warrant for our
own day of doom.

Our hope for creative living in this world house that we have inherited lies   16
in our ability to re-establish the moral ends of our lives in personal character
and social justice. Without this spiritual and moral reawakening we shall destroy ourselves in the misuse of our own instruments.

COMPREHENSION

1. What does the author mean by the concept of a world house? How is the
    modern era drawing the peoples of the world together? How does King
    explain the dangers confronting the world house? What is his proposal for
    creative living?
2. According to King, what are the two realms that we live in? How are these
    realms reflected in the content of this selection?
3. Explain the connection that King draws between oppression, freedom, and
    revolution.

RHETORIC

1. King, a compelling preacher and speaker (see his "I Have a Dream" speech
    earlier in this chapter, a contemporary classic delivered in 1963 at the end of
    the March on Washington), often delivered his prose in biblical and orator-
    ical rhythms. Find three examples of rhythmical, carefully balanced ca-
    dences in this essay, and explain their effect. Compare these rhythms with
    those in "I Have a Dream."
2. A second characteristic of King's oratorical and literary style is his fondness
    for figurative language. Locate and identify five examples of figurative
    language.
3. What is King's thesis? How does the key rhetorical strategy of analogy help
    advance it? What minor analogies exist in the essay?
4. Describe King's relationship with his reading audience. Identify words and
    phrases that clarify this relationship. Why, for example, does the author use
    the pronoun *we?*
5. How do the first and last paragraphs serve as a frame for this selection?
    How effective are they? Why?
6. What argumentative and persuasive techniques do you detect in this essay?
    How does King use illustration, comparison, and contrast to advance his
    proposition?

WRITING

1. Comment on the relevance of King's analogy to the 1990s.
2. Write a paper on the world house, using contemporary events, quotations from authorities, and your own ideas about today's conflicts to frame the analogy.
3. Using Whitehead's quotation (paragraph 7) as a guide, develop an argumentative essay on whether we are at a turning point in civilization.

Stranger in the Village

James Baldwin

James Baldwin (1924–1988), a major American essayist, novelist, short story writer, and playwright, was born and grew up in Harlem. He won a Eugene Saxon Fellowship and lived in Europe from 1948 to 1956. Always an activist in civil rights causes, Baldwin focused in his essays and fiction on the black search for identity in modern America and on the myth of white superiority. Among his principal works are Go Tell It on the Mountain *(1953),* Notes of a Native Son *(1955),* Giovanni's Room *(1956),* Nobody Knows My Name *(1961),* Another Country *(1962), and* If Beale Street Could Talk *(1974). One of the finest contemporary essayists, Baldwin had a rare talent for portraying the deepest concerns about civilization in an intensely personal style, as the following essay indicates.*

From all available evidence no black man had ever set foot in this tiny Swiss village before I came. I was told before arriving that I would probably be a "sight" for the village; I took this to mean that people of my complexion were rarely seen in Switzerland, and also that city people are always something of a "sight" outside of the city. It did not occur to me—possibly because I am an American—that there could be people anywhere who had never seen a Negro.

It is a fact that cannot be explained on the basis of the inaccessibility of the village. The village is very high, but it is only four hours from Milan and three hours from Lausanne. It is true that it is virtually unknown. Few people making plans for a holiday would elect to come here. On the other hand, the villagers are able, presumably, to come and go as they please—which they do: to another town at the foot of the mountain, with a population of approximately five thousand, the nearest place to see a movie or go to the bank. In the village there is no movie house, no bank, no library, no theater; very few radios, one jeep, one station wagon; and, at the moment, one typewriter, mine, an invention which the woman next door to me here had never seen. There are about six hundred people living here, all Catholic—I conclude this from the fact that the Catholic church is open all year round, whereas the Protestant chapel, set off on a hill a little removed from the village, is open only in the summertime when the tourists arrive. There are four or five hotels, all closed now, and four or five *bistros,* of which, however, only two do any business during the winter. These two do not do a great deal, for life in the village seems to end around nine or ten o'clock. There are a few stores, butcher, baker, *épicerie,* a hardware store, and a money-changer—who cannot change travelers' checks, but must send them down to the bank, an operation which takes two or three days. There is something called the *Ballet Haus,* closed in the winter and used for God knows what, certainly not ballet, during the summer. There seems to be only one schoolhouse in the village, and this for the quite young children; I suppose this to mean that their older brothers and sisters at some point descend from these mountains in order to complete their education—possibly, again, to the town just below. The landscape is absolutely forbidding, mountains towering on all four sides, ice and snow as far as the eye can reach. In this white wilderness, men and women and children move all day, carrying washing, wood, buckets of milk or water, sometimes skiing on Sunday afternoons. All week long boys and young men are to be seen shoveling snow off the rooftops, or dragging wood down from the forest in sleds.

The village's only real attraction, which explains the tourist season, is the hot spring water. A disquietingly high proportion of these tourists are cripples, or semi-cripples, who come year after year—from other parts of Switzerland, usually—to take the waters. This lends the village, at the height of the season, a rather terrifying air of sanctity, as though it were a lesser Lourdes. There is often something beautiful, there is always something awful, in the spectacle of a person who has lost one of his faculties, a faculty he never questioned until it was gone, and who struggles to recover it. Yet people remain people, on crutches or indeed on deathbeds; and wherever I passed, the first summer I was here, among the native villagers or among the lame, a wind passed with me— of astonishment, curiosity, amusement, and outrage. The first summer I stayed two weeks and never intended to return. But I did return in the winter, to work; the village offers, obviously, no distractions whatever and has the further advantage of being extremely cheap. Now it is winter again, a year later, and I am here again. Everyone in the village knows my name, though they scarcely ever use it, knows that I come from America—though this, apparently, they will never really believe: black men come from Africa—and everyone knows that I am the friend of the son of a woman who was born here, and that I am staying in their chalet. But I remain as much a stranger today as I was the first day I arrived, and the children shout *Neger! Neger!* as I walk along the streets.

It must be admitted that in the beginning I was far too shocked to have any real reaction. In so far as I reacted at all, I reacted by trying to be pleasant—it being a great part of the American Negro's education (long before he goes to school) that he must make people "like" him. This smile-and-the-world-smiles-with-you routine worked about as well in this situation as it had in the situation for which it was designed, which is to say that it did not work at all. No one, after all, can be liked whose human weight and complexity cannot be, or has not been, admitted. My smile was simply another unheard-of phenomenon which allowed them to see my teeth—they did not, really, see my smile and I began to think that, should I take to snarling, no one would notice any difference. All of the physical characteristics of the Negro which had caused me, in America, a very different and almost forgotten pain were nothing less than miraculous—or infernal—in the eyes of the village people. Some thought my hair was the color of tar, that it had the texture of wire, or the texture of cotton. It was jocularly suggested that I might let it all grow long and make myself a winter coat. If I sat in the sun for more than five minutes some daring creature was certain to come along and gingerly put his fingers on my hair, as though he were afraid of an electric shock, or put his hand on my hand, astonished that the color did not rub off. In all of this, in which it must be conceded there was the charm of genuine wonder and in which there was certainly no element of intentional unkindness, there was yet no suggestion that I was human: I was simply a living wonder.

I knew that they did not mean to be unkind, and I know it now; it is neces- 5
sary, nevertheless, for me to repeat this to myself each time I walk out of the chalet. The children who shout *Neger!* have no way of knowing the echoes this sound raises in me. They are brimming with good humor and the more daring swell with pride when I stop to speak with them. Just the same, there are days when I cannot pause and smile, when I have no heart to play with them; when, indeed, I mutter sourly to myself, exactly as I muttered on the streets of a city these children have never seen, when I was no bigger than these children are now: *Your* mother *was a nigger.* Joyce is right about history being a nightmare—but it may be the nightmare from which no one *can* awaken. People are trapped in history and history is trapped in them.

There is a custom in the village—I am told it is repeated in many villages— 6
of "buying" African natives for the purpose of converting them to Christianity. There stands in the church all year round a small box with a slot for money, decorated with a black figurine, and into this box the villagers drop their francs. During the *carnaval* which precedes Lent, two village children have their faces blackened—out of which bloodless darkness their blue eyes shine like ice—and fantastic horsehair wigs are placed on their blond heads; thus disguised, they solicit among the villagers for money for the missionaries in Africa. Between the box in the church and the blackened children, the village "bought" last year six or eight African natives. This was reported to me with pride by the wife of one of the *bistro* owners and I was careful to express astonishment and pleasure at the solicitude shown by the village for the souls of black folk. The *bistro* owner's wife beamed with a pleasure far more genuine than my own and seemed to feel that I might now breathe more easily concerning the souls of at least six of my kinsmen.

I tried not to think of these so lately baptized kinsmen, of the price paid for 7
them, or the peculiar price they themselves would pay, and said nothing about my father, who having taken his own conversion too literally never, at bottom, forgave the white world (which he described as heathen) for having saddled

him with a Christ in whom, to judge at least from their treatment of him, they themselves no longer believed. I thought of white men arriving for the first time in an African village, strangers there, as I am a stranger here, and tried to imagine the astounded populace touching their hair and marveling at the color of their skin. But there is a great difference between being the first white man to be seen by Africans and being the first black man to be seen by whites. The white man takes the astonishment as tribute, for he arrives to conquer and to convert the natives, whose inferiority in relation to himself is not even to be questioned; whereas I, without a thought of conquest, find myself among a people whose culture controls me, has even, in a sense, created me, people who have cost me more in anguish and rage than they will ever know, who yet do not even know of my existence. The astonishment with which I might have greeted them, should they have stumbled into my African village a few hundred years ago, might have rejoiced their hearts. But the astonishment with which they greet me today can only poison mine.

And this is so despite everything I may do to feel differently, despite my 8 friendly conversations with the *bistro* owner's wife, despite their three-year-old son who has at last become my friend, despite the *saluts* and *bonsoirs* which I exchange with people as I walk, despite the fact that I know that no individual can be taken to task for what history is doing, or has done. I say that the culture of these people controls me—but they can scarcely be held responsible for European culture. America comes out of Europe, but these people have never seen America nor have most of them seen more of Europe than the hamlet at the foot of their mountain. Yet they move with an authority which I shall never have; and they regard me, quite rightly, not only as a stranger in their village but as a suspect latecomer, bearing no credentials, to everything they have—however unconsciously—inherited.

For this village, even were it incomparably more remote and incredibly 9 more primitive, is the West, the West onto which I have been so strangely grafted. These people cannot be, from the point of view of power, strangers anywhere in the world; they have made the modern world, in effect, even if they do not know it. The most illiterate among them is related, in a way that I am not, to Dante, Shakespeare, Michelangelo, Aeschylus, Da Vinci, Rembrandt, and Racine; the cathedral at Chartres says something to them which it cannot say to me, as indeed would New York's Empire State Building, should anyone here ever see it. Out of their hymns and dances come Beethoven and Bach. Go back a few centuries and they are in their full glory—but I am in Africa, watching the conquerors arrive.

The rage of the disesteemed is personally fruitless, but it is also absolutely 10 inevitable; this rage, so generally discounted, so little understood even among the people whose daily bread it is, is one of the things that makes history. Rage can only with difficulty, and never entirely, be brought under the domination of the intelligence and is therefore not susceptible to any arguments whatever. This is a fact which ordinary representatives of the *Herrenvolk*, having never felt this rage and being unable to imagine it, quite fail to understand. Also, rage cannot be hidden, it can only be dissembled. This dissembling deludes the thoughtless, and strengthens rage and adds, to rage, contempt. There are, no doubt, as many ways of coping with the resulting complex of tensions as there are black men in the world, but no black man can hope ever to be entirely liberated from this internal warfare—rage, dissembling, and contempt having inevitably accompanied his first realization of the power of white men. What is crucial here is that, since white men represent in the black man's world so heavy a weight, white men have for black men a reality which is far from being reciprocal; and hence all black men have toward all white men an attitude which is designed, really, either to rob the white man of the jewel of his naïveté, or else to make it cost him dear.

The black man insists, by whatever means he finds at his disposal, that the white man cease to regard him as an exotic rarity and recognize him as a human being. This is a very charged and difficult moment, for there is a great deal of will power involved in the white man's naïveté. Most people are not naturally reflective any more than they are naturally malicious, and the white man prefers to keep the black man at a certain human remove because it is easier for him thus to preserve his simplicity and avoid being called to account for crimes committed by his forefathers, or his neighbors. He is inescapably aware, nevertheless, that he is in a better position in the world than black men are, nor can he quite put to death the suspicion that he is hated by black men therefore. He does not wish to be hated, neither does he wish to change places, and at this point in his uneasiness he can scarcely avoid having recourse to those legends which white men have created about black men, the most usual effect of which is that the white man finds himself enmeshed, so to speak, in his own language which describes hell, as well as the attributes which lead one to hell, as being as black as night. 11

Every legend, moreover, contains its residuum of truth, and the root function of language is to control the universe by describing it. It is of quite considerable significance that black men remain, in the imagination, and in overwhelming numbers in fact, beyond the disciplines of salvation; and this despite the fact the West has been "buying" African natives for centuries. There is, I should hazard, an instantaneous necessity to be divorced from this so visibly unsaved stranger, in whose heart, moreover, one cannot guess what dreams of vengeance are being nourished; and, at the same time, there are few things on earth more attractive than the idea of the unspeakable liberty which is allowed the unredeemed. When, beneath the black mask, a human being begins to make himself felt one cannot escape a certain awful wonder as to what kind of human being it is. What one's imagination makes of other people is dictated, of course, by the laws of one's own personality and it is one of the ironies of black-white relations that, by means of what the white man imagines the black man to be, the black man is enabled to know who the white man is. 12

I have said, for example, that I am as much a stranger in this village today as I was the first summer I arrived, but this is not quite true. The villagers wonder less about the texture of my hair than they did then, and wonder rather more about me. And the fact that their wonder now exists on another level is 13 reflected in their attitudes and in their eyes. There are the children who make those delightful, hilarious, sometimes astonishingly grave overtures of friendship in the unpredictable fashion of children; other children, having been taught that the devil is a black man, scream in genuine anguish as I approach. Some of the older women never pass without a friendly greeting, never pass, indeed, if it seems that they will be able to engage me in conversation; other women look down or look away or rather contemptuously smirk. Some of the men drink with me and suggest that I learn how to ski—partly, I gather, because they cannot imagine what I would look like on skis—and want to know if I am married, and ask questions about my *métier*. But some of the men have accused *le sale négre*—behind my back—of stealing wood and there is already in the eyes of some of them that peculiar, intent, paranoiac malevolence which one sometimes surprises in the eyes of American white men when, out walking with their Sunday girl, they see a Negro male approach.

There is a dreadful abyss between the streets of this village and the streets 14 of the city in which I was born, between the children who shout *Neger!* today and those who shouted *Nigger!* Yesterday—the abyss is experience, the American experience. The syllable hurled behind me today expresses, above all, wonder: I am a stranger here. But I am not a stranger in America and the same syllable riding on the American air expresses the war my presence has occasioned in the American soul.

For this village brings home to me this fact: that there was a day, and not 15 really a very distant day, when Americans were scarcely Americans at all but discontented Europeans, facing a great unconquered continent and strolling, say, into a marketplace and seeing black men for the first time. The shock this spectacle afforded is suggested, surely, by the promptness with which they decided that these black men were not really men but cattle. It is true that the necessity on the part of the settlers of the New World of reconciling their moral assumptions with the fact—and the necessity—of slavery enhanced immensely the charm of this idea, and it is also true that this idea expresses, with a truly American bluntness, the attitude which to varying extents all masters have had toward all slaves.

But between all former slaves and slave owners and the drama which be- 16 gins for Americans over three hundred years ago at Jamestown, there are at least two differences to be observed. The American Negro slave could not suppose, for one thing, as slaves in past epochs had supposed and often done, that he would ever be able to wrest the power from his master's hands. This was a supposition which the modern era, which was to bring about such vast changes in the aims and dimensions of power, put to death; it only begins, in unprecedented fashion, and with dreadful implications, to be resurrected today. But even had this supposition persisted with undiminished force, the American Negro slave could not have used it to lend his condition dignity, for the reason that this supposition rests on another: that the slave in exile yet remains related to his past, has some means—if only in memory—of revering and sustaining the forms of his former life, is able, in short, to maintain his identity.

This was not the case with the American Negro slave. He is unique among the black men of the world in that his past was taken from him, almost literally, at one blow. One wonders what on earth the first slave found to say to the first dark child he bore. I am told that there are Haitians able to trace their ancestry back to African kings, but any American Negro wishing to go back so far will find his journey through time abruptly arrested by the signature on the bill of sale which served as the entrance paper for his ancestor. At the time—to say nothing of the circumstances—of the enslavement of the captive black man who was to become the American Negro, there was not the remotest possibility that he would ever take power from his master's hands. There was no reason to suppose that his situation would ever change, nor was there, shortly, anything to indicate that his situation had ever been different. It was his necessity, in the words of E. Franklin Frazier, to find a "motive for living under American culture or die." The identity of the American Negro comes out of this extreme situation, and the evolution of this identity was a source of the most intolerable anxiety in the minds and the lives of his masters.

For the history of the American Negro is unique also in this: that the question of his humanity, and of his rights therefore as a human being, became a burning one for several generations of Americans, so burning a question that it ultimately became one of those used to divide the nation. It is out of this argument that the venom of the epithet *Nigger!* is derived. It is an argument which Europe has never had, and hence Europe quite sincerely fails to understand how or why the argument arose in the first place, why its effects are so frequently disastrous and always so unpredictable, why it refuses until today to be entirely settled. Europe's black possessions remained—and do remain—in Europe's colonies, at which remove they represented no threat whatever to European identity. If they posed any problem at all for the European conscience, it was a problem which remained comfortingly abstract: in effect, the black man, *as a man,* did not exist for Europe. But in America, even as a slave, he was an inescapable part of the general social fabric and no American could escape having an attitude toward him. Americans attempt until today to make an abstraction of the Negro, but the very nature of these abstractions reveals the tremendous effects the presence of the Negro has had on the American character.

When one considers the history of the Negro in America it is of the greatest importance to recognize that the moral beliefs of a person, or a people, are never really as tenuous as life—which is not moral—very often causes them to appear; these create for them a frame of reference and a necessary hope, the hope being that when life has done its worst they will be enabled to rise above themselves and to triumph over life. Life would scarcely be bearable if this hope did not exist. Again, even when the worst has been said, to betray a belief is not by any means to have put oneself beyond its power; the betrayal of a belief is not the same thing as ceasing to believe. If this were not so there would be no moral standards in the world at all. Yet one must also recognize that morality is based on ideas and that all ideas are dangerous—dangerous because ideas can only lead to action and where the action leads no man can say. And dangerous in this respect: that confronted with the impossibility of becoming free of them, one can be driven to the most inhuman excesses. The ideas on which American beliefs are based are not, though Americans often seem to think so, ideas which originated in America. They came out of Europe. And the establishment of democracy on the American continent was scarcely as radical a break with the past as was the necessity, which Americans faced, of broadening this concept to include black men.

This was, literally, a hard necessity. It was impossible, for one thing, for [20] Americans to abandon their beliefs, not only because these beliefs alone seemed able to justify the sacrifices they had endured and the blood that they had spilled, but also because these beliefs afforded them their only bulwark against a moral chaos as absolute as the physical chaos of the continent it was their destiny to conquer. But in the situation in which Americans found themselves, these beliefs threatened an idea which, whether or not one likes to think so, is the very warp and woof of the heritage of the West, the idea of white supremacy.

Americans have made themselves notorious by the shrillness and the bru- [21] tality with which they have insisted on this idea, but they did not invent it; and it has escaped the world's notice that those very excesses of which Americans have been guilty imply a certain, unprecedented uneasiness over the idea's life and power, if not, indeed, the idea's validity. The idea of white supremacy rests simply on the fact that white men are the creators of civilization (the present civilization, which is the only one that matters; all previous civilizations are simply "contributions" to our own) and are therefore civilization's guardians and defenders. Thus it was impossible for Americans to accept the black man as one of themselves, for to do so was to jeopardize their status as white men. But not so to accept him was to deny his human reality, his human weight and complexity, and the strain of denying the overwhelmingly undeniable forced Americans into rationalizations so fantastic that they approached the pathological.

At the root of the American Negro problem is the necessity of the American [22] white man to find a way of living with the Negro in order to be able to live with himself. And the history of this problem can be reduced to the means used by Americans—lynch law and law, segregation and legal acceptance, terrorization and concession—either to come to terms with this necessity, or to find a way around it, or (most usually) to find a way of doing both these things at once. The resulting spectacle, at once foolish and dreadful, led someone to make the quite accurate observation that "the Negro-in-America is a form of insanity which overtakes white men."

In this long battle, a battle by no means finished, the unforeseeable effects [23] of which will be felt by many future generations, the white man's motive was the protection of his identity; the black man was motivated by the need to establish an identity. And despite the terrorization which the Negro in America endured and endures sporadically until today, despite the cruel and totally inescapable ambivalence of his status in his country, the battle for his identity has long ago been won. He is not a visitor to the West, but a citizen there, an American; as American as the Americans who despise him, the Americans who fear him, the Americans who love him—the Americans who became less than themselves, or rose to be greater than themselves by virtue of the fact that the challenge he represented was inescapable. He is perhaps the only black man in the world whose relationship to white men is more terrible, more subtle, and more meaningful than the relationship of bitter possessed to uncertain possessor. His survival depended, and his development depends, on his ability to turn his peculiar status in the Western world to his own advantage and, it may be, to the very great advantage of that world. It remains for him to fashion out of his experience that which will give him sustenance, and a voice.

The cathedral at Chartres, I have said, says something to the people of this 24 village which it cannot say to me; but it is important to understand that this cathedral says something to me which it cannot say to them. Perhaps they are struck by the power of the spires, the glory of the windows; but they have known God, after all, longer than I have known him, and in a different way, and I am terrified by the slippery bottomless well to be found in the crypt, down which heretics were hurled to death, and by the obscene, inescapable gargoyles jutting out of the stone and seeming to say that God and the devil can never be divorced. I doubt that the villagers think of the devil when they face a cathedral because they have never been identified with the devil. But I must accept the status which myth, if nothing else, gives me in the West before I can hope to change the myth.

Yet, if the American Negro has arrived at his identity by virtue of the ab- 25 soluteness of his estrangement from his past, American white men still nourish the illusion that there is some means of recovering the European innocence, of returning to a state in which black men do not exist. This is one of the greatest errors Americans can make. The identity they fought so hard to protect has, by virtue of that battle, undergone a change: Americans are as unlike any other white people in the world as it is possible to be. I do not think, for example, that it is too much to suggest that the American vision of the world—which allows so little reality, generally speaking, for any of the darker forces in human life, which tends until today to paint moral issues in glaring black and white—owes a great deal to the battle waged by Americans to maintain between themselves and black men a human separation which could not be bridged. It is only now beginning to be borne in on us—very faintly, it must be admitted, very slowly, and very much against our will—that this vision of the world is dangerously inaccurate, and perfectly useless. For it protects our moral high-mindedness at the terrible expense of weakening our grasp of reality. People who shut their eyes to reality simply invite their own destruction, and anyone who insists on remaining in a state of innocence long after that innocence is dead turns himself into a monster.

The time has come to realize that the interracial drama acted out on the 26 American continent has not only created a new black man, it has created a new white man, too. No road whatever will lead Americans back to the simplicity of this European village where white men still have the luxury of looking on me as a stranger. I am not, really, a stranger any longer for any American alive. One of the things that distinguishes Americans from other people is that no other people has ever been so deeply involved in the lives of black men, and vice versa. This fact faced, with all its implications, it can be seen that the history of the American Negro problem is not merely shameful, it is also something of an achievement. For even when the worst has been said, it must also be added that the perpetual challenge posed by this problem was always, somehow, perpetually met. It is precisely this black-white experience which may prove of indispensable value to us in the world we face today. This world is white no longer, and it will never be white again.

COMPREHENSION

1. According to Baldwin, what distinguishes Americans from other people? What is his purpose in highlighting these differences?
2. What connections between Europe, Africa, and America emerge from this essay? What is the relevance of the Swiss village to this frame of reference?
3. In the context of the essay, explain what Baldwin means by his statement, "People are trapped in history and history is trapped in them" (paragraph 5).

RHETORIC

1. Analyze the effect of Baldwin's repetition of "there is" and "there are" constructions in paragraph 2. What does the parallelism at the start of paragraph 8 accomplish? Locate other examples of parallelism in the essay.
2. Analyze the image of winter in paragraph 3 and its relation to the rest of the essay.
3. Where in the essay is Baldwin's complex thesis condensed for the reader? What does this placement of thesis reveal about the logical method of development in the essay?
4. How does Baldwin create his introduction? What is the focus? What key motifs does the author present that will inform the rest of the essay? What is the relationship of paragraph 5 to paragraph 6?
5. What paragraphs constitute the second section of the essay? What example serves to unify this section? What major shift in emphasis occurs in the third part of the essay? Explain the cathedral of Chartres as a controlling motif between these two sections.
6. What comparisons and contrasts help structure and unify the essay?

WRITING

1. Examine the paradox implicit in Baldwin's statement in the last paragraph that the history of the American Negro problem is "something of an achievement."

2. Write an essay on civilization based on the last sentence in Baldwin's essay: "This world is white no longer, and it will never be white again."
3. Describe a time when you felt yourself a "stranger" in a certain culture.

Some Reflections on American Manners

Alexis de Tocqueville

Alexis Charles Henri Clerél de Tocqueville (1805–1859), descended from an aristocratic Norman family, was a French lawyer, politician, statesman, and historian. Sent to the United States in 1831 to study the American penal system, he wrote instead one of the most penetrating inquiries into the nature of the American system, Democracy in America *(1835). In this chapter from his study, Tocqueville compares and contrasts manners as manifested in the political and social contexts of democracy and aristocracy.*

Nothing, at first sight, seems less important than the external formalities of human behavior, yet there is nothing to which men attach more importance. They can get used to anything except living in a society which does not share their manners. The influence of the social and political system on manners is therefore worth serious examination.

Manners, speaking generally, have their roots in mores; they are also sometimes the result of an arbitrary convention agreed between certain men. They are both natural and acquired.

When some see that, without dispute or effort of their own, they stand first in society; when they daily have great aims in view which keep them occupied, leaving details to others; and when they live surrounded by wealth they have not acquired and do not fear to lose, one can see that they will feel a proud disdain for all the petty interests and material cares of life and that there will be a natural grandeur in their thoughts that will show in their words and manners.

In democracies there is generally little dignity of manner, as private life is very petty. Manners are often vulgar, as thoughts have small occasion to rise above preoccupation with domestic interests.

True dignity in manners consists in always taking one's proper place, not too high and not too low; that is as much within the reach of a peasant as of a prince. In democracies everybody's status seems doubtful; as a result, there is often pride but seldom dignity of manners. Moreover, manners are never well regulated or well thought out.

There is too much mobility in the population of a democracy for any definite group to be able to establish a code of behavior and see that it is observed.

So everyone behaves more or less after his own fashion, and a certain incoherence of manners always prevails, because they conform to the feelings and ideas of each individual rather than to an ideal example provided for everyone to imitate.

In any case, this is much more noticeable when an aristocracy has just fallen 7 than when it has long been destroyed.

New political institutions and new mores then bring together in the same 8 places men still vastly different in education and habits and compel them to a life in common; this constantly leads to the most ill-assorted juxtapositions. There is still some memory of the former strict code of politeness, but no one knows quite what it said or where to find it. Men have lost the common standard of manners but have not yet resolved to do without it, so each individual tries to shape, out of the ruins of former customs, some rule, however arbitrary and variable. Hence manners have neither the regularity and dignity frequent in aristocracies nor the qualities of simplicity and freedom which one sometimes finds in democracies; they are both constrained and casual.

But this is not a normal state of things.   9

When equality is complete and old-established, all men, having roughly the 10 same ideas and doing roughly the same things, do not need to come to an understanding or to copy each other in order to behave and talk in the same way; one sees a lot of petty variations in their manners but no great differences. They are never exactly alike, since they do not copy one pattern; they are never very unlike, because they have the same social condition. At first sight one might be inclined to say that the manners of all Americans are exactly alike, and it is only on close inspection that one sees all the variations among them.

The English make game of American manners, but it is odd that most of 11 those responsible for those comic descriptions belong themselves to the English middle classes, and the cap fits them very well too. So these ruthless critics generally themselves illustrate just what they criticize in America; they do not notice that they are abusing themselves, to the great delight of their own aristocracy.

Nothing does democracy more harm than its outward forms of behavior; 12 many who could tolerate its vices cannot put up with its manners.

But I will not admit that there is nothing to praise in democratic manners.   13

In aristocracies, all within reach of the ruling class are at pains to imitate it, 14 and very absurd and insipid imitations result. Democracies, with no models of high breeding before them, at least escape the necessity of daily looking at bad copies thereof.

In democracies manners are never so refined as among aristocracies, but 15 they are also never so coarse. One misses both the crude words of the mob and the elegant and choice phrases of the high nobility. There is much triviality of manner, but nothing brutal or degraded.

I have already said that a precise code of behavior cannot take shape in 16 democracies. That has its inconveniences and its advantages. In aristocracies rules of propriety impose the same demeanor on all, making every member of the same class seem alike in spite of personal characteristics; they bedizen and conceal nature. Democratic manners are neither so well thought out nor so regular, but they often are more sincere. They form, as it were, a thin, transparent veil through which the real feelings and personal thoughts of each man can be easily seen. Hence there is frequently an intimate connection between the form and the substance of behavior; we see a less decorative picture, but one truer to life. One may put the point this way: democracy imposes no particular manners, but in a sense prevents them from having manners at all.

Sometimes the feelings, passions, virtues, and vices of an aristocracy may 17 reappear in a democracy, but its manners never. They are lost and vanish past return when the democratic revolution is completed. It would seem that nothing is more lasting than the manners of an aristocratic class, for it preserves them for some time after losing property and power, nor more fragile, for as soon as they have gone, no trace of them is left, and it is even difficult to discover what they once were when they have ceased to exist. A change in the state of society works this marvel, and a few generations are enough to bring it about.

The principal characteristics of the aristocracy remain engraved in history 18 after its destruction, but the slight and delicate forms of its manners are lost to memory almost immediately after its fall. No one can imagine them when they are no longer seen. Their disappearance is unnoted and unfelt. For the heart needs an apprenticeship of custom and education to appreciate the refined pleasure derived from distinguished and fastidious manners; once the habit is lost, the taste for them easily goes too.

Thus, not only are democratic peoples unable to have aristocratic manners, 19 but they cannot even conceive or desire them. As they cannot imagine them, from their point of view it is as if they had never existed.

One should not attach too much importance to this loss, but it is permissible 20 to regret it.

I know it has happened that the same men have had very distinguished 21 manners and very vulgar feelings; the inner life of courts has shown well enough what grand appearances may conceal the meanest hearts. But though the manners of an aristocracy by no means create virtue, they may add grace to virtue itself. It was no ordinary sight to see a numerous and powerful class whose every gesture seemed to show a constant and natural dignity of feeling and thought, an ordered refinement of taste and urbanity of manners.

The manners of the aristocracy created a fine illusion about human nature; 22 though the picture was often deceptive, it was yet a noble satisfaction to look on it.

COMPREHENSION

1. Summarize Tocqueville's observations about American manners, and explain why he believes they got that way.
2. Explain the positive and negative aspects that Tocqueville finds in both aristocratic manners and democratic ones.

3. Why are manners the one element in the transition from an aristocracy to a democracy that cannot be transmitted?

RHETORIC

1. The author makes a number of points concerning the nature of manners. What method, if any, does he use to reach his conclusions?
2. The author seems quite concerned about the concepts of formality and informality. Would you rate his writing as formal or informal? What educational level does the author assume his intended audience has attained? Explain your answer.
3. Paragraph 3 is one long sentence. What punctuation devices does the author use to achieve this? How does his use of the word *when* help give the paragraph a logical structure?
4. We ordinarily think of rhythm as a component of music, yet, by mixing long and short sentences, the author is able to establish a rhythm to his prose. How do the short sentences help keep the prose moving? How do they function as transitional devices?
5. One commonly learns in school not to begin a sentence with the word *but*. Tocqueville breaks this convention three times in his essay—in paragraphs 9, 13, and 21. Explain why this is or is not effective.
6. The author uses comparison and contrast in many of his sentences. For example, in paragraph 15, he lists three distinctions between democratic manners and aristocratic ones. How often does he use this device in the essay? What is the total effect of using it so consistently?
7. Paragraph 13 offers the reader a rare example of the double negative in English. How does this reflect upon the style of the writing? How would the tone be different if the sentence were, "But I will admit there is something to praise in democratic manners"?

WRITING

1. Select an aspect of American behavior or perspective—such as language, attire, or taste—and write a brief essay explaining your subject, using Tocqueville's writing style.
2. For a research project, use anthropological, cultural, and historical source material in your library to write an essay about daily life in one American city during the early nineteenth century.
3. All cultures have rituals concerning things such as conversation, comfort zones, greeting and leave-taking signals. Browse through a book featuring photographs of a range of people from another era or culture, and write a brief descriptive essay describing their gestures or expressions.

CONNECTIONS FOR CRITICAL THINKING

1. Discuss whether the attributes of cyberspace as noted by Dyson can promote or discourage the ideas for a "World House" as proposed by King.
2. Discuss the views that Mukherjee and Baldwin have in common regarding the refusal of American culture to accept the "otherness" of those it perceives as not behaving like or looking like the conventional "American." Expand your discussion to present your own views about the similarities and differences in the ways "white" America views immigrants and African Americans.
3. Compare and contrast the diction, level of discourse, style, and vocabulary of Dyson and Baldwin.
4. Both Thomas Jefferson and Martin Luther King, Jr. made powerful appeals to the government in power on behalf of their people. Write a comparison and contrast essay that examines the language, style, and content of both essays.
5. Select the essays you find the most and the least appealing or compelling in this chapter. Discuss why you selected them, and explore the way you developed your viewpoint.
6. Compare and contrast the narrative style of Catton with the more analytical style of Machiavelli.
7. Compare and contrast the difficulties Orwell had in attempting to "fit in" to his role as a British police officer in a hostile culture with the experiences Mukherjee describes of a nonwhite American trying to assimilate into the dominant culture.
8. Create a "group" chat room with three students from different sections of your course, and discuss Dyson's views on cyberspace regulation. Provide a summary of your discussion to your classmates.
9. Interview five parents who have children under the age of 10, and ask them if and how they control the Internet content their children view. Report your findings to your class.
10. Discuss with a nonnative student de Tocqueville's "Reflections on American Manners." Explore to what degree your interviewee agrees with his classic assessment, and to what degree his views pertain today.

chapter **7**

Business and Economics
How Do We Earn Our Keep?

Work is central to the human experience; in fact, it is work and its economic and social outcomes that provide us with the keys to an understanding of culture and civilization. Work tells us much about scarcity and abundance, poverty and affluence, the haves and have-nots in any society, as well as a nation's economic imperatives. Whether it is the rise and fall of cities, the conduct of business and corporations, or the economic policies of government, we see in the culture of work an attempt to impose order on nature. Work is our handprint upon the world.

The work we perform and the careers we pursue also define us in very personal ways. "I'm a professor at Harvard" or "I work for IBM" serve as identity badges. (Robert Reich, a contributor to this chapter, did work at Harvard.) For what we do explains, at least in part, what and who we are. The very act of looking for work illuminates one's status in society, one's background, one's aspirations. Jonathan Swift, in his classic essay "A Modest Proposal," written in 1729, demonstrates how labor reveals economic and political configurations of power. Over 250 years later, Robert Reich tells us the same thing in his analysis of the changing nature of work and how these changes create an even broader gap between the rich and the poor.

Work is not merely an important human activity but an essential one for social and psychological health. You might like your work, or you might loathe it; be employed or unemployed; enjoy the reputation of a workaholic or a person who lives for leisure time; view work as a curse or as a duty. Regardless, it is work that occupies a central position in your relationship to society. In fact, Sigmund Freud spoke of work as the basis of one's social reality.

Regardless of your perspective on the issue, it is important to understand the multiple dimensions of work. In both traditional and modern societies, work prepares us for economic and social roles. It affects families, school curricula, public policy. Ultimately, as many authors here suggest, it determines our self-esteem. Through work we come to terms with ourselves and our environment. The nature and purpose of the work we do provide us with a powerful measure of our worth.

358

Previewing the Chapter

As you read the essays in this chapter and respond to them in discussion and writing, consider the following questions:

- What are the significant forms of support the author uses in viewing the world of work: observation, statistics, personal experience, history, and so on?
- What assumptions does the author make about the value of work?
- Does the author discuss work in general or focus on one particular aspect of work?
- How does the writer define *work?* In what ways, if any, does the author expand on the simple definition of *work* as "paid employment"?
- What issues of race, class, and gender does the author raise?
- What is the relationship of work to the changing social, political, and economic systems depicted in the author's essay?
- What tone does the writer take in his or her presentation of the work experience?
- What psychological insights does the author offer into the culture of work?
- What does the writer's style reveal about his or her attitude toward work?

Classic and Contemporary Images
WILL WORKERS BE DISPLACED BY MACHINES?

Using a Critical Perspective   Diego Rivera's mural and George Haling's photograph present industrial scenes that reveal the impact of technology on workers. What details are emphasized in each illustration? How are these two images similar and dissimilar? What, for example, is the relation of human beings to the machines that are the centerpiece of each photograph? Are the artist and photographer objective or subjective in the presentation of each scene? Explain.

Detroit Institute of Arts/The Bridgeman Art Library. Gift of Edsel Ford.

In the era known as the "Machine Age," 1918–1941, many artists, industrial designers, and architects in the United States and Europe evoked the mechanisms and images of industry in their works. During this time, the Mexican painter Diego Rivera (1886–1957) created a mural for the Detroit Institute of Arts (1932–33), a portion of which is reprinted here.

George Haling/Photo Researchers

Today, computers are used to help control assembly lines, as shown in this recent photo of a Chrysler assembly line.

Classic and Contemporary Essays

DOES EQUAL OPPORTUNITY EXIST?

Virginia Woolf's "Professions for Women" is ironic from the start as she readily admits she can speak expertly of only one profession, her own, which is writing. But her message is clear regarding the effect of living in a male-dominated society. Simply put, it is very difficult to break the shackles of conditioning that one acquires from being told over and over again by one's culture that gender is destiny, regardless of what one aspires to. The author—through personal experience—demonstrates how this discrimination has a profound effect on the ability to see with one's own eyes and to think with one's own head. Henry Louis Gates, Jr. presents an interesting variation on this theme. Although the outcome is the same, the premise is reversed. He demonstrates how correlating supposedly positive attributes to a group—that is, superior athletic performance and race—results in the same deadening of the sense of personal ambition, and a limiting of the scope of what one can aspire to. The thoughtful reader should be able to learn valuable lessons from comparing and contrasting these essays—one of which is that misguided perception all too often can be a self-fulfilling prophecy.

Professions for Women

Virginia Woolf

Virginia Woolf (1882–1941), novelist and essayist, was the daughter of Sir Leslie Stephen, a famous critic and writer on economics. An experimental novelist, Woolf attempted to portray consciousness through a poetic, symbolic, and concrete style. Her novels include Jacob's Room *(1922),* Mrs. Dalloway *(1925),* To the Lighthouse *(1927), and* The Waves *(1931). She was also a perceptive reader and critic; her criticism appears in* The Common Reader *(1925) and* The Second Common Reader *(1933). In the following essay, which was delivered originally as a speech to The Women's Service League in 1931, Woolf argues that women must overcome several "angels," or phantoms, in order to succeed in professional careers.*

When your secretary invited me to come here, she told me that your Society is   1
concerned with the employment of women and she suggested that I might tell you something about my own professional experiences. It is true I am a woman; it is true I am employed; but what professional experiences have I had? It is difficult to say. My profession is literature; and in that profession there are fewer experiences for women than in any other, with the exception of the stage— fewer, I mean, that are peculiar to women. For the road was cut many years ago—by Fanny Burney, by Aphra Behn, by Harriet Martineau, by Jane Austen, by George Eliot—many famous women, and many more unknown and forgotten, have been before me, making the path smooth, and regulating my steps. Thus, when I came to write, there were very few material obstacles in my way. Writing was a reputable and harmless occupation. The family peace was not broken by the scratching of a pen. No demand was made upon the family purse. For ten and sixpence one can buy paper enough to write all the plays of Shakespeare—if one has a mind that way. Pianos and models, Paris, Vienna and Berlin, masters and mistresses, are not needed by a writer. The cheapness of writing paper is, of course, the reason why women have succeeded as writers before they have succeeded in the other professions.

But to tell you my story—it is a simple one. You have only got to figure to   2
yourselves a girl in a bedroom with a pen in her hand. She had only to move that pen from left to right—from ten o'clock to one. Then it occurred to her to do what is simple and cheap enough after all—to slip a few of those pages into an envelope, fix a penny stamp in the corner, and drop the envelope into the red box at the corner. It was thus that I became a journalist; and my effort was rewarded on the first day of the following month—a very glorious day it was for me—by a letter from an editor containing a cheque for one pound ten shillings and sixpence. But to show you how little I deserve to be called a professional woman, how little I know of the struggles and difficulties of such lives, I have

to admit that instead of spending that sum upon bread and butter, rent, shoes and stockings, or butcher's bills, I went out and bought a cat—a beautiful cat, a Persian cat, which very soon involved me in bitter disputes with my neighbors.

What could be easier than to write articles and to buy Persian cats with the profits? But wait a moment. Articles have to be about something. Mine, I seem to remember, was about a novel by a famous man. And while I was writing this review, I discovered that if I were going to review books I should need to do battle with a certain phantom. And the phantom was a woman, and when I came to know her better I called her after the heroine of a famous poem, The Angel in the House. It was she who used to come between me and my paper when I was writing reviews. It was she who bothered me and wasted my time and so tormented me that at last I killed her. You who come of a younger and happier generation may not have heard of her—you may not know what I mean by the Angel in the House. I will describe her as shortly as I can. She was intensely sympathetic. She was immensely charming. She was utterly unselfish. She excelled in the difficult arts of family life. She sacrificed herself daily. If there was a chicken, she took the leg; if there was a draught she sat in it—in short she was so constituted that she never had a mind or a wish of her own, but preferred to sympathize always with the minds and wishes of others. Above all—I need not say it—she was pure. Her purity was supposed to be her chief beauty—her blushes, her great grace. In those days—the last of Queen Victoria— every house had its Angel. And when I came to write I encountered her with the very first words. The shadow of her wings fell on my page; I heard the rustling of her skirts in the room. Directly, that is to say, I took my pen in hand to review that novel by a famous man, she slipped behind me and whispered: "My dear, you are a young woman. You are writing about a book that has been written by a man. Be sympathetic; be tender; flatter; deceive; use all the arts and wiles of our sex. Never let anybody guess that you have a mind of your own. Above all, be pure." And she made as if to guide my pen. I now record the one act for which I take some credit to myself, though the credit rightly belongs to some excellent ancestors of mine who left me a certain sum of money—shall we say five hundred pounds a year—so that it was not necessary for me to depend solely on charm for my living. I turned upon her and caught her by the throat. I did my best to kill her. My excuse, if I were to be had up in a court of law, would be that I acted in self-defense. Had I not killed her she would have killed me. She would have plucked the heart out of my writing. For, as I found, directly I put pen to paper, you cannot review even a novel without having a mind of your own, without expressing what you think to be the truth about human relations, morality, sex. And all these questions, according to the Angel in the House, cannot be dealt with freely and openly by women; they must charm, they must conciliate, they must—to put it bluntly—tell lies if they are to succeed. Thus, whenever I felt the shadow of her wing or the radiance of her halo upon my page, I took up the inkpot and flung it at her. She died hard. Her fictitious nature was of great assistance to her. It is far harder to kill a phantom than a reality. She was always creeping back when I thought I had dispatched her. Though

I flatter myself that I killed her in the end, the struggle was severe; it took much time that had better have been spent upon learning Greek grammar; or in roaming the world in search of adventures. But it was a real experience; it was an experience that was bound to befall all women writers at that time. Killing the Angel in the House was part of the occupation of a woman writer.

But to continue my story. The Angel was dead; what then remained? You 4 may say that what remained was a simple and common object—a young woman in a bedroom with an inkpot. In other words, now that she had rid herself of falsehood, that young woman had only to be herself. Ah, but what is "herself"? I mean, what is a woman? I assure you, I do not know. I do not believe that you know. I do not believe that anybody can know until she has expressed herself in all the arts and professions open to human skill. That indeed is one of the reasons why I have come here—out of respect for you, who are in process of showing us by your experiments what a woman is, who are in process of providing us, by your failures and successes, with that extremely important piece of information.

But to continue the story of my professional experiences. I made one pound 5 ten and six by my first review; and I bought a Persian cat with the proceeds. Then I grew ambitious. A Persian cat is all very well, I said; but a Persian cat is not enough. I must have a motor car. And it was thus that I became a novelist— for it is a very strange thing that people will give you a motor car if you will tell them a story. It is a still stranger thing that there is nothing so delightful in the world as telling stories. It is far pleasanter than writing reviews of famous novels. And yet, if I am to obey your secretary and tell you my professional experiences as a novelist, I must tell you about a very strange experience that befell me as a novelist. And to understand it you must try first to imagine a novelist's state of mind. I hope I am not giving away professional secrets if I say that a novelist's chief desire is to be as unconscious as possible. He has to induce in himself a state of perpetual lethargy. He wants life to proceed with the utmost quiet and regularity. He wants to see the same faces, to read the same books, to do the same things day after day, month after month, while he is writing, so that nothing may break the illusion in which he is living—so that nothing may disturb or disquiet the mysterious nosings about, feelings round, darts, dashes and sudden discoveries of that very shy and illusive spirit, the imagination. I suspect that this state is the same both for men and women. Be that as it may, I want you to imagine me writing a novel in a state of trance. I want you to figure to yourselves a girl sitting with a pen in her hand, which for minutes, and indeed for hours, she never dips into the inkpot. The image that comes to my mind when I think of this girl is the image of a fisherman lying sunk in dreams on the verge of a deep lake with a rod held out over the water. She was letting her imagination sweep unchecked round every rock and cranny of the world that lies submerged in the depths of our unconscious being. Now came the experience, the experience that I believe to be far commoner with women writers than with men. The line raced through the girl's fingers. Her imagination had rushed away. It had sought the pools, the depths, the dark places where the largest fish slumber. And then there was a smash. There was an explosion. There was foam and confusion. The imagination had dashed itself against something hard. The girl was roused from her dream. She was indeed in a state of the most acute and difficult distress. To speak without figure she had thought of something, something about the body, about the passions which it was unfitting for her as a woman to say. Men, her reason told her, would be shocked. The consciousness of what men will say of a woman who speaks the truth about her passions had roused her from her artist's state of unconsciousness. She could write no more. The trance was over. Her imagination could work no longer. This I believe to be a very common experience with women writers—they are impeded by the extreme conventionality of the other sex. For though men sensibly allow themselves great freedom in these respects, I doubt that they realize or can control the extreme severity with which they condemn such freedom in women.

These then were two very genuine experiences of my own. These were two 6 of the adventures of my professional life. The first—killing the Angel in the House—I think I solved. She died. But the second, telling the truth about my own experiences as a body, I do not think I solved. I doubt that any woman has solved it yet. The obstacles against her are still immensely powerful—and yet they are very difficult to define. Outwardly, what is simpler than to write books? Outwardly, what obstacles are there for a woman rather than for a man? Inwardly, I think, the case is very different; she has still many ghosts to fight, many prejudices to overcome. Indeed it will be a long time still, I think, before a woman can sit down to write a book without finding a phantom to be slain, a rock to be dashed against. And if this is so in literature, the freest of all professions for women, how is it in the new professions which you are now for the first time entering?

Those are the questions that I should like, had I time, to ask you. And indeed, if I have laid stress upon these professional experiences of mine, it is because I believe that they are, though in different forms, yours also. Even when the path is nominally open—when there is nothing to prevent a woman from being a doctor, a lawyer, a civil servant—there are many phantoms and obstacles, as I believe, looming in her way. To discuss and define them is I think of great value and importance; for thus only can the labour be shared, the difficulties be solved. But besides this, it is necessary also to discuss the ends and the aims for which we are fighting, for which we are doing battle with these formidable obstacles. Those aims cannot be taken for granted; they must be perpetually questioned and examined. The whole position, as I see it—here in this hall surrounded by women practising for the first time in history I know not how many different professions—is one of extraordinary interest and importance. You have won rooms of your own in the house hitherto exclusively owned by men. You are able, though not without great labour and effort, to pay the rent. You are earning your five hundred pounds a year. But this freedom is only a beginning; the room is your own, but it is still bare. It has to be furnished; it has to be decorated; it has to be shared. How are you going to furnish it, how are you going to decorate it? With whom are you going to share it, and upon what terms? These, I think, are questions of the utmost importance and interest. For the first time in history you are able to ask for them; for the first time you are able to decide for yourselves what the answers should be. Willingly would I stay and discuss those questions and answers—but not tonight. My time is up; and I must cease.

COMPREHENSION

1. This essay was presented originally as a speech. What internal evidence indicates that it was intended as a talk? How do you respond to it today as a reader?
2. Who or what is the "angel" that Woolf describes in this essay? Why must she kill it? What other obstacles does a professional woman encounter?
3. Paraphrase the last two paragraphs of this essay. What is the essence of Woolf's argument?

RHETORIC

1. There is a significant amount of figurative language in the essay. Locate and explain examples. What does the figurative language contribute to the tone of the essay? Compare and contrast the figurative language in this essay and in Woolf's "The Death of the Moth" in Chapter 8.
2. How do we know that Woolf is addressing an audience of women? Why does she pose so many questions, and what does this strategy contribute to the rapport that she wants to establish? Explain the effect of the last two sentences.
3. How does Woolf use analogy to structure part of her argument?
4. Why does Woolf rely on personal narration? How does it affect the logic of her argument?
5. Evaluate Woolf's use of contrast to advance her argument.
6. Where does Woolf place her main proposition? How emphatic is it, and why?

WRITING

1. How effectively does Woolf use her own example as a professional writer to advance a broader proposition concerning all women entering professional life? Answer this question in a brief essay.
2. Explain the value of Woolf's essay for women today.
3. Discuss the problems and obstacles that you anticipate when you enter your chosen career.
4. Compare and contrast the essays by Steinem and Woolf.

Delusions of Grandeur

Henry Louis Gates, Jr.

Henry Louis Gates, Jr. (b. 1950) is an educator, writer, and editor. He was born in West Virginia and educated at Yale and at Clare College in Cambridge. Gates has had a varied career, working as a general anesthetist in Tanzania and as a staff correspondent for Time *magazine in London. His essays have appeared in such diverse publications as* Black American Literature Forum, Yale Review, The New York Times Book Review, *and* Sports Illustrated. *He is also the author of* Figures in Black: Words, Signs and the Racial Self *(1987) and* The Signifying Monkey: A Theory of Afro-American Literary Criticism *(1988) and is the editor, with Nellie Y. McKey, of* The Norton Anthology of African American Literature *(1996). In this article from* Sports Illustrated, *Gates turns his attention to the limited career choices presented as viable to African American youth and to public misconceptions about blacks in sports.*

Standing at the bar of an all-black VFW post in my hometown of Piedmont, 1 W.Va., I offered five dollars to anyone who could tell me how many African-American professional athletes were at work today. There are 35 million African-Americans, I said.

"Ten million!" yelled one intrepid soul, too far into his cups. 2

"No way . . . more like 500,000," said another. 3

"You mean *all* professional sports," someone interjected, "including golf 4 and tennis, but not counting the brothers from Puerto Rico?" Everyone laughed.

"Fifty thousand, minimum," was another guess. 5

Here are the facts: 6

There are 1,200 black professional athletes in the U.S.

There are 12 times more black lawyers than black athletes.

There are 2½ times more black dentists than black athletes.

There are 15 times more black doctors than black athletes.

Nobody in my local VFW believed these statistics; in fact, few people 7 would believe them if they weren't reading them in the pages of *Sports Illustrated*. In spite of these statistics, too many African-American youngsters still believe that they have a much better chance of becoming another Magic Johnson or Michael Jordan than they do of matching the achievements of Baltimore Mayor Kurt Schmoke or neurosurgeon Dr. Benjamin Carson, both of whom, like Johnson and Jordan, are black.

In reality, an African-American youngster has about as much chance of be- 8 coming a professional athlete as he or she does of winning the lottery. The tragedy for our people, however, is that few of us accept that truth.

Let me confess that I love sports. Like most black people of my genera- 9 tion—I'm 40—I was raised to revere the great black athletic heroes, and I never tired of listening to the stories of triumph and defeat that, for blacks, amount to a collective epic much like those of the ancient Greeks: Joe Louis's demolition of Max Schmeling; Satchel Paige's dazzling repertoire of pitches; Jesse Owens's in-your-face performance in Hitler's 1936 Olympics; Willie Mays's over-the-shoulder basket catch; Jackie Robinson's quiet strength when assaulted by racist taunts; and a thousand other grand tales.

Nevertheless, the blind pursuit of attainment in sports is having a devastat- 10 ing effect on our people. Imbued with a belief that our principal avenue to fame and profit is through sport, and seduced by a win-at-any-cost system that corrupts even elementary school students, far too many black kids treat basketball courts and football fields as if they were classrooms in an alternative school system. "O.K., I flunked English," a young athlete will say. "But I got an A plus in slamdunking."

The failure of our public schools to educate athletes is part and parcel of the 11 schools' failure to educate almost everyone. A recent survey of the Philadelphia school system, for example, stated that "more than half of all students in the third, fifth and eighth grades cannot perform minimum math and language tasks." One in four middle school students in that city fails to pass to the next grade each year. It is a sad truth that such statistics are repeated in cities throughout the nation. Young athletes—particularly young black athletes—are especially ill-served. Many of them are functionally illiterate, yet they are passed along from year to year for the greater glory of good old Hometown High. We should not be surprised to learn, then, that only 26.6% of black athletes at the collegiate level earn their degrees. For every successful educated black professional athlete, there are thousands of dead and wounded. Yet young blacks continue to aspire to careers as athletes, and it's no wonder why; when the University of North Carolina recently commissioned a sculptor to create archetypes of its student body, guess which ethnic group was selected to represent athletes?

Those relatively few black athletes who do make it in the professional ranks 12 must be prevailed upon to play a significant role in the education of all of our young people, athlete and nonathlete alike. While some have done so, many others have shirked their social obligations: to earmark small percentages of their incomes for the United Negro College Fund; to appear on television for educational purposes rather than merely to sell sneakers; to let children know the message that becoming a lawyer, a teacher or a doctor does more good for our people than winning the Super Bowl; and to form productive liaisons with educators to help forge solutions to the many ills that beset the black community. These are merely a few modest proposals.

A similar burden falls upon successful blacks in all walks of life. Each of us 13 must strive to make our young people understand the realities. Tell them to cheer Bo Jackson but to emulate novelist Toni Morrison or businessman Reginald Lewis or historian John Hope Franklin or Spelman College president Johnetta Cole—the list is long.

Of course, society as a whole bears responsibility as well. Until colleges stop 14 using young blacks as cannon fodder in the big-business wars of so-called non-professional sports, until training a young black's mind becomes as important as training his or her body, we will continue to perpetuate a system akin to that of the Roman gladiators, sacrificing a class of people for the entertainment of the mob.

COMPREHENSION

1. What is the general assumption made about African Americans in sports?
2. Why do American schools continue to perpetuate the myth that Gates is writing about?
3. According to Gates, what should successful African American athletes do to help guide the career choices of young black males?

RHETORIC

1. What is Gates's thesis? Where does it appear?
2. How does the introductory paragraph work to set up the writer's focus?
3. State Gates's purpose in using statistics in his essay.
4. What is the tone of Gates's essay? Cite specific sections where this tone seems strongest.
5. Examine the accumulation of facts in paragraph 11. How does this technique underscore Gates's point?
6. Explain Gates's allusion to Roman gladiators in his conclusion. How does it aid in emphasizing his main point?

WRITING

1. Write a brief essay in which you analyze your personal reaction to Gates's statistics. Were you surprised by them? What assumptions did you have about the number of black athletes? Why do you think most Americans share these assumptions?
2. Pretend you are addressing a group of young African Americans at an elementary school. What will you tell them about sports, their career choices, and education?
3. Write a biographical research paper on the life and career of an African American athlete.

Classic and Contemporary: Questions for Comparison

1. Examine the argumentative styles of Woolf and Gates. What are their main propositions? What are their minor propositions? What evidence do they provide?

2. Woolf first presented her paper as a speech before an audience of women. Gates wrote his essay as an opinion piece for *Sports Illustrated.* Write a comparative audience analysis of the two selections. Analyze purpose, tone, style, and any other relevant aspects of the two essays.
3. Argue for or against the proposition that white women and African American men face the same barriers to employment in today's professions. Refer to the essays by Woolf and Gates to support your position.

Men at Work

Anna Quindlen

Anna Quindlen was born in 1953 in Philadelphia. She has worked as a reporter and columnist for the New York Post *and* The New York Times *and is currently a columnist for* Newsweek *magazine. She published a novel entitled* Object Lessons *in 1991. In 1992, she received the Pulitzer Prize for commentary. An outspoken feminist, she stated in an interview in* Commonweal *that "I write for me . . . I tend to write about what we have come, unfortunately, to call women's issues. Those are issues that directly affect my life and those are issues that are historically underreported." The following is an essay about the contemporary father, published in a collection of her work entitled* Thinking Out Loud *(1993).*

Overheard in a Manhattan restaurant, one woman to another: "He's a terrific father, but he's never home."

The five o'clock dads can be seen on cable television these days, just after that time in the evening the stay-at-home moms call the arsenic hours. They are sixties sitcom reruns, Ward and Steve and Alex, and fifties guys. They eat dinner with their television families and provide counsel afterward in the den. Someday soon, if things keep going the way they are, their likenesses will be enshrined in a diorama in the Museum of Natural History, frozen in their recliner chairs. The sign will say, "Here sit lifelike representations of family men who worked only eight hours a day." 1

The five o'clock dad has become an endangered species. A corporate culture that believes presence is productivity, in which people of ambition are afraid to be seen leaving the office, has lengthened his workday and shortened his home-life. So has an economy that makes it difficult for families to break even at the end of the month. For the man who is paid by the hour, that means never saying no to overtime. For the man whose loyalty to the organization is measured in time at his desk, it means goodbye to nine to five. 2

To lots of small children it means a visiting father. The standard joke in one   3
large corporate office is that the dads always say their children look like angels
when they're sleeping because that's the only way they ever see them. A Gallup
survey taken several years ago showed that roughly 12 percent of the men surveyed with children under the age of six worked more than sixty hours a week,
and an additional 25 percent worked between fifty and sixty hours. (Less than
8 percent of the working women surveyed who had children of that age worked
those hours.)

No matter how you divide it up, those are twelve-hour days. When the   4
talk-show host Jane Wallace adopted a baby recently, she said one reason she
was not troubled by becoming a mother without becoming a wife was that
many of her married female friends were "functionally single," given the hours
their husbands worked. The evening commuter rush is getting longer. The 7:45
to West Backofbeyond is more crowded than ever before. The eight o'clock dad.
The nine o'clock dad.

There's a horribly sad irony to this, and it is that the quality of fathering is   5
better than it was when the dads left work at five o'clock and came home to cafe
curtains and tuna casserole. The five o'clock dad was remote, a "Wait till your
father gets home" kind of dad with a newspaper for a face. The roles he and his
wife had were clear: she did nurture and home, he did discipline and money.

The role fathers have carved out for themselves today is a vast improve-   6
ment, a muddling of those old boundaries. Those of us obliged to convert behavior into trends have probably been a little heavy-handed on the shared
childbirth and egalitarian diaper-changing. But fathers today do seem to be
more emotional with their children, more nurturing, more open. Many say, "My
father never told me he loved me," and so they tell their own children all the
time that they love them.

When they're home.   7

There are people who think that this is changing even as we speak, that   8
there is a kind of perestroika of home and work that we will look back on as beginning at the beginning of the 1990s. A nonprofit organization called the Families and Work Institute advises corporations on how to balance personal and
professional obligations and concerns, and Ellen Galinsky, its cofounder, says
she has noticed a change in the last year.

"When we first started doing this the groups of men and of women   9
sounded very different," she said. "If the men complained at all about long
hours, they complained about their wives' complaints. Now if the timbre of the
voice was disguised I couldn't tell which is which. The men are saying: 'I don't
want to live this way anymore. I want to be with my kids.' I think the corporate
culture will have to begin to respond to that."

This change can only be to the good, not only for women but especially for   10
men, and for kids, too. The stereotypical five o'clock dad belongs in a diorama,
with his "Ask your mother" and his "Don't be a crybaby." The father who believes hugs and kisses are sex-blind and a dirty diaper requires a change, not a
woman, is infinitely preferable. What a joy it would be if he were around more.

"This is the man's half of having it all," said Don Conway-Long, who 11
teaches a course at Washington University in St. Louis about men's relationships that drew 135 students this year for thirty-five places. "We're trying to do
what women want of us, what children want of us, but we're not willing to
transform the workplace." In other words, the hearts and minds of today's fathers are definitely in the right place. If only their bodies could be there, too.

COMPREHENSION

1. According to the author, contemporary fathers and traditional fathers both
   have faults. Describe the specific problems in each group.
2. What is the thesis of this essay? Where in the essay is this thesis most succinctly articulated?
3. Is this a regional essay? Does it address a particular class or geographic area
   of America? Would the examples need to be expanded if the author were to
   include *all* types of American fathers? Explain.

RHETORIC

1. The author uses some unique phrasing and vocabulary in her essay. What
   is the effect on the tone of the essay of expressions such as "arsenic hours,"
   "visiting father," "functionally single," "West Backofbeyond," and "perestroika"?
2. The opening paragraph of an essay often sets the tone for the rest. How
   does the tone of paragraph 1 help direct the tone of the essay's argument?
3. In paragraph 5, the author states that there is a "horribly sad irony" in the
   fact that fathers are better nurturers now but have less time to nurture.
   What other ironies does the author use to advance her argument?
4. What is the purpose of the rhetorical strategy of using the three-word paragraph "When they're home"? Does it add or detract from the coherence of
   the essay?
5. Paragraph 5 contains the rather oddly structured sentence. "The roles he
   and his wife had were clear: she did nurture and home, he did discipline
   and money." Conduct a grammatical analysis of the sentence. Does it make
   sense? Does it transgress any rules of grammar? Explain.
6. In paragraph 6, the author states, "fathers today do seem to be more emotional with their children, more nurturing, more open." Where in the essay
   does she provide documentation of this? Is this assertion argued sufficiently, or is it merely presented as an assumption without evidence?
7. Does the author provide a solution for or a recommendation on how to
   solve the problems she raises? Does its presence or absence strengthen or
   weaken the argument? Explain.

WRITING

1. Argue for or against the proposition that the author's description of the modern father is a narrow one, based on biases of class and culture.
2. The author cites television portraits of fifties fathers as her evidence for the family behavior of the traditional father. For a research project, explore whether her comparison between the contemporary father and the traditional one is accurate by comparing two books on family roles: one written during the 1950s, the other during the 1990s.
3. For a creative writing project, write an imaginary letter to a supervisor, stating your view that your work hours should be reduced so that you can spend more time with your family. Be sure to include appropriate supporting material.

Ambition

Perri Klass

Perri Klass (b. 1958) is a pediatrician, a mother of two, and the author of many books—two novels, Recombinations *(1985) and* Other Women's Children *(1990); a collection of short stories,* I Am Having an Adventure *(1986); and a collection of essays,* A Not Entirely Benign Procedure: Four Years as a Medical Student *(1987). In the following essay from the June 1990 issue of* Self, *Klass confesses her admiration of ambition as the necessary impetus to our dreams and our success. However, she advises us to tread cautiously because ambition has an ugly side too. We must be willing to understand what ambition is at its worst and its best and be ready to ask just how much is too much.*

In college, my friend Beth was very ambitious, not only for herself but for her   1
friends. She was interested in foreign relations, in travel, in going to law school. "I plan to be secretary of state someday," she would say matter-of-factly. One mutual friend was studying literature, planning to go to graduate school; he would be the chairman of the Yale English department. Another friend was interested in political journalism and would someday edit *Time* magazine. I was a biology major, which was a problem: Beth's best friend from childhood was also studying biology, and Beth had already decided *she* would win the Nobel Prize. This was resolved by my interest in writing fiction. I would win *that* Nobel, while her other friend would win for science.

It was a joke; we were all smart-ass college freshmen, pretending the world   2
was ours for the asking. But it was not entirely a joke. We were *smart* college freshmen, and why should we limit our ambitions?

I've always liked ambitious people, and many of my closest friends have ₃ had grandiose dreams. I like such people, not because I am desperate to be buddies with a future secretary of state but because I find ambitious people entertaining, interesting to talk to, fun to watch. And, of course, I like such people because I am ambitious myself, and I would rather not feel apologetic about it.

Ambition has gotten bad press. Back in the seventeenth century, Spinoza ₄ thought ambition and lust were "nothing but species of madness, although they are not enumerated among diseases." Especially in women, ambition has often been seen as a profoundly dislikable quality; the word "ambitious" linked to a "career woman" suggested that she was ruthless, hard as nails, clawing her way to success on top of the bleeding bodies of her friends.

Then, in the late Seventies and the Eighties, ambition became desirable, as ₅ books with titles like *How to Stomp Your Way to Success* became bestsellers. It was still a nasty sort of attribute, but nasty attributes were good because they helped you look out for number one.

But what I mean by ambition is dreaming big dreams, putting no limits on ₆ your expectations and your hopes. I don't really like very specific, attainable ambitions, the kind you learn to set in the career-strategy course taught by the author of *How to Stomp Your Way to Success,* I like big ambitions that suggest that the world could open up at any time, with work and luck and determination. The next book could hit it big. The next research project could lead to something fantastic. The next bright idea could change history.

Of course, eventually you have to stop being a freshman in college. You ₇ limit your ambitions and become more realistic, wiser about your potential, your abilities, the number of things your life can hold. Sometimes you get close to something you wanted to do, only to find it looks better from far away. Back when I was a freshman, to tell the truth, I wanted to be Jane Goodall, go into the jungle to study monkeys and learn things no one had ever dreamed of. This ambition was based on an interest in biology and several *National Geographic* television specials; it turned out that wasn't enough of a basis for a life. There were a number of other early ambitions that didn't pan out either. I was not fated to live a wild, adventurous life, to travel alone to all the most exotic parts of the world, to leave behind a string of broken hearts. Oh well, you have to grow up, at least a little.

One of the worst things ambition can do is tell you you're a failure. The ₈ world is full of measuring tapes, books and articles to tell you where you should be at your age, after so-and-so many years of doing what you do.

Almost all of us have to deal with the tremendous success of friends (or enemies), with those who somehow started out where we did but are now way in front. My college-alumni magazine arrives every two months without fail, so I can find out who graduated two years *after* I did but is now running a groundbreaking clinic at a major university hospital (and I'm only just finishing my residency!). Who is restoring a fabulous mansion in a highly desirable town by the sea. Who got promoted yet again, due to natural brilliance and industry.

I read an article recently about how one's twenties are the decade for de- 10
ciding on a career and finishing your training, and the thirties are for consoli-
dating your success and rising within your chosen job (and here I am in my
thirties, not even sure what I want to do yet!). With all these external yardsticks,
the last thing anyone needs is an internal voice as well, whispering irritably that
you were supposed to do it better, get further and that all you've actually accomplished is mush, since you haven't met your own goals.

The world is full of disappointed people. Some of them probably never had 11
much ambition to start with; they sat back and waited for something good and
feel cheated because it never happened. Some of them had very set, specific ambitions and, for one reason or another, never got what they wanted. Others got
what they wanted but found it wasn't exactly what they'd expected it to be.
Disappointed ambition provides fodder for both drama and melodrama: aspiring athletes (who coulda been contenders), aspiring dancers (all they ever
needed was the music and the mirror).

The world is also full of people so ambitious, so consumed by drive and 12
overdrive that nothing they pass on the way to success has any value at all. Life
becomes one long exercise in delayed gratification; everything you do, you're
doing only because it will one day get you where you want to be. Medical training is an excellent example of delayed gratification. You spend years in medical
school doing things with no obvious relationship to your future as a doctor, and
then you spend years in residency, living life on a miserable schedule, staying
up all night and slogging through the day, telling yourself that one day all this
will be over. It's what you have to do to become a doctor, but it's a lousy model
for life in general. There's nothing wrong with a little delayed gratification
every now and then, but a job you do only because of where it will get you—
and not because you like it—means a life of muttering to yourself, "Someday
this will be over." This is bad for the disposition.

As you grow up, your ambitions may come into conflict. Most prominently 13
nowadays, we have to hear about Women Torn Between Family and Career,
about women who make it to the top only to realize they left their ovaries behind. Part of growing up, of course, is realizing that there is only so much room
in one life, whether you are male or female. You can do one thing whole-heart-
edly and single-mindedly and give up some other things. Or you can be greedy
and grab for something new without wanting to give up what you already
have. This leads to a chaotic and crowded life in which you are always late, always overdue, always behind, but rarely bored. Even so, you have to come to
terms with limitations; you cannot crowd your life with occupations and then
expect to do each one as well as you might if it were all you had to do. I realize
this when I race out of the hospital, offending a senior doctor who had offered
to explain something to me, only to arrive late at the daycare center, annoying
the people who have been taking care of my daughter.

People consumed by ambition, living with ambition, get to be a little hu- 14
morless, a little one-sided. On the other hand, people who completely abrogate
their ambition aren't all fun and games either. I've met a certain number of

women whose ambitions are no longer for themselves at all; their lives are now dedicated to their offspring. I hope my children grow up to be nice people, smart people, people who use good grammar; and I hope they grow up to find things they love to do, and do well. But my ambitions are still for *me*.

Of course, I try to be mature about it all. I don't assign my friends Nobel 15 Prizes or top government posts. I don't pretend that there is room in my life for any and every kind of ambition I can imagine. Instead, I say piously that all I want are three things: I want to write as well as I can, I want to have a family and I want to be a good pediatrician. And then, of course, a voice inside whispers . . . to write a bestseller, to have ten children, to do stunning medical research. Fame and fortune, it whispers, fame and fortune. Even though I'm not a college freshman anymore, I'm glad to find that little voice still there, whispering sweet nothings in my ear.

COMPREHENSION

1. Why does Klass believe our personal concept of ambition should evolve as we grow older?
2. Why does Klass prefer ambitious people to unambitious people?
3. In what ways does Klass view ambition as a positive attribute? How can it become a negative one?

RHETORIC

1. Why does Klass begin her essay with personal anecdotes?
2. Who is the implied audience for this essay? To what degree does this audience determine the topic and examples the author uses?
3. What are the definitions of the following words: *grandiose* (paragraph 3), *fodder* (paragraph 11), *melodrama* (paragraph 11), and *abrogate* (paragraph 14)?
4. What is the author's purpose in writing the essay? What passages provide you with specific evidence as to its purpose? Explain.
5. In paragraphs 2, 7, and 15, the author alludes to college freshmen. What is the author implying about this period of life and her overall theme?
6. Examine paragraphs 11 and 12. What rhetorical strategies does the author use to develop a comparison-and-contrast structure between the two?
7. The word *ambition* is an abstract term. What strategies does the author use to make it more concrete and accessible?

WRITING

1. Choose an abstract concept like democracy, independence, power, morality. Write an extended definition for it by using examples, anecdotes, and comparison and contrast.

2. In an essay of at least 500 words, argue for or against the proposition that Klass's perspective on what constitutes an ambitious goal is limited by her own social milieu.
3. Write an expository essay explaining when ambition can be a dangerous or perverse human quality.
4. Write a personal essay in which you describe what ambition means to you.

Uncle Chul Gets Rich

Chang-Rae Lee

Chang-Rae Lee (b. 1967) was born in South Korea. When he was three years old, he and his family emigrated to the United States. He is a graduate of Yale University and received an MFA from the University of Oregon, where he now teaches creative writing. Lee's novel Native Speaker *(1996) won the Ernest Hemingway Foundation/PEN Award for First Fiction. He is also the author of another novel,* A Gesture Life *(1996). He has published short fiction in many magazines, among them* The New Yorker. *In the following essay, published in* The New York Times *in 1996, Lee narrates a familiar immigrant "rags-to-riches" story within a particular cultural context.*

My father's youngest brother, Uncle Chul, shared the Lees' famously bad reaction to liquor, which was to turn beet-red in the face, grow dizzy and finally get sick. In spite of this, he was always happy to stay up late at family gatherings. After a few Scotches he would really loosen up, and, with the notable exception of my mother, we all appreciated his rough language and racy stories. Only when Mother came in from the kitchen would his talk soften, for he knew he had always fallen short in her eyes. If they were ever alone together, say in the kitchen, after dinner, he would use the most decorous voice in asking for a glass or a fresh bucket of ice, and even offer to help load the dishwasher or run an errand to the store.

On one of those nights we sped off, both happy for a break in the long evening. He asked me about school, what sports I was playing, but the conversation inevitably turned toward my parents, and particularly my mother—how much she had invested in me, that I was her great hope. I thought it was odd that he was speaking this way, like my other relatives, and I answered with some criticism of her—that she was too anxious and overbearing. He stared at me and, with a hard solemnity I had not heard from him before, said that my mother was one of the finest people one could ever know. He kept a grip on the wheel and in the ensuing quiet of the drive I could sense how he must have both admired and despised her. In many respects, my mother was an unrelenting woman. She tended to measure people by the mark of a few principles of conduct: ask no help from anyone, always plan for the long run and practice (her own variation of) the golden rule, which was to treat others much better than oneself.

In her mind, Uncle Chul sorely lacked on all these accounts. In the weeks 3 following our drive, my father would be deciding whether to lend him $10,000 to start a business. As always after dinner, my parents sat in the kitchen (the scent of sesame oil and pickled vegetables still in the air) and spoke in Korean, under the light of a fluorescent ring. My mother, in many ways the director of the family, questioned my uncle's character and will. Hadn't he performed poorly in school, failed to finish college? Hadn't he spent most of his youth perfecting his skills as a black belt in taekwondo and his billiards game? Wasn't he a gambler in spirit?

My father could defend him only weakly. Uncle Chul had a history of 4 working hard only when reward was well within sight, like cash piled high on the end of a pool table. His older brothers were all respected professionals and academics. My father was a doctor, a psychiatrist who had taught himself English in order to practice in America. Uncle Chul had left Korea after a series of failed ventures and odd jobs, and found himself broke with a wife and new baby. How valuable were his taekwondo trophies now? What could he possibly do in this country?

My parents argued fiercely and my father left the kitchen. But as was my 5 mother's way, she kept on pushing her side of the issue, thinking aloud. My father was throwing away his hard-earned money on the naïve wish that his little brother had magically changed. Uncle Chul was a poor risk and even now was complaining about his present job, hauling and cleaning produce for a greengrocer in Flushing. He would get to the store at 4 A.M. to prepare vegetables for the day's selling. While he shared a sofa bed with his nephew in his older brother's tiny apartment, his wife and infant daughter were still in Seoul, waiting for him to make enough money to send for them.

But his wages were only $250 a week for 70 hours of work and he loathed 6 the job, the brutal effort that went into clearing a few cents a carrot, a quarter a soda, the niggling, daily accrual. The owners themselves would toil like slaves to see a till full of tattered ones and fives at day's end.

I knew Uncle Chul craved the big score, the quick hit, a rain of cash. For the 7 very reasons my mother had so little faith in him—his brashness, his flagrant ambitions—I admired him. Over Scotch and rice crackers, he would tell my father about the millions he was going to make by moving merchandise wholesale, in bigger-ticket items with decent margins. He would never touch another orange again. I remember my father absently nodding his head at each vague and grandiose idea, probably hearing my mothers' harangues.

The other men in my father's family were thick-lensed scribblers who 8 worked through their days from A to Z, assiduously removing uncertainty by paying close attention to the thousand details of each passing hour. My father worked long days at the hospital, and spent weekends pouring over volumes of Freud and Rank and Erickson in his second language, to "catch up" with the

American doctors. When my father decided to lend Uncle Chul the $10,000, making it clear that no further discussion was needed, my mother transferred her worrying energy squarely onto me. It seemed no accident that her latest criticism was that I was "always looking for the easy way." I had, in fact, been feeling moody and rebellious, weary of being a good student and good boy. I was in the eighth grade, and my friends were beginning to drink beer and smoke pot. I secretly resolved to join them.

I was also taking solo train trips from Pleasantville, N.Y., down to the city to 9 visit my older cousins on the weekends, prompting questions from my mother about what kind of fun we were having. I didn't tell her that what thrilled me most was riding the elevated trains between Flushing and Grand Central, shuttling back and forth with the multitude. My new comer's heart was fearful and enthralled, and I naïvely thought Uncle Chul felt the same way. He had quit working for the greengrocer after getting the money, and brought over his wife and child. He was busy scouting out stores for his first business in America.

But Uncle Chul found that the leases for even the smallest stores were 10 $4,000 a month, and he seemed tense and even a little scared. I felt a strange pang of guilt because of the extra pressure on him—the $10,000 and the tenuous faith behind it. The only thing worse than losing the money was what my mother would never have to mention again: that he started working a little too late.

But he did find a store, in the Bronx, and we drove down one Sunday to see 11 it in all its new glory. It seemed as if half the tenement buildings on the block were burned out or deserted, and the sidewalks were littered with garbage, broken glass and the rubble of bricks and mortar. My father pulled up behind Uncle Chul's car and we peered out to see if we had the right address. The shop couldn't have been more than eight feet wide. A single foot-wide corridor running its length was lined with accessories, odd-lot handbags and tie clips and lighters; the stuff hung on plastic grids on the walls and overhead. In the back, there was a hot plate on the floor, two stools and a carton of instant ramen noodles.

Uncle Chul proudly showed us the merchandise and, from a glass display 12 box, gave me a watch; my sister got a faux-pearl necklace. A customer peered in but waved her hand and scurried away. My mother said that we were disturbing the business, and after a rush of bows and goodbyes we were in the car, heading back to Westchester.

Uncle Chul had no choice but to be in that neighborhood, in that quarter- 13 size store, with the risk of crime and no insurance. The trade-off was the low rent, and it soon became clear that he had made an excellent choice. With little competition on the block, the money started coming in, and soon he moved to a larger store nearby, and then moved again. His volume and cash flow surged, and after selling each successive business, he staked his profit on the next store.

We didn't see him much during this time, but when we did he made sure to 14 show off his success to my parents. My aunt wore designer clothes, and Uncle Chul sported a fat gold Rolex. If we were out somewhere, he would casually pull out a rolled wad of $100's when a check arrived, proclaiming affably to his brothers that it was his turn to pay.

But I noticed, too, that he and my aunt looked haggard and pressed. They 15 spoke hurriedly and ate as quickly as they could. My mother would say something like, 'You've developed such expensive tastes,' and tell him that he was still frittering away his money on useless luxuries.

When Uncle Chul amassed the war chest he needed to open the wholesale 16 business he had hoped for, he moved away from New York. He had heard of opportunities in Texas, where goods could be imported across the border and sold at big profits. Within a few years he had more than 50 people working for him, selling, by containers and truckloads, the same purses and belts he started with years before.

He bought a sprawling ranch house, brand-new and fitted with jet-action 17 bathtubs and wide-screen televisions. He hired a team of Mexican maids to keep the place running. He traded in his Cadillacs for BMW's and sent his daughters to private school. One summer he paid my sister outrageous wages to sit in his air-conditioned office and practice her Spanish with the retailers. The business was on automatic pilot—effortless. Uncle Chul was now a millionaire several times over, richer than all his brothers combined.

I spent time with him again years later, when my mother became terminally 18 ill. He visited regularly, always bearing gifts for the family. To me, he simply gave money. He knew I had quit my first job to become a writer, which meant little to him, except that I would be poor forever. Maybe, someday, my name would be famous, and he invested in that possibility, slipping me a couple of $100's when my mother wasn't looking. He did this naturally, with an ease and power in his grip full of cash. His money was like a weight outside his body, which he could press upon others, like me. But in my mother's presence, his swagger vanished, and he was just Uncle Chul again, prodigal and bereft.

He was especially solemn on the day of her funeral. Of the many people 19 who made their way to the cemetery and later to the house, I suspect Uncle Chul knew he was among those she would be most closely watching. My mother's friends had brought food and electric rice cookers and the men were in the living room, drinking companionably, speaking in low voices. My mother had been dying for nearly two years, and now that it was over waves of exhaustion and relief were washing over everyone in the house.

I remember Uncle Chul padding softly about the house, wary of disturbing 20 even the layer of dust on her furniture. He was speaking in a soft register, his voice faltering, like a nervous young minister on his first encounter with the bereaved. He was nodding and bowing, even helping the ladies gather cups and plates, exercising until the last visitor left a younger brother's respect and obedience to the family and the dead.

In the Korean tradition, mourners brought offerings of money, all token 21 amounts, except for Uncle Chul's fat envelope, which held thousands of dollars. He would have given more, he said, but his wholesale business wasn't doing so well anymore. I knew that wasn't the real reason. He must have known what my mother would have said, perhaps was telling him now—that he couldn't help but be the flashy one again.

COMPREHENSION

1. In what way is Uncle Chul's success an example of living the "American Dream"? What are its positive and negative aspects?
2. The narrator compares and contrasts the values of his mother and those of Uncle Chul. Does he indicate a preference for one over the other? Explain your view.
3. How would you compare the lifestyle and values of Uncle Chul with those of the narrator's father? What is the attitude of the father toward Uncle Chul's goals?
4. What is the author's theme? Is the essay a narrative about the "American Dream," or is the author attempting to convey a message to the reader?

RHETORIC

1. Lee introduces his uncle by painting a picture of his behavior and personality. What is the purpose of beginning the essay this way rather than launching directly into an analysis of Chul's ambitions?
2. How does the author create a comparison and contrast between Chul and the other men in the family? What is the purpose of this comparison? Where else in the essay does Lee employ this comparison and contrast technique? What is its value and purpose?
3. Lee uses colloquial language to bring his narrative to life. How do the following expressions help enliven the writing: *the big score, the quick hit, rain of cash* (paragraph 7); *catch up* (paragraph 8); *scouting out* (paragraph 9); *war chest* (paragraph 16); and *automatic pilot* (paragraph 17)? How does this language lend an American flavor to the writing and to Uncle Chul's own quest for success?
4. What is the resolution that occurs in the final paragraph? How does it bring thematic and rhetorical closure to the essay? Explain.
5. Lee uses vivid imagery to bring Uncle Chul to life. How does the author achieve this in paragraph 20, particularly in his use of simile and attention to physical detail? Where else in the essay does the author demonstrate his descriptive powers?
6. Define the following words: *decorous* (paragraph 1), *niggling* and *accrual* (paragraph 6), *tenuous* (paragraph 10), and *prodigal* and *bereft* (paragraph 18).

WRITING

1. Write a 400- to 500-word biographical sketch of someone in your family, tracing his or her development over a period of a year and showing how he or she evolved through life experience.

2. Using the persona of Uncle Chul, write a letter to the author's mother, explaining the reasons behind your ambitions, actions, and attitudes toward success. As an alternative, write a letter from the perspective of the author's mother, expressing her views regarding Uncle Chul's goals, attitudes, and lifestyle.
3. Write an argumentative essay of 400 to 500 words arguing for or against the proposition that it is not important how one makes a living as long as one achieves financial security.

The Way to Wealth

Benjamin Franklin

Benjamin Franklin (1706–1790) was a statesman, printer, scientist, and writer. He was born in Boston, the son of a tallow chandler and soap maker. He left school at the age of 10 to help his father. His first profession was printing. He became the editor of a newspaper, the Pennsylvania Gazette, *in 1730 and began writing his common sense philosophy in that paper and also in* Poor Richard's Almanack *from 1732 to 1757. He was also known as an inventor; his most famous invention was the lightning rod. From 1753 to 1774, he held many distinguished public offices, including delegate to the Continental Congress and postmaster general. He was one of the signers of the Declaration of Independence in 1776 and shortly afterward became a diplomat, helping negotiate peace with Great Britain after the Revolutionary War. As a writer, he is best known for his autobiography, which is acknowledged as one of the finest autobiographies in any language. The following essay, taken from his* Almanack, *has its roots in "Poor Robin's," an almanac dating back in England to 1663. In this selection, Franklin provides homespun views on how to secure wealth and keep busy.*

Courteous Reader,

I have heard that nothing gives an author so great pleasure, as to find his works respectfully quoted by other learned authors. This pleasure I have seldom enjoyed; for though I have been, if I may say it without vanity, an eminent author of almanacs annually now a full quarter of a century, my brother authors in the same way, for what reason I know not, have ever been very sparing in their applauses, and no other author has taken the least notice of me, so that did not my writings produce me some solid pudding, the great deficiency of praise would have quite discouraged me.

I concluded at length, that the people were the best judges of my merit; for they buy my works; and besides, in my rambles, where I am not personally known, I have frequently heard one or other of my adages repeated, with "as Poor Richard says" at the end on 't; this gave me some satisfaction, as it showed

not only that my instructions were regarded, but discovered likewise some respect for my authority; and I own, that to encourage the practice of remembering and repeating those wise sentences, I have sometimes quoted myself with
great gravity.

Judge, then, how much I must have been gratified by an incident I am go- 3
ing to relate to you. I stopped my horse lately where a great number of people
were collected at a vendue[1] of merchant goods. The hour of sale not being come,
they were conversing on the badness of the times and one of the company
called to a plain clean old man, with white locks, "Pray, Father Abraham, what
think you of the times? Won't these heavy taxes quite ruin the country? How
shall we be ever able to pay them? What would you advise us to?" Father Abraham stood up, and replied, "If you'd have my advice, I'll give it you in short, for
a *word to the wise is enough, and many words won't fill a bushel,* as Poor Richard
says." They joined in desiring him to speak his mind, and gathering round him,
he proceeded as follows:

"Friends," says he, "and neighbors, the taxes are indeed very heavy, and if 4
those laid on by the government were the only ones we had to pay, we might
more easily discharge them; but we have many others, and much more grievous
to some of us. We are taxed twice as much by our idleness, three times as much
by our pride, and four times as much by our folly; and from these taxes the
commissioners cannot ease or deliver us by allowing an abatement. However,
let us hearken to good advice, and something may be done for us; *God helps
them that help themselves,* as Poor Richard says, in his Almanack of 1733.

"It would be thought a hard government that should tax its people one- 5
tenth part of their time, to be employed in its service. But idleness taxes many
of us much more, if we reckon all that is spent in absolute sloth, or doing of
nothing, with that which is spent in idle employments or amusements, that
amount to nothing. Sloth, by bringing on diseases, absolutely shortens life.
Sloth, like rust, consumes faster than labor wears; while the used key is always bright,
as Poor Richard says. *But dost thou love life, then do not squander time, for that's the
stuff life is made of,* as Poor Richard says. How much more than is necessary do
we spend in sleep, forgetting that *the sleeping fox catches no poultry* and that *there
will be sleeping enough in the grave,* as Poor Richard says.

"*If time be of all things the most precious, wasting time must be,* as Poor Richard 6
says, *the greatest prodigality;* since, as he elsewhere tells us, *lost time is never found
again; and what we call time enough, always proves little enough;* let us then up and
be doing, and doing to the purpose; so by diligence shall we do more with less
perplexity. *Sloth makes all things difficult, but industry all easy,* as Poor Richard
says; *and he that riseth late must trot all day, and shall scarce overtake his business at
night;* while *laziness travels so slowly, that poverty soon overtakes him,* as we read in
Poor Richard, who adds, *drive thy business, let not that drive thee,* and *early to bed,
and early to rise, makes a man healthy, wealthy, and wise.*

[1]A market.

"So what signifies wishing and hoping for better times. We may make 7 these times better ourselves. *Industry need not wish*, as Poor Richard says, *and he that lives upon hope will die fasting. There are no gains without pains; then help hands, for I have no lands,* or if I have, they are smartly taxed. And, as Poor Richard likewise observes, *he that hath a trade hath an estate; and he that hath a calling, hath an office of profit and honor;* but then the trade must be worked at, and the calling well followed, or neither the estate nor the office will enable us to pay our taxes. If we are industrious, we shall never starve, for, as Poor Richard says, *at the workingman's house hunger looks in, but dares not enter.* Nor will the bailiff or the constable enter, for *industry pays debts, while despair increases them*, says Poor Richard. What though you have found no treasure, nor has any rich relation left you a legacy, *diligence is the mother of goodluck*, as Poor Richard says, and *God gives all things to industry. Then plow deep, while sluggards sleep, and you shall have corn to sell and to keep,* says Poor Dick. Work while it is called today, for you know not how much you may be hindered tomorrow, which makes Poor Richard say, *one today is worth two tomorrows*, and farther, *have you somewhat to do tomorrow, do it today.* If you were a servant, would you not be ashamed that a good master should catch you idle? Are you then your own master, *be ashamed to catch yourself idle,* as Poor Dick says. When there is so much to be done for yourself, your family, your country, and your gracious king, be up by peep of day; *let not the sun look down and say, inglorious here he lies.* Handle your tools without mittens; remember *that the cat in gloves catches no mice,* as Poor Richard says. 'Tis true there is much to be done, and perhaps you are weak-handed, but stick to it steadily; and you will see great effects, for *constant dropping wears away stones,* and *by diligence and patience the mouse ate in two the cable;* and *little strokes fell great oaks,* as Poor Richard says in his Almanack, the year I cannot just now remember.

"Methinks I hear some of you say, "must a man afford himself no leisure?" 8 I will tell thee, my friend, what Poor Richard says, *employ thy time well if thou meanest to gain leisure; and, since thou art not sure of a minute, throw not away an hour.* Leisure is time for doing something useful; this leisure the diligent man will obtain, but the lazy man never; so that, as Poor Richard says *a life of leisure and a life of laziness are two things.* Do you imagine that sloth will afford you more comfort than labor? No, for as Poor Richard says, *trouble springs from idleness, and grievous toil from needless ease. Many without labor, would live by their wits only, but they break for want of stock.* Whereas industry gives comfort, and plenty, and respect: *fly pleasures, and they'll follow you. The diligent spinner has a large shift,*[2] *and now I have a sheep and a cow, everybody bids me good morrow;* all which is well said by Poor Richard.

"But with our industry, we must likewise be steady, settled, and careful, 9 and oversee our own affairs with our own eyes, and not trust too much to others, for, as Poor Richard says

---

[2]Supply of clothes.

> I never saw an oft-removed tree,
> Nor yet an oft-removed family,
> That throve so well as those that settled be.
> And again, *three removes*[3] *is as bad a fire;* and again, *keep thy shop, and
> thy shop will keep thee;* and again, *if you would have your business done, go;
> if not, send.* And again,
> He that by the plough would thrive,
> Himself must either hold or drive.

And again, *the eye of a master will do more work than both his hands;* and again, *want of care does us more damage than want of knowledge;* and again, *not to oversee workmen is to leave them your purse open.* Trusting too much to others' care is the ruin of many; for, as the Almanack says, *in the affairs of this world, men are saved, not by faith, but by the want of it;* but a man's own care is profitable; for, saith Poor Dick, *learning is to the studious,* and *riches to the careful,* as well as *power to the bold,* and *heaven to the virtuous,* and farther, *if you would have a faithful servant, and one that you like, serve yourself.* And again, he adviseth to circumspection and care, even in the smallest matters, because sometimes *a little neglect may breed great mischief;* adding, *for want of a nail the shoe was lost; for want of a shoe the horse was lost; and for want of a horse the rider was lost, being overtaken and slain by the enemy;* all for want of care about a horseshoe nail.

"So much for industry, my friends, and attention to one's own business; but to these we must add frugality, if we would make our industry more certainly successful. A man may, if he knows not how to save as he gets, keep his nose all his life to the grindstone, and die not worth a groat[4] at last. A *fat kitten makes a lean will,* as Poor Richard says; and

> Many estates are spent in the getting,
> Since women for tea forsook spinning and knitting,
> And men for punch forsook hewing and splitting.

If you would be wealthy, says he, in another Almanack, *think of saving as well as of getting: the Indies have not made Spain rich, because her outgoes are greater than her incomes.*

"Away then with your expensive follies, and you will not then have so much cause to complain of hard times, heavy taxes, and chargeable families; for, as Poor Dick says,

> Women and wine, game and deceit,
> Make the wealth small and the wants great.

And farther, *what maintains one vice would bring up two children.* You may think perhaps, that a little tea, or a little punch now and then, diet a little more costly, clothes a little finer, and a little entertainment now and then, can be no great matter; but remember what Poor Richard says, *many a little makes a mickle,*[5]

[3]Moves.
[4]A coin.
[5]Great deal.

and farther, *Beware of little expenses; a small leak will sink a great ship;* and again, *who dainties love shall beggars prove;* and moreover, *fools makes feasts, and wise men eat them.*

"Here you are all got together at this vendue of fineries and knicknacks. 13
You call them goods; but if you do not take care, they will prove evils to some of you. You expect they will be sold cheap, and perhaps they may for less than they cost; but if you have no occasion for them, they must be dear to you. Remember what Poor Richard says; *buy what thou hast no need of, and ere long thou shalt sell thy necessaries.* And again, *at a great pennyworth pause a while;* he means, that perhaps the cheapness is apparent only, and not real; or the bargain, by straightening thee in thy business, may do thee more harm than good. For in another place he says, *many have been ruined by buying good pennyworths.* Again, Poor Richard says, *'tis foolish to lay out money in a purchase of repentance;* and yet this folly is practiced every day at vendues, for want of minding the Almanack. *Wise men,* as Poor Dick says, *learn by others' harms, fools scarcely by their own;* but *felix quem faciunt aliena pericula cautum.*[6] Many a one, for the sake of finery on the back, have gone with a hungry belly, and half-starved their families. *Silks and satins, scarlet and velvets,* as Poor Richard says, *put out the kitchen fire.*

"These are not the necessaries of life; they can scarcely be called the conve- 14
niences; and yet only because they look pretty, how many want to have them! The artificial wants of mankind thus become more numerous than the natural; and, as Poor Dick says, *for one poor person, there are an hundred indigent.* By these, and other extravagancies, the genteel are reduced to poverty, and forced to borrow of those whom they formerly despised, but who through industry and frugality have maintained their standing; in which case it appears plainly, that *a plowman on his legs is higher than a gentleman on his knees,* as Poor Richard says. Perhaps they have had a small estate left them, which they knew not the getting of; they think, "'Tis day, and will never be night"; that a little to be spent out of so much is not worth minding; *a child and a fool,* as Poor Richard says, *imagine twenty shillings and twenty years can never be spent* but, *always taking out of the meal-tub, and never putting in, soon comes to the bottom;* as Poor Dick says, *when the well's dry, they know the worth of water.* But this they might have known before, if they had taken his advice; *if you would know the value of money, go and try to borrow some; for, he that goes a-borrowing goes a-sorrowing;* and indeed so does he that lends to such people, when he goes to get it in again. Poor Dick farther advises, and says,

> Fond pride of dress is sure a very curse;
> E'er fancy you consult, consult your purse.

And again, *price is as loud a beggar as want, and a great deal more saucy.* When you have bought one fine thing, you must buy ten more, that your appearance may be all of a piece; but Poor Dick says, *'tis easier to suppress the first desire, than to satisfy all that follow it.* And 'tis as truly folly for the poor to ape the rich, as for the frog to swell, in order to equal the ox.

[6]Latin for "what comes before."

Great estates may venture more,
But little boats should keep near shore.

'Tis, however, a folly soon punished; for *pride that dines on vanity sups on contempt,* as Poor Richard says. And in another place, *pride, breakfasted with plenty, dined with poverty, and supped with infamy.* And after all, of what use is this pride of appearance, for which so much is risked so much is suffered? It cannot promote health, or ease pain; it makes no increase of merit in the person, it creates envy, it hastens misfortune.

What is a butterfly? At best
He's but a caterpillar dressed
The gaudy fop's his picture just,

as Poor Richard says.

"But what madness must it be to run in debt for these superfluities! We are 15
offered, by the terms of this vendue, *six months' credit;* and that perhaps has induced some of us to attend it, because we cannot spare the ready money, and hope now to be fine without it. But, ah, think what you do when you run in debt: you give to another power over your liberty. If you cannot pay at the time, you will be ashamed to see your creditor; you will be in fear when you speak to him; you will make poor pitiful sneaking excuses, and by degrees come to lose your veracity, and sink into base downright lying; for, as Poor Richard says, *the second vice is lying, the first is running in debt.* And again, to the same purpose, *lying rides upon debt's back.* Whereas a free-born Englishman ought not to be ashamed or afraid to see or speak to any man living. But poverty often deprives a man of all spirit and virtue: *'tis hard for an empty bag to stand upright,* as Poor Richard truly says.

"What would you think of that prince, or that government, who should is- 16
sue an edict forbidding you to dress like a gentleman or a gentlewoman, on pain of imprisonment or servitude? Would you not say, that you were free, have a right to dress as you please, and that such an edict would be a breach of your privileges, and such a government tyrannical? And yet you are about to put yourself under that tyranny, when you run in debt for such dress! Your creditor has authority, at his pleasure to deprive you of your liberty, by confining you in gaol for life, or to sell you for a servant, if you should not be able to pay him! When you have got your bargain, you may, perhaps, think little of payment; but *creditors,* Poor Richard tells us, *have better memories than debtors;* and in another place says, *creditors are a superstitious sect, great observers of set days and times.* The day comes round before you are aware, and the demand is made before you are prepared to satisfy it, or if you bear your debt in mind, the term which at first seemed so long, will, as it lessens, appear extremely short. Time will seem to have added wings to his heels as well as shoulders. *Those have a short Lent,* said Poor Richard, *who owe money to be paid at Easter.* Then since, as he says, *The borrower is a slave to the lender, and the debtor to the creditor,* disdain the chain, preserve your freedom; and maintain your independency:

be industrious and free; be frugal and free. At present, perhaps, you may think yourself in thriving circumstances, and that you can bear a little extravagance without injury; but,

> For age and want, save while you may;
> No morning sun lasts a whole day,

as Poor Richard says. Gain may be temporary and uncertain, but ever while you live, expense is constant and entire; and *'tis easier to build two chimneys than to keep one in fuel*, as Poor Richard says. So, *rather go to bed supperless than rise in debt*.

> Get what you can, and what you get hold;
> 'Tis the stone that will turn all your lead into gold,

as Poor Richard says. And when you have got the philosopher's stone, sure you will no longer complain of bad times, or the difficulty of paying taxes.

"This doctrine, my friends, is reason and wisdom; but after all, do not de- 17 pend too much upon your own industry, and frugality, and prudence, though excellent things, for they may all be blasted without the blessing of heaven; and therefore, ask that blessing humbly, and be not uncharitable to those that at present seem to want it, but comfort and help them. Remember, job suffered, and was afterwards prosperous.

"And now to conclude, *experience keeps a dear school, but fools will learn in no* 18 *other, and scarce in that;* for it is true, *we may give advice, but we cannot give conduct*, as Poor Richard says: however, remember this, *they that won't be counseled, can't be helped*, as Poor Richard says: and farther, that, *if you will not hear reason, she'll surely rap your knuckles.*"

Thus the old gentleman ended his harangue. The people heard it, and ap- 19 proved the doctrine, and immediately practiced the contrary, just as if it had been a common sermon; for the vendue opened, and they began to buy extravagantly, notwithstanding, his cautions and their own fear of taxes. I found the good man had thoroughly studied my almanacs, and digested all I had dropped on these topics during the course of five and twenty years. The frequent mention he made of me must have tired any one else, but my vanity was wonderfully delighted with it, though I was conscious that not a tenth part of the wisdom was my own, which he ascribed to me, but rather the gleanings I had made of the sense of all ages and nations. However, I resolved to be the better for the echo of it; and though I had at first determined to buy stuff for a new coat, I went away resolved to wear my old one a little longer. Reader, if thou wilt do the same, thy profit will be as great as mine. I am, as ever, thine to serve thee.

Richard Saunders[7]
July 7, 1757

---

[7]The given name of the editor of *Apollo Angliccunus*, an English publication.

COMPREHENSION

1. What were the main concerns of the people who asked for Father Abraham's advice? How were his responses contrary to their inquiries?
2. Father Abraham distinguishes two categories of taxes. What are they? How are they different? Is one category more important than the other, or are they both of equal concern?
3. What is Father Abraham's advice for accumulating wealth?
4. Does the audience heed Father Abraham's advice? Explain your answer.

RHETORIC

1. Why does Franklin choose to inform his "audiences" (both his readership and the group assembled at the "vendue") through Father Abraham's narrative rather than speaking directly to them?
2. Franklin uses *aphorisms* throughout the essay. Why does he use them? How do they contribute to his purpose?
3. Who is Franklin's intended audience? How do you know? What does the letter format tell you about the intended audience?
4. The final paragraph changes the focus and tone of the essay. What point is Franklin making here? Explain.
5. Consider the length of Father Abraham's "sermon" and the number of aphorisms it contains. Is it realistic to think that a listening audience could absorb all his "wisdom" at one lecture? What does Franklin's literary device of providing the reader with a "recorded" speech suggest about the differences between oral and written language?
6. Some of Father Abraham's aphorisms are embedded within the body of the text; others are separated from it. What is the reason for this division?
7. What is Franklin's main purpose in composing this "letter"? How does the concluding paragraph help the reader understand his purpose?

WRITING

1. In an essay of approximately 500 words, define and classify the two major forms of taxes that Franklin considers. What are their differing attributes, causes, and consequences?
2. Create a mock "pamphlet" or "newsletter" of your own aphorisms. If you have access to a word-processing program with graphic capabilities, design it in the form of a pamphlet or newsletter, paying attention to typeface, columns, headlines, and so on. Include various categories of subjects such as leisure, work, laziness, wealth, and saving.
3. Write a letter of approximately 500 words to Benjamin Franklin to explain how the values of contemporary Americans would lead them to accept or reject some of the major suggestions he makes here.

Los Pobres

Richard Rodriguez

Richard Rodriguez, born in 1944 in San Francisco, received degrees from both Stanford University and Columbia University. He also did graduate study at the University of California, Berkeley, and at the Warburg Institute, London. He is a writer and editor for Pacifica News Service. *Rodriguez became a nationally known writer with the publication of his autobiography,* Hunger of Memory: The Education of Richard Rodriguez *(1982). In it, he describes the struggles of growing up biculturally—feeling alienated from his Spanish-speaking parents yet not wholly comfortable in the dominant culture of the United States. He opposes bilingualism and affirmative action as they are now practiced in the United States, and his stance has caused much controversy in educational and intellectual circles. Rodriguez continues to write about social issues such as acculturation, education, and language. In "Los Pobres," Rodriguez shows us how what starts off as a summer job ends with a personal revelation about social and personal identity.*

It was at Stanford, one day near the end of my senior year, that a friend told me 1 about a summer construction job he knew was available. I was quickly alert. Desire uncoiled within me. My friend said that he knew I had been looking for summer employment. He knew I needed some money. Almost apologetically he explained: It was something I probably wouldn't be interested in, but a friend of his, a contractor, needed someone for the summer to do menial jobs. There would be lots of shoveling and raking and sweeping. Nothing too hard. But nothing more interesting either. Still, the pay would be good. Did I want it? Or did I know someone who did?

I did. Yes, I said, surprised to hear myself say it. 2

In the weeks following, friends cautioned that I had no idea how hard 3 physical labor really is. ("You only *think* you know what it is like to shovel for eight hours straight.") Their objections seemed to me challenges. They resolved the issue. I became happy with my plan. I decided, however, not to tell my parents. I wouldn't tell my mother because I could guess her worried reaction. I would tell my father only after the summer was over, when I could announce that, after all, I did know what "real work" is like.

The day I met the contractor (a Princeton graduate, it turned out), he asked 4 me whether I had done any physical labor before. "In high school, during the summer," I lied. And although he seemed to regard me with skepticism, he decided to give me a try. Several days later, expectant, I arrived at my first construction site. I would take off my shirt to the sun. And at last grasp desired sensation. No longer afraid. At last become like a *bracero*. "We need those tree stumps out of here by tomorrow," the contractor said. I started to work.

I labored with excitement that first morning—and all the days after. The work was harder than I could have expected. But it was never as tedious as my friends had warned me it would be. There was too much physical pleasure in the labor. Especially early in the day, I would be most alert to the sensations of movement and straining. Beginning around seven each morning (when the air was still damp but the scent of weeds and dry earth anticipated the heat of the sun), I would feel my body resist the first thrusts of the shovel. My arms, tightened by sleep, would gradually loosen; after only several minutes, sweat would gather in beads on my forehead and then—a short while later—I would feel my chest silky with sweat in the breeze. I would return to my work. A nervous spark of pain would fly up my arm and settle to burn like an ember in the thick of my shoulder. An hour, two passed. Three. My whole body would assume regular movements. Even later in the day, my enthusiasm for primitive sensation would survive the heat and the dust and the insects pricking my back. I would strain wildly for sensation as the day came to a close. At three thirty, quitting time, I would stand upright and slowly let my head fall back, luxuriating in the feeling of tightness relieved.

Some of the men working nearby would watch me and laugh. Two or three of the older men took the trouble to teach me the right way to use a pick, the correct way to shovel. "You're doing it wrong, too fucking hard," one man scolded. Then proceeded to show me—what persons who work with their bodies all their lives quickly learn—the most economical way to use one's body in labor.

"Don't make your back do so much work," he instructed. I stood impatiently listening, half listening, vaguely watching, then noticed his work-thickened fingers clutching the shovel. I was annoyed. I wanted to tell him that I enjoyed shoveling the wrong way. And I didn't want to learn the right way. I wasn't afraid of back pain. I liked the way my body felt sore at the end of the day.

I was about to, but, as it turned out, I didn't say a thing. Rather it was at that moment I realized that I was fooling myself if I expected a few weeks of labor to gain me admission to the world of the laborer. I would not learn in three months what my father had meant by "real work." I was not bound to this job; I could imagine its rapid conclusion. For me the sensations of exertion and fatigue could be savored. For my father or uncle, working at comparable jobs when they were my age, such sensations were to be feared. Fatigue took a different toll on their bodies—and minds.

It was, I know, a simple insight. But it was with this realization that I took my first step that summer toward realizing something even more important about the "worker." In the company of carpenters, electricians, plumbers, and painters at lunch, I would often sit quietly, observant. I was not shy in such company. I felt easy, pleased by the knowledge that I was casually accepted, my presence taken for granted by men (exotics) who worked with their hands. Some days the younger men would talk and talk about sex, and they would howl at women who drove by in cars. Other days the talk at lunchtime was subdued; men gathered in separate groups. It depended on who was around. There were rough, good-natured workers. Others were quiet. The more I remember that summer, the more I realize that there was no single *type* of worker.

I am embarrassed to say I had not expected such diversity. I certainly had not expected to meet, for example, a plumber who was an abstract painter in his off hours and admired the work of Mark Rothko. Nor did I expect to meet so many workers with college diplomas. (They were the ones who were not surprised that I intended to enter graduate school in the fall.) I suppose what I really want to say here is painfully obvious, but I must say it nevertheless: The men of that summer were middle-class Americans. They certainly didn't constitute an oppressed society. Carefully completing their work sheets; talking about the fortunes of local football teams; planning Las Vegas vacations; comparing the gas mileage of various makes of campers—they were not *los pobres* my mother had spoken about.

On two occasions, the contractor hired a group of Mexican aliens. They 10 were employed to cut down some trees and haul off debris. In all, there were six men of varying age. The youngest in his late twenties; the oldest (his father?) perhaps sixty years old. They came and they left in a single old truck. Anonymous men. They were never introduced to the other men at the site. Immediately upon their arrival, they would follow the contractor's directions, start working—rarely resting—seemingly driven by a fatalistic sense that work which had to be done was best done as quickly as possible.

I watched them sometimes. Perhaps they watched me. The only time I saw 11 them pay me much notice was one day at lunchtime when I was laughing with the other men. The Mexicans sat apart when they ate, just as they worked by themselves. Quiet. I rarely heard them say much to each other. All I could hear were their voices calling out sharply to one another, giving directions. Otherwise, when they stood briefly resting, they talked among themselves in voices too hard to overhear.

The contractor knew enough Spanish, and the Mexicans—or at least the 12 oldest of them, their spokesman—seemed to know enough English to communicate. But because I was around, the contractor decided one day to make me his translator. (He assumed I could speak Spanish.) I did what I was told. Shyly I went over to tell the Mexicans that the patrón wanted them to do something else before they left for the day. As I started to speak, I was afraid with my old fear that I would be unable to pronounce the Spanish words. But it was a simple instruction I had to convey. I could say it in phrases.

The dark sweating faces turned toward me as I spoke. They stopped their 13 work to hear me. Each nodded in response. I stood there. I wanted to say something more. But what could I say in Spanish, even if I could have pronounced the words right? Perhaps I just wanted to engage in small talk, to be assured of their confidence, our familiarity. I thought for a moment to ask them where in Mexico they were from. Something like that. And maybe I wanted to tell them (a lie, if need be) that my parents were from the same part of Mexico.

I stood there. 14

Their faces watched me. The eyes of the man directly in front of me moved 15 slowly over my shoulder, and I turned to follow his glance toward *el patrón* some distance away. For a moment I felt swept up by that glance into the Mexicans' company. But then I heard one of them returning to work. And then the others went back to work. I left them without saying anything more.

When they had finished, the contractor went over to pay them in cash. (He 16
later told me that he paid them collectively—"for the job," though he wouldn't
tell me their wages. He said something quickly about the good rate of exchange
"in their own country.") I can still hear the loudly confident voice he used with
the Mexicans. It was the sound of the *gringo* I had heard as a very young boy.
And I can still hear the quiet, indistinct sounds of the Mexican, the oldest who
replied. At hearing that voice I was sad for the Mexicans. Depressed by their vulnerability. Angry at myself. The adventure of the summer seemed suddenly ludicrous. I would not shorten the distance I felt from *los pobres* with a few weeks of
physical labor. I would not become like them. They were different from me. . . .

In the end my father was right—though perhaps he did not know how right 17
or why—to say that I would never know what real work is. I will never know
what he felt at his last factory job. If tomorrow I worked at some kind of factory,
it would go differently for me. My long education would favor me. I could act as
a public person—able to defend my interests, to unionize, to petition, to speak
up—to challenge and demand. (I will never know what real work is.) I will never
know what the Mexicans knew, gathering their shovels and ladders and saws.

Their silence stays with me now. The wages those Mexicans received for 18
their labor were only a measure of their disadvantaged condition. Their silence
is more telling. They lack a public identity. They remain profoundly alien. Persons apart. People lacking a union obviously, people without grounds. They depend upon the relative good will or fairness of their employers each day. For
such people, lacking a better alternative, it is not such an unreasonable risk.

Their silence stays with me. I have taken these many words to describe its 19
impact. Only: the quiet. Something uncanny about it. Its compliance. Vulnerability. Pathos. As I heard their truck rumbling away, I shuddered, my face mir-
rored with sweat. I had finally come face to face with *los pobres.*

COMPREHENSION

1. How does Rodriguez set the scene for his narrative? What contrasts does he
   develop in the course of the essay?
2. What are the chief revelations Rodriguez receives from his work experience?
3. Why does Rodriguez focus on the silence of the Mexicans in the final two
   paragraphs? What is the relationship between this silence and the "real
   work" his father knows?

RHETORIC

1. In paragraph 9, Rodriguez puts quotation marks around *worker* and parentheses around *exotics,* and he italicizes *type.* What is the purpose of each
   choice of punctuation or style?
2. There are several fragments in each of the final two paragraphs. What is the
   effect of using this sentence structure? Where else are fragments employed
   in the essay?

3. Why are paragraphs 2 and 14 so short? How does the length of these paragraphs help delineate Rodriguez's mood?
4. What sensations does Rodriguez focus on in paragraph 5? Which words contribute most to evoking them?
5. In what way do the first three paragraphs prepare or fail to prepare you for the narrative that follows?
6. The opening sentence of paragraph 19 repeats that of paragraph 18. What is the purpose of this repetition?

WRITING

1. Imagine yourself in the same situation as Rodriguez. Would your presumptions about hard work and your co-workers have been the same? Would you be more or less naive than Rodriguez? Explain in a brief essay.
2. What are the major differences between the Mexican workers and the American workers in the essay? Write an essay focusing on these differences.
3. Write an essay explaining why Rodriguez feels excluded from each of the two groups.
4. Have you ever felt like an outsider in a social situation? Describe a time in your life when you were confronted with the desire to be accepted. How were you different from the others? How did you try to transcend this difference?

Why the Rich Are Getting Richer and the Poor, Poorer

Robert Reich

Robert Reich (b. 1946) is a University Professor in the Heller Graduate School at Brandeis University. He served as secretary of labor in the first Clinton administration, and before that, as a professor of economics at Harvard University. He has written numerous books on economics and has been a prominent lecturer for a dozen years. His books include The Next American Frontier *(1983) and* The Work of Nations *(1991), which takes its title from Adam Smith's classic work on economics* The Wealth of Nations, *written in 1776. Reich is known for his ability to "think outside the box," in other words, to see things from a unique and original perspective. Here he warns of what exists—perhaps in front of our very noses—but that we are too caught up in the moment to consider.*

The division of labour is limited by the extent of the market.

—Adam Smith,
An Inquiry into the Nature and Causes of the Wealth of Nations (1776)

Regardless of how your job is officially classified (manufacturing, service, man-   1
agerial, technical, secretarial, and so on), or the industry in which you work (automotive, steel, computer, advertising, finance, food processing), your real
competitive position in the world economy is coming to depend on the function
you perform in it. Herein lies the basic reason why incomes are diverging. The
fortunes of routine producers are declining. In-person servers are also becoming poorer, although their fates are less clear-cut. But symbolic analysts—who
solve, identify, and broker new problems—are, by and large, succeeding in the
world economy.

All Americans used to be in roughly the same economic boat. Most rose or   2
fell together as the corporations in which they were employed, the industries
comprising such corporations, and the national economy as a whole became
more productive—or languished. But national borders no longer define our economic fates. We are now in different boats, one sinking rapidly, one sinking
more slowly, and the third rising steadily.

The boat containing routine producers is sinking rapidly. Recall that by   3
mid-century routine production workers in the United States were paid relatively well. The giant pyramidlike organizations at the core of each major industry coordinated their prices and investments—avoiding the harsh winds of
competition and thus maintaining healthy earnings. Some of these earnings, in
turn, were reinvested in new plant and equipment (yielding ever-larger-scale
economies); another portion went to top managers and investors. But a large
and increasing portion went to middle managers and production workers.
Work stoppages posed such a threat to high-volume production that organized
labor was able to exact an ever-larger premium for its cooperation. And the pattern of wages established within the core corporations influenced the pattern
throughout the national economy. Thus the growth of a relatively affluent middle class, able to purchase all the wondrous things produced in high volume by
the core corporations.

But, as has been observed, the core is rapidly breaking down into global   4
webs which earn their largest profits from clever problem-solving, -identifying,
and brokering. As the costs of transporting standard things and of communicating information about them continue to drop, profit margins on high-volume, standardized production are thinning, because there are few barriers to
entry. Modern factories and state-of-the-art machinery can be installed almost
anywhere on the globe. Routine producers in the United States, then, are in direct competition with millions of routine producers in other nations. Twelve
thousand people are added to the world's population every hour, most of
whom, eventually, will happily work for a small fraction of the wages of routine
producers in America.[1]

---

[1]The reader should note, of course, that lower wages in other areas of the world are of no particular
attraction to global capital unless workers there are sufficiently productive to make the labor cost of
producing *each unit* lower there than in higher-wage regions. Productivity in many low-wage areas
of the world has improved due to the ease with which state-of-the-art factories and equipment can
be installed there.

The consequence is clearest in older, heavy industries, where high-volume, 5 standardized production continues its ineluctable move to where labor is cheapest and most accessible around the world. Thus, for example, the Maquiladora factories cluttered along the Mexican side of the U.S. border in the sprawling shanty towns of Tijuana, Mexicali, Nogales, Agua Prieta, and Ciudad Juárez— factories owned mostly by Americans, but increasingly by Japanese—in which more than a half million routine producers assemble parts into finished goods to be shipped into the United States.

The same story is unfolding worldwide. Until the late 1970s, AT&T had de- 6 pended on routine producers in Shreveport, Louisiana, to assemble standard telephones. It then discovered that routine producers in Singapore would perform the same tasks at a far lower cost. Facing intense competition from other global webs, AT&T's strategic brokers felt compelled to switch. So in the early 1980s they stopped hiring routine producers in Shreveport and began hiring cheaper routine producers in Singapore. But under this kind of pressure for ever lower high-volume production costs, today's Singaporean can easily end up as yesterday's Louisianan. By the late 1980s, AT&T's strategic brokers found that routine producers in Thailand were eager to assemble telephones for a small fraction of the wages of routine producers in Singapore. Thus, in 1989, AT&T stopped hiring Singaporeans to make telephones and began hiring even cheaper routine producers in Thailand.

The search for ever lower wages has not been confined to heavy industry. 7 Routine data processing is equally footloose. Keypunch operators located anywhere around the world can enter data into computers, linked by satellite or transoceanic fiber-optic cable, and take it out again. As the rates charged by satellite networks continue to drop, and as more satellites and fiber-optic cables become available (reducing communication costs still further), routine data processors in the United States find themselves in ever more direct competition with their counterparts abroad, who are often eager to work for far less.

By 1990, keypunch operators in the United States were earning, at most, 8 $6.50 per hour. But keypunch operators throughout the rest of the world were willing to work for a fraction of this. Thus, many potential American data-processing jobs were disappearing, and the wages and benefits of the remaining ones were in decline. Typical was Saztec International, a $20-million-a-year data-processing firm headquartered in Kansas City, whose American strategic brokers contracted with routine data processors in Manila and with American-owned firms that needed such data-processing services. Compared with the average Philippine income of $1,700 per year, data-entry operators working for Saztec earn the princely sum of $2,650. The remainder of Saztec's employees were American problem-solvers and -identifiers, searching for ways to improve the worldwide system and find new uses to which it could be put.[2]

---

[2]John Maxwell Hamilton, "A Bit Player Buys into the Computer Age," *New York Times Business World*, December 3, 1989, p. 14.

By 1990, American Airlines was employing over 1,000 data processors in 9
Barbados and the Dominican Republic to enter names and flight numbers from
used airline tickets (flown daily to Barbados from airports around the United
States) into a giant computer bank located in Dallas. Chicago publisher R. R.
Donnelley was sending entire manuscripts to Barbados for entry into computers in preparation for printing. The New York Life Insurance Company was dis-
patching insurance claims to Castleisland, Ireland, where routine producers,
guided by simple directions, entered the claims and determined the amounts
due, then instantly transmitted the computations back to the United States.
(When the firm advertised in Ireland for twenty-five data-processing jobs, it received six hundred applications.) And McGraw-Hill was processing subscription renewal and marketing information for its magazines in nearby Galway.
Indeed, literally millions of routine workers around the world were receiving
information, converting it into computer-readable form, and then sending it
back—at the speed of electronic impulses—whence it came.

The simple coding of computer software has also entered into world com- 10
merce. India, with a large English-speaking population of technicians happy to
do routine programming cheaply, is proving to be particularly attractive to
global webs in need of this service. By 1990, Texas Instruments maintained a
software development facility in Bangalore, linking fifty Indian programmers
by satellite to TI's Dallas headquarters. Spurred by this and similar ventures,
the Indian government was building a teleport in Poona, intended to make it
easier and less expensive for many other firms to send their routine software
design specifications for coding.[3]

This shift of routine production jobs from advanced to developing nations is a 11
great boon to many workers in such nations who otherwise would be jobless or
working for much lower wages. These workers, in turn, now have more money
with which to purchase symbolic-analytic services from advanced nations (often embedded within all sorts of complex products). The trend is also beneficial
to everyone around the world who can now obtain high-volume, standardized
products (including information and software) more cheaply than before.

But these benefits do not come without certain costs. In particular the bur- 12
den is borne by those who no longer have good-paying routine production jobs
within advanced economies like the United States. Many of these people used
to belong to unions or at least benefited from prevailing wage rates established
in collective bargaining agreements. But as the old corporate bureaucracies have
flattened into global webs, bargaining leverage has been lost. Indeed, the tacit
national bargain is no more.

Despite the growth in the number of new jobs in the United States, union 13
membership has withered. In 1960, 35 percent of all nonagricultural workers in
America belonged to a union. But by 1980 that portion had fallen to just under

[3]Udayan Gupta, "U.S.-Indian Satellite Link Stands to Cut Software Costs," *Wall Street Journal*, March
6, 1989, p. B2.

a quarter, and by 1989 to about 17 percent. Excluding government employees, union membership was down to 13.4 percent.[4] This was a smaller proportion even than in the early 1930s, before the National Labor Relations Act created a legally protected right to labor representation. The drop in membership has been accompanied by a growing number of collective bargaining agreements to freeze wages at current levels, reduce wage levels of entering workers, or reduce wages overall. This is an important reason why the long economic recovery that began in 1982 produced a smaller rise in unit labor costs than any of the eight recoveries since World War II—the low rate of unemployment during its course notwithstanding.

Routine production jobs have vanished fastest in traditional unionized industries (autos, steel, and rubber, for example), where average wages have kept up with inflation. This is because the jobs of older workers in such industries are protected by seniority; the youngest workers are the first to be laid off. Faced with a choice of cutting wages or cutting the number of jobs, a majority of union members (secure in the knowledge that there are many who are junior to them who will be laid off first) often have voted for the latter.   14

Thus the decline in union membership has been most striking among young men entering the work force without a college education. In the early 1950s, more than 40 percent of this group joined unions; by the late 1980s, less than 20 percent (if public employees are excluded, less than 10 percent).[5] In steelmaking, for example, although many older workers remained employed, almost half of all routine steelmaking jobs in America vanished between 1974 and 1988 (from 480,000 to 260,000). Similarly with automobiles: During the 1980s, the United Auto Workers lost 500,000 members—one-third of their total at the start of the decade. General Motors alone cut 150,000 American production jobs during the 1980s (even as it added employment abroad). Another consequence of the same phenomenon: the gap between the average wages of unionized and nonunionized workers widened dramatically—from 14.6 percent in 1973 to 20.4 percent by end of the 1980s.[6] The lesson is clear. If you drop out of high school or have no more than a high school diploma, do not expect a good routine production job to be awaiting you.   15

Also vanishing are lower- and middle-level management jobs involving routine production. Between 1981 and 1986, more than 780,000 foremen, supervisors, and section chiefs lost their jobs through plant closings and layoffs.[7] Large numbers of assistant division heads, assistant directors, assistant managers, and vice presidents also found themselves jobless. GM shed more than   16

[4]*Statistical Abstract of the United States* (Washington, D.C.: U.S. Government Printing Office, 1989), p. 416, table 684.
[5]Calculations from Current Population Surveys by L. Katz and A. Revenga, "Changes in the Structure of Wages: U.S. and Japan," National Bureau of Economic Research, September 1989.
[6]U.S. Department of Commerce, Bureau of Labor Statistics, "Wages of Unionized and Nonunionized Workers," various issues.
[7]U.S. Department of Labor, Bureau of Labor Statistics, "Reemployment Increases among Displaced Workers," *BLS News*, USDL 86-414, October 14,1986, table 6.

40,000 white-collar employees and planned to eliminate another 25,000 by the mid-1990s.[8] As America's core pyramids metamorphosed into global webs, many middle-level routine producers were as obsolete as routine workers on the line.

As has been noted, foreign-owned webs are hiring some Americans to do 17 routine production in the United States. Philips, Sony, and Toyota factories are popping up all over—to the self-congratulatory applause of the nation's governors and mayors, who have lured them with promises of tax abatements and new sewers, among other amenities. But as these ebullient politicians will soon discover, the foreign-owned factories are highly automated and will become far more so in years to come. Routine production jobs account for a small fraction of the cost of producing most items in the United States and other advanced nations, and this fraction will continue to decline sharply as computer-integrated robots take over. In 1977, it took routine producers thirty-five hours to assemble an automobile in the United States; it is estimated that by the mid-1990s, Japanese-owned factories in America will be producing finished automobiles using only eight hours of a routine producer's time.[9]

The productivity and resulting wages of American workers who run such 18 robotic machinery may be relatively high, but there may not be many such jobs to go around. A case in point: in the late 1980s, Nippon Steel joined with America's ailing Inland Steel to build a new $400 million cold-rolling mill fifty miles west of Gary, Indiana. The mill was celebrated for its state-of-the-art technology, which cut the time to produce a coil of steel from twelve days to about one hour. In fact, the entire plant could be run by a small team of technicians, which became clear when Inland subsequently closed two of its old cold-rolling mills, laying off hundreds of routine workers. Governors and mayors take note: your much-bally-hooed foreign factories may end up employing distressingly few of your constituents.

Overall, the decline in routine jobs has hurt men more than women. This is 19 because the routine production jobs held by men in high-volume metal bending manufacturing industries had paid higher wages than the routine production jobs held by women in textiles and data processing. As both sets of jobs have been lost, American women in routine production have gained more equal footing with American men—equally poor footing, that is. This is a major reason why the gender gap between male and female wages began to close during the 1980s.

The second of the three boats, carrying in-person servers, is sinking as well, but 20 somewhat more slowly and unevenly. Most in-person servers are paid at or just slightly above the minimum wage and many work only part-time, with the result that their take-home pay is modest, to say the least. Nor do they typically receive all the benefits (health care, life insurance, disability, and so forth) garnered by routine producers in large manufacturing corporations or by symbolic

---

[8]*Wall Street Journal,* February 16, 1990, p. A5.
[9]Figures from the International Motor Vehicles Program, Massachusetts Institute of Technology, 1989.

analysts affiliated with the more affluent threads of global webs.[10] In-person servers are sheltered from the direct effects of global competition and, like everyone else, benefit from access to lower-cost products from around the world. But they are not immune to its indirect effects.

For one thing, in-person servers increasingly compete with former routine 21 production workers, who, no longer able to find well-paying routine production jobs, have few alternatives but to seek in-person service jobs. The Bureau of Labor Statistics estimates that of the 2.8 million manufacturing workers who lost their jobs during the early 1980s, fully one-third were rehired in service jobs paying at least 20 percent less.[11] In-person servers must also compete with high school graduates and dropouts who years before had moved easily into routine production jobs but no longer can. And if demographic predictions about the American work force in the first decades of the twenty-first century are correct (and they are likely to be, since most of the people who will comprise the work force are already identifiable), most new entrants into the job market will be black or Hispanic men, or women—groups that in years past have possessed relatively weak technical skills. This will result in an even larger number of people crowding into in-person services. Finally, in-person servers will be competing with growing numbers of immigrants, both legal and illegal, for whom in-person services will comprise the most accessible jobs. (It is estimated that between the mid-1980s and the end of the century, about a quarter of all workers entering the American labor force will be immigrants.[12])

Perhaps the fiercest competition that in-person servers face comes from labor- 22 saving machinery (much of it invented, designed, fabricated, or assembled in other nations, of course). Automated tellers, computerized cashiers, automatic car washes, robotized vending machines, self-service gasoline pumps, and all similar gadgets substitute for the human beings that customers once encountered. Even telephone operators are fast disappearing, as electronic sensors and voice simulators become capable of carrying on conversations that are reasonably intelligent and always polite. Retail sales workers—among the largest groups of in-person servers—are similarly imperiled. Through personal computers linked to television screens, tomorrow's consumers will be able to buy furniture, appliances, and all sorts of electronic toys from their living rooms— examining the merchandise from all angles, selecting whatever color, size, special features, and price seem most appealing, and then transmitting the order instantly to warehouses from which the selections will be shipped directly to their homes. So, too, with financial transactions, airline and hotel reservations,

[10]The growing portion of the American labor force engaged in in-person services, relative to routine production, thus helps explain why the number of Americans lacking health insurance increased by at least 6 million during the 1980s.
[11]U.S. Department of Labor, Bureau of Labor Statistics, "Reemployment Increases among Disabled Workers," October 14, 1986.
[12]Federal Immigration and Naturalization Service, *Statistical Yearbook* (Washington, D.C.: U.S. Government Printing Office, 1986, 1987).

rental car agreements, and similar contracts, which will be executed between consumers in their homes and computer banks somewhere else on the globe.[13]

Advanced economies like the United States will continue to generate siz- 23 able numbers of new in-person service jobs, of course, the automation of older ones notwithstanding. For every bank teller who loses her job to an automated teller, three new jobs open for aerobics instructors. Human beings, it seems, have an almost insatiable desire for personal attention. But the intense competition nevertheless ensures that the wages of in-person servers will remain relatively low. In-person servers—working on their own, or else dispersed widely amid many small establishments, filling all sorts of personal-care niches—cannot readily organize themselves into labor unions or create powerful lobbies to limit the impact of such competition.

In two respects, demographics will work in favor of in-person servers, 24 buoying their collective boat slightly. First, as has been noted, the rate of growth of the American work force is slowing. In particular, the number of young workers is shrinking. Between 1985 and 1995, the number of the eighteen- to twenty-four-year-olds will have declined by 17.5 percent. Thus, employers will have more incentive to hire and train in-person servers whom they might previously have avoided. But this demographic relief from the competitive pressures will be only temporary. The cumulative procreative energies of the postwar baby-boomers (born between 1946 and 1964) will result in a new surge of workers by 2010 or thereabouts.[14] And immigration—both legal and illegal—shows every sign of increasing in years to come.

Next, by the second decade of the twenty-first century, the number of 25 Americans aged sixty-five and over will be rising precipitously, as the baby-boomers reach retirement age and live longer. Their life expectancies will lengthen not just because fewer of them will have smoked their way to their graves and more will have eaten better than their parents, but also because they will receive all sorts of expensive drugs and therapies designed to keep them alive—barely. By 2035, twice as many Americans will be elderly as in 1988, and the number of octogenarians is expected to triple. As these decaying baby-boomers ingest all the chemicals and receive all the treatments, they will need a great deal of personal attention. Millions of deteriorating bodies will require nurses, nursing-home operators, hospital administrators, orderlies, home-care providers, hospice aides, and technicians to operate and maintain all the expensive machinery that will monitor and temporarily stave off final disintegration. There might even be a booming market for euthanasia specialists. In-person servers catering to the old and ailing will be in strong demand.[15]

---

[13]See Claudia H. Deutsch, "The Powerful Push for Self-Service;" *New York Times,* April 9, 1989, section 3, p. 1.
[14]U.S. Bureau of the Census, Current Population Reports, Series P-23, no. 138, tables 2-1, 4-6. See W. Johnson, A. Packer, et al., *Workforce 2000: Work and Workers for the 21st Century* (Indianapolis: Hudson Institute, 1987).
[15]The Census Bureau estimates that by the year 2000, at least 12 million Americans will work in health services—well over 6 percent of the total work force.

One small problem: the decaying baby-boomers will not have enough   26
money to pay for these services. They will have used up their personal savings
years before. Their Social Security payments will, of course, have been used by
the government to pay for the previous generation's retirement and to finance
much of the budget deficits of the 1980s. Moreover, with relatively fewer young
Americans in the population, the supply of housing will likely exceed the demand, with the result that the boomers' major investments—their homes—will
be worth less (in inflation-adjusted dollars) when they retire than they planned
for. In consequence, the huge cost of caring for the graying boomers will fall on
many of the same people who will be paid to care for them. It will be like a great
sump pump: in-person servers of the twenty-first century will have an abundance of health-care jobs, but a large portion of their earnings will be devoted to
Social Security payments and income taxes, which will in turn be used to pay
their salaries. The net result: no real improvement in their standard of living.

The standard of living of in-person servers also depends, indirectly, on the   27
standard of living of the Americans they serve who are engaged in world commerce. To the extent that *these* Americans are richly rewarded by the rest of the
world for what they contribute, they will have more money to lavish upon in-
person services. Here we find the only form of "trickle-down" economics that
has a basis in reality. A waitress in a town whose major factory has just been
closed is unlikely to earn a high wage or enjoy much job security; in a swank resort populated by film producers and banking moguls, she is apt to do reasonably well. So, too, with nations. In-person servers in Bangladesh may spend
their days performing roughly the same tasks as in-person servers in the United
States, but have a far lower standard of living for their efforts. The difference
comes in the value that their customers add to the world economy.

Unlike the boats of routine producers and in-person servers, however, the   28
vessel containing America's symbolic analysts is rising. Worldwide demand for
their insights is growing as the ease and speed of communicating them steadily
increases. Not every symbolic analyst is rising as quickly or as dramatically as
every other, of course; symbolic analysts at the low end are barely holding their
own in the world economy. But symbolic analysts at the top are in such great
demand worldwide that they have difficulty keeping track of all their earnings.
Never before in history has opulence on such a scale been gained by people
who have earned it, and done so legally.

Among symbolic analysts in the middle range are American scientists and   29
researchers who are busily selling their discoveries to global enterprise webs.
They are not limited to American customers. If the strategic brokers in General
Motors' headquarters refuse to pay a high price for a new means of making
high-strength ceramic engines dreamed up by a team of engineers affiliated
with Carnegie Mellon University in Pittsburgh, the strategic brokers of Honda
or Mercedes-Benz are likely to be more than willing.

So, too, with the insights of America's ubiquitous management consultants,   30
which are being sold for large sums to eager entrepreneurs in Europe and Latin
America. Also, the insights of America's energy consultants, sold for even larger

sums to Arab sheikhs. American design engineers are providing insights to Olivetti, Mazda, Siemens, and other global webs; American marketers, techniques for learning what worldwide consumers will buy; American advertisers, ploys for ensuring that they actually do. American architects are issuing designs and blueprints for opera houses, art galleries, museums, luxury hotels, and residential complexes in the world's major cities; American commercial property developers, marketing these properties to worldwide investors and purchasers.

Americans who specialize in the gentle art of public relations are in demand 31 by corporations, governments, and politicians in virtually every nation. So, too, are American political consultants, some of whom, at this writing, are advising the Hungarian Socialist Party, the remnant of Hungary's ruling Communists, on how to salvage a few parliamentary seats in the nation's first free election in more than forty years. Also at this writing, a team of American agricultural consultants is advising the managers of a Soviet farm collective employing 1,700 Russians eighty miles outside Moscow. As noted, American investment bankers and lawyers specializing in financial circumnavigations are selling their insights to Asians and Europeans who are eager to discover how to make large amounts of money by moving large amounts of money.

Developing nations, meanwhile, are hiring American civil engineers to ad- 32 vise on building roads and dams. The present thaw in the Cold War will no doubt expand these opportunities. American engineers from Bechtel (a global firm notable for having employed both Caspar Weinberger and George Shultz for much larger sums than either earned in the Reagan administration) have begun helping the Soviets design and install a new generation of nuclear reactors. Nations also are hiring American bankers and lawyers to help them renegotiate the terms of their loans with global banks, and Washington lobbyists to help them with Congress, the Treasury, the World Bank, the IMF, and other politically sensitive institutions. In fits of obvious desperation, several nations emerging from communism have even hired American economists to teach them about capitalism.

Almost everyone around the world is buying the skills and insights of 33 Americans who manipulate oral and visual symbols—musicians, sound engineers, film producers, makeup artists, directors, cinematographers, actors and actresses, boxers, scriptwriters, songwriters, and set designers. Among the wealthiest of symbolic analysts are Steven Spielberg, Bill Cosby, Charles Schulz, Eddie Murphy, Sylvester Stallone, Madonna, and other star directors and performers—who are almost as well known on the streets of Dresden and Tokyo as in the Back Bay of Boston. Less well rewarded but no less renowned are the unctuous anchors on Turner Broadcasting's Cable News, who appear daily, via satellite, in places ranging from Vietnam to Nigeria. Vanna White is the world's most-watched game-show hostess. Behind each of these familiar faces is a collection of American problem-solvers, -identifiers, and brokers who train, coach, advise, promote, amplify, direct, groom, represent, and otherwise add value to their talents.[16]

---

[16]In 1989, the entertainment business summoned to the United States $5.5 billion in foreign earnings—making it among the nation's largest export industries, just behind aerospace. U.S. Department of Commerce, International Trade Commission, "Composition of U.S. Exports," various issues.

There are also the insights of senior American executives who occupy the ₃₄
world headquarters of global "American" corporations and the national or regional headquarters of global "foreign" corporations. Their insights are duly ex-
ported to the rest of the world through the webs of global enterprise. IBM does
not export many machines from the United States, for example. Big Blue makes
machines all over the globe and services them on the spot. Its prime American
exports are symbolic and analytic. From IBM's world headquarters in Armonk,
New York, emanate strategic brokerage and related management services
bound for the rest of the world. In return, IBM's top executives are generously
rewarded.

The most important reason for this expanding world market and increasing ₃₅
global demand for the symbolic and analytic insights of Americans has been the
dramatic improvement in worldwide communication and transportation technologies. Designs, instructions, advice, and visual and audio symbols can be
communicated more and more rapidly around the globe, with ever greater precision and at ever-lower cost. Madonna's voice can be transported to billions of
listeners, with perfect clarity, on digital compact discs. A new invention emanating from engineers in Battelle's laboratory in Columbus, Ohio, can be sent almost anywhere via modem, in a form that will allow others to examine it in
three dimensions through enhanced computer graphics. When face-to-face
meetings are still required—and videoconferencing will not suffice—it is relatively easy for designers, consultants, advisers, artists, and executives to board
supersonic jets and, in a matter of hours, meet directly with their worldwide
clients, customers, audiences, and employees.

With rising demand comes rising compensation. Whether in the form of li- ₃₆
censing fees, fees for service, salaries, or shares in final profits, the economic result is much the same. There are also nonpecuniary rewards. One of the
best-kept secrets among symbolic analysts is that so many of them enjoy their
work. In fact, much of it does not count as work at all, in the traditional sense.
The work of routine producers and in-person servers is typically monotonous;
it causes muscles to tire or weaken and involves little independence or discretion. The "work" of symbolic analysts, by contrast, often involves puzzles, experiments, games, a significant amount of chatter, and substantial discretion
over what to do next. Few routine producers or in-person servers would
"work" if they did not need to earn the money. Many symbolic analysts would
"work" even if money were no object.

At mid-century, when America was a national market dominated by core 37 ₃₇
pyramid-shaped corporations, there were constraints on the earnings of people
at the highest rungs. First and most obviously, the market for their services was
largely limited to the borders of the nation. In addition, whatever conceptual
value they might contribute was small relative to the value gleaned from large
scale—and it was dependent on large scale for whatever income it was to summon. Most of the problems to be identified and solved had to do with enhancing the efficiency of production and improving the flow of materials, parts,

assembly, and distribution. Inventors searched for the rare breakthrough revealing an entirely new product to be made in high volume; management consultants, executives, and engineers thereafter tried to speed and synchronize its manufacture, to better achieve scale efficiencies; advertisers and marketers sought then to whet the public's appetite for the standard item that emerged. Since white-collar earnings increased with larger scale, there was considerable incentive to expand the firm; indeed, many of America's core corporations grew far larger than scale economies would appear to have justified.

By the 1990s, in contrast, the earnings of symbolic analysts were limited neither by the size of the national market nor by the volume of production of the firms with which they were affiliated. The marketplace was worldwide, and conceptual value was high relative to value added from scale efficiencies. 38

There had been another constraint on high earnings, which also gave way by the 1990s. At mid-century, the compensation awarded to top executives and advisers of the largest of America's core corporations could not be grossly out of proportion to that of low-level production workers. It would be unseemly for executives who engaged in highly visible rounds of bargaining with labor unions, and who routinely responded to government requests to moderate prices, to take home wages and benefits wildly in excess of what other Americans earned. Unless white-collar executives restrained themselves, moreover, blue-collar production workers could not be expected to restrain their own demands for higher wages. Unless both groups exercised restraint, the government could not be expected to forbear from imposing direct controls and regulations. 39

At the same time, the wages of production workers could not be allowed to sink too low, lest there be insufficient purchasing power in the economy. After all, who would buy all the goods flowing out of American factories if not American workers? This, too, was part of the tacit bargain struck between American managers and their workers. 40

Recall the oft-repeated corporate platitude of the era about the chief executive's responsibility to carefully weigh and balance the interests of the corporation's disparate stakeholders. Under the stewardship of the corporate statesman, no set of stakeholders—least of all white-collar executives—was to gain a disproportionately large share of the benefits of corporate activity; nor was any stakeholder—especially the average worker—to be left with a share that was disproportionately small. Banal though it was, this idea helped to maintain the legitimacy of the core American corporation in the eyes of most Americans, and to ensure continued economic growth. 41

But by the 1990s, these informal norms were evaporating, just as (and largely because) the core American corporation was vanishing. The links between top executives and the American production worker were fading: an ever-increasing number of subordinates and contractees were foreign, and a steadily growing number of American routine producers were working for foreign-owned firms. An entire cohort of middle-level managers, who had once been deemed "white collar," had disappeared; and, increasingly, American executives were exporting their insights to global enterprise webs. 42

As the American corporation itself became a global web almost indistin- 43
guishable from any other, its stakeholders were turning into a large and diffuse
group, spread over the world. Such global stakeholders were less visible, and
far less noisy, than national stakeholders. And as the American corporation sold
its goods and services all over the world, the purchasing power of American
workers became far less relevant to its economic survival.

Thus have the inhibitions been removed. The salaries and benefits of Amer- 44
ica's top executives, and many of their advisers and consultants, have soared to
what years before would have been unimaginable heights, even as those of
other Americans have declined.

COMPREHENSION

1. To what does the title allude? Why is this allusion significant to the meaning of the title?
2. To whom does Reich refer when he mentions "symbolic analysts"? Regardless of their occupation, what do all symbolic analysts have in common regarding the nature of their work?
3. What has traditionally been the image of and the nature of work among the
white-collar workers to which Reich alludes? Why are they now one of the
groups in danger of losing employment opportunities?

RHETORIC

1. Reich uses the central metaphor of the "boat" in describing the state of economics and employment. Why? What connotations are associated with this
image in regard to financial security?
2. How does Reich's introduction prepare you for the major themes he addresses in the body of his essay?
3. Examine the section breaks at the start of paragraphs 3, 11, 20, and 37. How
does each section relate to the theme of the essay as a whole? What transitional devices does Reich use to bridge one section to the next?
4. Paragraphs 5, 6, 9, and 16 cite specific and detailed examples of the effects
of the changing global economy. How does this contribute to conveying Reich's authority regarding the subject he is discussing?
5. Reich describes a dire situation for the American worker. How would you
characterize the tone of this description? Is it angry, resigned, impartial, ac-
cusatory? You may use these or any other adjectives as long as you explain
your view.
6. Why has Reich opened his essay with an epigraph from Adam Smith? What
is the relationship of the quotation to the overall theme of the essay? How
does the tone of the epigraph contrast with the tone of the title?
7. What is the author's purpose? Is it to inform, to explain, to warn, to enlighten,
to offer solutions, or a combination of any of these? Explain your view.

WRITING

1. In a classification essay, describe three areas of academic concentration at your college or university that can help prepare one for a job as a symbolic analyst.
2. In an essay of 500 to 750 words, argue for or against the proposition that as long as one knows which careers command the highest salaries, it is up to the individual to decide whether he or she should pursue a job in those fields.
3. In an expository essay, explain whether you believe the discrepancy between high-wage and low-wage workers will increase, decrease, or remain the same.

The Market as God

Harvey Cox

Harvey Gallagher Cox (b. 1929) is a theologian. Born in Pennsylvania, he earned a BA from the University of Pennsylvania in 1951 and a PhD from Harvard in 1963. Since 1970, he has been the Victor Thomas Professor of Divinity at Harvard. He is the author and/or editor of over a dozen books on religion and theology. Among them are The Secular City *(1965),* Feast of Fools *(1969),* The Use and Misuse of People's Religion *(1973),* Turning East *(1977),* Many Mansions: A Christian's Encounter with Other Faiths *(1991), and* Fire from Heaven: The Rise of Pentecostal Spirituality and the Reshaping of Religion in the 21st Century *(1995). In this essay, originally published in the March 1999 issue of* Atlantic Monthly, *Cox demonstrates how the rhetoric of business writing mimics in style, vocabulary, and tone that of religious doctrine.*

A few years ago a friend advised me that if I wanted to know what was going on in the real world, I should read the business pages. Although my lifelong interest has been in the study of religion, I am always willing to expand my horizons; so I took the advice, vaguely fearful that I would have to cope with a new and baffling vocabulary. Instead I was surprised to discover that most of the concepts I ran across were quite familiar. 1

Expecting a *terra incognita*, I found myself instead in the land of *dèjá vu*. The lexicon of *The Wall Street Journal* and the business sections of *Time* and *Newsweek* turned out to bear a striking resemblance to Genesis, the Epistle to the Romans, and Saint Augustine's City of God. Behind descriptions of market reforms, monetary policy, and the convolutions of the Dow, I gradually made out the pieces of a grand narrative about the inner meaning of human history, why 2 things had gone wrong, and how to put them right. Theologians call these myths of origin, legends of the fall, and doctrines of sin and redemption. But here they were again, and in only thin disguise: chronicles about the creation of wealth, the seductive temptations of statism, captivity to faceless economic cycles, and, ultimately, salvation through the advent of free markets, with a small dose of ascetic belt tightening along the way, especially for the East Asian economies.

The East Asians' troubles, votaries argue, derive from their heretical devia- 3 tion from free-market orthodoxy—they were practitioners of "crony capitalism," of "ethnocapitalism," of "statist capitalism," not of the one true faith. The East Asian financial panics, the Russian debt repudiations, the Brazilian economic turmoil, and the U.S. stock market's $1.5 trillion "correction" momentarily shook belief in the new dispensation. But faith is strengthened by adversity, and the Market God is emerging renewed from its trial by financial "contagion." Since the argument from design no longer proves its existence, it is fast becoming a postmodern deity—believed in despite the evidence. Alan Greenspan vindicated this tempered faith in testimony before Congress last October. A leading hedge fund had just lost billions of dollars, shaking market confidence and precipitating calls for new federal regulation. Greenspan, usually Delphic in his comments, was decisive. He believed that regulation would only impede these markets, and that they should continue to be self-regulated. True faith, Saint Paul tells us, is the evidence of things unseen.

Soon I began to marvel at just how comprehensive the business theology is. 4 There were even sacraments to convey salvific power to the lost, a calendar of entrepreneurial saints, and what theologians call an "eschatology"—teaching about the "end of history." My curiosity was piqued. I began cataloguing these strangely familiar doctrines, and I saw that in fact there lies embedded in the business pages an entire theology, which is comparable in scope if not in profundity to that of Thomas Aquinas or Karl Barth. It needed only to be systematized for a whole new *Summa* to take shape.

At the apex of any theological system, of course, is its doctrine of God. In 5 the new theology this celestial pinnacle is occupied by The Market, which I capitalize to signify both the mystery that enshrouds it and the reverence it inspires in business folk. Different faiths have, of course, different views of the divine attributes. In Christianity, God has sometimes been defined as omnipotent (possessing all power), omniscient (having all knowledge), and omnipresent (existing everywhere). Most Christian theologies, it is true, hedge a bit. They teach that these qualities of the divinity are indeed *there,* but are hidden from human eyes both by human sin and by the transcendence of the divine itself. In "light inaccessible" they are, as the old hymn puts it, "hid from our eyes." Likewise, although The Market, we are assured, possesses these divine attributes, they are not always completely evident to mortals but must be trusted and affirmed by faith. "Further along," as another old gospel song says, "we'll understand why."

As I tried to follow the arguments and explanations of the economist- 6
theologians who justify The Market's ways to men; I spotted the same dialectics
I have grown fond of in the many years I have pondered the Thomists, the
Calvinists, and the various schools of modern religious thought. In particular,
the econologians' rhetoric resembles what is sometimes called "process theology," a relatively contemporary trend influenced by the philosophy of Alfred
North Whitehead. In this school although God *wills* to possess the classic attributes, He does not yet possess them in full, but is definitely moving in that direction. This conjecture is of immense help to theologians for obvious reasons.
It answers the bothersome puzzle of theodicy: why a lot of bad things happen
that an omnipotent, omnipresent, and omniscient God—especially a benevolent
one—would not countenance. Process theology also seems to offer considerable
comfort to the theologians of The Market. It helps to explain the dislocation,
pain, and disorientation that are the result of transitions from economic hetero-
doxy to free markets.

Since the earliest stages of human history, of course, there have been bazaars, 7
rialtos, and trading posts—all markets. But The Market was never God, because
there were other centers of value and meaning, other "gods." The Market operated within a plethora of other institutions that restrained it. As Karl Polanyi
has demonstrated in his classic work *The Great Transformation*, only in the past
two centuries has The Market risen above these demigods and chthonic spirits
to become today's First Cause.

Initially The Market's rise to Olympic supremacy replicated the gradual ascent 8
of Zeus above all the other divinities of the ancient Greek pantheon, an ascent that
was never quite secure. Zeus, it will be recalled, had to keep storming down from
Olympus to quell this or that threat to his sovereignty. Recently, however, The
Market is becoming more like the Yahweh of the Old Testament—not just one
superior deity contending with others but the Supreme Deity, the only true God,
whose reign must now be universally accepted and who allows for no rivals.

Divine *omnipotence* means the capacity to define what is real. It is the power 9
to make something out of nothing and nothing out of something. The willed-
but-not-yet-achieved omnipotence of The Market means that there is no conceivable limit to its inexorable ability to convert creation into commodities. But
again, this is hardly a new idea, though it has a new twist. In Catholic theology,
through what is called "transubstantiation," ordinary bread and wine become
vehicles of the holy. In the mass of The Market a reverse process occurs. Things
that have been held sacred transmute into interchangeable items for sale. Land
is a good example. For millennia it has held various meanings, many of them
numinous. It has been Mother Earth, ancestral resting place, holy mountain, enchanted forest, tribal homeland, aesthetic inspiration, sacred turf, and much
more. But when The Market's Sanctus bell rings and the elements are elevated,
all these complex meanings of land melt into one: real estate. At the right price
no land is not for sale, and this includes everything from burial grounds to the
cove of the local fertility sprite. This radical desacralization dramatically alters

the human relationship to land; the same happens with water, air, space, and soon (it is predicted) the heavenly bodies.

At the high moment of the mass the priest says, "This is my body," meaning the body of Christ and, by extension, the bodies of all the faithful people. Christianity and Judaism both teach that the human body is made "in the image of God." Now, however, in a dazzling display of reverse transubstantiation, the human body has become the latest sacred vessel to be converted into a commodity. The process began, fittingly enough, with blood. But now, or soon, all bodily organs—kidneys, skin, bone marrow, sperm, the heart itself—will be miraculously changed into purchasable items.

Still, the liturgy of The Market is not proceeding without some opposition from the pews. A considerable battle is shaping up in the United States, for example, over the attempt to merchandise human genes. A few years ago, banding together for the first time in memory, virtually all the religious institutions in the country, from the liberal National Council of Churches to the Catholic bishops to the Christian Coalition, opposed the gene mart, the newest theophany of The Market. But these critics are followers of what are now "old religions," which, like the goddess cults that were thriving when the worship of the vigorous young Apollo began sweeping ancient Greece, may not have the strength to slow the spread of the new devotion.

Occasionally backsliders try to bite the Invisible Hand that feeds them. On October 26, 1996, the German government ran an ad offering the entire village of Liebenberg, in what used to be East Germany, for sale—with no previous notice to its some 350 residents. Liebenberg's citizens, many of them elderly or unemployed, stared at the notice in disbelief. They had certainly loathed communism, but when they opted for the market economy that reunification promised, they hardly expected this. Liebenberg includes a thirteenth-century church, a Baroque castle, a lake, a hunting lodge, two restaurants, and 3,000 acres of meadow and forest. Once a favorite site for boar hunting by the old German nobility, it was obviously entirely too valuable a parcel of real estate to overlook. Besides, having been expropriated by the East German Communist government, it was now legally eligible for sale under the terms of German reunification. Overnight Liebenberg became a living parable, providing an invaluable glimpse of the Kingdom in which The Market's will is indeed done. But the outraged burghers of the town did not feel particularly blessed. They complained loudly, and the sale was finally postponed. Everyone in town realized, however, that it was not really a victory. The Market, like Yahweh, may lose a skirmish, but in a war of attrition it will always win in the end.

Of course, religion in the past has not been reluctant to charge for its services. Prayers, masses, blessings, healings, baptisms, funerals, and amulets have been hawked, and still are. Nor has religion always been sensitive to what the traffic would bear. When, in the early sixteenth century, Johann Tetzel jacked up the price of indulgences and even had one of the first singing commercials composed to push sales ("When the coin into the platter pings, the soul out of purgatory springs"), he failed to realize that he was overreaching. The customers balked, and a young Augustinian monk brought the traffic to a standstill with a placard tacked to a church door.

It would be a lot harder for a Luther to interrupt sales of The Market's 14 amulets today. As the people of Liebenberg discovered, everything can now be bought. Lakes, meadows, church buildings—everything carries a sticker price. But this practice itself exacts a cost. As everything in what used to be called creation becomes a commodity, human beings begin to look at one another, and at themselves, in a funny way, and they see colored price tags. There was a time when people spoke, at least occasionally, of "inherent worth"—if not of things, then at least of persons. The Liebenberg principle changes all that. One wonders what would become of a modern Luther who tried to post his theses on the church door, only to find that the whole edifice had been bought by an American billionaire who reckoned it might look nicer on his estate.

It is comforting to note that the *citizens* of Liebenberg, at least, were not put 15 on the block. But that raises a good question. What is the value of a human life in the theology of The Market? Here the new deity pauses, but not for long. The computation may be complex, but it is not impossible. We should not believe, for example, that if a child is born severely handicapped, unable to be "productive," The Market will decree its death. One must remember that the profits derived from medications, leg braces, and CAT-scan equipment should also be figured into the equation. Such a cost analysis might result in a close call—but the inherent worth of the child's life, since it cannot be quantified, would be hard to include in the calculation.

It is sometimes said that since everything is for sale under the rule of The 16 Market, nothing is sacred. But this is not quite true. About three years ago a nasty controversy erupted in Great Britain when a railway pension fund that owned the small jeweled casket in which the remains of Saint Thomas à Becket are said to have rested decided to auction it off through Sotheby's. The casket dates from the twelfth century and is revered as both a sacred relic and a national treasure. The British Museum made an effort to buy it but lacked the funds, so the casket was sold to a Canadian. Only last-minute measures by the British government prevented removal of the casket from the United Kingdom. In principle, however, in the theology of The Market, there is no reason why any relic, coffin, body, or national monument—including the Statue of Liberty and Westminster Abbey—should not be listed. Does anyone doubt that if the True Cross were ever really discovered, it would eventually find its way to Sotheby's? The Market is not omnipotent—yet. But the process is under way and it is gaining momentum.

Omniscience is a little harder to gauge than omnipotence. Maybe The Mar- 17 ket has already achieved it but is unable—temporarily—to apply its gnosis until its Kingdom and Power come in their fullness. Nonetheless, current thinking already assigns to The Market a comprehensive wisdom that in the past only the gods have known. The Market, we are taught, is able to determine what human needs are, what copper and capital should cost, how much barbers and

CEOs should be paid, and how much jet planes, running shoes, and hysterectomies should sell for. But how do we know The Market's will?

In days of old, seers entered a trance state and then informed anxious seekers what kind of mood the gods were in, and whether this was an auspicious time to begin a journey, get married, or start a war. The prophets of Israel repaired to the desert and then returned to announce whether Yahweh was feeling benevolent or wrathful. Today The Market's fickle will is clarified by daily reports from Wall Street and other sensory organs of finance. Thus we can learn on a day-to-day basis that The Market is "apprehensive," "relieved," "nervous," or even at times "jubilant." On the basis of this revelation awed adepts make critical decisions about whether to buy or sell. Like one of the devouring gods of old, The Market—aptly embodied in a bull or a bear—must be fed and kept happy under all circumstances. True, at times its appetite may seem excessive— a $35 billion bailout here, a $50 billion one there—but the alternative to assuaging its hunger is too terrible to contemplate. 18

The diviners and seers of The Market's moods are the high priests of its mysteries. To act against their admonitions is to risk excommunication and possibly damnation. Today, for example, if any government's policy vexes The Market, those responsible for the irreverence will be made to suffer. That The Market is not at all displeased by downsizing or a growing income gap, or can be gleeful about the expansion of cigarette sales to Asian young people, should not cause anyone to question its ultimate omniscience. Like Calvin's inscrutable deity, The Market may work in mysterious ways, "hid from our eyes," but ultimately it knows best. 19

Omniscience can sometimes seem a bit intrusive. The traditional God of the Episcopal Book of Common Prayer is invoked as one "unto whom all hearts are open, all desires known, and from whom no secrets are hid." Like Him, The Market already knows the deepest secrets and darkest desires of our hearts—or at least would like to know them. But one suspects that divine motivation differs in these two cases. Clearly The Market wants this kind of x-ray omniscience because by probing our inmost fears and desires and then dispensing across-the-board solutions, it can further extend its reach. Like the gods of the past, whose priests offered up the fervent prayers and petitions of the people, The Market relies on its own intermediaries: motivational researchers. Trained in the advanced art of psychology, which has long since replaced theology as the true "science of the soul," the modern heirs of the medieval confessors delve into the hidden fantasies, insecurities, and hopes of the populace. 20

One sometimes wonders, in this era of Market religion, where the skeptics and freethinkers have gone. What has happened to the Voltaires who once exposed bogus miracles, and the H. L. Menckens who blew shrill whistles on pious humbuggery? Such is the grip of current orthodoxy that to question the omniscience of The Market is to question the inscrutable wisdom of Providence. The metaphysical principle is obvious: If you *say* it's the real thing, then it must *be* the real thing. As the early Christian theologian Tertullian once remarked, *"Credo quia absurdum est"* ("I believe because it is absurd"). 21

Finally, there is the divinity's will to be *omnipresent*. Virtually every religion 22 teaches this idea in one way or another, and the new religion is no exception. The latest trend in economic theory is the attempt to apply market calculations to areas that once appeared to be exempt, such as dating, family life, marital relations, and child-rearing. Henri Lepage, an enthusiastic advocate of globalization, now speaks about a "total market." Saint Paul reminded the Athenians that their own poets sang of a God "in whom we live and move and have our being"; so now The Market is not only around us but inside us, informing our senses and our feelings. There seems to be nowhere left to flee from its untiring quest. Like the Hound of Heaven, it pursues us home from the mall and into the nursery and the bedroom.

It used to be thought—mistakenly, as it turns out—that at least the inner- 23 most, or "spiritual," dimension of life was resistant to The Market. It seemed unlikely that the interior castle would ever be listed by Century 21. But as the markets for material goods become increasingly glutted, such previously unmarketable states of grace as serenity and tranquillity are now appearing in the catalogues. Your personal vision quest can take place in unspoiled wildernesses that are pictured as virtually unreachable—except, presumably, by the other people who read the same catalogue. Furthermore, ecstasy and spirituality are now offered in a convenient generic form. Thus The Market makes available the religious benefits that once required prayer and fasting, without the awkwardness of denominational commitment or the tedious ascetic discipline that once limited their accessibility. All can now handily be bought without an unrealistic demand on one's time, in a weekend workshop at a Caribbean resort with a sensitive psychological consultant replacing the crotchety retreat master.

Discovering the theology of The Market made me begin to think in a differ- 24 ent way about the conflict among religions. Violence between Catholics and Protestants in Ulster or Hindus and Muslims in India often dominates the headlines. But I have come to wonder whether the real clash of religions (or even of civilizations) may be going unnoticed. I am beginning to think that for all the religions of the world, however they may differ from one another, the religion of The Market has become the most formidable rival, the more so because it is rarely recognized as a religion. The traditional religions and the religion of the global market, as we have seen, hold radically different views of nature. In Christianity and Judaism, for example, "the earth is the Lord's and the fullness thereof, the world and all that dwell therein." The Creator appoints human beings as stewards and gardeners but, as it were, retains title to the earth. Other faiths have similar ideas. In the Market religion, however, human beings, more particularly those with money, own anything they buy and—within certain limits—can dispose of anything as they choose. Other contradictions can be seen in ideas about the human body, the nature of human community, and the purpose of life. The older religions encourage archaic attachments to particular places. But in The Market's eyes all places are interchangeable. The Market prefers a homogenized world culture with as few inconvenient particularities as possible.

Disagreements among the traditional religions become picayune in com- 25
parison with the fundamental differences they all have with the religion of The
Market. Will this lead to a new jihad or crusade? I doubt it. It seems unlikely
that traditional religions will rise to the occasion and challenge the doctrines of
the new dispensation. Most of them seem content to become its acolytes or to be
absorbed into its pantheon, much as the old Nordic deities, after putting up a
game fight, eventually settled for a diminished but secure status as Christian
saints. I am usually a keen supporter of ecumenism. But the contradictions between the world views of the traditional religions on the one hand and the
world view of the Market religion on the other are so basic that no compromise
seems possible, and I am secretly hoping for a rebirth of polemics.

No religion, new or old, is subject to empirical proof, so what we have is a 26
contest between faiths. Much is at stake. The Market, for example, strongly
prefers individualism and mobility. Since it needs to shift people to wherever
production requires them, it becomes wrathful when people cling to local traditions. These belong to the older dispensations and—like the high places of the
Baalim—should be plowed under. But maybe not. Like previous religions, the
new one has ingenious ways of incorporating preexisting ones. Hindu temples,
Buddhist festivals, and Catholic saints' shrines can look forward to new incar-
nations. Along with native costumes and spicy food, they will be allowed to
provide local color and authenticity in what could otherwise turn out to be an
extremely bland Beulah Land.

There is, however, one contradiction between the religion of the Market 27
and the traditional religions that seems to be insurmountable. All of the traditional religions teach that human beings are finite creatures and that there are
limits to any earthly enterprise. A Japanese Zen master once said to his disciples as he was dying, "I have learned only one thing in life: how much is
enough." He would find no niche in the chapel of The Market, for whom the
First Commandment is "There is *never* enough." Like the proverbial shark that
stops moving, The Market that stops expanding dies. That could happen. If it
does, then Nietzsche will have been right after all. He will just have had the
wrong God in mind.

COMPREHENSION

1. What is the major difference between traditional religious values and the
   "religious" values of the "The Market"?
2. What does Cox mean by presenting "The Market as God"? Recall that a thesis statement must be in the form of a complete sentence. What is the thesis
   of the essay and how does it relate to the title?
3. Many professions have their own specialized vocabulary and concepts.
   From what field of study has Cox taken much of his descriptive and explanatory terminology?

RHETORIC

1. Cox introduces his essay with a simple anecdote. How does this help to set up the tone of the essay? What is the tone of the essay?
2. Cox makes a distinction between religion and a "theological system" (paragraph 5). In paragraphs 5 through 20, he analyzes "The Market's" theological system. How does he structure his analysis to create a clear system of classification for a rather complex model? How do the separations between sections help in demarcating the structure?
3. Cox uses a great deal of specialized vocabulary and makes references to historical events, personages, and abstract ideas. Considering this, who is his intended audience? How important is it to understand his many allusions to fully appreciate his argument? Where would you look up specific references he makes that are unknown to you?
4. If what Cox claims has truth, modern society has radically shifted its value system, and one would assume that the author, a respected theologian, would find this a serious matter. Is the tone of the essay serious? If so, why? If not, what is the tone of the piece? Provide evidence to support your view.
5. Cox claims to have a lifelong interest in theology but not necessarily expertise in business. Does he seem to speak with authority regarding the nature of business? Why or why not?
6. What is Cox's value position concerning "The Market as God"? Is his purpose to inform, explain, warn, entertain, or a combination of these? Explain your answer.
7. In his conclusion, the author suggests that "The Market" has the potential to die. Does his tone indicate whether he thinks this would be a good thing? Explain.

WRITING

1. Write an extended metaphor of 500 to 600 words, using terminology that will provide coherence to your argument. Some possible titles could be "The University as Community," "TV as Illicit Drug," "Cyberspace as Alternative Universe," "The Media as Religion," "Cars as Personalities," and so on.
2. Write an essay of approximately 750 to 1,000 words arguing for or against the proposition that Cox endows "The Market" with far more ethical and moral power than it has. Include personal experience and observation to support your argument.
3. If your instructor allows, use your e-mail account at your college or university to send a general e-mail to philosophy department and business department faculty members, inviting them to read Cox's article and to respond to a series of questions you develop to garner their responses to it. Explain that you are taking this survey for a school writing assignment. After you have secured three volunteers, interview them, collect your data, and write an expository essay, describing and reflecting on your research.

A Modest Proposal

Preventing the Children of Poor People in Ireland from Being a Burden to Their Parents or Country, and for Making Them Beneficial to the Public

Jonathan Swift

Jonathan Swift (1667–1745) is best known as the author of three satires: A Tale of a Tub *(1704),* Gulliver's Travels *(1726), and* A Modest Proposal *(1729). In these satires, Swift pricks the balloon of many of his contemporaries' and our own most cherished prejudices, pomposities, and delusions. He was also a famous churchman, an eloquent spokesman for Irish rights, and a political journalist. The following selection, perhaps the most famous satiric essay in the English language, offers modest advice to a nation suffering from poverty, overpopulation, and political injustice.*

It is a melancholy object to those who walk through this great town or travel in 1 the country, when they see the streets, the roads, and cabin doors, crowded with beggars of the female-sex, followed by three, four, or six children, all in rags and importuning every passenger for an alms. These mothers, instead of being able to work for their honest livelihood, are forced to employ all their time in strolling to beg sustenance for their helpless infants, who, as they grow up, either turn thieves for want of work, or leave their dear native country to fight for the Pretender in Spain, or sell themselves to the Barbadoes.

I think it is agreed by all parties that this prodigious number of children in the 2 arms, or on the backs, or at the heels of their mothers, and frequently of their fathers, is in the present deplorable state of the kingdom a very great additional grievance; and therefore whoever could find out a fair, cheap, and easy method of making these children sound, useful members of the commonwealth would deserve so well of the public as to have his statue set up for a preserver of the nation.

But my intention is very far from being confined to provide only for the 3 children of professed beggars; it is of a much greater extent, and shall take in the whole number of infants at a certain age who are born of parents in effect as little able to support them as those who demand our charity in the streets.

As to my own part, having turned my thoughts for many years upon this 4 important subject, and maturely weighted the several schemes of other projectors, I have always found them grossly mistaken in their computation. It is true, a child just dropped from its dam may be supported by her milk for a solar year, with little other nourishment; at most not above the value of two shillings, which the mother may certainly get, or the value in scraps, by her lawful occupation of begging; and it is exactly at one year old that I propose to provide for them in such a manner as instead of being a charge upon their parents or the parish, or wanting food and raiment for the rest of their lives, they shall on the contrary contribute to the feeding, and partly to the clothing, of many thousands.

There is likewise another great advantage in my scheme, that it will prevent 5 those voluntary abortions, and that horrid practice of women murdering their bastard children, alas, too frequent among us, sacrificing the poor innocent babes, I doubt, more to avoid the expense than the shame, which would move tears and pity in the most savage and inhuman breast.

The number of souls in this kingdom being usually reckoned one million 6 and a half, of these I calculate there may be about two hundred thousand couples whose wives are breeders; from which number I subtract thirty thousand couples who are able to maintain their own children, although I apprehend there cannot be so many under the present distresses of the kingdom; but this being granted, there will remain an hundred and seventy thousand breeders. I again subtract fifty thousand for those women who miscarry, or whose children die by accident or disease within the year. There only remain an hundred and twenty thousand children of poor parents annually born. The question therefore is, how this number shall be reared and provided for, which, as I have already said, under the present situation of affairs, is utterly impossible by all the methods hitherto proposed. For we can neither employ them in handicraft or agriculture; we neither build houses (I mean in the country) nor cultivate land. They can very seldom pick up a livelihood by stealing till they arrive at six years old, except where they are of towardly parts; although I confess they learn the rudiments much earlier, during which time they can however be looked upon only as probationers, as I have been informed by a principal gentleman in the county of Cavan, who protested to me that he never knew above one or two instances under the age of six, even in a part of the kingdom so renowned for the quickest proficiency in that art.

I am assured by our merchants that a boy or girl before twelve years old is 7 no salable commodity; and even when they come to this age they will not yield above three pounds, or three pounds and half a crown at most on the Exchange; which cannot turn to account either to the parents or the kingdom, the charge of nutriment and rags having been at least four times that value.

I shall now therefore humbly propose my own thoughts, which I hope will 8 not be liable to the least objection.

I have been assured by a very knowing American of my acquaintance in 9 London, that a young healthy child well nursed is at a year old a most delicious, nourishing, and wholesome food, whether stewed, roasted, baked or boiled; and I make no doubt that it will equally serve in a fricassee or a ragout.

I do therefore humbly offer it to public consideration that of the hundred 10 and twenty thousand children, already computed, twenty thousand may be reserved for breed, whereof only one fourth part to be males, which is more than we allow to sheep, black cattle, or swine; and my reason is that these children are seldom the fruits of marriage, a circumstance not much regarded by our savages, therefore one male will be sufficient to serve four females. That the remaining hundred thousand may at a year old be offered in sale to the persons of quality and fortune through the kingdom, always advising the mother to let them suck plentifully in the last month, so as to render them plump and fat for a good table. A child will make two dishes at an entertainment for friends; and when the family dines alone, the fore or hind quarter will make a reasonable dish, and seasoned with a little pepper or salt will be very good boiled on the fourth day, especially in winter.

I have reckoned upon a medium that a child just born will weigh twelve 11 pounds, and in a solar year if tolerably nursed increaseth to twenty-eight pounds.

I grant this food will be somewhat dear, and therefore very proper for land- 12 lords, who, as they have already devoured most of the parents, seem to have the best title to the children.

Infant's flesh will be in season throughout the year, but more plentiful in 13 March, and a little before and after. For we are told by a grave author, an eminent French physician, that fish being a prolific diet, there are more children born in Roman Catholic countries about nine months after Lent than at any other season: therefore, reckoning a year after Lent, the markets will be more glutted than usual, because the number of popish infants is at least three to one in this kingdom; and therefore it will have one other collateral advantage, by lessening the number of Papists among us.

I have already computed the charge of nursing a beggar's child (in which 14 list I reckon all cottagers, laborers, and four fifths of the farmers) to be about two shillings per annum, rags included: and I believe no gentleman would repine to give ten shillings for the carcass of a good fat child, which, as I have said, will make four dishes of excellent nutritive meat, when he hath only some particular friend or his own family to dine with him. Thus the squire will learn to be a good landlord, and grow popular among the tenants; the mother will have eight shillings net profit, and be fit for work till she produces another child.

Those who are more thrifty (as I must confess the times require) may flay 15 the carcass; the skin of which artificially dressed will make admirable gloves for ladies, and summer boots for fine gentlemen.

As to our city of Dublin, shambles may be appointed for this purpose in the 16 most convenient parts of it, and butchers we may be assured will not be wanting; although I rather recommend buying the children alive, and dressing them hot from the knife as we do roasting pigs.

A very worthy person, a true lover of his country, and whose virtues I highly 17 esteem, was lately pleased in discoursing on this matter to offer a refinement upon my scheme. He said that many gentlemen of this kingdom, having of late destroyed their deer, he conceived that the want of venison might be well supplied by the bodies of young lads and maidens, not exceeding fourteen years of age nor under twelve, so great a number of both sexes in every county being now ready to starve for want of work and service; and these to be disposed of by their parents, if alive, or otherwise by their nearest relations. But with due deference to so excellent a friend and so deserving a patriot, I cannot be altogether in his sentiments; for as to the males, my American acquaintance assured me from frequent experience that their flesh was generally tough and lean, like that of our schoolboys, by continual exercise, and their taste disagreeable; and to fatten them would not answer the charge. Then as to the females, it would, I think with humble submission, be a loss to the public, because they soon would become breeders themselves: and besides, it is not improbable that some scrupulous people might be apt to censure such a practice (although indeed very unjustly) as a little bordering upon cruelty; which, I confess, hath always been with me the strongest objection against any project, how well so ever intended.

But in order to justify my friend, he confessed that this expedient was put 18 into his head by the famous Psalmanazar, a native of the island Formosa, who came from thence to London above twenty years ago, and in conversation told my friend that in his country when any young person happened to be put to death, the executioner sold the carcass to persons of quality as a prime dainty; and that in his time the body of a plump girl of fifteen, who was crucified for an attempt to poison the emperor, was sold to his Imperial Majesty's prime minister of state, and other great mandarins of the court, in joints from the gibbet, at four hundred crowns. Neither indeed can I deny that if the same use were made of several plump young girls in this town, who without one single groat to their fortunes cannot stir abroad without a chair, and appear at the playhouse and assemblies in foreign fineries which they never will pay for, the kingdom would not be the worse.

Some persons of a desponding spirit are in great concern about that vast 19 number of poor people who are aged, diseased, or maimed, and I have been desired to employ my thoughts what course may be taken to ease the nation of so grievous an encumbrance. But I am not in the least pain upon that matter, because it is very well known that they are every day dying and rotting by cold and famine, and filth and vermin, as fast as can be reasonably expected. And as to the younger laborers, they are now in almost as hopeful a condition. They cannot get work, and consequently pine away for want of nourishment to a degree that if at any time they are accidentally hired to common labor, they have not strength to perform it; and thus the country and themselves are happily delivered from the evils to come.

I have too long digressed, and therefore shall return to my subject. I think 20 the advantages by the proposal which I have made are obvious and many, as well as of the highest importance.

For first, as I have already observed, it would greatly lessen the number of 21 Papists, with whom we are yearly overrun, being the principal breeders of the nation as well as our most dangerous enemies; and who stay at home on purpose to deliver the kingdom to the Pretender, hoping to take their advantage by the absence of so many good Protestants, who have chosen rather to leave their country than to stay at home and pay tithes against their conscience to an Episcopal curate.

Secondly, the poorer tenants will have something valuable of their own, 22 which by law may be made liable to distress, and help to pay their landlord's rent, their corn and cattle being already seized and money a thing unknown.

Thirdly, whereas the maintenance of an hundred thousand children, from 23 two years old and upwards, cannot be computed at less than ten shillings a piece per annum, the nation's stock will be thereby increased fifty thousand pounds per annum, besides the profit of a new dish introduced to the tables of all gentlemen of fortune in the kingdom who have any refinement in taste. And the money will circulate among ourselves, the goods being entirely of our own growth and manufacture.

Fourthly, the constant breeders, besides the gain of eight shillings sterling per annum by the sale of their children, will be rid of the charge of maintaining them after the first year.   24

Fifthly, this food would likewise bring great custom to taverns, where the vintners will certainly be so prudent as to procure the best receipts for dressing it to perfection, and consequently have their houses frequented by all the fine gentlemen, who justly value themselves upon their knowledge in good eating; and a skillful cook, who understands how to oblige his guests, will contrive to make it as expensive as they please.   25

Sixthly, this would be a great inducement to marriage, which all wise nations have either encouraged by rewards or enforced by laws and penalties. It would increase the care and tenderness of mothers toward their children, when they were sure of a settlement for life to the poor babes, provided in some sort by the public, to their annual profit instead of expense. We should see an honest emulation among the married women, which of them could bring the fattest child to the market. Men would become as fond of their wives during the time of their pregnancy as they are now of their mares in foal, their cows in calf, or sows when they are ready to farrow; nor offer to beat or kick them (as is too frequent a practice) for fear of a miscarriage.   26

Many other advantages might be enumerated. For instance, the addition of some thousand carcasses in our exportation of barreled beef, the propagation of swine's flesh, and improvement in the art of making good bacon, so much wanted among us by the great destruction of pigs, too frequent at our tables, which are no way comparable in taste or magnificence to a well-grown, fat yearling child, which roasted whole will make a considerable figure at a lord mayor's feast or any other public entertainment. But this and many others I omit, being studious of brevity.   27

Supposing that one thousand families in this city would be constant customers for infants' flesh, besides others who might have it at merry meetings, particularly weddings and christenings, I compute that Dublin would take off annually about twenty thousand carcasses, and the rest of the kingdom (where probably they will be sold somewhat cheaper) the remaining eighty thousand.   28

I can think of no one objection that will possibly be raised against this proposal, unless it should be urged that the number of people will be thereby much lessened in the kingdom. This I freely own, and it was indeed one principal design in offering it to the world. I desire the reader will observe, that I calculate my remedy for this one individual kingdom of Ireland and for no other that ever was, is, or I think ever can be upon earth. Therefore let no man talk to me of other expedients: of taxing our absentees at five shillings a pound: of using neither clothes nor household furniture except what is of our own growth and manufacture: of utterly rejecting the materials and instruments that promote   29 foreign luxury: of curing the expensiveness of pride, vanity, idleness, and gaming in our women: of introducing a vein of parsimony, prudence, and temperance: of learning to love our country, in the want of which we differ even from Laplanders and the inhabitants of Topinamboo: of quitting our animosities and factions, nor acting any longer like the Jews, who were murdering one another at the very moment their city was taken: of being a little cautious not to sell our country and conscience for nothing: of teaching landlords to have at least one degree of mercy toward their tenants: lastly, of putting a spirit of honesty, industry, and skill into our shopkeepers; who, if a resolution could be now taken to buy only our native goods, would immediately unite to cheat and exact upon us in the price, the measure and the goodness, nor could ever yet be brought to make one fair proposal of just dealing, though often and earnestly invited to it.

Therefore I repeat, let no man talk to me of these and the like expedients, till 30 he hath at least some glimpse of hope that there will ever be some hearty and sincere attempt to put them in practice.

But as to myself, having been wearied out for many years with offering 31 vain, idle, visionary thoughts, and at length utterly despairing of success, I fortunately fell upon this proposal, which, as it is wholly new, so it hath something solid and real, of no expense and little trouble, full in our own power, and whereby we can incur no danger in disobliging England. For this kind of commodity will not bear exportation, the flesh being of too tender a consistence to admit a long continuance in salt, although perhaps I could name a country which would be glad to eat up our whole nation without it.

After all, I am not so violently bent upon my own opinion as to reject any 32 offer proposed by wise men, which shall be found equally innocent, cheap, easy, and effectual. But before something of that kind shall be advanced in contradiction to my scheme, and offering a better, I desire the author or authors will be pleased maturely to consider two points. First, as things now stand, how they will be able to find food and raiment for an hundred thousand useless mouths and backs. And secondly, there being a round million of creatures in human figure throughout this kingdom, whose sole subsistence put into a common stock would leave them in debt two millions of pounds sterling, adding those who are beggars by profession to the bulk of farmers, cottagers, and laborers, with their wives and children who are beggars in effect; I desire those politicians who dislike my overture, and may perhaps be so bold to attempt an answer, that they will first ask the parents of these mortals whether they would not at this day think it a great happiness to have been sold for food at a year old in the manner I prescribe, and thereby have avoided such a perpetual scene of misfortunes as they have since gone through by the oppression of landlords, the impossibility of paying rent without money or trade, the want of common sustenance, with neither house nor clothes to cover them from the inclemencies of the weather, and the most inevitable prospect of entailing the like or greater miseries upon their breed forever.

I profess, in the sincerity of my heart, that I have not the least personal in- 33 terest in endeavoring to promote this necessary work, having no other motive than the public good of my country, by advancing our trade, providing for infants, relieving the poor, and giving some pleasure to the rich. I have no children by which I can propose to get a single penny; the youngest being nine years old, and my wife past childbearing.

COMPREHENSION

1. Who is Swift's audience for this essay? Defend your answer.
2. Describe the persona in this essay. How is the unusual narrative personality (as distinguished from Swift's personality) revealed by the author in degrees? How can we tell that the speaker's opinions are not shared by Swift?
3. What are the major propositions behind Swift's modest proposal? What are the minor propositions?

RHETORIC

1. Explain the importance of the word *modest* in the title. What stylistic devices does this "modesty" contrast with?
2. What is the effect of Swift's persistent reference to people as "breeders," "dams," "carcass," and the like? Why does he define *children* in economic terms? Find other words that contribute to this motif.
3. Analyze the purpose of the relatively long introduction, consisting of paragraphs 1 to 7. How does Swift establish his ironic-satiric tone in this initial section?
4. What contrasts and discrepancies are at the heart of Swift's ironic statement in paragraphs 9 and 10? Explain both the subtlety and savagery of the satire in paragraph 12.
5. Paragraphs 13 to 20 develop six advantages of Swift's proposal, while paragraphs 21 to 26 list them in enumerative manner. Analyze the progression of these propositions. What is the effect of the listing? Why is Swift parodying argumentative techniques?
6. How does the author both sustain and suspend the irony in paragraph 29? How is the strategy repeated in paragraph 32? How does the concluding paragraph cap his satiric commentary on human nature?

WRITING

1. Write a modest proposal—on, for example, how to end the drug problem—advancing an absurd proposition through various argumentative techniques.
2. Discuss Swift's social, political, religious, and economic views as they are revealed in the essay.
3. Write a comprehensive critique of America's failure to address the needs of its poor.

CONNECTIONS FOR CRITICAL THINKING

1. Using the essays of Quindlen and Rodriguez, compare the effects of work on human relationships.

2. Compare and contrast the social context and opportunities of the workers in the essay by Rodriguez with the college students in the essay by Klass.

3. Write a definition essay entitled "What Is Work?" Refer to any of the selections in this chapter to substantiate your opinions.

4. Describe the potential effect of the global marketplace as described by Reich on the "visiting father" mentioned by Quindlen.

5. Compare the writings of Swift, Rodriguez, and Reich in terms of the options of those on the lowest rungs of the economic system in Western society.

6. Locate the websites of three major newspapers in three different large cities in America. Review their classified sections, and compare and contrast the types of jobs advertised in the three cities. Do a similar search and comparison for federal and state government jobs.

7. Examine your own college or university's website, and review its philosophy regarding the relationship of college studies to the world of work.

8. Join a newsgroup with a special interest in the global economy. Post a general question to its members, asking whether they agree with Reich's analysis of the changing job market. Collect the responses.

9. Do a Web search using the keywords *immigration* and *employment*. Locate three websites that address the relationship between increased immigration and employment, and compare and contrast these three viewpoints.

10. Monitor and videotape three business news television shows that focus on analysis and commentary. Analyze the discourse of the moderators, hosts, and guests. Explore and discuss whether their use of terminology fits into Cox's perspective of "The Market as God." As an alternative method, review selected business news websites on the Internet, and subject them to the same process.

11. Locate several websites for job seekers, for example, Monster.com. Enter the job classification you are interested in, and compare and contrast the number and types of jobs advertised for three cities. Do a similar search and comparison for federal and state government jobs advertised on the Web.

12. Interview three people who founded small businesses, and compare their experiences with those of Uncle Chul.

13. Select at least five aphorisms from Franklin's essay that have become part of common parlance. Interview 10 college students and ask them to identify the author these aphorisms. Write a report in which you provide data indicating the results of your findings. Reflect on the reasons you believe your interviewees were either able or unable to identify the source of these aphorisms.

14. To what extent is American society guided by a business ethic? For example, do the selections by Benjamin Franklin and Chang-Rae Lee suggest a historical continuum in which Americans have been so preoccupied with

wealth that the quest for money actually becomes a distinguishing mark of the national character? Or when Harvey Cox employs the analogy of the stock market as some divine entity, do you think that the merging of business and religion (what social scientists term the Protestant work ethic) captures a uniquely American trait? Discuss these issues, with specific reference to the selections in this chapter, in an analytical and argumentative essay.

chapter *8*

Philosophy, Ethics, and Religion
What Do We Believe?

You do not have to be an academician in an ivory tower to think about religion and the destiny of humankind or about questions of right and wrong. All of us possess beliefs about human nature and conduct, about "rival conceptions of God" (to use C. S. Lewis's phrase), about standards of behavior and moral duty. In fact, as Robert Coles argues in an essay appearing in this chapter, even children make ethical choices every day and are attuned to the "moral currents and issues in the large society."

Most of us have a system of ethical and religious beliefs, a philosophy of sorts, although it may not be a fully logical and systematic philosophy and we may not be conscious that it determines what we do in everyday life. This system of beliefs and values is transmitted to us by family members, friends, educators, religious figures, and representatives of social groups. Such a philosophical system is not unyielding or unchanging, because our typical conflicts and the choices that we make often force us to test our ethical assumptions and our values. For example, you may believe in nonviolence, but what would you do if someone threatened physical harm to you or a loved one? Or you may oppose the death penalty but encounter an essay that causes you to reassess your position. Our beliefs about nonviolence, capital punishment, abortion, cheating, equality, and so on are often paradoxical and place us in a universe of ethical dilemmas.

Your ability to resolve such dilemmas and make complex ethical decisions depends on your storehouse of knowledge and experience and on how well formulated your philosophy or system of beliefs is. When you know what is truly important in your life, you can make choices and decisions carefully and responsibly. Growing up in a world with competing views on morality often makes these choices that much harder, for constellations of cultures, beliefs, and influences contribute to our own personal development. As Plato observes in his classic "The Allegory of the Cave," the idea of what is truly good and correct never appears without wisdom and effort.

In this context, religion is also intrinsically connected to our sense of morality and ethics. Our personal code of ethics often has a religious grounding. Our religion often determines the way in which we apply our ethics—for instance, it may determine our attitudes toward contraception, equality of the races or the sexes, and evolution. In all instances, competing religious and secular values may force us to make hard decisions about our positions on significant cultural issues.

In one essay in this section, Virginia Woolf contemplates a seemingly insignificant creature—a moth—that tells her (and us) a great deal about life and death. All authors in this chapter seek the essence of the values and ideas that we develop during our brief moment on this planet and that lend meaning and vitality to our lives.

Previewing the Chapter

As you read the essays in this chapter and respond to them in discussion and writing, consider the following questions:

- On what ethical or religious problem or conflict does the author focus?
- Is the author's view of life optimistic or pessimistic? Why?
- Do you agree or disagree with the philosophical or religious perspective that the author adopts?
- Is there a clear solution to the issue the author investigates?
- Does the author present rational arguments or engage in emotional appeals and weak reasoning?
- Does the author approach ethical, theological, and philosophical issues in an objective or in a subjective way?
- How significant is the ethical or philosophical subject addressed by the author?
- What social, political, or racial issues are raised by the author?
- Are there religious dimensions to the essay? If so, how does religion reinforce the author's philosophical inquiry?
- How do these essays encourage you to examine your own attitudes and values? In reading them, what do you discover about your own system of beliefs and the beliefs of society at large?

Classic and Contemporary Images
HOW DO WE VIEW ANGELS AND DEVILS?

Using a Critical Perspective Comment on the composition of each of these works of art. How does each artist present the supernatural beings depicted? What do you notice about the organization of the images? From what angle does the artist approach the depiction? What do the artists have in common? Is the overall impression or effect of each illustration the same or different? Explain.

From: Angels: Messengers of the Gods/Thames & Hudson/Indian Museum, Calcutta.

Angels, supernatural beings who serve as messengers from God, are found in the literature and imagery of Judaism, Christianity, and Islam from ancient times to the present, as in the Islamic painting from India shown here.

In more recent times, the sculptor Jacob Epstein (1880–1959) created a bronze statue of St. Michael for Coventry Cathedral in England. The ancient cathedral at Coventry was destroyed by German bombs in 1940. During the 1950s, a new cathedral was built near the ruins of the old one. With his spear in hand and his wings outstretched, St. Michael stands in triumph over the prone, chained figure of the devil.

Classic and Contemporary Essays

IS SUPERSTITION A SIGN OF WEAKNESS OR STRENGTH?

Although most contemporary individuals who consider themselves "educated" deny any strong influence of superstition in their lives, both Margaret Mead and Letty Cottin Pogrebin suggest in their respective essays that neither contemporary ideas, with their reliance on science, nor higher education, with its focus on rational thinking, insulate us from allowing at least a small amount of superstition into our lives. Mead discounts the notion that superstition is relegated to "primitive" societies or to the uneducated who have not been enlightened by a firm grounding in empiricism. The famed anthropologist suggests that we need superstition to provide coherence to our lives when other forms of belief and thought are not competent to satisfy us. For example, in facing the unknown, we may turn to superstition as a welcome friend. How many of your fellow schoolmates, for example, will cross their fingers before an exam or keep a good-luck charm attached to their computer? Simply put, very few of us are so secure that we can rely on our own inner fortitude to ward off occasional fears or feelings of helplessness. Superstition, therefore, provides a framework to maintain a private sanctuary against the unknown. Pogrebin admits to being a "very rational person" who also "happen[s] to be superstitious." Although the particular rituals that inform her superstition were learned from her mother, who used them as a means of "imposing order," the function of superstition in her own life, Pogrebin claims, is to maintain coherence with the past: to feel the connection between herself and her mother. In other words, like Mead, Pogrebin contends superstition helps us maintain a sense of protection in an environment where we do not have complete control. By keeping the same rituals as her mother, Pogrebin senses her mother's protection. Does this mean that humans are flawed, weak creatures? If we consider the vicissitudes and uncertainties of modern life, perhaps the tendency of humans to have a bit of superstition in their worldview is a sign of intelligence.

New Superstitions for Old

Margaret Mead

Margaret Mead (1901–1979), famed American anthropologist, was curator of ethnology at the American Museum of Natural History and a professor at Columbia University. Her field expeditions to Samoa, New Guinea, and Bali in the 1920s and 1930s produced several major studies, notably Coming of Age in Samoa *(1928),* Growing Up in New Guinea *(1930), and* Sex and Temperament in Three Primitive Societies *(1935). In this essay, first published in* A Way of Seeing *(1970), Mead discusses the role that superstition plays in our daily life.*

Once in a while there is a day when everything seems to run smoothly and even   1
the riskiest venture comes out exactly right. You exclaim, "This is my lucky day!" Then as an afterthought you say, "Knock on wood!" Of course, you do not really believe that knocking on wood will ward off danger. Still, boasting about your own good luck gives you a slightly uneasy feeling—and you carry out the little protective ritual. If someone challenged you at that moment, you would probably say, "Oh, that's nothing. Just an old superstition."

But when you come to think about it, what is superstition?   2

In the contemporary world most people treat old folk beliefs as superstitions—the belief, for instance, that there are lucky and unlucky days or numbers, that future events can be read from omens, that there are protective charms or that what happens can be influenced by casting spells. We have excluded magic from our current world view, for we know that natural events have natural causes.   3

In a religious context, where truths cannot be demonstrated, we accept   4
them as a matter of faith. Superstitions, however, belong to the category of beliefs, practices and ways of thinking that have been discarded because they are inconsistent with scientific knowledge. It is easy to say that other people are superstitious because they believe what we regard to be untrue. "Superstition" used in that sense is a derogatory term for the beliefs of other people that we do not share. But there is more to it than that. For superstitions lead a kind of half life in a twilight world where, sometimes, we partly suspend our disbelief and act as if magic worked.

Actually, almost every day, even in the most sophisticated home, something   5
is likely to happen that evokes the memory of some old folk belief. The salt spills. A knife falls to the floor. Your nose tickles. Then perhaps, with a slightly embarrassed smile, the person who spilled the salt tosses a pinch over his left shoulder. Or someone recites the old rhyme, "Knife falls, gentleman calls." Or as you rub your nose you think, That means a letter. I wonder who's writing? No one takes these small responses very seriously or gives them more than a

passing thought. Sometimes people will preface one of these ritual acts— walking around instead of under a ladder or hastily closing an umbrella that has been opened inside a house—with such remarks as "I remember my great-aunt used to . . ." or "Germans used to say you ought not . . ." And then, having placed the belief at some distance away in time or space, they carry out the ritual.

Everyone also remembers a few of the observances of childhood—wishing 6 on the first star; looking at the new moon over the right shoulder; avoiding the cracks in the sidewalk on the way to school while chanting, "Step on a crack, break your mother's back"; wishing on white horses, on loads of hay, on covered bridges, on red cars; saying quickly, "Bread-and-butter" when a post or a tree separated you from the friend you were walking with. The adult may not actually recite the formula "Star light, star bright . . ." and may not quite turn to look at the new moon, but his mood is tempered by a little of the old thrill that came when the observance was still freighted with magic.

Superstition can also be used with another meaning. When I discuss the re- 7 ligious beliefs of other peoples, especially primitive peoples, I am often asked, "Do they really have a religion, or is it all just superstition?" The point of contrast here is not between a scientific and a magical view of the world but between the clear, theologically defensible religious beliefs of members of civilized societies and what we regard as the false and childish views of the heathen who "bow down to wood and stone." Within the civilized religions, however, where membership includes believers who are educated and urbane and others who are ignorant and simple, one always finds traditions and practices that the more sophisticated will dismiss offhand as "just superstition" but that guide the steps of those who live by older ways. Mostly these are very ancient beliefs, some handed on from one religion to another and carried from country to country around the world.

Very commonly, people associate superstition with the past, with very old 8 ways of thinking that have been supplanted by modern knowledge. But new superstitions are continually coming into being and flourishing in our society. Listening to mothers in the park in the 1930s, one heard them say, "Now, don't you run out into the sun, or Polio will get you." In the 1940's elderly people explained to one another in tones of resignation, "It was the Virus that got him down." And every year the cosmetics industry offers us new magic—cures for baldness, lotions that will give every woman radiant skin, hair coloring that will restore to the middle-aged the charm and romance of youth—results that are promised if we will just follow the simple directions. Families and individuals also have their cherished, private superstitions. You must leave by the back door when you are going on a journey, or you must wear a green dress when you are taking an examination. It is a kind of joke, of course, but it makes you feel safe.

These old half-beliefs and new half-beliefs reflect the keenness of our wish 9 to have something come true or to prevent something bad from happening. We do not always recognize new superstitions for what they are, and we still follow the old ones because someone's faith long ago matches our contemporary hopes and fears. In the past people "knew" that a black cat crossing one's path was a bad omen, and they turned back home. Today we are fearful of taking a journey and would give anything to turn back—and then we notice a black cat running across the road in front of us.

Child psychologists recognize the value of the toy a child holds in his hand 10 at bedtime. It is different from his thumb, with which he can close himself in from the rest of the world, and it is different from the real world to which he is learning to relate himself. Psychologists call these toys—these furry animals and old, cozy baby blankets—"transitional objects"; that is, objects that help the child move back and forth between the exactions of everyday life and the world of wish and dream.

Superstitions have some of the qualities of these transitional objects. They 11 help people pass between the areas of life where what happens has to be accepted without proof and the areas where sequences of events are explicable in terms of cause and effect, based on knowledge. Bacteria and viruses that cause sickness have been identified; the cause of symptoms can be diagnosed and a rational course of treatment prescribed. Magical charms no longer are needed to treat the sick; modern medicine has brought the whole sequence of events into the secular world. But people often act as if this change had not taken place. Laymen still treat germs as if they were invisible, malign spirits, and physicians sometimes prescribe antibiotics as if they were magic substances.

Over time, more and more of life has become subject to the controls of 12 knowledge. However, this is never a one-way process. Scientific investigation is continually increasing our knowledge. But if we are to make good use of this knowledge, we must not only rid our minds of old, superseded beliefs and fragments of magical practice, but also recognize new superstitions for what they are. Both are generated by our wishes, our fears and our feeling of helplessness in difficult situations.

Civilized peoples are not alone in having grasped the idea of superstitions—beliefs and practices that are superseded but that still may evoke the different worlds in which we live—the sacred, the secular and the scientific. They allow us to keep a private world also, where, smiling a little, we can banish danger with a gesture and summon luck with a rhyme, make the sun shine in spite of storm clouds, force the stranger to do our bidding, keep an enemy at bay and straighten the paths of those we love.

COMPREHENSION

1. Explain in your own words the religious context for this essay.
2. What point is Mead making about superstition in modern life? Where does she state her main idea?
3. Where does Mead define *superstition?* How does it differ from folk beliefs?

RHETORIC

1. Explain what Mead means by "transitional objects." Why does she mention them?

2. Discuss the author's use of the pronouns *we* and *us* in the conclusion. Why does she state the conclusion in personal terms?
3. How does Mead use definition to differentiate *superstition* from *faith?* Explain the logic behind her distinction.
4. How does Mead use classification to describe the "worlds in which we live"? What are these worlds? What examples does she give of superstition in each of these worlds?
5. Look at paragraph 10. What is the purpose of this example? How does it figure in the context of Mead's essay?
6. Discuss the term "theologically defensible" as used in paragraph 7. Does Mead support this concept by example or evidence? Why?

WRITING

1. This article was published in 1966. Have we made any progress toward banishing superstition since then? Will we ever live in a culture free of superstition? Do we want to?
2. Write an essay about beliefs you once held that you have since abandoned. Why did you abandon them? What was the practical result?
3. Select a saying or phrase based in superstition or folk belief that you or a friend is fond of. Analyze its appeal.

Superstitious Minds

Letty Cottin Pogrebin

Letty Cottin Pogrebin (b. 1939) is deeply committed to women's issues, family politics, and the nonsexist rearing and education of children. A native of New York, she graduated from Brandeis University and from 1971 to 1987 was the editor of Ms. *magazine, for which she remains a contributing editor. She has also contributed to such publications as* The New York Times *and* The Nation *and has written a number of books, including* Among Friends *(1986);* Debra Golda and Me: Being Female and Jewish in America *(1991); and* Getting Over Getting Older *(1996). Pogrebin lectures frequently and is a founder of the Women's Political Caucus as well as president of the Authors' Guild. In the following essay, she reminisces about her fearful, superstitious mother, whom she understands much better since becoming a mother herself.*

I am a very rational person. I tend to trust reason more than feeling. But I also ₁ happen to be superstitious—in my fashion. Black cats and rabbits' feet hold no power for me. My superstitions are my mother's superstitions, the amulets and incantations she learned from her mother and taught me.

I don't mean to suggest that I grew up in an occult atmosphere. On the con- 2 trary, my mother desperately wanted me to rise above her immigrant ways and become an educated American. She tried to hide her superstitions, but I came to know them all: Slap a girl's cheeks when she first gets her period. Never take a picture of a pregnant woman. Knock wood when speaking about your good fortune. Eat the ends of bread if you want to have a boy. Don't leave a bride alone on her wedding day.

When I was growing up, my mother often would tiptoe in after I seemed to 3 be asleep and kiss my forehead three times, making odd noises that sounded like a cross between sucking and spitting. One night I opened my eyes and demanded an explanation. Embarrassed, she told me she was excising the "Evil Eye"—in case I had attracted its attention that day by being especially wonderful. She believed her kisses could suck out any envy or ill will that those less fortunate may have directed at her child.

By the time I was in my teens, I was almost on speaking terms with the Evil 4 Eye, a jealous spirit that kept track of those who had "too much" happiness and zapped them with sickness and misery to even the score. To guard against his mischief, my mother practiced rituals of interference. evasion, deference, and above all, avoidance of situations where the Evil Eye might feel at home.

This is why I wasn't allowed to attend funerals. This is also why my mother 5 hated to mend my clothes while I was wearing them. The only garment one should properly get sewn *into* is a shroud. To ensure that the Evil Eye did not confuse my pinafore with a burial outfit, my mother insisted that I chew a thread while she sewed, thus proving myself very much alive. Outwitting the Evil Eye also accounted for her closing the window shades above my bed whenever there was a full moon. The moon should only shine on cemeteries, you see; the living need protection from the spirits.

Because we were dealing with a deadly force, I also wasn't supposed to say 6 any words associated with mortality. This was hard for a 12-year-old who punctuated every anecdote with the verb "to die," as in "You'll die when you hear this!" or "If I don't get home by ten, I'm dead." I managed to avoid using such expressions in the presence of my mother until the day my parents brought home a painting I hated and we were arguing about whether it should be displayed on our walls. Unthinking, I pressed my point with a melodramatic idiom: "That picture will hang over my dead body!" Without a word, my mother grabbed a knife and slashed the canvas to shreds.

I understand all this now. My mother emigrated in 1907 from a small Hun- 7 garian village. The oldest of seven children, she had to go out to work before she finished the eighth grade. Experience taught her that life was unpredictable and often incomprehensible. Just as an athlete keeps wearing the same T-shirt in every game to prolong a winning streak, my mother's superstitions gave her a means of imposing order on a chaotic system. Her desire to control the fates sprung from the same helplessness that makes the San Francisco 49ers' defensive more superstitious than its offensive team. Psychologists speculate this is because the defense has less control; they don't have the ball.

Women like my mother never had the ball. She died when I was 15, leaving 8 me with deep regrets for what she might have been—and a growing understanding of who she was. *Superstitious* is one of the things she was. I wish I had a million sharp recollections of her, but when you don't expect someone to die, you don't store up enough memories. Ironically, her mystical practices are among the clearest impressions she left behind. In honor of this matrilineal heritage—and to symbolize my mother's effort to control her life as I in my way try to find order in mine—knock on wood and I do not let the moon shine on those I love. My children laugh at me, but they understand that these tiny rituals have helped keep my mother alive in my mind.

A year ago, I awoke in the night and realized that my son's window blinds 9 had been removed for repair. Smiling at my own compulsion, I got a bed sheet to tack up against the moonlight and I opened his bedroom door. What I saw brought tears to my eyes. There, hopelessly askew, was a blanket my son, then 18, had taped to his window like a curtain.

My mother never lived to know David, but he knew she would not want 10 the moon to shine upon him as he slept.

COMPREHENSION

1. What is the function of superstition in the writer's life? What purpose did it serve in her mother's life?
2. What was Pogrebin's reaction to her mother's behavior while she was growing up? How does the adult feel?
3. How does the writer use superstitions now as an adult? Has she passed on these beliefs to her children? Explain.

RHETORIC

1. Examine Pogrebin's first sentence. How does it prepare the reader for the content of the essay? How does its simplicity add to its force?
2. How do the accumulated examples in paragraph 2 illustrate the point of the paragraph?
3. What is the writer's tone? Justify your answer.
4. What is the point of paragraph 7? How does the metaphor work to support Pogrebin's point?
5. What is the purpose of the essay? Where does it become apparent? How do the other paragraphs reinforce it?
6. Comment on the author's final sentence. What effect does it have on the reader? How does it help to hold the essay together?

WRITING

1. Children are often annoyed or embarrassed by their parents' behavior or beliefs. Write an essay describing something your parents repeatedly said or did that caused you discomfort or confusion. Include how you now feel about their actions and any insight you may have since gained about their motives or feelings.
2. Write an essay about superstition. Consider the meaning of the word. What connection, if any, does it have with religion? How do superstitions affect the people who believe in them? Why do they believe? What is the role of superstition in your family? Provide examples of superstitions.
3. Write an essay in which you consider how your parents raised you—the values, opinions, beliefs they instilled in you. Would you want to pass these on to your children? Why, or why not?

Classic and Contemporary: Questions for Comparison

1. Mead presents her argument regarding the benefits of superstition through an anthropological analysis of the subject, while Pogrebin employs a more personal approach, focusing on the role of superstition in her own life. What are the merits of each approach? Do the two essays together contribute to a greater understanding of the nature of superstition than either one alone?
2. Both Mead and Pogrebin discuss the value of superstition in childhood. Why is childhood in particular a time in life when superstition can prove valuable? What is Mead's answer to this issue? How does it differ from Pogrebin's?
3. The tone of Mead's essay is objective, scientific, and critical. In addition, she never refers to personal experience, and we can assume she is writing from the perspective of someone who needs to maintain her professional status. Why would these factors influence her decision to contour her style so that she seems an observer of superstition rather than someone with superstitious leanings? On the other hand, why would Pogrebin choose to "personalize" her essay by referring to personal experience? Are these choices matters of style, audience, purpose, or a combination of these?
4. Mead seems more concerned with explicating her subject matter in academic terms. Note how she articulates the meaning of *folk beliefs, religion*, and *transitional objects*. How would you characterize the differences between an academically oriented argument such as Mead's and one intended for a more general audience such as Pogrebin's?

I Listen to My Parents and I Wonder What They Believe

Robert Coles

Robert Coles (b. 1929), author and psychologist, won the Pulitzer Prize in general nonfiction for volumes 1 and 2 of Children of Crisis, *in which he examines with compassion and intelligence the effects of the controversy over integration on children in the South. Walker Percy praised Coles because he "spends his time listening to people and trying to understand them." In its final form,* Children of Crisis *has five volumes, and Coles has widened its focus to include the children of the wealthy and the poor, the exploited and the exploiters. In collaboration with Jane Coles, he completed* Women in Crisis II *(1980). Below, Coles demonstrates his capacity to listen to and to understand children.*

Not so long ago children were looked upon in a sentimental fashion as "angels,"   1
or as "innocents." Today, thanks to Freud and his followers, boys and girls are understood to have complicated inner lives; to feel love, hate, envy and rivalry in various and subtle mixtures; to be eager participants in the sexual and emotional politics of the home, neighborhood and school. Yet some of us parents still cling to the notion of childhood innocence in another way. We do not see that our children also make ethical decisions every day in their own lives, or realize how attuned they may be to moral currents and issues in the larger society.

In Appalachia I heard a girl of eight whose father owns coal fields (and gas   2
stations, a department store and much timberland) wonder about "life" one day: "I'll be walking to the school bus, and I'll ask myself why there's some who are poor and their daddies can't find a job, and there's some who are lucky like me. Last month there was an explosion in a mine my daddy owns, and everyone became upset. Two miners got killed. My daddy said it was their own fault, because they'll be working and they get careless. When my mother asked if there was anything wrong with the safety down in the mine, he told her no and she shouldn't ask questions like that. Then the Government people came and they said it was the owner's fault—Daddy's. But he has a lawyer and the lawyer is fighting the Government and the union. In school, kids ask me what I think, and I sure do feel sorry for the two miners and so does my mother—I know that. She told me it's just not a fair world and you have to remember that. Of course, there's no one who can be sure there won't be trouble; like my daddy says, the rain falls on the just and the unjust. My brother is only six and he asked Daddy awhile back who are the 'just' and the 'unjust,' and Daddy said there are people who work hard and they live good lives, and there are lazy people and they're always trying to sponge off others. But I guess you have to feel sorry for anyone who has a lot of trouble, because it's poured-down, heavy rain."

Listening, one begins to realize that an elementary-school child is no 3
stranger to moral reflection—and to ethical conflict. This girl was torn between
her loyalty to her particular background, its values and assumptions, and to a
larger affiliation—her membership in the nation, the world. As a human being
whose parents were kind and decent to her, she was inclined to be thoughtful
and sensitive with respect to others, no matter what their work or position in
society. But her father was among other things a mineowner, and she had already learned to shape her concerns to suit that fact of life. The result: a moral
oscillation of sorts, first toward nameless others all over the world and then toward her own family. As the girl put it later, when she was a year older: "You
should try to have 'good thoughts' about everyone, the minister says, and our
teacher says that too. But you should honor your father and mother most of all;
that's why you should find out what they think and then sort of copy them. But
sometimes you're not sure if you're on the right track."

Sort of copy them. There could be worse descriptions of how children acquire 4
moral values. In fact, the girl understood how girls and boys all over the world
"sort of" develop attitudes of what is right and wrong, ideas of who the just and
the unjust are. And they also struggle hard and long, and not always with success, to find out where the "right track" starts and ends. Children need encouragement or assistance as they wage that struggle.

In home after home that I have visited, and in many classrooms, I have met 5
children who not only are growing emotionally and intellectually but also are
trying to make sense of the world morally. That is to say, they are asking themselves and others about issues of fair play, justice, liberty, equality. Those last
words are abstractions, of course—the stuff of college term papers. And there
are, one has to repeat, those in psychology and psychiatry who would deny elementary-school children access to that "higher level" of moral reflection. But
any parent who has listened closely to his or her child knows that girls and boys
are capable of wondering about matters of morality, and knows too that often it
is their grown-up protectors (parents, relatives, teachers, neighbors) who are
made uncomfortable by the so-called "innocent" nature of the questions children may ask or the statements they may make. Often enough the issue is not
the moral capacity of children but the default of us parents who fail to respond
to inquiries put to us by our daughters and sons—and fail to set moral standards for both ourselves and our children.

Do's and don't's are, of course, pressed upon many of our girls and boys. 6
But a moral education is something more than a series of rules handed down,
and in our time one cannot assume that every parent feels able—sure enough of
her own or his own actual beliefs and values—to make even an initial explanatory and disciplinary effect toward a moral education. Furthermore, for many
of us parents these days it is a child's emotional life that preoccupies us.

In 1963, when I was studying school desegregation in the South, I had ex- 7
tended conversations with Black and white elementary-school children caught up
in a dramatic moment of historical change. For longer than I care to remember,
I concentrated on possible psychiatric troubles, on how a given child was managing under circumstances of extreme stress, on how I could be of help—with

"support," with reassurance, with a helpful psychological observation or interpretation. In many instances I was off the mark. These children weren't "patients"; they weren't even complaining. They were worried, all right, and often enough they had things to say that were substantive—that had to do not so much with troubled emotions as with questions of right and wrong in the real-life dramas taking place in their worlds.

Here is a nine-year-old white boy, the son of ardent segregationists, telling ₈ me about his sense of what desegregation meant to Louisiana in the 1960s: "They told us it wouldn't happen—never. My daddy said none of us white people would go into schools with the colored. But then it did happen, and when I went to school the first day I didn't know what would go on. Would the school stay open or would it close up? We didn't know what to do; the teacher kept telling us that we should be good and obey the law, but my daddy said the law was wrong. Then my mother said she wanted me in school even if there were some colored kids there. She said if we all stayed home she'd be a 'nervous wreck.' So I went.

"After a while I saw that the colored weren't so bad. I saw that there are dif- ₉ ferent kinds of colored people, just like with us whites. There was one of the colored who was nice, a boy who smiled, and he played real good. There was another one, a boy, who wouldn't talk with anyone. I don't know if it's right that we all be in the same school. Maybe it isn't right. My sister is starting school next year, and she says she doesn't care if there's 'mixing of the races.' She says they told her in Sunday school that everyone is a child of God, and then a kid asked if that goes for the colored too and the teacher said yes, she thought so. My daddy said that it's true, God made everyone—but that doesn't mean we all have to be living together under the same roof in the home or the school. But my mother said we'll never know what God wants of us but we have to try to read His mind, and that's why we pray. So when I say my prayers I ask God to tell me what's the right thing to do. In school I try to say hello to the colored, because they're kids, and you can't be mean or you'll be 'doing wrong,' like my grandmother says."

Children aren't usually long-winded in the moral discussions they have ₁₀ with one another or with adults, and in quoting this boy I have pulled together comments he made to me in the course of several days. But everything he said was of interest to me. I was interested in the boy's changing racial attitudes. It was clear he was trying to find a coherent, sensible moral position too. It was also borne in on me that if one spends days, weeks in a given home, it is hard to escape a particular moral climate just as significant as the psychological one.

In many homes parents establish moral assumptions, mandates, priorities. ₁₁ They teach children what to believe in, what not to believe in. They teach children what is permissible or not permissible—and why. They may summon up the Bible, the flag, history, novels, aphorisms, philosophical or political sayings, personal memories—all in an effort to teach children how to behave, what and whom to respect and for which reasons. Or they may neglect to do so, and in so doing teach their children *that*—a moral abdication, of sorts—and in this way fail their children. Children need and long for words of moral advice, instruction, warning, as much as they need words of affirmation or criticism from their parents about other matters. They must learn how to dress and what to wear, how to eat and what to eat; and they must also learn how to behave under X or Y or Z conditions, and why.

All the time, in 20 years of working with poor children and rich children,   12
Black children and white children, children from rural areas and urban areas and in every region of this county, I have heard questions—thoroughly intelligent and discerning questions—about social and historical matters, about personal behavior, and so on. But most striking is the fact that almost all those questions, in one way or another, are moral in nature: Why did the Pilgrims leave England? Why didn't they just stay and agree to do what the king wanted them to do? . . . Should you try to share all you've got or should you save a lot for yourself? . . . What do you do when you see others fighting—do you try to break up the fight, do you stand by and watch or do you leave as fast as you can? . . . Is it right that some people haven't got enough to eat? . . . I see other kids cheating and I wish I could copy the answers too; but I won't cheat, though sometimes I feel I'd like to and I get all mixed up. I go home and talk with my parents, and I ask them what should you do if you see kids cheating—pay no attention, or report the kids or do the same thing they are doing?

Those are examples of children's concerns—and surely millions of Ameri-   13
can parents have heard versions of them. Have the various "experts" on childhood stressed strongly enough the importance of such questions—and the importance of the hunger we all have, no matter what our age or background, to examine what we believe in, are willing to stand up for, and what we are determined to ask, likewise, of our children?

Children not only need our understanding of their complicated emotional   14
lives; they also need a constant regard for the moral issues that come their way as soon as they are old enough to play with others and take part in the politics of the nursery, the back yard and the schoolroom. They need to be told what they must do and what they must not do. They need control over themselves and a sense of what others are entitled to from them—cooperation, thoughtfulness, an attentive ear and eye. They need discipline not only to tame their excesses of emotion but discipline also connected to stated and clarified moral values. They need, in other words, something to believe in that is larger than their own appetites and urges and, yes, bigger than their "psychological drives." They need a larger view of the world, a moral context, as it were—a faith that addresses itself to the meaning of this life we all live and, soon enough, let go of.

Yes, it is time for us parents to begin to look more closely at what ideas our   15
children have about the world; and it would be well to do so before they become teenagers and young adults and begin to remind us, as often happens, of how little attention we did pay to their moral development. Perhaps a nine-year-old girl from a well-off suburban home in Texas put it better than anyone else I've met:

I listen to my parents, and I wonder what they believe in more than anything else. I asked my mom and my daddy once: What's the thing that means most to you? They said they didn't know but I shouldn't worry my head too hard with questions like that. So I asked my best friend, and she said she wonders if there's a God and how do you know Him and what does He want you to do— I mean, when you're in school or out playing with your friends. They talk about God in church, but is it only in church that He's there and keeping an eye on you? I saw a kid steal in a store, and I know her father has a lot of money—because I hear my daddy talk. But stealing's wrong. My mother said she's a 'sick girl,' but it's still wrong what she did. Don't you think?

There was more—much more—in the course of the months I came to know   16
that child and her parents and their neighbors. But those observations and questions—a "mere child's"—reminded me unforgettably of the aching hunger for firm ethical principles that so many of us feel. Ought we not begin thinking about this need? Ought we not all be asking ourselves more intently what standards we live by—and how we can satisfy our children's hunger for moral values?

COMPREHENSION

1. How does the author's title capture the substance of his essay? What is his thesis?
2. According to Coles, why do parents have difficulty explaining ethics to their children? On what aspects of their children's development do they tend to concentrate? Why?
3. There is an implied contrast between mothers' and fathers' attitudes toward morality in Coles's essay. Explain this contrast, and cite examples for your explanation.

RHETORIC

1. What point of view does Coles use here? How does that viewpoint affect the tone of the essay?
2. Compare Coles's sentence structure with the sentence structure of the children he quotes. How do they differ?
3. Does this essay present an inductive or a deductive argument? Give evidence for your answer.
4. How does paragraph 13 differ from paragraphs 3, 10, and 16? How do all four paragraphs contribute to the development of the essay?
5. Explain the line of reasoning in the first paragraph. Why does Coles allude to Freud? How is that allusion related to the final sentence of the paragraph?
6. What paragraphs constitute the conclusion of the essay? Why? How do they summarize Coles's argument?

WRITING

1. Coles asserts the need for clear ethical values. How have your parents provided such values? What kind of values will you give your children? Answer these questions in a brief expository essay.
2. Write an essay describing conflict between your parents' ethical views and
your own.
3. Gather evidence, from conversations with your friends and relatives, about
an ethical issue such as poverty, world starvation, abortion, or capital punishment. Incorporate their opinions in your essay through direct and indirect quotation.

What Really Ails America

William J. Bennett

*William J. Bennett was born in 1943 and grew up in Brooklyn, New York. He re-
ceived a doctorate in political philosophy from the University of Texas and a law degree
from Harvard University. He served as secretary of education and director of the National Endowment for the Humanities under President Reagan and as director of the
Office of National Drug Control Policy under President Bush. He is a senior editor at
the magazine* National Review *and a fellow at the Heritage Foundation. In 1993, he
published* The Book of Virtues: A Treasury of Great Moral Stories, *which became a
best-seller. He often criticizes what he perceives to be a growing amorality in our society.*

A few months ago I lunched with a friend who now lives in Asia. During our 1
conversation the topic turned to America as seen through the eyes of foreigners.
My friend had observed that while the world still regards the United States as
the leading economic and military power on earth, this same world no longer
beholds us with the moral respect it once did, as a "shining city on a hill." Instead, it sees a society in decline.

Recently, a Washington, D.C., cabdriver—a graduate student from Africa— 2
told me that when he receives his degree, he is returning to his homeland. His
reason? He doesn't want his children to grow up in a country where his daughter will be an "easy target" for young men and where his son might also be a
target for violence at the hands of other young males. "It is more civilized where
I come from," he said.

Last year an article in the *Washington Post* described how exchange students 3
adopt the lifestyle of American teens. Paulina, a Polish high-school student
studying in the United States, said that when she first came here she was
amazed at the way teenagers spent their time. "In Warsaw, we would come

home after school, eat with our parents and then do four or five hours of home-work. Now, I go to Pizza Hut and watch TV and do less work in school. I can tell it is not a good thing to get used to."

I have an instinctive aversion to foreigners harshly judging my nation; yet,   4
I must concede that much of what they say is true. Something has gone wrong with us.

Yes, there are families, schools, churches and neighborhoods that work. But   5
there is a lot less virtue than there ought to be.

Last year I compiled *The Index of Leading Cultural Indicators,* a statistical por-   6
trait of American behavioral trends of the past three decades. Among the find-ings: Since 1960, while the gross domestic product has nearly tripled, violent crime has increased at least 560 percent. Divorces have more than doubled. The percentage of children in single-parent homes has tripled. And by the end of the decade 40 percent of all American births and 80 percent of minority births will occur out of wedlock.

These are not good things to get used to.   7

The United States leads the industrialized world in murder, rape and vio-   8
lent crime. At the same time, our elementary-school students rank at or near the bottom in tests of math and science skills. Since 1960, average SAT scores in our high schools have dropped 75 points.

In 1940, teachers identified the top problems in America's schools as: talk-   9
ing out of turn, chewing gum, making noise and running in the hall. In 1990, teachers listed drugs, alcohol, pregnancy, suicide, rape and assault.

These are not good things to get used to, either.   10

There is a coarseness, a callousness and a cynicism to our era. The worst of   11
it has to do with our children. Our culture seems almost dedicated to the cor-ruption of the young.

Last year, Snoop Doggy Dogg, indicted for murder, saw his rap album   12
"Doggystyle," which celebrates marijuana use and the degradation of women, debut at No. 1 on the pop chart. What will happen when young boys who grow up on mean streets, without fathers in their lives, are constantly exposed to such music?

On television, indecent exposure is celebrated by all ages as a virtue. There   13
was a time when personal failures, subliminal desires and perverse tastes were accompanied by guilt, or at least silence. Today they are tickets to appear as guests on talk shows. In one recent two-week period, these shows featured cross-dressing couples, a three-way love affair, a man who fools women into thinking he is using a condom during sex, and prostitutes who love their jobs. These shows present a two-edged problem: people want to expose themselves, and other people want to watch.

We have become inured to the cultural rot that is setting in. People are los-   14
ing their capacity for shock, disgust and outrage. During the 1992 Los Angeles riots, Damian Williams was filmed crushing an innocent man's skull with a brick, while Henry Watson held the victim down. When Williams was finished, he did a victory dance. Watson and Williams's lawyers then built a legal defense on the premise that people cannot be held accountable for getting caught up in

mob violence. ("I guess maybe they were in the wrong place at the wrong time," one juror told *The New York Times*.) When these men were acquitted on most counts, the sound you heard throughout the land was not outrage, but relief.

This is not a good thing to get used to.   15

What's to blame for this change? The hard fact is that it was not something 16 done to us; it is something we have done to ourselves. Thoughtful people have pointed to materialism, an overly permissive society, or the legacy of the 1960s. There is truth in almost all these accounts. But in my view our real crisis is spiritual, a corruption of the heart.

The ancients called our problem acedia, an aversion to spiritual things and 17 an undue concern for the external and the worldly. Acedia also is the seventh capital sin—sloth—but it does not mean mere laziness. The slothful heart is steeped in the worldly and carnal, hates the spiritual and wants to be free of its demands.

When the novelist Walker Percy was asked what concerned him most about 18 America's future, he answered, "Probably the fear of seeing America, with all its great strength and beauty and freedom ... gradually subside into decay through default and be defeated, not by the communist movement, but from within, from weariness, boredom, cynicism, greed and in the end helplessness before its great problems."

I realize this is a tough indictment. If my diagnosis is wrong, then why, 19 amid our economic prosperity and military security, do almost 70 percent of the public say we are off track? I submit that only when we turn to the right things—enduring, noble, spiritual things—will life get better.

During the last decade of the 20th century, there is a disturbing reluctance 20 to talk seriously about matters spiritual and religious. We have become used to not talking about the things that matter most. One will often hear that religious faith is a private matter. But whatever your faith—or even if you have none at all—it is a fact that when millions of people stop believing in God, enormous public consequences follow. Dostoyevsky reminded us in *The Brothers Karamazov* that "if God does not exist, everything is permissible." We are now seeing "everything."

What can be done? For one, we must once again connect public policies to 21 our deepest beliefs. Right now we say one thing and do another.

- We *say* we want law and order, but we allow violent criminals to return to 22 the streets.
- We *say* we want to stop illegitimacy, but we subsidize behavior that leads to 23 it.
- We *say* we want to discourage teenage sex, but educators across America 24 treat teenagers as if they were young animals in heat, and are more eager to dispense condoms than moral guidance.
- We *say* we want more families to stay together, but we make divorce easier 25 to attain.
- We *say* we want a colorblind society, but we continue to count people by 26 race and skin pigment.

Furthermore, America desperately needs to recover the purpose of educa- 27
tion, which is to provide for the intellectual *and* moral education of the young.
Plato made the point that good education makes good men, and good men act
nobly.

Until a quarter-century or so ago, this time-honored belief virtually went 28
unchallenged. But having departed from it, we are now reaping the whirlwind.
We say we desire more civility and responsibility from our children, but many
schools refuse to teach right and wrong. And so we talk about "skills facilita-
tion," "self-esteem" and being "comfortable with ourselves."

Most important, we must return religion to its proper place. Religion pro- 29
vides us with moral bearings, and the solution to our chief problem of spiritual
impoverishment depends on spiritual renewal. The surrendering of strong beliefs, in our private and public lives, has demoralized society.

Today, much of society ridicules and mocks those who are serious about 30
their faith. America's only respectable form of bigotry is bigotry against religious people. And the only reason for hatred of religion is that it forces us to
confront matters many would prefer to ignore.

Nobel Prize-winning author William Faulkner once declared, "I decline to 31
accept the end of man." Man will prevail because, as Faulkner said, he alone
among creatures "has a soul, a spirit capable of compassion and sacrifice and
endurance."

In our time, we have seen America make enormous gains—a standard of 32
living unimagined 50 years ago, with extraordinary advances in medicine, science and technology. Life expectancy has increased by more than 20 years in the
past seven decades. Opportunity has been extended to those who were once denied it. And, of course, America prevailed in our "long, twilight struggle"
against communism.

Today we must carry on a new struggle for the country we love. We must 33
push hard against an age that is pushing hard against us. If we have full employment and greater economic growth—if we have cities of gold and al-
abaster—but our children have not learned how to walk in goodness, justice
and mercy, then the American experiment, no matter how gilded, will have
failed.

Do not surrender. Get mad. Get in the fight.   34

COMPREHENSION

1. In one sentence, summarize what Bennett believes to be the major factor
   that "ails America." Where in the essay does Bennett most clearly express
   his general thesis?
2. In paragraph 11, the author states, "Our culture seems almost dedicated to
   the corruption of the young." What does he mean by the word *culture,* and
   what does he mean by the term *the young?*

3. What is the significance of using the word *really* in the title? How would the connotation of the title have changed if the word had not been included?
4. The author states, "The ancients called our problem acedia." To whom does the term *ancients* refer?

RHETORIC

1. The first three paragraphs include anecdotes. How does the juxtaposition of these anecdotes serve to benefit Bennett's argument that "what ails America" is pervasive?
2. What information does the author provide to directly or indirectly suggest that he is an authority on the essay's subject matter?
3. Bennett uses a one-sentence paragraph three times in the essay nearly verbatim. Locate the three sentences. What is their rhetorical effect, and how do they contribute toward asserting the author's polemical style?
4. The author uses the generic "we" in describing America's troubles; for example, "We have become inured to the cultural rot," "It is something we have done to ourselves," or "We say we want law and order." How does the repetition of this word emphasize his argument? Why would this method of repetition be particularly effective in a speech (from which this essay is condensed)?
5. What is the effect of the final paragraph? Does it provide closure to the essay? Does it provoke further thought on the subject? Does it seem abrupt and unsatisfying? Explain your view.
6. Where, if at all, does the author use *proof* to buttress his thesis? How does its presence or absence strengthen or weaken his argument?
7. The author makes direct or indirect references to historical figures and famous authors. Does he assume his audience is familiar with these references? What can you infer about the intended audience for this essay?

WRITING

1. Argue for or against the proposition that public policy can legislate morality. Use examples that directly affect *you*, such as rules and laws governing drinking, smoking, driving, sex, work, and school.
2. Bennett claims that America "hates the spiritual." For a research paper, investigate studies on church attendance, published studies on America's beliefs and values, the rise of religious programming in the media, the Christian Coalition, and so on. Then write an essay based on your research.
3. Many social critics blame unemployment and slow economic growth for many of our social ills, whereas the author implies in paragraph 33 that these are not such significant issues. Argue for or against Bennett's dismissal of them.

The Death of the Moth

Virginia Woolf

Virginia Woolf (1882–1941), English novelist and essayist, was the daughter of Sir Leslie Stephen, a famous critic and writer on economics. An experimental novelist, Woolf attempted to portray consciousness through a poetic, symbolic, and concrete style. Her novels include Jacob's Room *(1922),* Mrs. Dalloway *(1925),* To the Lighthouse *(1927), and* The Waves *(1931). She was also a perceptive reader and critic, and her criticism appears in* The Common Reader *(1925) and* The Second Common Reader *(1933). The following essay, which demonstrates Woolf's capacity to find profound meaning even in commonplace events, appeared in* The Death of the Moth and Other Essays *(1942).*

Moths that fly by day are not properly to be called moths; they do not excite that 1
pleasant sense of dark autumn nights and ivy-blossom which the commonest yellow-underwing asleep in the shadow of the curtain never fails to rouse in us. They are hybrid creatures, neither gay like butterflies nor sombre like their own species. Nevertheless the present specimen, with his narrow hay-coloured wings, fringed with a tassel of the same colour, seemed to be content with life. It was a pleasant morning, mid-September, mild, benignant, yet with a keener breath than that of the summer months. The plough was already scoring the field opposite the window, and where the share had been, the earth was pressed flat and gleamed with moisture. Such vigour came rolling in from the fields and the down beyond that it was difficult to keep the eyes strictly turned upon the book. The rooks too were keeping one of their annual festivities; soaring round the tree tops until it looked as if a vast net with thousands of black knots in it had been cast up into the air; which, after a few moments sank slowly down upon the trees until every twig seemed to have a knot at the end of it. Then, suddenly, the net would be thrown into the air again in a wider circle this time, with the utmost clamour and vociferation, as though to be thrown into the air and settle down upon the tree tops were a tremendously exciting experience.

The same energy which inspired the rooks, the ploughmen, the horses, and 2
even, it seemed, the lean bare-backed downs, sent the moth fluttering from side to side of his square of the windowpane. One could not help watching him. One was, indeed, conscious of a queer feeling of pity for him. The possibilities of pleasure seemed that morning so enormous and so various that to have only a moth's part in life, and a day moth's at that, appeared a hard fate, and his zest in enjoying his meagre opportunities to the full, pathetic. He flew vigorously to one corner of his compartment, and, after waiting there a second, flew across to the other. What remained for him but to fly to a third corner and then to a fourth? That was all he could do, in spite of the size of the downs, the width of

the sky, the far-off smoke of houses, and the romantic voice, now and then, of a steamer out at sea. What he could do he did. Watching him, it seemed as if a fibre, very thin but pure, of the enormous energy of the world had been thrust into his frail and diminutive body. As often as he crossed the pane, I could fancy that a thread of vital light became visible. He was little or nothing but life.

Yet, because he was so small, and so simple a form of the energy that was 3 rolling in at the open window and driving its way through so many narrow and intricate corridors in my own brain and in those of other human beings, there was something marvellous as well as pathetic about him. It was as if someone had taken a tiny bead of pure life and decking it as lightly as possible with down and feathers, had set it dancing and zigzagging to show us the true nature of life. Thus displayed one could not get over the strangeness of it. One is apt to forget all about life, seeing it humped and bossed and garnished and cumbered so that it has to move with the greatest circumspection and dignity. Again, the thought of all that life might have been had he been born in any other shape caused one to view his simple activities with a kind of pity.

After a time, tired by his dancing apparently, he settled on the window 4 ledge in the sun, and, the queer spectacle being at an end, I forgot about him. Then, looking up, my eye was caught by him. He was trying to resume his dancing, but seemed either so stiff or so awkward that he could only flutter to the bottom of the windowpane; and when he tried to fly across it he failed. Being intent on other matters I watched these futile attempts for a time without thinking, unconsciously waiting for him to resume his flight, as one waits for a machine, that has stopped momentarily, to start again without considering the reason of its failure. After perhaps a seventh attempt he slipped from the wooden ledge and fell, fluttering his wings, on to his back on the window sill. The helplessness of his attitude roused me. It flashed upon me that he was in difficulties; he could no longer raise himself; his legs struggled vainly. But, as I stretched out a pencil, meaning to help him to right himself, it came over me that the failure and awkwardness were the approach of death. I laid the pencil down again.

The legs agitated themselves once more. I looked as if for the enemy against 5 which he struggled. I looked out of doors. What had happened there? Presumably it was midday, and work in the fields had stopped. Stillness and quiet had replaced the previous animation. The birds had taken themselves off to feed in the brooks. The horses stood still. Yet the power was there all the same, massed outside, indifferent, impersonal, not attending to anything in particular. Somehow it was opposed to the little hay-coloured moth. It was useless to try to do anything. One could only watch the extraordinary efforts made by those tiny legs against an oncoming doom which could, had it chosen, have submerged an entire city, not merely a city, but masses of human beings; nothing, I knew, had any chance against death. Nevertheless after a pause of exhaustion the legs fluttered again. It was superb this last protest, and so frantic that he succeeded at last in righting himself. One's sympathies, of course, were all on the side of life. Also, when there was nobody to care or to know, this gigantic effort on the part of an insignificant little moth, against a power of such magnitude, to retain what no one else valued or desired to keep, moved one strangely. Again, somehow, one saw life, a pure bead. I lifted the pencil again, useless though I knew it to be. But even as I did so, the unmistakable tokens of death showed themselves. The body relaxed, and instantly grew stiff. The struggle was over. The insignificant little creature now knew death. As I looked at the dead moth, this minute wayside triumph of so great a force over so mean an antagonist filled me with wonder. Just as life had been strange a few minutes before, so death was now as strange. The moth having righted himself now lay most decently and uncomplainingly composed. O yes, he seemed to say, death is stronger than I am.

COMPREHENSION

1. Why is Woolf so moved by the moth's death? Why does she call the moth's protest (paragraph 5) "superb"?
2. What, according to Woolf, is the "true nature of life"?
3. What paradox is inherent in the death of the moth?

RHETORIC

1. Examine Woolf's use of simile in paragraph 1. Where else in the essay does she use similes? Are any of them similar to the similes used in paragraph 1?
2. Why does the author personify the moth?
3. What sentences constitute the introduction of this essay? What rhetorical device do they use?
4. Divide the essay into two parts. Now explain why you divided the essay where you did. How are the two parts different? How are they similar?
5. Explain the importance of description in this essay. Where, particularly, does Woolf describe the setting of her scene? How does that description contribute to the development of her essay? How does she describe the moth, and how does this description affect tone?
6. How is narration used to structure the essay?

WRITING

1. Woolf implicitly connects insect and human life. What else can we learn about human development by looking at other forms of life? Analyze this connection in an essay.
2. Write a detailed description of a small animal. Try to invest it with the importance that Woolf gives her moth.
3. Give an analysis of Woolf's use of figurative language in "The Death of the Moth."

The Allegory of the Cave

Plato

Plato (427–347 B.C.), pupil and friend of Socrates, was one of the greatest philosophers of the ancient world. Plato's surviving works are all dialogues and epistles, many of the dialogues purporting to be conversations of Socrates and his disciples. Two key aspects of his philosophy are the dialectical method—represented by the questioning and probing of the particular event to reveal the general truth—and the existence of Forms. Plato's best-known works include the Phaedo, Symposium, Phaedrus, *and* Timaeus. *The following selection, from the* Republic, *is an early description of the nature of Forms.*

And now, I said, let me show in a figure how far our nature is enlightened or 1 unenlightened: Behold! human beings living in an underground den, which has a mouth open towards the light and reaching all along the den; here they have been from their childhood, and have their legs and necks chained so that they cannot move, and can only see before them, being prevented by the chains from turning round their heads. Above and behind them a fire is blazing at a distance, and between the fire and the prisoners there is a raised way; and you will see, if you look, a low wall built along the way, like the screen which marionette players have in front of them, over which they show the puppets.

I see. 2

And do you see, I said, men passing along the wall carrying all sorts of ves- 3 sels, and statues and figures of animals made of wood and stone and various materials, which appear over the wall? Some of them are talking, others silent.

You have shown me a strange image, and they are strange prisoners. 4

Like ourselves, I replied; and they see only their own shadows, or the shad- 5 ows of one another, which the fire throws on the opposite wall of the cave?

True, he said; how could they see anything but the shadows if they were 6 never allowed to move their heads?

And of the objects which are being carried in like manner they would only 7 see the shadows?

Yes, he said. 8

And if they were able to converse with one another, would they not sup- 9 pose that they were naming what was actually before them?

Very true. 10

And suppose further that the prison had an echo which came from the 11 other side, would they not be sure to fancy when one of the passersby spoke that the voice which they heard came from the passing shadow?

No question, he replied. 12

To them, I said, the truth would be literally nothing but the shadows of the 13 images.

That is certain.   14

And now look again, and see what will naturally follow if the prisoners are   15
released and disabused of their error. At first, when any of them is liberated and
compelled suddenly to stand up and turn his neck round and walk and look towards the light, he will suffer sharp pains; the glare will distress him and he will
be unable to see the realities of which in his former state he had seen the shadows; and then conceive some one saying to him, that what he saw before was an
illusion, but that now, when he is approaching nearer to being and his eye is
turned towards more real existence, he has a clearer vision—what will be his
reply? And you may further imagine that his instructor is pointing to the objects
as they pass and requiring him to name them—will he not be perplexed? Will
he not fancy that the shadows which he formerly saw are truer than the objects
which are now shown to him?

Far truer.   16

And if he is compelled to look straight at the light, will he not have a pain   17
in his eyes which will make him turn away to take refuge in the objects of vision
which he can see, and which he will conceive to be in reality clearer than the
things which are now being shown to him?

True, he said.   18

And suppose once more, that he is reluctantly dragged up a steep and   19
rugged ascent, and held fast until he is forced into the presence of the sun himself, is he not likely to be pained and irritated? When he approaches the light his
eyes will be dazzled and he will not be able to see anything at all of what are
now called realities.

Not all in a moment, he said.   20

He will require to grow accustomed to the sight of the upper world. And   21
first he will see the shadows best, next the reflections of men and other objects
in the water, and then the objects themselves; then he will gaze upon the light of
the moon and the stars and the spangled heaven; and he will see the sky and the
stars by night better than the sun or the light of the sun by day?

Certainly.   22

Last of all he will be able to see the sun, and not mere reflections of him in   23
the water, but he will see him in his own proper place, and not in another; and
he will contemplate him as he is.

Certainly.   24

He will then proceed to argue that this is he who gives the season and the   25
years, and is the guardian of all that is in the visible world, and in a certain way
the cause of all things which he and his fellows have been accustomed to behold?

Clearly, he said, he would first see the sun and then reason about him.   26

And when he remembered his old habitation, and the wisdom of the den   27
and his fellow-prisoners, do you not suppose that he would felicitate himself on
the change, and pity them?

Certainly, he would.   28

And if they were in the habit of conferring honors among themselves on   29
those who were quickest to observe the passing shadows and to remark which

of them went before, and which followed after, and which were together; and who were therefore best able to draw conclusions as to the future, do you think that he would care for such honors and glories, or envy the possessors of them? Would he not say with Homer, Better to be the poor servant of a poor master, and to endure anything, rather than think as they do and live after their manner?

Yes, he said, I think that he would rather suffer anything than entertain 30 these false notions and live in this miserable manner.

Imagine once more, I said, such an one coming suddenly out of the sun to 31 be replaced in his old situation; would he not be certain to have his eyes full of darkness?

To be sure, he said. 32

And if there were a contest, and he had to compete in measuring the shad- 33 ows with the prisoners who had never moved out of the den, while his sight was still weak, and before his eyes had become steady (and the time which would be needed to acquire this new habit of sight might be very considerable) would he not be ridiculous? Men would say of him that up he went and down he came without his eyes; and that it was better not even to think of ascending; and if any one tried to loose another and lead him up to the light, let them only catch the offender, and they would put him to death.

No question, he said. 34

This entire allegory, I said, you may now append, dear Glaucon, to the pre- 35 vious argument; the prison-house is the world of sight, the light of fire is the sun, and you will not misapprehend me if you interpret the journey upwards to be the ascent of the soul into the intellectual world according to my poor belief, which, at your desire, I have expressed—whether rightly or wrongly God knows. But, whether true or false, my opinion is that in the world of knowledge the idea of good appears last of all, and is seen only with an effort; and, when seen, is also inferred to be the universal author of all things beautiful and right, parent of light and of the lord of light in this visible world, and the immediate source of reason and truth in the intellectual; and that this is the power upon which he who would act rationally either in public or private life must have his eye fixed.

I agree, he said, as far as I am able to understand you. 36

Moreover, I said, you must not wonder that those who attain to this beauti- 37 ful vision are unwilling to descend to human affairs; for their souls are ever hastening into the upper world where they desire to dwell; which desire of theirs is very natural, if our allegory may be trusted.

Yes, very natural. 38

And is there anything surprising in one who passes from divine contem- 39 plations to the evil state of man, misbehaving himself in a ridiculous manner; if, while his eyes are blinking and before he has become accustomed to the surrounding darkness, he is compelled to fight in courts of law, or in other places, about the images or the shadows of images of justice, and is endeavouring to meet the conceptions of those who have never yet seen absolute justice?

Anything but surprising, he replied. 40

Any one who has common sense will remember that the bewilderments of 41
the eyes are of two kinds, and arise from two causes, either from coming out of
the light or from going into the light, which is true of the mind's eye, quite as
much as of the bodily eye; and he who remembers this when he sees any one
whose vision is perplexed and weak, will not be too ready to laugh; he will first
ask whether that soul of man has come out of the brighter light, and is unable to
see because unaccustomed to the dark, or having turned from darkness to the
day is dazzled by excess of light. And he will count the one happy in his condition and state of being, and he will pity the other; or, if he have a mind to laugh
at the soul which comes from below into the light, there will be more reason in
this than in the laugh which greets him who returns from above out of the light
into the den.

That, he said, is a very just distinction. 42

COMPREHENSION

1. What does Plato hope to convey to readers of his allegory?
2. According to Plato, do human beings typically perceive reality? To what
   does he compare the world?
3. According to Plato, what often happens to people who develop a true idea
   of reality? How well do they compete with others? Who is usually considered superior? Why?

RHETORIC

1. Is the conversation portrayed here realistic? How effective is this conversational style at conveying information?
2. How do you interpret such details of this allegory as the chains, the cave,
   and the fire? What connotations do such symbols have?
3. How does Plato use conversation to develop his argument? What is Glaucon's role in the conversation?
4. Note examples of transition words that mark contrasts between the real and
   the shadow world. How does Plato use contrast to develop his idea of the
   true real world?
5. Plato uses syllogistic reasoning to derive human behavior from his allegory.
   Trace his line of reasoning, noting transitional devices and the development
   of ideas in paragraphs 5 to 14. Find and describe a similar line of reasoning.
6. In what paragraph does Plato explain his allegory? Why do you think he lo-
   cates his explanation where he does?

WRITING

1. Are Plato's ideas still influencing contemporary society? How do his ideas
   affect our evaluation of materialism, sensuality, sex, and love?

2. Write an allegory based on a sport, business, or space flight to explain how we act in the world.
3. Imagine an encounter with Plato. Report briefly on your conversation.

No Man Is an Island

John Donne

John Donne (1572–1631), English poet and priest, was a master of wit and devotion. Ben Jonson called him "the first poet in the world in some things." Donne's early career was threatened constantly by poverty, until he became dean of St. Paul's in 1621. He wrote richly complex poetry and sermons. Most of his works were published after his death by his son. Collections of his sermons appeared in 1640, 1649, and 1661; a collection of his poetry appeared in 1633. Donne was a superb inventor of metaphors, as the following essay, called a meditation, *indicates.*

Perchance he for whom this bell tolls may be so ill, as that he knows not it tolls for him; and perchance I may think myself so much better than I am, as that they who are about me, and see my state, may have caused it to toll for me, and I know not that. The church is Catholic, universal, so are all her actions; all that she does belongs to all. When she baptizes a child, that action concerns me; for that child is thereby connected to that body which is my head too, and ingrafted into that body whereof I am a member. And when she buries a man, that action concerns me: all mankind is of one author, and is one volume; when one man dies, one chapter is not torn out of the book, but translated into a better language; and every chapter must be so translated; God employs several translators; some pieces are translated by age, some by sickness, some by war, some by justice; but God's hand is in every translation, and his hand shall bind up all our scattered leaves again for that library where every book shall lie open to one another. As therefore the bell that rings to a sermon calls not upon the preacher only, but upon the congregation to come, so this bell calls us all; but how much more me, who am brought so near the door by this sickness. There was a contention as far as a suit (in which both poetry and dignity, religion and estimation, were mingled), which of the religious orders should ring to prayers first in the morning; and it was determined, that they should ring first that rose earliest. If we understand aright the dignity of this bell that tolls for our evening prayer, we would be glad to make it ours by rising early, in that application, that it might be ours as well as his, whose indeed it is. The bell doth toll for him that thinks it doth; and though it intermit again, yet from that minute that that occasion wrought upon him, he is united to God. Who casts not up his eye to the sun when it rises? But who takes off his eye from a comet when that breaks out? 1

Who bends not his ear to any bell which upon any occasion rings? but who can remove it from that bell which is passing a piece of himself out of this world? No man is an island, entire of itself; every man is a piece of the continent, a part of the main. If a clod be washed away by the sea, Europe is the less, as well as if a promontory were, as well as if a manor of thy friend's or of thine own were: any man's death diminishes me, because I am involved in mankind, and therefore never send to know for whom the bell tolls; it tolls for thee. Neither can we call this a begging of misery, or a borrowing of misery, as though we were not miserable enough of ourselves, but must fetch in more from the next house, in taking upon us the misery of our neighbors. Truly it were an excusable covetousness if we did, for affliction is a treasure, and scarce any man hath enough of it. No man hath affliction enough that is not matured and ripened by it, and made fit for God by that affliction. If a man carry treasure in bullion, or in a wedge of gold, and have none coined into current money, his treasure will not defray him as he travels. Tribulation is treasure in the nature of it, but it is not current money in the use of it, except we get nearer and nearer our home, heaven, by it. Another man may be sick too, and sick to death, and this affliction may lie in his Dowels, as gold in a mine, and be of no use to him; but this bell, that tells me of his affliction, digs out and applies that gold to me: if by this consideration of another's danger I take mine own into contemplation, and so secure myself, by making my recourse to my God, who is our only security.

COMPREHENSION

1. What is the theme of this essay?
2. The central metaphor in this essay is "bells." What do they signify?
3. Donne referred to his sermons as meditations. Upon what subject is this work a meditation?

RHETORIC

1. Standard punctuation has changed dramatically since the time this essay was written. Select one semicolon from each of five sentences in the essay. Explain the function of each semicolon within its context.
2. Read the essay aloud. What clues exist in the essay that it was meant to be recited rather than merely read?
3. The entire essay (or meditation) is one paragraph long. Many religions rely on repetitive prayer or chants to help the believer enter a sanctified state of mind. Discuss how the form of the essay can be considered part of the "rhetoric of the spiritual."
4. The author often joins ideas with coordinating conjunctions (*for, and, yet, but, so*) However there are few connecting words with more than one syllable—*nevertheless, however, because, moreover*—in the essay. How does this stylistic device contribute toward the tone of the writing?

5. A portion of one sentence reads, "Neither can we call this a begging of misery, or a borrowing of misery, as though we were not miserable enough of ourselves." Locate three other sentences with repetition of sounds and words. What is the effect of repetition as a rhetorical device?

6. Identify at least four other uses of metaphor besides the word *bells* in the essay. How does the author's frequent use of metaphor contribute to the effect of the essay?

7. Consider the statement, "The bell doth toll for him that thinks it doth." What aspects of this make it resemble poetry rather than prose?

WRITING

1. Argue for or against the proposition that no one is an island.

2. Write an imaginative essay in which you assume the persona of John Donne and examine today's society in terms of his philosophy.

3. Have a friend read the essay aloud. Afterward, write an essay describing the response you had while listening to the meditation.

The Mystery of Zen

Gilbert Highet

Gilbert Highet was born in Glasgow, Scotland, in 1906 and died in 1978. He was Anthon Professor of Latin Language and Literature at Columbia University, where he taught from 1938 to 1972. He wrote and edited critical works on poetry, satire, literary history, literary criticism, and classicism. Among his most popular works are The Classical Tradition: Greek and Roman Influences on Western Literature *(1949),* The Art of Teaching *(1953),* The Anatomy of Satire *(1962), and* The Immortal Profession *(1976). He was known for his personal, enthusiastic, and anecdotal perspective on the subjects upon which he wrote. In the following essay, he attempts an extraordinary feat of writing: namely, to describe and define a subject which by its very nature defies conscious understanding.*

The mind need never stop growing. Indeed, one of the few experiences which 1
never pall is the experience of watching one's own mind, and observing how it produces new interests, responds to new stimuli, and develops new thoughts, apparently without effort and almost independently of one's own conscious control. I have seen this happen to myself a hundred times; and every time it happens again, I am equally fascinated and astonished.

Some years ago a publisher sent me a little book for review. I read it, and 2
decided it was too remote from my main interests and too highly specialized. It

was a brief account of how a young German philosopher living in Japan had learned how to shoot with a bow and arrow, and how this training had made it possible for him to understand the esoteric doctrines of the Zen sect of Buddhism. Really, what could be more alien to my own life, and to that of everyone I knew, than Zen Buddhism and Japanese archery? So I thought, and put the book away.

Yet I did not forget it. It was well written, and translated into good English. 3 It was delightfully short, and implied much more than it said. Although its theme was extremely odd, it was at least highly individual; I had never read anything like it before or since. It remained in my mind. Its name was *Zen in the Art of Archery,* its author Eugen Herrigel, its publisher Pantheon of New York. One day I took it off the shelf and read it again; this time it seemed even stranger than before and even more unforgettable. Now it began to cohere with other interests of mine. Something I had read of the Japanese art of flower arrangement seemed to connect with it; and then, when I wrote an essay on the peculiar Japanese poems called *haiku,* other links began to grow. Finally I had to read the book once more with care, and to go through some other works which illuminated the same subject. I am still grappling with the theme; I have not got anywhere near understanding it fully; but I have learned a good deal, and I am grateful to the little book which refused to be forgotten.

The author, a German philosopher, got a job teaching philosophy at the 4 University of Tokyo (apparently between the wars), and he did what Germans in foreign countries do not usually do: he determined to adapt himself and to learn from his hosts. In particular, he had always been interested in mysticism— which, for every earnest philosopher, poses a problem that is all the more inescapable because it is virtually insoluble. Zen Buddhism is not the only mystical doctrine to be found in the East, but it is one of the most highly developed and certainly one of the most difficult to approach. Herrigel knew that there were scarcely any books which did more than skirt the edge of the subject, and that the best of all books on Zen (those by the philosopher D. T. Suzuki) constantly emphasize that Zen can never be learned from books, can never be studied as we can study other disciplines such as logic or mathematics. Therefore he began to look for a Japanese thinker who could teach him directly.

At once he met with embarrassed refusals. His Japanese friends explained 5 that he would gain nothing from trying to discuss Zen as a philosopher, that its theories could not be spread out for analysis by a detached mind, and in fact that the normal relationship of teacher and pupil simply did not exist within the sect, because the Zen masters felt it useless to explain things stage by stage and to argue about the various possible interpretations of their doctrine. Herrigel had read enough to be prepared for this. He replied that he did not want to dissect the teachings of the school, because he knew that would be useless. He wanted to become a Zen mystic himself. (This was highly intelligent of him. No one could really penetrate into Christian mysticism without being a devout Christian; no one could appreciate Hindu mystical doctrine without accepting the Hindu view of the universe.) At this, Herrigel's Japanese friends were more forthcoming. They told him that the best way, indeed the only way, for a European to approach Zen mysticism was to learn one of the arts which exemplified it. He was a fairly good rifle shot, so he determined to learn archery; and his wife cooperated with him by taking lessons in painting and flower arrangement. How any philosopher could investigate a mystical doctrine by learning to shoot with a bow and arrow and watching his wife arrange flowers, Herrigel did not ask. He had good sense.

A Zen master who was a teacher of archery agreed to take him as a pupil. 6 The lessons lasted six years, during which he practiced every single day. There are many difficult courses of instruction in the world: the Jesuits, violin virtuosi, Talmudic scholars, all have long and hard training, which in one sense never comes to an end; but Herrigel's training in archery equaled them all in intensity. If I were trying to learn archery, I should expect to begin by looking at a target and shooting arrows at it. He was not even allowed to aim at a target for the first four years. He had to begin by learning how to hold the bow and arrow, and then how to release the arrow; this took ages. The Japanese bow is not like our sporting bow, and the stance of the archer in Japan is different from ours. We hold the bow at shoulder level, stretch our left arm out ahead, pull the string and the nocked arrow to a point either below the chin or sometimes past the right ear, and then shoot. The Japanese hold the bow above the head, and then pull the hands apart to left and right until the left hand comes down to eye level and the right hand comes to rest above the right shoulder; then there is a pause, during which the bow is held at full stretch, with the tip of the three-foot arrow projecting only a few inches beyond the bow; after that, the arrow is loosed. When Herrigel tried this, even without aiming, he found it was almost impossible. His hands trembled. His legs stiffened and grew cramped. His breathing became labored. And of course he could not possibly aim. Week after week he practiced this, with the Master watching him carefully and correcting his strained attitude; week after week he made no progress whatever. Finally he gave up and told his teacher that he could not learn: it was absolutely impossible for him to draw the bow and loose the arrow.

To his astonishment, the Master agreed. He said, "Certainly you cannot. It 7 is because you are not breathing correctly. You must learn to breathe in a steady rhythm, keeping your lungs full most of the time, and drawing in one rapid inspiration with each stage of the process, as you grasp the bow, fit the arrow, raise the bow, draw, pause, and loose the shot. If you do, you will both grow stronger and be able to relax." To prove this, he himself drew his massive bow and told his pupil to feel the muscles of his arms: they were perfectly relaxed, as though he were doing no work whatever.

Herrigel now started breathing exercises; after some time he combined the 8 new rhythm of breathing with the actions of drawing and shooting; and, much to his astonishment, he found that the whole thing, after this complicated process, had become much easier. Or rather, not easier, but different. At times it became quite unconscious. He says himself that he felt he was not breathing, but being breathed; and in time he felt that the occasional shot was not being dispatched by him, but shooting itself. The bow and arrow were in charge; he had become merely a part of them.

All this time, of course, Herrigel did not even attempt to discuss Zen doc- 9 trine with his Master. No doubt he knew that he was approaching it, but he concentrated solely on learning how to shoot. Every stage which he surmounted appeared to lead to another stage even more difficult. It took him months to learn how to loosen the bowstring. The problem was this. If he gripped the string and arrowhead tightly, either he froze, so that his hands were slowly pulled together and the shot was wasted, or else he jerked, so that the arrow flew up into the air or down into the ground; and if he was relaxed, then the bowstring and arrow simply *leaked* out of his grasp before he could reach full stretch, and the arrow went nowhere. He explained this problem to the Master. The Master understood perfectly well. He replied, "You must hold the drawn bowstring like a child holding a grownup's finger. You know how firmly a child grips; and yet when it lets go, there is not the slightest jerk—because the child does not think of itself, it is not self-conscious, it does not say, 'I will now let go and do something else,' it merely acts instinctively. That is what you must learn to do. Practice, practice, and practice, and then the string will loose itself at the right moment. The shot will come as effortlessly as snow slipping from a leaf." Day after day, week after week, month after month, Herrigel practiced this; and then, after one shot, the Master suddenly bowed and broke off the lesson. He said "Just then it shot. Not you, but *it.*" And gradually thereafter more and more right shots achieved themselves; the young philosopher forgot himself, forgot that he was learning archery for some other purpose, forgot even that he was practicing archery, and became part of that unconsciously active complex, the bow, the string, the arrow, and the man.

Next came the target. After four years, Herrigel was allowed to shoot at the 10 target. But he was strictly forbidden to aim at it. The Master explained that even he himself did not aim; and indeed, when he shot, he was so absorbed in the act, so selfless and unanxious, that his eyes were almost closed. It was difficult, almost impossible, for Herrigel to believe that such shooting could ever be effective; and he risked insulting the Master by suggesting that he ought to be able to hit the target blindfolded. But the Master accepted the challenge, That night, after a cup of tea and long meditation, he went into the archery hall, put on the lights at one end and left the target perfectly dark, with only a thin taper burning in front of it. Then, with habitual grace and precision, and with that strange, almost sleepwalking, selfless confidence that is the heart of Zen, he shot two arrows into the darkness. Herrigel went out to collect them. He found that the first had gone to the heart of the bull's eye, and that the second had actually hit the first arrow and splintered it. The Master showed no pride. He said, "Perhaps, with unconscious memory of the position of the target, *I* shot the first arrow; but the second arrow? *It* shot the second arrow, and *it* brought it to the center of the target."

At last Herrigel began to understand. His progress became faster and faster; 11 easier, too. Perfect shots (perfect because perfectly unconscious) occurred at almost every lesson; and finally, after six years of incessant training, in a public display he was awarded the diploma. He needed no further instruction: he had himself become a Master. His wife meanwhile had become expert both in painting and in the arrangement of flowers—two of the finest of Japanese arts. (I wish she could be persuaded to write a companion volume, called *Zen in the Art of Flower Arrangement*—it would have a wider general appeal than her husband's work.) I gather also from a hint or two in his book that she had taken part in the archery lessons. During one of the most difficult periods in Herrigel's training, when his Master had practically refused to continue teaching him—because Herrigel had tried to cheat by *consciously* opening his hand at the moment of loosing the arrow—his wife had advised him against that solution, and sympathized with him when it was rejected. She in her own way had learned more quickly than he, and reached the final point together with him. All their effort had not been in vain: Herrigel and his wife had really acquired a new and valuable kind of wisdom. Only at this point, when he was about to abandon his lessons forever, did his Master treat him almost as an equal and hint at the innermost doctrines of Zen Buddhism. Only hints he gave; and yet, for the young philosopher who had now become a mystic, they were enough. Herrigel understood the doctrine, not with his logical mind, but with his entire being. He at any rate had solved the mystery of Zen.

Without going through a course of training as absorbing and as complete as   12
Herrigel's, we can probably never penetrate the mystery. The doctrine of Zen cannot be analyzed from without: it must be lived.

But although it cannot be analyzed, it can be hinted at. All the hints that the   13
adherents of this creed give us are interesting. Many are fantastic; some are practically incomprehensible, and yet unforgettable. Put together, they take us toward a way of life which is utterly impossible for westerners living in a western world, and nevertheless has a deep fascination and contains some values which we must respect.

The word Zen means "meditation." (It is the Japanese word, corresponding   14
to the Chinese Ch'an and the Hindu Dhyana.) It is the central idea of a special sect of Buddhism which flourished in China during the Sung period (between A.D. 1000 and 1300) and entered Japan in the twelfth century. Without knowing much about it, we might be certain that the Zen sect was a worthy and noble one, because it produced a quantity of highly distinguished art, specifically painting. And if we knew anything about Buddhism itself, we might say that Zen goes closer than other sects to the heart of Buddha's teaching: because Buddha was trying to found, not a religion with temples and rituals, but a way of life based on meditation. However, there is something eccentric about the Zen life which is hard to trace in Buddha's teaching; there is an active energy which he did not admire, there is a rough grasp on reality which he himself eschewed, there is something like a sense of humor, which he rarely displayed. The gravity and serenity of the Indian preacher are transformed, in Zen, to the earthy liveliness of Chinese and Japanese sages. The lotus brooding calmly on the water has turned into a knotted tree covered with spring blossoms.

In this sense, "meditation" does not mean what we usually think of when 15
we say a philosopher meditates: analysis of reality, a long-sustained effort to
solve problems of religion and ethics, the logical dissection of the universe. It
means something not divisive, but whole; not schematic, but organic; not long-
drawn-out, but immediate. It means something more like our words "intuition"
and "realization." It means a way of life in which there is no division between
thought and action; none of the painful gulf, so well known to all of us, between
the unconscious and the conscious mind; and no absolute distinction between
the self and the external world, even between the various parts of the external
world and the whole.

When the German philosopher took six years of lessons in archery in order 16
to approach the mystical significance of Zen, he was not given direct philosophical instruction. He was merely shown how to breathe, how to hold and
loose the bowstring, and finally how to shoot in such a way that the bow and arrow used him as an instrument. There are many such stories about Zen teachers. The strangest I know is one about a fencing master who undertook to train
a young man in the art of the sword. The relationship of teacher and pupil is
very important, almost sacred, in the Far East; and the pupil hardly ever thinks
of leaving a master or objecting to his methods, however extraordinary they
may seem. Therefore this young fellow did not at first object when he was made
to act as a servant, drawing water, sweeping floors, gathering wood for the fire,
and cooking. But after some time he asked for more direct instruction. The master agreed to give it, but produced no swords. The routine went on just as before, except that every now and then the master would strike the young man
with a stick. No matter what he was doing, sweeping the floor or weeding in
the garden, a blow would descend on him apparently out of nowhere; he had
always to be on the alert, and yet he was constantly receiving unexpected cracks
on the head or shoulders. After some months of this, he saw his master stoop-
ing over a boiling pot full of vegetables; and he thought he would have his revenge. Silently he lifted a stick and brought it down; but without any effort,
without even a glance in his direction, his master parried the blow with the lid
of the cooking pot. At last, the pupil began to understand the instinctive alertness, the effortless perception and avoidance of danger, in which his master had
been training him. As soon as he had achieved it, it was child's play for him to
learn the management of the sword: he could parry every cut and turn every
slash without anxiety, until his opponent, exhausted, left an opening for his
counterattack. (The same principle was used by the elderly samurai for selecting his comrades in the Japanese motion picture *The Magnificent Seven*.)

These stories show that Zen meditation does not mean sitting and thinking. 17
On the contrary, it means acting with as little thought as possible. The fencing
master trained his pupil to guard against every attack with the same immediate,
instinctive rapidity with which our eyelid closes over our eye when something
threatens it. His work was aimed at breaking down the wall between thought
and act, at completely fusing body and senses and mind so that they might all
work together rapidly and effortlessly. When a Zen artist draws a picture, he

does it in a rhythm almost the exact reverse of that which is followed by a Western artist. We begin by blocking out the design and then filling in the details, usually working more and more slowly as we approach the completion of the picture. The Zen artist sits down very calmly; examines his brush carefully; prepares his own ink; smoothes out the paper on which he will work; falls into a profound silent ecstasy of contemplation—during which he does not think anxiously of various details, composition, brushwork, shades of tone, but rather attempts to become the vehicle through which the subject can express itself in painting; and then, very quickly and almost unconsciously, with sure effortless strokes, draws a picture containing the fewest and most effective lines. Most of the paper is left blank; only the essential is depicted, and that not completely. One long curving line will be enough to show a mountainside; seven streaks will become a group of bamboos bending in the wind; and yet, though technically incomplete, such pictures are unforgettably clear. They show the heart of reality.

All this we can sympathize with, because we can see the results. The young ₁₈ swordsman learns how to fence. The intuitional painter produces a fine picture. But the hardest thing for us to appreciate is that the Zen masters refuse to teach philosophy or religion directly, and deny logic. In fact, they despise logic as an artificial distortion of reality. Many philosophical teachers are difficult to understand because they analyze profound problems with subtle intricacy: such is Aristotle in his *Metaphysics*. Many mystical writers are difficult to understand because, as they themselves admit, they are attempting to use words to describe experiences which are too abstruse for words, so that they have to fall back on imagery and analogy, which they themselves recognize to be poor media, far coarser than the realities with which they have been in contact. But the Zen teachers seem to deny the power of language and thought altogether. For example, if you ask a Zen master what is the ultimate reality, he will answer, without the slightest hesitation, "The bamboo grove at the foot of the hill" or "A branch of plum blossom." Apparently he means that these things, which we can see instantly without effort, or imagine in the flash of a second, are real with the ultimate reality; that nothing is more real than these; and that we ought to grasp ultimates as we grasp simple immediates. A Chinese master was once asked the central question, "What is the Buddha?" He said nothing whatever, but held out his index finger. What did he mean? It is hard to explain; but apparently he meant "Here. Now. Look and realize with the effortlessness of seeing. Do not try to use words. Do not think. Make no efforts toward withdrawal from the world. Expect no sublime ecstasies. Live. All *that* is the ultimate reality, and it can be understood from the motion of a finger as well as from the execution of any complex ritual, from any subtle argument, or from the circling of the starry universe."

In making that gesture, the master was copying the Buddha himself, who ₁₉ once delivered a sermon which is famous, but was hardly understood by his pupils at the time. Without saying a word, he held up a flower and showed it to the gathering. One man, one alone, knew what he meant. The gesture became renowned as the Flower Sermon.

In the annals of Zen there are many cryptic answers to the final question, 20
"What is the Buddha?"—which in our terms means "What is the meaning of
life? What is truly real?" For example, one master, when asked "What is the
Buddha?" replied, "Your name is Yecho." Another said, "Even the finest artist
cannot paint him." Another said, "No nonsense here." And another answered,
"The mouth is the gate of woe." My favorite story is about the monk who said
to a Master, "Has a dog Buddha-nature too?" The Master replied, "Wu"—which
is what the dog himself would have said.

Now, some critics might attack Zen by saying that this is the creed of a sav- 21
age or an animal. The adherents of Zen would deny that—or more probably
they would ignore the criticism, or make some cryptic remark which meant that
it was pointless. Their position—if they could ever be persuaded to put it into
words—would be this. An animal is instinctively in touch with reality, and so far
is living rightly, but it has never had a mind and so cannot perceive the Whole,
only that part with which it is in touch. The philosopher sees both the Whole and
the parts, and enjoys them all. As for the savage, he exists only through the
group; he feels himself as part of a war party or a ceremonial dance team or a
ploughing-and-sowing group or the Snake clan; he is not truly an individual at
all, and therefore is less than fully human. Zen has at its heart an inner solitude;
its aim is to teach us to live, as in the last resort we do all have to live, alone.

A more dangerous criticism of Zen would be that it is nihilism, that its pur- 22
pose is to abolish thought altogether. (This criticism is handled, but not fully
met, by the great Zen authority Suzuki in his *Introduction to Zen Buddhism*.) It
can hardly be completely confuted, for after all the central doctrine of Buddhism is—Nothingness. And many of the sayings of Zen masters are truly ni-
hilistic. The first patriarch of the sect in China was asked by the emperor what
was the ultimate and holiest principle of Buddhism. He replied, "Vast emptiness, and nothing holy in it." Another who was asked the searching question
"Where is the abiding place for the mind?" answered, "Not in this dualism of
good and evil, being and nonbeing, thought and matter." In fact, thought is an
activity which divides. It analyzes, it makes distinctions, it criticizes, it judges,
it breaks reality into groups and classes and individuals. The aim of Zen is to
abolish that kind of thinking, and to substitute—not unconsciousness, which
would be death, but a consciousness that does not analyze but experiences life
directly. Although it has no prescribed prayers, no sacred scriptures, no ceremonial rites, no personal god, and no interest in the soul's future destination,
Zen is a religion rather than a philosophy. Jung points out that its aim is to produce a religious conversion, a "transformation": and he adds, "The transformation process is incommensurable with intellect." Thought is always interesting,
but often painful; Zen is calm and painless. Thought is incomplete; Zen enlightenment brings a sense of completeness. Thought is a process; Zen illumi-
nation is a state. But it is a state which cannot be defined. In the Buddhist
scriptures there is a dialogue between a master and a pupil in which the pupil
tries to discover the exact meaning of such a state. The master says to him, 'If a
fire were blazing in front of you, would you know that it was blazing?'

"Yes, master."   23

"And would you know the reason for its blazing?"   24

"Yes, because it had a supply of grass and sticks."   25

"And would you know if it were to go out?"   26

"Yes, master."   27

"And on its going out, would you know where the fire had gone? To the   28
east, to the west, to the north, or to the south?"

"The question does not apply, master. For the fire blazed because it had a 29
supply of grass and sticks. When it had consumed this and had no other fuel,
then it went out."

"In the same way," replies the master, "no question will apply to the mean- 30
ing of Nirvana, and no statement will explain it."

Such, then, neither happy nor unhappy but beyond all divisive description, 31
is the condition which students of Zen strive to attain. Small wonder that they
can scarcely explain it to us, the unilluminated.

COMPREHENSION

1. The title of the essay uses the word *mystery*. Why is Zen a mystery?
2. The author claims Zen is not a philosophy but a religion. Why is it a religion? What are its basic tenets?
3. In paragraph 8, the author claims that Herrigel asserted that "he was not breathing, but being breathed." What is the difference between the two? Why is this experience so essential to the development of the Zen attitude?

RHETORIC

1. The opening paragraph makes no mention of Herrigel or of Zen itself. Assuming that the beginning of an essay is intended to capture the reader's attention, how does Highet achieve this in his introduction?
2. Why has Highet chosen the rhetorical strategy of using Herrigel's book to help explain the process of Zen? How would the essay have differed if he used solely his own knowledge?
3. What is the purpose of this essay: to describe, to analyze, to define, to instruct, to entertain, to encourage others to study Zen? Or is it a combination of these factors? Explain your view. Note that the author states that Zen masters believe Zen cannot be explained.
4. What is the author's tone? What is his emotional relationship to the reading of Herrigel's book and to Zen in general? Is he positive, negative, or neutral? Explain.
5. To what degree does the author appear to be a reliable source to learn about the topic? What clues does he provide that he is familiar with his subject matter beyond solely having read the book by Herrigel?

6. What is the implied audience for this essay: the general reader, individuals with an interest in religion, people who would be motivated to purchase the book *Zen in the Art of Archery*, readers who would be interested in becoming Zen disciples themselves? How did you reach your conclusion?

7. At times, Highet uses highly specific detail in describing the process of mastering the art of archery. For example, he describes how the Japanese bow is handled by the archer and how the archer must breathe when preparing to shoot the arrow. What function does such detail serve in providing the reader with a fuller image of the Zen process?

WRITING

1. Select an abstract term such as *intuition, motivation, satisfaction;* then write a definition of it, using both concepts and specific details.

2. Describe an activity that you do well and effortlessly. Explain how, when you are engaged in this activity, it seems to take on Zen-like characteristics.

3. Argue for or against the proposition that in a contemporary world that requires so much analysis, research, and experimentation, Zen consciousness is not particularly useful.

The Culture of Disbelief

Stephen L. Carter

Stephen L. Carter (b. 1954) received a BA from Stanford University in 1976 and graduated from Yale University Law School in 1979. He served as a law clerk for the U.S. Supreme Court and as a lawyer in private practice before becoming a professor of law at the Yale University Law School in 1982. An African American who is opposed to affirmative action, he has become a controversial figure among proponents of the policy. His first book, Reflections of an Affirmative Action Baby *(1991), outlines his views on the subject and draws on personal experience to show that, even though he was a beneficiary of affirmative action, such preference ultimately makes successful African Americans seem to have received preferential treatment. His second book,* The Culture of Disbelief: How American Law and Politics Trivialize Religious Devotion *(1993), addresses the ways he believes the law has recently operated against the spirit of American values in its effort to ban religion from political discourse and expression. The following essay succinctly sums up this argument.*

Contemporary American politics faces few greater dilemmas than deciding how to deal with the resurgence of religious belief. On the one hand, American ideology cherishes religion, as it does all matters of private conscience, which is why we justly celebrate a strong tradition against state interference with private religious choice. At the same time, many political leaders, commentators, scholars, and voters are coming to view any religious element in public moral discourse as a tool of the radical right for reshaping American society. But the effort to banish religion for politics' sake has led us astray: In our sensible zeal to keep religion from dominating our politics, we have created a political and legal culture that presses the religiously faithful to be other than themselves, to act publicly, and sometimes privately as well, as though their faith does not matter to them.

Recently, a national magazine devoted its cover story to an investigation of prayer: how many people pray, how often, why, how, and for what. A few weeks later came the inevitable letter from a disgruntled reader, wanting to know why so much space had been dedicated to such nonsense.[1]   2

Statistically, the letter writer was in the minority: by the magazine's figures, better than nine out of ten Americans believe in God and some four out of five pray regularly.[2] Politically and culturally, however, the writer was in the American mainstream, for those who do pray regularly—indeed, those who believe in God—are encouraged to keep it a secret, and often a shameful one at that. Aside from the ritual appeals to God that are expected of our politicians, for Americans to take their religions seriously, to treat them as ordained rather than chosen, is to risk assignment to the lunatic fringe.   3

Yet religion matters to people, and matters a lot. Surveys indicate that Americans are far more likely to believe in God and to attend worship services regularly than any other people in the Western world. True, nobody prays on prime-time television unless religion is a part of the plot, but strong majorities of citizens tell pollsters that their religious beliefs are of great importance to them in their daily lives. Even though some popular histories wrongly assert the contrary, the best evidence is that this deep religiosity has always been a facet of the American character and that it has grown consistently through the nation's history.[3] And today, to the frustration of many opinion leaders in both the legal and political cultures, religion, as a moral force and perhaps a political one too, is surging. Unfortunately, in our public life, we prefer to pretend that it is not.   4

Consider the following events: 5

- When Hillary Rodham Clinton was seen wearing a cross around her neck at some of the public events surrounding her husband's inauguration as President of the United States, many observers were aghast, and one television commentator asked whether it was appropriate for the First Lady to display so openly a religious symbol. But if the First Lady can't do it, then certainly the President can't do it, which would bar from ever holding the office an Orthodox Jew under a religious compulsion to wear a yarmulke.

---

[1]"Talking to God," *Newsweek,* Jan. 6, 1992, p. 38; Letter to the Editor, *Newsweek,* Jan. 1992, p. 10. The letter called the article a "theocratic text masquerading as a news article."
[2]"Talking to God," p. 39. The most recent Gallup data indicate that 96 percent of Americans say they believe in God, including 82 percent who describe themselves as Christians (56 percent Protestant, 25 percent Roman Catholic) and 2 percent who describe themselves as Jewish. (No other faith accounted for as much as 1 percent.) See Ari L. Goldman, "Religion Notes," *New York Times,* Feb. 27, 1993, p. 9.
[3]See, for example, Jon Butler, *Awash in a Sea of Faith* (Cambridge: Harvard University Press, 1990).

- Back in the mid-1980s, the magazine *Sojourners*—published by politically liberal Christian evangelicals—found itself in the unaccustomed position of defending the conservative evangelist Pat Robertson against secular liberals who, a writer in the magazine sighed, "see[m] to consider Robertson a dangerous neanderthal because he happens to believe that God can heal diseases."[4] The point is that the editors of *Sojourners*, who are no great admirers of Robertson, also believe that God can heal diseases. So do tens of millions of Americans. But they are not supposed to say so.

- In the early 1980s, the state of New York adopted legislation that, in effect, requires an Orthodox Jewish husband seeking a divorce to give his wife a *get*—a religious divorce—without which she cannot remarry under Jewish law. Civil libertarians attacked the statute as unconstitutional. Said one critic, the "barriers to remarriage erected by religious law . . . only exist in the minds of those who believe in the religion."[5] If the barriers are religious, it seems, then they are not real barriers, they are "only" in the woman's mind—perhaps even a figment of the imagination.

- When the Supreme Court of the United States, ostensibly the final refuge of religious freedom, struck down a Connecticut statute requiring employers to make efforts to allow their employees to observe the sabbath, one Justice observed that the sabbath should not be singled out because all employees would like to have "the right to select the day of the week in which to refrain from labor."[6] Sounds good, except that, as one scholar has noted, "It would come as some surprise to a devout Jew to find that he has 'selected the day of the week in which to refrain from labor,' since the Jewish people have been under the impression for some 3,000 years that this choice was made by God."[7] If the sabbath is just another day off, then religious choice is essentially arbitrary and unimportant; so if one sabbath day is inconvenient, the religiously devout employee can just choose another.

- When President Ronald Reagan told religious broadcasters in 1983 that all laws passed since biblical times "have not improved on the Ten Commandments one bit," which might once have been considered a pardonable piece of rhetorical license, he was excoriated by political pundits, including one who charged angrily that Reagan was giving "short shrift to the secular laws and institutions that a president is charged with protecting."[8] And as for the millions of Americans who consider the Ten Commandments the fundaments on which they build their lives, well, they are no doubt subversive of these same institutions.

[4]Collum, "The Kingdom and the Power," *Sojourners*, Nov. 1986, p. 4. Some 82 percent of Americans believe that God performs miracles today. George Gallup, Jr., and Jim Castelli, *The People's Religion: American Faith in the '90s* (New York: Macmillan, 1989), p. 58.
[5]Madeline Kochen, "Constitutional Implications of New York's 'Get' Statute," *New York Law Journal*, Oct. 27, 1983, p. 32.
[6]*Estate of Thornton v. Caldor, Inc.*, 472 U.S. 703, 711 (1985) (Justice Sandra Day O'Connor, concurring).
[7]Michael W. McConnell, "Religious Freedom at a Crossroads," *University of Chicago Law Review* 59 (1992):115.
[8]Robert G. Kaiser, "Hypocrisy: This Puffed-Up Piety Is Perfectly Preposterous," *Washington Post*, March 18, 1984, p. C1.

These examples share a common rhetoric that refuses to accept the notion 6 that rational, public-spirited people can take religion seriously. It might be argued that such cases as these involve threats to the separation of church and state, the durable and vital doctrine that shields our public institutions from religious domination and our religious institutions from government domination. I am a great supporter of the separation of church and state . . . but that is not what these examples are about.

What matters about these examples is the *language* chosen to make the 7 points. In each example, as in many more that I shall discuss, one sees a trend in our political and legal cultures toward treating religious beliefs as arbitrary and unimportant, a trend supported by a rhetoric that implies that there is something wrong with religious devotion. More and more, our culture seems to take the position that believing deeply in the tenets of one's faith represents a kind of mystical irrationality, something that thoughtful, public-spirited American citizens would do better to avoid. If you must worship your God, the lesson runs, at least have the courtesy to disbelieve in the power of prayer; if you must observe your sabbath, have the good sense to understand that it is just like any other day off from work.

The rhetoric matters. A few years ago, my wife and I were startled by a 8 teaser for a story on a network news program, which asked what was meant to be a provocative question: "When is a church more than just a place of worship?" For those to whom worship is significant, the subtle arrangement of words is arresting: *more than* suggests that what follows ("just a place of worship") is somewhere well down the scale of interesting or useful human activities, and certainly that whatever the story is about is *more than* worship; and *just*—suggests that what follows ("place of worship") is rather small potatoes.

A friend tells the story of how he showed his résumé to an executive search 9 consultant—in the jargon, a corporate headhunter—who told him crisply that if he was serious about moving ahead in the business world, he should remove from the resume any mention of his involvement with a social welfare organization that was connected with a church, but not one of the genteel mainstream denominations. Otherwise, she explained, a potential employer might think him a religious fanatic.

How did we reach this disturbing pass, when our culture teaches that reli- 10 gion is not to be taken seriously, even by those who profess to believe in it? Some observers suggest that the key moment was the Enlightenment, when the Western tradition sought to sever the link between religion and authority. One of the playwright Tom Stoppard's characters observes that there came "a calendar date—*a moment*—when the onus of proof passed from the atheist to the believer, when, quite suddenly, the noes had it."[9] To which the philosopher Jeffrey Stout appends the following comment: "If so, it was not a matter of majority

---

[9]Tom Stoppard, *Jumpers*, quoted in Jeffrey Stout, *The Flight from Authority: Religion, Morality and the Quest for Autonomy* (South Bend, Indiana: University of Notre Dame Press, 1981), p.150.

rule."[10] Maybe not—but a strong undercurrent of contemporary American politics holds that region must be kept in its proper place and, still more, in proper perspective. There are, we are taught by our opinion leaders, religious matters and important matters, and disaster arises when we confuse the two. Rationality, it seems, consists in getting one's priorities straight. (Ignore your religious law and marry at leisure.) Small wonder, then, that we have recently been treated to a book, coauthored by two therapists, one of them an ordained minister, arguing that those who would put aside, say, the needs of their families in order to serve their religions are suffering from a malady the authors called "toxic faith"—for no normal person, evidently, would sacrifice the things that most of us hold dear just because of a belief that God so intended it.[11] (One wonders how the authors would have judged the toxicity of the faith of Jesus, Moses, or Mohammed.)

We are trying, here in America, to strike an awkward but necessary balance, 11 one that seems more and more difficult with each passing year. On the one hand, a magnificent respect for freedom of conscience, including the freedom of religious belief, runs deep in our political ideology. On the other hand, our understandable fear of religious domination of politics presses us, in our public personas, to be wary of those who take their religion too seriously. This public balance reflects our private selves. We are one of the most religious nations on earth, in the sense that we have a deeply religious citizenry; but we are also perhaps the most zealous in guarding our public institutions against explicit religious influences. One result is that we often ask our citizens to split their public and private selves, telling them in effect that it is fine to be religious in private, but there is something askew when those private beliefs become the basis for public action.

We teach college freshmen that the Protestant Reformation began the 12 process of freeing the church from the state, thus creating the possibility of a powerful independent moral force in society. As defenders of the separation of church and state have argued for centuries, autonomous religions play a vital role as free critics of the institutions of secular society. But our public culture more and more prefers religion as something without political significance, less an independent moral force than a quietly irrelevant moralizer, never heard, rarely seen. "[T]he public sphere," writes the theologian Martin Marty, "does not welcome explicit Reformed witness—or any other particularized Christian witness."[12] Or, for that matter, any religious witness at all.

Religions that most need protection seem to receive it least. Contemporary 13 America is not likely to enact legislation aimed at curbing the mainstream Protestant, Roman Catholic, or Jewish faiths. But Native Americans, having

[10]Ibid.
[11]Stephen Arterburn and Jack Felton, *Toxic Faith: Understanding and Overcoming Religious Addiction* (Nashville, Tenn.: Oliver-Nelson Books, 1991).
[12]Martin E. Marry, "Reformed America and America Reformed," *Reformed Journal* (March 1989): 8, 10.

once been hounded from their lands, are now hounded from their religions, with the complicity of a Supreme Court untroubled when sacred lands are taken for road building or when Native Americans under a bona fide religious compulsion to use *peyote* in their rituals are punished under state antidrug regulations.[13] (Imagine the brouhaha if New York City were to try to take St. Patrick's Cathedral by eminent domain to build a new convention center, or if Kansas, a dry state, were to outlaw the religious use of wine.) And airports, backed by the Supreme Court, are happy to restrict solicitation by devotees of Krishna Consciousness, which travelers, including this one, find irritating.[14] (Picture the response should the airports try to regulate the wearing of crucifixes or yarmulkes on similar grounds of irritation.)

The problem goes well beyond our society's treatment of those who simply 14 want freedom to worship in ways that most Americans find troubling. An analogous difficulty is posed by those whose religious convictions move them to action in the public arena. Too often, our rhetoric treats the religious impulse to public action as presumptively wicked—indeed, as necessarily oppressive. But this is historically bizarre. Every time people whose vision of God's will moves them to oppose abortion rights are excoriated for purportedly trying to impose their religious views on others, equal calumny is implicitly heaped upon the mass protest wing of the civil rights movement, which was openly and unashamedly religious in its appeals as it worked to impose its moral vision on, for example, those who would rather segregate their restaurants.

One result of this rhetoric is that we often end up fighting the wrong battles. 15 Consider what must in our present day serve as the ultimate example of religion in the service of politics: the 1989 death sentence pronounced by the late Ayatollah Ruhollah Khomeini upon the writer Salman Rushdie for his authorship of *The Satanic Verses*, which was said to blaspheme against Islam. The death sentence is both terrifying and outrageous, and the Ayatollah deserved all the fury lavished upon him for imposing it. Unfortunately, for some critics the facts that the Ayatollah was a religious leader and that the "crime" was a religious one lends the sentence a particular monstrousness; evidently they are under the impression that writers who are murdered for their ideas are choosy about the motivations of their murderers, and that those whose writings led to their executions under, say, Stalin, thanked their lucky stars at the last instant of their lives that Communism was at least godless.

To do battle against the death sentence for Salman Rushdie—to battle 16 against the Ayatollah—one should properly fight against official censorship and intimidation, not against religion. We err when we presume that religious motives are likely to be illiberal, and we compound the error when we insist that the devout should keep their religious ideas—whether good or bad—to themselves. We do no credit to the ideal of religious freedom when we talk as though religious belief is something of which public-spirited adults should be ashamed.

---

[13]*Employment Division, Department of Human Resources v. Smith,* 494 U.S. 872 (1990).
[14]*International Society for Krishna Consciousness v. Lee,* 112 S. Ct. 2701 (1992).

The First Amendment to the Constitution, often cited as the place where [17] this difficulty is resolved, merely restates it. The First Amendment guarantees the "free exercise" of religion but also prohibits its "establishment" by the government. There may have been times in our history when we as a nation have tilted too far in one direction, allowing too much religious sway over politics. But in late-twentieth-century America, despite some loud fears about the influence of the weak and divided Christian right, we are upsetting the balance afresh by tilting too far in the other direction—and the courts are assisting in the effort. For example, when a group of Native Americans objected to the Forest Service's plans to allow logging and road building in a national forest area traditionally used by the tribes for sacred rituals, the Supreme Court offered the back of its hand. True, said the Justices, the logging "could have devastating effects on traditional Indian religious practices." But that was just too bad: "government simply could not operate if it were required to satisfy every citizen's religious needs and desires."[15]

A good point: but what, exactly, are the protesting Indians left to do? Pre- [18] sumably, now that their government has decided to destroy the land they use for their sacred rituals, they are free to choose new rituals. Evidently, a small matter like the potential destruction of a religion is no reason to halt a logging project. Moreover, had the government decided instead to prohibit logging in order to preserve the threatened rituals, it is entirely possible that the decision would be challenged as a forbidden entanglement of church and state. Far better for everyone, it seems, for the Native Americans to simply allow their rituals to go quietly into oblivion. Otherwise, they run the risk that somebody will think they actually take their rituals seriously.

THE PRICE OF FAITH

When citizens do act in their public selves as though their faith matters, they [19] risk not only ridicule, but actual punishment. In Colorado, a public school teacher was ordered by his superiors, on pain of disciplinary action, to remove his personal Bible from his desk where students might see it. He was forbidden to read it silently when his students were involved in other activities. He was also told to take away books on Christianity he had added to the classroom library, although books on Native American religious traditions, as well as on the occult, were allowed to remain. A federal appeals court upheld the instruction, explaining that the teacher could not be allowed to create a religious atmosphere in the classroom, which, it seems, might happen if the students knew he was a Christian.[16] One wonders what the school, and the courts, might do if, as many Christians do, the teacher came to school on Ash Wednesday with ashes in the shape of a cross imposed on his forehead—would he be required to wash

[15]*Lyng v. Northwest Indian Cemetery Protective Association*, 485 U.S. 439 (1988).
[16]*Roberts v. Madigan*, 921 F. 2d 1047 (10th Cir. 1990).

them off? He just might. Early in 1993, a judge required a prosecutor arguing a case on Ash Wednesday to clean the ashes from his forehead, lest the jury be influenced by its knowledge of the prosecutor's religiosity.

Or suppose a Jewish teacher were to wear a yarmulke in the classroom. If 20 the school district tried to stop him, it would apparently be acting within its authority. In 1986, after a Jewish Air Force officer was disciplined for wearing a yarmulke while on duty, in violation of a military rule against wearing headgear indoors, the Supreme Court shrugged: "The desirability of dress regulations in the military is decided by the appropriate military officials," the justices explained, "and they are under no constitutional mandate to abandon their considered professional judgment."[17] The Congress quickly enacted legislation permitting the wearing of religious apparel while in uniform as long as "the wearing of the item would [not] interfere with the performance of the member's military duties," and—interesting caveat—as long as the item is "neat and conservative."[18] Those whose faiths require them to wear dreadlocks and turbans, one supposes, need not apply to serve their country, unless they are prepared to change religions.

Consider the matter of religious holidays. One Connecticut town recently 21 warned Jewish students in its public schools that they would be charged with *six* absences if they missed two days instead of the officially allocated one for Yom Kippur, the holiest observance in the Jewish calendar. And Alan Dershowitz of Harvard Law School, in his controversial book *Chutzpah*, castigates Harry Edwards, a Berkeley sociologist, for scheduling an examination on Yom Kippur, when most Jewish students would be absent. According to Dershowitz's account, Edwards answered criticism by saying: "That's how I'm going to operate. If the students don't like it, they can drop the class." For Dershowitz, this was evidence that "Jewish students [are] second-class citizens in Professor Edwards's classes."[19] Edwards has heatedly denied Dershowitz's description of events, but even if it is accurate, it is possible that Dershowitz has identified the right crime and the wrong villain. The attitude that Dershowitz describes, if it exists, might reflect less a personal prejudice against Jewish students than the society's broader prejudice against religious devotion, a prejudice that masquerades as "neutrality." If Edwards really dared his students to choose between their religion and their grade, and if that meant that he was treating them as second-class citizens, he was still doing no more than the courts have allowed all levels of government to do to one religious group after another—Jews, Christians, Muslims, Sikhs, it matters not at all. The consistent message of modern American society is that whenever the demands of one's religion conflict with what one has to do to get ahead, one is expected to ignore the religious demands and act . . . well . . . *rationally.*

[17]*Goldman v Weinberger,* 475 U.S. 503 (1986).
[18]45 U.S.C. 774, as amended by Pub. L. No. 100-80, Dec. 4, 1987.
[19]Alan M. Dershowitz, *Chutzpah* (Boston: Little, Brown, 1991), pp. 329–30.

Consider Jehovah's Witnesses, who believe that a blood transfusion from 22
one human being to another violates the biblical prohibition on ingesting blood.
To accept the transfusion, many Witnesses believe, is to lose, perhaps forever, the
possibility of salvation. As the Witnesses understand God's law, moreover, the
issue is not whether the blood transfusion is given against the recipient's will,
but whether the recipient is, at the time of the transfusion, actively protesting.
This is the reason that Jehovah's Witnesses sometimes try to impede the physical
access of medical personnel to an unconscious Witness: lack of consciousness is
no defense. This is also the reason that Witnesses try to make the decisions on
behalf of their children: a child cannot be trusted to protest adequately.

The machinery of law has not been particularly impressed with these argu- 23
ments. There are many cases in which the courts have allowed or ordered transfusions to save the lives of unconscious Witnesses, even though the patient
might have indicated a desire while conscious not to be transfused.[20] The machinery of modern medicine has not been impressed, either, except with the
possibility that the Witnesses have gone off the deep end; at least one hospital's
protocol apparently requires doctors to refer protesting Witnesses to psychia-
trists.[21] Although the formal text of this requirement states as the reason the
need to be sure that the Witness knows what he or she is doing, the subtext is a
suspicion that the patient was not acting rationally in rejecting medical advice
for religious reasons. After all, there is no protocol for packing *consenting* patients off to see the psychiatrist. But then, patients who consent to blood transfusions are presumably acting rationally. Perhaps, with a bit of gentle
persuasion, the dissenting Witness can be made to act rationally too—even if it
means giving up an important tenet of the religion.

And therein lies the trouble. In contemporary American culture, the religions 24
are more and more treated as just passing beliefs—almost as fads, older, stuffier,
less liberal versions of so-called New Age—rather than as the fundaments upon
which the devout build their lives. (The noes have it!) And if religions *are* fundamental, well, too bad—at least if they're the *wrong* fundaments—if they're inconvenient, give them up! If you can't remarry because you have the wrong
religious belief, well, hey, believe something else! If you can't take your exam because of a Holy Day, get a new Holy Day! If the government decides to destroy
your sacred lands, just make some other lands sacred! If you must go to work on
your sabbath, it's no big deal! It's just a day off! Pick a different one! If you can't
have a blood transfusion because you think God forbids it, no problem! Get a
new God! And through all of this trivializing rhetoric runs the subtle but unmistakable message: pray if you like, worship if you must, but whatever you do, do
not on any account take your religion seriously.

[20]In every decided case that I have discovered involving efforts by Jehovah's Witness parents to prevent their children from receiving blood transfusions, the court has allowed the transfusion to proceed in the face of parental objection. I say more about transfusions of children of Witnesses, and
about the rights of parents over their children's religious lives, in chapter 11 [of my book].
[21]See Ruth Macklin, "The Inner Workings of an Ethics Committee: Latest Battle over Jehovah's Witnesses," *Hastings Center Report* 18 (February/March 1988): 15.

COMPREHENSION

1. Where does the author articulate the thesis of his essay?
2. The author cites the First Amendment as being a significant historical reference in raising the debate regarding the relationship between government and religion in the United States. What is the First Amendment to the Constitution? What does it mean that the Constitution was amended?
3. In your own words, what is the meaning of the essay's title?

RHETORIC

1. How does the opening line of the essay draw the reader into the concerns of the author?
2. What is the rhetorical function of the bulleted examples the author uses in paragraph 5?
3. In paragraphs 8 and 9, the author introduces a personal tone to his essay. Does this add to or diminish his argument?
4. In paragraph 7, Carter places the word *language* in italics; while in other places, he refers to the use of rhetoric as a way of demeaning the religious impulse. For example, in paragraph 14, where he states, "Too often, our rhetoric treats the religious impulse to public action as presumptively wicked." Why does Carter focus so much on the use of language as a tool in the attack on religion?
5. The author uses mainly anecdotal evidence to support his views, yet most social sciences claim that anecdotes are a poor form of evidence because they refer only to individual cases, and not to general trends. To what degree does Carter's strategy in using anecdotes strengthen or weaken his argument?
6. Carter devotes one section of his essay to "The Price of Faith." Why has he emphasized this religious issue by placing it in a separate category?
7. How does Carter use irony in his final paragraph? Why is this an effective way of both summing up his main points and drawing attention to them?

WRITING

1. Argue for or against the view that the strength of religious toleration among the America people renders any specific legislation regarding religion merely an academic exercise, with no true social effect.
2. In a research paper of approximately 1,000 words, compare and contrast court rulings regarding perceived governmental infringements on Christian rights of worship versus Native American rights of worship.
3. Assume the role of the CEO of a corporation. Write a policy statement in which you provide guidelines for acceptable and unacceptable displays of religious behavior and symbols.

The Rival Conceptions of God

C. S. Lewis

*Clive Staples Lewis (1898–1963) was born in Belfast, Ireland, but spent the most im-
portant years of his life as a lecturer in English at Oxford. His first book,* Dymer, *was
published in 1926, but it was not until the publication of* The Pilgrim's Regress *in
1933 that he addressed the central work of his life: a passionate defense of the Christian
faith. Lewis's immense output embraces science fiction, fantasy, children's books, theology, and literary criticism. Among his best-known works are* The Screwtape Letters
(1942), The Lion, the Witch, and the Wardrobe *(1950), and* The Chronicles of
Narnia *(1956). In this essay, Lewis describes the reasoning that led to his conversion.*

I have been asked to tell you what Christians believe, and I am going to begin   1
by telling you one thing that Christians do not need to believe. If you are a
Christian you do not have to believe that all the other religions are simply
wrong all through. If you are an atheist you do have to believe that the main
point in all the religions of the whole world is simply one huge mistake. If you
are a Christian, you are free to think that all these religions, even the queerest
ones, contain at least some hint of the truth. When I was an atheist I had to try
to persuade myself that most of the human race have always been wrong about
the question that mattered to them most; when I became a Christian I was able
to take a more liberal view. But, of course, being a Christian does mean thinking
that where Christianity differs from other religions, Christianity is right and
they are wrong. As in arithmetic—there is only one right answer to a sum, and
all other answers are wrong: but some of the wrong answers are much nearer
being right than others.

   The first big division of humanity is into the majority, who believe in some   2
kind of God or gods, and the minority who do not. On this point, Christianity
lines up with the majority—lines up with ancient Greeks and Romans, modern
savages, Stoics, Platonists, Hindus, Mohammedans, etc., against the modern
Western European materialist.

   Now I go on to the next big division. People who all believe in God can be   3
divided according to the sort of God they believe in. There are two very different ideas on this subject. One of them is the idea that He is beyond good and
evil. We humans call one thing good and another thing bad. But according to
some people that is merely our human point of view. These people would say
that the wiser you become the less you would want to call anything good or
bad, and the more clearly you would see that everything is good in one way
and bad in another, and that nothing could have been different. Consequently,
these people think that long before you got anywhere near the divine point of
view the distinction would have disappeared altogether. We call a cancer bad,
they would say, because it kills a man; but you might just as well call a successful

surgeon bad because he kills a cancer. It all depends on the point of view. The other and opposite idea is that God is quite definitely "good" or "righteous," a God who takes sides, who loves love and hates hatred, who wants us to behave in one way and not in another. The first of these views—the one that thinks God beyond good and evil—is called Pantheism. It was held by the great Prussian philosopher Hegel and, as far as I can understand them, by the Hindus. The other view is held by Jews, Mohammedans and Christians.

And with this big difference between Pantheism and the Christian idea of 4 God, there usually goes another. Pantheists usually believe that God, so to speak, animates the universe as you animate your body: that the universe almost *is* God, so that if it did not exist He would not exist either, and anything you find in the universe is a part of God. The Christian idea is quite different. They think God invented and made the universe—like a man making a picture or composing a tune. A painter is not a picture, and he does not die if his picture is destroyed. You may say, "He's put a lot of himself into it," but you only mean that all its beauty and interest has come out of his head. His skill is not in the picture in the same way that it is in his head, or even in his hands. I expect you see how this difference between Pantheists and Christians hangs together with the other one. If you do not take the distinction between good and bad very seriously, then it is easy to say that anything you find in this world is a part of God. But, of course, if you think some things really bad, and God really good, then you cannot talk like that. You must believe that God is separate from the world and that some of the things we see in it are contrary to His will. Confronted with a cancer or a slum the Pantheist can say, "If you could only see it from the divine point of view, you would realize that this also is God." The Christian replies, "Don't talk damned nonsense."[1] For Christianity is a fighting religion. It thinks God made the world—that space and time, heat and cold, and all the colours and tastes, and all the animals and vegetables, are things that God "made up out of His head" as a man makes up a story. But it also thinks that a great many things have gone wrong with the world that God made and that God insists, and insists very loudly, on our putting them right again.

And, of course, that raises a very big question. If a good God made the 5 world why has it gone wrong? And for many years I simply refused to listen to the Christian answers to this question, because I kept on feeling "whatever you say, and however clever your arguments are, isn't it much simpler and easier to say that the world was not made by any intelligent power? Aren't all your arguments simply a complicated attempt to avoid the obvious?" But then that threw me back into another difficulty.

My argument against God was that the universe seemed so cruel and un- 6 just. But how had I got this idea of *just* and *unjust*? A man does not call a line crooked unless he has some idea of a straight line. What was I comparing this universe with when I called it unjust? If the whole show was bad and senseless

---

[1]One listener complained of the word *damned* as frivolous swearing. But I mean exactly what I say— nonsense that is *damned* is under God's curse, and will (apart from God's grace) lead those who believe it to eternal death.

from A to Z, so to speak, why did I, who was supposed to be part of the show, find myself in such violent reaction against it? A man feels wet when he falls into water, because man is not a water animal: a fish would not feel wet. Of course I could have given up my idea of justice by saying it was nothing but a private idea of my own. But if I did that, then my argument against God collapsed too—for the argument depended on saying that the world was really unjust, not simply that it did not happen to please my private fancies. Thus in the very act of trying to prove that God did not exist—in other words, that the whole of reality was senseless—found I was forced to assume that one part of reality—namely my idea of justice—was full of sense. Consequently atheism turns out to be too simple. If the whole universe has no meaning, we should never have found out that it has no meaning: just as, if there were no light in the universe and therefore no creature with eyes, we should never know it was dark. *Dark* would be without meaning.

COMPREHENSION

1. Who is Lewis's audience? What is his purpose? How do you know?
2. Lewis divides humanity into a number of distinct categories. Name them, and discuss his purpose in establishing these categories.
3. What is Lewis's purpose in likening Christianity to arithmetic? In what sense is this apt? Where does he use a similar image?

RHETORIC

1. Look up the following words from paragraph 2 in a dictionary or an encyclopedia: *Stoics, Platonists, Hindus,* and *Mohammedans.* What are the major tenets of their beliefs?
2. Explain Lewis's use of the word *damned* (paragraph 4). What is specific about his use of this word? Is it appropriate?
3. How does Lewis develop his argument? What line of reasoning does he follow? What transition markers does Lewis use?
4. How does Lewis use definition to structure certain parts of his argument?
5. In which paragraph is Lewis making what he considers the one irrefutable argument in favor of the existence of God? Is this paragraph coherently reasoned in terms of the whole essay? Explain.
6. Why is Lewis's idea of justice critical to the evaluation of his thought? Is his use of the word *justice* idiosyncratic or objective? How does accepting his definition make an important difference to the response that a reader would give to this piece?

WRITING

1. The Western tradition is based, in large part, on the belief that Christianity is right and other religions are wrong. Is this belief as strong today as it was in the past? Does it still cohere as an argument?

2. Write an essay describing your religious beliefs and how they originated.
3. Argue for or against atheism.

CONNECTIONS FOR CRITICAL THINKING

1. How do writers like Plato, Donne, and Woolf use figurative language to make philosophical points? Use specific examples from these authors' works to formulate your answer.
2. Compare and contrast the way Plato presents his allegory to help the reader arrive at wisdom with the way the Zen master uses the "mystery" of his method to help the student arrive at a unique form of understanding. What is the main difference between the two? Is one preferable over another?
3. Explore the connection between Plato, the philosopher, and Donne, the theologian. How do their essays complement each other? How does Donne's attitude toward existence reflect Plato's philosophy of the cave?
4. What distinguishes a "true" religious belief from a superstition? What are their various functions? Is one more valid than the other? Explain your answer.
5. Coles argues that the moral education of children is essential to a well-functioning society. What function does superstition serve in the lives of children that a pure moral education may fail to provide?
6. Based on your reading of Lewis, explain whether you think he would consider Zen a religion.
7. What is the difference between philosophy and religion? Is it merely a matter of belief? Address this question in an essay, using support from writers in this chapter.
8. Write an essay entitled "The Purpose of Life." Using examples and evidence from their works, choose three writers in this chapter to develop this theme.
9. Join two religious newsgroups. Spend two weeks monitoring their messages. Compare and contrast their concerns, questions, perspectives, and beliefs.
10. Work with other class members in creating your own interactive Web site displaying an excerpt from Donne's "No Man Is an Island." Ask for personal responses from all its visitors, and report your findings.
11. Visit a Web site with summaries of judicial rulings by the Supreme Court. Using the keyword *religion,* study three case histories and the Court's ruling on each.
12. Research the role of cults in American society, particularly among young people. Focus on finding specific superstitions they have that can inflict self-harm or harm on others. Using the essays by Mead and Pogrebin as sources, explore the differences between "good" superstitions and "bad" superstitions.

chapter *9*

Communication, Film, and Media
How Do We Express Ourselves?

Imagine a world without fiction, poetry, or drama; music, art, or dance; radio, television, computers, or film. We are so accustomed to taking the arts in their totality for granted that it is hard for us to conceive of contemporary culture without them. Our fondness for stories or paintings or any other creative form might help us understand our culture or might even move us to action. Yet the value of various artistic forms doesn't derive exclusively from their ability to tell us something about life. The arts can also take us into an imaginative realm offering perhaps more intense experiences than anything we encounter in the "real" world.

Think of media and the arts as an exercise in imaginative freedom. You are free to select the books you read, the movies you see, the exhibitions and concerts you attend, and the entertainment software with which you interact. Some of your decisions might be serious and consequential to your education. Other decisions, perhaps to watch a few soap operas on a rainy afternoon or to buy something you see in a commercial, are less important. The way you view the arts—whether as a temporary escape from conventional reality or as a way to learn something about the temper of civilization—is entirely a matter of taste. Regardless of your purpose or intent, you approach the arts initially for the sheer exhilaration and pleasure they provide. Art, as Plato observed, is a dream for awakened minds.

The arts awaken you to the power and intensity of the creative spirit. At the same time, you make judgments and evaluations of the nature of your creative encounter. When you assert that you like this painting or dislike that movie, you are assessing the work or value of the artistic experience. It is clear that you develop taste and become more equipped to discern the more subtle elements of art the more you are exposed to it. Perhaps you prefer to keep your experience of literature and the other arts a pleasurable pastime or an escape from reality. Or you may wish to participate in them as a creative writer, musician, painter, or dancer. Ultimately you may come to view the arts as a transformational experience, a voyage of discovery in which you encounter diverse peoples and cultures, learn to see the world in creative terms, and begin to perceive your own creative potential in a new light.

Previewing the Chapter

As you read the essays in this chapter and respond to them in discussion and writing, consider the following questions:

- According to the author, what is the value of the art, media, or literary form under discussion?
- What function does literature or art serve?
- Is the writer's perspective subjective or objective and why?
- How does the author define his or her subject—whether it is poetry, fiction, art, or photography?
- Is the writer's experience of literature or art or film or other media similar to or different from your own?
- In what ways do gender and race influence the writer's perspective on the subject?
- What is the main idea that the author wants to present about literature, film, another form of media, or the arts? Do you agree or disagree with this key concept?
- What have you learned about the importance of literature, media, film, and the arts from reading these essays?

Classic and Contemporary Images
WHAT DO GANGSTER FILMS REVEAL ABOUT US?

Using a Critical Perspective   The best gangster films—like *Little Caesar* and *The Godfather*—challenge viewers to form ethical opinions about and interpretations of the tale of crime that unfolds. Even if you haven't seen these two films, what do you think is happening in each frame? What details do you focus on? Do the two characters capture the essence of the gangster life, and why? What aspects of film art—framing, the use of close-up or distance shots, the handling of light, shadow, and color—convey an ethical statement? More broadly, in what ways can film art serve as a commentary on American life?

Photofest

During the 1930s, the first decade of sound films, actors such as Edward G. Robinson, James Cagney, and Paul Muni created the classic portrait of the gangster as a tough-talking, violent outlaw in films such as *Little Caesar* (1930), *The Public Enemy* (1931), and *Scarface* (1932).

Photofest

In the 1970s, 1980s, and 1990s, Hollywood films provided a more nuanced portrait of the gangster as a member of a corrupt, and corrupting, organization with shifting loyalties. For example, Michael Corleone, the character played by Al Pacino in Francis Ford Coppola's three *Godfather* films (1972, 1974, and 1990), tries at first to resist his gangster heritage but is inevitably drawn in.

Classic and Contemporary Essays

WHY ARE WE FASCINATED BY OUTLAWS?

Both Robert Warshow and Roger Ebert examine the portrayal of the gangster in modern culture, although each has a somewhat different interpretive slant. Warshow sees the gangster as a "tragic hero" at odds with—although at times admired by—our value system. Ebert, on the other hand, sees him as a representation of a flawed mythology, a world doomed from the start owing to its own internal inadequacies. Warshow demonstrates that the gangster is ill-fated because he is compelled to operate in an "outlawed" system that ultimately must be squashed by the dominant one. Ebert demonstrates—through his analysis of the film *GoodFellas*—that the outlaw is destined to failure because at heart his system is intrinsically corrupt, and it is the very system to which he has pledged his allegiance that is responsible for his downfall. As Ebert states regarding Henry Hill and his wife, "They have made their lifetime commitment, and it was to the wrong life." Both critics acknowledge that the mythological gangster exists outside of "real time," and although he may be surrounded by acquaintances—in fact, embroiled with them in an alternative social structure—he is ultimately alone. Warshow's gangster is doomed because he must die, because as the author states, "The gangster's whole life is an effort to assert himself as an individual, to draw himself out of the crowd, and he always dies *because* he is an individual." For Ebert, the gangster must also die—if not literally at least figuratively, as Henry Hill does when he betrays the mob and enters the new universe of the "witness protection" program, thereby "dying" to his former life as a mobster. The reason is that in the end, corruption, by its very nature, cannot renew itself. Each of these highly articulate essays demonstrates that an observant writer can glean issues of major moral significance from what the general public views as mere "entertainment."

The Gangster as Tragic Hero

Robert Warshow

Robert Warshow (1917–1955) attended the University of Michigan and worked for the U.S. Army Security Agency from 1942 to 1946. After the war, he served as an editor of Commentary, *writing film criticism for this magazine and also for* Partisan Review. *Before his untimely death from a heart attack, Warshow had written several brilliant essays on film and on popular culture. Writing of Warshow, Lionel Trilling observed, "I believe that certain of his pieces establish themselves in the line of Hazlitt, a tradition in which I would place only one other writer of our time, George Orwell." One of these brilliant essays, focusing on the interrelation of film and society, is "The Gangster as Tragic Hero," which appeared in* The Immediate Experience: Movies, Games, Theatre and Other Aspects of Popular Culture *(1962).*

America, as a social and political organization, is committed to a cheerful view   1
of life. It could not be otherwise. The sense of tragedy is a luxury of aristocratic societies, where the fate of the individual is not conceived of as having a direct and legitimate political importance, being determined by a fixed and supra-political—that is, non-controversial—moral order or fate. Modern equalitarian societies, however, whether democratic or authoritarian in their political forms, always base themselves on the claim that they are making life happier; the avowed function of the modern state, at least in its ultimate terms, is not only to regulate social relations, but also to determine the quality and possibilities of human life in general. Happiness thus becomes the chief political issue—in a sense, the only political issue—and for that reason it can never be treated as an issue at all. If an American or a Russian is unhappy, it implies a certain reprobation of his society, and therefore, by a logic of which we can all recognize the necessity, it becomes an obligation of citizenship to be cheerful; if the authorities find it necessary, the citizen may even be compelled to make a public display of his cheerfulness on important occasions, just as he may be conscripted into the army in time of war.

Naturally, this civic responsibility rests most strongly upon the organs of   2
mass culture. The individual citizen may still be permitted his private unhappiness so long as it does not take on political significance, the extent of this tolerance being determined by how large an area of private life the society can accommodate. But every production of mass culture is a public act and must conform with accepted notions of the public good. Nobody seriously questions the principle that it is the function of mass culture to maintain public morale, and

certainly nobody in the mass audience objects to having his morale maintained.[1] At a time when the normal condition of the citizen is a state of anxiety, euphoria spreads over our culture like the broad smile of an idiot. In terms of attitudes towards life, there is very little difference between a "happy" movie like *Good News,* which ignores death and suffering, and a "sad" movie like *A Tree Grows in Brooklyn,* which uses death and suffering as incidents in the service of a higher optimism.

But, whatever its effectiveness as a source of consolation and a means of pressure for maintaining "positive" social attitudes, this optimism is fundamentally satisfying to no one, not even to those who would be most disoriented without its support. Even within the area of mass culture, there always exists a current of opposition, seeking to express by whatever means are available to it that sense of desperation and inevitable failure which optimism itself helps to create. Most often, this opposition is confined to rudimentary or semi-literate forms: in mob politics and journalism, for example, or in certain kinds of religious enthusiasm. When it does enter the field of art, it is likely to be disguised or attenuated: in an unspecific form of expression like jazz, in the basically harmless nihilism of the Marx Brothers, in the continually reasserted strain of hopelessness that often seems to be the real meaning of the soap opera. The gangster film is remarkable in that it fills the need for disguise (though not sufficiently to avoid arousing uneasiness) without requiring any serious distortion. From its beginnings, it has been a consistent and astonishingly complete presentation of the modern sense of tragedy.[2]

In its initial character, the gangster film is simply one example of the movies' constant tendency to create fixed dramatic patterns that can be repeated indefinitely with a reasonable expectation of profit. One gangster film follows another as one musical or one Western follows another. But this rigidity is not necessarily opposed to the requirements of art. There have been very successful types of art in the past which developed such specific and detailed conventions as almost to make individual examples of the type interchangeable. This is true, for example, of Elizabethan revenge tragedy and Restoration comedy.

For such a type to be successful means that its conventions have imposed themselves upon the general consciousness and become the accepted vehicles of a particular set of attitudes and a particular aesthetic effect. One goes to any individual example of the type with very definite expectations, and originality is to be welcomed only in the degree that it intensifies the expected experience

---

[1]In her testimony before the House Committee on Un-American Activities, Mrs. Leila Rogers said that the movie *None But the Lonely Heart* was un-American because it was gloomy. Like so much else that was said during the unhappy investigation of Hollywood, this statement was at once stupid and illuminating. One knew immediately what Mrs. Rogers was talking about; she had simply been insensitive enough to carry her philistinism to its conclusion.
[2]Efforts have been made from time to time to bring the gangster film into line with the prevailing optimism and social constructiveness of our culture; *Kiss of Death* is a recent example. These efforts are usually unsuccessful; the reasons for their lack of success are interesting in themselves, but I shall not be able to discuss them here.

without fundamentally altering it. Moreover, the relationship between the conventions which go to make up such a type and the real experience of its audience or the real facts of whatever situation it pretends to describe is of only secondary importance and does not determine its aesthetic force. It is only in an ultimate sense that the type appeals to its audience's experience of reality; much more immediately, it appeals to previous experience of the type itself: it creates its own field of reference.

Thus the importance of the gangster film, and the nature and intensity of its 6 emotional and aesthetic impact, cannot be measured in terms of the place of the gangster himself or the importance of the problem of crime in American life. Those European moviegoers who think there is a gangster on every corner in New York are certainly deceived, but defenders of the "positive" side of American culture are equally deceived if they think it relevant to point out that most Americans have never seen a gangster. What matters is that the experience of the gangster *as an experience of art* is universal to Americans. There is almost nothing we understand better or react to more readily or with quicker intelligence. The Western film, though it seems never to diminish in popularity, is for most of us no more than the folklore of the past, familiar and understandable only because it has been repeated so often. The gangster film comes much closer. In ways that we do not easily or willingly define, the gangster speaks for us, expressing that part of the American psyche which rejects the qualities and the demands of modern life, which rejects "Americanism" itself.

The gangster is the man of the city, with the city's language and knowledge, 7 with its queer and dishonest skills and its terrible daring, carrying his life in his hands like a placard, like a club. For everyone else, there is at least the theoretical possibility of another world—in that happier American culture which the gangster denies, the city does not really exist; it is only a more crowded and more brightly lit country—but for the gangster there is only the city; he must inhabit it in order to personify it: not the real city, but that dangerous and sad city of the imagination which is so much more important, which is the modern world. And the gangster—though there are real gangsters—is also, and primarily, a creature of the imagination. The real city, one might say, produces only criminals; the imaginary city produces the gangster: he is what we want to be and what we are afraid we may become.

Thrown into the crowd without background or advantages, with only those 8 ambiguous skills which the rest of us—the real people of the real city—can only pretend to have, the gangster is required to make his way, to make his life and impose it on others. Usually, when we come upon him, he has already made his choice or the choice has already been made for him, it doesn't matter which: we are not permitted to ask whether at some point he could have chosen to be something else than what he is.

The gangster's activity is actually a form of rational enterprise, involving, 9 fairly definite goals and various techniques for achieving them. But thus rationality is usually no more than a vague background; we know, perhaps, that the gangster sells liquor or that he operates a numbers racket; often we are not

given even that much information. So his activity becomes a kind of pure criminality: he hurts people. Certainly our response to the gangster film is most consistently and most universally a response to sadism; we gain the double
satisfaction of participating vicariously in the gangster's sadism and then seeing it turned against the gangster himself.

But on another level the quality of irrational brutality and the quality of ra- 10
tional enterprise become one. Since we do not see the rational and routine aspects of the gangster's behavior, the practice of brutality—the quality of
unmixed criminality—becomes the totality of his career. At the same time, we
are always conscious that the whole meaning of this career is a drive for success: the typical gangster film presents a steady upward progress followed by
a very precipitate fall. Thus brutality itself becomes at once the means to success and the content of success—a success that is defined in its most general
terms, not as accomplishment or specific gain, but simply as the unlimited
possibility of aggression. (In the same way, film presentations of businessmen
tend to make it appear that they achieve their success by talking on the telephone and holding conferences and that success *is* talking on the telephone
and holding conferences.)

From this point; of view, the initial contact between the film and its audi- 11
ence is an agreed conception of human life: that man is a being with the possibilities of success or failure. This principle, too, belongs to the city; one must
emerge from the crowd or else one is nothing. On that basis the necessity of the
action is established, and it progresses, by inalterable paths to the point where
the gangster lies dead and the principle has been modified: there is really only
one possibility—failure. The final meaning of the city is anonymity and death.

In the opening scene of *Scarface*, we are shown a successful man; we know 12
he is successful because he has just given a party of opulent proportions and
because he is called Big Louie. Through some monstrous lack of caution, he
permits himself to be alone for a few moments. We understand from this immediately that he is about to be killed. No convention of the gangster film is
more strongly established than this: it is dangerous to be alone. And yet the
very conditions of success make it impossible not to be alone, for success is always the establishment of an *individual* pre-eminence that must be imposed on
others, in whom it automatically arouses hatred; the successful man is an outlaw. The gangster's whole life is an effort to assert himself as an individual, to
draw himself out of the crowd, and he always dies *because* he is an individual;
the final bullet thrusts him back, makes him, after all, a failure. "Mother of
God," says the dying Little Caesar, "is this the end of Rico?"—speaking of himself thus in the third person because what has been brought low is not the un-
differentiated *man,* but the individual with a name, the gangster, the success;
even to himself he is a creature of the imagination. (T. S. Eliot has pointed out
that a number of Shakespeare's tragic heroes have this trick of looking at themselves dramatically; their true identity, the thing that is destroyed when they
die, is something outside themselves—not a man, but a style of life, a kind of
meaning.)

At bottom, the gangster is doomed because he is under the obligation to 13
succeed, not because the means he employs are unlawful. In the deeper layers
of the modern consciousness, *all* means are unlawful, every attempt to succeed
is an act of aggression, leaving one alone and guilty and defenseless among enemies: one is *punished* for success. This is our intolerable dilemma: that failure is
a kind of death and success is evil and dangerous, is—ultimately—impossible.
The effect of the gangster film is to embody this dilemma in the person of the
gangster and resolve it by his death. The dilemma is resolved because it is *his*
death, not ours. We are safe; for the moment, we can acquiesce in our failure, we
can choose to fail.

COMPREHENSION

1. What are the "organs of mass culture"? What properties do they all have in
   common?
2. Define the term *tragic hero* as Warshow uses it in his title.
3. Compare and contrast Warshow's concepts of the "real city" with those of
   the "imaginary city" as they relate to modern life and mass culture.

RHETORIC

1. Although the ultimate focus of the essay is on the "gangster," the subject is
   not referred to until paragraph 4. Why does the author need so much exposition before focusing on his main topic?
2. What do terms such as *supra-political* (paragraph 1), *harmless nihilism* (paragraph 3), and *general consciousness* (paragraph 5) suggest about the tone of
   the essay? What do they imply concerning the target audience for the essay?
3. Study the topic sentence of each paragraph. Are the topic sentences successful in setting up the material that follows? How does this strategy enhance or detract from the coherence of the author's argument?
4. Essayists usually provide their thesis at the beginning of their essays.
   Where does Warshow provide the thesis in his essay? What is the purpose
   and effect of placing it where it is?
5. The author explains the nature of the gangster film genre—its function,
   characters, themes, plots, meanings, and so on—*before* he cites specific films.
   Is this a rhetorical weakness in the essay, or does it give the essay particular
   potency? Explain.
6. Does the conclusion summarize the main points of the essay, bolster them,
   provide new insights into them, or does it do a combination of these things?
   Explain.
7. Study the introductory paragraph and the conclusion. What themes are re-
   iterated or complemented? How do these two paragraphs serve to provide
   both thematic and structural coherence?

WRITING

1. Select a genre of television show or movie. Analyze its conventions and to what degree these conventions transgress the implicit values of our society.
2. Select a contemporary gangster movie or television program. Using Warshow's criteria, demonstrate—via reference to its characters, plot, and theme—how your selection reinforces the author's thesis.
3. Argue for or against the proposition that genre movies are a form of escapism that distorts the individual's concept of the actual society he or she lives in and its citizens.

Review of *GoodFellas*

Roger Ebert

Roger Ebert (b. 1944) was born in Urbana, Illinois, graduated from the University of Illinois, and did graduate work at the Universities of Illinois, Cape Town (on a Rotary Fellowship), and Chicago. He has been film critic for the Chicago Sun-Times *since 1967 and in 1975 received the Pulitzer Prize for Distinguished Criticism. His reviews, interviews, and essays for the* Sun-Times *are distributed nationally to some 200 newspapers. He is also the best-selling author of the annual guide to films on video,* Roger Ebert's Video Companion. *Among his books are* A Kiss Is Still a Kiss *(1984) and* Two Weeks in the Midday Sun *(1987). He has co-authored other books, including* The Future of the Movies *(1991) and* The Computer Insectiary *(1994). He has been nominated for a TV Emmy award six times and is a member of numerous film and journalist societies and guilds. He has also taught at the University of Virginia and the University of Chicago. His writings have appeared in such magazines as* Wired, *Esquire,* Rolling Stone, Film Comment, *and the* Atlantic Monthly. *The following review of* GoodFellas, *first published in September 1990, in the* Chicago Sun-Times, *addresses the complex and comprehensive system of Mafia values that mixes violence and loyalty, with ultimately tragic results.*

For two days after I saw Martin Scorsese's new film, *GoodFellas,* the mood of the characters lingered within me, refusing to leave. It was a mood of guilt and regret, of quick stupid decisions leading to wasted lifetimes, of loyalty turned into betrayal. Yet at the same time there was an element of furtive nostalgia, for bad times that shouldn't be missed, but were.   1

Most films, even great ones, evaporate like mist once you've returned to the real world; they leave memories behind, but their reality fades fairly quickly. Not this film, which shows America's finest filmmaker at the peak of his form.   2

No finer film has ever been made about organized crime—not even *The Godfather*, although the two works are not really comparable.

"GoodFellas" is a memoir of life in the Mafia, narrated in the first person by 3 Henry Hill (Ray Liotta), an Irish-Italian kid whose only ambition, from his earliest teens, was to be a "wise guy," a Mafioso. There is also narration by Karen, the Jewish girl (Lorraine Bracco) who married him, and who discovered that her entire social life was suddenly inside the Mafia; mob wives never went anywhere or talked to anyone who was not part of that world, and eventually, she says, the values of the Mafia came to seem like normal values. She was even proud of her husband for not lying around the house all day, for having the energy and daring to go out and steal for a living.

There is a real Henry Hill, who disappeared into the anonymity of the fed- 4 eral government's witness protection program, and who over a period of four years told everything he knew about the mob to the reporter Nicholas Pileggi, whose *Wisequy: Life in a Mafia Family* was a best-seller. The screenplay by Pileggi and Scorsese distills those memories into a fiction that sometimes plays like a documentary, that contains so much information and feeling about the Mafia that finally it creates the same claustrophobic feeling Hill's wife talks about: The feeling that the mob world is the real world.

Scorsese is the right director—the only director—for this material. He 5 knows it inside out. The great formative experience of his life was growing up in New York's Little Italy as an outsider who observed everything—an asthmatic kid who couldn't play sports, whose health was too bad to allow him to lead a normal childhood, who was often overlooked, but never missed a thing.

There is a passage early in the film in which young Henry Hill looks out the 6 window of his family's apartment and observes with awe and envy the swagger of the low-level wise guys in the social club across the street, impressed by the fact that they got girls, drove hot cars, had money, that the cops never gave them tickets, that even when their loud parties lasted all night, nobody ever called the police.

That was the life he wanted to lead, the narrator tells us. The memory may 7 come from Hill and may be in Pileggi's book, but the memory also is Scorsese's, and in the 23 years I have known him, we have never had a conversation that did not touch at some point on that central image in his vision of himself—of the kid in the window, watching the neighborhood gangsters.

Like *The Godfather*, Scorsese's *GoodFellas* is a long movie, with the space and 8 leisure to expand and explore its themes. It isn't about any particular plot; it's about what it felt like to be in the Mafia—the good times and the bad times. At first, they were mostly good times, and there is an astonishing camera movement in which the point of view follows Henry and Karen on one of their first dates, to the Copacabana nightclub. There are people waiting in line at the door, but Henry takes her in through the service entrance, past the security guards and the off-duty waiters, down a corridor, through the kitchen, through the service area and out into the front of the club, where a table is literally lifted into the air and placed in front of all the others so that the young couple can be in the first row for the floor show. This is power.

Karen doesn't know yet exactly what Henry does. She finds out. The method   9
of the movie is a slow expansion through levels of the Mafia, with characters
introduced casually and some of them not really developed until later in the
story. We meet the don Paul Cicero (Paul Sorvino), and Jim (Jimmy the Gent)
Conway (Robert De Niro), a man who steals for the sheer love of stealing, and
Tommy DeVito (Joe Pesci), a likable guy except that his fearsome temper can explode in a second, with fatal consequences. We follow them through 30 years; at
first, through years of unchallenged power, then through years of decline (but
they have their own kitchen in prison, and boxes of thick steaks and crates of
wine), and then into betrayal and decay.

At some point, the whole wonderful romance of the Mafia goes sour for   10
Henry Hill, and that moment is when he and Jimmy and Tommy have to bury
a man whom Tommy kicked almost to death in a fit of pointless rage. First, they
have to finish killing him (they stop at Tommy's mother's house to borrow a
knife, and she feeds them dinner), then they bury him, then later they have to
dig him up again. The worst part is, their victim was a "made" guy, a Mafioso
who is supposed to be immune. So they are in deep, deep trouble, and this is
not how Henry Hill thought it was going to be when he started out on his life's
journey.

From the first shot of his first feature, *Who's That Knocking at My Door* (1967),   11
Scorsese has loved to use popular music as a counterpoint to the dramatic moments in his films. He doesn't simply compile a soundtrack of golden oldies; he
finds the precise sound to underline every moment, and in *GoodFellas*, the popular music helps to explain the transition from the early days when Henry sells
stolen cigarettes to guys at a factory gate, through to the frenetic later days
when he's selling cocaine in disobedience of Paul Cicero's orders, and using so
much of it himself that life has become a paranoid labyrinth.

In all of his work, which has included arguably the best film of the 1970s   12
(*Taxi Driver*) and of the 1980s (*Raging Bull*), Scorsese has never done a more
compelling job of getting inside someone's head as he does in one of the concluding passages of *GoodFellas*, in which he follows one day in the life of Henry
Hill, as he tries to do a cocaine deal, cook dinner for his family, placate his mistress and deal with the suspicion that he's being followed.

This is the sequence that imprinted me so deeply with the mood of the film.   13
It's not a straightforward narrative passage, and it has little to do with plot; it's
about the feeling of walls closing in, and the guilty feeling that the walls are deserved. The counterpoint is a sense of duty, of compulsion; the drug deal must
be made, but the kid brother also must be picked up, and the sauce must be
stirred, and meanwhile, Henry's life is careening wildly out of control.

Actors have a way of doing their best work—the work that lets us see them   14
clearly—in a Scorsese film. Robert De Niro emerged as the best actor of his
generation in *Taxi Driver*. Joe Pesci, playing De Niro's brother in *Raging Bull*,
created a performance of comparable complexity. Both De Niro and Pesci are
here in *GoodFellas*, essentially playing major and very challenging supporting
roles to Ray Liotta and Lorraine Bracco, who establish themselves here as

clearly two of our best new movie actors. Liotta was Melanie Griffith's late-arriving, disturbingly dangerous husband in *Something Wild*, and here he creates the emotional center for a movie that is not about the experience of being a Mafioso, but about the feeling. Bracco was the cop's wife from out in the suburbs in *Someone to Watch Over Me*, a film in which her scenes were so effective that it was with a real sense of loss that we returned to the main story. The sense of their marriage is at the heart of this film, especially in a shot where he clings to her, exhausted. They have made their lifetime commitment, and it was to the wrong life.

Many of Scorsese's best films have been poems about guilt. Think of *Mean* 15 *Streets*, with the Harvey Keitel character tortured by his sexual longings, or *After Hours*, with the Griffin Dunne character involved in an accidental death and finally hunted down in the streets by a misinformed mob, or think of *The Last Temptation of Christ*, in which even Christ is permitted to doubt.

GoodFellas is about guilt more than anything else. But it is not a straightfor- 16 ward morality play, in which good is established and guilt is the appropriate reaction toward evil. No, the hero of this film feels guilty for not upholding the Mafia code—guilty of the sin of betrayal. And his punishment is banishment, into the witness protection program, where nobody has a name and the headwaiter certainly doesn't know it.

What finally got to me after seeing this film—what makes it a great film— 17 is that I understood Henry Hill's feelings. Just as his wife Karen grew so completely absorbed by the Mafia inner life that its values became her own, so did the film weave a seductive spell. It is almost possible to think, sometimes, of the characters as really being good fellows. Their camaraderie is so strong, their loyalty so unquestioned. But the laughter is strained and forced at times, and sometimes it's an effort to enjoy the party, and eventually, the whole mythology comes crashing down, and then the guilt—the real guilt, the guilt a Catholic like Scorsese understands intimately—is not that they did sinful things, but that they want to do them again.

COMPREHENSION

1. In his introduction, Ebert refers to "an element of furtive nostalgia." What does he mean by this phrase? Is he referring to his own response to the film, the presumed response of the audience, or to an aspect within the characters themselves? Explain.

2. In paragraph 17, Ebert compares *GoodFellas* to a morality play. What is a morality play? What distinguishes *GoodFellas* from a traditional morality play?

3. In the conclusion, Ebert focuses on the issue of guilt and its relationship to the theme of the movie. Why does Ebert state that the guilt feelings Hill has about his actions are "the real guilt, the guilt a Catholic like Scorsese understands intimately"?

RHETORIC

1. The first two paragraphs of this review do not mention the plot, characters, actors, or setting of the movie, as do most film reviews. How do these two paragraphs set up the body of the review? Explain.
2. How does Ebert use references to his knowledge of filmmaking to give credibility to his position as a reviewer? What information does he disclose that the average filmgoer would not be likely to know?
3. In paragraph 2, Ebert refers to Martin Scorsese as "America's finest film-maker." What other adjectives does Ebert use in his review—when referring to Scorsese—that support his high regard for the director?
4. In paragraph 7, what is the implicit metaphor Ebert uses when describing Scorsese, the film's director, as "the kid in the window, watching the neighborhood gangsters"?
5. A topic sentence is usually considered to be the first sentence in a paragraph. Examine the final sentence in paragraph 8. What is its rhetorical function in the paragraph? How does Ebert structure the paragraph as a variation on the typical paragraph structure of going from the general to the specific?
6. Ebert makes a number of assertions in paragraph 14 regarding the quality of both the actors and the acting in the film. Are these facts or opinions? Explain your view.
7. In paragraph 15, Ebert claims that "Many of Scorsese's best films have been poems. . . ." Why would he describe a film as a poem? Do the two art forms have anything in common? Explain your answer.
8. Ebert refers to the "mood" of the film twice in the introductory paragraph and again in paragraph 13. What does he mean by the "mood" of the film? Why has Ebert used this element of rhetoric to describe the film? How does his description of the film's mood help to make the review comprehensive?

WRITING

1. In an expository essay, argue for or against the proposition that a film review augments one's appreciation of a film even after one has viewed it. Or, argue for or against the proposition that reading a film review can help you appreciate a film before viewing it. You may use *GoodFellas* as an example, either by recalling your experience of the film and then reflecting how the review has altered your response, or by reading the review and then viewing the film afterwards.
2. In paragraph 2, Ebert claims that *GoodFellas* and *The Godfather* "are not really comparable." View both films, and write a comparison and contrast paper in which you either support or refute Ebert's claim.
3. In the conclusion of his review, Ebert claims that *GoodFellas* is a "great film." See the film yourself and write an essay arguing for or against this point of view.

Classic and Contemporary: Questions for Comparison

1. Warshow critiques the function and role of the gangster in the popular media, while Ebert focuses on an analysis of one film in which the life of the gangster is articulated. How do these different focuses determine the themes of each essay? What are the positive and negative consequences of addressing the general issue of "The Gangster as Tragic Hero" without an in-depth explication of an example, as in the essay by Warshow, as opposed to the detailed analysis of one movie without a discussion of the gangster genre, as Ebert does in his review of *GoodFellas?*
2. Warshow explores the significance of the gangster film within the greater context of American culture. If you were to ascribe a genre to his essay, what would you call it: cultural criticism? media analysis? genre definition? There need not necessarily be one correct response, but be sure to support your answer with examples from the essay. On the other hand, is Ebert's essay a review, a critique, or an analysis of a movie, or is it more than one of these? Explain your view.
3. Ebert introduces his essay with a reflection on his personal response to viewing *GoodFellas*. Warshow, on the other hand, begins by making general observations on the nature of society, the modern state, and politics. How do these different rhetorical strategies set up the mode of analysis, tone, and purpose of the two essays?
4. Is it fair to say that Ebert's essay is about "film" while Warshow's is about "society at large"? Explain your view.

The Language of Discretion

Amy Tan

Amy Tan (b. 1952) is the daughter of a minister/electrical engineer and a vocational nurse. She was born in California and educated at San Jose State and the University of California, Berkeley. Tan has worked as a reporter and as a technical writer; her fiction focuses on the lives of Chinese-American women seeking to reconcile their traditional Chinese heritage with modern American culture. Her books are The Joy Luck Club *(1989),* The Kitchen God's Wife *(1991),* The Hundred Secret Senses *(1996), and* Bonesetter's Daughter *(2001). In this narrative essay from* The State of the Language, *Tan writes with both emotion and clarity about growing up with two languages, and she attacks some linguists who make hasty assumptions.*

At a recent family dinner in San Francisco, my mother whispered to me: "Sau- 1
sau [Brother's Wife] pretends too hard to be polite! Why bother? In the end, she
always takes everything."

My mother thinks like a *waixiao,* an expatriate, temporarily away from 2
China since 1949, no longer patient with ritual courtesies. As if to prove her
point, she reached across the table to offer my elderly aunt from Beijing the last
scallop from the Happy Family seafood dish.

Sau-sau scowled. *"B'vuo, zhen b'yao!"* (I don't want it, really I don't!) she 3
cried, patting her plump stomach.

"Take it! Take it!" scolded my mother in Chinese. 4

"Full, I'm already full," Sau-sau protested weakly, eyeing the beloved scallop. 5

"Ai!" exclaimed my mother, completely exasperated. "Nobody else wants 6
it. If you don't take it, it will only rot!"

At this point, Sau-sau sighed, acting as if she were doing my mother a big 7
favor by taking the wretched scrap off her hands.

My mother turned to her brother, a high-ranking communist official who was 8
visiting her in California for the first time: "In America a Chinese person could
starve to death. If you say you don't want it, they won't ask you again forever."

My uncle nodded and said he understood fully: Americans take things 9
quickly because they have no time to be polite.

I thought about this misunderstanding again—of social contexts failing in 10
translation—when a friend sent me an article from *The New York Times Magazine*
(24 April 1988). The article, on changes in New York's Chinatown, made passing reference to the inherent ambivalence of the Chinese language.

Chinese people are so "discreet and modest," the article stated, there aren't 11
even words for "yes" and "no."

That's not true. I thought, although I can see why an outsider might think 12
that. I continued reading.

If one is Chinese, the article went on to say. "One compromises, one doesn't 13
hazard a loss of face by an overemphatic response."

My throat seized. Why do people keep saying these things? As if we truly 14
were those little dolls sold in Chinatown tourist shops, heads bobbing up and
down in complacent agreement to anything said!

I worry about the effect of one-dimensional statements on the unwary and 15
guileless. When they read about this so-called vocabulary deficit, do they also
conclude that Chinese people evolved into a mild-mannered lot because the
language only allowed them to hobble forth with minced words?

Something enormous is always lost in translation. Something insidious 16
seeps into the gaps, especially when amateur linguists continue to compare,
one-for-one, language differences and then put forth notions wide open to mis-
interpretation: that Chinese people have no direct linguistic means to make decisions, assert or deny, affirm or negate, just say no to drug dealers, or behave
properly on the witness stand when told, "Please answer yes or no."

Yet one can argue, with the help of renowned linguists, that the Chinese are 17
indeed up a creek without "yes" and "no." Take any number of variations on
the old language-and-reality theory stated years ago by Edward Sapir: "Human

beings . . . are very much at the mercy of the particular language which has become the medium for their society. . . . The fact of the matter is that the 'real world' is to a large extent built up on the language habits of the group."[1]

This notion was further bolstered by the famous Sapir-Whorf hypothesis, 18 which roughly states that one's perception of the world and how one functions in it depends a great deal on the language used. As Sapir, Whorf, and new carriers of the banner would have us believe, language shapes our thinking, channels us along certain patterns embedded in words, syntactic structures, and intonation patterns. Language has become the peg and the shelf that enables us to sort out and categorize the world. In English, we see "cats" and "dogs"; what if the language had also specified *glatz*, meaning "animals that leave fur on the sofa," and *glotz*, meaning "animals that leave fur and drool on the sofa"? How would language, the enabler, have changed our perceptions with slight vocabulary variations?

And if this were the case—of language being the master of destined 19 thought—think of the opportunities lost from failure to evolve two little words, *yes* and *no*, the simplest of opposites! Ghenghis Khan could have been sent back to Mongolia. Opium wars might have been averted. The Cultural Revolution could have been sidestepped.

There are still many, from serious linguists to pop psychology cultists, who 20 view language and reality as inextricably tied, one being the consequence of the other. We have traversed the range from the Sapir-Whorf hypothesis to est and neurolinguistic programming, which tell us "you are what you say."

I too have been intrigued by the theories. I can summarize, albeit badly, 21 ages-old empirical evidence: of Eskimos and their infinite ways to say "snow," their ability to *see* the differences in snowflake configurations, thanks to the richness of their vocabulary, while non-Eskimo speakers like myself founder in "snow," "more snow," and "lots more where that came from."

I too have experienced dramatic cognitive awakenings via the word. Once I 22 added "mauve" to my vocabulary I began to see it everywhere. When I learned how to pronounce *prix fixe*, I ate French food at prices better than the easier-to-say *à la carte* choices.

But just how seriously are we supposed to take this? 23

Sapir said something else about language and reality. It is the part that of- 24 ten gets left behind in the dot-dot-dots of quotes: ". . . No two languages are ever sufficiently similar to be considered as representing the same social reality. The worlds in which different societies live are distinct worlds, not merely the same world with different labels attached."

When I first read this, I thought, Here at last is validity for the dilemmas I 25 felt growing up in a bicultural, bilingual family! As any child of immigrant parents knows, there's a special kind of double bind attached to knowing two languages. My parents, for example, spoke to me in both Chinese and English; I spoke back to them in English.

---

[1]Edward Sapir, *Selected Writings*, ed. D. G. Mandelbaum (Berkeley and Los Angeles, 1949).

"Amy-ah!" they'd call to me.   26

"What?" I'd mumble back.   27

"Do not question us when we call," they scolded me in Chinese. "It is not   28
respectful."

"What do you mean?"   29

"Ai! Didn't we just tell you not to question?"   30

To this day, I wonder which parts of my behavior were shaped by Chinese,   31
which by English. I am tempted to think, for example, that if I am of two minds
on some matter it is due to the richness of my linguistic experiences, not to any
personal tendencies toward wishy-washiness. But which mind says what?

Was it perhaps patience—developed through years of deciphering my   32
mother's fractured English—that had me listening politely while a woman
announced over the phone that I had won one of five valuable prizes? Was it
respect—pounded in by the Chinese imperative to accept convoluted explanations—that had me agreeing that I might find it worthwhile to drive seventy-
five miles to view a time-share resort? Could I have been at a loss for words
when asked, "Wouldn't you like to win a Hawaiian cruise or perhaps a fabulous
Star of India designed exclusively by Carter and Van Arpels?"

And when this same woman called back a week later, this time complaining   33
that I had missed my appointment, obviously it was my type A language that
kicked into gear and interrupted her. Certainly, my blunt denial—"Frankly I'm
not interested"—was as American as apple pie. And when she said, "But it's in
Morgan Hill," and I shouted, "Read my lips. I don't care if it's Timbuktu," you
can be sure I said it with the precise intonation expressing both cynicism and
disgust.

It's dangerous business, this sorting out of language and behavior. Which   34
one is English? Which is Chinese? The categories manifest themselves: passive
and aggressive, tentative and assertive, indirect and direct. And I realize they are
just variations of the same theme: that Chinese people are discreet and modest.

Reject them all!   35

If my reaction is overly strident, it is because I cannot come across as too   36
emphatic. I grew up listening to the same lines over and over again, like so
many rote expressions repeated in an English phrasebook. And I too almost
came to believe them.

Yet if I consider my upbringing more carefully, I find there was nothing dis-   37
creet about the Chinese language I grew up with. My parents made everything
abundantly clear. Nothing wishy-washy in their demands, no compromises accepted: "Of course you will become a famous neurosurgeon," they told me.
"And yes, a concert pianist on the side."

In fact, now that I remember, it seems that the more emphatic outbursts al-   38
ways spilled over into Chinese: "Not that way! You must wash rice so not a single grain spills out."

I do not believe that my parents—both immigrants from mainland China—   39
are an exception to the modest-and-discreet rule. I have only to look at the number of Chinese engineering students skewing minority ratios at Berkeley, MIT,

and Yale. Certainly they were not raised by passive mothers and fathers who said, "It is up to you, my daughter. Writer, welfare recipient, masseuse, or molecular engineer—you decide."

And my American mind says, See, those engineering students weren't able 40 to say no to their parents' demands. But then my Chinese remembers: Ah, but those parents all wanted their sons and daughters to be *pre-med*.

Having listened to both Chinese and English, I also tend to be suspicious of 41 any comparisons between the two languages. Typically, one language—that of the person doing the comparing—is often used as the standard, the benchmark for a logical form of expression. And so the language being compared is always in danger of being judged deficient or superfluous, simplistic or unnecessarily complex, melodious or cacophonous. English speakers point out that Chinese is extremely difficult because it relies on variations in tone barely discernible to the human ear. By the same token, Chinese speakers tell me English is extremely difficult because it is inconsistent, a language of too many broken rules, of Mickey Mice and Donald Ducks.

Even more dangerous to my mind is the temptation to compare both lan- 42 guage and behavior *in translation*. To listen to my mother speak English, one might think she has no concept of past or future tense, that she doesn't see the difference between singular and plural, that she is gender blind because she calls my husband "she." If one were not careful, one might also generalize that, based on the way my mother talks, all Chinese people take a circumlocutory route to get to the point. It is, in fact, my mother's idiosyncratic behavior to ramble a bit.

Sapir was right about differences between two languages and their realities. I 43 can illustrate why word-for-word translation is not enough to translate meaning and intent. I once received a letter from China which I read to non-Chinese speaking friends. The letter, originally written in Chinese, had been translated by my brother-in-law in Beijing. One portion described the time when my uncle at age ten discovered his widowed mother (my grandmother) had remarried— as a number three concubine, the ultimate disgrace for an honorable family. The translated version of my uncle's letter read in part:

> In 1925, I met my mother in Shanghai. When she came to me, I didn't have greeting to her as if seeing nothing. She pull me to a corner secretly and asked me why didn't have greeting to her. I couldn't control myself and cried, "Ma! Why did you leave us? People told me: one day you ate a beancake yourself. Your sister-in-law found it and sweared at you, called your names. So . . . is it true?" She clasped my hand and answered immediately, "It's not true, don't say what like this." After this time, there was a few chance to meet her.

"What!" cried my friends. "Was eating a beancake so terrible?"   44

Of course not. The beancake was simply a euphemism; a ten-year-old boy 45 did not dare question his mother on something as shocking as concubinage. Eating a beancake was his equivalent for committing this selfish act, something inconsiderate of all family members, hence, my grandmother's despairing response to what seemed like a ludicrous charge of gluttony. And sure enough, she was banished from the family, and my uncle saw her only a few times before her death.

While the above may fuel people's argument that Chinese is indeed a language of extreme discretion, it does not mean that Chinese people speak in secrets and riddles. The contexts are fully understood. It is only to those on the *outside* that the language seems cryptic, the behavior inscrutable.   46

I am, evidently, one of the outsiders. My nephew in Shanghai, who recently started taking English lessons, has been writing me letters in English. I had told him I was a fiction writer, and so in one letter he wrote, "Congratulate to you on your writing. Perhaps one day I should like to read it." I took it in the same vein as "Perhaps one day we can get together for lunch." I sent back a cheery note. A month went by and another letter arrived from Shanghai. "Last one perhaps I hadn't writing distinctly," he said. "In the future, you'll send a copy of your works for me."   47

I try to explain to my English-speaking friends that Chinese language use is more *strategic* in manner, whereas English tends to be more direct; an American business executive may say, "Let's make a deal," and the Chinese manager may reply, "Is your son interested in learning about your widget business?" Each to his or her own purpose, each with his or her own linguistic path. But I hesitate to add more to the pile of generalizations, because no matter how many examples I provide and explain, I fear that it appears defensive and only reinforces the image: that Chinese people are "discreet and modest"—and it takes an American to explain what they really mean.   48

Why am I complaining? The description seems harmless enough (after all, *The New York Times Magazine* writer did not say "slippery and evasive"). It is precisely the bland, easy acceptability of the phrase that worries me.   49

I worry that the dominant society may see Chinese people from a limited— and limiting—perspective. I worry that seemingly benign stereotypes may be part of the reason there are few Chinese in top management positions, in mainstream political roles. I worry about the power of language: that if one says anything enough times—in *any* language—it might become true.   50

Could this be why Chinese friends of my parents' generation are willing to accept the generalization?   51

"Why are you complaining?" one of them said to me. "If people think we are modest and polite, let them think that. Wouldn't Americans be pleased to admit they are thought of as polite?"   52

And I do believe anyone would take the description as a compliment—at first. But after a while, it annoys, as if the only things that people heard one say were phatic remarks: "I'm so pleased to meet you. I've heard many wonderful things about you. For me? You shouldn't have!"   53

These remarks are not representative of new ideas, honest emotions, or considered thought. They are what is said from the polite distance of social contexts: of greetings, farewells, wedding thank-you notes, convenient excuses, and the like.   54

It makes me wonder though. How many anthropologists, how many soci- 55
ologists, how many travel journalists have documented so-called "natural interactions" in foreign lands, all observed with spiral notebook in hand? How
many other cases are there of the long-lost primitive tribe, people who turned
out to be sophisticated enough to put on the stone-age show that ethnologists
had come to see?

And how many tourists fresh off the bus have wandered into Chinatown 56
expecting the self-effacing shopkeeper to admit under duress that the goods are
not worth the price asked? I have witnessed it.

"I don't know," the tourist said to the shopkeeper, a Cantonese woman in 57
her fifties. "It doesn't look genuine to me. I'll give you three dollars."

"You don't like my price, go somewhere else," said the shopkeeper. 58

"You are not a nice person," cried the shocked tourist, "not a nice person at all!" 59

"Who say I have to be nice," snapped the shopkeeper. 60

"So how does one say 'yes' and 'no' in Chinese?" ask my friends a bit warily. 61

And here I do agree in part with the *New York Times Magazine* article. There 62
is no one word for "yes" or "no"—but not out of necessity to be discreet. If anything, I would say the Chinese equivalent of answering "yes" or "no" is dis*crete*,
that is, specific to what is asked.

Ask a Chinese person if he or she has eaten, and he or she might say *chrle* 63
(eaten already) or perhaps *meiyou* (have not).

Ask, "So you had insurance at the time of the accident?" and the response 64
would be *dwei* (correct) or *meiyou* (did not have).

Ask, "Have you stopped beating your wife?" and the answer refers directly 65
to the proposition being asserted or denied: stopped already, still have not,
never beat, have no wife.

What could be clearer? 66

As for those who are still wondering how to translate the language of discre- 67
tion, I offer this personal example.

My aunt and uncle were about to return to Beijing after a three-month visit 68
to the United States. On their last night I announced I wanted to take them out
to dinner.

"Are you hungry?" I asked in Chinese. 69

"Not hungry," said my uncle promptly, the same response he once gave me 70
ten minutes before he suffered a low-blood-sugar attack.

"Not too hungry," said my aunt. "Perhaps you're hungry?" 71

"A little," I admitted. 72

"We can eat, we can eat," they both consented. 73

"What kind of food?" I asked. 74

"Oh, doesn't matter. Anything will do. Nothing fancy, just some simple 75
food is fine."

"Do you like Japanese food? We haven't had that yet," I suggested. 76

They looked at each other. 77

"We can eat it," said my uncle bravely, this survivor of the Long March. 78

"We have eaten it before," added my aunt. "Raw fish."   79
"Oh, you don't like it?" I said. "Don't be polite. We can go somewhere else." 80
"We are not being polite. We can eat it," my aunt insisted.   81
So I drove them to Japantown and we walked past several restaurants fea-   82
turing colorful plastic displays of sushi.

"Not this one, not this one either," I continued to say, as if searching for a 83
Japanese restaurant similar to the last. "Here it is," I finally said, turning into a
restaurant famous for its Chinese fish dishes from Shandong.

"Oh, Chinese food!" cried my aunt, obviously relieved.   84
My uncle patted my arm. "You think Chinese."   85
"It's your last night here in America," I said. "So don't be polite. Act like an 86
American."

And that night we ate a banquet.   87

COMPREHENSION

1. Why is the writer suspicious of any comparisons made between Chinese and English? What dangerous generalizations may be drawn?
2. What is meant by "the double bind attached to knowing two languages"?
3. In your own words, define Sapir's language theory.

RHETORIC

1. What tone does Tan use in her essay? Is her approach objective or subjective? Justify your response.
2. What is Tan's thesis? Is it implied or stated explicitly?
3. How do the anecdotes at the beginning and conclusion of the essay help frame what happens in between? How well do they illustrate or support the essay's body?
4. Cite specific examples of irony or humor in the essay. Is it used consistently throughout the piece? How does its use advance Tan's main ideas?
5. How does Tan employ comparison and contrast to structure this essay?
6. How many sections are there in this essay? What principles of writing and coherence govern each section?

WRITING

1. Tan writes about the generalizations made by "outsiders" about Chinese culture based on the language. Write an essay in which you explore this topic by focusing on misconceptions others may have about you or you may have about others based on language.
2. Linguistic theories are presented by both Tan, and Miller and Swift (pp. 532–538). Using support from either or both essays, consider the dangers of linking behavior to language. Can these theories be used to further racist or sexist notions? Are they valid, scientific attempts to study human behavior?

Loose Ends

Rita Dove

Rita Dove (b. 1953) grew up in Akron, Ohio, and graduated from Miami University of Ohio and the University of Iowa. She later studied at Tübingen University in West Germany on a Fulbright scholarship and received fellowships from the Guggenheim Foundation and the National Endowment for the Arts. In 1987, she received the Pulitzer Prize for her third book of poetry. In 1993, Dove was named Poet Laureate, the first African American and, at 40 years of age, the youngest person ever to hold that post. Rita Dove continues to write and to teach at the University of Virginia, where she is Commonwealth Professor of English. About her writing, she has said: "I am concerned with race but certainly not every poem of mine mentions the fact of being black. They are poems about humanity and sometimes humanity happens to be black. I cannot run from, I won't run from, any kind of truth." The following essay is from The Poet's World *(1995).*

For years the following scene would play daily at our house: Home from 1 school, my daughter would heave her backpack off her shoulder and let it thud to the hall floor, then dump her jacket on top of the pile. My husband would tell her to pick it up—as he did every day—and hang it in the closet. Begrudgingly with a snort and a hrrumph, she would comply. The ritual interrogation began:

"Hi, Aviva. How was school?"   2

"Fine."   3

"What did you do today?"   4

"Nothing."   5

And so it went, every day. We cajoled, we pleaded, we threatened with 6 rationed ice cream sandwiches and new healthy vegetable casseroles, we attempted subterfuges such as: "What was Ms. Boyers wearing today?" or: "Any new pets in science class?" but her answer remained the same: I dunno.

Asked, however, about that week's episodes of "MathNet," her favorite se- 7 ries on Public Television's "Square One," or asked for a quick gloss of a segment of "Lois and Clark" that we happened to miss, and she'd spew out the details of a complicated story, complete with character development, gestures, every twist and backflip of the plot.

Is TV greater than reality? Are we to take as damning evidence the soap 8 opera stars attacked in public by viewers who obstinately believe in the on-screen villainy of Erica or Jeannie's evil twin? Is an estrangement from real life the catalyst behind the escalating violence in our schools, where children imitate the gun-'em-down pyrotechnics of cop-and-robber shows?

Such a conclusion is too easy. Yes, the influence of public media on our per- 9 ceptions is enormous, but the relationship of projected reality—i.e., TV—to imagined reality—i.e., an existential moment—is much more complex. It is not that we confuse TV with reality, but that we prefer it to reality—the manageable struggle resolved in twenty-six minutes, the witty repartee within the family circle instead of the grunts and silence common to most real families; the sharpened conflict and defined despair instead of vague anxiety and invisible enemies. "Life, my friends, is boring. We must not say so," wrote John Berryman, and many years and "Dream Songs" later he leapt from a bridge in Minneapolis. But there is a devastating corollary to that statement: Life, friends, is ragged. Loose ends are the rule.

What happens when my daughter tells the television's story better than her own is simply this: the TV offers an easier tale to tell. The salient points are there for the plucking—indeed, they're the only points presented—and all she has to do is to recall them. Instant Nostalgia! Life, on the other hand, slithers about and runs down blind alleys and sometimes just fizzles at the climax. "The world is ugly, / And the people are sad," sings the country bumpkin in Wallace Stevens's "Gubinnal." Who isn't tempted to ignore the inexorable fact of our insignificance on a dying planet? We all yearn for our private patch of blue.   10

COMPREHENSION

1. What is the thesis of the essay?
2. What is the meaning of the title as it pertains to the essay's argument?
3. Define the following terms: *subterfuge, existential, salient,* and *corollary.*

RHETORIC

1. What is the tone of the essay? How does Dove's use of language suggest this tone?
2. Where and how does Dove make the transition from the opening anecdote to her more general conclusions about television?
3. The author uses dashes, semicolons, and colons in her essay. Locate them. What is their stylistic effect and function?
4. Dove talks of television shows as exhibiting only the "salient points." How can this same observation be made of her writing?
5. Dove states of television that "we prefer it to reality." Who is the "we" in that statement?

WRITING

1. Observe a family watching a television drama or comedy. Observe their body language, demeanor, responses, and gestures. Write an essay describing your observations.
2. Argue for or against the proposition that watching television is a passive pursuit.

3. Interview five students on your campus and ask them to write one-para-
graph responses to the question, "What is the function of television, and
what is your purpose for watching television?" Compare and contrast them
with Dove's argument regarding the purpose and function of television.

Television Addiction

Marie Winn

*Marie Winn was born in the mid-1930s in Prague, Czechoslovakia, and came to the
United States in 1939. She has been a prolific author of books for children. She has contributed many articles to publications such as* The New York Times Magazine, The
New York Times Book Review, *and* Parade. *But she gained national fame with her
book about the hazards of television,* The Plug-In Drug, *in 1977, followed by* Children
without Childhood *in 1983. The following is an excerpt from a chapter of her book on
television, one of the first to alert parents to the effects of the mass media on their children.*

The word "addiction" is often used loosely and wryly in conversation. People   1
will refer to themselves as "mystery book addicts" or "cookie addicts." E. B.
White writes of his annual surge of interest in gardening: "We are hooked and
are making an attempt to kick the habit." Yet nobody really believes that reading mysteries or ordering seeds by catalogue is serious enough to be compared
with addictions to heroin or alcohol. The word "addiction" is here used jokingly
to denote a tendency to overindulge in some pleasurable activity.

People often refer to being "hooked on TV." Does this, too, fall into the   2
lighthearted category of cookie eating and other pleasures that people pursue
with unusual intensity, or is there a kind of television viewing that falls into the
more serious category of destructive addiction?

When we think about addiction to drugs or alcohol, we frequently focus   3
on negative aspects, ignoring the pleasures that accompany drinking or drug-
taking. And yet the essence of any serious addiction is a pursuit of pleasure, a
search for a "high" that normal life does not supply. It is only the inability to
function without the addictive substance that is dismaying, the dependence of
the organism upon a certain experience and an increasing inability to function
normally without it. Thus a person will take two or three drinks at the end of
the day not merely for the pleasure drinking provides, but also because he
"doesn't feel normal" without them.

An addict does not merely pursue a pleasurable experience and need to   4
experience it in order to function normally. He needs to *repeat* it again and
again. Something about that particular experience makes life without it less
than complete. Other potentially pleasurable experiences are no longer possible,

for under the spell of the addictive experience, his life is peculiarly distorted. The addict craves an experience and yet he is never really satisfied. The organism may be temporarily sated, but soon it begins to crave again.

Finally a serious addiction is distinguished from a harmless pursuit of plea- 5 sure by its distinctly destructive elements. A heroin addict, for instance, leads a damaged life: his increasing need for heroin in increasing doses prevents him from working, from maintaining relationships, from developing in human ways. Similarly an alcoholic's life is narrowed and dehumanized by his dependence on alcohol.

Let us consider television viewing in the light of the conditions that define 6 serious addictions.

Not unlike drugs or alcohol, the television experience allows the participant 7 to blot out the real world and enter into a pleasurable and passive mental state. The worries and anxieties of reality are as effectively deferred by becoming absorbed in a television program as by going on a "trip" induced by drugs or alcohol. And just as alcoholics are only inchoately aware of their addiction, feeling that they control their drinking more than they really do ("I can cut it out any time I want—I just like to have three or four drinks before dinner"), people similarly overestimate their control over television watching. Even as they put off other activities to spend hour after hour watching television, they feel they could easily resume living in a different, less passive style. But somehow or other while the television set is present in their homes, the click doesn't sound. With television pleasures available, those other experiences seem less attractive, more difficult somehow.

A heavy viewer (a college English instructor) observes: 8

"I find television almost irresistible. When the set is on, I cannot ignore it. I 9 can't turn it off. I feel sapped, will-less, enervated. As I reach out to turn off the set, the strength goes out of my arms. So I sit there for hours and hours."

The self-confessed television addict often feels he "ought" to do other 10 things—but the fact that he doesn't read and doesn't plant his garden or sew or crochet or play games or have conversations means that those activities are no longer as desirable as television viewing. In a way a heavy viewer's life is as imbalanced by his television "habit" as a drug addict's or an alcoholic's. He is living in a holding pattern, as it were, passing up the activities that lead to growth or development or a sense of accomplishment. This is one reason people talk about their television viewing so ruefully, so apologetically. They are aware that it is an unproductive experience, that almost any other endeavor is more worthwhile by any human measure.

Finally it is the adverse effect of television viewing on the lives of so many 11 people that defines it as a serious addiction. The television habit distorts the sense of time. It renders other experiences vague and curiously unreal while taking on a greater reality for itself. It weakens relationships by reducing and sometimes eliminating normal opportunities for talking, for communicating.

And yet television does not satisfy, else why would the viewer continue to 12 watch hour after hour, day after day? "The measure of health," writes Lawrence

Kubie, "is flexibility . . . and especially the freedom to cease when sated."[1] But the television viewer can never be sated with his television experiences—they do not provide the true nourishment that satiation requires—and thus he finds that he cannot stop watching.

COMPREHENSION

1. Why does Winn consider television watching a true addiction?
2. Why does Winn consider television viewing hazardous to one's well-being?
3. What implicit assumption does Winn make concerning the purpose of human experience that leads her to conclude that television watching is harmful?

RHETORIC

1. What function does the question Winn poses in paragraph 2 serve in setting up her argument?
2. Study the introductory paragraph. Is it truly needed? Does it add strength to the author's argument? What is its function, if any?
3. In paragraph 3, Winn refers to a person as "the organism." From what branch of learning is she borrowing this term? What is the purpose of using this word within the context of her argument?
4. In paragraph 11, the author states several effects of television viewing. Are these based on fact or opinion? Does it matter for the sake of her argument?
5. What does paragraph 6 contribute to the structure and coherence of the essay?
6. In her concluding paragraph, the author cites the work of a psychologist. Does this support her main argument? Explain.
7. The author presents television addiction as a serious issue. How does the tone of her essay communicate how seriously she regards the subject?

WRITING

1. Argue for or against the view that watching television critically can be a positive educational experience.
2. Develop a manual for people who want to cut down on their television viewing. Model it after a weight-loss or smoking-cessation program.
3. It seems these days as though television is blamed for everything. Argue for the proposition that watching television is good for you.

---

[1]Lawrence Kubie, *Neurotic Distortion and the Creative Process* (Lawrence: University of Kansas Press, 1958).

2 Live Crew, Decoded

Henry Louis Gates Jr.

Henry Louis Gates Jr. was born in 1950 in Keyser, West Virginia, and was educated at Yale University and Clare College, Cambridge, where he received his PhD in 1979. He now teaches at Harvard University. Gates has edited numerous books addressing the issues of race, identity, and African American history and has contributed to over a dozen periodicals and journals, including Critical Inquiry, Black World, Yale Review, *and* Antioch Review, *among others. His work attempts to apply contemporary literary theories, such as structuralism and poststructuralism, to African and African American literature so that readers can develop a deep understanding of the structure, significance, methods, and meanings of this body of work. Much of his theoretical insights are summed up in his book* The Signifying Monkey: Towards a Theory of Afro-American Literary Criticism *(1988). Among his awards and honors have been a Carnegie Foundation fellowship, a MacArthur Prize fellowship, and a Mellon fellowship from Yale University. In the following essay, Gates offers a keen analysis of the rap music phenomenon.*

The rap group 2 Live Crew and their controversial hit recording, "As Nasty as 1
They Wanna Be," may well earn a signal place in the history of First Amendment rights. But just as important is how these lyrics will be interpreted and by whom.

For centuries, African Americans have been forced to develop coded ways 2
of communicating to protect them from danger. Allegories and double meanings, words redefined to mean their opposites ("bad" meaning "good," for instance), even neologisms ("bodacious") have enabled blacks to share messages only the initiated understand.

Many blacks were amused by the transcripts of Marion Barry's sting oper- 3
ation which reveals that he used the traditional black expression about one's "nose being opened." This referred to a love affair and not, as Mr. Barry's prosecutors have suggested, to the inhalation of drugs. Understanding this phrase could very well spell the difference (for the Mayor) between prison and freedom.

2 Live Crew is engaged in heavy-handed parody, turning the stereotypes of 4
black and white American culture on their heads. These young artists are acting out, to lively dance music, a parodic exaggeration of the age-old stereotypes of the oversexed black female and male. Their exuberant use of hyperbole (phantasmagoric sexual organs, for example) undermines—for anyone fluent in black cultural codes—a too literal-minded hearing of the lyrics.

This is the street tradition called "signifying" or "playing the dozens," 5
which has generally been risqué, and where the best signifier or "rapper" is the one who invents the most extravagant images, the biggest "lies," as the culture

says. (H. "Rap" Brown earned his nickname in just this way.) In the face of racist stereotypes about black sexuality, you can do one of two things: you can disavow them or explode them with exaggeration.

2 Live Crew, like many "hip-hop" groups, is engaged in sexual carnivalesque. Parody reigns supreme, from a take-off of standard blues to a spoof of the black power movement, their off-color nursery rhymes are part of a venerable Western tradition. The group even satirizes the culture of commerce when it appropriates popular advertising slogans ("Tastes great!" "Less filling!") and puts them in a bawdy context. 6

2 Live Crew must be interpreted within the context of black culture generally and of signifying specifically. Their novelty, and that of other adventuresome rap groups, is that their defiant rejection of euphemism now voices for the mainstream what before existed largely in the "race record" market—where the records of Redd Foxx and Rudy Ray Moore once were forced to reside. 7

Rock songs have always been about sex but have used elaborate subterfuges to convey that fact. 2 Live Crew uses Anglo-Saxon words and is self-conscious about it: a parody of a white voice in one song refers to "private personal parts," as a coy counterpart to the group's bluntness. 8

Much more troubling than its so-called obscenity is the group's overt sexism. Their sexism is so flagrant, however, that it almost cancels itself out in a hyperbolic war between the sexes. In this, it recalls the inter-sexual jousting in Zora Neale Hurston's novels. Still, many of us look toward the emergence of more female rappers to redress sexual stereotypes. And we must not allow ourselves to sentimentalize street culture: the appreciation of verbal virtuosity does not lessen one's obligation to critique bigotry in all of its pernicious forms. 9

Is 2 Live Crew more "obscene" than, say, the comic Andrew Dice Clay?[1] Clearly, this rap group is seen as more threatening than others that are just as sexually explicit. Can this be completely unrelated to the specter of the young black male as a figure of sexual and social disruption, the very stereotypes 2 Live Crew seem determined to undermine? 10

This question—and the very large question of obscenity and the First Amendment—cannot even be addressed until those who would answer them become literate in the vernacular traditions of African Americans. To do less is to censor through the equivalent of intellectual prior restraint—and censorship is to art what lynching is to justice. 11

COMPREHENSION

1. What is the author's thesis?
2. According to Gates, what must one know before engaging in a critique of 2 Live Crew?
3. Does Gates consider 2 Live Crew's music obscene? Why or why not?

---

[1]A controversial stand-up comedian popular in the late 1980s.

RHETORIC

1. The paragraphs in this essay are fairly short. How does this affect Gates's argument?
2. How does the author use definition to decode certain aspects of African American culture? Why is definition an important strategy in his argument?
3. Gates uses the word *hyperbole* in paragraph 4 and the word *hyperbolic* in paragraph 9. Why is it necessary for him to emphasize this concept to develop his argument?
4. Does the author appear to use a particular tone toward his subject matter? Does he appear to support the art of his subject, condemn it, explain it, or provide a mixture of all three approaches?
5. For whom is this essay written? What is its intended purpose? Explain your view.
6. Examine the final sentence of the essay. Does it provide an effective closure? Why is it particularly pertinent considering 2 Live Crew is an African American music group? Explain your view.

WRITING

1. Argue for or against the proposition that only after informed study and consideration can one legitimately judge the quality of a work of art or determine if something *is* art.
2. Argue for or against the proposition that 2 Live Crew is obscene, basing your argument on the points raised in the article by Gates.
3. For a research project, write a paper entitled "The Arts and Obscenity during the Twentieth Century."

My Creature from the Black Lagoon

Stephen King

Stephen King (b. 1947) was born in Portland, Maine. Raised by his mother, he spent parts of his childhood in Indiana, Connecticut, Massachusetts, and Maine. He graduated from the University of Maine at Orono in 1970 with a degree in English. During his early writing career, he sold several stories to mass market men's magazines and taught English in Hampden, Maine. In 1973, his novel Carrie *sold enough copies that he could devote his energies to writing full-time. He is the author of about 100 books, most focusing on horror and the occult. A number have been adapted for film and television, including* Carrie, The Dead Zone, The Shining, Christine, Pet Sematary, *and* Stand By Me, *among others. Besides writing, he belongs to an all-writers rock and roll band (with Dave Barry and Amy Tan) and is a major contributor to local and national charities. In the following selection, taken from* Danse Macabre *(1981), King compares and contrasts the responses of adults and children to horror movies.*

The first movie I can remember seeing as a kid was *Creature from the Black Lagoon.* 1 It was at the drive-in, and unless it was a second-run job I must have been about seven, because the film, which starred Richard Carlson and Richard Denning, was released in 1954. It was also originally released in 3-D, but I cannot remember wearing the glasses, so perhaps I did see a rerelease.

I remember only one scene clearly from the movie, but it left a lasting 2 impression. The hero (Carlson) and the heroine (Julia Adams, who looked absolutely spectacular in a one-piece white bathing suit) are on an expedition somewhere in the Amazon basin. They make their way up a swampy, narrow waterway and into a wide pond that seems an idyllic South American version of the Garden of Eden.

But the creature is lurking—naturally. It's a scaly, batrachian monster that is 3 remarkably like Lovecraft's half-breed, degenerate aberrations—the crazed and blasphemous results of liaisons between gods and human women (It's difficult to get away from Lovecraft). This monster is slowly and patiently barricading the mouth of the stream with sticks and branches, irrevocably sealing the party of anthropologists in.

I was barely old enough to read at that time, the discovery of my father's 4 box of weird fiction still years away. I have a vague memory of boyfriends in my mom's life during that period—from 1952 until 1958 or so; enough of a memory to be sure she had a social life, not enough to even guess if she had a sex life. There was Norville, who smoked Luckies and kept three fans going in his two-room apartment during the summer; and there was Milt, who drove a Buick and wore gigantic blue shorts in the summertime; and another fellow, very small, who was, I believe, a cook in a French restaurant. So far as I know, my mother came close to marrying none of them. She'd gone that route once. Also, that was a time when a woman, once married, became a shadow figure in the process of decision-making and bread-winning. I think my mom, who could be stubborn, intractable, grimly persevering and nearly impossible to discourage, had gotten a taste for captaining her own life. And so she went out with guys, but none of them became permanent fixtures.

It was Milt we were out with that night, he of the Buick and the large blue 5 shorts. He seemed to genuinely like my brother and me, and to genuinely not mind having us along in the back seat from time to time (it may be that when you have reached the calmer waters of your early forties, the idea of necking at the drive-in no longer appeals so strongly . . . even if you have a Buick as large as a cabin cruiser to do it in). By the time the Creature made his appearance, my brother had slithered down onto the floor of the back and had fallen asleep. My mother and Milt were talking, perhaps passing a Kool back and forth. They don't matter, at least not in this context; nothing matters except the big black-and-white images up on the screen, where the unspeakable Thing is walling the handsome hero and the sexy heroine into . . . into . . . the Black Lagoon!

I knew, watching, that the Creature had become *my* Creature; I had bought 6 it. Even to a seven-year-old, it was not a terribly convincing Creature. I did not know then it was good old Ricou Browning, the famed underwater stuntman, in a molded latex suit, but I surely knew it was some guy in some kind of a monster suit . . . just as I knew that, later on that night, he would visit me in the black lagoon of my dreams, looking much more realistic. He might be waiting in the closet when we got back; he might be standing slumped in the blackness of the bathroom at the end of the hall, stinking of algae and swamp rot, all ready for a post-midnight snack of small boy. Seven isn't old, but it is old enough to know that you get what you pay for. You own it, you bought it, it's yours. It is old enough to feel the dowser suddenly come alive, grow heavy, and roll over in your hands, pointing at hidden water.

My reaction to the Creature on that night was perhaps the perfect reaction, 7 the one every writer of horror fiction or director who has worked in the field hopes for when he or she uncaps a pen or a lens: total emotional involvement, pretty much undiluted by any real thinking process—and you understand, don't you, that when it comes to horror movies, the only thought process really necessary to break the mood is for a friend to lean over and whisper, "See the zipper running down his back?"

I think that only people who have worked in the field for some time truly 8 understand how fragile this stuff really is, and what an amazing commitment it imposes on the reader or viewer of intellect and maturity. When Coleridge spoke of "the suspension of disbelief" in his essay on imaginative poetry, I believe he knew that disbelief is not like a balloon, which may be suspended in air with a minimum of effort; it is like a lead weight, which has to be hoisted with a clean and a jerk and held up by main force. Disbelief isn't light; it's heavy. The difference in sales between Arthur Hailey and H. P. Lovecraft may exist because everyone believes in cars, and banks, but it takes a sophisticated and muscular intellectual act to believe, even for a little while, in Nyarlathotep, the Blind Faceless One, the Howler in the Night. And whenever I run into someone who expresses a feeling along the lines of, "I don't read fantasy or go to any of those movies; none of it's real," I feel a kind of sympathy. They simply can't lift the weight of fantasy. The muscles of the imagination have grown too weak.

In this sense, kids are the perfect audience for horror. The paradox is this: 9 children, who are physically quite weak, lift the weight of unbelief with ease. They are the jugglers of the invisible world—a perfectly understandable phenomenon when you consider the perspective they must view things from. Children deftly manipulate the logistics of Santa Claus's entry on Christmas Eve (he can get down small chimneys by making himself small, and if there's no chimney there's the letter slot, and if there's no letter slot there's always the crack under the door), the Easter Bunny, God (big guy, sorta old, white beard, throne), Jesus ("How do you think he turned the water into wine?" I asked my son Joe when he—Joe, not Jesus—was five; Joe's idea was that he had something "kinda like magic Kool-Aid, you get what I mean?"), the devil (big guy, red skin, horse feet, tail with an arrow on the end of it, Snidely Whiplash moustache), Ronald McDonald, the Burger King, the Keebler Elves, Dorothy and Toto, the Lone Ranger and Tonto, a thousand more.

Most parents think they understand this openness better than, in many 10 cases, they actually do, and try to keep their children away from anything that smacks too much of horror and terror—"Rated PG (or G in the case of *The Andromeda Strain*), but may be too intense for younger children," the ads for *Jaws* read—believing, I suppose, that to allow their kids to go to a real horror movie would be tantamount to rolling a live hand grenade into a nursery school.

But one of the odd Döppler effects that seems to occur during the selective 11 forgetting that is so much a part of "growing up" is the fact that almost *every-thing* has a scare potential for the child under eight. Children are literally afraid of their own shadows at the right time and place. There is the story of the four-year-old who refused to go to bed at night without a light on in his closet. His parents at last discovered he was frightened of a creature he had heard his father speak of often; this creature, which had grown large and dreadful in the child's imagination, was the "twi-night double-header."

Seen in this light, even Disney movies are minefields of terror, and the ani- 12 mated cartoons, which will apparently be released and rereleased even unto the end of the world,[*] are usually the worst offenders. There are adults today, who, when questioned, will tell you that the most frightening thing they saw at the movies as children was Bambi's father shot by the hunter, or Bambi and his mother running before the forest fire. Other Disney memories which are right up there with the batrachian horror inhabiting the Black Lagoon include the marching brooms that have gone totally out of control in *Fantasia* (and for the small child, the real horror inherent in the situation is probably buried in the implied father-son relationship between Mickey Mouse and the old sorcerer; those brooms are making a terrible mess, and when the sorcerer/father gets home, there may be PUNISHMENT. . . . This sequence might well send the child of strict parents into an ecstasy of terror); the night on Bald Mountain from the same film; the witches in *Snow White* and *Sleeping Beauty,* one with her enticingly red poisoned apple (and what small child is not taught early to fear the idea of POISON?), the other with her deadly spinning wheel; this holds all the way up to the relatively innocuous *One Hundred and One Dalmatians* which features the logical granddaughter of those Disney witches from the thirties and forties—the evil Cruella DeVille, with her scrawny, nasty face, her loud voice (grownups sometimes forget how terrified

---

[*]In one of my favorite Arthur C. Clarke stories, this actually happens. In this vignette, aliens from space land on earth after the Big One has finally gone down. As the story closes, the best brains of this alien culture are trying to figure out the meaning of a film they have found and learned how to play back. The film ends with the words *A Walt Disney Production.* I have moments when I really believe that there would be no better epitaph for the human race, or for a world where the only sentient being absolutely guaranteed of immortality is not Hitler, Charlemagne, Albert Schweitzer, or even Jesus Christ—but is, instead, Richard M. Nixon, whose name is engraved on a plaque placed on the airless surface of the moon.

young children are of loud voices, which come from the giants of their world, the adults), and her plan to kill all the dalmatian puppies (read "children," if you're a little person) and turn them into dogskin coats.

Yet it is the parents, of course, who continue to underwrite the Disney procedure of release and rerelease, often discovering goosebumps on their own arms as they rediscover what terrified them as children . . . because what the good horror film (or horror sequence in what may be billed a "comedy" or an "animated cartoon") does above all else is to knock the adult props out from under us and tumble us back down the slide into childhood. And there our own shadow may once again become that of a mean dog, a gaping mouth, or a beckoning dark figure.

Perhaps the supreme realization of this return to childhood comes in David Cronenberg's marvelous horror film *The Brood*, where a disturbed woman is literally producing "children of rage" who go out and murder the members of her family, one by one. About halfway through the film, her father sits dispiritedly on the bed in an upstairs room, drinking and mourning his wife, who has been the first to feel the wrath of the brood. We cut to the bed itself . . . and clawed hands suddenly reach out from beneath it and dig into the carpeting near the doomed father's shoes. And so Cronenberg pushes us down the slide; we are four again, and all of our worst surmises about what might be lurking under the bed have turned out to be true.

The irony of all this is that children are better able to deal with fantasy and terror *on its own terms* than their elders are. You'll note I've italicized the phrase "on its own terms." An adult is able to deal with the cataclysmic terror of something like *The Texas Chain Saw Massacre* because he or she understands that it is all make-believe, and that when the take is done the dead people will simply get up and wash off the stage blood. The child is not so able to make this distinction, and *Chainsaw Massacre* is quite rightly rated R. Little kids do not need this scene, any more than they need the one at the end of *The Fury* where John Cassavetes quite literally blows apart. But the point is, if you put a little kid of six in the front row at a screening of *The Texas Chainsaw Massacre* along with an adult who was temporarily unable to distinguish between make-believe and "real things" (as Danny Torrance, the little boy in *The Shining* puts it)—if, for instance, you had given the adult a hit of Yellow Sunshine LSD about two hours before the movie started—my guess is that the kid would have maybe a week's worth of bad dreams. The adult might spend a year or so in a rubber room, writing home with Crayolas.

A certain amount of fantasy and horror in a child's life seems to me a perfectly okay, useful sort of thing. Because of the size of their imaginative capacity, children are able to handle it, and because of their unique position in life, they are able to put such feelings to work They understand their position very well, too. Even in such a relatively ordered society as our own, they understand that their survival is a matter almost totally out of their hands. Children are "dependents" up until the age of eight or so in every sense of the word; dependent on mother and father (or some reasonable facsimile thereof) not only for food, clothing, and shelter, but dependent on them not to crash the car into a bridge abutment, to meet the school bus on time, to walk them home from Cub Scouts or Brownies, to buy medicines with childproof caps, dependent on them to make sure they don't electrocute themselves while screwing around with the toaster or while trying to play with Barbie's Beauty Salon in the bathtub.

Running directly counter to this necessary dependence is the survival directive built into all of us. The child realizes his or her essential lack of control, and I suspect it is this very realization which makes the child uneasy. It is the same sort of free-floating anxiety that many air travelers feel. They are not afraid because they believe air travel to be unsafe; they are afraid because they have surrendered control, and if something goes wrong all they can do is sit there clutching airsick bags or the in-flight magazine. To surrender control runs counter to the survival directive. Conversely, while a thinking, informed person may understand intellectually that travel by car is much more dangerous than flying, he or she is still apt to feel much more comfortable behind the wheel, because she/he has control . . . or at least an illusion of it. 17

This hidden hostility and anxiety toward the airline pilots of their lives may be one explanation why, like the Disney pictures which are released during school vacations in perpetuity, the old fairy tales also seem to go on forever. A parent who would raise his or her hands in horror at the thought of taking his/her child to see *Dracula* or *The Changeling* (with its pervasive imagery of the drowning child) would be unlikely to object to the baby sitter reading "Hansel and Gretel" to the child before bedtime. But consider: the tale of Hansel and Gretel begins with deliberate abandonment (oh yes, the stepmother masterminds that one, but she is the symbolic mother all the same, and the father is a spaghetti-brained nurd who goes along with everything she suggests even though he know it's wrong—thus we can see her as amoral, him as actively evil in the Biblical and Miltonian sense), it progresses to kidnapping (the witch in the candy house), enslavement, illegal detention, and finally justifiable homicide and cremation. Most mothers and fathers would never take their children to see *Survive*, that quickie Mexican exploitation flick about the rugby players who survived the aftermath of a plane crash in the Andes by eating their dead teammates, but these same parents find little to object to in "Hansel and Gretel," where the witch is fattening the children up so she can eat them. We give this stuff to the kids almost instinctively, understanding on a deeper level, perhaps, that such fairy stories are the perfect points of crystallization for those fears and hostilities. 18

Even anxiety-ridden air travelers have their own fairy tales—all those *Airport* movies, which, like "Hansel and Gretel" and all those Disney cartoons, show every sign of going on forever . . . but which should only be viewed on Thanksgivings, since all of them feature a large cast of turkeys. 19

My gut reaction to *Creature from the Black Lagoon* on that long-ago night was a kind of terrible, waking swoon. The nightmare was happening right in front of me; every hideous possibility that human flesh is heir to was being played out on that drive-in screen. 20

Approximately twenty-two years later, I had a chance to see *Creature from* 21
the Black Lagoon again—not on TV, with any kind of dramatic build and mood
broken up by adverts for used cars, K-Tel disco anthologies, and Underalls
pantyhose, thank God, but intact, uncut . . . and even in 3-D. Guys like me who
wear glasses have a hell of a time with 3-D, you know; ask anyone who wears
specs how they like those nifty little cardboard glasses they give you when you
walk in the door. If 3-D ever comes back in a big way, I'm going to take myself
down to the local Pearle Vision Center and invest seventy bucks in a special pair
of prescription lenses: one red, one blue. Annoying glasses aside, I should add
that I took my son Joe with me—he was then five, about the age I had been myself, that night at the drive-in (and imagine my surprise—my *rueful* surprise—
to discover that the movie which had so terrified me on that long-ago night had
been rated G by the MPAA . . . just like the Disney pictures).

As a result, I had a chance to experience that weird doubling back in time 22
that I believe most parents only experience at the Disney films with their children, or when reading them the Pooh books or perhaps taking them to the
Shrine or the Barnum & Bailey circus. A popular record is apt to create a particular "set" in a listener's mind, precisely because of its brief life of six weeks to
three months, and "golden oldies" continue to be played because they are the
emotional equivalent of freeze-dried coffee. When the Beach Boys come on the
radio singing "Help Me, Rhonda," there is always that wonderful second or
two when I can re-experience the wonderful, guilty joy of copping my first feel
(and if you do the mental subtraction from my present age of thirty-three, you'll
see that I was a little backward in that respect). Movies and books do the same
thing, although I would argue that the mental set, its depth and texture, tends
to be a little richer, a little more complex, when re-experiencing films and a lot
more complex when dealing with books.

With Joe that day I experienced *Creature from the Black Lagoon* from the other 23
end of the telescope, but this particular theory of set identification still applied;
in fact, it prevailed. Time and age and experience have all left their marks on
me, just as they have on you; time is not a river, as Einstein theorized—it's a big
. . . buffalo herd that runs us down and eventually mashes us into the ground,
dead and bleeding, with a hearing-aid plugged into one ear and a colostomy
bag instead of a .44 clapped on one leg. Twenty-two years later I knew that the
Creature was really good old Ricou Browning, the famed underwater stuntman,
in a molded latex suit, and the suspension of disbelief, that mental clean-and-
jerk, had become a lot harder to accomplish. But I did it, which may mean nothing, or which may mean (I hope!) that the buffalo haven't got me yet. But when
that weight of disbelief was finally up there, the old feelings came flooding in,
as they flooded in some five years ago when I took Joe and my daughter Naomi
to their first movie, a reissue of *Snow White and the Seven Dwarfs*. There is a scene
in that film where, after Snow White has taken a bite from the poisoned apple,
the dwarfs take her into the forest, weeping copiously. Half the audience of little kids was also in tears; the lower lips of the other half were trembling. The set
identification in that case was strong enough so that I was also surprised into
tears. I hated myself for being so blatantly manipulated, but manipulated I was,

and there I sat, blubbering into my beard over a bunch of cartoon characters. But it wasn't Disney that manipulated me; I did it myself. It was the kid inside who wept, surprised out of dormancy and into schmaltzy tears . . . but at least awake for awhile.

During the final two reels of *Creature from the Black Lagoon,* the weight of disbelief is nicely balanced somewhere above my head, and once again director Jack Arnold places the symbols in front of me and produces the old equation of the fairy tales, each symbol as big and as easy to handle as a child's alphabet block. Watching, the child awakes again and knows that this is what dying is like. Dying is when the Creature from the Black Lagoon dams up the exit. Dying is when the monster gets you. 24

In the end, of course, the hero and heroine, very much alive, not only survive but triumph—as Hansel and Gretel do. As the drive-in floodlights over the screen came on and the projector flashed its GOOD NIGHT, DRIVE SAFELY slide on that big white space (along with the virtuous suggestion that you ATTEND THE CHURCH OF YOUR CHOICE), there was a brief feeling of relief, almost of resurrection. But the feeling that stuck longest was the swooning sensation that good old Richard Carlson and Julia Adams were surely going down for the third time, and the image that remains forever after is of the creature slowly and patiently walling its victims into the Black Lagoon; even now I can see it peering over that growing wall of mud and sticks. 25

Its eyes. Its ancient eyes. 26

COMPREHENSION

1. Why does King claim that it is harder for an author to successfully bring a horror tale to life than a standard "realistic" one? What special skills does the horror writer need?
2. Why are children the "perfect audience for horror"? What exists in the structure of most horror films that make them suitable for children?
3. King titles his essay "My Creature from the Black Lagoon" rather than using the original title *The Creature from the Black Lagoon.* Why?
4. Why does King think it is ironic that many Disney movies are "G" rated while "horror" movies often contain warnings about content for children?
5. In paragraph 23, King remarks that he is pleased that he is still able to get a thrill from watching a horror movie even though he is an adult and understands the artifice behind the monster. Why does he feel this is a positive response? Why does he believe it would be beneficial for most adults to react this way?

RHETORIC

1. In paragraph 9, King attempts to reproduce the sense of what it is like to think like a child. How does he achieve this effect? What is his purpose?

2. How does King structure paragraph 18 to compare and contrast horror movies with "fairy tales"? What is his rhetorical intent?
3. What vocabulary choices does King use in his introduction to set up his conversational style of writing? What relationship does King intend to create between the writer and reader by employing this type of discourse?
4. In paragraphs 4 and 5, King recounts a childhood anecdote. What is the purpose of describing the outing to the drive-in theatre with his mother's boyfriend, Milt? How does King structure these two paragraphs so that they culminate rhetorically in a device similar to that employed in horror movies?
5. Although much of King's writing is informal, he does use references to popular culture, literature, and science in his writing. What is the significance and meaning of the following terms: *batrachian* (paragraph 3), *suspension of disbelief* (paragraph 8), *Doppler effects* (paragraph 11), *twi-night double-header* (paragraph 11), *possibility that human flesh is heir to* (paragraph 20), and *golden oldies* (paragraph 22).
6. The conclusion is only five words: two sentence fragments. Why has King chosen to end his essay this way?
7. King uses irony in his essay for comic effect; for example, in paragraph 25, what is the irony in the "sign-off" at the drive-in movie theatre that reads: ATTEND THE CHURCH OF YOUR CHOICE?

WRITING

1. Think of the first horror movie you recall vividly from your childhood. Write an expository essay of 500 words about how the film scared you. Include both the dramatic elements on the screen and your own state of mind while you watched.
2. In an essay of approximately 450 to 500 words, argue for or against the proposition that horror movies are scarier when viewed at the movie theater than on home video.
3. Select a horror or science fiction book you've read that has been adapted for the screen. Compare and contrast the effects of each version. Which was more captivating? More engaging? More horrifying? More believable? Explain your view.
4. Compare and contrast the benefits and/or drawbacks of an adult reading a story to a child versus taking a child to the movies.

Red, White, and Beer

Dave Barry

Dave Barry was born in Armonk, New York, in 1947. He graduated from Haverford College in 1969 and was a reporter and editor at the Daily Local News *from 1971 to 1975. Since 1983, he has been a columnist for* The Miami Herald. *Besides writing his columns, Barry has written numerous books, all with his unique, amusing point of view. His books include* Stay Fit and Healthy Until You're Dead *(1985),* Dave Barry's Greatest Hits *(1988),* Dave Barry Turns 40 *(1990), and* Dave Barry's Only Travel Guide You'll Ever Need *(1991). Barry won the 1988 Pulitzer Prize for commentary. In the piece below, he comments on the relation between television commercials and patriotism.*

Lately I've been feeling very patriotic, especially during commercials. Like, 1 when I see those strongly pro-American Chrysler commercials, the ones where the winner of the Bruce Springsteen Sound-Alike Contest sings about how The Pride Is Back, the ones where Lee Iacocca himself comes striding out and practically challenges the president of Toyota to a knife fight, I get this warm, proud feeling inside, the same kind of feeling I get whenever we hold routine naval maneuvers off the coast of Libya.

But if you want to talk about *real* patriotism, of course, you have to talk 2 about beer commercials. I would have to say that Miller is the most patriotic brand of beer. I grant you it tastes like rat saliva, but we are not talking about taste here. What we are talking about, according to the commercials, is that Miller is by God an *American* beer, "born and brewed in the U.S.A.," and the men who drink it are American men, the kind of men who aren't afraid to perspire freely and shake a man's hand. That's mainly what happens in Miller commercials: Burly American men go around, drenched in perspiration, shaking each other's hands in a violent and patriotic fashion.

You never find out exactly why these men spend so much time shaking 3 hands. Maybe shaking hands is just their simple straightforward burly masculine American patriotic way of saying to each other: "Floyd, I am truly sorry I drank all that Miller beer last night and went to the bathroom in your glove compartment." Another possible explanation is that, since there are never any women in the part of America where beer commercials are made, the burly men have become lonesome and desperate for any form of physical contact. I have noticed that sometimes, in addition to shaking hands, they hug each other. Maybe very late at night, after the David Letterman show, there are Miller commercials in which the burly men engage in slow dancing. I don't know.

I do know that in one beer commercial, I think this is for Miller—although 4 it could be for Budweiser, which is also a very patriotic beer—the burly men build a house. You see them all getting together and pushing up a brand-new wall. Me, I worry some about a house built by men drinking beer. In my experience, you run into trouble when you ask a group of beer-drinking men to perform any task more complex than remembering not to light the filter ends of cigarettes.

For example, in my younger days, whenever anybody in my circle of 5 friends wanted to move, he'd get the rest of us to help, and, as an inducement, he'd buy a couple of cases of beer. This almost always produced unfortunate results, such as the time we were trying to move Dick "The Wretch" Curry from a horrible fourth-floor walk-up apartment in Manhattan's Lower East Side to another horrible fourth-floor walk-up apartment in Manhattan's Lower East Side, and we hit upon the labor-saving concept of, instead of carrying The Wretch's possessions manually down the stairs, simply dropping them out the window, down onto the street, where The Wretch was racing around, gathering up the broken pieces of his life and shrieking at us to stop helping him move, his emotions reaching a fever pitch when his bed, which had been swinging wildly from a rope, entered the apartment two floors below his through what had until seconds earlier been a window.

This is the kind of thinking you get, with beer. So I figure what happens, in 6 the beer commercial where the burly men are building the house, is they push the wall up so it's vertical, and then, after the camera stops filming them, they just keep pushing, and the wall crashes down on the other side, possibly onto somebody's pickup truck. And then they all shake hands.

But other than that, I'm in favor of the upsurge in retail patriotism, which 7 is lucky for me because the airwaves are saturated with pro-American commercials. Especially popular are commercials in which the newly restored Statue of Liberty—and by the way, I say Lee Iacocca should get some kind of medal for that, or at least be elected president—appears to be endorsing various products, as if she were Mary Lou Retton[1] or somebody. I saw one commercial strongly suggesting that the Statue of Liberty uses Sure brand underarm deodorant.

I have yet to see a patriotic laxative commercial, but I imagine it's only a 8 matter of time. They'll show some actors dressed up as hard-working country folk, maybe at a church picnic, smiling at each other and eating pieces of pie. At least one of them will be a black person. The Statue of Liberty will appear in the background. Then you'll hear a country-style singer singing:

Folks 'round here they love this land;
They stand by their beliefs;
An' when they git themselves stopped up;
They want some quick relief.

Well, what do you think? Pretty good commercial concept, huh?   9

---

[1]A gymnast who won a gold medal for vaulting at the 1984 Olympics.

Nah, you're right. They'd never try to pull something like that. They'd put 10
the statue in the *foreground*.

COMPREHENSION

1. What does Barry mean by "retail patriotism"? How does the essay's title illustrate this concept?
2. According to Barry, what makes beer commercials, especially those for Miller, patriotic?
3. In Barry's opinion, what do sexism, patriotism, and beer have in common?

RHETORIC

1. Barry doesn't explicitly state his thesis anywhere in the essay. In your own words, what is his implied thesis? Use evidence from the essay to support your view.
2. Barry uses irony and humor very effectively in this piece. Cite some examples of his humor, and analyze how he achieves the desired effect.
3. The writer uses specific brand names in his essay. How does this device help strengthen his argument? Would eliminating them make the essay less persuasive? Why or why not?
4. Barry seems to digress from his point in paragraphs 4, 5, and 6. Why does he do this? How does this digression serve the purpose of the piece?
5. Does the anecdote Barry uses in paragraph 5 ring true? Why or why not? What purpose does it serve in the essay? Does its plausibility affect the strength of Barry's argument?
6. How does paragraph 10 function as a conclusion? Is it in keeping with the essay's tone and style? Is it an effective device? Justify your response.

WRITING

1. Barry's essay examines how television sells patriotism. Write an essay analyzing how television sells other abstract ideas, such as success, love, freedom, democracy. Pattern your essay after Barry's, using humor. Also, use specific television commercials you have seen as examples.
2. Write an essay entitled "Patriotism," using both denotative and connotative definitions of the word.
3. In an essay, examine the impact that television advertising has had on American consumers and its repercussions.

Politics and the English Language

George Orwell

George Orwell (1903–1950) was the pseudonym of Eric Arthur Blair, an English novelist, essayist, and journalist. Orwell served with the Indian Imperial Police from 1922 to 1927 in Burma, fought in the Spanish Civil War, and acquired from his experience a disdain of totalitarian and imperialistic systems. This attitude is reflected in the satiric fable Animal Farm *(1945) and in the bleak, futuristic novel* 1984 *(1949). This essay, one of the more famous of the twentieth century, relates sloppy thinking and writing with political oppression.*

Most people who bother with the matter at all would admit that the English 1 language is in a bad way, but it is generally assumed that we cannot by conscious action do anything about it. Our civilisation is decadent, and our language—so the argument runs—must inevitably share in the general collapse. It follows that any struggle against the abuse of language is a sentimental archaism, like preferring candles to electric light or hansom cabs to aeroplanes. Underneath this lies the half-conscious belief that language is a natural growth and not an instrument which we shape for our own purposes.

Now, it is clear that the decline of a language must ultimately have political 2 and economic causes: it is not due simply to the bad influence of this or that individual writer. But an effect can become a cause, reinforcing the original cause and producing the same effect in an intensified form, and so on indefinitely. A man may take to drink because he feels himself to be a failure, and then fail all the more completely because he drinks. It is rather the same thing that is happening to the English language. It becomes ugly and inaccurate because our thoughts are foolish, but the slovenliness of our language makes it easier for us to have foolish thoughts. The point is that the process is reversible. Modern English, especially written English, is full of bad habits which spread by imitation and which can be avoided if one is willing to take the necessary trouble. If one gets rid of these habits one can think more clearly, and to think clearly is a necessary first step towards political regeneration: so that the fight against bad English is not frivolous and is not the exclusive concern of professional writers. I will come back to this presently, and I hope that by that time the meaning of what I have said here will have become clearer. Meanwhile, here are five specimens of the English language as it is now habitually written.

These five passages have not been picked out because they are especially 3 bad—I could have quoted far worse if I had chosen—but because they illustrate various of the mental vices from which we now suffer. They are a little below the average, but are fairly representative samples. I number them so that I can refer back to them when necessary:

1. I am not, indeed, sure whether it is not true to say the Milton who once seemed not unlike a seventeenth-century Shelley had not become, out of an experience even more bitter in each year, more alien (sic) to the founder of that Jesuit sect which nothing could induce him to tolerate.

   —Professor Harold Laski (essay in *Freedom of Expression*)

2. Above all, we cannot play ducks and drakes with a native battery of idioms which prescribes such egregious collocations of vocables as the Basic *put up with* for *tolerate* or *put at a loss* for *bewilder*.

   —Professor Lancelot Hogben (*Interglossa*)

3. On the one side we have the free personality: by definition it is not neurotic, for it has neither conflict nor dream. Its desires, such as they are, are transparent, for they are just what institutional approval keeps in the forefront of consciousness; another institutional pattern would alter their number and intensity; there is little in them that is natural, irreducible, or culturally dangerous. But on the other side, the social bond itself is nothing but the mutual reflection of these self-secure integrities. Recall the definition of love. Is not this the very picture of a small academic? Where is there a place in this hall of mirrors for either personality or fraternity?

   —Essay on psychology in *Politics* (New York)

4. All the "best people" from the gentlemen's clubs, and all the frantic Fascist captains, united in common hatred of Socialism and bestial horror of the rising tide of the mass revolutionary movement, have turned to acts of provocation, to foul incendiarism, to medieval legends of poisoned wells, to legalise their own destruction to proletarian organisations, and rouse the agitated petty-bourgeoisie to chauvinistic fervour on behalf of the fight against the revolutionary way out of the crisis.

   —Communist pamphlet

5. If a new spirit is to be infused into this old country, there is one thorny and contentious reform which must be tackled, and that is the humanisation and galvanisation of the BBC. Timidity here will bespeak canker and atrophy for the soul. The heart of Britain may be sound and of strong beat, for instance, but the British lion's roar at present is like that of Bottom in Shakespeare's Midsummer Night's Dream—as gentle as any sucking dove. A virile new Britain cannot continue indefinitely to be traduced in the eyes, or rather ears, of the world by the effete languors of Langham Place, brazenly masquerading as "standard English." When the Voice of Britain is heard at nine o'clock, better far and infinitely less ludicrous to hear aitches honestly dropped than the present priggish, inflated, inhibited, schoolma'amish braying of blameless bashful mewing maidens!

   —Letter in *Tribune*

Each of these passages has faults of its own, but, quite apart from avoidable 4 ugliness, two qualities are common to all of them. The first is staleness of imagery: the other is lack of precision. The writer either has a meaning and cannot express it, or he inadvertently says something else, or he is almost indifferent as to whether his words mean anything or not. This mixture of vagueness and sheer incompetence is the most marked characteristic of modern English prose, and especially of any kind of political writing. As soon as certain topics are raised, the concrete melts into the abstract and no one seems able to think of turns of speech that are not hackneyed: prose consists less and less of *words* chosen for the sake of their meaning, and more of *phrases* tacked together like the sections of a prefabricated henhouse. I list below, with notes and examples, various of the tricks by means of which the work of prose construction is habitually dodged:

Dying Metaphors

A newly invented metaphor assists thought by evoking a visual image, while on the other hand a metaphor which is technically "dead" (e.g., *iron resolution*) has in effect reverted to being an ordinary word and can generally be used without loss of vividness. But in between these two classes there is a huge dump of wornout metaphors which have lost all evocative power and are merely used because they save people the trouble of inventing phrases for themselves. Examples are: *Ring the changes on, take up the cudgels for, toe the line, ride roughshod over, stand shoulder to shoulder with, play into the hands of, no axe to grind, grist to the mill, fishing in troubled waters, rift within the lute, on the order of the day, Achilles' heel, swan song, hotbed.* Many of these are used without knowledge of their meaning (what is a "rift," for instance?), and incompatible metaphors are frequently mixed, a sure sign that the writer is not interested in what he is saying. Some metaphors now current have been twisted out of their original meaning without those who use them even being aware of the fact. For example, *toe the line* is sometimes written *tow the line.* Another example is *the hammer and the anvil,* now always used with the implication that the anvil gets the worst of it. In real life it is always the anvil that breaks the hammer, never the other way about: a writer who stopped to think what he was saying would be aware of this, and would avoid perverting the original phrase.

Operators, or Verbal False Limbs

These save the trouble of picking out appropriate verbs and nouns, and at the same time pad each sentence with extra syllables which give it an appearance of symmetry. Characteristic phrases are: *render inoperative, militate against, prove unacceptable, make contact with, be subjected to, give rise to, give grounds for, have the effect of, play a leading part (rôle) in, make itself felt, take effect, exhibit a tendency to, serve the purpose of,* etc. etc. The keynote is the elimination of simple verbs. Instead of being a single word, such as *break, stop, spoil, mend, kill,* a verb becomes a *phrase,* made up of a noun or adjective tacked on to some general-purposes verb such as *prove, serve, form, play, render.* In addition, the passive voice is wherever possible used in preference to the active, and noun constructions are used instead of gerunds (*by examination of* instead of *by examining*). The range of verbs is further cut down by means of the *-ise* and *de-* formations, and banal statements are given an appearance of profundity by means of the *not un-* formation.

Simple conjunctions and prepositions are replaced by such phrases as *with respect to, having regard to, the fact that, by dint of, in view of, in the interests of, on the hypothesis that;* and the ends of sentences are saved from anti-climax by such resounding commonplaces as *greatly to be desired, cannot be left out of account, a development to be expected in the near future, deserving of serious consideration, brought to a satisfactory conclusion,* and so on and so forth.

Pretentious Diction

Words like *phenomenon, element, individual* (as noun), *objective, categorical, effec-* 7
tive, virtual, basic, primary, promote, constitute, exhibit, exploit, utilise, eliminate, liquidate, are used to dress up simple statements and give an air of scientific impartiality to biassed judgements. Adjectives like *epoch-making, epic, historic, unforgettable, triumphant, age-old, inevitable, inexorable, veritable,* are used to dignify the sordid processes of international politics, while writing that aims at glorifying war usually takes on an archaic colour, its characteristic words being: *realm, throne, chariot, mailed fist, trident, sword, shield, buckler, banner, jackboot, clarion.* Foreign words and expressions such as *cul de sac, ancien régime, deus ex machina, mutatis mutandis, status quo, Gleichschaltung, Weltanschauung,* are used to give an air of culture and elegance. Except for the useful abbreviations *i.e., e.g.,* and *etc.,* there is no real need for any of the hundreds of foreign phrases now current in English. Bad writers, and especially scientific, political and sociological writers, are nearly always haunted by the notion that Latin or Greek words are grander than Saxon ones, and unnecessary words like *expedite, ameliorate, predict, extraneous, deracinated, clandestine, subaqueous* and hundreds of others constantly gain ground from their Anglo-Saxon opposite numbers.[1] The jargon peculiar to Marxist writing (*hyena, hangman, cannibal, petty bourgeois, these gentry, lacquey, flunkey, mad dog, White Guard,* etc.) consists largely of words and phrases translated from Russian, German or French; but the normal way of coining a new word is to use a Latin or Greek root with the appropriate affix and, where necessary, the *–ise* formation. It is often easier to make up words of this kind (*deregionalise, impermissible, extramarital, non-fragmentatory* and so forth) than to think up the English words that will cover one's meaning. The result, in general, is an increase in slovenliness and vagueness.

Meaningless Words

In certain kinds of writing, particularly in art criticism and literary criticism, it 8
is normal to come across long passages which are almost completely lacking in meaning.[2] Words like *romantic, plastic, values, human, dead, sentimental, natural,*

---

[1]An interesting illustration of this is the way in which the English flower names which were in use till very recently are being ousted by Greek ones, *snapdragon* becoming *antirrhinum, forget-me-not* becoming *myosotis,* etc. It is hard to see any practical reason for this change of fashion: it is probably due to an instinctive turning-away from the more homely word and a vague feeling that the Greek word is scientific.

vitality, as used in art criticism, are strictly meaningless, in the sense that they not only do not point to any discoverable object, but are hardly even expected to do so by the reader. When one critic writes, "The outstanding features of Mr. X's work is its living quality," while another writes, "The immediately striking thing about Mr. X's work is its peculiar deadness," the reader accepts this as a simple difference of opinion. If words like *black* and *white* were involved, instead of the jargon words *dead* and *living,* he would see at once that language was being used in an improper way. Many political words are similarly abused. The word *Fascism* has now no meaning except in so far as it signifies "something not desirable." The words *democracy, socialism, freedom, patriotic, realistic, justice,* have each of them several different meanings which cannot be reconciled with one another. In the case of a word like *democracy,* not only is there no agreed definition, but the attempt to make one is resisted from all sides. It is almost universally felt that when we call a country democratic we are praising it: consequently the defenders of every kind of régime claim that it is a democracy, and fear that they might have to stop using the word if it were tied down to any one meaning. Words of this kind are often used in a consciously dishonest way. That is, the person who uses them has his own private definition, but allows his hearer to think he means something quite different. Statements like *Marshal Pétain was a true patriot, The Soviet press is the freest in the world, The Catholic Church is opposed to persecution,* are almost always made with intent to deceive. Other words used in variable meanings, in most cases more or less dishonestly, are: *class, totalitarian, science, progressive, reactionary, bourgeois, equality.*

Now that I have made this catalogue of swindles and perversions, let me give another example of the kind of writing that they lead to. This time it must of its nature be an imaginary one. I am going to translate a passage of good English into modern English of the worst sort. Here is a well-known verse from *Ecclesiastes:* 9

> I returned, and saw under the sun, that the race is not to the swift, nor the battle to the strong, neither yet bread to the wise, nor yet riches to men of understanding, not yet favour to men of skill; but time and chance happeneth to them all.

Here it is in modern English: 10

> Objective consideration of contemporary phenomena compels the conclusion that success or failure in competitive activities exhibits no tendency to be commensurate with innate capacity, but that a considerable element of the unpredictable must invariably be taken into account.

---

[2]*Example:* "Comfort's catholicity of perception and image, strangely Whitmanesque in range, almost the exact opposite in aesthetic compulsion, continues to evoke that trembling atmospheric accumulative hinting at a cruel, an inexorably serene timelessness. . . . Wrey Gardiner scores by aiming at simple bullseyes with precision. Only they are not so simple, and through this contented sadness runs more than the surface bittersweet of resignation." *(Poetry Quarterly).*

This is a parody, but not a very gross one. The passage on page 526, for 11 instance, contains several patches of the same kind of English. It will be seen that I have not made a full translation. The beginning and ending of the sentence follow the original meaning fairly closely, but in the middle the concrete illustrations—race, battle, bread—dissolve into the vague phrase "success or failure in competitive activities." This had to be so, because no modern writer of the kind I am discussing—no one capable of using phrases like "objective consideration of contemporary phenomena"—would ever tabulate his thoughts in that precise and detailed way. The whole tendency of modern prose is away from concreteness. Now analyse these two sentences a little more closely. The first contains 49 words but only 60 syllables, and all its words are those of everyday life. The second contains 38 words of 90 syllables: 18 of its words are from Latin roots, and one from Greek. The first sentence contains six vivid images, and only one phrase ("time and chance") that could be called vague. The second contains not a single fresh, arresting phrase, and in spite of its 90 syllables it gives only a shortened version of the meaning contained in the first. Yet without a doubt it is the second kind of sentence that is gaining ground in modern English. I do not want to exaggerate. This kind of writing is not yet universal, and outcrops of simplicity will occur here and there in the worst-written page. Still, if you or I were told to write a few lines on the uncertainty of human fortunes, we should probably come much nearer to my imaginary sentence than to the one from *Ecclesiastes*.

As I have tried to show, modern writing at its worst does not consist in 12 picking out words for the sake of their meaning and inventing images in order to make the meaning clearer. It consists in gumming together long strips of words which have already been set in order by someone else, and making the results presentable by sheer humbug. The attraction of this way of writing is that it is easy. It is easier—even quicker, once you have the habit—to say *In my opinion it is a not unjustifiable assumption that* than to say *I think*. If you use ready-made phrases, you not only don't have to hunt about for words; you also don't have to bother with the rhythms of your sentences, since these phrases are generally so arranged as to be more or less euphonious. When you are composing in a hurry—when you are dictating to a stenographer, for instance, or making a public speech—it is natural to fall into a pretentious, latinised style. Tags like *a consideration which we should do well to bear in mind* or *a conclusion to which all of us would readily assent* will save many a sentence from coming down with a bump. By using stale metaphors, similes and idioms, you save much mental effort, at the cost of leaving your meaning vague, not only for your reader but for yourself. This is the significance of mixed metaphors. The sole aim of a metaphor is to call up a visual image. When these images clash—as in *The Fascist octopus has sung its swan song, the jackboot is thrown into the melting-pot*—can be taken as certain that the writer is not seeing a mental image of the objects he is naming; in other words he is not really thinking. Look again at the examples I gave at the beginning of this essay. Professor Laski (1) uses five negatives in 53 words. One of these is superfluous, making nonsense of the whole passage, and in addition there is the slip *alien* for akin, making further nonsense, and several avoidable pieces of clumsiness which increase the general vagueness. Professor Hogben (2) plays ducks and drakes with a battery which is able to write prescriptions, and, while disapproving of the everyday phrase *put up with*, is unwilling to look *egregious* up in the dictionary and see what it means. In (3), if one takes an uncharitable attitude towards it, [it] is simply meaningless: probably one could work out its intended meaning by reading the whole of the article in which it occurs. In (4) the writer knows more or less what he wants to say, but an accumulation of stale phrases chokes him like tealeaves blocking a sink. In (5) words and meaning have almost parted company. People who write in this manner usually have a general emotional meaning—they dislike one thing and want to express solidarity with another—but they are not interested in the detail of what they are saying. A scrupulous writer, in every sentence that he writes, will ask himself at least four questions, thus: What am I trying to say? What words will express it? What image or idiom will make it clearer? Is this image fresh enough to have an effect? And he will probably ask himself two more: Could I put it more shortly? Have I said anything that is avoidably ugly? But you are not obliged to go to all this trouble. You can shirk it by simply throwing your mind open and letting the ready-made phrases come crowding in. They will construct your sentences for you—even think your thoughts for you, to a certain extent—and at need they will perform the important service of partially concealing your meaning even from yourself. It is at this point that the special connection between politics and the debasement of language becomes clear.

In our time it is broadly true that political writing is bad writing. Where it is 13
not true, it will generally be found that the writer is some kind of rebel, expressing his private opinions, and not a "party line." Orthodoxy, of whatever colour, seems to demand a lifeless, imitative style. The political dialects to be found in pamphlets, leading articles, manifestos, White Papers and the speeches of Under-Secretaries do, of course, vary from party to party, but they are all alike in that one almost never finds in them a fresh, vivid, home-made turn of speech. When one watches some tired hack on the platform mechanically repeating the familiar phrases—*bestial atrocities, iron heel, blood-stained tyranny, free peoples of the world, stand shoulder to shoulder*—one often has a curious feeling that one is not watching a live human being but some kind of dummy: a feeling which suddenly becomes stronger at moments when the light catches the speaker's spectacles and turns them into blank discs which seem to have no eyes behind them. And this is not altogether fanciful. A speaker who uses that kind of phraseology has gone some distance towards turning himself into a machine. The appropriate noises are coming out of his larynx, but his brain is not involved as it would be if he were choosing his words for himself. If the speech he is making is one that he is accustomed to make over and over again, he may be almost unconscious of what he is saying, as one is when one utters the responses in church. And this reduced state of consciousness, if not indispensable, is at any rate favourable to political conformity.

In our time, political speech and writing are largely the defence of the inde- 14
fensible. Things like the continuance of British rule in India, the Russian purges and deportations, the dropping of the atom bombs on Japan, can indeed be

defended, but only by arguments which are too brutal for most people to face, and which do not square with the professed aims of political parties. Thus political language has to consist largely of euphemism, question-begging and sheer cloudy vagueness. Defenceless villages are bombarded from the air, the inhabitants driven out into the countryside, the cattle machine-gunned, the huts set on fire with incendiary bullets: this is called *pacification*. Millions of peasants are robbed of their farms and sent trudging along the roads with no more than they can carry: this is called *transfer of population or rectification of frontiers*. People are imprisoned for years without trial, or shot in the back of the neck or sent to die of scurvy in Arctic lumber camps: this is called *elimination of unreliable elements*. Such phraseology is needed if one wants to name things without calling up mental pictures of them. Consider for instance some comfortable English professor defending Russian totalitarianism. He cannot say outright, "I believe in killing off your opponents when you can get good results by doing so." Probably, therefore, he will say something like this:

> While freely conceding that the Soviet régime exhibits certain features which the humanitarian may be inclined to deplore, we must, I think, agree that a certain curtailment of the right to political opposition is an unavoidable concomitant of transitional periods, and that the rigours which the Russian people have been called upon to undergo have been amply justified in the sphere of concrete achievement.

The inflated style is itself a kind of euphemism. A mass of Latin words falls 15 upon the facts like soft snow, blurring the outlines and covering up all the details. The great enemy of clear language is insincerity. When there is a gap between one's real and one's declared aims, one turns as it were instinctively to long words and exhausted idioms, like a cuttlefish squirting out ink. In our age there is no such thing as "keeping out of politics." All issues are political issues, and politics itself is a mass of lies, evasions, folly, hatred and schizophrenia. When the general atmosphere is bad, language must suffer. I should expect to find—this is a guess which I have not sufficient knowledge to verify—that the German, Russian and Italian languages have all deteriorated in the last ten or fifteen years, as a result of dictatorship.

But if thought corrupts language, language can also corrupt thought. A bad 16 usage can spread by tradition and imitation, even among people who should and do know better. The debased language that I have been discussing is in some ways very convenient. Phrases like *a not unjustifiable assumption, leaves much to be desired, would serve no good purpose, a consideration which we should do well to bear in mind*, are a continuous temptation, a packet of aspirins always at one's elbow. Look back through this essay, and for certain you will find that I have again and again committed the very faults I am protesting against. By this morning's post I have received a pamphlet dealing with conditions in Germany. The author tells me that he "felt impelled" to write it. I open it at random, and here is almost the first sentence that I see: "(The Allies) have an opportunity not only of achieving a radical transformation of Germany's social and political structure in such a way as to avoid a nationalistic reaction in Germany itself, but at the same time of laying the foundations of a cooperative and unified Europe." You see, he "feels impelled" to write—feels, presumably, that he has something new to say—and yet his words, like cavalry horses answering the bugle, group themselves automatically into the familiar dreary pattern. This invasion of one's mind by ready-made phrases (*lay the foundations, achieve a radical transformation*) can only be prevented if one is constantly on guard against them, and every such phrase anaesthetises a portion of one's brain.

I said earlier that the decadence of our language is probably curable. Those 17 who deny this would argue, if they produced an argument at all, that language merely reflects existing social conditions, and that we cannot influence its development by any direct tinkering with words and constructions. So far as the general tone or spirit of a language goes, this may be true, but it is not true in detail. Silly words and expressions have often disappeared, not through any evolutionary process but owing to the conscious action of a minority. Two recent examples were *explore every avenue* and *leave no stone unturned*, which were killed by the jeers of a few journalists. There is a long list of fly-blown metaphors which could similarly be got rid of if enough people would interest themselves in the job; and it should also be possible to laugh the *not un-* formation out of existence,[3] to reduce the amount of Latin and Greek in the average sentence, to drive out foreign phrases and strayed scientific words, and, in general, to make pretentiousness unfashionable. But all these are minor points. The defence of the English language implies more than this, and perhaps it is best to start by saying what it does *not* imply.

To begin with, it has nothing to do with archaism, with the salvaging of ob- 18 solete words and turns of speech, or with the setting up of a "standard English" which must never be departed from. On the contrary, it is especially concerned with the scrapping of every word or idiom which has outworn its usefulness. It has nothing to do with correct grammar and syntax, which are of no importance so long as one makes one's meaning clear, or with the avoidance of Americanisms, or with having what is called a "good prose style." On the other hand it is not concerned with fake simplicity and the attempt to make written English colloquial. Nor does it even imply in every case preferring the Saxon word to the Latin one, though it does imply using the fewest and shortest words that will cover one's meaning. What is above all needed is to let the meaning choose the word, and not the other way about. In prose, the worst thing one can do with words is to surrender to them. When you think of a concrete object, you think wordlessly, and then, if you want to describe the thing you have been visualising, you probably hunt about till you find the exact words that seem to fit it. When you think of something abstract you are more inclined to use words from the start, and unless you make a conscious effort to prevent it, the existing dialect will come rushing in and do the job for you, at the expense of blurring or even changing your meaning. Probably it is better to put off using words as

---

[3]One can cure oneself of the *not un-* formation by memorising this sentence: *A not unblack dog was chasing a not unsmall rabbit across a not ungreen field.*

long as possible and get one's meaning as clear as one can through pictures or sensations. Afterwards one can choose—not simply *accept*—the phrases that will best cover the meaning, and then switch around and decide what impression one's words are likely to make on another person. This last effort of the mind cuts out all stale or mixed images, all prefabricated phrases, needless repetitions, and humbug and vagueness generally. But one can often be in doubt about the effect of a word or a phrase, and one needs rules that one can rely on when instinct fails. I think the following rules will cover most cases:

   i. Never use a metaphor, simile or other figure of speech which you are used to seeing in print.

  ii. Never use a long word where a short one will do.

 iii. If it is possible to cut a word out, always cut it out.

 iv. Never use the passive where you can use the active.

  v. Never use a foreign phrase, a scientific word or a jargon word if you can think of an everyday English equivalent.

 vi. Break any of these rules sooner than say anything outright barbarous.

These rules sound elementary, and so they are, but they demand a deep change 19 of attitude in anyone who has grown used to writing in the style now fashionable. One could keep all of them and still write bad English, but one could not write the kind of stuff that I quoted in those five specimens at the beginning of this article.

    I have not here been considering the literary use of language, but merely 20 language as an instrument for expressing and not for concealing or preventing thought. Stuart Chase and others have come near to claiming that all abstract words are meaningless, and have used this as a pretext for advocating a kind of political quietism. Since you don't know what Fascism is, how can you struggle against Fascism? One need not swallow such absurdities as this, but one ought to recognise that the present political chaos is connected with the decay of language, and that one can probably bring about some improvement by starting at the verbal end. If you simplify your English, you are freed from the worst follies of orthodoxy. You cannot speak any of the necessary dialects, and when you make a stupid remark its stupidity will be obvious, even to yourself. Political language—and with variations this is true of all political parties, from Conservatives to Anarchists—is designed to make lies sound truthful and murder respectable, and to give an appearance of solidity to pure wind. One cannot change this all in a moment, but one can at least change one's own habits, and from time to time one can even, if one jeers loudly enough, send some worn-out and useless phrase—some *jackboot, Achilles' heel, hotbed, melting pot, acid test, veritable inferno* or other lump of verbal refuse—into the dustbin where it belongs.

COMPREHENSION

  1. What is Orwell's purpose? For what type of audience is he writing? Where does he summarize his concerns for readers?

2. According to Orwell, "thought corrupts language" and "language can also corrupt thought." Give examples of these assertions in the essay.
3. In what ways does Orwell believe that politics and language are related?

RHETORIC

1. Orwell himself uses similes and metaphors. Locate five of them, and explain their relationship to the author's analysis.
2. Orwell claims that concrete language is superior to abstract language. Give examples of Orwell's attempt to write concretely.
3. One of the most crucial rhetorical devices in this essay is definition. What important concepts does Orwell define? What methods of definition does he tend to use?
4. Identify an example of hypothetical reasoning in the essay. How does it contribute to the thesis of the essay?
5. After having given five examples of bad English, why does Orwell, in paragraph 10, give another example? How does this example differ from the others? What does it add to the essay?
6. Explain the use of extended analogy in paragraph 14.

WRITING

1. In an analytical essay, assess the state of language in politics today. Cite examples from newspapers and television reports.
2. Apply Orwell's advice on language to Roger Ebert's review of *Goodfellas*.
3. Prepare an essay analyzing the use and abuse of any word that sparks controversy today—for example, *abortion*, *AIDS*, or *greed*.

Who's in Charge of the English Language?

Casey Miller and Kate Swift

Casey Miller (1919–1997) and Kate Swift (b. 1923) worked as a writing team, focusing on issues addressing women and language. Miller received her BA degree from Smith College. Swift received her BA degree from the University of North Carolina. Their book Words and Women (1976) is an extensive look at the impact language has on the perception and identity of women. Both authors have worked in other areas. Miller served as an educational curriculum editor; Swift, as a journalist. The following essay is an adaptation of a talk given at the annual meeting of the Association of American Presses on June 26, 1990, in Philadelphia.

In order to encourage the use of language that is free of gender bias, it's obvi-   1
ously necessary to get authors to *recognize* gender bias in their writing. The reason that's so difficult is that our culture is steeped in unconscious attitudes and
beliefs about gender characteristics, a condition reflected in our use of words.

Every human society has recognized the relationship between power and   2
naming: that the *act of naming* confers power over the thing named. In the Book
of Genesis, Adam named all the animals and was given dominion over them,
and then, later, the story says "Adam called his wife's name Eve." Those who
have the power to name and define other things—animals, wives, whatever—
inevitably take themselves as the norm or standard, the measure of all things.

English is androcentric because for centuries it has been evolving in a soci-   3
ety where men have been dominant. They were the ones in charge of the major
social institutions: government, law, commerce, education, religion. They
shaped the course of history and were the subjects of history. It's natural that
the languages of patriarchal societies should come to express a male-centered
view. That's basic anthropology. Anthropologists know that the single best way
to understand the culture of any society is to study the lexicon of its language:
a people's words reflect their reality. But the question is: whose reality? The
English language still reflects a world in which the power to define gender characteristics is a male prerogative.

We all know that English contains a variety of words that identify and em-   4
phasize difference between the sexes. A number of English words actually express polarization of the sexes. Never mind that beyond having one or the other
set of biological features necessary for reproduction, every individual is distinct
in personality, combining in a unique way those polarized qualities called
"masculine" and "feminine." Never mind that virtually no one fits the mold at
either pole. It remains a cherished precept of our culture, semantically underlined in our lexicon and embraced by the purveyors of every commodity imaginable, that the sexes must be thought of as opposite.

Female-Negative-Trivial

This linguistic syndrome can be described as "female-negative-trivial" on the   5
one hand, and "male-positive-important" on the other. If that strikes you as
overly exaggerated, consider for a moment a group of people who are *not* in
charge of the English language—that is, lexicographers—and the definitions
they have come up with for a pair of words which relate to gender—the words
manly and *womanly*. These definitions are from the most recently updated edition of *Webster's Third New International Dictionary* (copyright 1986).

> **Manly** 1. a: having qualities appropriate to a man: not effeminate or timorous:
> bold, resolute, and open in conduct or bearing. . . . b. (1): belonging to or ap-
> propriate in character to man [*and they give as examples*] "manly sports," "beer is
> a manly drink," and "a big booming manly voice." (2): of undaunted courage:
> gallant, brave [*and among the quotations they give as examples*] "it seemed a big
> manly thing to say" and "a manly disregard of his enemies" . . .

Now compare the same dictionary's definition of *womanly*, remembering that lexicographers base their definitions on hundreds of examples of usage that have appeared in print.

> **Womanly** 1: marked by qualities characteristic of a woman, esp. marked by qualities becoming a well-balanced adult woman [*and their examples are*] "womanly manners" and "womanly advice." 2: possessed of the character or behavior befitting a grown woman: no longer childish or girlish: becoming to a grown woman [*and their example is from Charles Dickens*] "a little girl wearing a womanly sort of bonnet much too large for her" 3: characteristic of, belonging to, or suitable to women: conforming to or motivated by a woman's nature and attitudes rather than a man's. [*The first example here is*] "convinced that drawing was a waste of time, if not downright womanly, like painting on China." [*And another example*] "her usual womanly volubility."

What are these two supposedly parallel entries telling us? They're saying 6 that in addition to defining characteristics appropriate to a man, like vocal pitch, *manly* is synonymous with admirable qualities that all of us might wish we had. "Bold, resolute, open in conduct or bearing; of undaunted courage, gallant, brave." And where is the list of comparable synonyms for *womanly*? There aren't any. Instead, *womanly* is defined only in a circular way—through characteristics seen to be appropriate or inappropriate to women, not to human beings in general. And the examples of usage cited give a pretty good picture of what is considered appropriate to, or characteristic of, a well-balanced adult woman: she's concerned with manners, advice, and hat styles (as distinguished from sports and beer, which are felt to be manly); she wastes time in trivial pursuits like painting on china; and she talks too much.

The Slippery Slope

Most writers and editors today recognize that the female-negative-trivial syn- 7 drome is clearly evident in the use of so-called feminine suffixes with nouns of common gender. In 1990 no publishable author would identify someone as "a poetess," except in ridicule. (Adrienne Rich says the word brings out the "terroristress" in her.) But respectable writers are still using *heroine, suffragette,* and *executrix* when referring to a hero, a suffragist, or an executor who is a woman.

These words illustrate what Douglas Hofstadter calls "the slippery slope" 8 of meaning. In his book *Metamagical Themas,* Hofstadter shows diagramatically how the slippery slope works. A triangle represents the idea of, let's say, a heroic person. At one base angle of this triangle is the word *heroine,* representing the female heroic person. At the other base angle is the word *hero,* representing the male heroic person. And at the apex is the generic word, again *hero,* encompassing both. But because the *hero* at the apex and the *hero* at one base angle are identical in name, their separate meanings slip back and forth along one side of the triangle, the slippery slope. The meanings blend and absorb each other. They bond together on the slope. And *heroine,* at the other base angle, remains outside that bond.

Another word that comes to mind in this connection is *actress*. It's our im- 9
pression that women performers in the theater and films today are tending
more and more to refer to themselves and one another as "actors." It may be deliberate, conscious usage on the part of some. Considering that their union is
called Actors Equity, and that they may have trained at Actors Studio, and performed at Actors Playhouse, they simply accept that the generic word for their
profession is *actor*. But when this word appears in juxtaposition with *actress*, the
generic meaning of *actor* is absorbed into the gender-specific meaning, and
women are identified as nonactors, as being outside or marginal, in de Beau-
voir's phrase, as "the other."

Many people will undoubtedly go on feeling that *actress* is a term without 10
bias, but we would like to suggest that it is on its way to becoming archaic, or at
least quaint, simply because people it has identified are abandoning it by a
process that may be more visceral than cerebral. In a sense it's their word, it has
defined them, and, whether intentionally or not, they are taking charge of it,
perhaps dumping it. We'll see.

Because linguistic changes reflect changes in our ways of thinking, a living 11
language is constantly being created and re-created by the people who speak it.
Linguistic changes spring from nothing less than new perceptions of the world
and of ourselves.

Obviously we all know that over time the "rules" of grammar have 12
changed, and we know that words themselves change their meanings: they lose
some and acquire others; new words come into existence and old ones disappear into that word heaven, the *Oxford English Dictionary*. Nevertheless, most
people resist change, especially, it seems, changes in grammar and the meanings of words. What we tend to forget—or choose to forget—is that the only languages which don't change are the ones no one speaks any more, like classical
Greek and Latin.

Take the narrowing process that turned the Old English word *man* into a 13
synonym for "adult male human being." As long ago as 1752 the philosopher
David Hume recognized how ambiguous that word had already become: "All
men," he wrote, and then added, "both male and female." And you are probably familiar with the numerous experimental studies done in the last few years,
primarily by psychologists and sociologists rather than linguists, which show
that most native speakers of English simply do not conceptualize women and
girls when they encounter *man* and *mankind* used generically. In fact the narrowing process is felt so strongly, at least at an existential level, that a growing
number of women today strongly object to being subsumed under those male-
gender terms. "We aren't men," they're saying; "we're women, and we're tired
of being made invisible."

Yet despite women's objections, and despite the slippery, ambiguous nature 14
of generic *man*, lots of people, especially formally educated people, have a hard
time giving it up. They forget, it seems, that words have a power of their own—
the power of taking over meaning. A writer starts out talking about the species
as a whole and, more often than we'll ever know, ends up talking about males.

Listen to this well-known author, for example, who was discussing aggressive behavior in human beings—all of us, *Homo sapiens*. "[M]an," he wrote, "can do several things which the animal cannot do. . . . Eventually, his vital interests are not only life, food, access to females, etc., but also values, symbols, institutions."

Resistance to Change and the Problem of Precision

It's probably helpful, once in a while, to look back at the way some of the most familiar and accepted words in use today were greeted when they were newcomers. 15

Back in 1619, for example, the London schoolmaster Alexander Gil described what he called "the new mange in speaking and writing." What he was deploring was the introduction of newly coined, Latin-derived words to replace older English ones. According to him, the "new mange" included such terms as *virtue, justice, pity, compassion,* and *grace.* And he asked, "Whither have you banished those words our forefathers used for these new-fangled ones?" Alexander Gil was headmaster of St. Paul's school at the time, and it might be noted that one of his students was an eleven-year-old named John Milton who—fortunately—was not persuaded to reject Gil's "new-fangled" words. 16

And how about old terms that have lost favor, like the once-accepted use of the pronoun *they* with a singular referent, as in "If a person is born of a gloomy temper, they cannot help it." That was written in 1759 by none other than the very correct, well-educated British statesman, Lord Chesterfield. However, since most academics are not yet ready to revive that convenient usage—despite precedents ranging from Shakespeare to Shaw—it still isn't surprising to come across a recently published book about, let's say, the psychology of children, in which the distinguished author uses *he* and its inflected forms as all-purpose pronouns, leaving readers to guess whether a particular problem or development applies to boys only or to children of both sexes. We submit that such writing is not just unfortunate. It's inexcusable. 17

These days more and more writers acknowledge that *he* used generically is, like *man* used generically, both ambiguous and insidious, and they take the time and trouble to write more precisely. But sometimes, even after several polite but probably exhausting battles between author and editor, all the author will agree to do is add a disclaimer. Disclaimers can be helpful, of course (for example, those providing guidance as to what a writer of some previous century may have meant by a now-ambiguous term). More often, however, they are nothing but excuses for sloppiness. 18

There is also an element here which we don't think should be ignored: the deep if often unacknowledged *psychological* impact of the grammatical "rule" mandating masculine-gender pronouns for indefinite referents. As long ago as the 1950s, Lynn White, Jr., then the president of Mills College, described with great perception the harm that rule can do to children when he wrote: 19

> The penetration of this habit of language into the minds of little girls as they grow up to be women is more profound than most people, including most women, have recognized; for it implies that personality is really a male

attribute, and that women are a human subspecies. . . . It would be a miracle if a girl-baby, learning to use the symbols of our tongue, could escape some un-verbalized wound to her self-respect; whereas a boy-baby's ego is bolstered by the pattern of our language.

Obviously many literate men (and some literate women) must find the [20] truth of White's perception difficult to accept, or we wouldn't still be battling the generic use of masculine-gender pronouns. But since accuracy and precision are what we're talking about today, let us ask this question: what is one to make of a scholar—a professor of communications with a special interest in seman-tics, as a matter of fact—who dismissed the problem of sexist language as fol-lows: "I tend to avoid 'gender-exclusive' words," he wrote, "except when in so doing, I would injure the rhythm of a sentence."

Has it never occurred to him that in writing a sentence, any sentence, he [21] must choose both its words and the way those words, in their infinite variety, are put together? That the choice isn't between exclusionary language on the one hand and rhythm on the other? (Surely it's possible to write with style and still communicate accurately what it is you want to say.) The choice is between settling for an ambiguous or inaccurate term because it "sounds good"—and finding the exact combination of words to convey one's message with clarity and precision. It seems to us that editors have every right to expect nothing less than the latter.

English is a vigorously alive tongue, and it reflects a vigorously alive, dynamic [22] society that is capable of identifying its ills and thereby trying to cope with them. Neither the term *sexism* nor the term *racism* existed fifty years ago—which, as you know, isn't the same as saying that the attitudes and practices they define didn't exist before; of course they did. But those attitudes and prac-tices came to be widely examined and questioned, and finally to be widely ac-knowledged within the dominant culture, only after they were put into words.

Without precision, language can betray everything we stand for. As George [23] Orwell put it in his essay "Politics and the English Language," we must "Let the meaning choose the word and not the other way about." And Orwell went on, "In prose the worst thing you can do with words is surrender to them."

With George Orwell giving us courage, may we be so bold, in closing, as to [24] adapt his wisdom to the occasion by adding this final thought? In publishing, the worst thing you can do is surrender to some tyrannical author who lets the *word* choose the *meaning* rather than the other way about.

COMPREHENSION

1. The authors pose a question in their title. Where, if at all, do they answer it in the essay?
2. In your own words, explain what is meant by "the slippery slope."
3. Define these specialized words: *androcentric, lexicon, lexicographer, generic,* and *inflected.*

4. What overriding issues—issues that transcend matters solely pertaining to the English language—concern the authors?

RHETORIC

1. The authors devote one section to each of three major reasons for the resistance to altering gender-biased language. Does this method create a solid foundation for their argument? Explain.
2. Identify at least two cases of each of the following methods of argumentation: example, definition, explanation, and appeal to authority.
3. The authors place quotation marks around the expressions "masculine," "feminine," and "rules of grammar." What is the function of these quotation marks?
4. Describe the intended audience for this essay. Where do they fit in the social, political, and educational scale of society? Explain your view.
5. The authors refer to the historical record in making a case for altering sexist language in writing. For what type of audience would this be a particularly strong argument?
6. In paragraph 13, the authors state: "And you are probably familiar with the numerous experimental studies done in the last few years, primarily by psychologists and sociologists rather than linguists." To whom does the *you* in this sentence refer? Is this a fair assumption on the part of the writers? What, if anything, does it imply about the relationship of the writers to their audience?
7. A final section is set off by space. What is the purpose of this division? How does it distinguish the final section from the rest of the essay?

WRITING

1. Write an argumentative essay entitled, "Why Gender Writing Bias Bothers Me" or the alternative, "Why So-Called Gender Writing Bias Doesn't Bother Me."
2. As a research assignment, compare and contrast a chapter from a book on child development written in the 1950s and one written in the 1990s. Compare and contrast the chapters in terms of gender-biased language.
3. For a creative writing project, write two identical short mystery stories. In one, use feminine-inflected words for the major character; in the other, use masculine-inflected ones. When you are finished, read each, and note the differences in your psychological reactions to the hero.

CONNECTIONS FOR CRITICAL THINKING

1. Examine the role of the media in society and the responsibilities or duties to humanity of individuals associated with the media. Use at least three essays from this chapter to illustrate or support your thesis.

2. Define *popular culture,* using the essays of Barry and Gates as reference points, along with any additional essays that you consider relevant.

3. Compare and contrast Rita Dove's views on television with those of Marie Winn.

4. Use the essays of Warshow and Ebert to explore the connections of media representations to American cultural experience. What strategies do these writers use? Are their goals similar?

5. Use the essays of Gates and Barry to explore the importance of both the causes and effects of the media promoting particular lifestyles to the public.

6. Gates refers to the African American "style" of communicating through music; Tan refers to the Asian-American style of communication through conversation; and Barry presents beer commercials as communicating the traditional "patriotic symbols" of America. Do these authors have similar or differing points of view regarding the issues they address? Refer specifically to selections in each essay to support your view.

7. Select one essay about art and another about popular culture. Explain any major differences between these two forms of cultural expression.

8. Search the Internet using the keywords *television* AND *teenagers.* Select three or four sites, and write an expository paper describing the various ways the authors interpret any of the major themes.

9. After reading the essays of Warshow, Ebert, Gates, and King, research the issue of the difference between popular entertainment and art. Based on your research, discuss whether there are legitimate criteria that distinguish the two forms. Apply these criteria to gangster films, rap music, and horror films.

10. Compare the use of gender-biased language from an archival issue of a well-known newsweekly such as *Time* or *Newsweek* or a gender-targeted magazine such as *Cosmopolitan* or *Esquire* from the year 1960 to a current issue of the same magazine. Are there any differences you can detect regarding such gender-specific or gender-neutral phrasings as *he* versus *he or she, man* versus *people* or *human?* Do writers and editors employ different gender-biased adjectives to describe emotional traits, for example, *womanly, manly, feminine, masculine,* and so on? Note for example, that a best-selling photo-essay book about world culture published during the 1960s was entitled *The Family of Man.*

11. Select several images of real "gangsters" from magazines or print out images of true gangsters from the Internet. Compare and contrast them with advertisements depicting gangsters from contemporary crime movies such as *Pulp Fiction.* What are the similarities and differences in the subjects' dress, demeanor, facial expression, and so on? What can you conclude from your comparisons?

chapter *10*

Science and Technology
What Can Science Teach Us?

Contrary to popular assumptions, contemporary science and mathematics are not dry subjects but rather bodies of specialized knowledge concerned with the great how and why questions of our time. In fact, we are currently in the midst of a whole series of scientific revolutions that will radically transform our lives as we enter the 21st century. The essential problem for humankind is to make sense of all this revolutionary scientific and mathematical knowledge, invest it with value, use it ethically, and make it serve our cultural and global needs.

As you will see in the essays assembled for this chapter, human beings are always the ultimate subject of scientific investigation. Science and mathematics attempt to understand the physical, biological, and chemical events that shape our lives. Whenever we switch on a light or turn on a computer, take an aspirin or start the car, we see that science and technology have intervened effectively in our lives. Often the specialized knowledge of science forces us to make painful decisions, and the misuse of science can have disastrous results. As Terry Tempest Williams demonstrates in her highly personal essay "The Clan of the One-breasted Women," science can have dire, unforeseen ethical implications.

The technology that arises from science affects everyday decisions as well as the larger contours of culture. Nowhere is the impact of science more apparent than in medicine and health. As Stephen Jay Gould observes in his essay on AIDS, medical science is intended to serve us, to help us with our common dilemmas. At the same time, medical science reminds us that despite advances, we are still mortal. Even as knowledge flows from research laboratories, these mortal paradoxes tend to perplex and goad us as we seek scientific solutions to the complex problems of our era.

Science and technology as specialized bodies of knowledge can send contradictory messages because science and mathematics are socially constructed and reflect the contours of culture. How we manage the revolution in science— how we harness nuclear power or battle the ravages of AIDS—will determine the health of civilization in the next century.

Previewing the Chapter

As you read the essays in this chapter and respond to them in discussion and writing, consider the following questions:

- Does the author take a personal or an objective approach to the subject? What is the effect?
- What area of scientific or mathematical inquiry does the writer focus on?
- What scientific conflicts arise in the course of the essay?
- Is the writer a specialist, a layperson, a journalist, or a commentator? How does the background of the writer affect the tone of the essay?
- What assumptions does the author make about his or her audience? How much specialized knowledge must you bring to the essay?
- How do social issues enter into the author's presentation?
- What gender issues are raised by the author?
- How have your perceptions of the author's topic been changed or enhanced? What new knowledge have you gained? Does the writer contradict any of your assumptions or beliefs?
- Is the writer optimistic or pessimistic about the state of technology or science? How do you know?

Classic and Contemporary Images
WHERE IS SCIENCE TAKING US?

Using a Critical Perspective   Make a series of observations about each of these images. Where does your eye rest in each one? How many objects and details do you see? What reasonable inferences can you draw about the relationship of the artist who created the 15th-century image to the culture and historical period? What purpose did the scientists who created and control the Hubble Space Telescope have? What purposes do the 15th-century artist and 20th-century scientist have in common? Argue for or against the proposition that art can actually capture the advances in science, technology, and humanity that we have experienced over time.

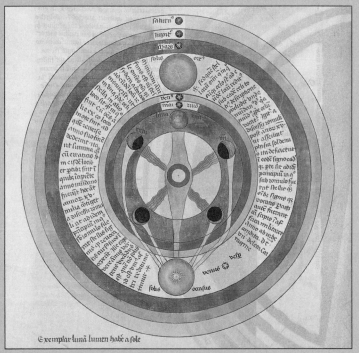

Musse Conde, Chantilly, France/The Bridgeman Art Library.

During the Renaissance in Europe, scientists such as Nicolaus Copernicus (1473–1543) and Galileo Galilei (1564–1642) revolutionized the way Europeans viewed the universe and their place in it by proving that the earth and the planets revolve around the sun, thus changing forever the worldview exemplified by the 15th-century Flemish depiction of the movements of the sun and moon shown here.

Space Telescope Science Institute/Science Photo Library/Photo Researchers.

Galileo's primitive telescope was a distant forerunner of the powerful Hubble Space Telescope, launched in 1990, which is able to take photographs of extremely distant stars and other phenomenon, such as the gaseous pillars shown here, as it orbits the earth.

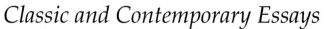

Classic and Contemporary Essays
WHAT IS TECHNOLOGICAL PROGRESS?

Progress: Is it the answer to humankind's problems, or does it create a whole new set of them? This question seems to be more highly and hotly debated each year as technology becomes more sophisticated and as we are faced with the problem of what each new invention is designed to do and what it is replacing. The term *future shock,* coined over 25 years ago, summarized this dilemma, suggesting that the human mind was not capable of dealing with the ever-increasing changes in technology and their effects. In Lewis Mumford's "The Monastery and the Clock," excerpted from his 1934 book *Technics and Civilization*, the author demonstrates how once a significant technology—in this case, the clock—dominates an aspect of daily life, it changes the nature of life forever. Does Mumford consider the clock a machine that marked the progress of human civilization, or does he perceive it as a step backward for civilization? Does the clock, like so many other inventions, require trade-offs in terms of relinquishing aspects of the past by introducing new structures into the relationship of humans with nature? Unlike the clock, which is obviously here to stay, the technology Jeremy Rifkin addresses is still developing today: electronic machines that simulate human communication. It is undeniable that computers and television are here to stay. But should they be regulated? Do they present dangers to our way of living? Can they alienate us from our relationship with experience? Consider these issues in terms of their impact on your own life before you read Rifkin's "The Age of Simulation." Also, you may wish to consider how far simulation of experience has come from the era Mumford describes to the present.

The Monastery and the Clock

Lewis Mumford

Lewis Mumford (1895–1990) was an American sociologist, writer, and critic, whose major interests were architecture and urban planning. Technics and Civilization *(1934),* The Culture of Cities *(1938),* The Conduct of Life *(1951), and* The City in History *(1961), which won a National Book Award, all reveal his interest in the relationship between human need and technology. The following selection is from* Technics and Civilization.

Where did the machine first take form in modern civilization? There was 1 plainly more than one point of origin. Our mechanical civilization represents the convergence of numerous habits, ideas, and modes of living, as well as technical instruments; and some of these were, in the beginning, directly opposed to the civilization they helped to create. But the first manifestation of the new order took place in the general picture of the world: during the first seven centuries of the machine's existence the categories of time and space underwent an extraordinary change, and no aspect of life was left untouched by this transformation. The application of quantitative methods of thought to the study of nature had its first manifestation in the regular measurement of time; and the new mechanical conception of time arose in part out of the routine of the monastery. Alfred Whitehead has emphasized the importance of the scholastic belief in a universe ordered by God as one of the foundations of modern physics: but behind that belief was the presence of order in the institutions of the Church itself.

The technics of the ancient world were still carried on from Constantinople 2 and Baghdad to Sicily and Cordova: hence the early lead taken by Salerno in the scientific and medical advances of the Middle Age. It was, however, in the monasteries of the West that the desire for order and power, other than that expressed in the military domination of weaker men, first manifested itself after the long uncertainty and bloody confusion that attended the breakdown of the Roman Empire. Within the walls of the monastery was sanctuary: under the rule of the order surprise and doubt and caprice and irregularity were put at bay. Opposed to the erratic fluctuations and pulsations of the worldly life was the iron discipline of the rule. Benedict added a seventh period to the devotions of the day, and in the seventh century, by a bull of Pope Sabinianus, it was decreed that the bells of the monastery be rung seven times in the twenty-four hours. These punctuation marks in the day were known as the canonical hours, and some means of keeping count of them and ensuring their regular repetition became necessary.

According to a now discredited legend, the first modern mechanical clock, 3 worked by falling weights, was invented by the monk named Gerbert who afterwards became Pope Sylvester II, near the close of the tenth century. This clock was probably only a water clock, one of those bequests of the ancient world either left over directly from the days of the Romans, like the water-wheel itself, or coming back again into the West through the Arabs. But the legend, as so often happens, is accurate in its implications if not in its facts. The monastery was the seat of a regular life, and an instrument for striking the hours at intervals or for reminding the bell-ringer that it was time to strike the bells, was an almost inevitable product of this life. If the mechanical clock did not appear until the cities of the thirteenth century demanded an orderly routine, the habit of order itself and the earnest regulation of time-sequences had become almost second nature in the monastery. Coulton agrees with Sombart in looking upon the Benedictines, the great working order, as perhaps the original founders of modern capitalism: their rule certainly took the curse off work and their vigorous engineering enterprises may even have robbed warfare of some of its glamour. So one is not straining the facts when one suggests that the monasteries—at one time there were 40,000 under the Benedictine rule—helped to give human enterprise the regular collective beat and rhythm of the machine; for the clock is not merely a means of keeping track of the hours, but of synchronizing the actions of men.

Was it by reason of the collective Christian desire to provide for the welfare 4 of souls in eternity by regular prayers and devotions that time keeping and the habits of temporal order took hold of men's minds: habits that capitalist civilization presently turned to good account? One must perhaps accept the irony of this paradox. At all events, by the thirteenth century there are definite records of mechanical clocks, and by 1370 a well-designed "modern" clock had been built by Heinrich von Wyck at Paris. Meanwhile, bell towers had come into existence, and the new clocks, if they did not have, till the fourteenth century, a dial and a hand that translated the movement of time into a movement through space, at all events struck the hours. The clouds that could paralyze the sundial, the freezing that could stop the water clock on a winter night, were no longer obstacles to time-keeping: summer or winter, day or night, one was aware of the measured clank of the clock. The instrument presently spread outside the monastery; and the regular striking of the bells brought a new regularity into the life of the workman and the merchant. The bells of the clock tower almost defined urban existence. Time-keeping passed into time-serving and time-accounting and time-rationing. As this took place, Eternity ceased gradually to serve as the measure and focus of human actions.

The clock, not the steam-engine, is the key machine of the modern indus- 5 trial age. For every phase of its development the clock is both the outstanding fact and the typical symbol of the machine: even today no other machine is so ubiquitous. Here, at the very beginning of modern technics, appeared prophetically the accurate automatic machine which, only after centuries of further effort, was also to prove the final consummation of this technics in every department of industrial activity. There had been power-machines, such as the water-mill, before the clock; and there had also been various kinds of automata, to awaken the wonder of the populace in the temple, or to please the idle fancy of some Moslem caliph: machines one finds illustrated in Hero and Al-Jazari. But here was a new kind of power-machine, in which the source of power and the transmission were of such a nature as to ensure the even flow of energy throughout the works and to make possible regular production and a standardized product. In its relationship to determinable quantities of energy, to standardization, to automatic action, and finally to its own special product, accurate timing, the clock has been the foremost machine in modern technics; and at each period it has remained in the lead: it marks a perfection toward which other machines aspire. The clock, moreover, served as a model for many other kinds of mechanical works, and the analysis of motion that accompanied the perfection of the clock, with the various types of gearing and transmission that were elaborated, contributed to the success of quite different kinds of machine. Smiths could have hammered thousands of suits of armor or thousands of iron cannon, wheelwrights could have shaped thousands of great water-wheels or crude gears, without inventing any of the special types of movement developed in clockwork, and without any of the accuracy of measurement and fineness of articulation that finally produced the accurate eighteenth-century chronometer.

The clock, moreover, is a piece of power-machinery whose "product" is seconds and minutes: by its essential nature it dissociated time from human events and helped to create the belief in an independent world of mathematically measurable sequences: the special world of science. There is relatively little foundation for this belief in common human experience: throughout the year the days are of uneven duration, and not merely does the relation between day and night steadily change, but a slight journey from East to West alters astronomical time by a certain number of minutes. In terms of the human organism itself, mechanical time is even more foreign: while human life has regularities of its own, the beat of the pulse, the breathing of the lungs, these change from hour to hour with mood and action, and in the longer span of days, time is measured not by the calendar but by the events that occupy it. The shepherd measures from the time the ewes lambed; the farmer measures back to the day of sowing or forward to the harvest: if growth has its own duration and regularities, behind it are not simply matter and motion but the facts of development: in short, history. And while mechanical time is strung out in a succession of mathematically isolated instants, organic time—what Bergson calls duration—is cumulative in its effects. Though mechanical time can, in a sense, be speeded up or run backward, like the hands of a clock or the images of a moving picture, organic time moves in only one direction—through the cycle of birth, growth, development, decay, and death—and the past that is already dead remains present in the future that has still to be born. 6

Around 1345, according to Thorndike, the division of hours into sixty minutes and of minutes into sixty seconds became common: it was this abstract framework of divided time that became more and more the point of reference for both action and thought, and in the effort to arrive at accuracy in this department, the astronomical exploration of the sky focused attention further 7 upon the regular implacable movements of the heavenly bodies through space. Early in the sixteenth century a young Nuremberg mechanic, Peter Henlein, is supposed to have created "many-wheeled watches out of small bits of iron" and by the end of the century the small domestic clock had been introduced in England and Holland. As with the motor car and the airplane, the richer classes first took over the new mechanism and popularized it: partly because they alone could afford it, partly because the new bourgeoisie were the first to discover that, as Franklin later put it, "time is money." To become "as regular as clock-work" was the bourgeois ideal, and to own a watch was for long a definite symbol of success. The increasing tempo of civilization led to a demand for greater power: and in turn power quickened the tempo.

Now, the orderly punctual life that first took shape in the monasteries is not 8 native to mankind, although by now Western peoples are so thoroughly regimented by the clock that it is "second nature" and they look upon its observance as a fact of nature. Many Eastern civilizations have flourished on a loose basis in time: the Hindus have in fact been so indifferent to time that they lack even an authentic chronology of the years. Only yesterday, in the midst of the industrializations of Soviet Russia, did a society come into existence to further the carrying of watches there and to propagandize the benefits of punctuality. The popularization of time-keeping, which followed the production of the cheap standardized watch, first in Geneva, then in America around the middle of the last century, was essential to a well-articulated system of transportation and production.

To keep time was once a peculiar attribute of music: it gave industrial value 9 to the workshop song or the tattoo or the chantey of the sailors tugging at a rope. But the effect of the mechanical clock is more pervasive and strict: it presides over the day from the hour of rising to the hour of rest. When one thinks of the day as an abstract span of time, one does not go to bed with the chickens on a winter's night: one invents wicks, chimneys, lamps, gaslights, electric lamps, so as to use all the hours belonging to the day. When one thinks of time, not as a sequence of experiences, but as a collection of hours, minutes, and seconds, the habits of adding time and saving time come into existence. Time took on the character of an enclosed space: it could be divided, it could be filled up, it could even be expanded by the invention of labor-saving instruments.

Abstract time became the new medium of existence. Organic functions 10 themselves were regulated by it: one ate, not upon feeling hungry, but when prompted by the clock: one slept, not when one was tired, but when the clock sanctioned it. A generalized time-consciousness accompanied the wider use of clocks: dissociating time from organic sequences, it became easier for the men of the Renaissance to indulge the fantasy of reviving the classic past or of reliving the splendors of antique Roman civilization: the cult of history, appearing first in daily ritual, finally abstracted itself as a special discipline. In the seventeenth century journalism and periodic literature made their appearance: even in dress, following the lead of Venice as fashion-center, people altered styles every year rather than every generation.

The gain in mechanical efficiency through co-ordination and through 11 the closer articulation of the day's events cannot be overestimated: while this increase cannot be measured in mere horsepower, one has only to imagine its absence today to foresee the speedy disruption and eventual collapse of our entire society. The modern industrial régime could do without coal and iron and steam more easily than it could do without the clock.

COMPREHENSION

1. What is the major theme of the essay? Explain how you arrived at your conclusion.
2. How is the "product" of the clock different in kind from products of other machinery?
3. What external world events catalyzed the development of the clock?
4. Define the following words: *caprice* (paragraph 2), *ubiquitous* (paragraph 5), *automata* (paragraph 5), and *bourgeois* (paragraph 7).

RHETORIC

1. Mumford begins his inquiry with a question. Why?
2. What types of support does Mumford use to back up his theme? How well does the author integrate them within the context of his essay?
3. Does Mumford seem to be an authority on his subject matter? Explain your view.
4. Owing to the originality of his thinking, Mumford creates his own compound nouns to assist him in explaining his theme. What do the following terms from paragraph 4 mean: *time-serving, time-accounting,* and *time-rationing?* Also, what does the term *abstract time* in the next to the last paragraph mean?
5. Where in the essay does Mumford explore the cognitive and technological changes that the clock influenced? Why has he located this information where he does?
6. Does Mumford take a value position regarding his topic; that is, does he see it as positive, negative, or neutral? Explain your view.
7. Review the final sentence in the essay. Is it fact or opinion? Explain your view.

WRITING

1. Does Mumford satisfactorily demonstrate his thesis? Write an essay of 500 to 750 words explaining why you believe he does or does not.
2. Argue for or against the proposition that the needs of society are catalysts to the development of new technologies. Use any appropriate example, such as the Apollo spaceship, the traffic light, the automated teller machine.
3. Describe an event whose activities are not dictated by clock time. Explain how the divisions of the event are determined.

The Age of Simulation

Jeremy Rifkin

Jeremy Rifkin was born in 1935 in Denver, Colorado. He received his BA degree from the University of Pennsylvania and his MA degree from the Fletcher School of Law and Diplomacy. He is an internationally known commentator, activist, and lecturer on the social impact of science and technology and the author of many books, including Biosphere Politics *(1991),* Entropy: A New World View *(1980), and* The End of Work *(1996). His book* Beyond Beef *(1992) took a critical look at the American agriculture industry and called for a revolution in the way it operates. The following excerpt is from his book* Biosphere Politics *(1991).*

The separation of human beings from nature and the parallel detachment of human consciousness from the human body has transformed Western man into an   1
alien on his own planet. Much of the outside world has become a kind of "no man's land," a scarred and polluted terrain full of danger—a foreboding environment where wars are fought, animals are slaughtered, forests are razed and burned, and human refugees wander aimlessly from place to place in search of safe havens. In the new indoor world, modern man and woman attempt to escape their last connection with the outside world by suppressing their own animal senses and freeing themselves from their own physical nature. A marvelous array of machines, big and small, have been invented to replace nearly every part of our bodies, providing us with mechanical surrogates from head to toe.

Our deep yearning for a mechanical analogue to nature was first expressed in the construction of automata, elaborate mechanized toys that mimicked living creatures, even human beings, in bodily function, movement, and gesture.   2
The most elaborate of the automata were the brain-children of a brilliant and imaginative French engineer, Jacques de Vaucanson. In 1738, Vaucanson amazed his fellow countrymen with the introduction of a fully automated flutist. The mechanized miniature of a human being "possessed lips that moved, a moving tongue that served as the airflow valve, and movable fingers whose leather tips opened and closed the stops of the flute." Voltaire was so taken by the sight of the lifelike, remarkable little creature that he dubbed Vaucanson "Prometheus's rival." Vaucanson's greatest work was a mechanical duck, an automata of such great versatility that it has not been surpassed in design to this day. The duck could drink puddle water with its bill, eat bits of grain, and within a special chamber visible to admiring spectators, duplicate the process of digestion. "Each of its wings contained four hundred moving pieces and could open and close like that of a living duck."[1]

Automata were the rage of Europe during the early industrial era. Engineers built little mechanical boys who wrote out poems and prose, petite   3
mechanical maidens who danced to music, and animals of every kind and

description performing wondrous feats. The toys, which became a favorite of princes and kings, were toured and put on exhibition throughout Europe. The automata provided a kind of proof to many that nature, like the automata that mimicked it, must indeed be animated by principles of mechanism just as Descartes and his contemporaries had argued. The visible presence of these strange little automated creatures could not help but excite the scientific and popular imagination and add impetus to the drive to find mechanized surrogates for everything in nature, even the human body.

During the first stage of the Industrial Revolution, machines of all kinds were invented to substitute for the human body. With the invention of electricity at the turn of the nineteenth century, a new category of machines was created to amplify and even replace human consciousness. Marshall McLuhan summed up the "bodily" impact of the two stages of invention:

> During the mechanical age we had extended our bodies in space. Today, after more than a century of electronic technology, we have extended our central nervous system itself in a global embrace. . . .[2]

McLuhan's now famous aphorism that "electronic man has no physical body" is fast becoming a reality in a world in which electronic communication has increasingly substituted for face-to-face communication between people. Today, electronic media have even eclipsed print in importance. Less than 20 percent of all the words delivered in America today are printed. Over 80 percent of all communications now go through the airwaves and telephone wires.[3]

Electronic technology represents the final disembodiment of the senses. The more intimate senses, smell and touch, are eliminated altogether. Sight and sound are disembodied by machines, turned into invisible waves and pulses, transported over great distances with lightning speed, and then reembodied by other machines in the form of facsimiles, artificially reconstructed versions of the originals.

Television is today's electronic sequel to the mechanized automata of the early industrial period. The mechanical representations of life have been replaced by electronic representations. With television, cinema, radio, stereos, cassette-disc players, and the like, modern man and woman can surround themselves with a second creation, an artificially conceived electronic environment that is virtually sealed off from the world of living nature.

Over 99 percent of the homes in the United States now have at least one television set. On any given evening, over 80 million people are watching television. It is not uncommon for 100 million people to all watch the same show at the same time.[4] Never before in history have so many human beings collectively experienced the same event simultaneously. Ironically, it is anything but a shared experience, in that each viewer is witnessing the events in the privacy of his or her own home, far removed from neighbors.

The average American household watches over six hours of television each day. The average viewer watches over four hours of television daily. Most Americans are spending nearly half their nonworking, nonsleeping hours in front of a machine watching "the phosphorescent glow of three hundred thousand tiny dots" flicker on and off at thirty times per second, creating electronic images of people, places, and things.[5] While the images entertain, inform, and educate, we tend to forget that they are not "real" experiences. They are simulations. In his book *Four Arguments for the Elimination of Television*, Jerry Mander points to the profound anthropological significance of this powerful and ubiquitous new presence in our life: "America has become the first culture to have substituted secondary, mediated versions of experience for direct experience of the world."[6]

Television is the ultimate technological surrogate for real life. It represents   10
the final separation from nature, a retreat into a private domain where, cut off from the outside world, the individual can view artificial electronic recreations of reality. Millions of people have become voyeurs, passive spectators of experience. They can watch in horror as wars unfold before their eyes, be entertained by swashbuckling adventures, be romanced and beguiled by torrid love stories, tickled and amused by comedic antics, and saddened by the tragic accounts of others' misfortunes. All of the human emotions and feelings are aroused daily by television—millions of people reacting not to other flesh-and-blood people, not to a living environment, but rather to a machine pulsing electronic images into a semidarkened room.

The electronic images cannot be touched, smelled, or tasted. They are visual   11
and only secondarily aural, and even then both senses are narrowly circumscribed, diminished in size, range, and volume. Television cannot begin to capture the color, resolution, pitch, and tones of real images and sounds in the outside world. The flicker of illuminated dots conveys a one-dimensional silhouette, a distorted and disembodied representation of life.

Television distorts temporal and spatial reality in other, even more funda-   12
mental ways. The images of people, places, and events are cut into seven- or eight-second frames or sound bites. The viewer is asked to suspend reality and accept cutaway shots in which the past, present, and future intermix, follow each other out of sequence, dovetail and parallel each other in a confusing array of combinations that bear no resemblance to the temporal and spatial realities of the real world.

Then, too, the medium has become so pervasive in our lives that it has be-   13
come much of our experience of life. We often talk about television characters and situations as if they were an intimate part of our lives. So much of our waking experience is consumed by television that many viewers are unable to distinguish clearly the artificial from the real. Indeed, the artificial becomes the most real part of our lives, since it takes up so much of our time.

Television blurs the distinction between artificial and real as no other   14
medium in history, creating a fundamental distortion in human consciousness that for many borders on dysfunctional pathology. "Marcus Welby, M.D." received over 250,000 letters from viewers during the five-year run of the show asking the fictional doctor for medical advice.[7]

In a study prepared for the National Institute of Mental Health, Dr. George   15
Grebner, dean of the Annenberg School of Communications at the University of Pennsylvania, and Dr. Larry Gross found that television watchers form much of

their view of the world from what they see and experience on the screen. Among other things, the researchers found that:

> heavy viewers of television were more likely to overestimate the percentage of the world population that lives in America: they seriously overestimated the percentage of the population that have professional jobs; and they drastically overestimated the number of police in the U.S. and the amount of violence. In all these cases, the overestimate matched a distortion that exists in television programming. The more television people watched, the more their view of the world matched television reality.[8]

As both a medium and a technology, television incorporates many of the 16 operative principles of Enlightenment thinking. It separates people from the natural world, isolates them from their neighbors, suppresses some bodily senses and narrows others, emphasizes the artificial over the real, and reinforces the illusion of an autonomous, secure existence. From the safe haven of the television room, one can experience the outside world vicariously, without having to risk intimate participation or bodily contact.

While television helped further enclose human consciousness from the world of 17 nature by conditioning the mind to live within an artificial environment, computer technology is creating a second artificial enclosure, which "promises" to replace living nature altogether. With computer technology, human civilization enters what may best be characterized as the age of simulation. At the Massachusetts Institute of Technology, Carnegie-Mellon University, and other elite schools of engineering, scientists are working feverishly on a new generation of computers that they say will create totally artificial environments. They call these new environments "virtual reality" to distinguish them from the kind of reality we have experienced up to now in our evolutionary history.[9]

At the advanced media lab at MIT, scientists are creating prototypes of com- 18 puting machines that can simulate aspects of reality. Their goal is to construct an artificial "vivarium," a totally enclosed environment in which they can create and sustain facsimiles of life in isolation from the outside world. In the new world of simulation, the computer is not only used to create the simulated world of virtual reality but also becomes a machine surrogate for human companionship. Nicholas Negroponte of MIT states unabashedly that he regards his relationship to the computer not as "one of master and slave but rather of two associates that have a potential and a desire for self-fulfillment."[10] Negroponte, like many of his engineering colleagues, envisions the computing machines of the future more as personalized companions than work tools or mechanized forms of entertainment. He writes in his book *The Architecture Machine:*

> Imagine a machine that can follow your design technology and at the same time discern and assimilate your conversational idiosyncrasies. The same machine, after observing your behavior, could build a predictive model of your conversational performance. . . . The dialogue would be so intimate—even exclusive—that only mutual persuasion and compromise would bring about ideas. Ideas unrealizable by either conversant alone.[11]

The goal of advanced computing design extends far beyond the obvious [19] and banal considerations of commerce, military preparedness, or even more lofty goals like education and discovery. After spending several months interviewing scientists at MIT and other engineering schools, futurist Stewart Brand concluded in his book *Media Lab* that what scientists really desire with their mechanical creation is "companionship" and the security of a predictable artificial environment to wrap around them. Daniel Hillis of the media lab at MIT fantasized: "I would like to build a machine that can be proud of me," to which he added, "Thinking machines will be grateful to their creators."[12] The notion of an intimate mechanized companion that, while not completely predictable, is at least somewhat controllable and, of course, replaceable—to wit, an artificial surrogate to living creatures—reinforces the vision of Descartes, Bacon, and other early Enlightenment thinkers.

In his second book, *Soft Architecture Machines*, Negroponte turns the final [20] screw on the age of modernity, envisioning the ultimate vivarium, or enclosed environment:

> The last chapter is my view of the distant future of architecture machines: they won't help us design; instead, we will live in them. . . . While proposing that a room might giggle at a funny gesture or be reluctant to be transformed into something else seems so unserious today, it does expose some of the questions associated with possible cognitive environments of tomorrow.[13]

Negroponte's vivarium is almost alive. It is virtual reality and, like the natural [21] world, it can be silly, even obstinate. Still, it is a creation of human beings and therefore seems more easily manipulated and exploitable.

The autonomous interactive vivarium is years, if not decades, away. Scien- [22] tists, however, have already successfully created limited virtual reality environments. At the Japanese government's mechanical engineering laboratory, scientists are experimenting in a new field of simulation called "teleoperations." Japanese scientists have already created a successful visual model with teleoperations, a robotized camera that allows the viewer to scan an environment hundreds or thousands of miles away with the help of a mobile robot. The observer can send the robot to distant places and then scan the terrain with his own eyes, as if he were actually there experiencing it firsthand. The observer places his head in a black-velvet-lined box equipped with two television receivers, one for each eye:

> The receivers are gauged so that the image that is reflected against the retina of each eye is exactly the same as if you were looking at the world unaided. Further, every movement of your head is duplicated on the robot, where two precisely placed video cameras transmit a human range of what is seen.[14]

Researchers are working on other teleoperation devices, including one that [23] allows an individual to manipulate an artificial environment on a computer screen in the control room and have his actions duplicated precisely and virtually simultaneously by a robot working miles away in the real environment.

Scientists working in the new field of virtual reality are experimenting with   24
high-technology systems that can simulate all of the senses, enabling people to
affect the outside world by way of an array of artificial experiences. The Data
Glove was pioneered in the 1980s by Thomas G. Zimmerman and Lyoring
Haivell. The glove, which contains fiber-optic cables tucked inside the fingers
and thumbs, is connected to a computer terminal. The glove allows someone in
a central control room to work with the mechanical hands of a robot in the outside world. As the human hand clenches, grasps, squeezes, and turns, the pressures are transmitted electronically to the robot's hands, which mimics each
gesture. In the not-too-distant future, researchers say they will be able to reverse the tactile experience. As the robot takes hold of an object or even a living creature in the outside world, the tactile feeling will be transmitted inside,
to the controller's hand, allowing him to experience touch by way of electronic
stimulation.[15]

Computer synthesizing machines using advanced digital design techniques   25
can already simulate the sound of an entire orchestra. One person sitting at a
console can electronically reproduce the sound of virtually any musical instrument with the kind of precision that a musician cannot hope to duplicate.

Scientists are even working on techniques that will simulate smells, provid-   26
ing the vivariums of the future with preprogrammed odoriferous releases designed to incite, soothe, energize, and divert. Aroma therapists are
experimenting with scent machines that can time a steady release of odors
through ventilation systems into enclosed work environments or households.
Researchers at Duke and Yale universities are studying the impact of various
odors on blood pressure, brain waves, and other physiological processes. The
new developments in olfactory science, says Yale psychologist William Cain, are
likely to have extraordinary impacts on human civilization in the coming
decades. "We'll gain tremendous understanding of the basic neurophysiologi-
cal ways in which odors regulate the body and influence the mind. And after
we've mapped the hidden pathways of olfactory nerves, we'll be able to influence behavior, modulate mood, and alleviate pain."[16] Some scientists hope to
simulate smell electronically, over distances, just as they've begun to do with
touch. One could smell flowers or a sea breeze hundreds or even thousands of
miles away by way of artificially transmitted electronic pulses.

Proponents of virtual reality are eager to simulate every aspect of the hu-   27
man environment in hopes of creating a totally artificial living space. With each
new technological marvel, reality becomes more ephemeral and further removed from anything that might be thought of as natural. With laser-generated
holography, scientists hope to fashion new artificial environments that are mere
illusions, transporting us into a world lacking any semblance of physicality.
Holographically furnished homes might include paintings and other artifacts
that are no more real than the electronic images on the television screen.

Virtual reality represents the final retreat from organic reality and the last   28
chapter in the modern drive for security. The substitution of artificial experiences for natural ones masks an almost pathological fear of the living world.

Grant Fjermedal, in *The Tomorrow Makers*, recounts the dreams and goals of ₂₉
scientists he interviewed at Carnegie-Mellon. Their vision of the future captures
much of the artificiality of the modern sojourn.

> At Carnegie-Mellon University, Hans Moravec and Mike Blackwell had talked
> of the day when experiences could be simulated so well that you could sit in a
> chair wearing a headset to captivate your eyes, ears, and nose and have sensors
> attached to hands and legs, which would enable you to visit the world from the
> safety and comfort of your home.[17]

The relentless pursuit of a mechanized form of autonomous existence, ₃₀
seemingly free from the hold of nature and the death sentence it imposes on all
living creatures, has led scientists like Hans Moravec to experiment with the
idea of "downloading" human consciousness. Moravec, who is a senior research scientist at Carnegie-Mellon's Autonomous Mobile Robot Laboratory, explains the process in a theoretical paper entitled "Robots That Rove." Using
ultrasonic radar, phased array radio encephalography, and high-resolution,
three-dimensional nuclear magnetic resonance holography, researchers might
be able to scan parts of the human brain in order to develop a three-dimensional
picture of its chemical makeup. A computer program could be written to simulate the behavior of each section of the brain. After each section of the brain has
been "downloaded" into a written program, the entire simulation could be
transferred into a computerized brain, which would think and act as the living
original, complete with an identical set of memories.[18]

Many researchers in the new field of artificial intelligence believe that ₃₁
downloading is indeed possible. MIT's Marvin Minsky says, "If a person is a
machine and you get a wiring diagram of it, then you can make copies."[19] Like
the alchemists who dreamed of discovering the elixir for everlasting life, and
the mechanical engineers of the industrial age who dreamed of inventing a perpetual motion machine, the new computer scientists of the age of simulation
dream of replacing the organic brain with a simulated computer model in an effort to defeat the inevitability of death.

MIT professor Gerald Jay Sussman expressed the hopes and expectations of ₃₂
many of his colleagues:

> "If you can make a machine that contains the contents of your mind, then the
> machine is you. To hell with the rest of your physical body, it's not very inter-
> esting. Now, the machine can last forever. Even if it doesn't last forever, you can
> always dump it onto tape and make backups, then load it up on some other
> machine if the first one breaks. . . . Everyone would like to be immortal. . . . I'm
> afraid, unfortunately, that I am the last generation to die."[20]

The idea of downloading human consciousness should not really surprise ₃₃
us. It stands as the last unexplored terrain in a five-hundred-year odyssey to find
a mechanical elixir. With thoughts of downloading dancing in their heads, scientists have crossed the final boundary separating the secular from the sacred, the
artificial from the real world. The modern journey ends in the laboratories of

MIT and Carnegie-Mellon, where some of the best minds of science are currently devoting their energies and their lives to creating a mechanical surrogate for eternal salvation.

In the age of simulation, security and immortality are no longer sought in 34 Christ on Judgment Day, or in unlimited material progress, or even in the specter of a classless society at the end of history. The new immortality is information, which can be collected, stored, edited, and preserved in perpetuity. Unlike living creatures, information does not rot and decay. Because it is mathematically derived and immaterial in nature, information can be transferred from one program to another and from one computing machine to another forever, without risk of diminution. While the software and hardware will eventually run down, the information will not and needs merely to be downloaded periodically to preserve its contents. Yoneji Masuda, a principal figure in the Japanese plan to become the first fully simulated information society, expresses unbridled enthusiasm for the new immortality:

> Unlike material goods, information does not disappear by being consumed, and even more important, the value of information can be amplified indefinitely by constant additions of new information to the existing information. People will thus continue to utilize information which they and others have created, even after it has been used.[21]

For some, the notion of transferring human consciousness to electronic pro- 35 grams that can be tucked inside automated computing machines is a chilling prospect. For others, like Moravec and his colleagues, downloading represents the long-sought-after fulfillment of Descartes's grand vision, the final reaffirmation of the modern quest for total autonomy from nature and absolute security for humankind.

Notes

1. Vaucanson's automata were first described in the *Encyclopédie* of 1751. See also Siegfried Giedion, *Mechanization Takes Command: A Contribution to Anonymous History*, p. 35: Michael Uhl. "Living Dolls," *Geo*, July 1984, p. 86.
2. Herbert Marshall McLuhan, *Understanding Media: The Extensions of Man*, p. 53.
3. Stewart Brand, *The Media Lab, Inventing the Future at MIT*, pp. 18, 58.
4. Jerry Mander, *Four Arguments for the Elimination of Television*, p. 24.
5. Ibid., p. 192.
6. Ibid., p. 24.
7. Ibid., p. 255.
8. Ibid.
9. See Brand, *The Media Lab*, pp. 97–99, 112–13.
10. Nicholas Negroponte, quoted in Brand, *The Media Lab*, p. 149.
11. Nicholas Negroponte, *The Architecture Machine*, pp. 11–13.
12. Daniel Hillis, quoted in Grant Fjermedal, *The Tomorrow Makers*, p. 94.

13. Quoted in Brand, *The Media Lab*, p. 152.
14. Fjermedal, *Tomorrow Makers*, p. 233; see also Jeremy Rifkin, *Time Wars: The Primary Conflict in Human History*, pp. 173–74.
15. James D. Foley, "Interfaces for Advanced Computing," p. 130.
16. Quoted in Pamela Weintraub, "Sentimental Journeys," *Omni*, April 1986, p. 48.
17. Fjermedal, *Tomorrow Makers*, p. 229.
18. Ibid., p. 4.
19. Marvin Minsky, quoted in ibid., p. 7.
20. Gerald Jay Sussman, quoted in ibid., p. 8.
21. Yoneji Masuda, *The Information Society*, p. 150.

COMPREHENSION

1. Why is Rifkin particularly troubled by the latest developments in technology?
2. What does Rifkin mean by "The Age of Simulation"?
3. How does Rifkin define *virtual reality?*

RHETORIC

1. What is Rifkin's value position toward the latest technologies: positive, negative, or neutral? Explain your view.
2. What organizational plan does Rifkin use in his essay: chronology, division, cause and effect, comparison and contrast? Explain your view.
3. Who is the implied audience for the essay? Explain your view.
4. Does Rifkin have a rhetorical goal? If so, what is it? And does he achieve it?
5. What types of evidence does Rifkin provide in his criticism of television? Is his evidence adequate to defend his view? Explain.
6. Is the opening sentence of the essay a fact or an opinion? Explain your view.
7. In the concluding paragraph of the essay, Rifkin presents two views of the logical conclusion to the development of virtual reality. What is the rhetorical strategy behind ending the essay with this comparison-and-contrast device?

WRITING

1. Argue for or against the proposition that "downloading human consciousness" would be a good thing.
2. Explain why human beings are or are not destined to develop more sophisticated virtual reality technologies.
3. Argue for or against the proposition that Rifkin is misguided when he states that "autonomous, secure existence" is an "illusion" (paragraph 16).

Classic and Contemporary: Questions for Comparison

1. How do Mumford and Rifkin approach the subject of technology? Do they have different priorities? Are they writing for similar audiences? Use examples from both writers to support your ideas.
2. Analyze the language used in the two essays. What is similar or different about the style and diction of the two pieces? Is one essay more accessible to the modern reader? If so, why? How does each use details?
3. What are the similarities and differences between the technologies and the effects of the technologies that Mumford and Rifkin write about? Has one made a greater impact on civilization than the other? Explain.

Natural Selection

Charles Darwin

Charles Darwin (1809–1882) was born in England and studied medicine at Edinburgh. He also studied for the ministry at Cambridge but soon turned his interest to natural history. Through his friendship with a well-known botanist, he was given the opportunity to take a five-year cruise around the world (1831–1836) aboard the H.M.S. Beagle, *serving as a naturalist. This started Darwin on a career of accumulating and assimilating data that resulted in the formulation of his concept of evolution. He spent the remainder of his life carefully and methodically working over the information from his copious notes. He first published his findings in 1858 and a year later published his influential* Origin of Species. *This seminal work was supplemented and elaborated in many later books, including* The Descent of Man *(1871). The following selection demonstrates the methodical and meticulous method Darwin used in developing his concepts.*

In order to make it clear how, as I believe, natural selection acts, I must beg permission to give one or two imaginary illustrations. Let us take the case of a wolf, which preys on various animals, securing some by craft, some by strength, and some by fleetness; and let us suppose that the fleetest prey, a deer for instance, had from any change in the country increased in numbers, or that other prey had decreased in numbers, during that season of the year when the wolf is hardest pressed for food. I can under such circumstances see no reason to doubt that the swiftest and slimmest wolves would have the best chance of surviving, and so be preserved or selected, provided always that they retained strength to master their prey at this or at some other period of the year, when they might be compelled to prey on other animals. I can see no more reason to doubt this, than that man can improve the fleetness of his greyhounds by careful and methodical selection, or by that unconscious selection which results from each man trying to keep the best dogs without any thought of modifying the breed.

Even without any change in the proportional numbers of the animals on 2 which our wolf preyed, a cub might be born with an innate tendency to pursue certain kinds of prey. Nor can this be thought very improbable; for we often observe great differences in the natural tendencies of our domestic animals; one cat, for instance, taking to catch rats, another mice; one cat, according to Mr. St. John, bringing home winged game, another hares or rabbits, and another hunting on marshy ground and almost nightly catching woodcocks or snipes. The tendency to catch rats rather than mice is known to be inherited. Now, if any slight innate change of habit or of structure benefited an individual wolf, it would have the best chance of surviving and of leaving offspring. Some of its young would probably inherit the same habits or structure, and by the repetition of this process, a new variety might be formed which would either supplant or coexist with the parent-form of wolf. Or, again, the wolves inhabiting a mountainous district, and those frequenting the lowlands, would naturally be forced to hunt different prey; and from the continued preservation of the individuals best fitted for the two sites, two varieties might slowly be formed. These varieties would cross and blend where they met; but to this subject of intercrossing we shall soon have to return. I may add, that, according to Mr. Pierce, there are two varieties of the wolf inhabiting the Catskill Mountains in the United States, one with a light greyhound-like form, which pursues deer, and the other more bulky, with shorter legs, which more frequently attacks the shepherd's flocks.

Let us now take a more complex case. Certain plants excrete a sweet juice, 3 apparently for the sake of eliminating something injurious from their sap; this is effected by glands at the base of the stipules in some Leguminosae, and at the back of the leaf of the common laurel. This juice, though small in quantity, is greedily sought by insects. Let us now suppose a little sweet juice or nectar to be excreted by the inner bases of the petals of a flower. In this case insects in seeking the nectar would get dusted with pollen, and would certainly often transport the pollen from one flower to the stigma of another flower. The flowers of two distinct individuals of the same species would thus get crossed; and the act of crossing, we have good reason to believe (as will hereafter be more fully alluded to), would produce very vigorous seedlings, which consequently would have the best chance of flourishing and surviving. Some of these seedlings would probably inherit the nectar-excreting power. Those individual flowers which had the largest glands or nectaries, and which excreted most nectar, would be oftenest visited by insects, and would be oftenest crossed; and so in the long-run would gain the upper hand. Those flowers, also, which had their stamens and pistils placed, in relation to the size and habits of the particular insects which visited them, so as to favor in any degree the transportal of their pollen from flower to flower, would likewise be favored or selected. We might have taken the case of insects visiting flowers for the sake of collecting

pollen instead of nectar; and as pollen is formed for the sole object of fertiliza-
tion, its destruction appears a simple loss to the plant; yet if a little pollen were
carried, at first occasionally and then habitually, by the pollen-devouring insects
from flower to flower, and a cross thus effected, although nine-tenths of the
pollen were destroyed, it might still be a great gain to the plant; and those individuals which produced more and more pollen, and had larger and larger anthers, would be selected.

When our plant, by this process of the continued preservation or natural se- 4
lection of more and more attractive flowers, had been rendered highly attractive
to insects, they would, unintentionally on their part, regularly carry pollen from
flower to flower; and that they can most effectually do this, I could easily show
by many striking instances. I will give only one—not as a very striking case, but
as likewise illustrating one step in the separation of the sexes of plants,
presently to be alluded to. Some holly-trees bear only male flowers, which have
four stamens producing rather a small quantity of pollen, and a rudimentary
pistil; other holly-trees bear only female flowers; these have a full-sized pistil,
and four stamens with shriveled anthers, in which not a grain of pollen can be
detected. Having found a female tree exactly sixty yards from a male tree, I put
the stigmas of twenty flowers, taken from different branches, under the microscope, and on all, without exception, there were pollen-grains, and on some a
profusion of pollen. As the wind had set for several days from the female to the
male tree, the pollen could not thus have been carried. The weather had been
cold and boisterous, and therefore not favorable to bees; nevertheless every female flower which I examined had been effectually fertilized by the bees, accidentally dusted with pollen, having flown from tree to tree in search of nectar.
But to return to our imaginary case: as soon as the plant had been rendered so
highly attractive to insects that pollen was regularly carried from flower to
flower, another process might commence. No naturalist doubts the advantage
of what has been called the "physiological division of labor"; hence we may believe that it would be advantageous to a plant to produce stamens alone in one
flower or on one whole plant, and pistils alone in another flower or on another
plant. In plants under culture and placed under new conditions of life, sometimes the male organs and sometimes the female organs become more or less
impotent; now if we suppose this to occur in ever so slight a degree under nature, then as pollen is already carried regularly from flower to flower, and as a
more complete separation of the sexes of our plant would be advantageous on
the principle of the division of labor, individuals with this tendency more and
more increased, would be continually favored or selected, until at last a complete separation of the sexes would be effected.

Let us now turn to the nectar-feeding insects in our imaginary case: we may 5
suppose the plant of which we have been slowly increasing the nectar by continued selection, to be a common plant; and that certain insects depended in
main part on its nectar for food. I could give many facts, showing how anxious
bees are to save time; for instance, their habit of cutting holes and sucking the
nectar at the bases of certain flowers, which they can, with a very little more

trouble, enter by the mouth. Bearing such facts in mind, I can see no reason to doubt that an accidental deviation in the size and form of the body, or in the curvature and length of the proboscis, etc., far too slight to be appreciated by us, might profit a bee or other insect, so that an individual so characterized would be able to obtain its food more quickly, and so have a better chance of living and leaving descendants. Its descendants would probably inherit a tendency to a similar slight deviation of structure. The tubes of the corollas of the common red and incarnate clovers (Trifolium pratense and incarnatum) do not on a hasty glance appear to differ in length; yet the hive-bee can easily suck the nectar out of the incarnate clover, but not out of the common red clover, which is visited by humble-bees alone; so that the whole fields of the red clover offer in vain an abundant supply of precious nectar to the hive-bee. Thus it might be a great advantage to the hive-bee to have a slightly longer or differently constructed proboscis. On the other hand, I have found by experiment that the fertility of clover greatly depends on bees visiting and moving parts of the corolla, so as to push the pollen on to the stigmatic surface. Hence, again, if humble-bees were to become rare in any country, it might be a great advantage to the red clover to have a shorter or more deeply divided tube to its corolla, so that the hive-bee could visit its flowers. Thus I can understand how a flower and a bee might slowly become, either simultaneously or one after the other, modified and adapted in the most perfect manner to each other, by the continued preservation of individuals presenting mutual and slightly favorable deviations of structure.

I am well aware that this doctrine of natural selection, exemplified in the 6 above imaginary instances, is open to the same objections which were at first urged against Sir Charles Lyell's noble views on "the modern changes of the earth, as illustrative of geology"; but we now very seldom hear the action, for instance, of the coast-waves, called a trifling and insignificant cause, when applied to the excavation of gigantic valleys or to the formation of the longest lines of inland cliffs. Natural selection can act only by the preservation and accumulation of infinitesimally small inherited modifications, each profitable to the preserved being; and as modern geology has almost banished such views as the excavation of a great valley by a single diluvial wave, so will natural selection, if it be a true principle, banish the belief of the continued creation of new organic beings, or of any great and sudden modification in their structure.

COMPREHENSION

1. What does Darwin mean by the term *natural selection?*
2. What is Darwin attempting to refute by his concept of natural selection? Where in the essay is this refutation articulated?
3. Explain what Darwin means by the "physiological division of labor."
4. Define the following terms: *innate* (paragraph 2), *stamens* (paragraph 3), *pistils* (paragraph 3), *rudimentary* (paragraph 4), *incarnate* (paragraph 5), and *doctrine* (paragraph 6).

RHETORIC

1. In the introduction, Darwin makes an analogy between the needs of humans and those of nature. What is this analogy, and why is it important in devising his argument?
2. What is the tone of the essay? Consider such phrases as "beg permission" (paragraph 1) and "Let us now" (paragraph 3).
3. Darwin uses two "imaginary illustrations" in an attempt to prove his point. What are they, and why are these hypothetical illustrations more effective than real-life ones for his purpose?
4. Darwin tends to use extremely long sentences when he wishes to illustrate a process. For example, the sentence in paragraph 3 that begins "We might have taken" is 101 words long. Deconstruct this sentence by paying special attention to its punctuation, its logical succession of clauses, and its effect on the reader of describing so many processes within its boundaries. What is the relationship between rhetorical style and its purpose?
5. Who is the implied audience for the essay? Cite specific aspects of the rhetoric that led you to your conclusion.
6. What gives Darwin his authority? Specifically, how is his authority linked to the specialized vocabulary of the essay and to the way Darwin uses language to articulate natural processes?
7. Darwin uses the argumentative technique of disarming potential critics in the final paragraph. What is the rhetorical function of this device? Does it strengthen or weaken his argument? Explain your view.

WRITING

1. In an essay of 500 to 750 words, argue for or against the proposition that in order to agree with or attempt to refute Darwin's ideas of natural selection, one would have to have at least as much experience in observing nature as Darwin obviously had.
2. Argue for or against the view that Darwin's theory can have disastrous consequences for the human species if applied to politics, sociology, or economics.
3. Write a précis of the essay, focusing on the major points Darwin is trying to assert in his theory of natural selection.

Sarcophagus

Richard Selzer

Richard Selzer (b. 1928) is a professional surgeon who started writing for several hours each night after he had already established a successful medical career. His first book of essays, Mortal Essays: Notes on the Art of Surgery *(1974), established him as a prominent essayist specializing in the world of medicine and surgery. Selzer employs his elegant prose style in describing the often tragic, unpleasant, and painful world of medical patients. He is a contributor to popular magazines, and his essays have been collected in several books, among them* Confessions of a Knife *(1979),* Letters to a Young Doctor *(1982),* Taking the World in for Repairs *(1997), and* The Exact Location of the Soul *(2001). He has also contributed to a number of anthologies and wrote a book of stories,* Imagine a Woman *(1997). The following essay demonstrates Selzer's experience and expertise as a surgeon as well as his unique ability to describe the world of medicine in poetic and graceful terms.*

We are six who labor here in the night. No . . . seven! For the man horizontal   1
upon the table strives as well. But we do not acknowledge his struggle. It is our
own that preoccupies us.

I am the surgeon.   2

David is the anesthesiologist. You will see how kind, how soft he is. Each   3
patient is, for him, a preparation respectfully controlled. Blood pressure, pulse,
heartbeat, flow of urine, loss of blood, temperature, whatever is measurable,
David measures. And he is a titrator, adding a little gas, drug, oxygen, fluid,
blood in order to maintain the dynamic equilibrium that is the only state compatible with life. He is in the very center of the battle, yet he is one step removed; he has not known the patient before this time, nor will he deal with the
next of kin. But for him, the occasion is no less momentous.

Heriberto Paz is an assistant resident in surgery. He is deft, tiny, mercurial.   4
I have known him for three years. One day he will be the best surgeon in Mexico.

Evelyn, the scrub nurse, is a young Irish woman. For seven years we have   5
worked together. Shortly after her immigration, she led her young husband into
my office to show me a lump on his neck. One year ago he died of Hodgkin's
disease. For the last two years of his life, he was paralyzed from the waist down.
Evelyn has one child, a boy named Liam.

Brenda is a black woman of forty-five. She is the circulating nurse, who will   6
conduct the affairs of this room, serving our table, adjusting the lights, counting
the sponges, ministering to us from the unsterile world.

Roy is a medical student who is beginning his surgical clerkship. He has been   7
assigned to me for the next six weeks. This is his first day, his first operation.

David is inducing anesthesia. In cases where the stomach is not empty   8
through fasting, the tube is passed into the windpipe while the patient is awake.

Such an "awake" intubation is called crashing. It is done to avoid vomiting and the aspiration of stomach contents into the lungs while the muscles that control coughing are paralyzed.

We stand around the table. To receive a tube in the windpipe while fully ⁹ awake is a terrifying thing.

"Open your mouth wide," David says to the man. The man's mouth opens ¹⁰ slowly to its fullest, as though to shriek. But instead, he yawns. We smile down at him behind our masks.

"OK. Open again. Real wide." ¹¹

David sprays the throat of the man with a local anesthetic. He does this ¹² three times. Then, into the man's mouth. David inserts a metal tongue depressor which bears a light at the tip. It is called a laryngoscope. It is to light up the throat, reveal the glottic chink through which the tube must be shoved. All this while, the man holds his mouth agape, submitting to the hard pressure of the laryngoscope. But suddenly, he cannot submit. The man on the table gags, struggles to free himself, to spit out the instrument. In his frenzy his lip is pinched by the metal blade.

There is little blood. ¹³

"Suction," says David. ¹⁴

Secretions at the back of the throat obscure the view. David suctions them ¹⁵ away with a plastic catheter.

"Open," commands David. More gagging. Another pass with the scope. ¹⁶ Another thrust with the tube. Violent coughing informs us that the tube is in the right place. It has entered the windpipe. Quickly the balloon is inflated to snug it against the wall of the trachea. A bolus of Pentothal is injected into a vein in the man's arm. It takes fifteen seconds for the drug to travel from his arm to his heart, then on to his brain. I count them. In fifteen seconds, the coughing stops, the man's body relaxes. He is asleep.

"All set?" I ask David. ¹⁷

"Go ahead," he nods. ¹⁸

A long incision. You do not know how much room you will need. This part ¹⁹ of the operation is swift, tidy. Fat . . . muscle . . . fascia . . . the peritoneum is snapped open and a giant shining eggplant presents itself. It is the stomach, black from the blood it contains and that threatens to burst it. We must open that stomach, evacuate its contents, explore.

Silk sutures are placed in the wall of the stomach as guidelines between ²⁰ which the incision will be made. They are like the pitons of a mountaineer. I cut again. No sooner is the cavity of the stomach achieved, than a columnar geyser of blood stands from the small opening I have made. Quickly, I slice open the whole front of the stomach. We scoop out handfuls of clot, great black gelatinous masses that shimmy from the drapes to rest against our own bellies as though, having been evicted from one body, they must find another in which to dwell. Now and then we step back to let them slither to the floor. They are under our feet. We slip in them. "Jesus," I say. "He is bleeding all over North America." Now my hand is inside the stomach, feeling, pressing. There! A tumor spreads across the back wall of this stomach. A great hard craterous plain, the dreaded linitis plastica (leather bottle) that is not content with seizing one area, but infiltrates between the layers until the entire organ is stiff with cancer. It is that, of course, which is bleeding. I stuff wads of gauze against the tumor. I press my fist against the mass of cloth. The blood slows. I press harder. The bleeding stops.

A quick glance at Roy. His gown and gloves, even his mask, are sprinkled 21 with blood. Now is he dipped; and I, his baptist.

David has opened a second line into the man's veins. He is pumping blood 22 into both tubings.

"Where do we stand?" I ask him. 23

"Still behind. Three units." He checks the blood pressure. 24

"Low, but coming up," he says. 25

"Shall I wait 'til you catch up?" 26

"No. Go ahead. I'll keep pumping." 27

I try to remove my fist from the stomach, but as soon as I do, there is a fresh 28 river of blood.

"More light," I say. "I need more light." 29

Brenda stands on a platform behind me. She adjusts the lamps. 30

"More light," I say, like a man going blind. 31

"That's it," she says. "There is no more light." 32

"We'll go around from the outside," I say. Heriberto nods agreement. "Free 33 up the greater curvature first, then the lesser, lift the stomach up and get some control from behind."

I must work with one hand. The other continues as the compressor. It is the 34 tiredest hand of my life. One hand, then, inside the stomach, while the other creeps behind. Between them . . . a ridge of tumor. The left hand fumbles, gropes toward its mate. They swim together. I lift the stomach forward to find that *nothing* separates my hands from each other. The wall of the stomach has been eaten through by the tumor. One finger enters a large tubular structure. It is the aorta. The incision in the stomach has released the tamponade of blood and brought us to this rocky place.

"Curved aortic clamp." 35

A blind grab with the clamp, high up at the diaphragm. The bleeding slack- 36 ens, dwindles. I release the pressure warily. A moment later there is a great bang of blood. The clamp has bitten through the cancerous aorta.

"Zero silk on a big Mayo needle." 37

I throw the heavy sutures, one after the other, into the pool of blood, hoping 38 to snag with my needle some bit of tissue to close over the rent in the aorta, to hold back the blood. There is no tissue. Each time, the needle pulls through the crumble of tumor. I stop. I repack the stomach. Now there is a buttress of packing both outside and inside the stomach. The bleeding is controlled. We wait. Slowly, something is gathering here, organizing. What had been vague and shapeless before is now declaring itself. All at once, I know what it is. There is nothing to do.

For what tool shall I ask? With what device fight off this bleeding? A knife?   39
There is nothing here to cut. Clamps? Where place the jaws of a hemostat? A
scissors? Forceps? Nothing. The instrument does not exist that knows such deep
red jugglery. Not all my clever picks, my rasp . . . A miner's lamp, I think, to cast
a brave glow.

David has been pumping blood steadily.   40
    "He is stable at the moment," he says. "'Where do we go from here?'"   41
    "No place. He's going to die. The minute I take away my pressure, he'll   42
bleed to death."
    I try to think of possibilities, alternatives. I cannot; there are none. Minutes   43
pass. We listen to the cardiac monitor, the gassy piston of the anesthesia
machine.
    "More light!" I say. "Fix the light."   44
    The light seems dim, aquarial, a dilute beam slanting through a green sea.   45
At such a fathom the fingers are clumsy. There is pressure. It is cold.
    "Dave," I say, "stop the transfusion." I hear my voice coming as from a   46
great distance. "Stop it," I say again.
    David and I look at each other, standing among the drenched rags, the   47
smeared equipment.
    "I can't," he says.   48
    "Then I will," I say, and with my free hand I reach across the boundary that   49
separates the sterile field from the outside world, and I close the clamp on the
intravenous tubing. It is the act of an outlaw, someone who does not know right
from wrong. But I know. I know that this is right to do.
    "The oxygen." I say. "Turn it off."   50
    "You want it turned off, you do it," he says.   51
    "Hold this," I say to Heriberto, and I give over the packing to him. I step   52
back from the table, and go to the gas tanks.
    "This one?" I have to ask him.   53
    "Yes," David nods.   54
    I turn it off. We stand there, waiting, listening to the beeping of the electro-   55
cardiograph. It remains even, regular, relentless. Minutes go by, and the sound
continues. The man will not die. At last, the intervals on the screen grow longer,
the shape of the curve changes, the rhythm grows wild, furious. The line
droops, flattens. The man is dead.
    It is silent in the room. Now we are no longer a team, each with his circum-   56
scribed duties to perform. It is Evelyn who speaks first.
    "It is a blessing," she says. I think of her husband's endless dying.   57
    "No," says Brenda. "Better for the family if they have a few days . . . to get   58
used to the idea of it."
    "But, look at all the pain he's been spared."   59
    "Still, for the ones that are left, it's better to have a little time."   60
    I listen to the two women murmuring, debating without rancor, speaking in   61
hushed tones of the newly dead as women have done for thousands of years.

"May I have the name of the operation?" It is Brenda, picking up her duties. 62
She is ready with pen and paper.

"Exploratory laparotomy. Attempt to suture malignant aorto-gastric fistula." 63

"Is he pronounced?" 64

"What time is it?" 65

"Eleven-twenty." 66

"Shall I put that down?" 67

"Yes." 68

"Sew him up," I say to Heriberto. "I'll talk to the family." 69

To Roy I say, "You come with me." 70

Roy's face is speckled with blood. He seems to me a child with the measles. 71
What, in God's name, is he doing here?

From the doorway, I hear the voices of the others, resuming. 72

"Stitch," says Heriberto. 73

Roy and I go to change our bloody scrub suits. We put on long white coats. In 74
the elevator, we do not speak. For the duration of the ride to the floor where the
family is waiting, I am reasonable. I understand that in its cellular wisdom, the
body of this man had sought out the murderous function of my scalpel, and
stretched itself upon the table to receive the final stabbing. For this little time, I
know that it is not a murder committed but a mercy bestowed. Tonight's knife
is no assassin, but the kind scythe of time.

We enter the solarium. The family rises in unison. There are so many! How 75
ruthless the eyes of the next of kin.

"I am terribly sorry . . .," I begin. Their faces tighten, take guard. "There was 76
nothing we could do."

I tell them of the lesion, tell of how it began somewhere at the back of the 77
stomach; how, long ago, no one knows why, a cell lost the rhythm of the body,
fell out of step, sprang, furious, into rebellion. I tell of how the cell divided and
begat two of its kind, which begat four more and so on, until there was a whole
race of lunatic cells, which is called cancer.

I tell of how the cancer spread until it had replaced the whole back of the 78
stomach, invading, chewing until it had broken into the main artery of the body.
Then it was, I tell them, that the great artery poured its blood into the stomach.
I tell of how I could not stop the bleeding, how my clamps bit through the
crumbling tissue, how my stitches would not hold, how there was nothing to be
done. All of this I tell.

A woman speaks. She has not heard my words, only caught the tone of my 79
voice.

"Do you mean he is dead?" 80

Should I say "passed away" instead of "died"? No. I cannot. 81

"Yes," I tell her, "he is dead." 82

Her question and my answer unleash their anguish. Roy and I stand among 83
the welter of bodies that tangle, grapple, rock, split apart to form new cou-
plings. Their keening is exuberant, wild. It is more than I can stand. All at once,
a young man slams his fist into the wall with great force.

"Son of a bitch!" he cries.   84

"Stop that!" I tell him sharply. Then, more softly, "Please try to control   85
yourself."

The other men crowd about him, patting, puffing, grunting. They are all fat,   86
with huge underslung bellies. Like their father's. A young woman in a nun's
habit hugs each of the women in turn.

"Shit!" says one of the men.   87

The nun hears, turns away her face. Later, I see the man apologizing to her.   88

The women, too, are fat. One of them has a great pile of yellowish hair that   89
has been sprayed and rendered motionless. All at once, she begins to whine. A
single note, coming louder and louder. I ask a nurse to bring tranquilizer pills.
She does, and I hand them out, one to each, as though they were the wafers of
communion. They urge the pills upon each other.

"Go on, Theresa, take it. Make her take one."   90

Roy and I are busy with cups of water. Gradually it grows quiet. One of the   91
men speaks.

"What's the next step?"   92

"Do you have an undertaker in mind?"   93

They look at each other, shrug. Someone mentions a name. The rest nod.   94

"Give the undertaker a call. Let him know. He'll take care of everything."   95

I turn to leave.   96

"Just a minute," one of the men calls. "Thanks, Doc. You did what you   97
could."

"Yes," I say.   98

Once again in the operating room. Blood is everywhere. There is a wild smell,   99
as though a fox had come and gone. The others, clotted about the table, work
on. They are silent, ravaged.

"How did the family take it?"   100

"They were good, good."   101

Heriberto has finished reefing up the abdomen. The drapes are peeled back.   102
The man on the table seems more than just dead. He seems to have gone beyond that, into a state where expression is possible—reproach and scorn. I
study him. His baldness had advanced beyond the halfway mark. The remaining strands of hair had been gallantly dyed. They are, even now, neatly combed
and crenellated. A stripe of black moustache rides his upper lip. Once, he had
been spruce!

We all help lift the man from the table to the stretcher.   103

"On three," says David. "One. . . two . . . three."   104

And we heft him over, using the sheet as a sling. My hand brushes his   105
shoulder. It is cool. I shudder as though he were infested with lice. He has
become something that I do not want to touch.

More questions from the women.   106

"Is a priest coming?"   107

"Does the family want to view him?"   108

"Yes. No. Don't bother me with these things."   109

"Come on," I say to Roy. We go to the locker room and sit together on a   110
bench. We light cigarettes.

"Well?" I ask him.   111

"When you were scooping out the clots, I thought I was going to swoon."   112

I pause over the word. It is too quaint, too genteel for this time. I feel, at that   113
moment, a great affection for him.

"But you fought it."   114

"Yes. I forced it back down. But, almost . . ."   115

"Good," I say. Who knows what I mean by it? I want him to know that I   116
count it for something.

"And you?" he asks me. The students are not shy these days.   117

"It was terrible, his refusal to die."   118

I want him to say that it was right to call it quits, that I did the best I could.   119
But he says nothing. We take off our scrub suits and go to the shower. There are
two stalls opposite each other. They are curtained. But we do not draw the curtains. We need to see each other's healthy bodies. I watch Roy turn his face directly upward into the blinding fall of water. His mouth is open to receive it. As
though it were milk flowing from the breasts of God. For me, too, this water is
like a well in a wilderness.

In the locker room, we dress in silence.   120

"Well, goodnight."   121

Awkwardly our words come out in unison.   122

"In the morning . . ."   123

"Yes, yes, later."   124

"Goodnight."   125

I watch him leave through the elevator door.   126

For the third time I go to that operating room. The others have long since   127
finished and left. It is empty, dark. I turn on the great lamps above the table that
stands in the center of the room. The pediments of the table and the floor have
been scrubbed clean. There is no sign of the struggle. I close my eyes and see
again the great pale body of the man, like a white bullock, bled. The line of
stitches on his abdomen is a hieroglyph. Already, the events of this night are
hidden from me by these strange untranslatable markings.

COMPREHENSION

1. What has the author implied by choosing his title for the essay? How is the
   title reinforced by the final paragraph?
2. Based upon Selzer's description of the surgeon's work, to what other profession does the author draw analogies? Explain.
3. Why do the other members of the operating team refuse to tamper with the
   medical apparatus, even after being ordered to do so by the surgeon?

RHETORIC

1. What is the dramatic effect of telling the story in the present tense?
2. The author often eschews conventional sentence structure. For example in paragraph 16, he employs fragments: "Another pass with the scope. Another thrust with the tube." In paragraph 21, he uses odd syntax, "Now is he dipped; and I, his baptist." And some sentences are extremely short, such as paragraph 96: "I turn to leave." What is the cumulative effect of using such innovative sentence structure?
3. Why has the author divided his essay into six parts? What is the function of each part? How does the author create drama via the juxtaposition of one section to the next?
4. Dialogue is used frequently in the essay. What is the function and effect of the dialogue?
5. Selzer's imagery is often vivid and original. How do the following excerpts contribute to the tone of the essay: "I understand that in its cellular wisdom, the body of this man had sought out the murderous function of my scalpel"; "Tonight's knife is no assassin, but the kind scythe of time" (paragraph 74). "There is a wild smell, as though a fox had come and gone" (paragraph 99).
6. There are several references to religion in the essay. Locate them, and explain what their cumulative effect is on the tone of the essay.
7. Mystery plays a significant part in the author's mood; for example, the final sentence reads, "Already, the events of this night are hidden from me by these strange untranslatable markings." What other passages reflect this mood of mystery in the essay? How does this mood affect the description of the essay's events, which are supposedly based on science?

WRITING

1. We take for granted many things which are mysterious to us; for example, the act of reading, writing, and breathing. Write a descriptive essay of 500 words in which you reflect upon some basic activity that you have never analyzed before.
2. Write a 400-word critique of Selzer's essay, entitling it "Religious Imagery in Selzer's 'Sarcophagus.'"
3. Create a metaphor or simile for a particular profession, such as "a professional athlete is superhuman" or "a rock star is like a god (or goddess)." Extend your metaphor in a 400-word essay, using analogies to fit your central metaphor.

Can We Know the Universe?
Reflections on a Grain of Salt

Carl Sagan

Carl Edward Sagan (1931–1996) received his BA, BS, MA, and PhD degrees from the University of Chicago. Probably the most popular scientist in America in the 1970s and 1980s, he was the host of several television series on science and wrote a number of best-selling books on science, including The Dragons of Eden *(1977) and* Broca's Brain *(1979). The former earned him a Pulitzer Prize for general nonfiction in 1978. He also contributed hundreds of papers to scientific journals. Besides writing, Sagan served as a full-time professor at Cornell University and a visiting professor at dozens of other in-stitutions of higher learning in the United States and abroad. He was also an activist for many philanthropic causes, and served as an adviser to groups such as the Council for a Livable World Education Fund, the Children's Health Fund, and the American Committee on U.S.-Soviet Relations. Despite controversies surrounding the speculative nature of his work, Carl Sagan was one of modern science's most popular spokespersons. Sagan's philosophy may be summed up in a statement he made in a* Time *magazine interview. "We make our world significant by the courage of our questions and by the depth of our answers."*

Nothing is rich but the inexhaustible wealth of nature. She shows us only surfaces, but she is a million fathoms deep.

—Ralph Waldo Emerson

Science is a way of thinking much more than it is a body of knowledge. Its goal 1
is to find out how the world works, to seek what regularities there may be, to penetrate to the connections of things—from subnuclear particles, which may be the constituents of all matter, to living organisms, the human social community, and thence to the cosmos as a whole. Our intuition is by no means an infallible guide. Our perceptions may be distorted by training and prejudice or merely because of the limitations of our sense organs, which, of course, perceive directly but a small fraction of the phenomena of the world. Even so straightforward a question as whether in the absence of friction a pound of lead falls faster than a gram of fluff was answered incorrectly by Aristotle and almost everyone else before the time of Galileo. Science is based on experiment, on a willingness to challenge old dogma, on an openness to see the universe as it really is. Accordingly, science sometimes requires courage—at the very least the courage to question the conventional wisdom.

Beyond this the main trick of science is to *really* think of something: the 2
shape of clouds and their occasional sharp bottom edges at the same altitude everywhere in the sky; the formation of a dewdrop on a leaf; the origin of a

name or a word—Shakespeare, say, or "philanthropic"; the reason for human social customs—the incest taboo, for example; how it is that a lens in sunlight can make paper burn; how a "walking stick" got to look so much like a twig; why the Moon seems to follow us as we walk; what prevents us from digging a hole down to the center of the Earth; what the definition is of "down" on a spherical Earth; how it is possible for the body to convert yesterday's lunch into today's muscle and sinew; or how far is up—does the universe go on forever, or if it does not, is there any meaning to the question of what lies on the other side? Some of these questions are pretty easy. Others, especially the last, are mysteries to which no one even today knows the answer. They are natural questions to ask. Every culture has posed such questions in one way or another. Almost always the proposed answers are in the nature of "Just So Stories," attempted explanations divorced from experiment, or even from careful comparative observations.

But the scientific cast of mind examines the world critically as if many alternative worlds might exist, as if other things might be here which are not. Then we are forced to ask why what we see is present and not something else. Why are the Sun and the Moon and the planets spheres? Why not pyramids, or cubes, or dodecahedra? Why not irregular, jumbly shapes? Why so symmetrical, worlds? If you spend any time spinning hypotheses, checking to see whether they make sense, whether they conform to what else we know, thinking of tests you can pose to substantiate or deflate your hypotheses, you will find yourself doing science. And as you come to practice this habit of thought more and more you will get better and better at it. To penetrate into the heart of the thing—even a little thing, a blade of grass, as Walt Whitman said—is to experience a kind of exhilaration that, it may be, only human beings of all the beings on this planet can feel. We are an intelligent species and the use of our intelligence quite properly gives us pleasure. In this respect the brain is like a muscle. When we think well, we feel good. Understanding is a kind of ecstasy.

But to what extent can we *really* know the universe around us? Sometimes this question is posed by people who hope the answer will be in the negative, who are fearful of a universe in which everything might one day be known. And sometimes we hear pronouncements from scientists who confidently state that everything worth knowing will soon be known—or even is already known—and who paint pictures of a Dionysian or Polynesian age in which the zest for intellectual discovery has withered, to be replaced by a kind of subdued languor, the lotus eaters drinking fermented coconut milk or some other mild hallucinogen. In addition to maligning both the Polynesians, who were intrepid explorers (and whose brief respite in paradise is now sadly ending), as well as the inducements to intellectual discovery provided by some hallucinogens, this contention turns out to be trivially mistaken.

Let us approach a much more modest question: not whether we can know the universe or the Milky Way Galaxy or a star or a world. Can we know, ultimately and in detail, a grain of salt? Consider one microgram of table salt, a speck just barely large enough for someone with keen eyesight to make out without a microscope. In that grain of salt there are about 10^{16} sodium and chlorine atoms. This is a 1 followed by 16 zeros, 10 million billion atoms. If we wish to know a grain of salt, we must know at least the three-dimensional positions of each of these atoms. (In fact, there is much more to be known—for example, the nature of the forces between the atoms—but we are making only a modest calculation.) Now, is this number more or less than the number of things which the brain can know?

How much *can* the brain know? There are perhaps 10^{11} neurons in the brain, 6 the circuit elements and switches that are responsible in their electrical and chemical activity for the functioning of our minds. A typical brain neuron has perhaps a thousand little wires, called dendrites, which connect it with its fellows. If, as seems likely, every bit of information in the brain corresponds to one of these connections, the total number of things knowable by the brain is no more than 10^{14}, one hundred trillion. But this number is only one percent of the number of atoms in our speck of salt.

So in this sense the universe is intractable, astonishingly immune to any hu- 7 man attempt at full knowledge. We cannot on this level understand a grain of salt, much less the universe.

But let us look a little more deeply at our microgram of salt. Salt happens to 8 be a crystal in which, except for defects in the structure of the crystal lattice, the position of every sodium and chlorine atom is predetermined. If we could shrink ourselves into this crystalline world, we would see rank upon rank of atoms in an ordered array, a regularly alternating structure—sodium, chlorine, sodium, chlorine, specifying the sheet of atoms we are standing on and all the sheets above us and below us. An absolutely pure crystal of salt could have the position of every atom specified by something like 10 bits of information.[1] This would not strain the information-carrying capacity of the brain.

If the universe had natural laws that governed its behavior to the same de- 9 gree of regularity that determines a crystal of salt, then, of course, the universe would be knowable. Even if there were many such laws, each of considerable complexity, human beings might have the capability to understand them all. Even if such knowledge exceeded the information-carrying capacity of the brain, we might store the additional information outside our bodies—in books, for example, or in computer memories—and still, in some sense, know the universe.

Human beings are, understandably, highly motivated to find regularities, 10 natural laws. The search for rules, the only possible way to understand such a vast and complex universe, is called science. The universe forces those who live in it to understand it. Those creatures who find everyday experience a muddled

---

[1]Chlorine is a deadly poison gas employed on European battlefields in World War I. Sodium is a corrosive metal which burns upon contact with water. Together they make a placid and unpoisonous material, table salt. Why each of these substances has the properties it does is a subject called chemistry, which requires more than 10 bits of information to understand.

jumble of events with no predictability, no regularity, are in grave peril. The universe belongs to those who, at least to some degree, have figured it out.

It is an astonishing fact that there *are* laws of nature, rules that summarize 11 conveniently—not just qualitatively but quantitatively—how the world works. We might imagine a universe in which there are no such laws, in which the 10^{80} elementary particles that make up a universe like our own behave with utter and uncompromising abandon. To understand such a universe we would need a brain at least as massive as the universe. It seems unlikely that such a universe could have life and intelligence, because beings and brains require some degree of internal stability and order. But even if in a much more random universe there were such beings with an intelligence much greater than our own, there could not be much knowledge, passion or joy.

Fortunately for us, we live in a universe that has at least important parts 12 that are knowable. Our common-sense experience and our evolutionary history have prepared us to understand something of the workaday world. When we go into other realms, however, common sense and ordinary intuition turn out to be highly unreliable guides. It is stunning that as we go close to the speed of light our mass increases indefinitely, we shrink toward zero thickness in the direction of motion, and time for us comes as near to stopping as we would like. Many people think that this is silly, and every week or two I get a letter from someone who complains to me about it. But it is a virtually certain consequence not just of experiment but also of Albert Einstein's brilliant analysis of space and time called the Special Theory of Relativity. It does not matter that these effects seem unreasonable to us. We are not in the habit of traveling close to the speed of light. The testimony of our common sense is suspect at high velocities.

Or consider an isolated molecule composed of two atoms shaped some- 13 thing like a dumbbell—a molecule of salt, it might be. Such a molecule rotates about an axis through the line connecting the two atoms. But in the world of quantum mechanics, the realm of the very small, not all orientations of our dumbbell molecule are possible. It might be that the molecule could be oriented in a horizontal position, say, or in a vertical position, but not at many angles in between. Some rotational positions are forbidden. Forbidden by what? By the laws of nature. The universe is built in such a way as to limit, or quantize, rotation. We do not experience this directly in everyday life; we would find it startling as well as awkward in sitting-up exercises, to find arms outstretched from the sides or pointed up to the skies permitted but many intermediate positions forbidden. We do not live in the world of the small, on the scale of 10^{-13} centimeters, in the realm where there are twelve zeros between the decimal place and the one. Our common-sense intuitions do not count. What does count is experiment—in this case observations from the far infrared spectra of molecules. They show molecular rotation to be quantized.

The idea that the world places restrictions on what humans might do is 14 frustrating. Why *shouldn't* we be able to have intermediate rotational positions? Why *can't* we travel faster than the speed of light? But so far as we can tell, this is the way the universe is constructed. Such prohibitions not only press us toward a little humility; they also make the world more knowable. Every restriction corresponds to a law of nature, a regularization of the universe. The more restrictions there are on what matter and energy can do, the more knowledge human beings can attain. Whether in some sense the universe is ultimately knowable depends not only on how many natural laws there are that encompass widely divergent phenomena, but also on whether we have the openness and the intellectual capacity to understand such laws. Our formulations of the regularities of nature are surely dependent on how the brain is built, but also, and to a significant degree, on how the universe is built.

For myself, I like a universe that includes much that is unknown and, at the   15 same time, much that is knowable. A universe in which everything is known would be static and dull, as boring as the heaven of some weak-minded theologians. A universe that is unknowable is no fit place for a thinking being. The ideal universe for us is one very much like the universe we inhabit. And I would guess that this is not really much of a coincidence.

COMPREHENSION

1. What is the thesis of the essay? In what paragraph is this thesis most clearly expressed?
2. Why does the author say, in paragraph 12, that in many circumstances, "common sense and ordinary intuition turn out to be highly unreliable guides"?
3. Why does Sagan say, in his conclusion, that "The ideal universe for us is one very much like the universe we inhabit"?

RHETORIC

1. What is the function of the epigram by Emerson? How does it relate to the essay proper?
2. Many of the paragraphs in the essay begin with coordinating conjunctions (a structure frowned on by many high school English teachers). What is Sagan's rhetorical purpose in using them as connecting devices?
3. What specific clues are there in the essay that Sagan's tone is one of excitement and celebration regarding science?
4. Sagan refers often to what he calls "a law of nature." Where and how in the essay does he explain, describe, or define this term?
5. The essay begins abruptly with an explanation of the concept of science. What purpose is served by diving into the subject so dramatically?
6. What is the intended effect of combining the terms *universe* and *grain of salt* in the title and subtitle? How does the author exploit this juxtaposition in his essay?
7. Examine the italicized words in the essay. Why has Sagan chosen to italicize these words? Explain.

WRITING

1. Argue for or against the proposition that scientific knowledge takes the mystery out of life.
2. For a research paper, select one of the items Sagan enumerates in paragraph 2, such as "the formation of a dewdrop on a leaf," the origin of the name *Shakespeare* or the word *philanthropic*, "the incest taboo," or "how a 'walking stick' got to look so much like a twig." Write a 500- to 600-word expository essay on your topic.
3. Write a personal essay in which you describe how you felt when you suddenly understood a particular topic in school that had previously eluded you.

Macho

Perri Klass

Perri Klass (b. 1958) is a pediatrician, a mother of two, and the author of many books, including two novels, Recombinations *(1985) and* Other Women's Children *(1990); a collection of short stories,* I Am Having an Adventure *(1986); and a collection of essays,* A Not Entirely Benign Procedure: Four Years as a Medical Student *(1987). In the following essay from the latter publication, she demonstrates that the medical profession and personality types have very strong ties.*

Purely by coincidence, our team has four women and one man. The two interns and the two medical students are female, and the resident, who leads the team, is male. We are clattering up the stairs one morning in approved hospital fashion, conveying by our purposeful demeanor: out of the way, doctors coming, decisions to make, lives to save. (In fact, what we are actually trying to do is to rush through morning rounds in time to get to breakfast before the cafeteria stops serving hot food, but never mind that now.) We barrel through the door into the intensive care unit, and some other resident, standing by, announces, "Here comes The A-Team." Immediately our resident swings around to respond to some undertone he has detected: 1

"Are you saying my team is weak? Huh? You saying my team is weak?" 2

We continue on our rounds, the resident occasionally prompting one of the interns, "You should be pushing me out of the way, you know. Go on, push me out of the way." He means that since she is on call that day, she should be first through every door, first to lay hands on every patient. 3

My fellow medical student and I trail along in the rear, a position that accurately reflects our place in the hierarchy and also my energy level (this is, after 4 all, 7:00 A.M.) She whispers to me, "Straighten your back! Suck in your stomach! This is war!" And as we start to clatter down the stairs to breakfast, our morning mission successfully accomplished, she and I are both singing under our breaths, "Macho macho doc, I wanna be a macho doc. . . ."

Macho in medicine can mean a number of things. Everyone knows it's out 5 there as a style, either an ideal or an object of ridicule. You hear echoes of it in the highest praise one can receive in the hospital, "Strong work," which may be said to an intern who got a very sick patient through the night or to a medical student who successfully fielded some obscure questions on rounds. And the all-purpose term of disparagement is "Weak." They're being really weak down in the emergency room tonight, admitting people who could just as well be sent home. Dr. So-and-so is being weak with that patient—why doesn't he just tell him he *has* to have the surgery? You were pretty weak this morning when they were asking you about rheumatic heart disease—better read up on it.

Macho can refer to your willingness to get tough with your patients, to 6 keep them from pushing you around. It can refer to your eagerness to do invasive procedures—"The hell with radiology, I wanna go for the biopsy." Talk like that and they'll call you a cowboy, and generally mean it as a compliment. Macho can mean territoriality: certain doctors resent calling in expert consultations and, when they finally have to, await the recommendations with truculent eagerness to disregard them. "These are *our* patients and *we* make all the decisions," I heard over and over from one resident I worked under. The essence of macho, any kind of macho, after all, is that life is a perpetual contest. You must not let others intrude on your stamping grounds. You must not let anyone tell you what to do. And of course, the most basic macho fear is the fear of being laughed at; whatever you do, you must not let anyone mock you— or our team.

A medical student once said to me when I teased him about not being able 7 to work the Addressograph machine after six weeks in the hospital, "That's secretarial work. I can draw a blood gas blindfolded, from thirty feet away!"

Life in the hospital is full of opportunities to prove yourself, if you want to 8 look at it that way. "I want you guys to be able to get blood from a stone," announced our new resident on his first day as our leader. The "guys," the other female medical student and I, must have looked a little dubious, because he continued, "Okay, it may mean the patient gets stuck a few extra times, but I don't want you giving up just because of that." And sure enough, when I came to tell him that I had stuck one particular woman six times without success, and could he please come show me where he thought a decent vein might be, he sent me back in to try her ankles. "Blood from a stone!" he called after me, and when I finally got a tube of this unfortunate woman's blood, he patted me on the back and said, "Strong work."

If we are at war, then who is the enemy? Rightly the enemy is disease, and 9 even if that is not your favorite metaphor, it is a rather common way to think of medicine: we are combating these deadly processes for the bodies of our patients. They become battlefields, lying there passively in bed while the evil armies of pathology and the resplendent forces of modern medicine fight it out. Still, there are very good doctors who seem to think that way, who take disease as a personal enemy and battle it with fury and dedication. The real problem arises because all too often the patient comes to personify the disease, and somehow the patient becomes the enemy.

We don't say, or think, "Mrs. Hawthorne's cancer is making her sicker." We   10 say, "Mrs. Hawthorne's crumping on me," and Mrs. Hawthorne represents the challenge we cannot meet, the disease we cannot cure. And instead of hating her cancer, it's not hard to start hating Mrs. Hawthorne—especially if she has an irritating personality, and most especially of all if she somehow seems to be blaming us. That is, if every day the doctor sees the challenge again in the patient's eye, hears it in the patient's voice: "You can't do anything for me, can you, despite all the tests and all the medicines?"

The patient may want the doctor to continue fighting, may even take re-   11 newed hope as new therapies are instituted, but the doctor, knowing them to be essentially futile, may become angrier and angrier. When the disease has essentially won and the patient continues to present the challenge, the macho doctor is left with no appropriate response. He cannot sidestep the challenge by offering comfort rather than combat, because comfort is not in his repertoire. And unable to do battle against the disease to any real effect, he may feel almost ready to battle the patient.

I have been talking as if macho medicine is a male preserve, and to a large   12 extent that's true. Certainly there are some female doctors who end up being fairly macho and, much more important, many men who are not macho at all. Some of the gentlest, most reasonable doctors I worked with were male, good teachers and superb healers. But there are also many macho docs, and certainly it is pervasive as a style in the hospital. I don't believe that would be the case if the majority of doctors up to now had been female, and perhaps it will change over time as more women become doctors. The tradition of medical training is partly a tradition of hazing, boot camp, basic training. New buzzwords are now being muttered, like "nurturing" or "supportive," but there are many doctors riding the range out there to whom you wouldn't dare mutter any such words.

"Sup-por-tive," you can almost hear The Duke drawl as the doctor looks   13 down at the newest sissy in town. At which point you tuck your hypodermic needle back into its holster and march, on the double, back into that pesky varmint's room to let him know who's boss in this here hospital.

COMPREHENSION

1. What does Klass mean by the term *macho?* What actions constitute macho behavior?
2. What specific negative effects does Klass see as a result of doctors' macho behavior? Does she see any advantages?

3. Klass states that members of the medical profession have their own vernacular, such as "strong work," "cowboy," and "weak." What do they mean within the context of Klass's work environment? What do they say about the attitude of the doctors who use them?

RHETORIC

1. What is Klass's purpose in the essay? Where is the purpose best articulated? Explain.
2. Klass has chosen to quote some of her colleagues directly. What is the rhetorical purpose of using these quotations?
3. Why is the essay divided into two sections? What change in tone or mood occurs in the second section?
4. Klass uses irony in describing the world of her internship. For example, in paragraph 1, she states that the reason they are rushing through morning rounds is to get a hot breakfast before the cafeteria stops serving. What other examples of irony can you find in the essay? What is the overall purpose of Klass's irony?
5. Klass uses two references to popular culture: one in paragraph 4 where she parodies a popular song by using the lyrics "Macho macho doc" and the other, in paragraph 13, where she refers to "The Duke." What are the origins of these references, and what is their rhetorical purpose in the essay?
6. What seems to be Klass's attitude toward macho medical behavior? What is the relationship between her attitude and the tone of the essay?
7. Klass uses an extended metaphor in paragraph 9 by comparing the treatment of disease to waging war. Where else does she use this metaphor?

WRITING

1. Write an essay in which you argue that medical practice has either changed for the better, changed for the worse, or remained the same since 1987, when Klass's essay was written. You may consult your parents and other older adults to assist you.
2. Drawing upon personal experience, argue for or against the proposition that women in the medical field are gentler and more sympathetic than their male counterparts.
3. Select a profession such as law, teaching, the arts, or business, and find an attitude among members of that profession that can be used conceptually to explain how members of the profession perceive their roles.

The Technology of Medicine

Lewis Thomas

Lewis Thomas (1913–1993) was born in Flushing, New York, and was educated at Princeton University and Harvard University Medical School. He held appointments at numerous research hospitals and medical schools before assuming his last position as president of the Sloan-Kettering Cancer Center in New York City. Thomas's early writing, on the subject of pathology, appeared in scientific journals. In 1971 he began contributing a popular column, "Notes of a Biology Watcher," to the New England Journal of Medicine. *In 1974 his collection of these essays,* The Lives of a Cell: Notes of a Biology Watcher, *won the National Book Award for Arts and Letters. His other books include* The Medusa and the Snail: More Notes of a Biology Watcher *(1979),* The Youngest Science *(1983),* Late Night Thoughts on Listening to Mahler's Ninth Symphony *(1983), and* The Fragile Species *(1992). In the following essay, from* The Lives of the Cell, *Thomas classifies "three quite different levels of technology in medicine."*

Technology assessment has become a routine exercise for the scientific enterprises on which the country is obliged to spend vast sums for its needs. Brainy committees are continually evaluating the effectiveness and cost of doing various things in space, defense, energy, transportation, and the like, to give advice about prudent investments for the future.

Somehow medicine, for all the $80-odd billion that it is said to cost the nation, has not yet come in for much of this analytical treatment. It seems taken for granted that the technology of medicine simply exists, take it or leave it, and the only major technologic problem which policy-makers are interested in is how to deliver today's kind of health care, with equity, to all the people.

When, as is bound to happen sooner or later, the analysts get around to the technology of medicine itself, they will have to face the problem of measuring the relative cost and effectiveness of all the things that are done in the management of disease. They make their living at this kind of thing, and I wish them well, but I imagine they will have a bewildering time. For one thing, our methods of managing disease are constantly changing—partly under the influence of new bits of information brought in from all corners of biologic science. At the same time, a great many things are done that are not so closely related to science, some not related at all.

In fact, there are three quite different levels of technology in medicine, so unlike each other as to seem altogether different undertakings. Practitioners of medicine and the analysts will be in trouble if they are not kept separate.

1. First of all, there is a large body of what might be termed "nontechnol- 5
ogy," impossible to measure in terms of its capacity to alter either the natural
course of disease or its eventual outcome. A great deal of money is spent on this.
It is valued highly by the professionals as well as the patients. It consists of what
is sometimes called "supportive therapy." It tides patients over through diseases that are not, by and large, understood. It is what is meant by the phrases
"caring for" and "standing by." It is indispensable. It is not, however, a technology in any real sense, since it does not involve measures directed at the underlying mechanism of disease.

It includes the large part of any good doctor's time that is taken up with 6
simply providing reassurance, explaining to patients who fear that they have
contracted one or another lethal disease that they are, in fact, quite healthy.

It is what physicians used to be engaged in at the bedside of patients with 7
diphtheria, meningitis, poliomyelitis, lobar pneumonia, and all the rest of the
infectious diseases that have since come under control.

It is what physicians must now do for patients with intractable cancer, se- 8
vere rheumatoid arthritis, multiple sclerosis, stroke, and advanced cirrhosis.
One can think of at least twenty major diseases that require this kind of supportive medical care because of the absence of an effective technology. I would
include a large amount of what is called mental disease, and most varieties of
cancer, in this category.

The cost of this nontechnology is very high, and getting higher all the time. 9
It requires not only a great deal of time but also very hard effort and skill on the
part of physicians; only the very best of doctors are good at coping with this
kind of defeat. It also involves long periods of hospitalization, lots of nursing,
lots of involvement of nonmedical professionals in and out of the hospital. It
represents, in short, a substantial segment of today's expenditures for health.

2. At the next level up is a kind of technology best termed "halfway tech- 10
nology." This represents the kinds of things that must be done after the fact, in
efforts to compensate for the incapacitating effects of certain diseases whose
course one is unable to do very much about. It is a technology designed to make
up for disease, or to postpone death.

The outstanding examples in recent years are the transplantations of hearts, 11
kidneys, livers, and other organs, and the equally spectacular inventions of artificial organs. In the public mind, this kind of technology has come to seem like
the equivalent of the high technologies of the physical sciences. The media tend
to present each new procedure as though it represented a breakthrough and
therapeutic triumph, instead of the makeshift that it really is.

In fact, this level of technology is, by its nature, at the same time highly so- 12
phisticated and profoundly primitive. It is the kind of thing that one must continue to do until there is a genuine understanding of the mechanisms involved
in disease. In chronic glomerulonephritis, for example, a much clearer insight
will be needed into the events leading to the destruction of glomeruh by the im-
munologic reactants that now appear to govern this disease, before one will
know how to intervene intelligently to prevent the process, or turn it around.

But when this level of understanding has been reached, the technology of kidney replacement will not be much needed and should no longer pose the huge problem of logistics, cost, and ethics that it poses today.

An extremely complex and costly technology for the management of coronary heart disease has evolved—involving specialized ambulances and hospital units, all kinds of electronic gadgetry, and whole platoons of new professional personnel—to deal with the end results of coronary thrombosis. Almost everything offered today for the treatment of heart disease is at this level of technology, with the transplanted and artificial hearts as ultimate examples. When enough has been learned to know what really goes wrong in heart disease, one ought to be in a position to figure out ways to prevent or reverse the process, and when this happens the current elaborate technology will probably be set to one side. 13

Much of what is done in the treatment of cancer, by surgery, irradiation, and chemotherapy, represents halfway technology, in the sense that these measures are directed at the existence of already established cancer cells, but not at the mechanisms by which cells become neoplastic. 14

It is a characteristic of this kind of technology that it costs an enormous amount of money and requires a continuing expansion of hospital facilities. There is no end to the need for new, highly trained people to run the enterprise. And there is really no way out of this, at the present state of knowledge. If the installation of specialized coronary-care units can result in the extension of life for only a few patients with coronary disease (and there is no question that this technology is effective in a few cases), it seems to me an inevitable fact of life that as many of these as can be will be put together, and as much money as can be found will be spent. I do not see that anyone has much choice in this. The only thing that can move medicine away from this level of technology is new information, and the only imaginable source of this information is research. 15

3. The third type of technology is the kind that is so effective that it seems to attract the least public notice; it has come to be taken for granted. This is the genuinely decisive technology of modern medicine, exemplified best by modern methods for immunization against diphtheria, pertussis, and the childhood virus diseases, and the contemporary use of antibiotics and chemotherapy for bacterial infections. The capacity to deal effectively with syphilis and tuberculosis represents a milestone in human endeavor, even though full use of this potential has not yet been made. And there are, of course, other examples: the treatment of endocrinologic disorders with appropriate hormones, the prevention of hemolytic disease of the newborn, the treatment and prevention of various nutritional disorders, and perhaps just around the corner the management of Parkinsonism and sickle-cell anemia. There are other examples, and everyone will have his favorite candidates for the list, but the truth is that there are nothing like as many as the public has been led to believe. 16

The point to be made about this kind of technology—the real high technology of medicine—is that it comes as the result of a genuine understanding of disease mechanisms, and when it becomes available, it is relatively inexpensive, and relatively easy to deliver. 17

Offhand, I cannot think of any important human disease for which medi- 18
cine possesses the outright capacity to prevent or cure where the cost of the
technology is itself a major problem. The price is never as high as the cost of
managing the same diseases during the earlier stages of no-technology or
halfway technology. If a case of typhoid fever had to be managed today by the
best methods of 1935, it would run to a staggering expense. At, say, around fifty
days of hospitalization, requiring the most demanding kind of nursing care,
with the obsessive concern for details of diet that characterized the therapy of
that time, with daily laboratory monitoring, and, on occasion, surgical inter-
vention for abdominal catastrophe, I should think $10,000 would be a conserv-
ative estimate for the illness, as contrasted with today's cost of a bottle of
chloramphenicol and a day or two of fever. The halfway technology that was
evolving for poliomyelitis in the early 1950s, just before the emergence of the
basic research that made the vaccine possible, provides another illustration of
the point. Do you remember Sister Kenny, and the cost of those institutes for rehabilitation, with all those ceremonially applied hot fomentations, and the debates about whether the affected limbs should be totally immobilized or kept in
passive motion as frequently as possible, and the masses of statistically tormented data mobilized to support one view or the other? It is the cost of that
kind of technology, and its relative effectiveness, that must be compared with
the cost and effectiveness of the vaccine.

Pulmonary tuberculosis had similar episodes in its history. There was a 19
sudden enthusiasm for the surgical removal of infected lung tissue in the early
1950s, and elaborate plans were being made for new and expensive installations
for major pulmonary surgery in tuberculosis hospitals, and then INH and strep-
tomycin came along and the hospitals themselves were closed up.

It is when physicians are bogged down by their incomplete technologies, by 20
the innumerable things they are obliged to do in medicine when they lack a
clear understanding of disease mechanisms, that the deficiencies of the health-
care system are most conspicuous. If I were a policy-maker, interested in saving
money for health care over the long haul, I would regard it as an act of high prudence to give high priority to a lot more basic research in biologic science. This
is the only way to get the full mileage that biology owes to the science of medicine, even though it seems, as used to be said in the days when the phrase still
had some meaning, like asking for the moon.

COMPREHENSION

1. What is the thesis of the essay? Does Thomas explicitly state it or is it implied in the text? Explain your answer.
2. Why does Thomas support "basic research in biologic science" (paragraph
20)? Why would this support be financially beneficial for "health care over
the long haul"?
3. What are the author's views on the second category in his taxonomy of
medical technology, that is, "halfway technology" (paragraph 10)? What

does he mean when he claims it is "at the same time highly sophisticated and profoundly primitive (paragraph 12)?

RHETORIC

1. How do Thomas's three categories—nontechnology, halfway technology, and effective technology—clarify the principle behind his establishment of this classification system? What does this system imply about the dual role of the physician?
2. Is Thomas's main purpose to explain, argue, or both? Explain your answer.
3. Does Thomas's statement in paragraph 20, "If I were a policy-maker, interested in saving money for health care over the long haul . . ." imply that his audience consists of medical professionals, politicians, consumers of medical services, or a combination of these audiences? Explain your view.
4. Without knowing Thomas's professional status, what elements in his essay gives his voice authority? Explain your answer.
5. Thomas is known for his ability to create a style that is both conversational and academic. For example, compare and contrast the discourse of the first two sentences of the essay: "Technological assessment has become a routine exercise for the scientific enterprises on which the country is obliged to spend vast sums for its needs" versus "Brainy committees are continually evaluating the effectiveness and cost of doing various things in space . . ." What other examples of contrasting levels of discourse can you find in the essay? What is the possible effect of this technique on the author's purpose and audience?
6. Analyze the concluding paragraph and note that it consists of only three sentences, albeit long ones. How is Thomas able to pack so much information and opinion into the conclusion without confusing the reader? Pay particular attention to syntax and punctuation.
7. What is the tone of the essay, particularly in regards to Thomas's view of modern medicine and doctors? Explain your answer.

WRITING

1. Thomas uses the terms *technology* and *medicine* repeatedly in his essay but mentions *science* only four times. Using an encyclopedia as your source, write a 500-word essay comparing and contrasting the concepts of *technology* and *science*.
2. As an exercise in paraphrasing, paraphrase the three types of technology Thomas enumerates in his taxonomy, devoting one paragraph to each category. Be sure to follow paraphrasing guidelines in Chapter 1 to ensure you do not plagiarize.
3. In an essay of approximately 500 words, argue for or against the proposition that medical students should be required to take a course in expository writing so that they can better articulate their views on their profession for their colleagues and patients.

The Bird and the Machine

Loren Eiseley

Loren Eiseley (1907–1997) was born in Lincoln, Nebraska, and had ambitions to become a science writer from the time he attended high school. Because of his family's isolation from the town (his mother was deaf), Eiseley became enamored of caves and creeks around his yard. Owing to illness and the death of his father, he did not receive his BS degree in English and Geology/Anthropology until 1933. He went on to receive a PhD from the University of Pennsylvania in 1937. He began teaching at the University of Kansas but in 1947 moved to the anthropology department at the University of Pennsylvania. His book The Immense Journey *(1946) established him as a writer of immense talent, combining the themes of science and humanism. Among his better known books are* Darwin's Century *(1958),* The Night Country *(1973), and* All the Strange Hours *(1977). In the following essay, taken from* The Immense Journey, *Eiseley combines personal experience, observation, reflection, and philosophy to meditate upon the relationship between humans and their environment.*

I suppose their little bones have years ago been lost among the stones and winds of those high glacial pastures. I suppose their feathers blew eventually into the piles of tumbleweed beneath the straggling cattle fences and rotted there in the mountain snows, along with dead steers and all the other things that drift to an end in the corners of the wire. I do not quite know why I should be thinking of birds over the *New York Times* at breakfast, particularly the birds of my youth half a continent away. It is a funny thing what the brain will do with memories and how it will treasure them and bring them into odd juxtapositions with other things, as though it wanted to make a design, or get some meaning out of them, whether you want it or not, or even see it.

It used to seem marvelous to me, but I read now that there are machines that can do these things in a small way, machines that can crawl about like animals, and that it may not be long now until they do more things—maybe even make themselves—I saw that piece in the *Times* just now. And then they will, maybe—well, who knows—but you read about it more and more with no one making any' protest, and already they can add better than we and reach up and hear things through the dark and finger the guns over the night sky.

This is the new world that I read about at breakfast. This is the world that confronts me in my biological books and journals, until there are times when I sit quietly in my chair and try to hear the little purr of the cogs in my head and the tubes flaring and dying as the messages go through them and the circuits snap shut or open. This is the great age, make no mistake about it; the robot has been born somewhat appropriately along with the atom bomb, and the brain they say now is just another type of more complicated feedback system. The engineers have its basic principles worked out; it's mechanical, you know; nothing to get superstitious about; and man can always improve on nature once he gets the idea. Well, he's got it all right and that's why, I guess, that I sit here in my chair, with the article crunched in my hand, remembering those two birds and that blue mountain sunlight. There is another magazine article on my desk that reads "Machines Are Getting Smarter Every Day." I don't deny it, but I'll still stick with the birds. It's life I believe in, not machines.

Maybe you don't believe there is any difference. A skeleton is all joints and   4
pulleys, I'll admit. And when man was in his simpler stages of machine building in the eighteenth century, he quickly saw the resemblances. "What," wrote Hobbes, "is the heart but a spring, and the nerves but so many strings, and the joints but so many wheels, giving motion to the whole body?" Tinkering about in their shops it was inevitable in the end that men would see the world as a huge machine "subdivided into an infinite number of lesser machines."

The idea took on with a vengeance. Little automatons toured the country— 5
dolls controlled by clockwork. Clocks described as little worlds were taken on tours by their designers. They were made up of moving figures, shifting scenes and other remarkable devices. The life of the cell was unknown. Man, whether he was conceived as possessing a soul or not, moved and jerked about like these tiny puppets. A human being thought of himself in terms of his own tools and implements. He had been fashioned like the puppets he produced and was only a more clever model made by a greater designer.

Then in the nineteenth century, the cell was discovered, and the single ma- 6
chine in its turn was found to be the product of millions of infinitesimal machines—the cells. Now, finally; the cell itself dissolves away into an abstract chemical machine—and that into some intangible, inexpressible flow of energy. The secret seems to lurk all about, the wheels get smaller and smaller, and they turn more rapidly, but when you try to seize it the life is gone—and so, by popular definition, some would say that life was never there in the first place. The wheels and the cogs are the secret and we can make them better in time— machines that will run faster and more accurately than real mice to real cheese.

I have no doubt it can be done, though a mouse harvesting seeds on an au- 7
tumn thistle is to me a fine sight and more complicated, I think, in his multiform activity, than a machine "mouse" running a maze. Also, I like to think of the possible shape of the future brooding in mice, just as it brooded once in a rather ordinary mousy insectivore who became a man. It leaves a nice fine indeterminate sense of wonder that even an electronic brain hasn't got, because you know perfectly well that if the electronic brain changes, it will be because of something man has done to it. But what man will do to himself he doesn't really know. A certain scale of time and a ghostly intangible thing called change are ticking in him. Powers and potentialities like the oak in the seed, or a red and awful ruin. Either way, it's impressive; and the mouse has it, too. Or those birds, I'll never forget those birds—yet before I measured their significance, I learned the lesson of time first of all. I was young then and left alone in a great desert— part of an expedition that had scattered its men over several hundred miles in

order to carry on research more effectively. I learned there that time is a series of planes existing superficially in the same universe. The tempo is a human illusion, a subjective clock ticking in our own kind of protoplasm.

As the long months passed, I began to live on the slower planes and to observe 8 more readily what passed for life there. I sauntered, I passed more and more slowly up and down the canyons in the dry baking heat of midsummer. I slumbered for long hours in the shade of huge brown boulders that had gathered in tilted companies out on the flats. I had forgotten the world of men and the world had forgotten me. Now and then I found a skull in the canyons, and these justified my remaining there. I took a serene cold interest in these discoveries. I had come, like many a naturalist before me, to view life with a wary and subdued attention. I had grown to take pleasure in the divested bone.

I sat once on a high ridge that fell away before me into a waste of sand 9 dunes. I sat through hours of a long afternoon. Finally, as I glanced beside my boot an indistinct configuration caught my eye. It was a coiled rattlesnake, a big one. How long he had sat with me I do not know. I had not frightened him. We were both locked in the sleep-walking tempo of the earlier world, baking in the same high air and sunshine. Perhaps he had been there when I came. He slept on as I left, his coils, so ill discerned by me, dissolving once more among the stones and gravel from which I had barely made him out.

Another time I got on a higher ridge, among some tough little wind- 10 warped pines half covered over with sand in a basin-like depression that caught everything carried by the air up to those heights. There were a few thin bones of birds, some cracked shells of indeterminable age, and the knotty fingers of pine roots bulged out of shape from their long and agonizing grasp upon the crevices of the rock. I lay under the pines in the sparse shade and went to sleep once more.

It grew cold finally, for autumn was in the air by then, and the few things 11 that lived thereabouts were sinking down into an even chillier scale of time. In the moments between sleeping and waking I saw the roots about me and slowly, slowly, a foot in what seemed many centuries, I moved my sleep-stiffened hands over the scaling bark and lifted my numbed face after the vanishing sun. I was a great awkward thing of knots and aching limbs, trapped up there in some long, patient endurance that involved the necessity of putting living fingers into rock and by slow, aching expansion bursting those rocks asunder. I suppose, so thin and slow was the time of my pulse by then, that I might have stayed on to drift still deeper unto the lower cadences of the frost, or the crystalline life that glistens pebbles, or shines in a snowflake, or dreams in the meteoric iron between the worlds.

It was a dim descent, but time was present in it. Somewhere far down in 12 that scale the notion struck me that one might come the other way. Not many months thereafter I joined some colleagues heading higher into a remote windy tableland where huge bones were reputed to protrude like boulders from the turf. I had drowsed with reptiles and moved with the century-long pulse of trees; now, lethargically, I was climbing back up some invisible ladder of quickening hours. There had been talk of birds in connection with my duties. Birds are intense, fast-living creatures—reptiles, I suppose one might say, that have escaped out of the heavy sleep of time, transformed fairy creatures dancing over sunlit meadows. It is a youthful fancy, no doubt, but because of something that happened up there among the escarpments of that range, it remains with me a lifelong impression. I can never bear to see a bird imprisoned.

We came into that valley through the trailing mists of a spring night. It was 13 a place that looked as it might never have known the foot of man, but our scouts had been ahead of us and we knew all about the abandoned cabin of stone that lay far up on one hillside. It had been built in the land rush of the last century and then lost to the cattlemen again as the marginal soils failed to take to the plow.

There were spots like this all over that country. Lost graves marked by un- 14 lettered stones and old corroding rim-fire cartridge cases lying where somebody had made a stand among the boulders that rimmed the valley. They are all that remain of the range wars; the men are under the stones now. I could see our cavalcade winding in and out through the mist below us: torches, the reflection of the truck lights on our collecting tins, and the far-off bumping of a loose dinosaur thigh bone in the bottom of a trailer. I stood on a rock a moment looking down and thinking what it cost in money and equipment to capture the past.

We had, in addition, instructions to lay hands on the present. The word had 15 come through to get them alive—birds, reptiles, anything. A zoo somewhere abroad needed restocking. It was one of those reciprocal matters in which science involves itself. Maybe our museum needed a stray ostrich egg and this was the payoff. Anyhow, my job was to help capture some birds and that was why I was there before the trucks.

The cabin had not been occupied for years. We intended to clean it out and 16 live in it, but there were holes in the roof and the birds had come in and were roosting in the rafters. You could depend on it in a place like this where everything blew away, and even a bird needed some place out of the weather and away from coyotes. A cabin going back to nature in a wild place draws them till they come in, listening at the eaves, I imagine, pecking softly among the shingles till they find a hole and then suddenly the place is theirs and man is forgotten.

Sometimes of late years I find myself thinking the most beautiful sight in 17 the world might be the birds taking over New York after the last man has run away to the hills. I will never live to see it, of course, but I know just how it will sound because I've lived up high and I know the sort of watch birds keep on us. I've listened to sparrows tapping tentatively on the outside of air conditioners when they thought no one was listening, and I know how other birds test the vibrations that come up to them through the television aerials.

"Is he gone?" they ask, and the vibrations come up from below, "Not yet, 18 not yet."

Well, to come back, I got the door open softly and I had the spotlight all   19
ready to turn on and blind whatever birds there were so they couldn't see to get
out through the roof. I had a short piece of ladder to put against the far wall
where there was a shelf on which I expected to make the biggest haul. I had all
the information I needed just like any skilled assassin. I pushed the door open,
the hinges squeaking only a little. A bird or two stirred—I could hear them—but
nothing flew and there was a faint starlight through the holes in the roof.

I padded across the floor, got the ladder up and the light ready, and slith-   20
ered up the ladder till my head and arms were over the shelf. Everything was
dark as pitch except for the starlight at the little place back of the shelf near the
eaves. With the light to blind them, they'd never make it. I had them. I reached
my arm carefully over in order to be ready to seize whatever was there and I
put the flash on the edge of the shelf where it would stand by itself when I
turned it on. That way I'd be able to use both hands.

Everything worked perfectly except for one detail—I didn't know what   21
kind of birds were there. I never thought about it at all, and it wouldn't have
mattered if I had. My orders were to get something interesting. I snapped on the
flash and sure enough there was a great beating and feathers flying, but instead
of my having them, they, or rather he, had me. He had my hand, that is, and for
a small hawk not much bigger than my fist he was doing all right. I heard him
give one short metallic cry when the light went on and my hand descended on
the bird beside him; after that he was busy with his claws and his beak was
sunk in my thumb. In the struggle I knocked the lamp over on the shelf, and his
mate got her sight back and whisked neatly through the hold in the roof and off
among the stars outside. It all happened in fifteen seconds and you might think
I would have fallen down the ladder, but no, I had a professional assassin's reputation to keep up, and the bird, of course, made the mistake of thinking the
hand was the enemy and not the eyes behind it. He chewed my thumb up
pretty effectively and lacerated my hand with his claws, but in the end I got
him, having my two hands up to work with.

He was a sparrow hawk and a fine young male in the prime of life. I was   22
sorry not to catch the pair of them, but as I dripped blood and folded his wings
carefully, holding him by the back so that he couldn't strike again, I had to admit the two of them might have been more than I could have handled under the
circumstances. The little fellow had saved his mate by diverting me, and that
was that. He was born to it, and made no outcry now, resting in my hand hopelessly, but peering toward me in the shadows behind the lamp with a fierce, almost indifferent glance. He neither gave nor expected mercy and something out
of the high air passed from him to me, stilling a faint embarrassment.

I quit looking into that eye and managed to get my huge carcass with its fist   23
full of prey back down the ladder. I put the bird in a box too small to allow him
to injure himself by struggle and walked out to welcome the arriving trucks. It
had been a long day, and camp still to make in the darkness. In the morning that
bird would be just another episode. He would go back with the bones in the
truck to a small cage in a city where he would spend the rest of his life. And a

good thing, too. I sucked my aching thumb and spat out some blood. An assassin has to get used to these things. I had a professional reputation to keep up.

In the morning, with the change that comes on suddenly in that high country, 24 the mist that had hovered below us in the valley was gone. The sky was a deep blue, and one could see for miles over the high outcroppings of stone. I was up early and brought the box in which the little hawk was imprisoned out onto grass where I was building a cage. A wind as cool as a mountain spring ran over the grass and stirred my hair. It was a fine day to be alive. I looked up and around and at the hole in the cabin roof out of which the other little hawk had fled. There was no sign of her anywhere that I could see.

"Probably in the next county by now," I thought cynically, but before be- 25 ginning work I decided I'd have a look at my last night's capture.

Secretively, I looked again all around the camp and up and down and 26 opened the box. I got him right out in my hand with his wings folded properly and I was careful not to startle him. He lay limp in my grasp and I could feel his heart pound under the feathers but he only looked beyond me and up.

I saw him look that last look away beyond me into a sky so full of light that 27 I could not follow his gaze. The little breeze flowed over me again, and nearby a mountain aspen shook all its tiny leaves. I suppose I must have had an idea then of what was I going to do, but I never let it come up into consciousness. I just reached over and laid the hawk on the grass.

He lay there a long minute without hope, unmoving, his eyes still fixed on that blue vault above him. It must have been that he was already so far away in heart that he never felt the release from my hand. He never even stood. He just lay with his breast against the grass.

In the next second after that long minute he was gone. Like a flicker of light, 28 he had vanished with my eyes full on him, but without actually seeing even a premonitory wing beat. He was gone straight into that towering emptiness of light and crystal that my eyes could scarcely bear to penetrate. For another long moment there was silence. I could not see him. The light was too intense. Then from far up somewhere a cry came ringing down.

I was young then and had seen little of the world, but when I heard that 29 cry my heart turned over. It was not the cry of the hawk I had captured; for, by shifting my position against the sun, I was now seeing further up. Straight out of the sun's eye, where she must have been soaring restlessly above us for untold hours, hurtled his mate. And from far up, ringing from peak to peak of the summits over us, came a cry of such unutterable and ecstatic joy that it sounds down across the years and tingles among the cups on my quiet breakfast table.

I saw them both now. He was rising fast to meet her. They met in a great 30 soaring gyre that turned to a whirling circle and a dance of wings. Once more, just once, their two voices, joined in a harsh wild medley of question and response, struck and echoed against the pinnacles of the valley. Then they were gone forever somewhere into those upper regions beyond the eyes of men.

I am older now, and sleep less, and have seen most of what there is to see and am not very much impressed any more, I suppose, by anything. "What Next in the Attributes of Machines?" my morning headline runs. "It Might Be the Power to Reproduce Themselves."

I lay the paper down and across my mind a phrase floats insinuatingly: "It 31 does not seem that there is anything in the construction, constituents, or behavior of the human being which it is essentially impossible for science to duplicate and synthesize. On the other hand . . ."

All over the city the cogs in the hard, bright mechanisms have begun to 32 turn. Figures move through computers, names are spelled out, a thoughtful machine selects the fingerprints of a wanted criminal from an array of thousands. In the laboratory an electronic mouse runs swiftly through a maze toward the cheese it can neither taste nor enjoy. On the second run it does better than a living mouse.

"On the other hand . . ." Ah, my mind takes up, on the other hand the ma- 33 chine does not bleed, ache, hang for hours in the empty sky in a torment of hope to learn the fate of another machine, nor does it cry out with joy nor dance in the air with the fierce passion of a bird. Far off, over a distance greater than space, that remote cry from the heart of heaven makes a faint buzzing among my breakfast dishes and passes on and away.

COMPREHENSION

1. Why does Eiseley refer to himself as an assassin in paragraph 20? How does this comparison serve to explain his role leading up to the event with the sparrow hawk? Explain your answer as it pertains to the implications of his role during his service in the "field."

2. Eiseley states at the conclusion of paragraph 3, "It's life I believe in, not machines." What does he mean by this remark? Does he have more than one meaning? Explain by citing specific references in the text.

3. What is the particular purpose of his excursion? Why does he feel ambivalent about it?

4. Eiseley makes a comparison that is summarized in the title of his essay. He also makes an implied comparison between reading (which he is doing in the opening paragraph) and working directly in nature (as he begins to describe in the second section of the essay). What is the difference between the two activities?

RHETORIC

1. Some critics have commented that Eiseley has an elliptical style of writing. Note how long he takes before he mentions "birds" in the opening paragraph, although he refers to them at the very beginning of the introduction. What is the rhetorical effect of this strategy?

2. In paragraphs 4 through 6, Eiseley admits that there are certain similarities between living creatures and machines. Why does he take the time to point out these similarities when he ultimately believes there is a primary and primal difference? Explain.

3. Both the essay's rhetorical mode and the author's tone change in the second section. How would you characterize these two changes? Refer to specific phrases, words, and levels of abstraction that mark these changes.

4. In paragraphs 8 through 13, the author describes a landscape with many vestiges of death, desolation, and abandonment. What is the purpose of this extended description, and how does it add rhetorical strength to his argument when he states, "It's life I believe in, not machines"?

5. In paragraph 14, Eiseley says, "We had, in addition, instructions to lay hands on the present." How does this statement foreshadow a major event in the narrative? Why does it turn out to be an ironic remark?

6. In the third section of the essay, beginning with paragraph 21, Eiseley notes the passage of time. What emotional change is effected by the events in the third section? Why so?

7. In paragraph 26, we learn that Eiseley is describing events that took place many years before his recollection of them. What rhetorical purpose does this serve? What clues at the beginning of the final section suggest the answer?

8. In the final paragraph, Eiseley makes reference to "heaven." Is he using this term literally, figuratively, or both? Does it ultimately matter? Explain your response.

WRITING

1. Nature has often been considered hostile by humans, reflected for example, in such terms as "survival of the fittest" and "eat or be eaten." In 500 to 750 words, write an essay based on personal experience and observation that argues for or against the proposition that Eiseley romanticizes nature.

2. In an essay of 500 words, argue for or against the proposition that technology actually allows us to appreciate nature more fully, for example, in the use of binoculars, telescopes, sophisticated camping equipment, protected nature preserves, and so on.

3. Write a narrative/descriptive essay of 500 to 750 words discussing your experience when you spent time in a "natural" setting. Be sure to use details that bring to life both the place and your emotional responses.

4. After researching issues pertaining to contemporary zoos, write a research paper of 1,000 to 1,500 words in which you argue for or against the proposition that modern zoos and zoo-keeping practices have a positive role in our society because they allow many people who would not ordinarily experience nature the opportunity to do so, and, at the same time, protect endangered species from extinction. Be sure to use at least three secondary sources to support your views.

The Terrifying Normalcy of AIDS

Stephen Jay Gould

*Stephen Jay Gould (b. 1941), an acclaimed contemporary science writer, teaches biol-
ogy, geology, and the history of science at Harvard University. He also writes a
monthly column, "This View of Life," for* Natural History *and is the author of* Ever
Since Darwin *(1977),* Ontogeny and Phylogeny *(1977),* The Panda's Thumb
(1980), Wonderful Life *(1989), and* Bully for Brontosaurus *(1991). In this 1987 essay, Gould explains in clear, precise language why AIDS is a "natural phenomenon"
and warns against viewing it in moral terms.*

Disney's Epcot Center in Orlando, Fla., is a technological tour de force and a   1
conceptual desert. In this permanent World's Fair, American industrial giants
have built their versions of an unblemished future. These masterful entertainments convey but one message, brilliantly packaged and relentlessly expressed:
progress through technology is the solution to all human problems. G.E.
proclaims from Horizons: "If we can dream it, we can do it." A.T.&T. speaks
from on high within its giant golf ball: We are now "unbounded by space and
time." United Technologies bubbles from the depths of Living Seas: "With
the help of modern technology, we feel there's really no limit to what can be
accomplished."

Yet several of these exhibits at the Experimental Prototype Community of   2
Tomorrow, all predating last year's space disaster, belie their stated message
from within by using the launch of the shuttle as a visual metaphor for technological triumph. The Challenger disaster may represent a general malaise, but it
remains an incident. The AIDS pandemic, an issue that may rank with nuclear
weaponry as the greatest danger of our era, provides a more striking proof that
mind and technology are not omnipotent and that we have not canceled our
bond to nature.

In 1984, John Platt, a biophysicist who taught at the University of Chicago   3
for many years, wrote a short paper for private circulation. At a time when most
of us were either ignoring AIDS, or viewing it as a contained and peculiar affliction of homosexual men, Platt recognized that the limited data on the origin
of AIDS and its spread in America suggested a more frightening prospect: we
are all susceptible to AIDS, and the disease has been spreading in a simple exponential manner.

Exponential growth is a geometric increase. Remember the old kiddy prob-   4
lem: if you place a penny on square one of a checkerboard and double the number of coins on each subsequent square—2, 4, 8, 16, 32 . . .—how big is the stack
by the sixty-fourth square? The answer: about as high as the universe is wide.
Nothing in the external environment inhibits this increase, thus giving to expo-

nential processes their relentless character. In the real, noninfinite world, of course, some limit will eventually arise, and the process slows down, reaches a steady state, or destroys the entire system: the stack of pennies falls over, the bacterial cells exhaust their supply of nutrients.

Platt noticed that data for the initial spread of AIDS fell right on an expo- 5 nential curve. He then followed the simplest possible procedure of extrapolating the curve unabated into the 1990's. Most of us were incredulous, accusing Platt of the mathematical gamesmanship that scientists call "curve fitting." After all, aren't exponential models unrealistic? Surely we are not all susceptible to AIDS. Is it not spread only by odd practices to odd people? Will it not, therefore, quickly run its short course within a confined group?

Well, hello 1987—worldwide data still match Platt's extrapolated curve. This 6 will not, of course, go on forever. AIDS has probably already saturated the African areas where it probably originated, and where the sex ratio of afflicted people is 1-to-1, male-female. But AIDS still has far to spread, and may be moving exponentially, through the rest of the world. We have learned enough about the cause of AIDS to slow its spread, if we can make rapid and fundamental changes in our handling of that most powerful part of human biology—our own sexuality. But medicine, as yet, has nothing to offer as a cure and precious little even for palliation.

This exponential spread of AIDS not only illuminates its, and our, biology, 7 but also underscores the tragedy of our moralistic misperception. Exponential processes have a definite time and place of origin, an initial point of "inoculation"—in this case, Africa. We didn't notice the spread at first. In a population of billions, we pay little attention when one increases to two, or eight to sixteen, but when one million becomes two million, we panic, even though the *rate* of doubling has not increased.

The infection has to start somewhere, and its initial locus may be little more 8 than an accident of circumstance. For a while, it remains confined to those in close contact with the primary source, but only by accident of proximity, not by intrinsic susceptibility. Eventually, given the power and lability of human sexuality, it spreads outside the initial group and into the general population. And now AIDS has begun its march through our own heterosexual community.

What a tragedy that our moral stupidity caused us to lose precious time, the 9 greatest enemy in fighting an exponential spread, by down-playing the danger because we thought that AIDS was a disease of three irregular groups of minorities: minorities of life style (needle users), of sexual preference (homosexuals) and of color (Haitians). If AIDS had first been imported from Africa into a Park Avenue apartment, we would not have dithered as the exponential march began.

The message of Orlando—the inevitability of technological solutions—is 10 wrong, and we need to understand why.

Our species has not won its independence from nature, and we cannot do 11 all that we can dream. Or at least we cannot do it at the rate required to avoid tragedy, for we are not unbounded from time. Viral diseases are preventable in principle, and I suspect that an AIDS vaccine will one day be produced. But how will this discovery avail us if it takes until the millennium, and by then AIDS has fully run its exponential course and saturated our population, killing a substantial percentage of the human race? A fight against an exponential enemy is primarily a race against time.

We must also grasp the perspective of ecology and evolutionary biology   12
and recognize, once we reinsert ourselves properly into nature, that AIDS represents the ordinary workings of biology, not an irrational or diabolical plague with a moral meaning. Disease, including epidemic spread, is a natural phenomenon, part of human history from the beginning. An entire subdiscipline of my profession, paleopathology, studies the evidence of ancient diseases preserved in the fossil remains of organisms. Human history has been marked by episodic plagues. More native peoples died of imported disease than ever fell before the gun during the era of colonial expansion. Our memories are short, and we have had a respite, really, only since the influenza pandemic at the end of World War I, but AIDS must be viewed as a virulent expression of an ordinary natural phenomenon.

I do not say this to foster either comfort or complacency. The evolutionary   13
perspective is correct, but utterly inappropriate for our human scale. Yes, AIDS is a natural phenomenon, one of a recurring class of pandemic diseases. Yes, AIDS may run through the entire population, and may carry off a quarter or more of us. Yes, it may make no *biological* difference to Homo sapiens in the long run: there will still be plenty of us left and we can start again. Evolution cares as little for its agents—organisms struggling for reproductive success—as physics cares for individual atoms of hydrogen in the sun. But we care. These atoms are our neighbors, our lovers, our children and ourselves. AIDS is both a natural phenomenon and, potentially, the greatest natural tragedy in human history.

The cardboard message of Epcot fosters the wrong attitudes: we must both rein-   14
sert ourselves into nature and view AIDS as a natural phenomenon in order to fight properly. If we stand above nature and if technology is all-powerful, then AIDS is a horrifying anomaly that must be trying to tell us something. If so, we can adopt one of two attitudes, each potentially fatal. We can either become complacent, because we believe the message of Epcot and assume that medicine will soon generate a cure, or we can panic in confusion and seek a scapegoat for something so irregular that it must have been visited upon us to teach us a moral lesson.

But AIDS is not irregular. It is part of nature. So are we. This should galva-   15
nize us and give us hope, not prompt the worst of all responses: a kind of "new-age" negativism that equates natural with what we must accept and cannot, or even should not, change. When we view AIDS as natural, and when we recognize both the exponential property of its spread and the accidental character of its point of entry into America, we can break through our destructive tendencies to blame others and to free ourselves of concern.

If AIDS is natural, then there is no message in its spread. But by all that science ₁₆ has learned and all that rationality proclaims, AIDS works by a *mechanism*—and we can discover it. Victory is not ordained by any principle of progress, or any slogan of technology, so we shall have to fight like hell, and be watchful. There is no message, but there is a mechanism.

COMPREHENSION

1. What does Gould mean when he defines AIDS as a "natural phenomenon"? How does the title support this definition?
2. What does Gould mean by "our moral stupidity" in paragraph 9?
3. What connection does Gould make between our reaction to the AIDS crisis and our alienation from nature?

RHETORIC

1. What is Gould's main idea? Where in the essay is it stated?
2. What is the purpose of paragraphs 1 and 2? How do they contribute to Gould's argument? How do they help establish the tone of the essay? What *is* the tone? What is the importance of Epcot Center to Gould's thesis?
3. Gould uses scientific terminology in his essay. Define the words *exponential* in paragraph 3 and *pandemic* and *phenomenon* in paragraph 13. Is this essay intended for a specialized audience? Justify your response.
4. Trace the progression of ideas in paragraphs 2, 3, 4, and 5. What transitions does Gould employ?
5. Does Gould use rhetorical strategies besides argument in his essay? Cite evidence of this varied rhetorical approach.
6. Explain the final sentence in Gould's conclusion. What is its relation to the paragraph as a whole?

WRITING

1. Write an essay in which you expand on Gould's belief that our moral stupidity has not only hindered society's recognition of the AIDS threat but continues to impede AIDS research and treatment.
2. Gould states that we must "reinstate ourselves into nature." What does he mean by this? How would this affect the way in which we deal with disease and death in our society? Explore this issue in a brief essay.

The Clan of One-breasted Women

Terry Tempest Williams

Terry Tempest Williams (b. 1955) is the author of many books of nonfiction, including A Journey to Navajoland *(1984),* Coyote's Canyon *(1989),* Refuge: An Unnatural History of Family and Place *(1991),* An Unspoken Hunger *(1994), and* Desert Quartet *(1995). Williams was identified by* Newsweek *magazine as someone who will have "a considerable impact on the political, economic and environmental issues facing the western states in this decade." She is the recipient of a Lannan Fellowship in creative nonfiction and was chosen by the periodical* UTNE *Reader as a "visionary," one of the UTNE 100 "who could change your life." She is Naturalist-in-Residence at the Utah Museum of Natural History in Salt Lake City. The following essay—published in 1989 in* Witness—*describes the pernicious intergenerational effects of nuclear testing.*

I belong to a Clan of One-breasted Women. My mother, my grandmothers, and   1
six aunts have all had mastectomies. Seven are dead. The two who survive have
just completed rounds of chemotherapy and radiation.

I've had my own problems: two biopsies for breast cancer and a small tu-   2
mor between my ribs diagnosed as "a border-line malignancy."

This is my family history.   3

Most statistics tell us breast cancer is genetic, hereditary, with rising per-   4
centages attached to fatty diets, childlessness, or becoming pregnant after thirty.
What they don't say is living in Utah may be the greatest hazard of all.

We are a Mormon family with roots in Utah since 1847. The word-of-   5
wisdom, a religious doctrine of health, kept the women in my family aligned
with good foods: no coffee, no tea, tobacco, or alcohol. For the most part, these
women were finished having their babies by the time they were thirty. And only
one faced breast cancer prior to 1960. Traditionally, as a group of people, Mormons have a low rate of cancer.

Is our family a cultural anomaly? The truth is we didn't think about it.   6
Those who did, usually the men, simply said, "bad genes." The women's attitude was stoic. Cancer was part of life. On February 16, 1971, the eve before my
mother's surgery, I accidentally picked up the telephone and overheard her ask
my grandmother what she could expect.

"Diane, it is one of the most spiritual experiences you will ever encounter."   7

I quietly put down the receiver.   8

Two days later, my father took my three brothers and me to the hospital to   9
visit her. She met us in the lobby in a wheelchair. No bandages were visible. I'll
never forget her radiance, the way she held herself in a purple velour robe and
how she gathered us around her.

"Children, I am fine. I want you to know I felt the arms of God around me." 10

We believed her. My father cried. Our mother, his wife, was thirty-eight 11 years old.

Two years ago, after my mother's death from cancer, my father and I were 12 having dinner together. He had just returned from St. George where his construction company was putting in natural gas lines for towns in southern Utah. He spoke of his love for the country: the sandstoned landscape, bare-boned and beautiful. He had just finished hiking the Kolob trail in Zion National Park. We got caught up in reminiscing, recalling with fondness our walk up Angel's Landing on his fiftieth birthday and the years our family had vacationed there. This was a remembered landscape where we had been raised.

Over dessert, I shared a recurring dream of mine. I told my father that for 13 years, as long as I could remember, I saw this flash of light in the night in the desert. That this image had so permeated my being, I could not venture south without seeing it again, on the horizon, illuminating buttes and mesas.

"You did see it," he said.   14

"Saw what?" I asked, a bit tentative.   15

"The bomb. The cloud. We were driving home from Riverside, California. 16 You were sitting on your mother's lap. She was pregnant. In fact, I remember the date, September 7, 1957. We had just gotten out of the Service. We were driving north, past Las Vegas. It was an hour or so before dawn, when this explosion went off. We not only heard it, but felt it. I thought the oil tanker in front of us had blown up. We pulled over and suddenly, rising from the desert floor, we saw it, clearly, this golden-stemmed cloud, the mushroom. The sky seemed to vibrate with an eerie pink glow. Within a few minutes, a light ash was raining on the car."

I stared at my father. This was new information to me.   17

"I thought you knew that," my father said. "It was a common occurrence in 18 the fifties."

It was at this moment I realized the deceit I had been living under. Children 19 growing up in the American Southwest, drinking contaminated milk from contaminated cows, even from the contaminated breasts of their mother, my mother—members, years later, of the Clan of One-breasted Women.

It is a well-known story in the Desert West, "The Day We Bombed Utah," or 20 perhaps, "The Years We Bombed Utah."[1] Above ground atomic testing in Nevada took place from January 27, 1951, through July 11, 1962. Not only were the winds blowing north, covering "low use segments of the population" with fallout and leaving sheep dead in their tracks, but the climate was right.[2] The United States of the 1950s was red, white, and blue. The Korean War was raging. McCarthyism was rampant. Ike was in and the Cold War was hot. If you were against nuclear testing, you were for a Communist regime.

[1]Fuller, John G., *The Day We Bombed Utah* (New York: New American Library, 1984).
[2]Discussion on March 14, 1988, with Carole Gallagher, photographer and author, *Nuclear Towns: The Secret War in the American Southwest,* published by Doubleday, Spring, 1990.

Much has been written about this "American nuclear tragedy." Public 21 health was secondary to national security. The Atomic Energy Commissioner, Thomas Murray said, "Gentlemen, we must not let anything interfere with this series of tests, nothing."[3]

Again and again, the American public was told by its government, in spite 22 of burns, blisters, and nausea, "It has been found that the tests may be conducted with adequate assurance of safety under conditions prevailing at the bombing reservations."[4] Assuaging public fears was simply a matter of public relations. "Your best action," an Atomic Energy Commission booklet read, "is not to be worried about fallout." A news release typical of the times stated, "We find no basis for concluding that harm to any individual has resulted from radioactive fallout."[5]

On August 30, 1979, during Jimmy Carter's presidency, a suit was filed en- 23 titled "Irene Allen vs. the United States of America." Mrs. Allen was the first to be alphabetically listed with twenty-four test cases, representative of nearly 1200 plaintiffs seeking compensation from the United States government for cancers caused from nuclear testing in Nevada.

Irene Allen lived in Hurricane, Utah. She was the mother of five children 24 and had been widowed twice. Her first husband with their two oldest boys had watched the tests from the roof of the local high school. He died of leukemia in 1956. Her second husband died of pancreatic cancer in 1978.

In a town meeting conducted by Utah Senator Orrin Hatch, shortly before 25 the suit was filed, Mrs. Allen said, "I am not blaming the government, I want you to know that, Senator Hatch. But I thought if my testimony could help in any way so this wouldn't happen again to any of the generations coming up after us . . . I am really happy to be here this day to bear testimony of this."[6]

God-fearing people. This is just one story in an anthology of thousands.   26

On May 10, 1984, Judge Bruce S. Jenkins handed down his opinion. Ten of 27 the plaintiffs were awarded damages. It was the first time a federal court had determined that nuclear tests had been the cause of cancers. For the remaining fourteen test cases, the proof of causation was not sufficient. In spite of the split decision, it was considered a landmark ruling.[7] It was not to remain so for long.

In April 1987, the 10th Circuit Court of Appeals overturned Judge Jenkins' 28 ruling on the basis that the United States was protected from suit by the legal doctrine of sovereign immunity, the centuries-old idea from England in the days of absolute monarchs.[8]

---

[3]Szasz, Ferenc M., "Downwind from the Bomb," *Nevada Historical Society Quarterly*, Fall, 1987 Vol. XXX, No. 3, p. 185.
[4]Fradkin, Philip L., *Fallout* (Tucson: University of Arizona Press, 1989), 98.
[5]Ibid., 109.
[6]Town meeting held by Senator Orrin Hatch in St. George, Utah, April 17, 1979, transcript, 26–28.
[7]Fradkin, Op. Cit., 228.
[8]U.S. vs. Allen, 816 Federal Reporter, 2d/1417 (10th Circuit Court 1987), cert. denied, 108 S. CT. 694 (1988).

In January 1988, the Supreme Court refused to review the Appeals Court 29 decision. To our court system, it does not matter whether the United States Government was irresponsible, whether it lied to its citizens or even that citizens died from the fallout of nuclear testing. What matters is that our government is immune. "The King can do no wrong."

In Mormon culture, authority is respected, obedience is revered, and independent thinking is not. I was taught as a young girl not to "make waves" or "rock the boat." 30

"Just let it go—"my mother would say. "You know how you feel, that's what counts." 31

For many years, I did just that—listened, observed, and quietly formed my own opinions within a culture that rarely asked questions because they had all the answers. But one by one, I watched the women in my family die common, heroic deaths. We sat in waiting rooms hoping for good news, always receiving the bad. I cared for them, bathed their scarred bodies and kept their secrets. I watched beautiful women become bald as cytoxan, cisplatin and adriamycin were injected into their veins. I held their foreheads as they vomited green-black bile and I shot them with morphine when the pain became inhuman. In the end, I witnessed their last peaceful breaths, becoming a midwife to the rebirth of their souls. But the price of obedience became too high. 32

The fear and inability to question authority that ultimately killed rural communities in Utah during atmospheric testing of atomic weapons was the same fear I saw being held in my mother's body. Sheep. Dead sheep. The evidence is buried. 33

I cannot prove that my mother, Diane Dixon Tempest, or my grandmothers, Lettie Romney Dixon and Kathryn Blackett Tempest, along with my aunts contracted cancer from nuclear fallout in Utah. But I cant prove they didn't. 34

My father's memory was correct, the September blast we drove through in 1957 was part of Operation Plumbbob, one of the most intensive series of bomb tests to be initiated. The flash of light in the night in the desert I had always thought was a dream developed into a family nightmare. It took fourteen years, from 1957 to 1971, for cancer to show up in my mother—the same time, Howard L. Andrews, an authority on radioactive fallout at the National Institutes of Health, says radiation cancer requires to become evident.[9] The more I learn about what it means to be a "downwinder," the more questions I drown in. 35

What I do know, however, is that as a Mormon woman of the fifth generation of "Latter-Day-Saints," I must question everything, even if it means losing my faith, even if it means becoming a member of a border tribe among my own people. Tolerating blind obedience in the name of patriotism or religion ultimately takes our lives. 36

[9]Fradkin, Op. cit. 116.

When the Atomic Energy Commission described the country north of the 37 Nevada Test Site as "virtually uninhabited desert terrain," my family members were some of the "virtual uninhabitants."

One night, I dreamed women from all over the world circling a blazing fire in 38 the desert. They spoke of change, of how they hold the moon in their bellies and wax and wane with its phases. They mocked at the presumption of even-tempered beings and made promises that they would never fear the witch inside themselves. The women danced wildly as sparks broke away from the flames and entered the night sky as stars.

And they sang a song given to them by Shoshoni grandmothers: 39

Ah ne nah, nah
nin nah nah—
Ah ne nah, nah
nin nah nah—
Nyaga mutzi
oh ne nay—
Nyaga mutzi
oh ne nay—[10]

The women danced and drummed and sang for weeks, preparing them- 40 selves for what was to come. They would reclaim the desert for the sake of their children, for the sake of the land.

A few miles downwind from the fire circle, bombs were being tested. Rab- 41 bits felt the tremors. Their soft leather pads on paws and feet recognized the shaking sands while the roots of mesquite and sage were smoldering. Rocks were hot from the inside out and dust devils hummed unnaturally. And each time there was another nuclear test, ravens watched the desert heave. Stretch marks appeared. The land was losing its muscle.

The women couldn't bear it any longer. They were mothers. They had suf- 42 fered labor pains but always under the promise of birth. The red hot pains beneath the desert promised death only as each bomb became a stillborn. A contract had been broken between human beings and the land. A new contract was being drawn by the women who understood the fate of the earth as their own.

Under the cover of darkness, ten women slipped under the barbed wire 43 fence and entered the contaminated country. They were trespassing. They walked toward the town of Mercury in moonlight, taking their cues from coyote, kit fox, antelope squirrel, and quail. They moved quietly and deliberately through the maze of Joshua trees. When a hint of daylight appeared they rested,

---

[10]This song was sung by the Western Shoshone women as they crossed the line at the Nevada Test Site on March 18, 1988, as part of their "Reclaim the Land" action. The translation they gave was: "Consider the rabbits how gently they walk on the earth. Consider the rabbits how gently they walk on the earth. We remember them. We can walk gently also. We remember them. We can walk gently also."

drinking tea and sharing their rations of food. The women closed their eyes. The time had come to protest with the heart, that to deny one's genealogy with the earth was to commit treason against one's soul.

At dawn, the women draped themselves in mylar, wrapping long stream- 44 ers of silver plastic around their arms to blow in the breeze. They wore clear masks that became the faces of humanity. And when they arrived on the edge of Mercury, they carried all the butterflies of a summer day in their wombs. They paused to allow their courage to settle.

The town which forbids pregnant women and children to enter because of 45 radiation risks to their health was asleep. The women moved through the streets as winged messengers, twirling around each other in slow motion, peeking inside homes and watching the easy sleep of men and women. They were astonished by such stillness and periodically would utter a shrill note or low cry just to verify life.

The residents finally awoke to what appeared as strange apparitions. Some 46 simply stared. Others called authorities, and in time, the women were apprehended by wary soldiers dressed in desert fatigues. They were taken to a white, square building on the other edge of Mercury. When asked who they were and why they were there, the women replied, "We are mothers and we have come to reclaim the desert for our children."

The soldiers arrested them. As the ten women were blindfolded and hand- 47 cuffed, they began singing:

> You can't forbid us everything
> You can't forbid us to think—
> You can't forbid our tears to flow
> And you can't stop the songs that we sing.

The women continued to sing louder and louder, until they heard the 48 voices of their sisters moving across the mesa.

> Ah ne nah, nah
> nin nah nah—
> Ah ne nah, nah
> nin nah nah—
> Nyaga mutzi
> oh ne nay—
> Nyaga mutzi
> oh ne nay—

"Call for re-enforcement," one soldier said.   49

"We have," interrupted one woman. "We have—and you have no idea of 50 our numbers."

On March 18, 1988, I crossed the line at the Nevada Test Site and was arrested 51 with nine other Utahns for trespassing on military lands. They are still conducting nuclear tests in the desert. Ours was an act of civil disobedience. But as

I walked toward the town of Mercury, it was more than a gesture of peace. It was a gesture on behalf of the Clan of One-breasted Women.

As one officer cinched the handcuffs around my wrists, another frisked my 52 body. She found a pen and a pad of paper tucked inside my left boot.

"And these?" she asked sternly. 53

"Weapons," I replied. 54

Our eyes met. I smiled. She pulled the leg of my trousers back over my boot. 55

"Step forward, please," she said as she took my arm. 56

We were booked under an afternoon sun and bussed to Tonapah, Nevada. 57 It was a two-hour ride. This was familiar country to me. The Joshua trees standing their ground had been named by my ancestors who believed they looked like prophets pointing west to the promised land. These were the same trees that bloomed each spring, flowers appearing like white flames in the Mojave. And I recalled a full moon in May when my mother and I had walked among them, flushing out mourning doves and owls.

The bus stopped short of town. We were released. The officials thought it 58 was a cruel joke to leave us stranded in the desert with no way to get home. What they didn't realize is that we were home, soul-centered and strong, women who recognized the sweet smell of sage as fuel for our spirits.

COMPREHENSION

1. What is the theme of the essay? How did you arrive at your answer?
2. The credo of the United States promotes "life, liberty, and the pursuit of happiness." In her essay, what does Williams imply is the major antagonist to this philosophy?
3. Define the following words and terms: *doctrine* (paragraph 5), *anomaly* (paragraph 6), *buttes* (paragraph 12), *mesas* (paragraph 12), *plaintiffs* (paragraph 23), and *sovereign* (paragraph 28).

RHETORIC

1. Williams often uses quotation marks to signal irony in her writing. What is the perverse irony in the following expressions: "low use segments of the population," "downwinder," and "virtually uninhabited desert terrain"?
2. Although this is a highly personal essay and reveals a profound and emotional personal experience, Williams also relies on evidence from secondary source material to support her theme. What is the effect of using such sources in terms of the author's authority and believability?
3. The essay is divided into four segments. What is the main subject of each one?
4. Williams uses extended metaphor, personification, and comparison and contrast in paragraphs 41 and 42. Explain how she incorporates these three rhetorical devices, and their relevance to the overarching theme of the essay.

5. Williams provides a revelation to the reader in paragraph 16 that determines to a large degree the focus of her essay. What was the rhetorical purpose in waiting so long to reveal it?
6. Literary critics often state that one of the essential elements of powerful drama is some profound change that the major protagonist undergoes. What change in perspective did Williams undergo, and what was its implication for her attitudes and actions toward society?
7. Despite profound tragedy and continuous frustration in her life, Williams ends her essay on a positive note. Where is this change in tone most evident? What images reflect her ultimate triumph?

WRITING

1. Argue for or against the proposition that in any action that results from public policy, there will always be "winners" and "losers."
2. For a research project, study public policy in the 1950s and 1960s regarding aboveground nuclear testing, and report on whether or not the American government foresaw that there was a good degree of certainty that some individuals would suffer dire physical infirmities as a result of such procedures.
3. Argue for or against the proposition that technology is never value-free.

CONNECTIONS FOR CRITICAL THINKING

1. Using the essays of Gould and Williams, discuss the need for strict ethics among the government and medical establishments in regards to their concern over the well-being of the general populace.
2. Using any of the essays in this chapter, write an essay advancing the rationale for scientists and technocrats to be more sensitive to the emotional needs of people.
3. Compare the tone of Williams and Klass with the tone of any two male writers in this chapter. Are there any significant differences between the genders?
4. Make a connection between views on natural selection and Gould's view that "Our species has not won its independence from nature." How alienated are we from other animal societies? What do we share with them? How can we use this knowledge to save ourselves and our planet?
5. Compare the process of natural selection as advanced by Darwin with the "evolution" of the clock and its effects on human society as claimed by Mumford.
6. Search the Web for two sites: one promoting the idea of evolution, the other promoting the idea of creationism. Compare and contrast the approach of each site as well as responses made by the visitors to each site.
7. Have your class create a private chat room with screen names that do not divulge the gender of the participants. Discuss the pros and cons of the macho ideology of the medical profession as described by Klass. Have a host tally the nature of the responses, reveal the gender of the students who participated, and discuss any differences that were found between the responses of the male and female students.
8. Do a search of the Web using the keywords *medicine* and *virtual reality*. Analyze three hits to see how virtual reality technology is being used in hospitals in your region of the country.
9. Rent the videotape version of the television series *Cosmos*, which was based on a novel by Carl Sagan. Compare the ideas set forth in the film with those in Sagan's essay "Can We Know the Universe? Reflections on a Grain of Salt."
10. Compare and contrast the expository methods Darwin uses to explain the process of natural selection and the narrative technique Selzer uses to describe a surgical operation.
11. Argue for or against the proposition that Rifkin's meditation on the ultimate effects of "The Age of Simulation" demonstrate that Eiseley was correct in his much earlier critique of the evolution of machines.

12. Using Williams's essay on the pernicious effects of technology and Thomas's views on the benefits of technology as prompts for meditation and thought on the subject, explore how technology can be either a friend or a foe of humankind.

chapter 11

Nature and the Environment

How Do We Relate to the Natural World?

We are at a point in the history of civilization where consciousness of our fragile relationship to nature and the environment is high. Even as you spend an hour reading a few of the essays in this chapter, it is estimated that we are losing 3,000 acres of rain forest around the world and four species of plants or animals. From pollution to the population explosion to the depletion of the ozone layer, we seem to be confronted with ecological catastrophe. Nevertheless, as Rachel Carson reminds us, we have "an obligation to endure," to survive potential natural catastrophe by understanding and managing our relationship with the natural world.

Ecology, or the study of nature and the environment, as many of the essayists in this chapter attest, involves us in the conservation of the earth. It moves us to suppress our rapacious destruction of the planet. Clearly, the biological stability of the planet is increasingly precarious. More plants, insects, birds, and animals became extinct in the 20th century than in any era since the Cretaceous catastrophe more than 65 million years ago that led to the extinction of the dinosaurs. Within this ecological context, writers like Thoreau and Carson become our literary conscience, reminding us of how easily natural processes can break down unless we insist on a degree of ecological economy.

Of course, any modification of human behavior in an effort to conserve nature is a complex matter. To save the spotted owl in the Pacific Northwest, we must sacrifice the jobs of people in the timber industry. To reduce pollution, we must forsake gas and oil for alternate energy sources that are costly to develop. To reduce the waste stream, we must shift from a consumption to a conservation society. The ecological debate is complicated, but it is clear that the preservation of the myriad life cycles on earth is crucial, for we, too, could become an endangered species.

The language of nature is as enigmatic as the sounds of dolphins and whales communicating with their respective species. Writers like Gretel Ehrlich, John Steinbeck, and Alice Walker, and the language found in the letter of Chief Seattle help us decipher the language of our environment. These writers

608

encourage us to converse with nature, learn from it, and even revere it. All of us are guests on this planet; the natural world is our host. If we do not protect the earth, how can we guarantee the survival of global civilization?

Previewing the Chapter

As you read the essays in this chapter and respond to them in discussion and writing, consider the following questions:

- According to the author, what should our relationship to the natural world be?
- What claims or arguments does the author make about the importance of nature? Do you agree or disagree with these claims and arguments?
- What specific ecological problem does the author investigate?
- How does the author think that nature influences human behavior?
- What cultural factors are involved in our approach to the environment?
- Is the writer optimistic, pessimistic, or neutral in the assessment of our ability to conserve nature?
- Do you find that the author is too idealistic or sentimental in the depiction of nature? Why?
- Based on the author's essay, how does he or she qualify as a nature writer?
- How have you been challenged or changed by the essays in this chapter?

Classic and Contemporary Images:
ARE WE DESTROYING OUR NATURAL WORLD?

Using a Critical Perspective Imagine yourself to be part of each of the scenes depicted in these two illustrations. How do you feel, and why? Now examine the artistic purpose of each illustration. What details do the artists emphasize to convey their statement about our relationship to the natural world? What images does each artist create to capture your attention and direct your viewing and thinking toward a specific, dominant impression?

Smithsonian American Art Museum/Art Resource

The painters of the Hudson River School such as John Frederick Kensett (1816–1872) celebrated American landscapes in their art, painting breathtaking scenes in meticulous detail. In *Along the Hudson* (1852), the beauty of the river is unspoiled.

Michael Brophy

Starting in the late nineteenth century naturalists such as John Muir (1838–1914) and, later, Rachel Carson (1907–1964) began to warn of the danger to the environment posed by our industrial society. Michael Brophy's *Powerline* (1998) is a vivid illustration of a different kind of landscape: one marked by the powerlines that make our information age possible.

Classic and Contemporary Essays
DO WE OWN NATURE?

The simple yet passionate reflections of Chief Seattle regarding the destruction of a worldview are complemented by the more scholarly and learned meditation written nearly a century and a half later by the esteemed naturalist and writer Barry Lopez. Chief Seattle mourns the death of a way of life, a way of thinking, and a way of being as he tragically accepts that the cultural world of his people is doomed to disappear with the encroachment of "civilization." The white man exploits nature, uses nature, and perhaps most radically of all, perceives himself as apart from nature. This is in profound contrast to the ways of Chief Seattle's people, who saw themselves in harmony with nature, or more specifically inseparable from it, as inseparable perhaps as from a part of their own bodies. Chief Seattle's address is simple. And so perhaps is his message, although one should not confuse simplicity with lack of profundity. Lopez, writing from the perspective of a 21st-century academic and naturalist, informs the reader of humans' ongoing "feud" with nature—not only by reflecting on his own experience and perceptions—but by drawing on his "book" knowledge as well. He relates many relevant tales from other cultures and mythologies, and excavates the historical record when reflecting on the "stone horse" he finds hidden in the wilderness, a symbol of that union with nature that Chief Seattle spoke of so eloquently. Although they speak in very different levels of discourse and from different perspectives, it is evident that the awe of nature has not been demolished despite many deliberate and random attempts to extinguish it.

Letter to President Pierce, 1855

Chief Seattle

Chief Seattle (1786–1866) was the leader of the Dewamish and other Pacific North-west tribes. The city of Seattle, Washington, bears his name. In 1854, Chief Seattle reluctantly agreed to sell tribal lands to the United States government and move to the government-established reservations. The authenticity of the following speech has been challenged by many scholars. However, most specialists agree it contains the substance and perspective of Chief Seattle's attitude toward nature and the white race.

We know that the white man does not understand our ways. One portion of the land is the same to him as the next, for he is a stranger who comes in the night and takes from the land whatever he needs. The earth is not his brother, but his enemy, and when he has conquered it, he moves on. He leaves his fathers' graves, and his children's birthright is forgotten. The sight of your cities pains the eyes of the red man. But perhaps it is because the red man is a savage and does not understand.

There is no quiet place in the white man's cities. No place to hear the leaves of spring or the rustle of insect's wings. But perhaps because I am a savage and do not understand, the clatter only seems to insult the ears. The Indian prefers the soft sound of the wind darting over the face of the pond, the smell of the wind itself cleansed by a mid-day rain, or scented with the piñon pine. The air is precious to the red man. For all things share the same breath—the beasts, the trees, the man. Like a man dying for many days, he is numb to the stench.

What is man without the beasts? If all the beasts were gone, men would die from great loneliness of spirit, for whatever happens to the beasts also happens to man. All things are connected. Whatever befalls the earth befalls the sons of the earth.

It matters little where we pass the rest of our days; they are not many. A few more hours, a few more winters, and none of the children of the great tribes that once lived on this earth, or that roamed in small bands in the woods, will be left to mourn the graves of a people once as powerful and hopeful as yours.

The whites, too, shall pass—perhaps sooner than other tribes. Continue to contaminate your bed, and you will one night suffocate in your own waste. When the buffalo are all slaughtered, the wild horses all tamed, the secret corners of the forest heavy with the scent of many men, and the view of the ripe hills blotted by talking wires, where is the thicket? Gone. Where is the eagle? Gone. And what is it to say goodbye to the swift and the hunt, the end of living and the beginning of survival? We might understand if we knew what it was that the white man dreams, what he describes to his children on the long winter nights, what visions he burns into their minds, so they will wish for tomorrow. But we are savages. The white man's dreams are hidden from us.

COMPREHENSION

1. What does Chief Seattle suggest is the major difference between the white man's relationship with nature and that of the red man?
2. Chief Seattle claims that perhaps the red man would understand the white man better if he understood better the "dreams" and "visions" of the white man. What does Chief Seattle suggest by these terms?
3. Chief Seattle refers to Native Americans as "savages." Why?

RHETORIC

1. The author uses a number of sensory details in describing both nature and the white man's crimes against nature. How does the eliciting of sensations help determine the relationship between writer, text, and reader?
2. The letter is written simply, with simply constructed paragraphs and sentences. What does this style suggest about the writer's voice?
3. There is a noted absence of transitional expressions in the writing, that is, such linking words as *in addition, furthermore, nevertheless, moreover.* How does this absence contribute to the directness of the writing?
4. The author uses the convention of the series, as in the following examples: "For all things share the same breath—the beasts, the trees, the man" (paragraph 2) and "When the buffalo are all slaughtered, the wild horses all tamed, the secret corners of the forest heavy with the scent of many men, and the view of the ripe hills blotted by talking wires" (paragraph 5). What is the rhetorical effect of this device?
5. Note the opening and closing sentences of the letter. How do they frame the letter? What do they suggest about one of the major themes of the letter?
6. Some scholars dispute the authenticity of the letter, attributing it to a white man who was attempting to articulate the essence of Chief Seattle's oratory in an effort to champion Native American causes. What elements of the letter resemble the rhetorical elements of a speech?

WRITING

1. Write a 250-word summary in which you compare and contrast the major differences between the white man's and the red man's perception of and relationship to nature as conceived by Chief Seattle.
2. Argue for or against the view that the charge by Chief Seattle that the white man is contemptuous of nature is still valid today. Use at least three points to support your thesis.
3. For a research project, trace the use of the word *savage* as it has been used to describe Native Americans.

The Stone Horse

Barry Lopez

Barry Lopez (b. 1945) was born in New York but spent much of his childhood in southern California. He received a BA from the University of Notre Dame and an MAT from the University of Oregon in 1968. His early writings appeared in such magazines as National Geographic, Antaeus, Wilderness, Science, *and* Harper's. *He has written both fiction and nonfiction including* Desert Notes: Reflections in the Eye of a Raven *(1976),* Of Wolves and Men *(1978),* Arctic Dreams: Imagination and Desire in a Northern Landscape *(1986),* Crossing Open Ground *(1988),* The Rediscovery of North America *(1991),* Crow & Weasel *(1999), and an autobiography,* About This Life *(1999). Lopez sees his role as a storyteller, someone who has the responsibility to create an atmosphere in which the wisdom of the work can reveal itself and "make the reader feel a part of something." In the following piece, from* Crossing Open Ground, *he focuses on an archaeological landmark to make a philosophical and moral inquiry into the way humans regard nature.*

I

The deserts of southern California, the high, relatively cooler and wetter Mojave 1 and the hotter, dryer Sonoran to the south of it, carry the signatures of many cultures. Prehistoric rock drawings in the Mojave's Coso Range, probably the greatest concentration of petroglyphs in North America, are at least three thousand years old. Big-game-hunting cultures that flourished six or seven thousand years before that are known from broken spear tips, choppers, and burins left scattered along the shores of great Pleistocene lakes, long since evaporated. Weapons and tools discovered at China Lake may be thirty thousand years old; and worked stone from a quarry in the Calico Mountains is, some argue, evidence that human beings were here more than 200,000 years ago.

Because of the long-term stability of such arid environments, much of this 2 prehistoric stone evidence still lies exposed on the ground, accessible to anyone who passes by—the studious, the acquisitive, the indifferent, the merely curious. Archaeologists do not agree on the sequence of cultural history beyond about twelve thousand years ago, but it is clear that these broken bits of chalcedony, chert, and obsidian, like the animal drawings and geometric designs etched on walls of basalt throughout the desert, anchor the earliest threads of human history, the first record of human endeavor here.

Western man did not enter the California desert until the end of the eigh- 3 teenth century, 250 years after Coronado brought his soldiers into the Zuni pueblos in a bewildered search for the cities of Cibola. The earliest appraisals of the land were cursory, hurried. People traveled *through* it, en route to Santa Fe or the California coastal settlements. Only miners tarried. In 1823 what had been Spain's became Mexico's, and in 1848 what had been Mexico's became America's; but the bare, jagged mountains and dry lake beds, the vast and uniform plains of creosote bush and yucca plants, remained as obscure as the northern Sudan until the end of the nineteenth century.

Before 1940 the tangible evidence of twentieth-century man's passage here 4 consisted of very little—the hard tracery of travel corridors; the widely scattered, relatively insignificant evidence of mining operations; and the fair expanse of irrigated fields at the desert's periphery. In the space of a hundred years or so the wagon roads were paved, railroads were laid down, and canals and high-tension lines were built to bring water and electricity across the desert to Los Angeles from the Colorado River. The dark mouths of gold, talc, and tin mines yawned from the bony flanks of desert ranges. Dust-encrusted chemical plants stood at work on the lonely edges of dry lake beds. And crops of grapes, lettuce, dates, alfalfa, and cotton covered the Coachella and Imperial valleys, north and south of the Salton Sea, and the Palo Verde Valley along the Colorado.

These developments proceeded with little or no awareness of earlier human 5 occupations by cultures that preceded those of the historic Indians—the Mohave, the Chemehuevi, the Quechan. (Extensive irrigation began actually to change the climate of the Sonoran Desert, and human settlements, the railroads, and farming introduced many new, successful plants into the region.)

During World War II, the American military moved into the desert in great 6 force, to train troops and to test equipment. They found the clear weather conducive to year-round flying, the dry air and isolation very attractive. After the war, a complex of training grounds, storage facilities, and gunnery and test ranges was permanently settled on more than three million acres of military reservations. Few perceived the extent or significance of the destruction of the aboriginal sites that took place during tank maneuvers and bombing runs or in the laying out of highways, railroads, mining districts, and irrigated fields. The few who intuited that something like an American Dordogne Valley lay exposed here were (only) amateur archaeologists; even they reasoned that the desert was too vast for any of this to matter.

After World War II, people began moving out of the crowded Los Angeles 7 basin into homes in Lucerne, Apple, and Antelope valleys in the western Mojave. They emigrated as well to a stretch of resort land at the foot of the San Jacinto Mountains that included Palm Springs, and farther out to old railroad and military towns like Twenty-nine Palms and Barstow. People also began exploring the desert, at first in military-surplus jeeps and then with a variety of all-terrain and off-road vehicles that became available in the 1960s. By the mid-1970s, the number of people using such vehicles for desert recreation had increased exponentially. Most came and went in innocent curiosity; the few who didn't wreaked a havoc all out of proportion to their numbers. The disturbance of previously isolated archaeological sites increased by an order of magnitude. Many sites were vandalized before archaeologists, themselves late to the desert, had any firm grasp of the bounds of human history in the desert. It was as though in the same moment an Aztec library had been discovered intact various lacunae had begun to appear.

The vandalism was of three sorts: the general disturbance usually caused 8 by souvenir hunters and by the curious and the oblivious; the wholesale stripping of a place by professional thieves for black-market sale and trade; and outright destruction, in which vehicles were actually used to ram and trench an area. By 1980, the Bureau of Land Management estimated that probably 35 percent of the archaeological sites in the desert had been vandalized. The destruction at some places by rifles and shotguns, or by power winches mounted on vehicles, was, if one cared for history, demoralizing to behold.

In spite of public education, land closures, and stricter law enforcement in 9 recent years, the BLM estimates that, annually, about 1 percent of the archaeological record in the desert continues to be destroyed or stolen.

II

A BLM archaeologist told me, with understandable reluctance, where to find 10 the intaglio. I spread my Automobile Club of Southern California map of Imperial County out on his desk, and he traced the route with a pink felt-tip pen. The line crossed Interstate 8 and then turned west along the Mexican border.

"You can't drive any farther than about here," he said, marking a small X. 11 "There's boulders in the wash. You walk up past them."

On a separate piece of paper he drew a route in a smaller scale that would 12 take me up the arroyo to a certain point where I was to cross back east, to another arroyo. At its head, on higher ground just to the north, I would find the horse.

"It's tough to spot unless you know it's there. Once you pick it up . . ." He 13 shook his head slowly, in a gesture of wonder at its existence.

I waited until I held his eye. I assured him I would not tell anyone else how 14 to get there. He looked at me with stoical despair, like a man who had been robbed twice, whose belief in human beings was offered without conviction.

I did not go until the following day because I wanted to see it at dawn. I ate 15 breakfast at four A.M. in El Centro and then drove south. The route was easy to follow, though the last section of road proved difficult, broken and drifted over with sand in some spots. I came to the barricade of boulders and parked. It was light enough by then to find my way over the ground with little trouble. The contours of the landscape were stark, without any masking vegetation. I worried only about rattlesnakes.

I traversed the stone plain as directed, but, in spite of the frankness of the 16 land, I came on the horse unawares. In the first moment of recognition I was without feeling. I recalled later being startled, and that I held my breath. It was laid out on the ground with its head to the east, three times life size. As I took in its outline I felt a growing concentration of all my senses, as though my attentiveness to the pale rose color of the morning sky and other peripheral images had now ceased to be important. I was aware that I was straining for sound in the windless air, and I felt the uneven pressure of the earth hard against my feet. The horse, outlined in a standing profile on the dark ground, was as vivid before me as a bed of tulips.

I've come upon animals suddenly before, and felt a similar tension, a pre- 17 cipitate heightening of the senses. And I have felt the inexplicable but sharply boosted intensity of a wild moment in the bush, where it is not until some minutes later that you discover the source of electricity—the warm remains of a grizzly bear kill, or the still moist tracks of a wolverine.

But this was slightly different. I felt I had stepped into an unoccupied corri- 18 dor. I had no familiar sense of history, the temporal structure in which to think: This horse was made by Quechan people three hundred years ago. I felt instead a headlong rush of images: people hunting wild horses with spears on the Pleistocene veld of southern California; Cortés riding across the causeway into Montezuma's Tenochtitlán; a short-legged Comanche, astride his horse like some sort of ferret, slashing through cavalry lines of young men who rode like farmers; a hood exploding past my face one morning in a corral in Wyoming. These images had the weight and silence of stone.

When I released my breath, the images softened. My initial feeling, of fac- 19 ing a wild animal in a remote region, was replaced with a calm sense of antiquity. It was then that I became conscious, like an ordinary tourist, of what was before me, and thought: this horse was probably laid out by Quechan people. But when? I wondered. The first horses they saw, I knew, might have been those that came north from Mexico in 1692 with Father Eusebio Kino. But Cocopa people, I recalled, also came this far north on occasion, to fight with their neighbors, the Quechan. And *they* could have seen horses with Melchior Diaz, at the mouth of the Colorado River in the fall of 1540. So, it could be four hundred years old. (No one in fact knows.)

I still had not moved. I took my eyes off the horse for a moment to look 20 south over the desert plain into Mexico, to look east past its head at the brightening sunrise, to situate myself. Then, finally, I brought my trailing foot slowly forward and stood erect. Sunlight was running like a thin sheet of water over the stony ground and it threw the horse into relief. It looked as though no hand had ever disturbed the stones that gave it its form.

The horse had been brought to life on ground called desert pavement, a 21 tight, flat matrix of small cobbles blasted smooth by sand-laden winds. The uniform, monochromatic blackness of the stones, a patina of iron and magnesium oxides called desert varnish, is caused by long-term exposure to the sun. To make this type of low-relief ground glyph, or intaglio, the artist either selectively turns individual stones over to their lighter side or removes areas of stone to expose the lighter soil underneath, creating a negative image. This horse, about eighteen feet from brow to rump and eight feet from withers to hoof, had been made in the latter way, and its outline was bermed at certain points with low ridges of stone a few inches high to enhance its three-dimensional qualities. (The left side of the horse was in full profile; each leg was extended at 90 degrees to the body and fully visible, as though seen in three-quarter profile.)

I was not eager to move. The moment I did I would be back in the flow of   22
time, the horse no longer quivering in the same way before me. I did not want
to feel again the sequence of quotidian events—to be drawn off into deliberation and analysis. A human being, a four-footed animal, the open land. That
was all that was present—and a "thoughtless" understanding of the very old
desires bearing on this particular animal: to hunt it, to render it, to fathom it, to
subjugate it, to honor it, to take it as a companion.

What finally made me move was the light. The sun now filled the shallow   23
basin of the horse's body. The weighted line of the stone berm created the illusion of a mane and the distinctive roundness of an equine belly. The change in
definition impelled me. I moved to the left, circling past its rump, to see how the
light might flesh the horse out from various points of view. I circled it completely before squatting on my haunches. Ten or fifteen minutes later I chose another view. The third time I moved, to a point near the rear hooves, I spotted a
stone tool at my feet. I stared at it a long while, more in awe than disbelief, before reaching out to pick it up. I turned it over in my left palm and took it between my fingers to feel its cutting edge. It is always difficult, especially with
something so portable, to rechannel the desire to steal.

I spent several hours with the horse. As I changed positions and as the an-   24
gle of the light continued to change I noticed a number of things. The angle at
which the pastern carried the hoof away from the ankle was perfect. Also,
stones had been placed within the image to suggest at precisely the right spot
the left shoulder above the foreleg. The line that joined thigh and hock was similarly accurate. The muzzle alone seemed distorted—but perhaps these stones
had been moved by a later hand. It was an admirably accurate representation,
but not what a breeder would call perfect conformation. There was the suggestion of a bowed neck and an undershot jaw, and the tail, as full as a winter coyote's, did not appear to be precisely to scale.

The more I thought about it, the more I felt I was looking at an individual   25
horse, a unique combination of generic and specific detail. It was easy to imagine one of Kino's horses as a model, or a horse that ran off from one of Coronado's columns. What kind of horses would these have been? I wondered. In the
sixteenth century the most sought-after horses in Europe were Spanish, the offspring of Arabian stock and Barbary horses that the Moors brought to Iberia
and bred to the older, eastern European strains brought in by the Romans. The
model for this horse, I speculated, could easily have been a palomino, or a descendant of horses trained for lion hunting in North Africa.

A few generations ago, cowboys, cavalry quartermasters, and draymen   26
would have taken this horse before me under consideration and not let up their
scrutiny until they had its heritage fixed to their satisfaction. Today, the distinction between draft and harness horses is arcane knowledge, and no image may
come to mind for a blue roan or a claybank horse. The loss of such refinement in
everyday conversation leaves me unsettled. People praise the Eskimo's ability to
distinguish among forty types of snow but forget the skill of others who routinely
differentiate between overo and tobiano pintos. Such distinctions are made for the
same reason. You have to do it to be able to talk clearly about the world.

For parts of two years I worked as a horse wrangler and packer in 27
Wyoming. It is dim knowledge now; I would have to think to remember if a
buckskin was a kind of dun horse. And I couldn't throw a double-diamond
hitch over a set of panniers—the packer's basic tie-down—without guidance.
As I squatted there in the desert, however, these more personal memories
seemed tenuous in comparison with the sweep of this animal in human time.
My memories had no depth. I thought of the Hittite cavalry riding against the
Syrians 3,500 years ago. And the first of the Chinese emperors, Ch'in Shih
Huang, buried in Shensi Province in 210 B.C. with thousands of life-size horses
and soldiers, a terra-cotta guardian army. What could I know of what was
in the mind of whoever made this horse? Was there some racial memory of it as
an animal that had once fed the artist's ancestors and then disappeared from
North America? And then returned in this strange alliance with another race
of men?

Certainly, whoever it was, the artist had observed the animal very closely. 28
Certainly the animal's speed had impressed him. Among the first things the
Quechan would have learned from an encounter with Kino's horses was that
their own long-distance runners—men who could run down mule deer—were
no match for this animal.

From where I squatted I could look far out over the Mexican plain. Juan 29
Bautista de Anza passed this way in 1774, extending El Camino Real into Alta
California from Sinaloa. He was followed by others, all of them astride the magical horse; *gente de razón*, the people of reason, coming into the country of *los
primitivos*. The horse, like the stone animals of Egypt, urged these memories
upon me. And as I drew them up from some forgotten corner of my mind—
huge horses carved in the white chalk downs of southern England by an Iron
Age people; Spanish horses rearing and wheeling in fear before alligators in
Florida—the images seemed tethered before me. With this sense of proportion,
a memory of my own—the morning I almost lost my face to a horse's hoof—
now had somewhere to fit.

I rose up and began to walk slowly around the horse again. I had taken the 30
first long measure of it and was now looking for a way to depart, a new angle
of light, a fading of the image itself before the rising sun, that would break its
hold on me. As I circled, feeling both heady and serene at the encounter, I realized again how strangely vivid it was. It had been created on a barren bajada
between two arroyos, as nondescript a place as one could imagine. The only
plant life here was a few wands of ocotillo cactus. The ground beneath my shoes
was so hard it wouldn't take the print of a heavy animal even after a rain. The
only sounds I heard here were the voices of quail.

The archaeologist had been correct. For all its forcefulness, the horse is 31
inconspicuous. If you don't care to see it you can walk right past it. That pleases
him, I think. Unmarked on the bleak shoulder of the plain, the site signals to no
one; so he wants no protective fences here, no informative plaque, to act as bea-
cons. He would rather take a chance that no motorcyclist, no aimless wanderer
with a flair for violence and a depth of ignorance, will ever find his way here.

The archaeologist had given me something before I left his office that now ₃₂ seemed peculiar—an aerial photograph of the horse. It is widely believed that an aerial view of an intaglio provides a fair and accurate depiction. It does not. In the photograph the horse looks somewhat crudely constructed; from the ground it appears far more deftly rendered. The photograph is of a single moment, and in that split second the horse seems vaguely impotent. I watched light pool in the intaglio at dawn; I imagine you could watch it withdraw at dusk and sense the same animation I did. In those prolonged moments its shape and so, too, its general character change—noticeably The living quality of the image, its immediacy to the eye, was brought out by the light-in-time, not, at least here, in the camera's frozen instant.

Intaglios, I thought, were never meant to be seen by gods in the sky above. ₃₃ They were meant to be seen by people on the ground, over a long period of shifting light. This could even be true of the huge figures on the Plain of Nazca in Peru, where people could walk for the length of a day beside them. It is our own impatience that leads us to think otherwise.

This process of abstraction, almost unintentional, drew me gradually away ₃₄ from the horse. I came to a position of attention at the edge of the sphere of its influence. With a slight bow I paid my respects to the horse, its maker, and the history of us all, and departed.

III

A short distance away I stopped the car in the middle of the road to make a few ₃₅ notes. I could not write down what I was thinking when I was with the horse. It would have seemed disrespectful, and it would have required another kind of attention. So now I patiently drained my memory of the details it had fastened itself upon. The road I'd stopped on was adjacent to the All American Canal, the major source of water for the Imperial and Coachella valleys. The water flowed west placidly. A disjointed flock of coots, small, dark birds with white bills, was paddling against the current, foraging in the rushes.

I was peripherally aware of the birds as I wrote, the only movement in the ₃₆ desert, and of a series of sounds from a village a half-mile away. The first sounds from this collection of ramshackle houses in a grove of cottonwoods were the distracted dawn voices of dogs. I heard them intermingled with the cries of a rooster. Later, the high-pitched voices of children calling out to each other came disembodied through the dry desert air. Now, a little after seven, I could hear someone practicing on the trumpet, the same rough phrases played over and over. I suddenly remembered how as children we had tried to get the rhythm of a galloping horse with hands against our thighs, or by fluttering our tongues against the roofs of our mouths.

After the trumpet, the impatient calls of adults summoning children. Sun- ₃₇ day morning. Wood smoke hung like a lens in the trees. The first car starts—a cold eight-cylinder engine, of Chrysler extraction perhaps, goosed to life, then throttled back to murmur through dual mufflers, the obbligato music of a shade-tree mechanic. The rote bark of mongrel dogs at dawn, the jagged out-cries of men and women, an engine coming to life. Like a thousand villages from West Virginia to Guadalajara.

I finished my notes—where was I going to find a description of the horses 38 that came north with the conquistadors? Did their manes come forward promi-nently over the brow, like this one's, like the forelocks of Blackfeet and Assini-boin men in nineteenth-century paintings? I set the notes on the seat beside me.

The road followed the canal for a while and then arced north, toward Inter- 39 state 8. It was slow driving and I fell to thinking how the desert had changed since Anza had come through. New plants and animals—the MacDougall cot-tonwood, the English house sparrow, the chukar from India—have about them now the air of the native born. Of the native species, some—no one knows how many—are extinct. The populations of many others, especially the animals, have been sharply reduced. The idea of a desert impoverished by agricultural poisons and varmint hunters, by off-road vehicles and military operations, did not seem as disturbing to me, however, as this other horror, now that I had been those hours with the horse. The vandals, the few who crowbar rock art off the desert's walls, who dig up graves, who punish the ground that holds intaglios, are people who devour history. Their self-centered scorn, their disrespect for ideas and images beyond their ken, create the awful atmosphere of loose ends in which totalitarianism thrives, in which the past is merely curious or wrong.

I thought about the horse sitting out there on the unprotected plain. I enu- 40 merated its qualities in my mind until a sense of its vulnerability receded and it became an anchor for something else. I remembered that history, a history like this one, which ran deeper than Mexico, deeper than the Spanish, was a kind of medicine. It permitted the great breadth of human expression to reverberate, and it did not urge you to locate its apotheosis in the present.

Each of us, individuals and civilizations, has been held upside down like 41 Achilles in the River Styx. The artist mixing his colors in the dim light of Al-tamira; an Egyptian ruler lying still now, wrapped in his byssus, stored against time in a pyramid; the faded Dorset culture of the Arctic; the Hmong and Sam-buru and Walbiri of historic time; the modern nations. This great, imperfect stretch of human expression is the clarification and encouragement, the urging and the reminder, we call history. And it is inscribed everywhere in the face of the land, from the mountain passes of the Himalayas to a nameless bajada in the California desert.

Small birds rose up in the road ahead, startled, and flew off. I prayed no 42 infidel would ever find that horse.

COMPREHENSION

1. What is Lopez's primary purpose in this essay? How does its title relate to the purpose?

2. Does Lopez assume his audience has the same value position as he does? Does he assume it has a commensurate background in anthropology, history, and ecology? Explain your answer.

3. What provides Lopez with the most compelling evidence that humans have a history? Base your answer on the author's statement in paragraph 41: "This great, imperfect stretch of human expression is the clarification and encouragement, the origin and the reminder, we call history."

RHETORIC

1. How would you characterize the tone of this essay? Does the tone remain constant or does it change? Can you connect the tone with Lopez's thesis?

2. Lopez has chosen to divide his essay into three sections. Why is that decision appropriate to his strategy? How does the structure relate to the overall development of his theme?

3. While Lopez inspects the "horse," he describes it in detail. Next, he experiences a change in emotion and thinking. How does his erudition concerning history and anthropology enrich his emotional response? Explain the rhetorical progression from description to response and reflection in paragraphs 19 to 28.

4. Define the following terms: *petroglyphs* (paragraph 1), *intaglio* (paragraph 10), *arroyo* (paragraph 12), *glyph* (paragraph 21), *pastern* (paragraph 24), *conquistadors* (paragraph 38), and *totalitarianism* (paragraph 39).

5. Why does Lopez end this substantial essay with such a brief conclusion? Why has the author juxtaposed the presence of "birds" and the fear of the "infidel" in his conclusion?

6. There is a marked change in "atmosphere" between sections 2 and 3. What is this change? How does Lopez express it? What does it signify?

7. How does Lopez demonstrate a sense of authority on his subject matter? Does it stem naturally from the flow of his writing or is it superimposed? Explain your response.

WRITING

1. Write a descriptive/narrative essay about a personal experience in an environment that made you feel as though you were experiencing a place with implications greater than yourself, for example, a setting in nature, a church, sports arena or stadium during a game, a concert, and so on.

2. Write an essay in which you argue for or against the public's right to gain access to archeological sites for study.

3. Argue for or against the proposition that the American system of values encourages people to despoil, destroy, or neglect historical sites and structures.

Classic and Contemporary:
Questions for Comparison

1. Chief Seattle and Barry Lopez decry the destruction of nature as a physical and spiritual presence. In what ways are their stakes in this destruction the same? In what ways are they different? Does either writer have more power to effect a transformation in our attitude toward nature? Explain.
2. It has often been said that intellectual knowledge changes one's relationship with the world environment. In what ways has Lopez's "book learning" and erudition made him a different person from Chief Seattle? Base your response on the style and tone of each author.
3. Chief Seattle is literally the leader and spokesperson of a defeated nation. How does he preserve his dignity in the face of being conquered? How does he indicate to the white man that his "victory" is temporary? Lopez, on the other hand, is a successful member of his society: esteemed naturalist, award-winning writer, popular lecturer. What prevents him from reaping the benefits of his accomplishments? Explain by referring to the text.

The Obligation to Endure

Rachel Carson

Rachel Carson (1907–1964) was a seminal figure in the environmental movement. Born in Pennsylvania, she awakened public consciousness to environmental issues through her writing. Her style was both literary and scientific as she described nature's riches in such books as The Sea Around Us *(1951) and* The Edge of the Sea *(1954). Her last book,* Silent Spring *(1962), aroused controversy and concern with its indictment of insecticides. In the following excerpt from that important book, Carson provides compelling evidence of the damage caused by indiscriminate use of insecticides and the danger of disturbing the earth's delicate balance.*

The history of life on earth has been a history of interaction between living things and their surroundings. To a large extent, the physical form and the habits of the earth's vegetation and its animal life have been molded by the environment. Considering the whole span of earthly time, the opposite effect, in which life actually modifies its surroundings, has been relatively slight. Only within the moment of time represented by the present century has one species—man—acquired significant power to alter the nature of his world.

During the past quarter century this power has not only increased to one of disturbing magnitude but it has changed in character. The most alarming of all man's assaults upon the environment is the contamination of air, earth, rivers, and sea with dangerous and even lethal materials. This pollution is for the most part irrecoverable; the chain of evil it initiates not only in the world that must support life but in living tissues is for the most part irreversible. In this now universal contamination of the environment, chemicals are the sinister and little-recognized partners of radiation in changing the very nature of the world—the very nature of its life. Strontium 90, released through nuclear explosions into the air, comes to earth in rain or drifts down as fallout, lodges in soil, enters into the grass or corn or wheat grown there, and in time takes up its abode in the bones of a human being, there to remain until his death. Similarly, chemicals sprayed on croplands or forests or gardens lie long in soil, entering into living organisms, passing from one to another in a chain of poisoning and death. Or they pass mysteriously by underground streams until they emerge and, through the alchemy of air and sunlight, combine into new forms that kill vegetation, sicken cattle, and work unknown harm on those who drink from once pure wells. As Albert Schweitzer has said, "Man can hardly even recognize the devils of his own creation."

It took hundreds of millions of years to produce the life that now inhabits 3 the earth—eons of time in which that developing and evolving and diversifying life reached a state of adjustment and balance with its surroundings. The environment, rigorously shaping and directing the life it supported, contained elements that were hostile as well as supporting. Certain rocks gave out dangerous radiation; even within the light of the sun, from which all life draws its energy, there were shortwave radiations with power to injure. Given time—time not in years but in millennia—life adjusts, and a balance has been reached. For time is the essential ingredient; but in the modern world there is no time.

The rapidity of change and the speed with which new situations are created 4 follow the impetuous and heedless pace of man rather than the deliberate pace of nature. Radiation is no longer merely the background radiation of rocks, the bombardment of cosmic rays, the ultraviolet of the sun that have existed before there was any life on earth; radiation is now the unnatural creation of man's tampering with the atom. The chemicals to which life is asked to make its adjustment are no longer merely the calcium and silica and copper and all the rest of the minerals washed out of the rocks and carried in rivers to the sea; they are the synthetic creations of man's inventive mind, brewed in his laboratories, and having no counterparts in nature.

To adjust to these chemicals would require time on the scale that is nature's; 5 it would require not merely the years of a man's life but the life of generations. And even this, were it by some miracle possible, would be futile, for the new chemicals come from our laboratories in an endless stream; almost five hundred annually find their way into actual use in the United States alone. The figure is staggering and its implications are not easily grasped—500 new chemicals to which the bodies of men and animals are required somehow to adapt each year, chemicals totally outside the limits of biologic experience.

Among them are many that are used in man's war against nature. Since the 6 mid-1940's over 200 basic chemicals have been created for use in killing insects, weeds, rodents, and other organisms described in the modern vernacular as "pests"; and they are sold under several thousand different brand names.

These sprays, dusts, and aerosols are now applied almost universally to farms, gardens, forests, and homes—nonselective chemicals that have the power to kill every insect, the "good" and the "bad," to still the song of birds and the leaping of fish in the streams, to coat the leaves with a deadly film, and to linger on in soil—all this though the intended target may be only a few weeds or insects. Can anyone believe it is possible to lay down such a barrage of poisons on the surface of the earth without making it unfit for all life? They should not be called "insecticides," but "biocides." 7

The whole process of spraying seems caught up in an endless spiral. Since DDT was released for civilian use, a process of escalation has been going on in which ever more toxic materials must be found. This has happened because insects, in a triumphant vindication of Darwin's principle of the survival of the fittest, have evolved super races immune to the particular insecticide used, hence a deadlier one has always to be developed—and then a deadlier one than that. It has happened also because, for reasons to be described later, destructive insects often undergo a "flareback," or resurgence, after spraying in numbers greater than before. Thus the chemical war is never won, and all life is caught in its violent crossfire. 8

Along with the possibility of the extinction of mankind by nuclear war, the central problem of our age has therefore become the contamination of man's total environment with such substances of incredible potential for harm—substances that accumulate in the tissues of plants and animals and even penetrate the germ cells to shatter or alter the very material of heredity upon which the shape of the future depends. 9

Some would-be architects of our future look toward a time when it will be possible to alter the human germ plasm by design. But we may easily be doing so now by inadvertence, for many chemicals, like radiation, bring about gene mutations. It is ironic to think that man might determine his own future by something so seemingly trivial as the choice of an insect spray. 10

All this has been risked—for what? Future historians may well be amazed by our distorted sense of proportion. How could intelligent beings seek to control a few unwanted species by a method that contaminated the entire environment and brought the threat of disease and death even to their own kind? Yet this is precisely what we have done. We have done it, moreover, for reasons that collapse the moment we examine them. We are told that the enormous and expanding use of pesticides is necessary to maintain farm production. Yet is our real problem not one of *overproduction*? Our farms, despite measures to remove acreages from production and to pay farmers *not* to produce, have yielded such a staggering excess of crops that the American taxpayer in 1962 is paying out more than one billion dollars a year as the total carrying cost of the surplus-food storage program. And is the situation helped when one branch of the Agriculture Department tries to reduce production while another states, as it did in 1958, "It is believed generally that reduction of crop acreages under provisions 11 of the Soil Bank will stimulate interest in use of chemicals to obtain maximum production on the land retained in crops."

All this is not to say there is no insect problem and no need of control. I am 12 saying, rather, that control must be geared to realities, not to mythical situations, and that the methods employed must be such that they do not destroy us along with the insects.

The problem whose attempted solution has brought such a train of disaster in 13 its wake is an accompaniment of our modern way of life. Long before the age of man, insects inhabited the earth—a group of extraordinarily varied and adaptable beings. Over the course of time since man's advent, a small percentage of the more than half a million species of insects have come into conflict with human welfare in two principal ways: as competitors for the food supply and as carriers of human disease.

Disease-carrying insects become important where human beings are 14 crowded together, especially under conditions where sanitation is poor, as in times of natural disaster or war or in situations of extreme poverty and deprivation. Then control of some sort becomes necessary. It is a sobering fact, however, as we shall presently see, that the method of massive chemical control has had only limited success, and also threatens to worsen the very conditions it is intended to curb.

Under primitive agricultural conditions the farmer had few insect prob- 15 lems. These arose with the intensification of agriculture—the devotion of immense acreages to a single crop. Such a system set the stage for explosive increases in specific insect populations. Single-crop farming does not take advantage of the principles by which nature works; it is agriculture as an engineer might conceive it to be. Nature has introduced great variety into the landscape, but man has displayed a passion for simplifying it. Thus he undoes the built-in checks and balances by which nature holds the species within bounds. One important natural check is a limit on the amount of suitable habitat for each species. Obviously then, an insect that lives on wheat can build up its population to much higher levels on a farm devoted to wheat than on one in which wheat is intermingled with other crops to which the insect is not adapted.

The same thing happens in other situations. A generation or more ago, the 16 towns of large areas of the United States lined their streets with the noble elm tree. Now the beauty they hopefully created is threatened with complete destruction as disease sweeps through the elms, carried by a beetle that would have only limited chance to build up large populations and to spread from tree to tree if the elms were only occasional trees in a richly diversified planting.

Another factor in the modern insect problem is one that must be viewed 17 against a background of geologic and human history: the spreading of thousands of different kinds of organisms from their native homes to invade new territories. This worldwide migration has been studied and graphically described by the British ecologist Charles Elton in his recent book *The Ecology of Invasions.* During the Cretaceous Period, some hundred million years ago, flooding seas cut many land bridges between continents and living things found themselves confined in what Elton calls "colossal separate nature reserves." There, isolated from others of their kind, they developed many new species. When some of the land masses were joined again, about 15 million years ago, these species began to move out into new territories—a movement that is not only still in progress but is now receiving considerable assistance from man.

The importation of plants is the primary agent in the modern spread of 18 species, for animals have almost invariably gone along with the plants, quarantine being a comparatively recent and not completely effective innovation. The United States Office of Plant Introduction alone has introduced almost 200,000 species and varieties of plants from all over the world. Nearly half of the 180 or so major insect enemies of plants in the United States are accidental imports from abroad, and most of them have come as hitchhikers on plants.

In new territory, out of reach of the restraining hand of the natural enemies 19 that kept down its numbers in its native land, an invading plant or animal is able to become enormously abundant. Thus it is no accident that our most troublesome insects are introduced species.

These invasions, both the naturally occurring and those dependent on 20 human assistance, are likely to continue indefinitely. Quarantine and massive chemical campaigns are only extremely expensive ways of buying time. We are faced, according to Dr. Elton, "with a life-and-death need not just to find new technological means of suppressing this plant or that animal"; instead we need the basic knowledge of animal populations and their relations to their surroundings that will "promote an even balance and damp down the explosive power of outbreaks and new invasions."

Much of the necessary knowledge is now available but we do not use it. We 21 train ecologists in our universities and even employ them in our governmental agencies but we seldom take their advice. We allow the chemical death rain to fall as though there were no alternative, whereas in fact there are many, and our ingenuity could soon discover many more if given opportunity.

Have we fallen into a mesmerized state that makes us accept as inevitable 22 that which is inferior or detrimental, as though having lost the will or the vision to demand that which is good? Such thinking, in the words of the ecologist Paul Shepard, "idealizes life with only its head out of water, inches above the limits of toleration of the corruption of its own environment. . . . Why should we tolerate a diet of weak poisons, a home in insipid surroundings, a circle of acquaintances who are not quite our enemies, the noise of motors with just enough relief to prevent insanity? Who would want to live in a world which is just not quite fatal?"

Yet such a world is pressed upon us. The crusade to create a chemically sterile, insect-free world seems to have engendered a fanatic zeal on the part of 23 many specialists and most of the so-called control agencies. On every hand there is evidence that those engaged in spraying operations exercise a ruthless power. "The regulatory entomologists . . . function as prosecutor, judge and jury, tax assessor and collector and sheriff to enforce their own orders," said Connecticut entomologist Neely Turner. The most flagrant abuses go unchecked in both state and federal agencies.

It is not my contention that chemical insecticides must never be used. I do contend that we have put poisonous and biologically potent chemicals indiscriminately into the hands of persons largely or wholly ignorant of their potentials for harm. We have subjected enormous numbers of people to contact with these poisons, without their consent and often without their knowledge. If the Bill of Rights contains no guarantee that a citizen shall be secure against lethal poisons distributed either by private individuals or by public officials, it is surely only because our forefathers, despite their considerable wisdom and foresight, could conceive of no such problem.

I contend, furthermore, that we have allowed these chemicals to be used with little or no advance investigation of their effect on soil, water, wildlife, and man himself. Future generations are unlikely to condone our lack of prudent concern for the integrity of the natural world that supports all life.

There is still very limited awareness of the nature of the threat. This is an era of specialists, each of whom sees his own problem and is unaware of or intolerant of the larger frame into which it fits. It is also an era dominated by industry, in which the right to make a dollar at whatever cost is seldom challenged. When the public protests, confronted with some obvious evidence of damaging results of pesticide applications, it is fed little tranquilizing pills of half truth. We urgently need an end to these false assurances, to the sugar coating of unpalatable facts. It is the public that is being asked to assume the risks that the insect controllers calculate. The public must decide whether it wishes to continue on the present road, and it can do so only when in full possession of the facts. In the words of Jean Rostand, "The obligation to endure gives us the right to know."

COMPREHENSION

1. What does Carson mean by "the obligation to endure"?
2. What reasons does the author cite for the overpopulation of insects?
3. What remedies does Carson propose?

RHETORIC

1. What tone does Carson use in her essay? Does she seem to be a subjective or an objective speaker? Give specific support for your response.
2. How does the use of words such as *dangerous, evil, irrevocable,* and *sinister* help shape the reader's reaction to the piece?
3. Examine the ordering of ideas in paragraph 4, and consider how such an order serves to reinforce Carson's argument.
4. Paragraph 9 consists of only one sentence. What is its function in the essay's scheme?

5. Examine Carson's use of expert testimony. How does it help strengthen her thesis?
6. How effectively does the essay's conclusion help tie up Carson's points? What is the writer's intent in this final paragraph? How does she accomplish this aim?

WRITING

1. Write an essay in which you suggest solutions to the problems brought up in Carson's piece. You may want to suggest measures that the average citizen can take to eliminate the casual use of insecticides to control the insect population.
2. Write an essay entitled "Insects Are Not the Problem; Humanity Is." In this essay, argue that it is humanity's greed that has caused such an imbalance in nature as to threaten the planet's survival.
3. Write a biographical research paper on Rachel Carson that focuses on her involvement with nature and environmental issues.

Am I Blue?

Alice Walker

Alice Walker (b. 1944) was born in Eatonton, Georgia, attended Spellman College, and graduated from Sarah Lawrence College. Besides being a prolific novelist, short story writer, poet, and essayist, she has also been active in the civil rights movement. She often draws on both her own history and historical records to reflect on the African American experience. Some of her well-known books are The Color Purple *(1976),* You Can't Keep a Good Woman Down *(1981),* Living in the World: Selected Writings, 1973–1987 *(1987),* The Temple of My Familiar *(1989),* By the Light of My Father's Smile *(1999), and* The Way Forward Is with a Broken Heart *(2001). In the following essay from* Living in the World, *Walker questions the distinctions commonly made between human and animal.*

For about three years my companion and I rented a small house in the country   1
that stood on the edge of a large meadow that appeared to run from the end of
our deck straight into the mountains. The mountains, however, were quite far
away, and between us and them there was, in fact, a town. It was one of the
many pleasant aspects of the house that you never really were aware of this.

It was a house of many windows, low, wide, nearly floor to ceiling in the   2
living room, which faced the meadow, and it was from one of these that I first

saw our closest neighbor, a large white horse, cropping grass, flipping its mane, and ambling about—not over the entire meadow, which stretched well out of sight of the house, but over the five or so fenced-in acres that were next to the twenty-odd that we had rented. I soon learned that the horse, whose name was Blue, belonged to a man who lived in another town, but was boarded by our neighbors next door. Occasionally, one of the children, usually a stocky teenager, but sometimes a much younger girl or boy, could be seen riding Blue. They would appear in the meadow, climb up on his back, ride furiously for ten or fifteen minutes, then get off, slap Blue on the flanks, and not be seen again for a month or more.

There were many apple trees in our yard, and one by the fence that Blue ₃ could almost reach. We were soon in the habit of feeding him apples, which he relished, especially because by the middle of summer the meadow grasses—so green and succulent since January—had dried out from lack of rain, and Blue stumbled about munching the dried stalks half-heartedly. Sometimes he would stand very still just by the apple tree, and when one of us came out he would whinny, snort loudly, or stamp the ground. This meant, of course: I want an apple.

It was quite wonderful to pick a few apples, or collect those that had fallen ₄ to the ground overnight, and patiently hold them, one by one, up to his large, toothy mouth. I remained as thrilled as a child by his flexible dark lips, huge, cubelike teeth that crunched the apples, core and all, with such finality, and his high, broad-breasted *enormity*; beside which, I felt small indeed. When I was a child, I used to ride horses, and was especially friendly with one named Nan until the day I was riding and my brother deliberately spooked her and I was thrown, head first, against the trunk of a tree. When I came to, I was in bed and my mother was bending worriedly over me; we silently agreed that perhaps horseback riding was not the safest sport for me. Since then I have walked, and prefer walking to horseback riding—but I had forgotten the depth of feeling one could see in horses' eyes.

I was therefore unprepared for the expression in Blue's. Blue was lonely. ₅ Blue was horribly lonely and bored. I was not shocked that this should be the case; five acres to tramp by yourself, endlessly, even in the most beautiful of meadows—and his was—cannot provide many interesting events, and once the rainy season turned to dry that was about it. No, I was shocked that I had forgotten that human animals and nonhuman animals can communicate quite well; if we are brought up around animals as children we take this for granted. By the time we are adults we no longer remember. However, the animals have not changed. They are in fact *completed* creations (at least they seem to be, so much more than we) who are not likely *to* change; it is their nature to express themselves. What else are they going to express? And they do. And, generally speaking, they are ignored.

After giving Blue the apples, I would wander back to the house, aware that ₆ he was observing me. Were more apples not forthcoming then? Was that to be his sole entertainment for the day? My partner's small son had decided he wanted to learn how to piece a quilt; we worked in silence on our respective squares as I thought . . .

Well, about slavery: about white children, who were raised by black people, who knew their first all-accepting love from black women, and then, when they were twelve or so, were told they must "forget" the deep levels of communication between themselves and "mammy" that they knew. Later they would be able to relate quite calmly, "My old mammy was sold to another good family." "My old mammy was _____." Fill in the blank. Many more years later a white woman would say: "I can't understand these Negroes, these blacks. What do they want? They're so different from us." 7

And about the Indians, considered to be "like animals" by the "settlers" (a very benign euphemism for what they actually were), who did not understand their description as a compliment. 8

And about the thousands of American men who marry Japanese, Korean, Filipina, and other non-English-speaking women and of how happy they report they are, "blissfully," until their brides learn to speak English, at which point the marriages tend to fall apart. What then did the men see, when they looked into the eyes of the women they married, before they could speak English? Apparently only their own reflections. 9

I thought of society's impatience with the young. "Why are they playing the music so loud?" Perhaps the children have listened to much of the music of oppressed people their parents danced to before they were born, with its passionate but soft cries for acceptance and love, and they have wondered why their parents failed to hear. 10

I do not know how long Blue had inhabited his five beautiful, boring acres before we moved into our house; a year after we had arrived—and had also traveled to other valleys, other cities, other worlds—he was still there. 11

But then, in our second year at the house, something happened in Blue's life. One morning, looking out the window at the fog that lay like a ribbon over the meadow, I saw another horse, a brown one, at the other end of Blue's field. Blue appeared to be afraid of it, and for several days made no attempt to go near. We went away for a week. When we returned, Blue had decided to make friends and the two horses ambled or galloped along together, and Blue did not come nearly as often to the fence underneath the apple tree. 12

When he did, bringing his new friend with him, there was a different look in his eyes. A look of independence, of self-possession, of inalienable *horse*ness. His friend eventually became pregnant. For months and months there was, it seemed to me, a mutual feeling between me and the horses of justice, of peace. I fed apples to them both. The took in Blue's eyes was one of unabashed "this is *it*ness." 13

It did not, however, last forever. One day, after a visit to the city, I went out to give Blue some apples. He stood waiting, or so I thought, though not beneath the tree. When I shook the tree and jumped back from the shower of apples, he made no move. I carried some over to him. He managed to half-crunch one. The rest he let fall to the ground. I dreaded looking into his eyes—because I had of course noticed that Brown, his partner, had gone—but I did look. If I had been 14 born into slavery, and my partner had been sold or killed, my eyes would have looked like that. The children next door explained that Blue's partner had been "put with him" (the same expression that old people used, I had noticed, when speaking of an ancestor during slavery who had been impregnated by her owner) so that they could mate and she conceive. Since that was accomplished, she had been taken back by her owner, who lived somewhere else.

Will she be back? I asked.   15

They didn't know.   16

Blue was like a crazed person. Blue *was*, to me, a crazed person. He gal- 17 loped furiously, as if he were being ridden, around and around his five beautiful acres. He whinnied until he couldn't. He tore at the ground with his hooves. He butted himself against his single shade tree. He looked always and always toward the road down which his partner had gone. And then, occasionally, when he came up for apples, or I took apples to him, he looked at me. It was a look so piercing, so full of grief, a look so *human*, I almost laughed (I felt too sad to cry) to think there are people who do not know that animals suffer. People like me who have forgotten, and daily forget, all that animals try to tell us. "Everything you do to us will happen to you; we are your teachers, as you are ours. We are one lesson" is essentially it, I think. There are those who never once have even considered animals' rights: those who have been taught that animals actually want to be used and abused by us, as small children "love" to be frightened, or women "love" to be mutilated and raped. . . . They are the great-grandchildren of those who honestly thought, because someone taught them this: "Woman can't think" and "niggers can't faint." But most disturbing of all, in Blue's large brown eyes was a new look, more painful than the look of despair: the look of disgust with human beings, with life; the look of hatred. And it was odd what the look of hatred did. It gave him, for the first time, the look of a beast. And what that meant was that he had put up a barrier within to protect himself from further violence; all the apples in the world wouldn't change that fact.

And so Blue remained, a beautiful part of our landscape, very peaceful to 18 look at from the window, white against the grass. Once a friend came to visit and said, looking out on the soothing view: "And it *would* have to be a *white* horse; the very image of freedom." And I thought, yes, the animals are forced to become for us merely "images" of what they once so beautifully expressed. And we are used to drinking milk from containers showing "contented" cows, whose real lives we want to hear nothing about, eating eggs and drumsticks from "happy" hens, and munching hamburgers advertised by bulls of integrity who seem to command their fate.

As we talked of freedom and justice one day for all, we sat down to steaks. 19 I am eating misery, I thought, as I took the first bite. And spit it out.

COMPREHENSION

1. What is the major thesis of the essay? Is it stated explicitly in the text or does one have to infer it? Explain.

2. In paragraph 5, Walker states that animals are *"completed* creations (at least they seem to be, so much more than we) who are not likely to change." What does she mean by making this distinction between animals and humans?
3. What is the significance of the title of the essay? Does it have more than one meaning? Explain your answer.

RHETORIC

1. In paragraph 4, Walker creates a vivid description of Blue. How does she achieve this?
2. In paragraph 7, Walker makes a cognitive association between the relationship between humans and animals and the relationship between whites and blacks during slavery. Does this transition seem too abrupt, or is there a rhetorical reason for the immediate comparison? Explain.
3. Explore the other analogies she makes in paragraphs 7 and 8. Are they pertinent? What is the rhetorical effect of juxtaposing seemingly different realms to convey one central idea?
4. Walker often breaks the conventions of "college English." For example, paragraphs 8 and 9 both begin with the coordinating conjunction "and." Paragraph 12 begins with the coordinating conjunction "but." Paragraphs 15 and 16 are only one line each. Explain the effect of each of these rhetorical devices. Find three other unusual rhetorical strategies—either on the paragraph or sentence level—and explain their effects.
5. In paragraphs 17 and 18, Walker speeds up the tempo of her writing by beginning many of the sentences with the conjunction "and." What is the purpose and rhetorical effect of this strategy and how does it mimic—in linguistic terms—Blue's altered emotional state?
6. Walker seems to have a profound empathy for animals, yet it is only at the end that she is repulsed by the thought of eating meat. What rhetorical strategy is she employing in the conclusion that helps bring closure to her meditation on Blue? Does it matter whether the culminating event actually occurred in her experience, or is it all right for an essayist to use "poetic license" for stylistic purposes?

WRITING

1. Write a personal essay in which you describe your relationship with a favorite pet. Include your observations of, responses to, and attitude toward your pet. Compare and contrast this relationship to those you have with humans.
2. Some writers have argued that it matters little if certain "nonessential" endangered species become extinct if they interfere with "human progress." Argue for or against this proposition.

3. Argue for or against one of the following practices:
   a. Hunting for the sake of the hunt.
   b. Eating meat.
   c. Keeping animals in zoos.

The Greenest Campuses: An Idiosyncratic Guide

Noel Perrin

Noel Perrin (b. 1927) was born in New York City and worked as an editor before start-ing a career as a college instructor at the University of North Carolina and then Dart-mouth College, where he has taught since 1959. He has been awarded two Guggenheim Fellowships, has been a contributor to numerous periodicals, and has authored over 10 books. His subject matter has ranged from the scholarly, such as Dr. Bowdler's Legacy *(1969) and* Giving Up the Gun: Japan's Reversion to the Sword, 1543–1879 *(1979), to his experiences as a part-time farmer. Among the latter are* First Person Plural *(1978),* Second Person Plural *(1980),* Third Person Plural *(1983), and* Last Person Plural *(1991). His concerns about the environment have made him a popular speaker on ecological issues. In the following essay, first published in* The Chronicle of Higher Education *in April 2001, Perrin creates his own "best" college guide by ranking institutions of higher learning according to their environmental awareness.*

About 1,100 American colleges and universities run at least a token environ- 1
mental-studies program, and many hundreds of those programs offer well-designed and useful courses. But only a drastically smaller number practice even a portion of what they teach. The one exception is recycling. Nearly every institution that has so much as one lonely environmental-studies course also does a little halfhearted recycling. Paper and glass, usually.

There are some glorious exceptions to those rather churlish observations, 2
I'm glad to say. How many? Nobody knows. No one has yet done the necessary research (though the National Wildlife Federation's Campus Ecology program is planning a survey).

Certainly *U.S. News & World Report* hasn't. Look at the rankings in their an- 3
nual college issue. The magazine uses a complex formula something like this: Institution's reputation, 25 percent; student-retention rate, 20 percent; faculty re-sources, 20 percent; and so on, down to alumni giving, 5 percent. The lead cri-terion may help explain why Harvard, Yale, and Princeton Universities so frequently do a little dance at the top of the list.

But *U.S. News* has nothing at all to say about the degree to which a college 4
or university attempts to behave sustainably—that is, to manage its campus and
activities in ways that promote the long-term health of the planet. The magazine
is equally mum about which of the institutions it is ranking can serve as models
to society in a threatened world.

And, of course, the world *is* threatened. When the Royal Society in London 5
and the National Academy of Sciences in Washington issued their first-ever
joint statement, it ended like this: "The future of our planet is in the balance.
Sustainable development can be achieved, but only if irreversible degradation
of the environment can be halted in time. The next 30 years may be crucial."
They said that in 1992. If all those top scientists are right, we have a little more
than 20 years left in which to make major changes in how we live.

All this affects colleges. I have one environmentalist friend who loves to 6
point out to the deans and trustees she meets that if we don't make such
changes, and if the irreversible degradation of earth does occur, Harvard's huge
endowment and Yale's lofty reputation will count for nothing.

But though *U.S. News* has nothing to say, fortunately there is a fairly good 7
grapevine in the green world. I have spent considerable time in the past two
years using it like an organic cell phone. By that means I have come up with a
short, idiosyncratic list of green colleges, consisting of six that are a healthy
green, two that are greener still, and three that I believe are the greenest in the
United States.

Which approved surveying techniques have I used? None at all. Some of 8
my evidence is anecdotal, and some of my conclusions are affected by my personal beliefs, such as that electric and hybrid cars are not just a good idea, but
instruments of salvation.

Obviously I did not examine, even casually, all 1,100 institutions. I'm sure I 9
have missed some outstanding performers. I hope I have missed a great many.

Now, here are the 11, starting with **Brown University.** 10

It is generally harder for a large urban university to move toward sustain- 11
able behavior than it is for a small-town college with maybe a thousand students. But it's not impossible. Both Brown, in the heart of Providence, R.I., and
Yale University (by no means an environmental leader in other respects), in the
heart of New Haven, Conn., have found a country way of dealing with food
waste. Pigs. Both rely on pigs.

For the past 10 years, Brown has been shipping nearly all of its food waste 12
to a Rhode Island piggery. Actually, not shipping it—just leaving it out at dawn
each morning. The farmer comes to the campus and gets it. Not since Ralph
Waldo Emerson took food scraps out to the family pig have these creatures enjoyed such a high intellectual connection.

But there is a big difference in scale. Where Emerson might have one pail of 13
slops now and then, Brown generates 700 tons of edible garbage each year.
Haulage fee: $0. Tipping fee: $0. (That's the cost of dumping the garbage into
huge cookers, where it is heated for the pigs.) Annual savings to Brown: about

$50,000. Addition to the American food supply: many tons of ham and bacon each year.

Of course, Brown does far more than feed a balanced diet to a lot of pigs. 14 That's just the most exotic (for an urban institution) of its green actions "Brown is Green" became the official motto of the university in August 1990. It was accurate then, and it remains accurate now.

Yale is the only other urban institution I'm aware of that supports a pig 15 population. Much of the credit goes to Cyril May, the university's environmental coordinator, just as much of the credit at Brown goes to its environmental coordinator, Kurt Teichert.

May has managed to locate two Connecticut piggeries. The one to which he 16 sends garbage presents problems. The farmer has demanded—and received—a collection fee. And he has developed an antagonistic relationship with some of Yale's food-service people. (There are a lot of them: The campus has 16 dining facilities.) May is working on an arrangement with the second piggery. But if it falls through, he says, "I may go back on semibended knee to the other."

Yale does not make the list as a green college, for reasons you will learn 17 later in this essay. But it might in a few more years

Carleton College is an interesting example of an institution turning green almost overnight. No pig slops here; the dining halls are catered by Marriott. But change is coming fast.

In the summer of 1999, Carleton appointed its first-ever environmental co- 18 ordinator, a brand-new graduate named Rachel Smit. The one-year appointment was an experiment, with a cobbled-together salary and the humble title of "fifth-year intern." The experiment worked beyond anyone's expectation.

Smit began publishing an environmental newsletter called *The Green Bean* 19 and organized a small committee of undergraduates to explore the feasibility of composting the college's food waste, an effort that will soon begin. A surprised Marriott has already found itself serving organic dinners on Earth Day.

Better yet, the college set up an environmental-advisory committee of three 20 administrators, three faculty members, and three students to review all campus projects from a green perspective. Naturally, many of those projects will be buildings, and to evaluate them, Carleton is using the Minnesota Sustainable Design Guide, itself cowritten by Richard Strong, director of facilities.

The position of fifth-year intern is now a permanent one-year position, and 21 its salary is a regular part of the budget.

What's next? If Carleton gets a grant it has applied for, there will be a mas- 22 sive increase in environmental-studies courses and faculty seminars and, says the dean of budgets, "a whole range of green campus projects under the rubric of 'participatory learning.'"

And if Carleton doesn't get the grant? Same plans, slower pace. 23

Twenty years ago, **Dartmouth College** would have been a contender for the 24 title of greenest college in America, had such a title existed. It's still fairly green. It has a large and distinguished group of faculty members who teach environmental studies, good recycling, an organic farm that was used last summer in six courses, years of experience with solar panels, and a fair number of midlevel administrators (including three in the purchasing office) who are ardent believers in sustainability.

But the college has lost ground. Most troubling is its new $50-million library, which has an actual anti-environmental twist: A portion of the roof requires steam from the power plant to melt snow off of it. The architect, Robert Venturi, may be famous, but he's no environmentalist. 25

Dartmouth is a striking example of what I shall modestly call Perrin's Law: No college or university can move far toward sustainability without the active support of at least two senior administrators. Dartmouth has no such committed senior administrators at all. It used to. James Hornig, a former dean of sciences, and Frank Smallwood, a former provost, were instrumental in creating the environmental-studies program, back in 1970. They are now emeriti. The current senior administrators are not in the least hostile to sustainability; they just give a very low priority to the college's practicing what it preaches. 26

Emory University is probably further into the use of nonpolluting and lowpolluting motor vehicles than any other college in the country. According to Eric Gaither, senior associate vice president for business affairs, 60 percent of Emory's fleet is powered by alternative fuels. The facilities-management office has 40 electric carts, which maintenance workers use for getting around campus. The community-service office (security and parking) has its own electric carts and an electric patrol vehicle. There are five electric shuttle buses and 14 compressed–natural-gas buses on order, plus one natural-gas bus in service. 27

Bill Chace, Emory's president, has a battery-charging station for electric cars in his garage, and until recently an electric car to charge. Georgia Power, which lent the car, has recalled it, but Chace hopes to get it back. Meanwhile, he rides his bike to work most of the time. 28

How has Emory made such giant strides? "It's easy to do," says Gaither, "when your president wants you to." 29

If Carleton is a model of how a small college turns green, the **University of Michigan at Ann Arbor** is a model of how a big university does. Carleton is changing pretty much as an entity, while Michigan is more like the Electoral College—50 separate entities. The School of Natural Resources casts its six votes for sustainability, the English department casts its 12 for humanistic studies, the recycling coordinator casts her 1, the electric-vehicle program casts its 2, and so on. An institution of Michigan's size changes in bits and pieces. 30

Some of the bits show true leadership. For example, the university is within weeks of buying a modest amount of green power. It makes about half of its own electricity (at its heating plant) and buys the other half. Five percent of that other half soon will come from renewable sources: hydro (water power) and biomass (so-called fuel crops, which are grown specifically to be burned for power). 31

The supporters of sustainability at Michigan would like to see the university adopt a version of what is known as the Kyoto Protocol. The agreement, which the United States so far has refused to sign, requires that by 2012 each 32 nation reduce its emission of greenhouse gases to 7 percent below its 1990 figure. Michigan's version of the protocol, at present a pipe dream, would require the university to do what the government won't—accept that reduction as a goal.

The immediate goal of "sustainabilists" at Ann Arbor is the creation of a 33 universitywide environmental coordinator, who would work either in the president's or the provost's office.

Giants are slow, but they are also strong. 34

Tulane University has the usual programs, among green institutions, in re- 35 cycling, composting, and energy efficiency. But what sets it apart is the Tulane Environmental Law Clinic, which is staffed by third-year law students. The director is a faculty member, and there are three law "fellows," all lawyers, who work with the students. The clinic does legal work for environmental organizations across Louisiana and "most likely has had a greater environmental impact than all our other efforts combined," says Elizabeth Davey, Tulane's first-ever environmental coordinator.

At least two campuses of the **University of California** (Berkeley is not 36 among them) have taken a first and even a second step toward sustainable behavior. First step: symbolic action, like installing a few solar panels, to produce clean energy and to help educate students. With luck, one of those little solar arrays might produce as much as a 20th of a percent of the electricity the university uses. It's a start.

The two campuses are Davis and Santa Cruz, and I think Davis nudges 37 ahead of Santa Cruz. That is primarily because Davis the city and Davis the university have done something almost miraculous. They have brought car culture at least partially under control, greatly reducing air pollution as a result.

The city has a population of about 58,000, which includes 24,000 students. 38 According to reliable estimates, there are something over 50,000 bikes in town or on the campus, all but a few hundred owned by their riders. Most of the bikes are used regularly on the city's 45 miles of bike paths (closed to cars) and the 47 miles of bike lanes (cars permitted in the other lanes). The university maintains an additional 14 miles of bike paths on its large campus

What happens on rainy days? "A surprising number continue to bike," says 39 David Takemoto-Weerts, coordinator of Davis's bicycle program.

If every American college in a suitable climate were to behave like Davis, 40 we could close a medium-sized oil refinery. Maybe we could even get rid of one coal-fired power plant, and thus seriously improve air quality.

The **University of New Hampshire** is trying to jump straight from sym- 41 bolic gestures, like installing a handful of solar panels, to the hardest task of all for an institution trying to become green—establishing a completely new mindset among students, administrators, and faculty and staff members. It may well succeed.

Campuses that have managed to change attitudes are rare. Prescott College, 42 in Prescott, Ariz., and Sterling College, in Craftsbury Common, Vt., are rumored to have done so, and there may be two or three others. They're not on my list—

because they're so small, because their students tend to be bright green even before they arrive, and because I have limited space.

New Hampshire has several token green projects, including a tiny solar array, able to produce one kilowatt at noon on a good day. And last April it inaugurated the Yellow Bike Cooperative. It is much smaller than anything that happens at Davis, where a bike rack might be a hundred yards long. But it's also more original and more communitarian. Anyone in Durham—student, burger flipper, associate dean—can join the Yellow Bike program by paying a $5 fee. 43

What you get right away is a key that unlocks all 50 bikes owned by the cooperative. (They are repaired and painted by student volunteers.) Want to cross campus? Just go to the nearest bike rack, unlock a Yellow, and pedal off. The goal, says Julie Newman, of the Office of Sustainability Programs, is "to greatly decrease one-person car trips on campus." 44

But the main thrust at New Hampshire is consciousness-raising. When the subject of composting food waste came up, the university held a. seminar for its food workers. 45

New Hampshire's striking vigor is partly the result of a special endowment—about $12.8-million—exclusively for the sustainability office. Tom Kelly, the director, refuses to equate sustainability with greenness. Being green, in the sense of avoiding pollution and promoting reuse, is just one aspect of living sustainably, which involves "the balancing of economic viability with ecological health and human well-being," he says. 46

Oberlin College is an exception to Perrin's Law. The college has gotten deeply into environmental behavior without the active support of two or, indeed, any senior administrators. As at Dartmouth, the top people are not hostile; they just have other priorities. 47

Apparently, until this year, Oberlin's environmental-studies program was housed in a dreary cellar. Now it's in the $8.2-million Adam Joseph Lewis Environmental Studies Center, which is one of the most environmentally benign college buildings in the world. The money for it was raised as a result of a deal that the department chairman, David Orr, made with the administration: He could raise money for his own program, provided that he approached only people and foundations that had never shown the faintest interest in Oberlin. 48

It's too soon for a full report on the building. It is loaded with solar panels— 690 of them, covering the roof (for a diagram of the building, see www.oberlin.edu/newserv/esc/escabout.html). In about a year, data will be available on how much energy the panels have saved and whether, as Orr hopes, the center will not only make all its own power, but even export some. 49

Northland College, in Wisconsin, also goes way beyond tokenism. Its McLean Environmental Living and Learning Center, a two-year-old residence hall for 114 students, is topped by a 120-foot wind tower that, with a good breeze coming off Lake Superior, can generate 20 kilowatts of electricity. The building also includes three arrays of solar panels. They are only token-size, generating a total of 3.2 kilowatts at most. But one array does heat most of the water for one wing of McLean, while the other three form a test project. 50

One test array is fixed in place—it can't be aimed. Another is like that sun- 51
flower in Blake's poem—it countest the steps of the sun. Put more prosaically, it
tracks the sun across the sky each day. The third array does that and can also be
tilted to get the best angle for each season of the year.

Inside the dorm is a pair of composting toilets—an experiment, to see if stu- 52
dents will use them. Because no one is forced to try the new ones if they don't
want to—plenty of conventional toilets are close by—it means something when
James Miller, vice president and dean of student development and enrollment,
reports, "Students almost always choose the composting bathrooms."

From the start, the college's goal has been to have McLean operate so effi- 53
ciently that it consumes 40 percent less outside energy than would a conventional dormitory of the same dimensions. The building didn't reach that goal in
its first year; energy use dropped only 34.2 percent. But anyone dealing with a
new system knows to expect bugs at the beginning. There were some at Northland, including the wind generator's being down for three months. (As I write,
it's turning busily.) Dean Miller is confident that the building will meet or
exceed the college's energy-efficiency goal.

There is no room here to talk about the octagonal classroom structure made 54
of bales of straw, built largely by students. Or about the fact that Northland's
grounds are pesticide- and herbicide-free.

If Oberlin is a flagrant exception to Perrin's Law, **Middlebury College** is a 55
strong confirmation. Middlebury is unique, as far as I know, in having not only
senior administrators who strongly back environmentalism, but one senior administrator right inside the program. What Michigan wants, Middlebury has.

Nan Jenks-Jay, director of environmental affairs, reports directly to the 56
provost. She is responsible for both the teaching side and the living-sustainably
side of environmentalism. Under her are an environmental coordinator, Amy
Self, and an academic-program coordinator, Janet Wiseman.

The program has powerful backers, including the president, John M. 57
McCardell Jr.; the provost and executive vice president, Ronald D. Liebowitz;
and the executive vice president for facilities planning, David W. Ginevan. But
everyone I talked with at Middlebury, except for the occasional student who
didn't want to trouble his mind with things like returnable bottles—to say nothing of acid rain—seemed at least somewhat committed to sustainable living.

Middlebury has what I think is the oldest environmental-studies program 58
in the country; it began back in 1965. It has the best composting program I've
ever seen. And, like Northland, it is pesticide- and herbicide-free.

Let me end as I began, with Harvard, Yale, and Princeton. And with *U.S.* 59
News's consistently ranking them in the top five, accompanied from time to
time by the California Institute of Technology, Stanford University, and the
Massachusetts Institute of Technology.

What if *U.S. News* did a green ranking? What if it based the listings on one 60
of the few bits of hard data that can be widely compared: the percentage of
waste that a college recycles?

Harvard would come out okay, though hardly at the top. The university re- 61
cycled 24 percent of its waste last year, thanks in considerable part to the presence of Rob Gogan, the waste manager. He hopes to achieve 28 percent this
year. That's feeble compared with Brown's 35 percent, and downright puny
against Middlebury's 64 percent.

But compared with Yale and Princeton, it's magnificent. Most of the infor- 62
mation I could get from Princeton is sadly dated. It comes from the 1995 report
of the Princeton Environmental Reform Committee, whose primary recommendation was that the university hire a full-time waste manager. The university
has not yet done so. And if any administrators on the campus know the current
recycling percentage, they're not telling.

And Yale—poor Yale! It does have a figure. Among the performances of the 63
20 or so other colleges and universities whose percentages I'm aware of, only
Carnegie Mellon's is worse. Yale: 19 percent. Carnegie Mellon: 11 percent.

What should universities—and society—be shooting for? How can you 64
ask? One-hundred-percent retrieval of everything retrievable, of course.

COMPREHENSION

1. Why does Perrin call his essay an "idiosyncratic guide" when environmentalism has become a major issue in most municipalities, regions, and
   countries?
2. Is Perrin's purpose to inform, argue, or both? Does he have a clear-cut thesis, or does he leave it up to the reader to infer the thesis? Explain.
3. What information is Perrin's informal "guide" providing that is not offered
   in more conventional college rankings? Is Perrin suggesting that parents
   and students consider "green rankings" in choosing which college to apply
   to? Explain.

RHETORIC

1. What purpose might Perrin have for choosing to create a "green guide" for
   colleges when there are so many other institutions or items he could have
   selected for review, such as corporations, towns, cities, automobiles, and
   numerous household products? What makes colleges and universities a
   particularly apt target?
2. Usually, Ivy League colleges are at the top of college guide lists as most
   desirable. Where do they place on Perrin's list? What ironic statement is
   Perrin making by providing their rankings on the "green scale"? What
   is he implying about American values, particularly as they pertain to
   education?
3. Colleges and universities often pride themselves on the renown of their faculties. Who are the people Perrin cites as models of academic worth? Why
   has he chosen them?

4. What is the ironic purpose behind the author mentioning "Perrin's Law"? Is it a true "law," like the law of gravity? What body of knowledge is the author satirizing by invoking such a law?
5. Perrin is not didactic, since he does not recommend that other colleges adopt the environmental measures his model colleges have chosen. Would more direct advocacy on his part have strengthened his argument or weakened it, or not have had any effect? Explain.
6. In Perrin's conclusion, he changes his purpose from providing a purely informational assessment to offering a strong reprimand and recommendation. Why does he wait until the concluding paragraph to do so?

WRITING

1. Describe an environmentally friendly practice conducted at your college or university. Is it truly helpful for the environment, or is it largely symbolic?
2. Compare and contrast the academically oriented courses and programs offered at your school with what your institution actually does in the way of helping the environment. Discuss which of the two priorities is more prominent, and why.
3. Argue for or against the proposition that a magazine such as *U.S. News & World Report* should include environmental awareness and practice in their formula for assessing the rankings of colleges.

The Solace of Open Spaces

Gretel Ehrlich

Gretel Ehrlich was born in California in 1949 and educated at Bennington College, UCLA, and The New School for Social Research. She currently lives on a ranch in Shell, Wyoming. She has worked as a professional documentary filmmaker. Her essays have appeared in The New York Times, Atlantic, Harper's, *and the* New Age Journal. *She has also published two books of poetry and a novel,* Heart Mountain *(1987). Ehrlich has received awards from the National Endowment for the Arts and the Wyoming Council for the Arts. In the following selection from* The Solace of Open Spaces *(1985), with the eyes and ears of an anthropologist and the knowledge of a historian, Ehrlich provides us with a comprehensive view of a life most Americans are no longer familiar with.*

It's May, and I've just awakened from a nap, curled against sagebrush the way   1
my dog taught me to sleep-sheltered from wind. A weather front is pulling the
huge sky over me, and from the dark a hailstone has hit me on the head.

I'm trailing a band of 2000 sheep across a stretch of Wyoming badland, a 50- 2
mile trip that takes five days because sheep shade up in the hot sun and won't
budge until it cools. Bunched together now, and excited into a run by the storm,
they drift across dry land, tumbling into draws like water and surging out again
onto the rugged, choppy plateaus that are the building blocks of this state.

The name "Wyoming" comes from an Indian word meaning "at the great 3
plains," but the plains are really valleys, great arid valleys, 1600 square miles'
worth of them, with the horizon bending up on all sides into mountain ranges.
This gives the vastness a sheltering look.

Winter lasts six months here. Prevailing winds spill snowdrifts to the east, 4
and new storms from the northwest replenish them. This white bulk is sometimes dizzying, even nauseating, to look at. At 20, 30, 40 degrees below zero, it
is not only your car that doesn't work but also your mind and body.

The landscape hardens into a dungeon of space. During the winter, while I 5
was riding to find a new calf, my legs half froze to the saddle, and in the silence
that such cold creates, I felt like the first person on earth, or the last.

Today the sun is out—only a few clouds billowing. In the east, where the 6
sheep have started off without me, the benchland tilts up in a series of red-
earthed, eroded mesas, planed flat on top by a million years of water. Behind
them, a bold line of muscular scraps rears up 10,000 feet to become the Big Horn
Mountains. A tidal pattern is engraved into the ground, as if left by the sea that
once covered this state. Canyons curve down like galaxies to meet the oncoming rush of flat land.

To live and work in this kind of open country, with its 100-mile views, is to 7
lose the distinction between background and foreground. When I asked an
older ranch hand to describe Wyoming's openness, he said, "It's all a bunch of
nothing—wind and rattlesnakes—and so much of it you can't tell where you're
going or where you've been and it don't make much difference."

John, a sheepman I know, is tall and handsome and has an explosive tem- 8
perament. He has a perfect intuition about people and sheep. They call him
"Highpockets" because he's so long-legged; his graceful stride matches the distances he has to cover.

"Open space hasn't affected me at all. It's all the people moving in on it," he 9
said. The huge ranch he was born on takes up much of one county and spreads
into another state. For him to put 100,000 miles on his pickup in three years and
never leave home is not unusual.

Most of Wyoming has a "lean-to" look. Instead of big, roomy barns and Vic- 10
torian houses, there are dugouts, low sheds, log cabins, sheep camps and fence
lines that look like driftwood blown haphazardly into place. People in
Wyoming still feel pride because they live in such a harsh place, part of the
glamorous cowboy past, and they are determined not to be the victims of a min-
ing-dominated future.

Most characteristic of the state's landscape is what a developer euphemisti- 11
cally describes as "indigenous growth right up to your front door"—a reference
to waterless stands of salt sage, snakes, jack-rabbits, deerflies, red dust, a brief
respite of wildflowers, dry washes and no trees.

Sagebrush covers 58,000 square miles of Wyoming. The biggest city has a 12 population of 50,000, and there are only five settlements that could be called cities in the whole state. The rest are towns, scattered across the expanse with as much as 60 miles between them, their populations 2000, 50 or 10. They are fugitive-looking, perched on a barren, windblown bench, or tagged onto a river or a railroad, or laid out straight in a farming valley with implement stores and a block-long Mormon church.

In the eastern part of the state, which slides down into the Great Plains, the 13 new mining settlements are boomtowns, trailer cities, metal knots on flat land.

Despite the desolate look, there's a coziness to living in this state. 14

There are so few people (only 470,000) that ranchers who buy and sell cattle 15 know each other statewide. The kids who choose to go to college usually go to the state's one university, in Laramie. Hired hands work their way around Wyoming in a lifetime of hirings and firings. And, despite the physical separation, people stay in touch, often driving two or three hours to another ranch for dinner.

Seventy-five years ago, when travel was by buckboard or horseback, cow- 16 boys who were temporarily out of work rode the grub line—drifting from ranch to ranch, mending fences or milking cows, and receiving in exchange a bed and meals. Gossip and messages traveled this slow circuit with them, creating an intimacy among ranchers who were three and four weeks' ride apart.

One old-time couple I know, whose turn-of-the-century homestead was 17 used by an outlaw gang as a relay station for stolen horses, recall that if you were traveling, desperado or not, any lighted ranch house was a welcome sign.

Even now, for someone who lives in a remote spot, arriving at a ranch or 18 coming to town for supplies is cause for celebration. To emerge from isolation can be disorienting. Everything looks bright, new, vivid. After I had been herding sheep for only three days, the sound of the camp-tender's pickup flustered me. Longing for human company, I felt a foolish grin take over my face, yet I had to resist an urgent temptation to run and hide.

Things happen suddenly in Wyoming: the change of seasons and weather; 19 for people, the violent swings into and out of isolation. But goodnaturedness goes hand in hand with severity. Friendliness is a tradition. Strangers passing on the road wave hello.

A common sight is two pickups stopped side by side far out on a range, on 20 a dirt track winding through the sage. The drivers will share a cigarette, uncap their Thermos bottles, and pass a battered cup, steaming with coffee, between windows. These meetings summon up the details of several generations, because in Wyoming private histories are largely public knowledge.

In most parts of Wyoming, the human population is visibly out-numbered 21 by the animal. Not far from my town of 50, I rode into a narrow valley and startled a herd of 200 elk. Eagles look like small people as they eat car-killed deer by the road. Antelope, moving in small, graceful bands, travel at 60 m.p.h., their mouths open as if drinking in the space.

The solitude in which Westerners live makes them quiet. They telegraph 22 thoughts and feelings by the way they tilt their heads and listen; pulling their Stetsons into a steep dive over their eyes or pigeon-toeing one boot over the other, they lean against a fence and take the whole scene in. These detached looks of quiet amusement are sometimes cynical, but they can also come from a dry-eyed humility as lucid as the air is clear.

Conversation goes on in what sounds like a private code. A few phrases im- 23 ply a complex of meanings. Asking directions you get a curious list of details. While trailing sheep, I was told to "ride up to that kinda upturned rock, follow the pin wash, turn left at the dump, and then you'll see the waterhole."

I've spent hours riding to sheep camp at dawn in a pickup when nothing 24 was said and eaten meals in the cookhouse when the only words spoken were a mumbled "Thank you, ma'am" at the end of dinner. The silence is profound. Instead of talking, we seem to share one eye. The landscape is engorged with detail, every movement on it chillingly sharp. The air between people is charged.

Spring weather is capricious and mean. It snows, then blisters with heat. 25 There have been tornadoes. They lay their elephant trunks out in the sage until they find houses, then slurp everything up and leave. I've noticed that melting snowbanks hiss and rot, viperous, then drip into calm pools where ducklings hatch and livestock, being trailed to summer range, drink.

With the ice cover gone, rivers churn a milkshake brown, taking culverts 26 and small bridges with them. Water in such an arid place (the average annual rainfall where I live is less than eight inches) is like blood. It festoons drab land with green veins: a line of cottonwoods following a stream; a strip of alfalfa, and on ditchbanks, wild asparagus growing.

I try to imagine a world of uncharted land, in which one could look over an 27 uncompleted map and ride a horse past where all the lines have stopped. There is no real wilderness left; wilderness, yes, but true wilderness has been gone on this continent since the time of Lewis and Clark's overland journey.

Two hundred years ago, the Crow, Shoshone, Arapaho, Cheyenne, and 28 Sioux roamed the intermountain West, orchestrating their movements according to hunger, season, and warfare. Once they acquired horses, they traversed the spines of all the big Wyoming ranges—the Absarokas, the Wind Rivers, the Tetons, the Big Horns—and wintered on the unprotected plains that fan out from them. Space was life. The world was their home.

What was life-giving to native Americans was often nightmarish to sod- 29 busters who arrived encumbered with families and ethnic pasts to be transplanted in nearly uninhabitable land. The great distances, the shortage of water and trees, and the loneliness created unexpected hardships for them.

In her book *O Pioneers!* Willa Cather gives a settler's version of the bleak 30 landscape: "The little town behind them had vanished as if it had never been, had fallen behind the swell of the prairie, and the stern frozen country received them into its bosom. The homesteads were few and far apart; here and there a windmill gaunt against the sky, a sod house crouching in a hollow."

The emptiness of the West was for others a geography of possibility. Men 31 and women who amassed great chunks of land and struggled to preserve unfenced empires were, despite their self-serving motives, unwitting geographers. They understood the lay of the land.

But by the 1850s, the Oregon and Mormon trails sported bumper-to- 32 bumper traffic. Wealthy landowners, many of them aristocratic absentee land-lords, known as remittance men because they were paid to come West and get out of their families' hair, overstocked the range with more than a million head of cattle. By 1885, the feed and water were desperately short, and the winter of 1886 laid out the gaunt bodies of dead animals so closely together that when the thaw came, one rancher from Kaycee claimed to have walked on cowhide all the way to Crazy Woman Creek, 20 miles away.

Territorial Wyoming was a boy's world. The land was generous with every- 33 thing but water. At first there was room enough and food enough for everyone. And, as with all beginnings, an expansive mood set in. The young cowboys, drifters, shopkeepers, and schoolteachers were heroic, lawless, generous, rowdy, and tenacious. The individualism and optimism generated during those times have endured.

Cattle barons tried to control all the public grazing land by restricting mem- 34 bership in the Wyoming Stock Growers Association, as if it were a country club. They ostracized from roundups and brandings cowboys and ranchers who were not members, then denounced them as rustlers.

One cold-blooded murder of a small-time stockman kicked off the Johnson 35 County cattle war, which was no simple good guy–bad guy shootout but a complicated class struggle between landed gentry and less affluent settlers—a shocking reminder that the West was not an egalitarian sanctuary after all.

Fencing ultimately enforced boundaries, but barbed wire abolished space. 36 It was stretched across the beautiful valleys, into mountains, over desert bad-lands, through buffalo grass.

The "anything is possible" fever—the lure of any place—was constricted. 37 The integrity of the land as a geographical body, and the freedom to ride any-where on it, was lost.

I punched cows with a young man named Martin, who is the greatgrand- 38 son of John Tisdale. His inheritance is not the open land that Tisdale knew and prematurely lost but a rage against restraint.

In all this open space, values crystalize quickly. People are strong on scru- 39 ples but tenderhearted about quirky behavior. A friend and I found one ranch hand, who's "not right in the head," sitting in front of the badly decayed carcass of a cow, shaking his finger and saying, "Now, I don't want you to do this ever again!"

When I asked what was wrong with him, I was told, "He's goofier than hell, 40 just like the rest of us."

Perhaps because the West is historically new, conventional morality is still 41 felt to be less important than rock-bottom truths. Though there's always a lot of teasing and sparring around, people are blunt with each other, sometimes even cruel, believing honesty is stronger medicine than sympathy, which may con-sole but often conceals.

The formality that goes hand in hand with the rowdiness is known as "the 42 Western Code." It's a list of practical do's and don'ts, faithfully observed. A friend, Cliff, who runs a trapline in the winter, cut off half his foot while axing a hole in the ice. Alone, he dragged himself to his pickup and headed for town, stopping to open the ranch gate as he left, and getting out to close it again, thus losing, in his observance of rules, precious time and blood.

Later, he commented, "How would it look, them having to come to the hos- 43 pital to tell me their cows had gotten out?"

The roominess of the state has affected political attitudes. Ranchers keep up 44 with world politics and the convulsions of the economy but are basically isolationists. Used to running their own small empires of land and livestock, they're suspicious of big government.

It's a "don't fence me in" holdover from a century ago. They still want the 45 elbow room their grandfathers had, so they're strongly conservative, but with a populist twist.

Summer is the season when we get our "cowboy tans"—on the lower parts 46 of our faces and on three fourths of our arms. Excessive heat, in the 90s and higher, sends us outside with the mosquitoes.

After the brief lushness of summer, the sun moves south. The range grass is 47 brown. Livestock has been trailed back down from the mountains. Waterholes begin to frost over at night. Last fall Martin asked me to accompany him on a pack trip. With five horses, we followed a river into the mountains behind the tiny Wyoming town of Meeteetse. Groves of aspen, red and orange, gave off a light that made us look toasted.

One of our evening entertainments was to watch the night sky. My dog, 48 who also came on the trip, a dingo bred to herd sheep, is so used to the silence and empty skies that when an airplane flies over he always looks up and eyes the distant intruder quizzically.

The sky, lately, seems to be much more crowded than it used to be. Satellites 49 make their silent passes in the dark with great regularity. We counted 18 in one hour's viewing. How odd to think that while they circumnavigated the planet, Martin and I had moved only six miles into our local wilderness, and had seen no other human for the two weeks we stayed there.

At night, by moonlight, the land is whittled to slivers—a ridge, a river, a 50 strip of grassland stretching to the mountains, then the huge sky. One morning a full moon was setting in the west just as the sun was rising. I felt precariously balanced between the two as I loped across a meadow. For a moment, I could believe that the stars, which were still visible, work like cooper's bands, holding everything above Wyoming together.

Space has a spiritual equivalent, and can heal what is divided and burden- 51 some in us. My grandchildren will probably use space shuttles for a honeymoon trip or to recover from heart attacks, but closer to home we might also learn how to carry space inside ourselves in the effortless way we carry our skins. Space represents sanity, not a life purified, dull, or "spaced out" but one that might accommodate intelligently any idea or situation.

COMPREHENSION

1. What is Wyoming's predominant appeal to the author? Why has she chosen to live in its rather inhospitable climate?
2. Explain the ways in which Wyoming, for Ehrlich, symbolizes the American West.
3. In the concluding paragraph, Ehrlich says, "Space has a spiritual equivalent." What does she mean by this? How do the Wyoming natives display this spirituality? How has it affected the author?

RHETORIC

1. How do the following descriptions help create the nature of Wyoming space: "This gives the vastness a sheltering look" (paragraph 3); "The landscape hardens into a dungeon of space" (paragraph 5); and "Canyons curve down like galaxies" (paragraph 6)?
2. None of the direct speech in this essay is in the form of dialogue. How is this indicative of the Westerner's attitude toward speech? How does it support the idea that "A few phrases imply a complex of meanings" (paragraph 23)?
3. How does Ehrlich's introductory comment that "my dog taught me to sleep" (paragraph 1) set the general tone for the bond between humans and nature in Wyoming? What other evidence is there in the essay of this special relationship?
4. Paragraphs 28 through 37 describe Wyoming's history. What function does this serve in the essay? How does it explain life in present-day Wyoming?
5. In the conclusion, Ehrlich suggests that the relationship of humans to space as it exists in Wyoming may be dying out. What references are there in the essay that seem to move toward this conclusion?

WRITING

1. How can one's environment affect the nature of one's relationship with others? How can it affect one's communicative style? For example, do city dwellers speak differently from rural ones? Do people from one region—for example, the South—relate differently toward one another than do people from another region? Explore these issues in an essay, focusing on a locale you are familiar with. Your topics don't have to be limited to speech but may include body language, dress, jewelry, and so forth.
2. Compare and contrast the sense of space in this essay with that of the place where you grew up.
3. Think about some quality that is important to you—for example, solitude or brightness—and then write an essay about a place or environment that captures this quality.

Two Views of the Mississippi

Mark Twain

Mark Twain (1835–1910) was the pseudonym of Samuel Langhorne Clemens, perhaps America's most famous humorist, narrator, and social observer. Many critics consider his book The Adventures of Huckleberry Finn *(1884) the most significant and influential American novel ever written. Apprenticed to a printer in Hannibal, Missouri, at the age of 13, Twain quickly turned to life on the river, eventually becoming a pilot on riverboats. This job required him to measure and announce the depth of the river at each point to avoid accidents. From his experience as riverboat pilot, Clemens drew his pseudonym, Mark Twain, which means "two fathoms deep." After the Civil War put an end to river traffic, Twain went to Nevada, where he attempted and failed at several get-rich-quick schemes before turning to work as a newspaperman. His tales and anecdotes soon won him fame as a writer. His more famous books include* The Adventures of Tom Sawyer *(1876),* The Prince and the Pauper *(1882), and* A Connecticut Yankee in King Arthur's Court *(1889). His later life had bitter and tragic aspects, including heavy debt and the deaths of two of his daughters. His keen powers of observation and natural ability to create metaphors are evident in the following excerpt from* Life on the Mississippi *(1885).*

The face of the water, in time, became a wonderful book—a book that was a   1
dead language to the uneducated passenger, but which told its mind to me without reserve, delivering its most cherished secrets as clearly as if it uttered them with a voice. And it was not a book to be read once and thrown aside, for it had a new story to tell every day. Throughout the long twelve hundred miles there was never a page that was void of interest, never one that you could leave unread without loss, never one that you would want to skip, thinking you could find higher enjoyment in some other thing. There never was so wonderful a book written by man; never one whose interest was so absorbing, so unflagging, so sparklingly renewed with every re-perusal. The passenger who could not read it was charmed with a peculiar sort of faint dimple on its surface (on the rare occasions when he did not overlook it altogether); but to the pilot that was an *italicized* passage; indeed, it was more than that, it was a legend of the largest capitals, with a string of shouting exclamation points at the end of it; for it meant that a wreck or a rock was buried there that could tear the life out of the strongest vessel that ever floated. It is the faintest and simplest expression the water ever makes, and the most hideous to a pilot's eye. In truth, the passenger who could not read this book saw nothing but all manner of pretty pictures in it, painted by the sun and shaded by the clouds, whereas to the trained eye these were not pictures at all, but the grimmest and most dead-earnest of reading-matter.

Now when I had mastered the language of this water and had come to ₂
know every trifling feature that bordered the great river as familiarly as I knew
the letters of the alphabet, I had made a valuable acquisition. But I had lost
something, too. I had lost something which could never be restored to me while
I lived. All the grace, the beauty, the poetry had gone out of the majestic river! I
still keep in mind a certain wonderful sunset which I witnessed when steam-
boating was new to me. A broad expanse of the river was turned to blood; in the
middle distance the red hue brightened into gold, through which a solitary log
came floating, black and conspicuous; in one place a long, slanting mark lay
sparkling upon the water; in another the surface was broken by boiling, tumbling rings, that were as many-tinted as an opal; where the ruddy flush was
faintest, was a smooth spot that was covered with graceful circles and radiating
lines, ever so delicately traced; the shore on our left was densely wooded, and
the sombre shadow that fell from this forest was broken in one place by a long,
ruffled trail that shone like silver; and high above the forest wall a clean-
stemmed dead tree waved a single leafy bough that glowed like a flame in the
unobstructed splendor that was flowing from the sun. There were graceful
curves, reflected images, woody heights, soft distances; and over the whole
scene, far and near, the dissolving lights drifted steadily, enriching it, every
passing moment, with new marvels of coloring.

I stood like one bewitched. I drank it in, in a speechless rapture. The world ₃
was new to me, and I had never seen anything like this at home. But as I have
said, a day came when I began to cease from noting the glories and the charms
which the moon and the sun and the twilight wrought upon the river's face; another day came when I ceased altogether to note them. Then, if that sunset scene
had been repeated, I should have looked upon it without rapture, and should
have commented upon it, inwardly, after this fashion: This sun means that we
are going to have wind to-morrow; that floating log means that the river is rising, small thanks to it; that slanting mark on the water refers to a bluff reef
which is going to kill somebody's steamboat one of these nights, if it keeps on
stretching out like that; those tumbling "boils" show a dissolving bar and a
changing channel there; the lines and circles in the slick water over yonder are
a warning that the troublesome place is shoaling up dangerously; that silver
streak in the shadow of the forest is the "break" from a new snag, and he has located himself in the very best place he could have found to fish for steamboats;
that tall dead tree, with a single living branch, is not going to last long, and then
how is a body ever going to get through this blind place at night without the
friendly old landmark?

No, the romance and the beauty were all gone from the river. All the value ₄
any feature of it had for me now was the amount of usefulness it could furnish
toward compassing the safe piloting of a steamboat. Since those days, I have
pitied doctors from my heart. What does the lovely flush in a beauty's cheek
mean to a doctor but a "break" that ripples above some deadly disease? Are not
all her visible charms sown thick with what are to him the signs and symbols of
hidden decay? Does he ever see her beauty at all, or doesn't he simply view her

professionally, and comment upon her unwholesome condition all to himself? And doesn't he sometimes wonder whether he has gained most or lost most by learning his trade?

COMPREHENSION

1. According to the author, what are the two Mississippis?
2. What is the author's attitude toward the "uneducated passenger"?
3. What does the author mean when he writes that he had "mastered the language" of the river (paragraph 2)?

RHETORIC

1. What is the central metaphor the author uses to describe the river? How does he divide the central metaphor into components?
2. From what time perspective is the author musing on the river? How does this perspective influence the tone of the essay?
3. Study the number and placement of semicolons in paragraphs 2 and 3. What is their rhetorical function? How would the mood of the paragraphs change if the semicolons were replaced with periods?
4. In general, the sentences in this essay are much longer than the standard English sentence. How does this alter the overall coherence of the essay? Why are long sentences uniquely suited for the subject matter?
5. The author uses descriptive passages such as "graceful curves, reflected images, woody heights, soft distances," and many other descriptors denoting and suggesting space and visual imagery. How do they contribute to the tone of the essay?
6. What is the author's purpose in posing four questions in the concluding paragraph of the essay? What is the rhetorical effect of ending the essay with a question?
7. The author paints a mental picture of the Mississippi in the following sentence: "A broad expanse of the river was turned to blood; in the middle distance the red hue brightened into gold, through which a solitary log came floating, black and conspicuous." What function does color serve in this sentence? Cite other instances of Twain's use of color. How do they affect the relationship between you, the reader, and the subject matter?

WRITING

1. Write an essay comparing and contrasting your emotions and perceptual responses on your first day of college with your current perceptions and emotions.

2. Create a central metaphor out of a familiar place; for example, "school is a jail," "the street is a jungle," "the library is a house of ghosts," or "the park is an oasis." Describe the place you have selected, using vocabulary that reflects your central metaphor.
3. Write a critical essay on the subject of Twain's use of metaphor in this selection.

High Tide in Tucson

Barbara Kingsolver

*Barbara Kingsolver (b. 1955) was born in Annapolis, Maryland, and raised in eastern Kentucky. She studied biology at DePauw University (BA, 1977) and the University of Arizona (MS, 1981) and worked as a scientist and scientific writer before beginning her career as a writer of fiction and essays. Her highly acclaimed books include novels—*The Bean Trees *(1988),* Animal Dreams *(1990),* Pigs in Heaven *(1993), and* The Poisonwood Bible *(1998); stories—*Homeland and Other Stories *(1989); poetry—*Another America *(1992); and essays—*High Tide in Tucson: Essays from Now or Never *(1996). The following essay is from the latter volume and provides a hopeful analogy regarding ourselves and the animal world.*

A hermit crab lives in my house. Here in the desert he's hiding out from local 1
animal ordinances, at minimum, and maybe even the international laws of native-species transport. For sure, he's an outlaw against nature. So be it.

He arrived as a stowaway two Octobers ago. I had spent a week in the Ba- 2
hamas, and while I was there, wishing my daughter could see those sparkling blue bays and sandy covers, I did exactly what she would have done: I collected shells. Spiky murexes, smooth purple moon shells, ancient-looking whelks sand-blasted by the tide—tucked them in the pockets of my shirt and shorts until my lumpy, suspect hemlines gave me away, like a refugee smuggling the family fortune. When it was time to go home, I rinsed my loot in the sink and packed it carefully into a plastic carton, then nested it deep in my suitcase for the journey to Arizona.

I got home in the middle of the night, but couldn't wait till morning to 3
show my hand. I set the carton on the coffee table for my daughter to open. In the dark living room her face glowed, in the way of antique stories about children and treasure. With perfect delicacy she laid the shells out on the table, counting, sorting, designating scientific categories like yellow-striped pinky, Barnacle Bill's pocketbook . . . Yeek! She let loose a sudden yelp, dropped her booty, and ran to the far end of the room. The largest, knottiest whelk had begun to move around. First it extended one long red talon of a leg, tap-tap-tapping

like a blind man's cane. Then came half a dozen more red legs, plus a pair of eyes on stalks, and a purple claw that snapped open and shut in a way that could not mean We come in Friendship.

Who could blame this creature? It had fallen asleep to the sound of the 4 Caribbean tide and awakened on a coffee table in Tucson, Arizona, where the nearest standing water source of any real account was the municipal sewage-treatment plant.

With red stiletto legs splayed in all directions, it lunged and jerked its huge 5 shell this way and that, reminding me of the scene I make whenever I'm moved to rearrange the living-room sofa by myself. Then, while we watched in stunned reverence, the strange beast found its bearings and began to reveal a determined, crabby grace. It felt its way to the edge of the table and eased itself over, not falling bang to the floor but hanging suspended underneath within the long grasp of its ice-tong legs, lifting any two or three at a time while many others still held in place. In this remarkable fashion it scrambled around the underside of the table's rim, swift and sure and fearless like a rock climber's dream.

If you ask me, when something extraordinary shows up in your life in the 6 middle of the night, you give it a name and make it the best home you can.

The business of naming involved a grasp of hermit-crab gender that was 7 way out of our league. But our household had a deficit of males, so my daughter and I chose Buster, for balance. We gave him a terrarium with clean gravel and a small cactus plant dug out of the yard and a big cockleshell full of tap water. All this seemed to suit him fine. To my astonishment our local pet store carried a product called Vitaminized Hermit Crab Cakes. Tempting enough (till you read the ingredients) but we passed, since our household leans more toward the recycling ethic. We give him leftovers. Buster's rapture is the day I drag the unidentifiable things in cottage cheese containers out of the back of the fridge.

We've also learned to give him a continually changing assortment of 8 seashells, which he tries on and casts off like Cinderella's stepsisters preening for the ball. He'll sometimes try to squeeze into ludicrous outfits too small to contain him (who can't relate?). In other moods, he will disappear into a conch the size of my two fists and sit for a day, immobilized by the weight of upward mobility. He is in every way the perfect housemate: quiet, entertaining, and willing to eat up the trash. He went to school for first-grade show-and-tell, and was such a hit the principal called up to congratulate me (I think) for being a broad-minded mother.

It was a long time, though, before we began to understand the content of 9 Buster's character. He required more patient observation than we were in the habit of giving to a small, cold-blooded life. As months went by, we would periodically notice with great disappointment that Buster seemed to be dead. Or not entirely dead, but ill, or maybe suffering the crab equivalent of the blues. He would burrow into a gravelly corner, shrink deep into his shell, and not move, for days and days. We'd take him out to play, dunk him in water, offer him a new frock—nothing. He wanted to be still.

Life being what it is, we'd eventually quit prodding our sick friend to cheer 10 up, and would move on to the next stage of a difficult friendship: neglect. We'd ignore him wholesale, only to realize at some point later on that he'd lapsed into hyperactivity. We'd find him ceaselessly patrolling the four corners of his world, turning over rocks, rooting out and dragging around truly disgusting pork-chop bones, digging up his cactus and replanting it on its head. At night when the household fell silent I would lie in bed listening to his methodical pebbly racket from the opposite end of the house. Buster was manic-depressive.

I wondered if he might be responding to the moon. I'm partial to lunar cy- 11 cles, ever since I learned as a teenager that human females in their natural state—which is to say, sleeping outdoors—arrive at menses in synchrony and ovulate with the full moon. My imagination remains captive to that primordial village: the comradely grumpiness of new-moon days, when the entire world at once would go on PMS alert. And the compensation that would turn up two weeks later on a wild wind, under that great round headlamp, driving both men and women to distraction with the overt prospect of conception. The sur-face of the land literally rises and falls—as much as fifty centimeters—as the moon passes over, and we clay-footed mortals fall like dominoes before the swell. It's no surprise at all if a full moon inspires lyricists to corny love songs, or inmates to slamming themselves against barred windows. A hermit crab hardly seems this impetuous, but animals are notoriously responsive to the full moon: wolves howl; roosters announce daybreak all night. Luna moths, Arctic loons, and lunatics have a sole inspiration in common. Buster's insomniac rest-lessness seemed likely to be a part of the worldwide full-moon fellowship.

But it wasn't, exactly. The full moon didn't shine on either end of his cycle, 12 the high or the low. We tried to keep track, but it soon became clear: Buster marched to his own drum. The cyclic force that moved him remained as myste-rious to us as his true gender and the workings of his crustacean soul.

Buster's aquarium occupies a spot on our kitchen counter right next to the 13 coffeepot, and so it became my habit to begin mornings with chin in hands, pondering the oceanic mysteries while awaiting percolation. Finally, I remem-bered something. Years ago when I was a graduate student of animal behavior, I passed my days reading about the likes of animals' internal clocks. Tempera-ture, photoperiod, the rise and fall of hormones—all these influences have been teased apart like so many threads from the rope that pulls every creature to its regulated destiny. But one story takes the cake. F. A. Brown, a researcher who is more or less the grandfather of the biological clock, set about in 1954 to track the cycles of intertidal oysters. He scooped his subjects from the clammy coast of Connecticut and moved them into the basement of a laboratory in landlocked Illinois. For the first fifteen days in their new aquariums, the oysters kept right up with their normal intertidal behavior: they spent time shut away in their shells, and time with their mouths wide open, siphoning their briny bath for the plankton that sustained them, as the tides ebbed and flowed on the distant Connecticut shore. In the next two weeks, they made a mystifying shift. They still carried out their cycles in unison, and were regular as the tides, but their high-tide behavior didn't coincide with high tide in Connecticut, or for that matter California, or any other tidal charts known to science. It dawned on the researchers after some calculations that the oysters were responding to high tide in Chicago. Never mind that the gentle mollusks lived in glass boxes in the basement of a steel-and-cement building. Nor that Chicago has no ocean. In the circumstances, the oysters were doing their best.

When Buster is running around for all he's worth, I can only presume it's 14 high tide in Tucson. With or without evidence, I'm romantic enough to believe it. This is the lesson of Buster, the poetry that camps outside the halls of science: Jump for joy, hallelujah. Even a desert has tides.

When I was twenty-two, I donned the shell of a tiny yellow Renault and 15 drove with all I owned from Kentucky to Tucson. I was a typical young American, striking out. I had no earthly notion that I was bringing on myself a calamity of the magnitude of the one that befell poor Buster. I am the commonest kind of North American refugee: I believe I like it here, far-flung from my original home. I've come to love the desert that bristles and breathes and sleeps outside my windows. In the course of seventeen years I've embedded myself in a family here—neighbors, colleagues, friends I can't foresee living without, and a child who is native to this ground, with loves of her own. I'm here for good, it seems.

And yet I never cease to long in my bones for what I left behind. I open my 16 eyes on every new day expecting that a creek will run through my backyard under broad-leafed maples, and that my mother will be whistling in the kitchen. Behind the howl of coyotes, I'm listening for meadowlarks, I sometimes ache to be rocked in the bosom of the blood relations and busybodies of my childhood. Particularly in my years as a mother without a mate, I have deeply missed the safety net of extended family.

In a city of half a million I still really look at every face, anticipating recog- 17 nition, because I grew up in a town where every face meant something to me. I have trouble remembering to lock the doors. Wariness of strangers I learned the hard way. When I was new to the city, I let a man into my house one hot afternoon because he seemed in dire need of a drink of water; when I turned from the kitchen sink I found sharpened steel shoved against my belly. And so I know, I know. But I cultivate suspicion with as much difficulty as I force tomatoes to grow in the drought-stricken hardpan of my strange backyard. No creek runs here, but I'm still listening to secret tides, living as if I belonged to an earlier place: not Kentucky, necessarily, but a welcoming earth and a human family. A forest. A species.

In my life I've had frightening losses and unfathomable gifts: A knife in my 18 stomach. The death of an unborn child. Sunrise in a rain forest. A stupendous column of blue butterflies rising from a Greek monastery. A car that spontaneously caught fire while I was driving it. The end of a marriage, followed by a year in which I could barely understand how to keep living. The discovery, just weeks ago when I rose from my desk and walked into the kitchen, of three strangers industriously relieving my house of its contents.

I persuaded the strangers to put down the things they were holding (what 19
a bizarre tableau of anti-Magi they made, these three unwise men, bearing a
camera, an electric guitar, and a Singer sewing machine), and to leave my home,
pronto. My daughter asked excitedly when she got home from school, "Mom,
did you say bad words?" (I told her this was the very occasion that bad words
exist for.) The police said, variously, that I was lucky, foolhardy, and "a brave
lady." But it's not good luck to be invaded, and neither foolish nor brave to
stand your ground. It's only the way life goes, and I did it, just as years ago I
fought off the knife; mourned the lost child; bore witness to the rain forest;
claimed the blue butterflies as Holy Spirit in my private pantheon; got out of the
burning car; survived the divorce by putting one foot in front of the other and
taking good care of my child. On most important occasions, I cannot think how
to respond, I simply do. What does it mean, anyway, to be an animal in human
clothing? We carry around these big brains of ours like the crown jewels, but
mostly I find that millions of years of evolution have prepared me for one thing
only: to follow internal rhythms. To walk upright, to protect my loved ones, to
cooperate with my family group—however broadly I care to define it—to do
whatever will help us thrive. Obviously, some habits that saw us through the
millennia are proving hazardous in a modern context: for example, the yen to
consume carbohydrates and fat whenever they cross our path, or the proclivity
for unchecked reproduction. But it's surely worth forgiving ourselves these
tendencies a little, in light of the fact that they are what got us here. Like Buster,
we are creatures of inexplicable cravings. Thinking isn't everything. The way I
stock my refrigerator would amuse a level-headed interplanetary observer, who
would see I'm responding not to real necessity but to the dread of famine honed
in the African savannah. I can laugh at my Rhodesian Ridgeback as she
furtively sniffs the houseplants for a place to bury bones, and circles to beat
down the grass before lying on my kitchen floor. But she and I are exactly the
same kind of hairpin.

We humans have to grant the presence of some past adaptations, even in 20
their unforgivable extremes, if only to admit they are permanent rocks in the
stream we're obliged to navigate. It's easy to speculate and hard to prove, ever,
that genes control our behaviors. Yet we are persistently, excruciatingly adept at
many things that seem no more useful to modern life than the tracking of tides
in a desert. At recognizing insider/outsider status, for example, starting with
white vs. black and grading straight into distinctions so fine as to baffle the by-
stander—Serb and Bosnian, Hutu and Tutsi, Crip and Blood. We hold that children learn discrimination from their parents, but they learn it fiercely and well,
world without end. Recite it by rote like a multiplication table. Take it to heart,
though it's neither helpful nor appropriate, anymore than it is to hire the taller
of two men applying for a position as bank clerk, though statistically we're
likely to do that too. Deference to the physical superlative, a preference for the
scent of our own clan: a thousand anachronisms dance down the strands of our
DNA from a hidebound tribal past, guiding us toward the glories of survival,
and some vainglories as well. If we resent being bound by these ropes, the best

hope is to seize them out like snakes, by the throat, look them in the eye and own up to their venom.

But we rarely do, silly egghead of a species that we are. We invent the most 21 outlandish intellectual grounds to justify discrimination. We tap our toes to chaste love songs about the silvery moon without recognizing them as hymns to copulation. We can dress up our drives, put them in three-piece suits or ballet slippers, but still they drive us. The wonder of it is that our culture attaches almost unequivocal shame to our animal nature, believing brute urges must be hurtful, violent things. But it's no less an animal instinct that leads us to marry (species that benefit from monogamy tend to practice it); to organize a neighborhood cleanup campaign (rare and doomed is the creature that fouls its nest); to improvise and enforce morality (many primates socialize their young to be cooperative and ostracize adults who won't share food).

It's starting to look as if the most shameful tradition of Western civilization 22 is our need to deny we are animals. In just a few centuries of setting ourselves apart as landlords of the Garden of Eden, exempt from the natural order and entitled to hold dominion, we have managed to behave like so-called animals anyway, and on top of it to wreck most of what took three billion years to assemble. Air, water, earth, and fire—so much of our own element so vastly contaminated, we endanger our own future. Apparently we never owned the place after all. Like every other animal, we're locked into our niche: the mercury in the ocean, the pesticides on the soybean fields; all comes home to our breastfed babies. In the silent spring we are learning it's easier to escape from a chain gang than a food chain. Possibly we will have the sense to begin a new century by renewing our membership in the Animal Kingdom.

Not long ago I went backpacking in the Eagle Tail Mountains. This range 23 is a trackless wilderness in western Arizona that most people would call God-forsaken, taking for granted God's preference for loamy topsoil and regular precipitation. Whoever created the Eagle Tails had dry heat on the agenda, and a thing for volcanic rock. Also cactus, twisted mesquites, and five-alarm sunsets. The hiker's program in a desert like this is dire and blunt: carry in enough water to keep you alive till you can find a water source: then fill your bottles and head for the next one, or straight back out. Experts warn adventurers in this region, without irony, to drink their water while they're still alive, as it won't help later.

Several canyons looked promising for springs on our topographical map, 24 but turned up dry. Finally, at the top of a narrow, overgrown gorge we found a blessed tinaja, a deep, shaded hollow in the rock about the size of four or five claw-foot tubs, holding water. After we drank our fill, my friends struck out again, but I opted to stay and spend the day in the hospitable place that had slaked our thirst. On either side of the natural water tank, two shallow caves in the canyon wall faced each other, only a few dozen steps apart. By crossing from one to the other at noon, a person could spend the whole day here in shady comfort—or in colder weather, follow the winter sun. Anticipating a morning of reading, I pulled *Angle of Repose* out of my pack and looked for a place to settle on the flat, dusty floor of the west-facing shelter. Instead, my eyes were startled by a smooth corngrinding stone. It sat in the exact center of its rock bowl, as if the Hohokam woman or man who used this mortar and pestle had walked off and left them there an hour ago. The Hohokam disappeared from the earth in A.D. 1450. It was inconceivable to me that no one had been here since then, but that may have been the case—that is the point of trackless wilderness. I picked up the grinding stone. The size and weight and smooth, balanced perfection of it in my hand filled me at once with a longing to possess it. In its time, this excellent stone was the most treasured thing in a life, a family, maybe the whole neighborhood. To whom it still belonged. I replaced it in the rock depression, which also felt smooth to my touch. Because my eyes now understood how to look at it, the ground under my feet came alive with worked flint chips and pottery shards. I walked across to the other cave and found its floor just as lively with historic debris. Hidden under brittlebush and catclaw I found another grinding stone, this one some distance from the depression in the cave floor that once answered its pressure daily, for the grinding of corn or mesquite beans.

For a whole day I marveled at this place, running my fingers over the knife edges of dark flint chips, trying to fit together thick red pieces of shattered clay jars, biting my lower lip like a child concentrating on a puzzle. I tried to guess the size of whole pots from the curve of the broken pieces: some seemed as small as my two cupped hands, and some maybe as big as a bucket. The sun scorched my neck, reminding me to follow the shade across to the other shelter. Bees hummed at the edge of the water hole, nosing up to the water, their abdomens pulsing like tiny hydraulic pumps; by late afternoon they rimmed the pool completely, a collar of busy lace. Off and on, the lazy hand of a hot breeze shuffled the white leaves of the brittlebush. Once I looked up to see a screaming pair of red-tailed hawks mating in midair, and once a clatter of hooves warned me to hold still. A bighorn ram emerged through the brush, his head bent low under his hefty cornice, and ambled by me with nothing on his mind so much as a cool drink.

How long can a pestle stone lie still in the center of its mortar? That long ago—that recently—people lived here. *Here,* exactly, and not one valley over, or two, or twelve, because this place had all a person needs: shelter, food, and permanent water. They organized their lives around a catchment basin in a granite boulder, conforming their desires to the earth's charities; they never expected the opposite. The stories I grew up with lauded Moses for striking the rock and bringing forth the bubbling stream. But the stories of the Hohokam—oh, how they must have praised that good rock.

At dusk my friends returned with wonderful tales of the ground they had covered. We camped for the night, refilled our canteens, and hiked back to the land of plumbing and a fair guarantee of longevity. But I treasure my memory of the day I lingered near water and covered no ground. I cant think of a day in my life in which I've had such a clear fix on what it means to be human.

Want is a thing that unfurls unbidden like fungus, opening large upon itself, stopless, filling the sky. But *needs* from one day to the next, are few enough to fit in a bucket, with room enough left to rattle like brittlebush in a dry wind.

For each of us—furred, feathered, or skinned alive—the whole earth bal- 29
ances on the single precarious point of our own survival. In the best of times, I
hold in mind the need to care for things beyond the self: poetry, humanity,
grace. In other times, when it seems difficult merely to survive and be happy
about it, the condition of my thought tastes as simple as this: let me be a good
animal today. I've spent months at a stretch, even years, with that taste in my
mouth, and have found that it serves.

But it seems a wide gulf to cross, from the raw, green passion for survival to 30
the dispassionate, considered state of human grace. How does the animal mind
construct a poetry for the modern artifice in which we now reside? Often I feel
as disoriented as poor Buster, unprepared for the life that zooms headlong past
my line of sight. This clutter of human paraphernalia and counterfeit necessi-
ties—what does it have to do with the genuine business of life on earth? It feels
strange to me to be living in a box, hiding from the steadying influence of the
moon; wearing the hide of a cow, which is supposed to be dyed to match God-
knows-what, on my feet; making promises over the telephone about things I
will do at a precise hour next *year*. (I always feel the urge to add, as my grandmother does, "Lord willing and the creeks don't rise!") I find it impossible to
think, with a straight face, about what colors ought not to be worn after Labor
Day. I can become hysterical over the fact that someone, somewhere, invented a
thing called the mushroom scrubber, and that many other people undoubtedly
feel they *need* to possess one. It's completely usual for me to get up in the morning, take a look around, and laugh out loud.

Strangest of all, I am carrying on with all of this in a desert, two thousand 31
miles from my verdant childhood home. I am disembodied. No one here remembers how I was before I grew to my present height. I'm called upon to rein-
vent my own childhood time and again; in the process, I wonder how I can ever
know the truth about who I am. If someone had told me what I was headed for
in that little Renault—that I was stowing away in a shell, bound to wake up to
an alien life on a persistently foreign shore—I surely would not have done it.
But no one warned me. My culture, as I understand it, values independence
above all things—in part to ensure a mobile labor force, grease for the machine
of a capitalist economy. Our fairy tale commands: Little Pig, go out and seek
your fortune! So I did.

Many years ago I read that the Tohono O'odham, who dwell in the deserts 32
near here, traditionally bury the umbilicus of a newborn son or daughter somewhere close to home and plant a tree over it, to hold the child in place. In a sentimental frame of mind, I did the same when my own baby's cord fell off. I'm
staring at the tree right now, as I write—a lovely thing grown huge outside my
window, home to woodpeckers, its boughs overarching the house, as dissimilar
from the sapling I planted seven years ago as my present life is from the tidy future I'd mapped out for us all when my baby was born. She will roam light-
years from the base of that tree. I have no doubt of it. I can only hope she's
growing as the tree is, absorbing strength and rhythms and a trust in the seasons, so she will always be able to listen for home.

I feel remorse about Buster's monumental relocation; it's a weighty respon- 33 sibility to have thrown someone else's life into permanent chaos. But as for my own, I cant be sorry I made the trip. Most of what I learned in the old place seems to suffice for the new: if the seasons like Chicago tides come at ridiculous times and I have to plant in September instead of May, and if I have to make up family from scratch, what matters is that I do have sisters and tomato plants, the essential things. Like Buster, I'm inclined to see the material backdrop of my life as mostly immaterial, compared with what moves inside of me. I hold on to my adopted shore, chanting private vows: wherever I am, let me never forget to distinguish *want* from *need*. Let me be a good animal today. Let me dance in the waves of my private tide, the habits of survival and love.

Every one of us is called upon, probably many times, to start a new life. A 34 frightening diagnosis, a marriage, a move, loss of a job or a limb or a loved one, a graduation, bringing a new baby home: it's impossible to think at first how this all will be possible. Eventually, what moves it all forward is the subterranean ebb and flow of being alive among the living.

In my own worst seasons I've come back from the colorless world of de- 35 spair by forcing myself to look hard, for a long time, at a single glorious thing: a flame of red geranium outside my bedroom window. And then another: my daughter in a yellow dress. And another: the perfect outline of a full, dark sphere behind the crescent moon. Until I learned to be in love with my life again. Like a stroke victim retraining new parts of the brain to grasp lost skills, I have taught myself joy, over and over again.

It's not such a wide gulf to cross, then, from survival to poetry. We hold fast 36 to the old passions of endurance that buckle and creak beneath us, dovetailed, tight as a good wooden boat to carry us onward. And onward full tilt we go, pitched and wrecked and absurdly resolute, driven in spite of everything to make gold on a new shore. To be hopeful, to embrace one possibility after another—that is surely the basic instinct. Baser even than hate, the thing with teeth, which can be stilled with a tone of voice or stunned by beauty. If the whole world of the living has to turn on the single point of remaining alive, that pointed endurance is the poetry of hope. The thing with feathers.

What a stroke of luck. What a singular brute feat of outrageous fortune: to 37 be born to citizenship in the Animal Kingdom. We love and we lose, go back to the start and do it right over again. For every heavy forebrain solemnly cataloging the facts of a harsh landscape, there's a rush of intuition behind it crying out: High tide! Time to move out into the glorious debris. Time to take this life for what it is.

COMPREHENSION

1. What is the thesis of the essay? Is it expressed explicitly, or does the reader have to infer it? Explain your view.

2. In paragraph 22, Kingsolver says, "It's starting to look as if the most shameful tradition of Western civilization is our need to deny we are animals." In what ways, according to the essay, are we like other animals?
3. Paragraphs 15 through 19 describe some of the disruptions and problems created by contemporary life. What responses to these problems does the writer offer?

RHETORIC

1. Kingsolver uses an overarching analogy between herself and the hermit crab. Where does this first occur in the essay?
2. The writer divides the essay into four parts. What is the content and purpose of each part?
3. How does the contrast between "wants" and "needs" at the end of paragraph 28 serve as a transition to the next paragraph and to those that follow?
4. The title of the essay is enigmatic, as there is no ocean or sea in Tucson. What is the rhetorical purpose of choosing the title "High Tide in Tucson" for the essay?
5. Kingsolver is a noted fiction writer with a singular poetic style of writing. How does this sentence from paragraph 16 demonstrate her writer's voice: "I sometimes ache to be rocked in the bosom of the blood relations and busybodies of my childhood"?
6. Personification is the attribution of human qualities to nonhuman beings or things. Explain how Kingsolver uses personification in the introduction.
7. Kingsolver compares and contrasts human behavior with animal nature in paragraph 21. What is the main similarity between the two? The main difference?

WRITING

1. In an expository essay, describe and examine at least three technological devices that have alienated humans from their animal nature.
2. Argue for or against the view that human intelligence is so developed that our quest for knowledge, such as exploration of space, understanding of the laws of physics, and creating labor-saving devices, is far stronger than our primitive animal natures.
3. Argue for or against the proposition that our human flaws keep us from finding harmony with the world and are the causes behind wars, racial and ethnic strife, and environmental pollution—elements that do not exist within the animal kingdom.

Economy

Henry David Thoreau

Henry David Thoreau (1817–1862), author of the masterpiece Walden *(1854), is one of the most important figures in American thought and literature. A social and political activist, he opposed the Mexican War, protested slavery, and refused to pay his poll taxes. As a naturalist, he believed in the preeminence of individualism and nature over technology, materialism, and nationalism. In 1845, Thoreau went to live at Walden Pond, "living deep and sucking out all the marrow of life." Walden, describing his life at the pond, is one of the most challenging, exuberant, and innovative works of American literature. This account from Thoreau's masterpiece, tracing the construction of his dwelling, reflects his preoccupation with economy, natural process, and self-reliance.*

Near the end of March, 1845, I borrowed an axe and went down to the woods   1
by Walden Pond, nearest to where I intended to build my house, and began to
cut down some tall arrowy white pines, still in their youth, for timber. It is difficult to begin without borrowing, but perhaps it is the most generous course
thus to permit your fellow-men to have an interest in your enterprise. The
owner of the axe, as he released his hold on it, said that it was the apple of his
eye; but I returned it sharper than I received it. It was a pleasant hillside where
I worked, covered with pine woods, through which I looked out on the pond,
and a small open field in the woods where pines and hickories were springing
up. The ice in the pond was not yet dissolved, though there were some open
spaces, and it was all dark colored and saturated with water. There were some
slight flurries of snow during the days that I worked there; but for the most part
when I came out onto the railroad, on my way home, its yellow sand heap
stretched away gleaming in the hazy atmosphere, and the rails shone in the
spring sun, and I heard the lark and pewee and other birds already come to
commence another year with us. They were pleasant spring days, in which the
winter of man's discontent was thawing as well as the earth, and the life that
had lain torpid began to stretch itself. One day, when my axe had come off and
I had cut a green hickory for a wedge, driving it with a stone, and had placed
the whole to soak in a pond hole in order to swell the wood, I saw a striped
snake run into the water, and he lay on the bottom, apparently without inconvenience, as long as I stayed there, or more than a quarter of an hour; perhaps
because he had not yet fairly come out of the torpid state. It appeared to me that
for a like reason men remain in their present low and primitive condition; but if
they should feel the influence of the spring of springs arousing them, they
would of necessity rise to a higher and more ethereal life. I had previously seen
the snakes in frosty mornings in my path with portions of their bodies still
numb and inflexible, waiting for the sun to thaw them. On the 1st of April it

rained and melted the ice, and in the early part of the day, which was very foggy, I heard a stray goose groping about over the pond and cackling as if lost, or like the spirit of the fog.

So I went on for some days cutting and hewing timber, and also studs and ₂ rafters, all with my narrow axe, not having many communicable or scholarlike thoughts, singing to myself.

Men say they know many things;
But lo! they have taken wings—
The arts and sciences,
And a thousand appliances;
The wind that blows
Is all that anybody knows.

I hewed the main timber six inches square, most of the studs on two sides only, ₃ and the rafters and floor timbers on one side, leaving the rest of the bark on, so that they were just as straight and much stronger than sawed ones. Each stick was carefully mortised or tenoned by its stump, for I had borrowed other tools by this time. My days in the woods were not very long ones; yet I usually carried my dinner of bread and butter, and read the newspaper in which it was wrapped, at noon, sitting amid the green pine boughs which I had cut off, and to my bread was imparted some of their fragrance, for my hands were covered with a thick coat of pitch. Before I was done I was more the friend than the foe of the pine tree, though I had cut down some of them, having become better acquainted with it. Sometimes a rambler in the wood was attracted by the sound of my axe, and we chatted pleasantly over the chips which I had made.

By the middle of April, for I made no haste in my work, but rather made the ₄ most of it, my house was framed and ready for the raising. I had already bought the shanty of James Collins, an Irishman who worked on the Fitchburg Railroad, for boards. James Collins' shanty was considered an uncommonly fine one. When I called to see it he was not at home. I walked about the outside, at first unobserved from within, the window was so deep and high. It was of small dimensions, with a peaked cottage roof, and not much else to be seen, the dirt being raised five feet all around as if it were a compost heap. The roof was the soundest part, though a good deal warped and made brittle by the sun. Doorsill there was none, but a perennial passage for the hens under the door board. Mrs. C. came to the door and asked me to view it from the inside. The hens were driven in by my approach. It was dark, and had a dirt floor for the most part, dank, clammy, and aguish, only here a board and there a board which would not bear removal. She lighted a lamp to show me the inside of the roof and the walls, and also that the board floor extended under the bed, warning me not to step into the cellar, a sort of dust hole two feet deep. In her own words, they were "good boards overhead, good boards all around, and a good window"—of two whole squares originally, only the cat had passed out that way lately. There was a stove, a bed, and a place to sit, an infant in the house where it was born, a silk parasol, gilt-framed looking-glass, and a patent new coffee-mill nailed to an oak sapling, all told. The bargain was soon concluded, for James had in the meanwhile returned. I to pay four dollars and twenty-five cents tonight, he to vacate at five tomorrow morning, selling to nobody else meanwhile: I to take possession at six. It were well, he said, to be there early, and anticipate certain indistinct but wholly unjust claims on the score of ground rent and fuel. This he assured me was the only encumbrance. At six I passed him and his family on the road. One large bundle held their all—bed, coffee-mill, looking-glass, hens—all but the cat; she took to the woods and became a wild cat and, as I learned afterward, trod in a trap set for woodchucks, and so became a dead cat at last.

I took down this dwelling the same morning, drawing the nails, and re- 5 moved it to the pond side by small cartloads, spreading the boards on the grass there to bleach and warp back again in the sun. One early thrush gave me a note or two as I drove along the woodland path. I was informed treacherously by a young Patrick that neighbor Seeley, an Irishman, in the intervals of the carting, transferred the still tolerable, straight, and drivable nails, staples, and spikes to his pocket, and then stood when I came back to pass the time of day, and look freshly up, unconcerned, with spring thoughts, at the devastation; there being a dearth of work, as he said. He was there to represent spectatordom, and help make this seemingly insignificant event one with the removal of the gods of Troy.

I dug my cellar in the side of a hill sloping to the south, where a woodchuck 6 had formerly dug his burrow, down through sumach and blackberry roots, and the lowest stain of vegetation, six feet square by seven deep, to a fine sand where potatoes would not freeze in any winter. The sides were left shelving, and not stoned; but the sun having never shone on them, the sand still keeps its place. It was but two hours' work. I took particular pleasure in this breaking of ground, for in almost all latitudes men dig into the earth for an equable temperature. Under the most splendid house in the city is still to be found the cellar where they store their roots as of old, and long after the superstructure had disappeared posterity remark its dent in the earth. The house is still but a sort of porch at the entrance of a burrow.

At length, in the beginning of May, with the help of some of my acquain- 7 tances, rather to improve so good an occasion for neighborliness than from any necessity, I set up the frame of my house. No man was ever more honored in the character of his raisers than I. They are destined, I trust, to assist at the raising of loftier structures one day. I began to occupy my house on the 4th of July, as soon as it was boarded and roofed, for the boards were carefully feather-edged and lapped, so that it was perfectly impervious to rain, but before boarding I laid the foundation of a chimney at one end, bringing two cartloads of stones up the hill from the pond in my arms. I built the chimney after my hoeing in the fall, before a fire became necessary for warmth, doing my cooking in the meanwhile out of doors on the ground, early in the morning: which mode I still think is in some respects more convenient and agreeable than the usual one. When it stormed before my bread was baked, I fixed a few boards over the fire, and sat under them to watch my loaf, and passed some pleasant hours in that way. In those days, when my hands were much employed, I read but little, but the least scraps of paper which lay on the ground, my holder, or tablecloth, afforded me as much entertainment, in fact answered the same purpose as the Iliad.

COMPREHENSION

1. Explain the process by which Thoreau builds his house. What are the main steps in this process?
2. What is Thoreau's attitude toward economy in this selection? Which of the details Thoreau has included most successfully reveal this attitude?
3. Compare Thoreau's evocation of place in this essay with Ehrlich's presentation of place in "The Solace of Open Spaces." Are the two authors addressing readers in the same way? Justify your response.

RHETORIC

1. In paragraph 1, what connotation does the author develop for the word *borrowing?* How do words related to economics serve as a motif in the essay?
2. What is the analogy in paragraph 1?
3. How does Thoreau use process analysis? Why is this rhetorical technique reinforced by the natural processes depicted in the essay?
4. How does Thoreau particularize the generalizations he makes in the essay?
5. What is the tone of the essay? Does an implied thesis for the essay emerge? Justify your answer.
6. What is the relationship of the last two sentences in paragraph 6 to the rest of the selection?

WRITING

1. Analyze Thoreau's poem in paragraph 2. Identify the poem's theme. Then write a brief essay explaining its relevance to "Economy."
2. Using Thoreau's method, write an essay in which you trace the process of building or creating something that was important to you.
3. Write a letter to the editor of your college newspaper arguing the need to economize in some aspect of personal or public life. Refer to Thoreau in this letter.

Americans and the Land

John Steinbeck

John Steinbeck (1902–1968) was born in California, the setting for some of his best fiction. Steinbeck's fiction of the 1930s, including The Pastures of Heaven *(1932),* Tortilla Flat *(1935),* In Dubious Battle *(1936),* Of Mice and Men *(1937), and the Pulitzer Prize–winning epic,* The Grapes of Wrath *(1939), offers one of the best imaginative presentations of the American Depression. Steinbeck won the Nobel Prize in Literature in 1962 for "realistic and imaginative writings, distinguished as they are by a sympathetic humor and a social perception." In this section from* America and Americans *(1966), Steinbeck offers a probing, critical appraisal of American social development.*

I have often wondered at the savagery and thoughtlessness with which our 1 early settlers approached this rich continent. They came at it as though it were an enemy, which of course it was. They burned the forests and changed the rainfall; they swept the buffalo from the plains, blasted the streams, set fire to the grass, and ran a reckless scythe through the virgin and noble timber. Perhaps they felt that it was limitless and could never be exhausted and that a man could move on to new wonders endlessly. Certainly there are many examples to the contrary, but to a large extent the early people pillaged the country as though they hated it, as though they held it temporarily and might be driven off at any time.

This tendency toward irresponsibility persists in very many of us today; 2 our rivers are poisoned by reckless dumping of sewage and toxic industrial wastes, the air of our cities is filthy and dangerous to breathe from the belching of uncontrolled products from combustion of coal, coke, oil, and gasoline. Our towns are girdled with wreckage and the debris of our toys—our automobiles and our packaged pleasures. Through uninhibited spraying against one enemy we have destroyed the natural balances our survival requires. All these evils can and must be overcome if America and Americans are to survive; but many of us still conduct ourselves as our ancestors did, stealing from the future for our clear and present profit.

Since the river-polluters and the air-poisoners are not criminal or even bad 3 people, we must presume that they are heirs to the early conviction that sky and water are unowned and that they are limitless. In the light of our practices here at home it is very interesting to me to read of the care taken with the carriers of our probes into space to make utterly sure that they are free of pollution of any kind. We would not think of doing to the moon what we do every day to our own dear country.

When the first settlers came to America and dug in on the coast, they hud- 4
dled in defending villages hemmed in by the sea on one side and by endless
forests on the other, by Red Indians and, most frightening, the mystery of an unknown land extending nobody knew how far. And for a time very few cared or
dared to find out. Our first Americans organized themselves and lived in a state
of military alertness; every community built its blockhouse for defense. By law
the men went armed and were required to keep their weapons ready and available. Many of them wore armor, made here or imported; on the East Coast, they
wore the cuirass and helmet, and the Spaniards on the West Coast wore both
steel armor and heavy leather to turn arrows.

On the East Coast, and particularly in New England, the colonists farmed 5
meager lands close to their communities and to safety. Every man was permanently on duty for the defense of his family and his village; even the hunting
parties went into the forest in force, rather like raiders than hunters, and their
subsequent quarrels with the Indians, resulting in forays and even massacres,
remind us that the danger was very real. A man took his gun along when he
worked the land, and the women stayed close to their thick-walled houses and
listened day and night for the signal of alarm. The towns they settled were permanent, and most of them exist today with their records of Indian raids, of
slaughter, of scalpings, and of punitive counter-raids. The military leader of the
community became the chief authority in time of trouble, and it was a long time
before danger receded and the mystery could be explored.

After a time, however, brave and forest-wise men drifted westward to hunt, 6
to trap, and eventually to bargain for the furs which were the first precious ne-
gotiable wealth America produced for trade and export. Then trading posts
were set up as centers of collection and the exploring men moved up and down
the rivers and crossed the mountains, made friends for mutual profit with the
Indians, learned the wilderness techniques, so that these explorer-traders soon
dressed, ate, and generally acted like the indigenous people around them. Suspicion lasted a long time, and was fed by clashes sometimes amounting to full-
fledged warfare; but by now these Americans attacked and defended as the
Indians did.

For a goodly time the Americans were travelers, moving about the country 7
collecting its valuables, but with little idea of permanence; their roots and their
hearts were in the towns and the growing cities along the eastern edge. The few
who stayed, who lived among the Indians, adopted their customs and some
took Indian wives and were regarded as strange and somehow treasonable
creatures. As for their half-breed children, while the tribe sometimes adopted
them they were unacceptable as equals in the eastern settlements.

Then the trickle of immigrants became a stream, and the population began 8
to move westward—not to grab and leave but to settle and live, they thought.
The newcomers were of peasant stock, and they had their roots in a Europe
where they had been landless, for the possession of land was the requirement
and the proof of a higher social class than they had known. In America they
found beautiful and boundless land for the taking—and they took it.

It is little wonder that they went land-mad, because there was so much of it. 9
They cut and burned the forests to make room for crops; they abandoned their
knowledge of kindness to the land in order to maintain its usefulness. When
they had cropped out a piece they moved on, raping the country like invaders.
The topsoil, held by roots and freshened by leaffall, was left helpless to the
spring freshets, stripped and eroded with the naked bones of clay and rock exposed. The destruction of the forests changed the rainfall, for the searching
clouds could find no green and beckoning woods to draw them on and milk
them. The merciless nineteenth century was like a hostile expedition for loot
that seemed limitless. Uncountable buffalo were killed, stripped of their hides,
and left to rot, a reservoir of permanent food supply eliminated. More than that,
the land of the Great Plains was robbed of the manure of the herds. Then the
plows went in and ripped off the protection of the buffalo grass and opened the
helpless soil to quick water and slow drought and the mischievous winds that
roamed through the Great Central Plains. There has always been more than
enough desert in America; the new settlers, like overindulged children, created
even more.

The railroads brought new hordes of land-crazy people, and the new 10
Americans moved like locusts across the continent until the western sea put a
boundary to their movements. Coal and copper and gold drew them on; they
savaged the land, gold-dredged the rivers to skeletons of pebbles and debris.
An aroused and fearful government made laws for the distribution of public
lands—a quarter section, one hundred and sixty acres, per person—and a
claim had to be proved and improved; but there were ways of getting around
this, and legally. My own grandfather proved out a quarter section for himself,
one for his wife, one for each of his children, and, I suspect, acreage for children he hoped and expected to have. Marginal lands, of course, suitable only
for grazing, went in larger pieces. One of the largest land-holding families in
California took its richest holdings by a trick: By law a man could take up all
the swamp or water-covered land he wanted. The founder of this great holding
mounted a scow on wheels and drove his horses over thousands of acres of the
best bottom land, then reported that he had explored it in a boat, which was
true, and confirmed his title. I need not mention his name; his descendants will
remember.

Another joker with a name still remembered in the West worked out a 11
scheme copied many times in after years. Proving a quarter section required a
year of residence and some kind of improvement—a fence, a shack—but once
the land was proved the owner was free to sell it. This particular princely character went to the stews and skid rows of the towns and found a small army of
hopeless alcoholics who lived for whiskey and nothing else. He put these men
on land he wanted to own, grubstaked them and kept them in cheap liquor until the acreage was proved, then went through the motions of buying it from his
protégés and moved them and their one-room shacks on sled runners to new
quarter sections. Bums of strong constitution might prove out five or six homesteads for this acquisitive hero before they died of drunkenness.

It was full late when we began to realize that the continent did not stretch   12
out to infinity; that there were limits to the indignities to which we could subject it. Engines and heavy mechanical equipment were allowing us to ravage it
even more effectively than we had with fire, dynamite, and gang plows. Conservation came to us slowly, and much of it hasn't arrived yet. Having killed the
whales and wiped out the sea otters and most of the beavers, the market
hunters went to work on game birds; ducks and quail were decimated, and the
passenger pigeon eliminated. In my youth I remember seeing a market hunter's
gun, a three-gauge shotgun bolted to a frame and loaded to the muzzle with
shingle nails. Aimed at a lake and the trigger pulled with a string, it slaughtered
every living thing on the lake. The Pacific Coast pilchards were once the raw
material for a great and continuing industry. We hunted them with aircraft far
at sea until they were gone and the canneries had to be closed. In some of the
valleys of the West, where the climate makes several crops a year available,
which the water supply will not justify, wells were driven deeper and deeper
for irrigation, so that in one great valley a million acre feet more of water was
taken out than rain and melting snow could replace, and the water table went
down and a few more years may give us a new desert.

The great redwood forests of the western mountains early attracted atten-   13
tion. These ancient trees, which once grew everywhere, now exist only where
the last Ice Age did not wipe them out. And they were found to have value. The
Sempervirens and the Gigantea, the two remaining species, make soft, straight-
grained timber. They are easy to split into planks, shakes, fenceposts, and railroad ties, and they have a unique virtue: they resist decay, both wet and dry rot,
and an inherent acid in them repels termites. The loggers went through the
great groves like a barrage, toppling the trees—some of which were two thousand years old—and leaving no maidens, no seedlings or saplings on the de-
nuded hills.

Quite a few years ago when I was living in my little town on the coast of   14
California a stranger came in and bought a small valley where the Sempervirens
redwoods grew, some of them three hundred feet high. We used to walk among
these trees, and the light colored as though the great glass of the Cathedral at
Chartres had strained and sanctified the sunlight. The emotion we felt in this
grove was one of awe and humility and joy; and then one day it was gone,
slaughtered, and the sad wreckage of boughs and broken saplings left like nonsensical spoilage of the battle-ruined countryside. And I remember that after
our rage there was sadness, and when we passed the man who had done this
we looked away, because we were ashamed for him.

From early times we were impressed and awed by the fantastic accidents of   15
nature, like the Grand Canyon and Yosemite and Yellowstone Park. The Indians
had revered them as holy places, visited by the gods, and all of us came to have
somewhat the same feeling about them. Thus we set aside many areas of astonishment as publicly owned parks; and though this may to a certain extent have
been because there was no other way to use them as the feeling of preciousness
of the things we had been destroying grew in Americans, more and more areas

were set aside as national and state parks, to be looked at but not injured. Many people loved and were in awe of the redwoods; societies and individuals bought groves of these wonderful trees and presented them to the state for preservation.

No longer do we Americans want to destroy wantonly, but our newfound 16 sources of power—to take the burden of work from our shoulders, to warm us, and cool us, and give us light, to transport us quickly, and to make the things we use and wear and eat—these power sources spew pollution on our country, so that the rivers and streams are becoming poisonous and lifeless. The birds die for the lack of food; a noxious cloud hangs over our cities that burns our lungs and reddens our eyes. Our ability to conserve has not grown with our power to create, but this slow and sullen poisoning is no longer ignored or justified. Almost daily, the pressure of outrage among Americans grows. We are no longer content to destroy our beloved country. We are slow to learn; but we learn. When a superhighway was proposed in California which would trample the redwood trees in its path, an outcry arose all over the land, so strident and fierce that the plan was put aside. And we no longer believe that a man, by owning a piece of America, is free to outrage it.

But we are an exuberant people, careless and destructive as active children. 17 We make strong and potent tools and then have to use them to prove that they exist. Under the pressure of war we finally made the atom bomb, and for reasons which seemed justifiable at the time we dropped it on two Japanese cities—and I think we finally frightened ourselves. In such things, one must consult himself because there is no other point of reference. I did not know about the bomb, and certainly I had nothing to do with its use, but I am horrified and ashamed; and nearly everyone I know feels the same thing. And those who loudly and angrily justify Hiroshima and Nagaski—why, they must be the most ashamed of all.

COMPREHENSION

1. What is Steinbeck's purpose in writing this essay? State his thesis in your own words.
2. According to Steinbeck, how did the American attitude toward the land evolve?
3. Does Steinbeck think that the American attitude toward the land can be changed? Cite evidence from the essay to support your answer.

RHETORIC

1. Analyze Steinbeck's use of figurative language in paragraphs 1, 2, 9, and 14.
2. Locate images and vocabulary relating to rape and destruction in the essay. What is the relevance of this motif to the development of Steinbeck's thesis?

3. How does Steinbeck use examples in paragraphs 1 and 2 to establish the subject and thesis of his essay?
4. Analyze the relationship between the patterns of description and example in the essay. What types of illustrations does Steinbeck employ? How does he achieve concreteness through examples? Where does he employ extended examples? Does he use examples subjectively or objectively? Explain.
5. How does Steinbeck employ process analysis to highlight his thesis?
6. Explain the relationship between paragraph 16 and paragraph 17 in the essay.

WRITING

1. Analyze the way in which description and figurative language advance Steinbeck's thesis.
2. Write an essay entitled "Americans and the Land," using examples to support your thesis.
3. Write an essay on the relationship between ecology and the state of civilization.

CONNECTIONS FOR CRITICAL THINKING

1. Using support from the works of Steinbeck, Carson, Chief Seattle, and others, write a causal-analysis essay tracing our relationship to the land. To what extent have history, greed, and fear helped shape our attitude? Can this attitude be changed? How?
2. Consider the empathy and sensitivity Walker has toward animals. How do her attitude and perceptions coincide with the view expressed by Chief Seattle concerning the natural world?
3. Write a letter to the op-ed page of a newspaper objecting to a governmental ruling harmful to the environment. State the nature of the policy, its possible dangers, and your reasons for opposing it. Use support from any of the writers in this chapter. Extra reading or research may be necessary.
4. Consider why we fear nature. Why do we consider it an enemy, an alien, something to be destroyed? How would Steinbeck, Walker, Lopez, and Chief Seattle respond to this question? Do you agree or disagree with them?
5. Both Steinbeck and Ehrlich use historical data and description to explore our relationship to the land. How do they approach their subject in terms of language, attitude, and style?
6. Choose an author in this chapter whose essay, in your opinion, romanticizes nature. Compare his or her attitude with that of a writer with a more pragmatic approach to the subject. Compare the two views, and specify the

elements in their writing that contribute to the overall strength of their arguments.

7. Thoreau uses process analysis to structure his essay; Perrin uses enumeration and illustration. What are some of the strengths and weaknesses of employing traditional and orderly means of presenting one's thoughts?

8. Write an essay entitled "Nature's Revenge" in which you examine the consequences of environmental abuse. Consider the short- as well as the long-term effects on the quality of life. Use support from any writer in this chapter to defend your opinion.

9. Write specifically about our relationship to other living creatures on our planet. Is it one of exploitation, cooperation, or tyranny? How does this relationship influence how we treat each other? Explore the answers to these questions in an essay. Use the works of Lopez, Steinbeck, and Chief Seattle to support your thesis.

10. Join a newsgroup on the Web devoted to addressing a specific environmental issue, for example, atomic waste, overdevelopment, environmental regulations and deregulations. Follow the conversation of the newsgroup for one month. Write an essay describing the chief concerns of the newsgroup members, how they address issues regarding the environment, and what specific actions they recommend or take over the course of your membership.

11. Visit the Web site of the Environmental Protection Agency. Write a report describing the agency's announcements, speeches, activities, and proposals.

12. Create your own interactive Web site focusing on the environment. Present, in its headline, this request: "In a statement of 100 words, please explain whether we are doing enough to reverse the destruction to our environment." Check back in a month, and write a report summarizing the responses.

chapter *12*

A Guide to Research and Documentation

A research paper is a report in which you synthesize information on your topic, contributing your own analysis and evaluation to the subject. Research writing is a form of problem solving. You identify a problem, form a hypothesis (an unproven thesis, theory, or argument), gather and organize information from various sources, assess and interpret data, evaluate alternatives, reach conclusions, and provide documentation.

Research writing is both exciting and demanding. American essayist and novelist Joan Didion states, "The element of discovery takes place, in nonfiction, not during the writing but during the research." Nowhere is the interplay of the stages in the composing process more evident than in writing research papers. Prewriting is an especially important stage, for the bulk of your research and bibliographical spadework is done before you actually sit down to draft your report. Moreover, strategic critical thinking skills are required at every step of research writing. Here you sense the active, questioning, reflective activity of the mind as it confronts a problem, burrows into it, and moves through the problem to a solution, proof, or conclusion. Developing the ability to do research writing thus represents an integration of problem-solving and composing talents.

Research writing should be treated as a skill to be developed rather than a trial to be borne. Unfortunately, there are many misconceptions about it. Contrary to conventional wisdom, research does not begin boringly with the library catalog and end with the final period that you add to a bibliographic entry. (In fact, electronic searches and word processing have taken much of the drudgery out of writing research papers.) Nor does research writing exclusively report information, even though some writers tackle a research paper as a bland and boring recitation of facts.

Research actually means the careful investigation of a subject in order to discover or revise facts, theories, or applications. Your purpose is to demonstrate how other researchers approach a problem and how you treat that problem. A good research paper subtly blends your ideas and the attitudes or findings of others. In research writing you are dealing with ideas that are already in the public domain, but you are also contributing to knowledge.

RESEARCH WRITING:
PRECONCEPTIONS AND PRACTICE

When your ideas—rather than the ideas of others—become the center of the research process, writing a research paper becomes dynamic instead of static. The standard preconception about preparing a research paper is that a researcher simply finds a subject and then assembles information from sources usually found in a library. This strategy does teach disciplined habits of work and thought, and it is a traditional way to conduct research for college courses. Yet, does this conventional preconception match the practices of professional researchers?

Consider the following tasks:

- Evaluate critical responses to a best-selling novel, a book of poetry, a CD, or an award-winning film.
- Analyze the impact of the South, the West, or another region on presidential politics during a recent decade.
- Investigate a literary, political, or scientific scandal of the last century.
- Assess the effectiveness of urban, suburban, and rural schools, comparing specific measures of student success.
- Discuss the practical consequences of economic theory, examining work opportunities for men, women, recent immigrants, young people entering the workforce, former welfare recipients, or some other group of workers.
- Define a popular medical, dietary, or health-related term, examining how it contributes to or relates to a healthy life.

How would a professional researcher view these projects? First, the researcher sees a subject as a *problem* rather than a mere topic. Often this problem is authorized or designated by a collaborator, an editor, or a person in authority. The researcher has the task of developing or testing a hypothesis stemming from the particular problem: for example, whether or not a vegetarian diet effectively wards off cancer. *Hypothesis formation* is at the heart of professional research.

Second, the researcher often has to engage in primary as well as secondary research. *Primary research* relies on your analysis of texts, letters, manuscripts, and other materials, whether written, visual, or aural. *Secondary research* relies on sources that comment on the primary sources. For example, a critic's commentary on *Citizen Kane* or an historian's analysis of the cold war politics of the 1950s would be secondary sources; the film itself or a speech delivered by Senator Joseph McCarthy in 1950 would be primary sources. Because primary sources are not necessarily more reliable than secondary sources, you must always evaluate the reliability of both types of material. Critics can misinterpret, and experts often disagree, forcing you to weigh evidence and reach your own conclusions.

Third, all researchers face deadlines of a few days, a week, a month, or more. Confronted with deadlines, professional researchers learn to *telescope* their efforts in order to obtain information quickly. Common strategies include telephoning, networking (using personal and professional contacts as well as guides to organizations), browsing or searching on-line, conducting computerized or automated bibliographical searches, and turning to annotated bibliographies (listing articles on the topic with commentaries on each item) and specialized indexes (focusing on a particular field or discipline). Other strategies include turning to review articles, which evaluate other resources, and browsing through current articles, which may provide useful background as well as the most current thinking about the topic. These sources, many of which are found in the reference room of a library, permit the researcher to dive into the middle of a problem, rather than tread water in front of a library catalog.

Finally, much professional researching does not fall neatly into one academic content area. Typically, it cuts across subjects and disciplines, perhaps touching on literature, history, politics, psychology, economics, or more. The interdisciplinary nature of many research projects creates special problems for the researcher, especially in the use of bibliographical materials, which do tend to be subject-oriented. Good researchers know that they cannot be ghettoized into one subject area, such as history of physics. Knowledge in the contemporary era tends increasingly toward interdisciplinary concerns, and you must develop the critical thinking skills needed to operate effectively in an increasingly complex world.

Training, discipline, and strong critical thinking skills are necessary for any form of college research. Such research is not beyond your talents and abilities. Learn how to use library and electronic sources selectively and efficiently, but also learn how to view the world outside your library as a vast laboratory to be used fruitfully in order to solve your research problems.

THE RESEARCH PROCESS

The research process involves thinking, searching, reading, writing, and rewriting. The final product—the research paper—is the result of your discoveries in and contributions to the realm of ideas about your topic. More than any other form of college writing, however, the research paper evolves gradually through a series of stages.

This does not mean you proceed step-by-step through a rigid series of phases. Instead, the act of composing moves back and forth over a series of activities, and the actual act of writing remains unique to the individual researcher. For example, some writers prefer to draft an essay on some problem or issue that they know well and then fill in the research component. This procedure works especially well if you have been assigned a researched essay, requiring a limited number of sources, rather than a full research project. Other researchers are more cautious and conduct research before writing anything. Some writers take notes on note cards; some store information in their computers; others, in the tradition of the journalist, jot down information in loose-leaf notebooks. And there are some writers who, with a good internal sense of organization, manage to get by with seemingly chaotic ramblings recorded on any scrap of paper available.

Writers with little experience in developing research papers do have to be more methodical than experienced researchers who streamline and adjust the composing process to the scope and design of their projects. Despite the idiosyncrasies of writers, however, the research process tends to move through several interrelated stages or phases.

Phases in the Research Process

Phase I: Defining Your Objective

Choose a *researchable* topic.

Identify a *problem* inherent in the topic that gives you the reason for writing about the topic.

Examine the *purpose* of or the benefits to be gained from conducting research on the topic.

Think about the assumptions, interests, and needs of your *audience*.

Decide how you are going to *limit* your topic.

Establish a working *hypothesis* to guide and control the scope and direction of your research.

Phase 2: Locating Your Sources

Decide on your *methodology*—the types or varieties of primary and secondary research you plan to conduct. Determine the method of collecting data.

Go to the library and skim a general article or conduct a computer search to *determine if your topic is researchable* and if your hypothesis is likely to stand up.

Develop a *tentative working bibliography*, a file listing sources that seem relevant to your topic.

Review your bibliography, and *reassess your topic and hypothesis*.

Phase 3: Gathering and Organizing Data

Obtain your sources, taking notes on all information related directly to your thesis.

Analyze and organize your information. Design a *preliminary outline* with a tentative thesis if your findings support your hypothesis.

Revise your thesis if your findings suggest alternative conclusions.

(*Phases in the Research Process* continued)

Phase 4: Writing and Submitting the Paper

Write a *rough draft* of the paper, concentrating on the flow of thoughts and integrating research findings into the texture of the report.

Write a *first revision* to tighten organization, improve style, and check on the placement of data. Prepare citations that identify the sources of your information. Assemble a list of the references you have cited in your paper.

Prepare the manuscript using the format called for by the course, the discipline, or the person authorizing the research project.

Phase 1: Defining Your Objective

The first step in research writing is to select a researchable topic. You certainly do not want to discover that your topic for a 1,500-word term paper requires a book to handle it adequately. Nor do you want to risk spending fruitless days investigating a topic that lacks enough available information. Like the bear in the Goldilocks tale, you are in quest of something that is "just right"—a topic that is appropriate in scope for your assignment, a topic that promises an adventure for you in the realm of ideas, and a topic that will interest, if not excite, your audience.

You reduce wasted time and effort if you approach the research project as a problem to be investigated and solved, a controversy to take a position on, or a question to be answered. As a basis, you need a strong hypothesis or working thesis (which may be little more than a hunch or a calculated guess). The point of your investigation is to identify, illustrate, explain, argue, or prove that thesis. Start with a hypothesis before you actually begin to conduct research; otherwise, you will discover that you are simply reading in or about a topic, instead of reading toward the objective of substantiating your thesis or proposition.

Of course, before you can formulate a hypothesis, you need to start with a general idea of what subject you want to explore, what your purpose is going to be, and how you plan to select and limit a topic from your larger subject area. Prewriting strategies can help you find and limit topics for your research project. At the same time, a topic lends itself to research and to hypothesis formation if (1) it strongly interests you, (2) you already know something about it, (3) it raises the sort of questions that require primary and secondary research, and (4) you already have formed some opinions about problems related to it. If you are free to choose a topic in which you are already expert, it will be relatively easy to arrive at a strong, working thesis to serve as the basis for a rewarding research effort. On the other hand, if a professor assigns a topic about which you know little or nothing, you might have to do some background reading before you can develop your hypothesis.

The trick at the outset of the research process is to fit your topic and hypothesis to the demands of the assignment. Your purpose is to solve a *specific* problem, shed light on a *specific* topic, state an opinion on a *specific* controversy, offer *specific* proofs or solutions. Your audience does not want a welter of general information, a bland summary of the known and the obvious, or free associations or meditations on an issue or problem. You know that your audience wants answers; consequently, a way to locate your ideal topic is to ask questions about it.

You may want to ask a series of specific questions about your subject and ultimately combine related questions. Remember to ask your questions in such a way as to pose problems that demand answers. Then try to determine which topic best fits the demands of the assignment and lends itself to the most fruitful and economical method of research.

Phase 2: Locating Your Sources

You have only a certain amount of time in which to locate information for any research project. If you have a sufficiently narrowed topic and a working hypothesis, you at least know what type of information will be most useful for your report. Not all information on a topic is relevant, of course; with a hypothesis you can distinguish between useful and irrelevant material.

To use your time efficiently, you have to *streamline* your method for collecting data. Most research writing for college courses relies heavily on secondary research material available in libraries or on-line. To develop a preliminary list of sources, you should go directly to general reference works if you have to do background reading. If you are already knowledgeable about the subject, begin with resources that permit you to find a continuing series of articles and books on a single issue, specifically, periodical indexes, newspaper indexes, and card catalogs. Again, you should be moving as rapidly as possible from the general to the specific.

Using the Library Catalog The library on-line or card catalog lists information by author, title, subject, and keyword. Of the four, the subject listings are the best place to look for sources, but they are not necessarily the place to start your research. Begin by determining what your library offers. For instance, the on-line catalog may include all library materials or only holdings acquired fairly recently. The catalog also may or may not supply up-to-date information because books may take several years to appear in print and some weeks to be cataloged. Thus you may need to turn to separate indexes of articles, primary documents, and on-line materials for the most current material. Remember also that when you search by subject, you are searching the subject fields that are assigned by the cataloger. This differs from a keyword search in which the researcher—you the writer—selects key terms that describe the research situation and enters them into a search engine that will find these key terms anywhere within the item record—whether they happen to be in the title, comments, notes, or subject fields.

On the other hand, if your library has a consolidated on-line system, you may have immediate access to materials available regionally and to extensive on-line databases. You may be able to use the same terminal to search for books shelved in your own library, materials available locally through the city or county library, and current periodicals listed in specialized databases. Such access can simplify and consolidate your search.

Subject indexing can be useful when you are researching a topic around which a considerable body of information and analysis has already developed. Identify as many key words (terms that identify and describe your subject) or relevant subject classifications as possible. Use these same terms as you continue your search for sources, and add additional terms identified in the entries you find. The following example illustrates a key word search for materials on gender issues and advertising.

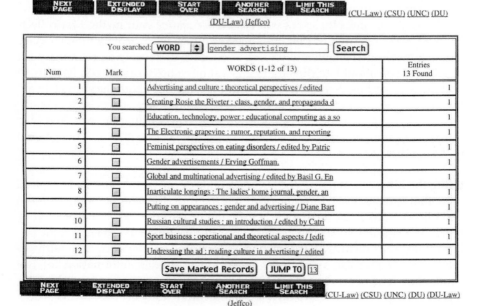

AURARIA LIBRARY

GENDER is in 1561 titles.
ADVERTISING is in 1270 titles.
Both "ADVERTISING" and "GENDER" are in 13 titles.
There are 13 entries with ADVERTISING & GENDER.

| NEXT PAGE | EXTENDED DISPLAY | START OVER | ANOTHER SEARCH | LIMIT THIS SEARCH | (CU-Law) (CSU) (UNC) (DU) |

(DU-Law) (Jeffco)

You searched: WORD ⬍ gender advertising   [Search]

Num	Mark	WORDS (1-12 of 13)	Entries 13 Found
1	☐	Advertising and culture : theoretical perspectives / edited	1
2	☐	Creating Rosie the Riveter : class, gender, and propaganda d	1
3	☐	Education, technology, power : educational computing as a so	1
4	☐	The Electronic grapevine : rumor, reputation, and reporting	1
5	☐	Feminist perspectives on eating disorders / edited by Patric	1
6	☐	Gender advertisements / Erving Goffman.	1
7	☐	Global and multinational advertising / edited by Basil G. En	1
8	☐	Inarticulate longings : The ladies' home journal, gender, an	1
9	☐	Putting on appearances : gender and advertising / Diane Bart	1
10	☐	Russian cultural studies : an introduction / edited by Catri	1
11	☐	Sport business : operational and theoretical aspects / [edit	1
12	☐	Undressing the ad : reading culture in advertising / edited	1

[Save Marked Records]   [JUMP TO] [13]

| NEXT PAGE | EXTENDED DISPLAY | START OVER | ANOTHER SEARCH | LIMIT THIS SEARCH | (CU-Law) (CSU) (UNC) (DU) (DU-Law) |

(Jeffco)

Search Other Regional Libraries:

 Denver Public Library   Colorado State Publications

Clicking on the Extended Display option for an item supplies full bibliographic information as well as the location of the book in the library and its availability. Following is the information for the fourth item listed below.

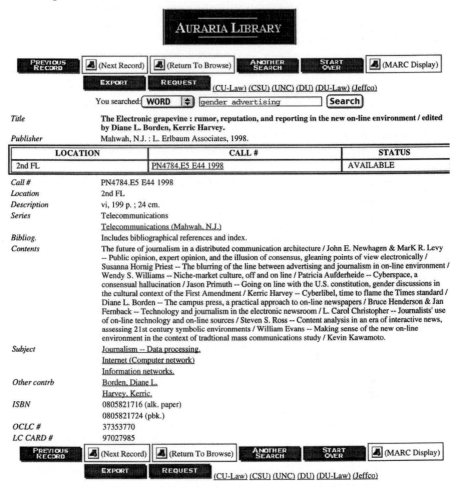

There are two ways to make this search GENDER and ADVERTISING more complete: (1) Think of alternate terms that might come into play; for example, *sex* is an synonym for *gender,* and *advertising* is only one form of the verb *to advertise.* A searcher would probably want to include "advertise" or "advertisement." Using the truncation symbol (in this case, * but it varies in different library catalogs) would help to catch these variations. The best idea is to review the search tips that nearly always accompany any public catalog. (2) Select one of the titles you feel is most closely related to your subject and pull up that record. For example "Sex in advertising" and "Sex role in advertising" could yield fruitful links, directing you to other materials that have been assigned the same headings. This strategy is a much more direct search than thumbing through the red Library of Congress Subject Headings volumes to find out what an appropriate subject heading might be, and it will catch those titles you might have missed when selecting your key words.

Checking General Reference Sources   General reference sources include encyclopedias, dictionaries, handbooks, atlases, biographies, almanacs, year-books, abstracts, and annual reviews of scholarship within a field. Many of these sources are available both in print and in an electronic format, on CD-ROM or on-line. Begin your search for these sources in your library's reference room. General reference sources can be useful for background reading and for an introduction to your topic. The bibliographies they contain (such as those that end articles in an encyclopedia) are generally limited, however, and frequently out-of-date. If you want to be a professional researcher, you should not rely exclusively on general reference sources to solve your research problems.

Searching Indexes and Databases   Electronic and print indexes and databases can efficiently lead you to up-to-date articles in journals, magazines, and news-papers. Indexes usually list materials that you will then need to locate. Some databases, however, may include complete texts of articles or even books. Ask a reference librarian about the terminals available in your library for accessing materials on CD-ROM or on-line. If you need historical information or want to trace a topic backwards in time, however, you may need to use print indexes as well because electronic sources may date back only a few years or cover only a certain number of years.

The following indexes and databases are just a few of the many resources that are widely available. Some are general; others are specialized by discipline or field. Such indexes supply ready access to a wide array of useful materials, including articles, books, newspaper stories, statistics, and government docu-ments. Ask the librarian in the reference area or the catalog area whether these are available in print or on-line.

General Resources

American Statistics Index

Congressional Information Service Index

Expanded Academic Index

FirstSearch Catalog

Magazine Index

National Newspaper Index

New York Times Index

Specialized Resources

Applied Science and Technology Index

Biological and Agricultural Index

Business Periodicals Index

Education Index

ERIC (Educational Resources Information Center)

General BusinessFile

Humanities Index

Index Medicus or Medline

MLA (Modern Language Association) International Bibliography

PsychLit

Public Affairs Information Service (PAIS)

Social Sciences Index

Each index or database restricts the sources it lists in specific ways, based on the particular topics covered or the types of sources included. For example, the full title of the *MLA Bibliography* indicates that it lists "Books and Articles on the Modern Languages and Literatures." Besides books and articles, however, it includes essays or chapters collected in a book, conference papers, films, recordings, and other similar sources, but it does not list summaries or encyclopedia articles. Its primary subjects include literary criticism, literary themes and genres, linguistics, and folklore. Thus, you can search for an author's name, a title, a literary period, or subjects as varied as hoaxes, metaphysical poetry, and self-knowledge, all in relationship to studies in language and literature. This bibliography is available in print, on CD-ROM, on-line, or in other electronic versions. The print version is published every year, but the on-line version is updated 10 times during the year. A search of the *MLA Bibliography* 1/91–4/01 on CD-ROM for information on gender issues in advertising would turn up items such as the following:

```
TI: Gender Issues in Advertising Language
AU: Artz,-Nancy; Munizer,-Jeanne; Purdy,-Warren
SO: Women-and-Language, Fairfax, VA (W&Lang). 1999 Fall, 22:2, 20-26.
AN: 1999095570

TI: Anglicisms in German Car Advertising: The Problem of Gender
Assignment
AU: Vesterhus,-Sverre-A..
SO: Moderna-Sprak, Goteborg, Sweden (MSpr). 1998, 92:2, 160-70.
AN: 1999091717
```

```
TI: Ready or Not: Clothing, Advertising, and Gender in Late
Nineteenth-Century America
AU: Schorman,-Rob
SO: Dissertation-Abstracts-International,-Section-A:-The-
Humanities-and-Social-Sciences, Ann Arbor, MI (DAIA). 1999 Mar,
59:9, 3619 DAI No.: DA9907365. Degree granting institution:
Indiana U, 1998.
AN: 1999079868
```

As your search progresses and your hypothesis evolves, you will find resources even more specifically focused on your interests.

Finding On-Line Materials   Your library, your college Web site, or your instructor's home page may list useful sites on the World Wide Web, organized by discipline or interest area. On-line clearinghouses and print materials about the Web also identify especially useful sites for researchers. Depending on your topic, there are subject-specific Web pages on the Internet that link you to everything you could want, including both primary and secondary sources. "Findlaw" is a good example for law; most of the sciences and many of the liberal arts have useful pages like this. Once you have located an Internet address—a URL (universal resource locator)—for a site on the World Wide Web, you can go directly to that location. The end of the address can help you assess the kind of location you will reach.

.org = nonprofit organizations, including professional groups

.edu = colleges, universities, and other educational institutions

.com = businesses and commercial enterprises

.gov = government branches and agencies

.mil = branches of the military

.net = major computer networks

If you need to search the Internet for sources, try using one of the search engines supplied by your Internet access program. Search engines such as Google, AltaVista, Excite, Infoseek, Lycos, HotBot, or Yahoo! hunt through vast numbers of pages at Web sites, seeking those that mention key words that you specify. The search engine then supplies you with a list, usually 10 items at a time, of those sites. Given the enormous number of Web sites and their component pages, you need to select your search items carefully so that you locate reasonable numbers of pertinent sources.

A Web page may supply links to other useful sites. If you click on the link, usually highlighted or in color, you can go directly to that related site. For example, the following site (*http://www.fedworld.gov/*), sponsored by the federal government, includes links to federal databases and two forms of key word searches that can lead to particular resources.

Site Revised 1999 May 18
File, Jobs and Web Databases Updated Daily

Browse the FedWorld Information Network
Pick From List:

| List FedWorld Databases | ⇕ | Go! |

Search Web Pages on the FedWorld Information Network
Enter some keywords:

| | Search |

Search for U.S. Government Reports
Enter some keywords:

| | Search |

Explore U.S. Government Web Sites

About FedWorld   About NTIS   FedWorld Services For U.S. Government Agencies

Points of Contact at FedWorld   Privacy   Security

 National Technical Information Service
Technology Administration
U.S. Department of Commerce
Springfield, VA 22161
703-605-6000
Send comments to webmaster@fedworld.gov

Hammer Award Winner

Following a chain of links requires critical thinking to assess whether each link seems reliable and current. This kind of research also can take a great deal of time, especially if you explore each link and then follow it to the next. As you move from link to link, keep your hypothesis in mind so that you are not distracted from your central purpose.

In order to gain expert information, you may wish to contact an informed individual directly by e-mail, following up on contact information supplied at a Web site or through other references. If your topic is of long-term interest to you and you have plenty of time to do your research, you may want to join a *listserv* or *e-mail conference,* a group of people interested in a particular topic, whose messages are sent automatically to all participants. Exchanges among those interested in a topic may also be posted on a *bulletin board server* or a *newsgroup,* where you can read both past and ongoing messages and exchanges. The information you receive from others may be very authoritative and reliable, but it may also represent the biased viewpoint of the individual. Assess it carefully by comparing it with information from other sources—print as well as electronic.

Using Nonprint Sources   In the library and on-line, you have access to potentially useful nonprint materials of all kinds—videos, CD-ROMs, films, slides, works of art, records of performances, or other sources that might relate to your topic. When you search for these sources, you may find them in your library's main catalog or in a separate listing. In the catalog entry, be sure to note the location of the source and its access hours, especially if they are limited. If you need a projector or other equipment to use the material, ask the reference librarian where you go to find such equipment.

Developing Field Resources   You may want to *interview* an expert, *survey* the opinions of other students, *observe* an event or situation, or examine it over a long period of time as a *case study*. Ask your instructor's advice as you design questions for an interview or a survey or procedures for a short- or long-term observation. Also be sure to find out whether you need permission to conduct this kind of research on campus or in the community.

The questions you ask will determine the nature and extent of the responses that you receive; as a result, your questions should be developed after you have established clear objectives for your field research. You also need to plan how you will analyze the answers before, not after, you administer the questionnaire or conduct the interview. Once you have drafted interview or survey questions, test them by asking your friends or classmates to respond. Use these preliminary results to revise any ambiguous questions and to test your method of analysis. If you are an observer, establish in advance what you will observe, how you will record your observations, and how you will analyze them. Get permission, if needed, from the site where you will conduct your observation. Your field sources can help you expand your knowledge of the topic, see its applications or discover real-world surprises, or locate more sources, whether print, electronic, or field.

Preparing a Working Bibliography   The purpose of compiling a working bibliography is to keep track of possible sources, to determine the nature and extent of the information available, to provide a complete and accurate list of sources to be presented in the paper, and to make preparing the final bibliography much easier. Include in your working bibliography all sources that you have a hunch are potentially useful. After all, you may not be able to obtain all the items listed, and some material will turn out to be useless, repetitious, or irrelevant to your topic. Such entries can easily be eliminated at a later stage when you prepare your final bibliography.

One way to simplify the task of preparing your final Works Cited or References section is to use a standard form for your working bibliography, whether you use cards or computer entries. The models given later in this chapter are based on two guides, abbreviated as MLA and APA. The *MLA Handbook for Writers of Research Papers* (New York: Modern Language Association of America, 1999; 5th ed.) is generally followed in English, foreign languages, and other fields in the humanities. Instructors in the social sciences, natural sciences, education, and business are likely to favor the style presented in the *Publication Manual of the American Psychological Association* (Washington, DC: American Psychological Association, 1994; 4th ed.). Because the preferred form of citation of sources varies considerably from field to field, check with your instructors to determine which of these two formats they prefer or if they recommend another style. Follow any specific directions from an instructor carefully.

As you search for relevant articles and books, you should take down complete information on each item on a 3 × 5 note card or start a bibliographic file on your computer. Complete information, properly recorded, will save you the trouble of having to scurry back to the library or back to a Web page for missing data when typing your final bibliography. Be sure to list the item's call number and location in the library or its URL; then you can easily find the material once

---

INFORMATION FOR A WORKING BIBLIOGRAPHY

Record the following information for a book:
1. Name(s) of author(s)
2. Title of book, underlined
3. Place of publication
4. Publisher's name
5. Date of publication
6. Call number or location in library
7. URL and date of access on-line

Record the following information for an article in a periodical:
1. Name(s) of author(s)
2. Title of article, in quotation marks
3. Title of periodical, underlined
4. Volume number or issue number
5. Date of publication
6. Page numbers on which article appears
7. Call number or location in library
8. URL and date of access on-line

you are ready to begin reading and relocate it if you need to refer to it again. When preparing bibliography cards for entries listed in annotated bibliographies, citation indexes, and abstracts, you might want to jot down notes from any pertinent summaries that are provided. Complete a separate card or file entry for each item that you think is promising.

Author	Dávidházi, Péter
Title	The Romantic Cult of Shakespeare: Literary Reception in Anthropological Perspective
Place of publication	New York St. Martin's Press
Date of publication	1998
Location	Call Number: PR 2979.H8.D38.1998

If you use your computer to record bibliographic information, you may want to find software designed for this purpose. Your software may provide database categories or options from which you can select the categories required by the style guide you need to use. You also can use the requirements of your style guide to help you develop your own, such as these for a book.

Author's last name:	Pinker
Author's first name:	Steven
Book title:	The Language Instinct: How the Mind Creates Language
Publisher's location:	New York
Publisher (imprint):	HarperCollins Publishers (HarperPerennial)
Date published (original date):	1995 (1994)

Once you begin to build a bibliographic database, you can refer to your listings and supplement them each time you are assigned a paper.

Reassessing Your Topic   Once you have compiled your working bibliography, take the time to reassess the entire project before you get more deeply involved in it. Analyze your bibliography cards carefully to determine whether you should proceed to the next stage of information gathering.

Your working bibliography should send out signals that help you shape your thinking about the topic. The dominant signal should indicate that your topic is not too narrow or too broad. Generally, a bibliography of 10 to 15 promising entries for a 1,500-word paper indicates that your topic might be properly limited at this stage. A listing of only three or four entries signals that you must expand the topic or consider discarding it. Conversely, a listing of a hundred entries warns that you might be working yourself into a research swamp.

Another signal from your working bibliography should help you decide whether your hypothesis is on target or could be easily recast to make it more precise. Entry titles, abstracts, and commentaries on articles are excellent sources of confirmation. If established scholarship does not support your hypothesis, it would be best to discard your hypothesis and begin again.

Finally, the working bibliography should provide signals about the categories or parts of your research. Again, titles, abstracts, and commentaries are useful. In other words, as you compile the entries, you can begin to think through the problem and to perceive contours of thought that will dictate the organization of the paper even before you begin to do detailed research. Your working bibliography should be alive with such signals.

Phase 3: Gathering and Organizing Data

If your working bibliography confirms the value, logic, and practicality of your research project, you can then move to the next phase of the research process: taking notes and organizing information. Information shapes and refines your thinking; you move from an overview to a more precise understanding, analysis, and interpretation of the topic. By the end of this third phase, you should be able to transform your hypothesis into a thesis and your assembled notes into an outline.

Evaluating Sources   Your preliminary task as you move into the third phase is to immerse yourself in articles, books, and perhaps primary research sources, but not to drown in them. Begin by skimming your sources. Skimming is not random reading or casual perusal, but a careful examination of the material to sort out the valuable sources from the not-so-valuable ones. For a book, check the table of contents and index for information on your topic; then determine whether the information is relevant to your problem. For an article, see if the abstract or topic sentences in the body of the essay confirm your research interests. The guidelines below can help you determine if a source will be useful.

CRITERIA FOR ASSESSING THE VALUE OF A SOURCE FOR YOUR PROJECT

---

1. Is the source directly relevant to your topic?
2. Does it discuss the topic extensively, uniquely, and with good authority?
3. Does it bear on your hypothesis, supporting, qualifying, or contradicting it?
4. Does it present relatively current information, especially for research in the social and natural sciences?

CRITERIA FOR EVALUATING SOURCES FOR YOUR PROJECT

Evaluating Print Sources

1. Is the author a credible authority? Does the book jacket, preface, or byline indicate the author's background, education, or other publications? Do other writers refer to this source and accept it as reliable? Is the publisher or publication reputable?

2. Does the source provide information comparable to that in other reputable sources?

3. Does the source seem accurate and authoritative, or does it make claims that are not generally accepted?

4. Does the source seem unbiased, or does it seem to promote a particular business, industry, organization, political position, or philosophy?

5. Does the source supply notes, a bibliography, or other information to document its sources?

6. If the source has been published recently, does it include current information? Are its sources current or dated?

7. Does the source seem carefully edited and printed?

Evaluating Web Sites or Other Electronic Sources

1. Is the author identified? Is the site sponsored by a reputable business, agency, or organization? Does the site supply information so that you can contact the author or the sponsor?

2. Does the site provide information comparable to that in other reputable sources, including print sources?

3. Does the site seem accurate and authoritative or quirky and idiosyncratic?

4. Does the site seem unbiased, or is it designed to promote a particular business, industry, organization, political position, or philosophy?

5. Does the site supply appropriate, useful links? Do these links seem current and relevant? Do most of them work? Does the site document sources for the information it supplies directly?

6. Has the site been updated or revised recently?

7. Does the site seem carefully designed? Is it easy and logical to navigate? Are its graphics well integrated and related to the site's overall purpose or topic? Is the text carefully edited?

Besides being pertinent to your research problem, a source needs to be reliable. Books and articles in print have generally been reviewed by editors and experts in the field, but materials located on the World Wide Web or elsewhere on the Internet may or may not have been examined by unbiased or authoritative experts. The guidelines on page 690 can help you determine the reliability of a source.

Taking Notes   Once you have a core of valuable material, you can begin to read these sources closely and take detailed notes. Skillful note taking requires a subtle blend of critical thinking skills. It is not a matter of recording all the information available or simply copying long quotes. You want to select and summarize the general ideas that will form the outline of your paper, to record specific evidence to support your ideas, and to copy exact statements you plan to quote for evidence or interest. You also want to add your own ideas and evaluation of the material. All the notes you take must serve the specific purpose of your paper as it is stated in your hypothesis. (See pages 11–13 for more information on paraphrase, summary, and quotation.)

Alternatives for taking notes include using 5 × 8 note cards, setting up a computer file for your notes, writing on one side of separate pages in a notebook, or combining these systems with on-line and library printouts. In any case, take brief and precise notes. Look for the crisp quotation, the telling statistic, the insight by a leading authority, the sound original idea. Always keep your hypothesis in mind to limit your note taking.

GUIDELINES FOR TAKING NOTES
ABOUT YOUR TOPIC

1.   Write the author's last name, the title of the source, and the page number at the top of each card or entry. (Complete information on the source should already have been recorded on a bibliography card or listed in an entry in a computer file.)

2.   Record only one idea or a group of closely related facts on each card or in each entry.

3.   List a subtopic at the top of the card or entry. This will permit you to arrange your cards or entries from various sources into groups, and these groups can then serve as the basis of your outline.

4.   List three types of information: (a) summaries of material; (b) paraphrases of material, in which you recast the exact words of the author; and (c) direct quotations, accurately transcribed (see pages 11–13).

5.   Add your own ideas at the bottom of the card or following specific notes.

The sample note cards printed below illustrate useful arrangements of research information.

Topic label	cult-definition
Author of book or article	Dávidházi
Relevant page numbers	pp. 8–21
Direct quotation	8: Defines "cult and culture in terms of their specific attitudes, their different ritual and their respective ways of using language."
Student's commentary	Is this a matter of degree? (How do you tell the difference?)

Topic label	cult-definition
Author of book or article	Dávidházi
Relevant page numbers	pp. 8–21
Paraphrase	8: The first criteria for a literary cult is an attitude that is worshipful, a feeling like religious reverence. The next lies in behavior that celebrates the literary figure, including both verbalizing praise and attending ritual events, such as festivals and trips to Stratford. Finally, the glorified language used to describe the figure is extreme.
Student's commentary	(Useful list—does it relate to the Shakespeare festival on campus during the summer?)

The following example illustrates how you might enter notes in a computer file. The nature and scope of your paper may help you figure out how to organize your files. For example, you could set up a separate file for each source or for each main topic. Each note might start at the top of a new page. Once your notes are entered, you can easily copy quotations from your note file to your paper or use your computer's search system to hunt for a key word.

Topic:	language community
Source:	Pinker
Page numbers:	pp. 15-16
Quotation/ Summary/ Paraphrase:	Q. 16: "In any natural history of the human species, language would stand out as the preeminent trait. [. . .] A common language connects the members of a community into an information-sharing network with formidable collective powers."
Comment:	I like the book's example of the Tower of Babel as a key story. It shows what happens if people work on communicating with each other.

When you have completed all your research, organize your notes under the various subtopics or subheadings that you have established. If possible or desirable, try to combine some subtopics and eliminate others so that you have between three and five major categories for analysis and development. You are now ready to develop an outline for the research essay.

Designing an Outline   Because you must organize a lot of material in a clear way, an outline is especially valuable in a research essay. Some experts actually recommend that you develop an outline before you conduct research, but this is possible only if your bibliographical search and your own general knowledge of the topic permit establishing subtopics at that early stage.

Most importantly, now is the time to establish your thesis. By reviewing your notes and assessing the data, you should be able to transform the calculated guess that was your hypothesis into a much firmer thesis. Focus your attention on your thesis by stating it at the top of the page where you are working on your outline.

Spend as much time as is reasonable drafting an outline. For a rough outline, you can simply list your general subheadings and their supporting data. However, the recommended strategy is to work more systematically through your notes and compile as full an outline as possible, one that develops each point logically and in detail. If you are required to submit an outline with your research paper, you should begin to develop a full, formal outline at this stage. Such an outline would look like this:

I.
   A.
   B.
      1.
      2.
      3.
         a.
         b.
II.

Use roman numerals for your most important points, capital letters for the next most important points, arabic numbers for supporting points, and lowercase letters for pertinent details or minor points.

Phase 4: Writing and Submitting the Paper

As you enter the fourth and final phase of the research process, keep in mind that a research paper is a formal essay, not a jagged compilation of notes. You should be prepared to take your research effort through several increasingly polished versions, most likely at least a rough draft, a revised draft, and a final manuscript.

Writing the Rough Draft   For your rough draft, concentrate on filling in the shape of your outline. If your notes are out of sequence or scattered to the four corners of your room, take the time to rearrange them in the topic order that your outline assumes. In this way you will be able to integrate notes and writing more efficiently and effectively.

Even as you adhere to your formal outline in beginning the rough draft, you should also be open to better possibilities and prospects for presenting ideas and information. Often you discover that an outline is too rigid, that a minor idea needs greater emphasis, that something important has been left out entirely, even that your thesis needs further adjustment. There are potentially dozens of shifts, modifications, and improvements that you can make as you transfer the form of an outline to an actual written paper. Although your primary effort in writing a first draft is to rough out the shape and content of your paper, the flow of your ideas will often be accompanied by self-adjusting operations of your mind, all aimed at making your research effort even better than you thought it could be at the outline stage.

Whether or not you incorporate quotations from your notes into the rough draft is a matter of preference. Some writers prefer to transcribe quotations and paraphrases at this point in order to save time at a later stage. Other writers copy and insert these materials directly from entries in a computer file for notes. Still others feel their thought processes are interrupted by having to write out quoted and paraphrased material and to design transitions between their own writing and the transcribed material. They simply write "insert" in the draft with a reference to the appropriate notes.

The need to integrate material from several sources tests your reasoning ability during the writing of the rough draft. For any given subtopic in your outline, you will be drawing together information from a variety of sources. To an extent, your outline will tell you how to arrange some of this information. At the same time, you must contribute your own commentary, arrange details in an effective order, and sort out conflicting claims and interpretations. A great deal of thinking as well as writing goes into the design of your first draft.

It is critical thinking and problem solving as much as the act of writing that makes for a successful rough draft. As you draft, you are actually solving a complex research problem in your own words. For the moment, you do not have to worry about the polished state of your words. You do, however, have to be certain that the intelligence that you are bringing to bear on the design of your paper is adequate to the challenge. You are not involved in a dull tran-scription of material when writing the rough draft of a research paper. Instead, you are engaged in a demanding effort to think your way through a problem of considerable magnitude, working in a logical way from the introduction and the statement of your thesis, through the evidence, to the outcome or conclusion that supports everything that has come before.

Revising the Draft   If you can put your rough draft away for a day or two, you can return to it with the sharpened and objective eye of a critical reviewer. In the rough draft you thought and wrote your way through the problem. Now you must rethink and rewrite in order to give better form and expression to your ideas.

Use the guidelines outlined below to approach your revision. Consider every aspect of your paper, from the most general to the most specific. Look again at the organization of the whole paper, key topics, paragraphs, and sentences; read through for clarity of expression and details of grammar, punctuation, and spelling. A comprehensive revision effort will result in a decidedly more polished version of your paper.

GUIDELINES FOR REVISING YOUR RESEARCH WRITING

1. Does my title illuminate the topic of the essay and capture the reader's interest?

2. Have I created the proper tone to meet the expectations of my audience?

3. Does my opening paragraph hook the reader? Does it clearly establish and limit the topic? Is my thesis statement clear, limited, and interesting?

(continued)

4. Do all my body paragraphs support the thesis? Is there a single topic and main idea for each paragraph? Do I achieve unity, coherence, and proper development? Is there sufficient evidence in each paragraph to support the main idea?

5. Are there clear and effective transitions linking my ideas within and between paragraphs?

6. Have I selected the best strategies to meet the demands of the assignment and the expectations of my audience?

7. Are all my assertions clearly stated, defined, and supported? Do I use sound logic and avoid faulty reasoning? Do I acknowledge other peoples' ideas properly?

8. Is my conclusion strong and effective?

9. Are my sentences grammatically correct? Have I avoided errors in the use of verbs, pronouns, adjectives, and prepositions? Have I corrected errors of agreement?

10. Are my sentences complete? Have I corrected all fragments, comma splices, and fused sentences?

11. Have I varied my sentences effectively? Have I employed clear coordination and subordination? Have I avoided awkward constructions?

12. Is my use of periods, commas, semicolons, and other forms of punctuation correct?

13. Are all words spelled correctly? Do my words mean what I think they mean? Are they specific? Are they concrete? Is my diction appropriate to college writing? Is my language free of clichés, slang, jargon, and euphemism? Do I avoid needless abstractions? Is my usage sound?

14. Have I carefully attended to such mechanical matters as apostrophes, capitals, numbers, and word divisions?

15. Does my manuscript conform to acceptable guidelines for submitting typewritten work?

Preparing the Final Manuscript   Leave time in your research effort to prepare a neat, clean, attractively designed manuscript using a typewriter or computer. Store your word processor file on a backup disk, and print or duplicate an extra copy of the report. Submit a neat, clear version, and keep the second copy. Consult your instructor for the desired format, and carefully follow the guidelines for manuscript preparation in your final version. Look also at the sample paper at the end of this chapter, which illustrates how to present the final version of a paper in accordance with MLA style (see pages 712–725). Having invested so much time and effort in a research project, you owe it to yourself as well as to the reader to submit a manuscript that has been prepared with extreme care.

DOCUMENTING SOURCES

Documentation is an essential part of any research paper. Documenting your sources throughout the paper and in a section called Works Cited or References tells your audience just how well you have conducted your research. It offers readers the opportunity to check on authorities, to do further reading, and to assess the originality of your contribution to an established body of opinion. Neglect of proper documentation can destroy your research effort. It can also be *plagiarism*—the use of material without giving credit to the source, or, put more seriously, the theft of material that properly belongs to other thinkers, writers, and researchers.

Quotations, paraphrases, and summaries obviously require credit, for they are the actual words or the theories or interpretations of others. Paraphrases and summaries also frequently offer statistics or data that are not well known, and this type of information also requires documentation. Facts in a controversy (facts open to dispute or to varying interpretations) also fall within the realm of documentation.

Besides giving appropriate credit to others for their words and ideas, be careful either to quote exactly or to paraphrase or summarize using your own words and your own sentence structures. For example, avoid a paraphrase that simply replaces a few key words in a sentence. Like wording copied directly without giving credit to its source, such a paraphrase may be considered plagiarism. Even if you do credit your source, such a close paraphrase makes your research seem sloppy and poorly conducted. Aim instead at recasting the writer's ideas in your own words.

MATERIALS THAT REQUIRE DOCUMENTATION

1. Direct quotations
2. Paraphrased material
3. Summarized material
4. Any key idea or opinion adapted and incorporated into your paper
5. Specific data (whether quoted, paraphrased, or tabulated)
6. Disputed facts

Parenthetical documentation—briefly identifying sources within parentheses in the text—is the most common method of indicating sources. The purpose of a parenthetical citation is to identify a source briefly yet clearly enough that it can be located in the list of references at the end of the paper. In MLA style, the author's last name and the page number in the source are included. APA style uses the author's last name and the year of publication; page numbers are included primarily for direct quotations. Then complete information is listed, alphabetically by author or title (if a source has no specific author), in the Words Cited or References section following the text of the paper. The bibliographic information you have collected should provide you with the details needed for the preparation of both parenthetical documentation and a list of sources.

GENERAL GUIDELINES FOR PARENTHETICAL DOCUMENTATION

1. Give enough information so that the reader can readily identify the source in the Works Cited (MLA) or References (APA) section of your paper.
2. Supply the citation information in parentheses placed where the material occurs in your text.
3. Give the specific information required by the documentation system you are using, especially when dealing with multivolume works, editions, newspapers, and legal documents.
4. Make certain that the complete sentence containing the parenthetical documentation is readable and grammatically correct.

With your parenthetical documentation prepared, turn your attention next to a final Works Cited or References section. To prepare this list of sources, you simply have to transcribe those bibliography cards or entries that you actually used to write your paper, following the appropriate format.

GENERAL GUIDELINES FOR PREPARING A LIST OF SOURCES

1. Use the title *Works Cited* (MLA) or *References* (APA).
2. Include only works actually cited in the research paper unless directed otherwise by your instructor.
3. Arrange all works alphabetically according to author's last name or according to the title of a work if there is no author. Ignore *A, An,* or *The.*
4. Begin each entry at the left margin. Indent everything in an entry that comes after the first line by five spaces or 1/2 inch (MLA style) or by five to seven spaces (following APA style for students, unless your instructor directs otherwise).
5. Double-space every line.
6. Punctuate with periods after the three main divisions in most entries—author, title, and publishing information.

In the following sections, you will find examples of MLA and APA documentation forms. Use these examples to help you cite your sources efficiently and clearly.

MLA (MODERN LANGUAGE ASSOCIATION) DOCUMENTATION

The following examples illustrate how to cite a source in the text and in the list of works cited at the end of a paper.

MLA Parenthetical Documentation   The simplest MLA entry includes the author's last name and the page number, identifying exactly where the quotation or information is located. If the author's name is included in the text, it does not need to be repeated in the citation.

Page Number(s) for a Book
    The play offers what many audiences have found a satisfying conclusion (Hansberry 265–76).

    Garcia Marquez uses another particularly appealing passage as the opening of the story (105).

Volume and Page Number(s) for One Volume of a Multivolume Work
    A strong interest in this literature in the 1960s and 1970s inevitably led to "a significant reassessment of the aesthetic and humanistic achievements of black writers" (Inge, Duke, and Bryer 1: v).

Page Number(s) for an Article in a Journal or Magazine
    Barlow's description of the family members includes "their most notable strengths and weaknesses" (18).

Section and Page Number(s) for a Newspaper Article
A report on achievement standards for high school courses found "significant variation among schools" (Mallory B1).

Page Number(s) for a Work without an Author
Computerworld has developed a thoughtful editorial on the issue of government and technology ("Uneasy Silence" 54).

Page Number(s) for a Work by a Group or an Organization
The Commission on the Humanities has concluded that "the humanities are inescapably bound to literacy" (69).

Page Number(s) for Several Works by One Author
In The Coming Fury, Catton identifies the "disquieting omens" (6) which precede the Civil War.

As Catton concludes his history of the Civil War, he notes that "it began with one act of madness and it ended with another" (Never Call Retreat 457).

Page Number(s) for One Work Quoted in Another
Samuel Johnson praises She Stoops to Conquer because Goldsmith's play achieves "the great end of comedy—making an audience merry" (qtd. in Boswell 171).

MLA List of Works Cited   Following your paper, list the references you have cited in alphabetical order on a separate page entitled "Works Cited." See the Works Cited page of the sample paper (page 725) for an illustration of how you should prepare this page. Use the following sample entries to help you format your references in MLA style. Pay special attention to abbreviated names of publishers, full names of authors, details of punctuation, and other characteristic features of MLA citations.

Work with One Author
Notice the punctuation and underlining in the basic entry for a book.

Aldrich, Marcia. Girl Rearing. New York: Norton, 1998.

Muller, Eddie. Dark City: The Lost World of Film Noir. New York: St. Martin's-Griffin, 1998.

Several Works by One Author
If you use several books or articles by one author, list the author's name in the initial entry. In the next entry or entries, replace the name with three hyphens.

Aldrich, John Herbert. Why Parties? The Origin and Transformation of Political Parties in America. Chicago: U of Chicago P, 1995.

—. Before the Convention: Strategies and Choices in Presidential Nomination Campaigns. Chicago: U of Chicago P, 1980.

Work with Two or Three Authors or Editors

List the names of several authors in the sequence in which they appear in the book or article. Begin with the last name of the author listed first because it is used to determine the alphabetical order for entries. Then identify the other authors by first and last names.

> Oakes, Jill, and Rick Riewe. Spirit of Siberia: Traditional Native Life, Clothing, and Footwear. Washington: Smithsonian Inst. P, 1998.

> Trueba, Henry T., Grace Pung Guthrie, and Kathryn Hu-Pei Au, eds. Culture and the Bilingual Classroom: Studies in Classroom Ethnography. Rowley: Newbury, 1981.

Work with More than Three Authors or Editors

Name all those involved, or list only the first author or editor with *et al.*, for "and others."

> Nordhus, Inger, Gary R. VandenBos, Stig Berg, and Pia Fromholt, eds. Clinical Geropsychology. Washington: APA, 1998.

> Nordhus, Inger, et al., eds. Clinical Geropsychology. Washington: APA, 1998.

Work with Group or an Organization as Author

> National PTA. National Standards for Parent/Family Involvement Programs. Chicago: National PTA, 1997.

Work without an Author

> A Visual Dictionary of Art. Greenwich, CT: New York Graphic Society, 1974.

Work in a Collection of Pieces All by the Same Author

> Malamud, Bernard. "The Assistant." A Malamud Reader. New York: Farrar, 1967. 750–95.

Work in a Collection of Pieces by Different Authors

> McCorkle, Jill. "Final Vinyl Days." It's Only Rock and Roll: An Anthology of Rock and Roll Short Stories. Ed. Janice Eidus and John Kastan. Boston: Godine, 1998. 19–33.

Collection of Pieces Cited as a Whole

> Weston-Lews, Aidan, ed. Effigies and Ecstasies: Roman Baroque Sculpture and Design in the Age of Bernini. Edinburgh: Natl. Gallery of Scotland, 1998.

Work in Several Volumes

> Walther, Ingo F. Art of the 20th Century. 2 vols. Cologne: Taschen, 1998.

Work Translated from Another Language

The first entry on page 702 emphasizes the work of the original author by placing his name first. The next example shifts emphasis to the work of the translators by identifying them first.

Rostand, Edmund. <u>Cyrano de Bergerac</u>. Trans. Anthony Burgess. New York: Applause, 1998.

Young, David, and Jiann I. Lin, trans. <u>The Clouds Float North: The Complete Poems of Du Xuanji</u>. Bilingual Edition. Hanover: Wesleyan UP, 1998.

Work Appearing as Part of a Series

Rohn, Suzanne. <u>The Wizard of Oz: Shaping an Imaginary World</u>. Twayne's Masterwork Studies 167. New York: Twayne-Simon, 1998.

New Edition of an Older Book

Wharton, Edith. <u>The Custom of the Country</u>. 1913. NY Public Library Collector's Edition. New York: Doubleday, 1998.

Entry from a Reference Volume

Treat less common reference books like other books, including place of publication, publisher, and date. For encyclopedias, dictionaries, and other familiar references, simply note the edition and its date. No page numbers are needed if the entries appear in alphabetical order in the reference volume.

"Fox, Luke." <u>Encyclopedia Americana: International Edition</u>. 1996 ed.

Minton, John. "Worksong." <u>American Folklore: An Encyclopedia</u>. Ed. Jan Harold Brunvold. New York: Garland, 1996.

Work Issued by a Federal, State, or Other Government Agency

Depending on the emphasis you intend, you can start with either the writer or the government agency responsible for the publication. "GPO" stands for "Government Printing Office," the publisher of most federal documents.

Brock, Dan W. "An Assessment of the Ethical Issues Pro and Con." <u>Cloning Human Beings</u>. National Bioethics Advisory Commission. Vol. 2. Rockville, MD: GPO, 1997. E1–E23.

National Bioethics Advisory Commission. <u>Cloning Human Beings</u>. 2 vols. Rockville, MD: GPO, 1997.

United States. Cong. House. Subcommittee on Oversight and Investigations of the Committee on Education and the Workforce. <u>Education at a Crossroads: What Works and What's Wasted in Education Today</u>. 105th Cong., 2nd sess. Washington: GPO, 1998.

US Const. Art. 9.

Reference to a Legal Document

When you discuss court cases in your paper, underline their names. In your Works Cited, do not underline them.

Aguilar v. Felton. 473 US 402.1985.

Article in a Journal with Pagination Continuing through Each Volume

Pistol, Todd A. "Unfinished Business: Letters from a Father to His Son, 1922–1928." <u>Journal of Men's Studies</u> 7 (1999): 215–31.

Article in a Journal with Pagination Continuing Only through Each Issue
Add the issue number after the volume number.

> Guyer, Jane I. "Traditions of Invention in Equatorial Africa." <u>African Studies Review</u> 39.3 (1996): 1–28.

Article in a Weekly or Biweekly Periodical

> Cowley, Geoffrey. "Cancer and Diet." <u>Newsweek</u> 30 Nov. 1998: 60–66.

> Lemonick, Michael D. "The Biological Mother Lode." <u>Time</u> 16 Nov. 1998: 96–97.

Article in a Monthly or Bimonthly Periodical
If an article in a magazine or a newspaper does not continue on consecutive pages, follow the page number on which it begins with a plus sign.

> Blow, Richard. "The Great American Whale Hunt." <u>Mother Jones</u> Sept.–Oct. 1998: 49+.

Article in a Daily Newspaper

> Morson, Berny. "Tuft-eared Cats Make Tracks in Colorado." <u>Denver Rocky Mountain News</u> 4 Feb. 1999: 5A+.

Article with No Author

> "Iguanas Cruise the Caribbean." <u>New Scientist</u> 10 Oct. 1998: 25.

> "People in the News." <u>US News and World Report</u> 11 Jan. 1999:16.

Editorial in a Periodical

> Fogarty, Robert W. "Fictional Families." Editorial. <u>Antioch Review</u> 56 (1998): 388.

Letter Written to the Editor of a Periodical

> Paley, James A. Letter. "New Haven Renaissance." <u>New York Times</u> 30 Jan. 1999: A26.

Review Article
If a review article has a title, add it after the author's name.

> Swain, William N. Rev. of <u>Getting Hits: The Definitive Guide to Promoting Your Website</u>, by Don Sellers. <u>Public Relations Review</u> 24 (1998): 403–09.

Presentation at a Professional Meeting or Conference

> Ciardi, John. Address. National Council of Teachers of English Convention. Hilton Hotel, Washington. 19 Nov. 1982.

Film, Slides, Videotape
Start with any actor, producer, director, or other person whose work you wish to emphasize. Otherwise, simply begin with the title of the recording. Note the form cited—videocassette, filmstrip, and so forth.

America in the Depression Years. Slide program. Laurel: Instructional Resources, 1979.

Olivier, Laurence, prod. and dir. Richard III. By William Shakespeare. Videocassette. London Film Productions, 1955.

Richard III. By William Shakespeare. Prod. and dir. Laurence Olivier. Videocassette. London Film Productions, 1955.

Visions of the Spirit: A Portrait of Alice Walker. By Elena Featherston. Videocassette. Women Make Films, 1989.

Programs on Radio or Television
"Alone on the Ice." The American Experience. PBS. KRMA, Denver. 8 Feb. 1999.

The Life and Adventures of Nicholas Nickleby. By Charles Dickens. Adapt. David Edgar. Dir. Trevor Nunn and John Caird. Royal Shakespeare Co. Mobile Showcase Network. WNEW, New York. 10–13 Jan. 1983.

CD or Other Recording
Identify the format if the recording is not on a compact disk.

Basie, Count. "Sunday at the Savoy." 88 Basie Street. Rec. 11–12 May 1983. LP. Pablo Records, 1984.

Cherry, Don. "When Will the Blues Leave?" Art Deco. A&M Records, 1989.

Published or Personal Letter
Lasswell, Harold. Letter to the author. 15 July 1976.

Schneider, Alan. "To Sam from Alan." 3 Sept. 1972. No Author Better Served: The Correspondence of Samuel Beckett and Alan Schneider. Ed. Maurice Harmon. Cambridge: Harvard UP, 1998. 278–82.

Thackeray, William Makepeace. "To George Henry Lewes." 6 Mar. 1848. Letter 452 of Letters and Private Papers of William Makepeace Thackery. Ed. Gordon N. Ray. Cambridge: Harvard UP, 1946. 335–354.

Published or Personal Interview
Freund, Nancy. Telephone interview. 18 June 1998.

Gerard, William. Personal interview. 16 May 1999.

Previn, Andre. Interview. "A Knight at the Keyboard." By Jed Distler. Piano and Keyboard. Jan.–Feb. 1999: 24–29.

Computer Software
Biblio-Link II for Windows: Powerful Data Transfer for ProCit. Diskette. Ann Arbor: Personal Bibliographic Software, 1993.

Schwartz, Howard F., Robert Hamblen, and Mark S. McMillan, eds. AG Photo CD-1. Diskette. Fort Collins: Colorado State U and Advanced Digital Imaging, 1996.

Database Available On-line
Bartleby Library. Ed. Steven van Leeuwen. 1999. 5 May 1999 <http://www.bartleby.com>.

Book, Article, or Other Source Available On-line

Besides author and title, add any translator or editor and the date of electronic publication or last update. Conclude with the date on which you visited the electronic site where the source is located and the site's address.

> Land-Webber, Ellen. To Save a Life: Stories of Jewish Rescue. 1999. 5 Feb. 1999 <http://sorrel.humboldt/edu/~rescuers/>.
>
> Latham, Ernest. "Conducting Research at the National Archives into Art Looting, Recovery, and Restitution." National Archives Library. 4 Dec. 1998. National Archives and Records Administration. 5 Feb. 1999 <http://www.nara.gov/research/assets/sympaper/latham.html>.
>
> Marvell, Andrew. Last Instructions to a Painter. Poet's Corner. 11 Nov. 1997. 5 Feb. 1999 <http://www.geocities.com/~spanoudi/poems/marvel04.html>.
>
> Wollstonecraft, Mary. "A Vindication of the Rights of Women: With Strictures on Political and Moral Subjects." Project Bartleby Archive. Ed. Steven van Leeuwen. Jan. 1996. Columbia U. 5 Feb. 1999 <http://www.cc.columbia.edu/acis/bartleby/wollstonecraft>.

Magazine Article Available On-line

> Chatsky, Jean Sherman. "Grow Your Own Employee Benefits." Money.com 30–31 Jan. 1999. 7 Feb. 1999 <http://www.pathfinder.com/money/moneytalk>.

Newspaper Article Available On-line

> Wolf, Mark. "Finding Art in Albums."@ The Post: World Wide Web Edition of the Cincinnati Post 5 Feb. 1999. 5 Feb. 1999 <http://www.cincypost.com/living/album020599.html>.

Article from an Electronic Journal

> Warren, W. L. "Church and State in Angevin Ireland." Chronicon: An Electronic History Journal 1 (1997): 6 pars. 6 Feb. 1999 <http://www.ucc.ie/chronicon/warren.htm>.

Electronic Posting to a Group

> Faris, Tommy L. "Tiger Woods." Online posting. 3 Sept. 1996. H-Net: Humanities & Social Sciences Online Posting. 7 Feb. 1999 <http://www.h-net.msu.edu/~arete/archives/threads/tiger.html>.

Review Available On-line

> Holden, Stephen. Rev. of Anne Frank Remembered. 22 Feb. 1996. 5 Feb. 1999 <http://www.english.upenn.edu/~afilreis/Holocaust/anne-frank-film.html>.

Public Web Site with Organizational Message

> Raab, Jennifer J. "Greeting from Chairman Jennifer J. Raab." Landmarks Preservation Commission New York City. 8 Sept. 1998. 7 Feb. 1999 <http://www.ci.nyc.ny.us/html/lpc/home.html>.

Database or Other Source Available on CD-ROM

Use "n.p." to indicate either "no place" or "no publisher" if such information is not available. Use "n.d." to indicate "no date."

> "Landforms of the Earth: Cause, Course, Effect, Animation." <u>Phenomena of the Earth</u>. CD-ROM. n.p.: Springer Electronic Media/MMCD, 1998.

> <u>Life in Tudor Times</u>. CD-ROM. Princeton: Films for the Humanities and Sciences, 1996.

APA (AMERICAN PSYCHOLOGICAL ASSOCIATION) DOCUMENTATION

The samples below show how to use APA style for citing a source in the text and in the References section at the end of a paper.

APA Parenthetical Documentation   The basic APA parenthetical citation includes the author's last name and the date of publication, information generally sufficient to identify a source in the reference list. Although researchers in the social sciences often cite works as a whole, the page number can be added to identify exactly where a quotation or other specific information is located. If the author's name is included in the text, it does not need to be repeated in the citation.

Single Author
> The city's most current traffic flow analysis (Dunlap, 1998) proposed two alternatives.

> Nagle (1998) compared the costs and benefits of both designs.

Two Authors
Use both names each time the source is cited. Use the word *and* to join them in the text; use an ampersand (&) in parentheses and the reference list.

> Moll and Greenberg (1990) outline the advantages of a more flexible approach to social context.

> An earlier study (Moll & Diaz, 1987) proposed classroom change as one research objective.

Three to Five Authors
Supply all the names the first time the source is cited. If it is cited again, use only the name of the first author and et al., for "and others."

> Greene, Rucker, Zauss, and Harris (1998) maintain that anxiety is an important factor in communication.

> Greene et al. (1998) address anxiety and communication directly.

More than Five Authors
Use only the name of the first author with *et al.* in the paper. Supply the names of the first six authors in the list of references followed by *et al.* for any additional authors.

> Heath et al. (1988) continue to address the problems involved in implementing this methodology.

Group or Organization as Author
The Ford Foundation (1988) outlined several efforts to change decision-making processes.

Work without an Author
"Challenging the Myths" (1995) identifies several traditional beliefs about teacher training.

Page Numbers for a Work
The characteristics of successful charter schools follow an opening definition of the "charter school challenge" (Rowe, 1995, p. 34).

Two or More Works in the Same Citation
If several citations are grouped in one pair of parentheses, arrange them alphabetically.

Recent studies of small groups (Laramie & Nader, 1997; McGrew, 1996; Tiplett, 1999) concentrate on their interactions rather than their context.

Letters, Telephone Calls, E-mail Messages, and Similar Communications
These communications are personal and thus are cited only in the text, not in the references.

This staffing pattern for nurses is used at four of the six major metropolitan hospitals (G. N. Prescott, personal communication, August 23, 1999).

APA List of References   As you examine the following illustrations, notice how capitalization, italics, punctuation, and other features change with the type of source noted. (If italics are not available, you may use underlining.) Note also that authors' names are listed with surnames first, followed by initials only. Although the entries in an APA reference list follow very specific patterns, references in your paper—to titles, for instance—should use standard capitalization. Similarly, the word *and* should be spelled out in your paper (except in parenthetical citations) even though the ampersand (&) is used in the references.

Book with One Author
Blau, T. H. (1998). *The psychologist as expert witness* (2nd ed.). New York: Wiley.

Nuckalls, C. W. (1998). *Culture: A problem that cannot be solved.* Madison: University of Wisconsin Press.

Several Works by One Author
List the works by year of publication, with the earliest first.
Muller, N. J. (1998). *Mobile telecommunications factbook.* New York: McGraw-Hill.

Muller, N. J. (1999). *Desktop encyclopedia of the Internet.* Boston: Artech House.

Book with Two Authors
Arden, H., & Wall, S. (1998). *Travels in a stone canoe: The return to the wisdomkeepers.* New York: Simon & Schuster.

Book with More than Two Authors or Editors

Greenfield, L. A., Rand, M. R., Craven, D., Klaus, P. A., Perkins, C. A., Ringel, et al. (1998). *Violence by intimates: Analysis of data on crimes by current or former spouses, boyfriends, and girlfriends* (NCJ-167237). Bureau of Justice Statistics Factbook. Washington: U.S. Department of Justice.

Hair, J. F., Jr., Anderson, R. E., Tatham, R. L., & Black, W. C. (1998). *Multivariate data analysis* (5th ed.). Upper Saddle River, NJ: Prentice Hall, 1998.

Work with a Group or an Organization as Author

When the author is also the publisher, "Author" is used as the publisher's name.

American Public Transit Association. (1986). *The 1986 rail transit report.* Washington, DC: Author.

Amnesty International. (1998). *Children in South Asia: Securing their rights.* New York: Author.

Book without an Author

Ultimate visual dictionary of science. (1998). New York: Dorling Kindersley.

Work in a Collection of Pieces by Different Authors

Ombaka, C. (1998). War and environment in African literature. In P. D. Murphy (Ed.), *Literature of nature: An international sourcebook* (pp. 327–336). Chicago: Fitzroy Dearborn.

Collection of Pieces Cited as a Whole

Young, C. (Ed.). (1998). *Ethnic diversity and public policy.* New York: St. Martin's.

Work in Several Volumes

AFL-CIO. (1960). *American Federation of Labor: History, encyclopedia, and reference book* (Vols. 1–3). Washington, DC: Author.

Work Translated from Another Language

When you cite a translation in your paper, include both its original publication date and the date of the translation you have used, as in (Rousseau, 1762/1954).

Rousseau, J. J. (1954). *The social contract.* (W. Kendall, Trans.) Chicago: Regnery. (Original work published 1762)

Work Appearing as Part of a Series

Frith, K. T. (Vol. Ed.). (1997). *Counterpoints: Vol. 54. Undressing the ad: Reading culture in advertising.* New York: Peter Lang.

New Edition of an Older Book

When you cite an older source in your paper, include the original publication date and the date of the new edition, as in (Packard, 1866/1969).

Packard, F. A. (1969). *The daily public school in the United States.* New York: Arno Press. (Original work published 1866)

Article in a Reference Volume
Breadfruit (1994) In Crystal D. (Ed.), *The Cambridge encyclopedia* (2nd ed., p. 175). Cambridge: Cambridge University Press.

Work Issued by a Federal, State, or Other Government Agency
Nelson, R. E., Ziegler, A. A., Serino, D. F., & Basner, P. J. (1987). Radioactive waste processing apparatus. *Energy research abstracts* Vol. 12, (Abstract No. 34680.) Washington, D.C.: U.S. Department of Energy, Office of Scientific and Technical Information.

Reference to a Legal Document
Individuals with Disabilities Education Act (IDEA), 20 U.S.C. § 1400 *et seq.* (1996).

Turner Broadcasting System Inc. v. Federal Communications Commission, 95 U.S. 992 (1997).

Article in a Journal with Pagination Continuing through Each Volume
Dinerman, T. (1998). The case for an American manned Mars mission. *The Journal of Social, Political and Economic Studies, 23*, 369–378.

Greene, J. O., Rucker, M. P., Zauss, E. S., & Harris, A. A. (1998). Communication anxiety and the acquisition of message-production skill. *Communication Education, 47*, 337–347.

Article in a Journal with Pagination Continuing Only through Each Issue
Brune, L. H. (1998). Recent scholarship and findings about the Korean War. *American Studies International, 36(3)*, 4–16.

Special Issue of a Periodical
Larsen, C. S. (1994). In the wake of Columbus: Native population biology in the postcontact Americas. In A. T. Steegmann, Jr. (Ed.), *Yearbook of Physical Anthropology: Vol. 37* (pp. 109–154). New York: Wiley-Liss.

Riley, P., & Morse, P. R. (Eds.). (1998). Communication in the global community [Special issue]. *Communication Research, 25(2)*.

Article in a Weekly or Biweekly Periodical
Greenwald, J. (1998, November 23). Herbal healing. *Time, 152*, 58–67.

Article in a Monthly or Bimonthly Periodical
Glausiusz, J. (1999, June). Creatures from the bleak lagoon. *Discover, 20*, 76–79.

Gordon, J. S. (1999, May/June). The great crash (of 1792). *American Heritage. 50*, 20–24.

Article in a Daily Newspaper
Levine, S. (1999, January 30). Hearing loss touches a younger generation. *The Washington Post*, pp. A1, A8.

Article with No Author
Fire and lightning. (1998, October 10). *New Scientist*, 25.

Editorial in a Periodical
Zuckerman, M. B. (1999, February 8). Coming to Russia's rescue. *U.S. News and World Report*, p. 68.

Letter Written to the Editor of a Periodical
Triebold, M. (1998, July/August). Digging bones for fun and $$$ [Letter to the editor]. *The Sciences*, 5.

Review Article
Glaeser, E. L. (1997). [Review of the book *Policing space: Territoriality and the Los Angeles Police Department*]. *Contemporary Sociology: A Journal of Reviews, 26*, 750–751.

Presentation at a Professional Meeting or Conference
Achilles, C. M., Keedy, J. L., & Zaharias, J. B. (1996, October). *If we're rebuilding education, let's start with a firm foundation*. Paper presented at the annual meeting of the University Council for Educational Administration, Louisville, KY.

Film, Videotape
If sources do not mention a place of publication, use *n.p.* If no date is mentioned, use *n.d.*

CityTV and Sleeping Giant Productions (Producers). (1994). *Dalai Lama: A portrait in the first person* [Motion picture]. n.p.: Films for the Humanities and Sciences.

Programs on Radio and Television
If appropriate, add the names of contributors or a specific episode before the series title.

The New Detectives: Case Studies in Forensic Science. (1999, February 9). Bethesda, MD: Discovery.

CD or Other Recording
Use *n.d.* and *n.p.* if you need to indicate that a recording or other source does not note the date or place of publication.

Cleveland, J. (1993). Marching to Zion. On *The great gospel men* [CD]. Newton, NJ: Shanachie Records.

Jamal, A. (1961). Night mist blues. On *Ahmad Jamal at the Blackhawk* [Record]. Chicago: Argo.

Letters, Interviews, and Personal Messages
If you have used a communication such as a letter in a print or other medium, follow the form for that type of citation. If the communication is a message or call not available to other researchers, cite it only in your text, not in your list of references. (See page 707.)

Computer Software
Weiss, H. J. (1990). PC-POM: Software for Production and Operations Management (Version 2.10) [Computer software]. Boston: Allyn and Bacon.

Database Available On-line

Academic Info: Your Gateway to Quality Internet Resources. (1999, February 4). Retrieved February 5, 1999 from http://www.academicinfo.net

Book, Article, or Other Source Available On-line

Hornbeck, D. (1999, January 22). The past in California's landscape. Retrieved February 7, 1999 from California Mission Studies Association: http://www.ca-missions.org/hornbeck.html

1695: Northwestern Indians at Quebec: Huron intrigues. Retrieved February 5, 1999 from State Historical Society of Wisconsin, http://memory.loc.gov/cgibin/query/r?ammem/lhbum:@field (DOCID+Alit(M7689e42)

Magazine Article Available On-line

All hope gone for Hussein, power is passing to Abdullah. (1999, February 7). *Time Daily.* Retrieved February 7, 1999 from http://cgi.pathfinder.com/time/daily/0,2960,19381-101990206,00.html

Spragins, E. E. (1999, February 7). Patient power: How to beat job lock. *Newsweek.* Retrieved February 7, 1999 from http://www.newsweek.com/nw-srv/focus/he/fohe0224_1.htm

Newspaper Article Available On-line

Harden, C., & Long, P. A. (1998, October 28). Grand jury begins work in bid probe. *The Kentucky Post.* Retrieved February 5, 1999 from http://www.kypost.com/news/bids102989.html

Sack, K. On the bipartisan bayou, a brouhaha. (1999, February 5). *New York Times.* Retrieved February 5, 1999 from http://www.nytimes.com/yr/mo/day/news/washpol/la-cooperate.html

Article from an Electronic Journal

Peiss, K. L. (1998, Fall). American women and the making of modern consumer culture. *Journal for MultiMedia History, 1*(1). Retrieved February 5, 1999 from http://www.albany.edu/jmmh/ vol1no1/peiss.html

Abstract Available On-line

Gay, H. (1998 August). East end, west end: Science education, culture and class in mid-Victorian London. *Canadian Journal of History, 33.* Retrieved February 5, 1999 from http://www.asask.ca/history/cjh/ABS_897.HTM

Electronic Posting to a Group

French, M. (1996, February 21). Erie Canal? Message posted to http://www.h-net.msu.edu/~aseh/archives/threads/eriecanal.html

Database or Other Source Available on CD-ROM

Real facts about the sun. (2000). *The Dynamic Sun.* Retrieved October 27, 2001, from NASA database.

Sample Student Paper (MLA Style)

Last name and
page number 1/2
inch below top of
page

Heading 1 inch
below top of page

All lines double-
spaced, including
heading and title

Title centered
Title defines topic

Paragraph indented
1/2 inch or 5 spaces

1-inch side
margins

Opening interests
reader with detail
from film

Quotation from
electronic source

Support from print
source

Lee 1

Clara Lee

Professor Paul Smith

Writing Workshop II

5 May 2002

The Courage of Intimacy:

Movie Masculinity in the Nineties

Mike Newell's 1997 film Donnie Brasco begins and ends
with an extreme close-up of Johnny Depp's eyes. Shot in wide-
screen so that the eyes literally span the entire screen, the image is a black-and-white snapshot that appears during the
opening credits and returns as a full-color close-up at the end
of the movie. Depp's lustrous eyes are large and black and
beautiful, and gazing at them up close gives the viewer a surprisingly intimate sensation. Even within the conventional narrative that makes up the body of the movie, they become
noticeably important; Web-site critic Rob Blackwelder observes
that "Depp has [the central conflict of the movie] in his eyes in
every scene," and Susan Wloszczyna of USA Today notes, "It's
all in the eyes. Depp's intense orbs focus like surveillance cam-
eras, taking in each crime and confrontation. He's sucked into
the brutal, bullying lifestyle, and so are we." The close-up image
at the beginning and end is one of the few instances in which
the film draws blatant attention to its own style, but the device

Lee 2

calls attention to the film's central focus, its constant probing

into the character at the center of the movie.

Somehow, without restricting the film to a first-person narration by Depp's undercover FBI agent, the audience comes to identify with him and understand the many pressures increasing inside his head simply by watching his eyes. They reflect his watchfulness, his uncertainty, his frustration, and his guilt—all without drawing too much attention to himself from his unsuspecting wise guy companions. He is guarded with his words, causing his closest Mafioso friend to remark, "You never say anything without thinking about it first." His quietness invites viewers to read his looks and expressions, to become intimately acquainted with a character who constantly has to hide part of himself from the people around him, until they can virtually feel every twinge of fear or regret that the character feels. Seeing this man trapped in situations in which he faces crisis after crisis, unwillingly alienated from his family and eventually his employers, trying only to protect the people he loves, viewers can ultimately recognize him as a more sensitive, struggling, and courageous hero than those celebrated in the past.

Over the decades, Hollywood has glorified the gruff masculinity of actors from Humphrey Bogart to Sylvester Stallone. Joan Mellen notes in her 1977 book <u>Big Bad Wolves: Masculinity in the American Film</u> that in traditional Hollywood films,

---

Margin notes (right column):

1-inch margin at the top

Heading 1/2 inch below top of page continues last name and page numbering

Quotation from film

Thesis stated

Past contrasted with present

Source identified in text

Lee 3

Quotation from book with page number

especially the stoic action films of the 1970s, "physical action unencumbered by effeminate introspection is what character-izes the real man" (5). In the 1990s, it seems that much has changed; introspection has become a central part of leading-male roles. Character-driven films of the past year alone have won accolades for such intimate roles as Robert Duvall's tor-

Other examples noted

mented evangelical preacher in The Apostle, Matt Damon's emotionally needy genius and Robin William's mourning thera-pist in Good Will Hunting, and the unemployed guys struggling over issues like impotence and child custody in The Full Monty.

Background tied to thesis

Thoughtfulness, vulnerability, and the ability to handle relation-ships have become virtual requirements for the male "hero" in the 1990s. The old-fashioned masculinity of characters played by Clint Eastwood or John Wayne in the past has come to be regarded as emotionally repressed and overly macho.

The change is partly cyclical. Mellen cites the 1930s and 1950s as eras in film in which leading men were given

Clarification added in brackets

greater depth. She says, "despite the limitations imposed by a repressive society [in the fifties], film recovered for men an

Quotation with two page numbers

individual self with a distinctive identity and a flourishing ego" (191–92). Actors like Marion Brando and James Dean, in particular, played insecure, emotionally torn rebels who express tenderness in their relationships with women and with other men. However, in the sixties, "as the Vietnam War progressed

Lee 4

[. . .] maleness itself appeared under siege and in need of defense," and "traumatic events of the sixties induced the Hollywood hero to tighten up, reveal as little about himself as possible, and to find comfort in his own recalcitrance" (248–49). Things scarcely got better when "glorification of the vigilante male [became] the dominant masculine myth of the seventies" (295) with films like <u>Dirty Harry</u> and <u>Taxi Driver</u>. "In the seventies film, people are allowed no option: they must meet force with force" (307). Following two decades of grim testosterone, there was a definite reaction in the bubble gum pop culture of the eighties, with flashy cartoon violence starring Sylvester Stallone or Arnold Schwarzeneggar presenting highly unrealistic images of masculinity, and lighter portrayals like Marty McFly and Indiana Jones gaining in popularity. By the nineties, American audiences were no longer taking tough guy masculinity seriously, leading to a trend of ironic humor in action films from <u>True Lies</u> to <u>Independence Day</u>. It is doubtful that Will Smith would have been a favorite action hero in any other era but the 1990s.

However, the crucial underlying shift in American culture is the debilitation of the conventional white male hero in a country he once monopolized. Trends in society within the last thirty years have led to greater freedom for women, minorities, and homosexuals, and as pride and power among these groups have increased, there has been a backlash against the white

Ellipses for words omitted added in brackets

Quotations and summary from source

Transition back to present day

male. Today's hero has to prove that he is sensitive and completely respectful of every group mentioned above in order to
remain sympathetic, forcing his previous role of unquestioned
dominance to change drastically. In addition, now that women
are going to work and less is expected of men in terms of being
the provider and protector of the family and society, more is expected of them in their personal relationships. As noted recently
by Sylvester Stallone, a fitting symbol of the old macho masculinity who is now trying to change his image to a more sensi-

Quotation from published interview

tive one, "I think the leading man of the future will be one who
is beleaguered by the need to constantly define on film the
male-female relationship." He also notes, "People want to nurture the underdog. The day of the strongman is over" (94). The
themes of inefficacy in society, sensitivity in relationships, and a
reaction to the old strongman ideal show up clearly in <u>Donnie
Brasco</u>.

Analysis of film

    In the movie, FBI agent Joe Pistone, alias Donnie Brasco,
goes undercover in the belief that he is on the side of law and
order, with the simple goal of booking some major criminals; instead he finds a bunch of endearing but disturbingly violent
men who become his closest companions for several years.

Plot summary and interpretation

Particularly perplexing is his relationship with Benjamin "Lefty"
Ruggiero, the trod-upon hitman whose thirty years of faithful
service are rewarded with dirty-work assignments while

Lee 6

younger wise guys are promoted over him. Lefty is the one who notices Donnie and recruits him into the organization, and from the start his faith in Donnie is clear; as Pistone smugly reports to a contact early in the movie, "I got my hooks in this guy." However, Pistone's smugness wears off as Lefty repeatedly invites him into his home, confides in him with his complaints and his dreams, and says unexpectedly one day waiting in the hospital where his own son is in the E.R. for a drug overdose, "I love you, Donnie." It is appropriate that the fictional Donnie Brasco is an orphan, because Lefty essentially becomes a surrogate father to him. Pistone, concerned for Lefty's fate, becomes more and more reluctant to "pull out" of his undercover assignment, revealing Donnie Brasco as a spy and leaving the blame (and death sentence) on Lefty. At one point he stops meeting his FBI contacts because they are pressuring him to pull out. Instead, he lets himself take on his mob alter ego more and more, tearing both his professional and personal lives apart.

Character analysis

In a way, the film is an interesting commentary on how ideals have changed, because it is set in the 1970s but made with a 1990s ideology. Because it is based on a book by the real agent Joe Pistone, who is currently living under the Witness Protection Program, one might think the portrayal would be strictly fact-based and would not be affected by the recent obsession with the sensitive male; but of course, one must never underestimate the power of filmmakers in any era to interpret their material with their own contemporary vision (note the portrayal of the Three Musketeers as aging and vulnerable in the recent screen adaptation of <u>The Man in the Iron Mask</u>; the seventies version of the same book depicted the Musketeers as brash and irreverent). There is plenty of traditional macho posturing in the Mafia sequences of <u>Donnie Brasco</u>, but director Mike Newell places special emphasis on Pistone's sensitive relationship with Lefty Ruggiero, his mentor in the mob, and on his imperiled relationship with his wife. Newell, a British director most famous for his vastly different romantic comedy <u>Four Weddings and a Funeral</u>, also boasted about <u>Donnie Brasco</u>'s "absolutely novel point of view about the Mob," focusing on "the lowest rung, the have-nots" (Schickel), rather than the rich and powerful men at the top so often depicted in mob movies. The film focuses on the soulful side of a male protagonist in a genre in which sensitivity is rare.

Electronic source cited by author's name only

In fact, <u>Donnie Brasco</u> has been recognized as "a different take on the mob," an evolutionary step in the genre of gangster films. <u>Time</u> calls it a "neo-Scorsesian study of lowlife Mob life" (Schickel), and Blackwelder says that it "rises above the mire of its shopworn genre by showing the cracks in its characters' armor." Chris Grunden sums up the difference when he says, "Newell eschews fancy camera-work and visual flair to remain tightly focused on the human drama—he's made an actors' picture in a genre obsessed with style (<u>GoodFellas</u>, <u>Heat</u>)." Conventional gangster films usually depict the rise and fall of a charismatic criminal. The gangster movies of the thirties and forties featured fast-talking tough guys like James Cagney and Humphrey Bogart; Francis Ford Coppola's 1972 epic <u>The Godfather</u>, which revived the genre, depicted the same glamour, ruthlessness, and power of the Mafia, on an even greater romanticized scale. But after a spate of stylized mob movies in the past twenty years, many reviewers of <u>Donnie Brasco</u> welcomed a new approach in a genre that was growing old and stale. Put another way, <u>Donnie Brasco</u> is the film that finally brings its genre into the nineties by replacing its tough, glamorous hero with a real guy who can't live up to the stereotypes.

Contrasts lead back to thesis

Almost in direct response to the ideal of masculinity presented in the past, Newell shows that although at first Pistone is doing everything right—fitting perfectly into his undercover persona, doing top-rate work for the FBI, and sending checks home regularly to his family—he cannot "be the man in the f—kin' white hat" that he thought he could be, as he puts it late in the movie. He knows how impossible it is to fulfill his male responsibilities in all three of his very different worlds after he has ditched the FBI, almost lost his marriage, and realized that his undercover work, once revealed, will be the cause of Lefty's

Analysis of main character

death. He has failed his own expectations of himself to save the day and make everything right. The contemporary audience recognizes the realism of the situation. As Stallone stated in his interview, "The male is [only] the illusion of the protector and guardian, [. . . b]ecause in this day and age, there is no security he can offer" (94). By now the audience realizes that a hero cannot always save the day in a conventional sense. In an odd way, viewers even appreciate his failure because it has knocked all of his arrogance out of him and left only an exposed, vulnerable character.

A contemporary audience can especially relate to the issues of family breakdown, recognizing in Donnie's situation the roots of the culture of estrangement and divorce which is so widespread today. Violating the conventional lone male gangster/cop figure, Joe Pistone has not only a wife but three small daughters hidden away in suburbia, and he can't tell them anything about his job without putting them at risk. His visits home are less and less frequent, sometimes months apart, due to the consuming nature of his "job." Although viewers can see from the start the tenderness and love he has for his wife and daughters, his prolonged absences and broken promises (he misses his daughter's first Communion) lead to intensifying arguments between him and his wife. As she constantly reminds him, his job is tearing their home apart, and not knowing what

Analysis of relationships with other characters

Lee 10

he is doing makes it all the more unbearable. Pistone knows, as his identification with the Mafia grows deeper and deeper, that his involvement has serious consequences for his family, and this mounting pressure becomes impossible to resolve when weighed against the life of Lefty Ruggiero.

Regarding the role of women in Mafia movies, Mellen points out that "Well into the seventies the male protagonist of films from The Godfather (I or II) to Serpico uses women solely to discard them" (327). Wives in The Godfather are cheated on, lied to, and in one case, violently beaten. At a pivotal moment at the end of the movie, the wife of Michael Corleone tearfully asks him if he has ordered the death of his sister's husband, and he looks directly into her eyes and lies, saying he did not. She smiles and believes him. Her character is, in fact, constantly under the thumb of her husband who misleads her, ignores her, and coaxes her into marrying him after not contacting her for over a year. She and the other women in the movie are not once consulted or listened to, no matter how much their husbands' actions affect their lives.

Contrasting example

Donnie Brasco could have been made in precisely the same way. Pistone's wife Maggie is, after all, left at home for months at a time while her husband is off doing his job for the FBI. However, Newell makes the relationship between them a pivotal storyline in the movie. Repeatedly in the course of the

Contrasting example related to film

narrative, interrupting the Mafia sequences, the audience sees Pistone call or visit home, reinforcing his identity as a husband and father. Viewers also note the progression as his relationship

Incident from film substantiates interpretation

begins to sour. The lowest point comes when Pistone shows up at his home in the middle of the night to retrieve a bag containing $3 million in cash and confronts Maggie, who has found it and hidden it. When she tells him that he has become "like one of them," he strikes her, and both recoil in surprise, less shocked at the blow than at the realization of what their marriage has become. At this critical moment, he tries to tell her the truth. He awkwardly explains the situation with Lefty and his fear of being responsible for his death. He tells her that he is not

Quotation from film

sure of what is right anymore. He tells her, "I'm not like them. I am them." It is evident that the troubles of Pistone's marriage hurt himself as much as his wife, and in a sense, dealing with them takes more courage than risking his life as an undercover agent in the Mafia. The film treats this relationship delicately, and the woman here is not merely discarded or lied to, but confronted and confided in, with her concerns presented as clearly as his own.

What makes Pistone's situation so compelling is that he starts out believing that he can be one of the traditional "solitary

Source identified in citation

heroes who solve all problems for themselves" (Mellen 23) and instead comes up against situations that are too difficult to handle. Joe Pistone slaps his wife, not to exert his male domi-

nance, but because he has lost control. When he tries to make

things right, he doesn't sweep her into his arms (and probably

have his way with her, in the true tradition of male heroes); he is

almost frightened to make a move and instead makes a ges-

ture—kissing the back of her head—to try and reestablish the

emotional (not sexual) intimacy between them. In his early

scenes with Lefty, Pistone is noticeably on his guard and de-

tached from the affection Lefty is developing for him; later,

when he has the opportunity to be promoted within the ranks of

the mob and Lefty feels betrayed, Pistone tries to express his

devotion by visiting him at the hospital where his son has over-

dosed. When Lefty orders him to leave, he refuses.

Detail from film supports interpretation

These gestures are some of Pistone's most heroic acts, at

least as Newell presents it. Although he is given a medal and a

check for $500 at the end of the movie for his undercover work

(which is enough to secure scores of convictions), his feelings

about it are clearly mixed; his loyalty to the FBI has been disin-

tegrating as he has lost faith in their good guy/bad guy rhetoric,

and his primary concern—Lefty's safety—is now uncertain. His

success in infiltrating a group of depressed Brooklyn wise guys

is now a cause for guilt. It is at this point at the end of the

movie, as Pistone accepts his reward and his wife tells him it's

all over, that Newell returns to the extreme close-up of Depp's

Return to detail used in first paragraph

eyes, and the audience sees how troubled they are. Viewers are left with that image, indicating that Newell intended for them to leave the theater asking themselves what it was all for—whether doing his job was really the right thing or not. True to life, there is no easy, happy ending, in which a man can die in battle or save the day and thus fulfill his "masculine" duties. What matters, however, as viewers return to that close-up, is that they have seen Joe Pistone/Donnie Brasco's vulnerability and his devotion within his relationships. If he feels confused or uncertain at the end, it is because he has faced these emotional issues, which are far more subtle than the challenges related to

Return to thesis

his job. The audience has seen him show more courage in his private struggles than John Wayne ever did out on the frontier and can applaud him for that.

Lee 14

Works Cited

Blackwelder, Rob. "<u>Donnie Brasco</u>." Rev. of <u>Donnie Brasco</u>, dir.

Mike Newell. <u>The Fairfield [CA] Daily Republic</u> 3 Mar. 1997:

D5+. <u>Spliced Online</u> Archives Mar. 1977. 23 Sept. 1998

<*http://www.splicedonline.com*>.

<u>Donnie Brasco.</u> Dir. Mike Newell. Tristar, 1997.

Grunden, Chris. "<u>Donnie Brasco</u>." Rev. of <u>Donnie Brasco</u>, dir.

Mike Newell. <u>Film Journal International Online</u> Mar. 1997.

20 Sept. 1998 <*http://www.filmjournal.com/reviews/html/*

mar977.html>.

Mellen, Joan. <u>Big Bad Wolves: Masculinity in American Film</u>.

New York: Pantheon, 1977.

Schickel, Richard. "Depp Charge." <u>Time Magazine Online</u> 3

Mar. 1977. 22 Sept. 1998 <*http://cgi.pathfinder.com/time/*

magazine/1997/dom/970303/deppcharge.html>.

Stallone, Sylvester. "Masculine Mystique." Interview. <u>Esquire.</u>

Dec. 1996: 89–96.

Wloszczyna, Susan. "<u>Donnie Brasco</u>: A High Point for Lowlifes."

Rev. of <u>Donnie Brasco,</u> dir. Mike Newell. <u>USA Today</u> 28

Feb. 1997: 1D.

All lines double-spaced, including title and entries

Title 1 inch below top of page and centered

First line at margin

Next lines indented 1/2 inch or 5 spaces

Entries in alphabetical order

Article title in quotation marks

Movie title underlined

Glossary of Terms

Abstract/concrete patterns of language reflect an author's word choice. Abstract words (for example, *wisdom, power, beauty*) refer to general ideas, qualities, or conditions. Concrete words name material objects and items associated with the five senses—words like *rock, pizza,* and *basketball.* Both abstract and concrete language are useful in communicating ideas. Generally you should not be too abstract in writing. It is best to employ concrete words, naming things that can be seen, touched, smelled, heard, or tasted in order to support generalizations, topic sentences, or more abstract ideas.

Acronym is a word formed from the first or first few letters of several words, as in OPEC (Organization of Petroleum Exporting Countries).

Action in narrative writing is the sequence of happenings or events. This movement of events may occupy just a few minutes or extend over a period of years or centuries.

Alliteration is the repetition of initial consonant sounds in words placed closely next to each other, as in "what a *t*ale of *t*error now their *t*urbulency *t*ells." Prose that is highly rhythmical or "poetic" often makes use of this method.

Allusion is a literary, biographical, or historical reference, whether real or imaginary. It is a "figure of speech" (a fresh, useful comparison) employed to illuminate an idea. A writer's prose style can be made richer through this economical method of evoking an idea or emotion, as in E. M. Forster's biblical allusion in this sentence: "Property produces men of weight, and it was a man of weight who failed to get into the Kingdom of Heaven."

Analogy is a form of comparison that uses a clear illustration to explain a difficult idea or function. It is unlike a formal comparison in that its subjects of comparison are from different categories or areas. For example, an analogy likening "division of labor" to the activity of bees in a hive makes the first concept more concrete by showing it to the reader through the figurative comparison with the bees. Analogy in exposition can involve a few sentences, a paragraph or set of paragraphs, or an entire essay. Analogies can also be used in argumentation to heighten an appeal to emotion, but they cannot actually *prove* anything.

Analysis   is a method of exposition in which a subject is broken up into its parts to explain their nature, function, proportion, or relationship. Analysis thus explores connections and processes within the context of a given subject. (See *Causal analysis* and *Process analysis.*)

Anecdote   is a brief, engaging account of some happening, often historical, biographical, or personal. As a technique in writing, anecdote is especially effective in creating interesting essay introductions and also in illuminating abstract concepts in the body of the essay.

Antecedent   in grammar refers to the word, phrase, or clause to which a pronoun refers. In writing, antecedent also refers to any happening or thing that is prior to another, or to anything that logically precedes a subject.

Antithesis   is the balancing of one idea or term against another for emphasis.

Antonym   is a word whose meaning is opposite to that of another word.

Aphorism   is a short, pointed statement expressing a general truism or an idea in an original or imaginative way. Marshall McLuhan's statement that "the medium is the message" is a well-known contemporary aphorism.

Archaic   language is vocabulary or usage that belongs to an early period and is old-fashioned today. The word *thee* for *you* is an archaism still in use in certain situations.

Archetypes   are special images or symbols that, according to Carl Jung, appeal to the total racial or cultural understanding of a people. Such images or symbols as the mother archetype, the cowboy in American film, a sacred mountain, or spring as a time of renewal tend to trigger the "collective unconscious" of the human race.

Argumentation   is a formal variety of writing that offers reasons for or against something. Its goal is to persuade or convince the reader through logical reasoning and carefully controlled emotional appeal. Argumentation as a formal mode of writing contains many properties that distinguish it from exposition. (See *Assumption, Deduction, Evidence, Induction, Logic, Persuasion, Proposition,* and *Refutation.*)

Assonance   defined generally as likeness or rough similarity of sound. Its specific definition is a partial rhyme in which the stressed vowel sounds are alike but the consonant sounds are unlike, as in *late* and *make*. Although more common to poetry, assonance can also be detected in highly rhythmic prose.

Assumption   in argumentation is anything taken for granted or presumed to be accepted by the audience and therefore unstated. Assumptions in argumentative writing can be dangerous because the audience might not always accept the idea implicit in them. (See *Begging the question.*)

Audience   is that readership toward which an author directs his or her essay. In composing essays, writers must acknowledge the nature of their expected readers—whether specialized or general, minimally educated or highly educated, sympathetic or unsympathetic toward the writer's opinions, and so forth. Failure to focus on the writer's true audience can lead to confusions in language and usage, presentation of inappropriate content, and failure to appeal to the expected reader.

Balance   in sentence structure refers to the assignment of equal treatment in the arrangement of coordinate ideas. It is often used to heighten a contrast of ideas.

Begging the question   is an error or a fallacy in reasoning and argumentation in which the writer assumes as a truth something for which evidence or proof is actually needed.

Causal analysis   is a form of writing that examines causes and effects of events or conditions as they relate to a specific subject. Writers can investigate the causes of a particular effect or the effects of a particular cause or combine both methods. Basically, however, causal analysis looks for connections between things and reasons behind them.

Characterization   especially in narrative or descriptive writing is the creation of people involved in the action. Authors use techniques of dialogue, description, reportage, and observation in attempting to present vivid and distinctive characters.

Chronology or chronological order   is the arrangement of events in the order in which they happened. Chronological order can be used in such diverse narrative situations as history, biography, scientific process, and personal account. Essays that are ordered by chronology move from one step or point to the next in time.

Cinematic technique   in narration, description, and occasionally exposition is the conscious application of film art to the development of the contemporary essay. Modern writers often are aware of such film techniques as montage (the process of cutting and arranging film so that short scenes are presented in rapid succession), zoom (intense enlargement of subject), and various forms of juxtaposition, and use these methods to enhance the quality of their essays.

Classification   is a form of exposition in which the writer divides a subject into categories and then groups elements in each of those categories according to their relationships with one another. Thus a writer using classification takes a topic, divides it into several major groups, and then often subdivides those groups, moving always from larger categories to smaller ones.

Cliché   is an expression that once was fresh and original but has lost much of its vitality through overuse. Because terms like "as quick as a wink" and "blew her stack" are trite or common today, they should be avoided in writing.

Climactic ordering   is the arrangement of a paragraph or essay so that the most important items are saved for last. The effect is to build slowly through a sequence of events or ideas to the most critical part of the composition.

Coherence   is a quality in effective writing that results from the careful ordering of each sentence in a paragraph and each paragraph in the essay. If an essay is coherent, each part will grow naturally and logically from those parts that come before it. Following careful chronological, logical, spatial, or sequential order is the most natural way to achieve coherence in writing. The main devices used in achieving coherence are transitions, which help connect one thought with another.

Colloquial language   is conversational language used in certain types of informal and narrative writing but rarely in essays, business writing, or research writing. Expressions like "cool," "pal," or "I can dig it" often have a place in conversational settings. However, they should be used sparingly in essay writing for special effects.

Comparison/contrast   as an essay pattern treats similarities and differences between two subjects. Any useful comparison involves two items from the same class. Moreover, there must be a clear reason for the comparison or contrast. Finally, there must be a balanced treatment of the various comparative or contrasting points between the two subjects.

Conclusions   are the endings of essays. Without a conclusion, an essay would be incomplete, leaving the reader with the feeling that something important has been left out. There are numerous strategies for conclusions available to writers: summarizing main points in the essay, restating the main idea, using an effective quotation to bring the essay to an end, offering the reader the climax to a series of events, returning to the beginning and echoing it, offering a solution to a problem, emphasizing the topic's significance, or setting a new frame of reference by generalizing from the main thesis. A conclusion should end the essay in a clear, convincing, or emphatic way.

Concrete   (see *abstract/concrete.*)

Conflict   in narrative writing is the clash or opposition of events, characters, or ideas that makes the resolution of action necessary.

Connotation/denotation   are terms specifying the way a word has meaning. Connotation refers to the "shades of meaning" that a word might have because of various emotional associations it calls up for writers and readers alike. Words like *patriotism, pig,* and *rose* have strong connotative overtones to them. Denotation refers to the "dictionary" definition of a word—its exact meaning. Good writers understand the connotative and denotative value of words and must control the shades of meaning that many words possess.

Context   is the situation surrounding a word, group of words, or sentence. Often the elements coming before or after a certain confusing or difficult construction will provide insight into the meaning or importance of that item.

Coordination   in sentence structure refers to the grammatical arrangement of parts of the same order or equality in rank.

Declarative sentences   make a statement or assertion.

Deduction   is a form of logic that begins with a generally stated truth or principle and then offers details, examples, and reasoning to support the generalization. In other words, deduction is based on reasoning from a known principle to an unknown principle, from the general to the specific, or from a premise to a logical conclusion. (See *syllogism.*)

Definition   in exposition is the extension of a word's meaning through a paragraph or an entire essay. As an extended method of explaining a word, this type of definition relies on other rhetorical methods, including detail, illustration, comparison and contrast, and anecdote.

Denotation   (see *connotation/denotation.*)

Description   in the prose essay is a variety of writing that uses details of sight, sound, color, smell, taste, and touch to create a word picture and to explain or illustrate an idea.

Development   refers to the way a paragraph or an essay elaborates or builds upon a topic or theme. Typical development proceeds either from general illustrations to specific ones or from one generalization to another. (See *horizontal/vertical.*)

Dialogue   is the reproduction of speech or conversation between two or more persons in writing. Dialogue can add concreteness and vividness to an essay and can also help reveal character. A writer who reproduces dialogue in an essay must use it for a purpose and not simply as a decorative device.

Diction   is the manner of expression in words, choice of words, or wording. Writers must choose vocabulary carefully and precisely to communicate a message and also to address an intended audience effectively; this is good diction.

Digression   is a temporary departure from the main subject in writing. Any digression in the essay must serve a purpose or be intended for a specific effect.

Discourse (forms of)   relates conventionally to the main categories of writing—narration, description, exposition and argumentation. In practice, these forms of discourse often blend or overlap. Essayists seek the ideal fusion of forms of discourse in the treatment of their subject.

Division   is that aspect of classification in which the writer divides some large subject into categories. Division helps writers split large and potentially complicated subjects into parts for orderly presentation and discussion.

Dominant impression   in description is the main impression or effect that writers attempt to create for their subject. It arises from an author's focus on a single subject and from the feelings the writer brings to that subject.

Editorialize   is to express personal opinions about the subject of the essay. An editorial tone can have a useful effect in writing, but at other times an author might want to reduce editorializing in favor of a better balanced or more objective tone.

Effect   is a term used in causal analysis to describe the outcome or expected result of a chain of happenings.

Emphasis   indicates the placement of the most important ideas in key positions in the essay. As a major principle, emphasis relates to phrases, sentences, paragraphs—the construction of the entire essay. Emphasis can be achieved by repetition, subordination, careful positioning of thesis and topic sentences, climactic ordering, comparison and contrast, and a variety of other methods.

Episodic   relates to that variety of narrative writing that develops through a series of incidents or events.

Essay   is the name given to a short prose work on a limited topic. Essays take many forms, ranging from personal narratives to critical or argumentative treatments of a subject. Normally an essay will convey the writer's personal ideas about the subject.

Etymology   is the origin and development of a word—tracing a word back as far as possible.

Evidence   is material offered to support an argument or a proposition. Typical forms of evidence are facts, details, and expert testimony.

Example   is a method of exposition in which the writer offers illustrations in order to explain a generalization or a whole thesis. (See *illustration*.)

Exclamatory sentences   in writing express surprise or strong emotion.

Expert testimony   as employed in argumentative essays and in expository essays is the use of statements by authorities to support a writer's position or idea. This method often requires careful quotation and acknowledgment of sources.

Exposition   is a major form of discourse that informs or explains. Exposition is the form of expression required in much college writing, for it provides facts and information, clarifies ideas, and establishes meaning. The primary methods of exposition are illustration, comparison and contrast, analogy, definition, classification, causal analysis, and process analysis (see entries).

Extended metaphor   is a figurative comparison that is used to structure a significant part of the composition or the whole essay. (See *figurative language* and *metaphor*.)

Fable   is a form of narrative containing a moral that normally appears clearly at the end.

Fallacy   in argumentation is an error in logic or in the reasoning process. Fallacies occur because of vague development of ideas, lack of awareness on the part of writers of the requirements of logical reasoning, or faulty assumptions about the proposition.

Figurative language   as opposed to literal language is a special approach to writing that departs from what is typically a concrete, straightforward style. It is the use of vivid, imaginative statements to illuminate or illustrate an idea. Figurative language adds freshness, meaning, and originality to a writer's style. Major figures of speech include allusion, hyperbole, metaphor, personification, and simile (see entries).

Flashback   is a narrative technique in which the writer begins at some point in the action and then moves into the past in order to provide crucial information about characters and events.

Foreshadow   is a technique that indicates beforehand what is to occur at a later point in the essay.

Frame   in narration and description is the use of a key object or pattern—typically at the start and end of the essay—that serves as a border or structure to contain the substance of the composition.

General/specific words   are the basis of writing, although it is wise in college composition to keep vocabulary as specific as possible. General words refer to broad categories and groups, whereas specific words capture with force and clarity the nature of the term. General words refer to large classes, concepts, groups, and emotions; specific words are more particular in providing meanings. The distinction between general and specific language is always a matter of degree.

Generalization   is a broad idea or statement. All generalizations require particulars and illustrations to support them.

Genre   is a type or form of literature—for example, short fiction, novel, poetry, drama.

Grammatical structure   is a systematic description of language as it relates to the grammatical nature of a sentence.

Horizontal/vertical   paragraph and essay development refers to the basic way a writer moves either from one generalization to another in a carefully related series of generalizations (horizontal) or from a generalization to a series of specific supporting examples (vertical).

Hortatory style   is a variety of writing designed to encourage, give advice, or urge to good deeds.

Hyperbole   is a form of figurative language that uses exaggeration to overstate a position.

Hypothesis   is an unproven theory or proposition that is tentatively accepted to explain certain facts. A working hypothesis provides the basis for further investigation or argumentation.

Hypothetical examples   are illustrations in the form of assumptions that are based on the hypothesis. As such, they are conditional rather than absolute or certain facts.

Identification   as a method of exposition refers to focusing on the main subject of the essay. It involves the clear location of the subject within the context or situation of the composition.

Idiomatic language   is the language or dialect of a people, region, or class—the individual nature of a language.

Ignoring the question   in argumentation is a fallacy that involves the avoidance of the main issue by developing an entirely different one.

Illustration   is the use of one or more examples to support an idea. Illustration permits the writer to support a generalization through particulars or specifics.

Imagery   is clear, vivid description that appeals to the sense of sight, smell, touch, sound, or taste. Much imagery exists for its own sake, adding descriptive flavor to an essay. However, imagery (especially when it involves a larger pattern) can also add meaning to an essay.

Induction   is a method of logic consisting of the presentation of a series of facts, pieces of information, or instances in order to formulate or build a likely generalization. The key is to provide prior examples before reaching a logical conclusion. Consequently, as a pattern of organization in essay writing, the inductive method requires the careful presentation of relevant data and information before the conclusion is reached at the end of the paper.

Inference   involves arriving at a decision or opinion by reasoning from known facts or evidence.

Interrogative sentences   are sentences that ask or pose a question.

Introduction   is the beginning or opening of an essay. The introduction should alert the reader to the subject by identifying it, set the limits of the essay, and indicate what the thesis (or main idea) will be. Moreover, it should arouse the reader's interest in the subject. Among the devices available in the creation of good introductions are making a simple statement of thesis; giving a clear, vivid description of an important setting; posing a question or series of questions; referring to a relevant historical event; telling an anecdote; using comparison and contrast to frame the subject; using several examples to reinforce the statement of the subject; and presenting a personal attitude about a controversial issue.

Irony   is the use of language to suggest the opposite of what is stated. Writers use irony to reveal unpleasant or troublesome realities that exist in life or to poke fun at human weaknesses and foolish attitudes. In an essay there may be verbal irony, in which the result of a sequence of ideas or events is the opposite of what normally would be expected. A key to the identification of irony in an essay is our ability to detect where the author is stating the opposite of what he or she actually believes.

Issue   is the main question upon which an entire argument rests. It is the idea that the writer attempts to prove.

Jargon   is the use of special words associated with a specific area of knowledge or a particular profession. Writers who employ jargon either assume that readers know specialized terms or take care to define terms for the benefit of the audience.

Juxtaposition   as a technique in writing or essay organization is the placing of elements—either similar or contrasting—close together, positioning them side by side in order to illuminate the subject.

Levels of language   refer to the kinds of language used in speaking and writing. Basically there are three main levels of language—formal, informal, and colloquial. Formal English, used in writing or speech, is the type of English employed to address special groups and professional people. Informal English is the sort of writing found in newspapers, magazines, books, and essays. It is popular English for an educated audience but still more formal than conversational English. Finally, colloquial

English is spoken (and occasionally written) English used in conversations with friends, employees, and peer group members; it is characterized by the use of slang, idioms, ordinary language, and loose sentence structure.

Linear order   in paragraph development means the clear line of movement from one point to another.

Listing   is a simple technique of illustration in which facts or examples are used in order to support a topic or generalization.

Logic   as applied to essay writing is correct reasoning based on induction or deduction. The logical basis of an essay must offer reasonable criteria or principles of thought, present these principles in an orderly manner, avoid faults in reasoning, and result in a complete and satisfactory outcome in the reasoning process.

Metaphor   is a type of figurative language in which an item from one category is compared briefly and imaginatively with an item from another area. Writers use such implied comparisons to assign meaning in a fresh, vivid, and concrete way.

Metonymy   is a figure of language in which a thing is not designated by its own name but by another associated with or suggested by it, as in "The Supreme Court has decided" (meaning that the judges of the Supreme Court have decided).

Mood   is the creation of atmosphere in descriptive writing.

Motif   in an essay is any series of components that can be detected as a pattern. For example, a particular detail, idea, or image can be elaborated upon or designed to form a pattern or motif in the essay.

Myth   in literature is a traditional story or series of events explaining some basic phenomenon of nature; the origin of humanity; or the customs, institutions, and religious rites of a people. Myth often relates to the exploits of gods, goddesses, and heroes.

Narration   as a form of essay writing is the presentation of a story in order to illustrate an idea.

Non sequitur   in argumentation is a conclusion or inference that does not follow from the premises or evidence on which it is based. The non sequitur thus is a type of logical fallacy.

Objective/subjective   writing refers to the attitude that writers take toward their subject. When writers are objective, they try not to report their personal feelings about the subject; they attempt to be detached, impersonal, and unbiased. Conversely, subjective writing reveals an author's personal attitudes and emotions. For many varieties of college writing, such as business or laboratory reports, term papers, and literary analyses, it is best to be as objective as possible. But for many personal essays in composition courses, the subjective touch is fine. In the hands of skilled writers, the objective and subjective tones often blend.

Onomatopoeia   is the formation of a word by imitating the natural sound associated with the object or action, as in *buzz* or *click*.

Order   is the arrangement of information or materials in an essay. The most common ordering techniques are *chronological order* (time in sequence); *spatial order* (the arrangement of descriptive details); *process order* (a step-by-step approach to an activity); *deductive order* (a thesis followed by information to support it); and *inductive order* (evidence and examples first, followed by the thesis in the form of a conclusion). Some rhetorical patterns, such as comparison and contrast, classification, and argumentation, require other ordering methods. Writers should select those ordering principles that permit them to present materials clearly.

Overstatement is an extravagant or exaggerated claim or statement

Paradox is a statement that seems to be contradictory but actually contains an element of truth.

Paragraph is a unit in an essay that serves to present and examine one aspect of a topic. Composed normally of a group of sentences (one-sentence paragraphs can be used for emphasis or special effect), the paragraph elaborates an idea within the larger framework of the essay and the thesis unifying it.

Parallelism is a variety of sentence structure in which there is balance or coordination in the presentation of elements. "I came, I saw, I conquered" is a standard example of parallelism, presenting both pronouns and verbs in a coordinated manner. Parallelism can appear in a sentence, a group of sentences, or an entire paragraph.

Paraphrase as a literary method is the process of rewording the thought or meaning expressed in something that has been said or written before.

Parenthetical refers to giving qualifying information or explanation. This information normally is marked off or placed within parentheses.

Parody is ridiculing the language or style of another writer or composer. In parody, a serious subject tends to be treated in a nonsensical manner.

Periphrasis is the use of many words where one or a few would do; it is a roundabout way of speaking or writing.

Persona is the role or characterization that writers occasionally create for themselves in a personal narrative.

Personification is giving an object, a thing, or an idea lifelike or human characteristics, as in the common reference to a car as "she." Like all forms of figurative language, personification adds freshness to description and makes ideas vivid by setting up striking comparisons.

Persuasion is the form of discourse, related to argumentation, that attempts basically to move a person to action or to influence an audience toward a particular belief.

Point of view is the angle from which a writer tells a story. Many personal and informal essays take the *first-person* (or "i") point of view, which is natural and fitting for essays in which the author wants to speak in a familiar way to the reader. On the other hand, the *third-person* point of view ("he," "she," "it," "they") distances the reader somewhat from the writer. The third-person point of view is useful in essays in which the writers are not talking exclusively about themselves, but about other people, ideas, and events.

Post hoc, ergo propter hoc in logic is the fallacy of thinking that a happening that follows another must be its result. It arises from a confusion about the logical causal relationship.

Process analysis is a pattern of writing that explains in a step-by-step way how something is done, how it is put together, how it works, or how it occurs. The subject can be a mechanical device, a product, an idea, a natural phenomenon, or a historical sequence. However, in all varieties of process analysis, the writer traces all important steps, from beginning to end.

Progression   is the forward movement or succession of acts, events, or ideas presented in an essay.

Proportion   refers to the relative emphasis and length given to an event, an idea, a time, or a topic within the whole essay. Basically, in terms of proportion the writer gives more emphasis to a major element than to a minor one.

Proposition   is the main point of an argumentative essay—the statement to be defended, proved, or upheld. It is like a *thesis* (see entry) except that it presents an idea that is debatable or can be disputed. The *major proposition* is the main argumentative point; *minor propositions* are the reasons given to support or prove the issue.

Purpose   is what the writer wants to accomplish in an essay. Writers having a clear purpose will know the proper style, language, tone, and materials to utilize in designing an effective essay.

Refutation   in argumentation is a method by which you recognize and deal effectively with the arguments of your opponents. Your own argument will be stronger if you refute—prove false or wrong—all opposing arguments.

Repetition   is a simple method of achieving emphasis by repeating a word, a phrase, or an idea.

Rhetoric   is the art of using words effectively in speaking or writing. It is also the art of literary composition, particularly in prose, including both figures of speech and such strategies as comparison and contrast, definition, and analysis.

Rhetorical question   is a question asked only to emphasize a point, introduce a topic, or provoke thought, but not to elicit an answer.

Rhythm   in prose writing is a regular recurrence of elements or features in sentences, creating a patterned emphasis, balance, or contrast.

Sarcasm   is a sneering or taunting attitude in writing, designed to hurt by evaluating or criticizing. Basically, sarcasm is a heavy-handed form of *irony* (see entry). Writers should try to avoid sarcastic writing and to use more acceptable varieties of irony and satire to criticize their subject.

Satire   is the humorous or critical treatment of a subject in order to expose the subject's vices, follies, stupidities, and so forth. The intention of such satire is to reform by exposing the subject to comedy or ridicule.

Sensory language   is language that appeals to any of the five senses—sight, sound, touch, taste, or smell.

Sentimentality   in prose writing is the excessive display of emotion, whether intended or unintended. Because sentimentality can distort the true nature of a situation or an idea, writers should use it cautiously, or not at all.

Series   as a technique in prose is the presentation of several items, often concrete details or similar parts of grammar such as verbs or adjectives, in rapid sequence.

Setting   in narrative and descriptive writing is the time, place, environment, background, or surroundings established by an author.

Simile   is a figurative comparison using *like* or *as*.

Slang   is a kind of language that uses racy or colorful expressions associated more often with speech than with writing. It is colloquial English and should be used in essay writing only to reproduce dialogue or to create a special effect.

Spatial order   in descriptive writing is the careful arrangement of details or materials in space—for example, from left to right, top to bottom, or near to far.

Specific words   (see *general/specific words.*)

Statistics   are facts or data of a numerical kind, assembled and tabulated to present significant information about a given subject. As a technique of illustration, statistics can be useful in analysis and argumentation.

Style   is the specific or characteristic manner of expression, execution, construction, or design of an author. As a manner or mode of expression in language, it is the unique way each writer handles ideas. There are numerous stylistic categories—literary, formal, argumentative, satiric—but ultimately, no two writers have the same style.

Subjective   (see *objective/subjective.*)

Subordination   in sentence structure is the placing of a relatively less important idea in an inferior grammatical position to the main idea. It is the designation of a minor clause that is dependent upon a major clause.

Syllogism   is an argument or form of reasoning in which two statements or premises are made and a logical conclusion drawn from them. As such, it is a form of deductive logic—reasoning from the general to the particular. The *major premise* presents a quality of class ("All writers are mortal"). The *minor premise* states that a particular subject is a member of that class ("Ernest Hemingway was a writer."). The conclusion states that the qualities of the class and the member of the class are the same. ("Hemingway was mortal.").

Symbol   is something—normally a concrete image—that exists in itself but also stands for something else or has greater meaning. As a variety of figurative language, the symbol can be a strong feature in an essay, operating to add depth of meaning and even to unify the composition.

Synonym   is a word that means roughly the same as another word. In practice, few words are exactly alike in meaning. Careful writers use synonyms to vary word choice without ever moving too far from the shade of meaning intended.

Theme   is the central idea in an essay; it is also termed the *thesis*. Everything in an essay should support the theme in one way or another.

Thesis   is the main idea in an essay. The *thesis sentence,* appearing only in the essay (normally somewhere in the first paragraph) serves to convey the main idea to the reader in a clear and emphatic manner.

Tone   is the writer's attitude toward his or her subject or material. An essay writer's tone may be objective, subjective, comic, ironic, nostalgic, critical, or a reflection of numerous other attitudes. Tone is the voice that writers give to an essay.

Topic sentence   is the main idea that a paragraph develops. Not all paragraphs contain topic sentences; often the topic is implied.

Transition   is the linking of ideas in sentences, paragraphs, and larger segments of an essay in order to achieve *coherence* (see entry). Among the most common techniques to achieve smooth transitions are: (1) repeating a key word or phrase; (2) using a pronoun to refer to a key word or phrase; (3) relying on traditional connectives such as *thus, however, moreover, for example, therefore, finally,* and *in conclusion;* (4) using parallel structure (see *parallelism*); and (5) creating a sentence or paragraph that serves as a bridge from one part of an essay to another. Transition is best achieved when a writer presents ideas and details carefully and in logical order.

Understatement   is a method of making a weaker statement than is warranted by truth, accuracy, or importance.

Unity   is a feature in an essay whereby all material relates to a central concept and contributes to the meaning of the whole. To achieve a unified effect in an essay, the writer must design an effective introduction and conclusion, maintain consistent tone or point of view, develop middle paragraphs in a coherent manner, and above all stick to the subject, never permitting unimportant or irrelevant elements to enter.

Usage   is the way in which a word, phrase, or sentence is used to express a particular idea; it is the customary manner of using a given language in speaking or writing.

Vertical   (see *horizontal/vertical.*)

Voice   is the way you express your ideas to the reader, the tone you take in addressing your audience. Voice reflects your attitude toward both your subject and your readers. (See *tone.*)

Credits

The McGraw-Hill Reader, 8th Edition

Adler, Mortimer J. From "How to Mark a Book" by Mortimer J. Adler. Reprinted by permission of the author.

Angelou, Maya. "Graduation" from *I Know Why the Caged Bird Sings* by Maya Angelou. Copyright © 1969 and renewed 1997 by Maya Angelou. Reprinted by permission of Random House, Inc.

Angier, Natalie. "Why Men Don't Last." *The New York Times,* 2/17/99. Copyright © 1999 by The New York Times Co. Reprinted by permission.

Atwood, Margaret. "The Female Body" by Margaret Atwood. © O.W. Toad Ltd., 1992. Reprinted from *Good Bones* with permission of Coach House Press.

Baldwin, James. "Stranger in the Village" from *Notes of a Native Son* by James Baldwin. Copyright © 1955, renewed 1983 by James Baldwin. Reprinted by permission of Beacon Press, Boston.

Barber, Benjamin R. "America Skips School." Copyright © 1993 by *Harper's* Magazine. All rights reserved. Reproduced from the November issue by special permission.

Barry, Dave. "Red, White & Beer" from *Dave Barry's Greatest Hits.* Copyright © 1988 by Dave Barry. Reprinted by permission of the author.

Bennett, William J. "What Really Ails America" by William Bennett as appeared in *Reader's Digest,* August 1984. Reprinted by permission of the author.

Carson, Rachel. "The Obligation to Endure" from *Silent Spring* by Rachel Carson. Copyright © 1962 by Rachel L. Carson. Copyright © renewed 1990 by Roger Christie. Reprinted by permission of Houghton Mifflin Company. All rights reserved.

Carter, Stephen L. From *The Culture of Disbelief* by Stephen L. Carter. Reprinted by permission of Basic Books, a member of Perseus Books, L.L.C.

Cofer, Judith Ortiz. "Silent Dancing" by Judith Ortiz Cofer is reprinted with permission from the publisher of *Silent Dancing.* (Houston: Arte Publico Press—University of Houston, 1990). Originally published in *Georgia Review,* 1991.

Mencken, H. L. "The Penalty of Death" from *A Mencken Chrestomathy* by H. L. Mencken. Copyright © 1926 by Alfred A. Knopf Inc. and renewed 1954 by H. L. Mencken. Reprinted by permission of the publisher.

Miller, Casey and Kate Swift. "Who's in Charge of the English Language?" Copyright © 1990 by Casey Miller and Kate Swift. Reprinted by permission of Kate Swift.

Mirikitani, Janice. "Breaking Silences" excerpted from *Shedding Silence*. Copyright © 1987 by Janice Mirikitani. Reprinted by permission of Celestial Arts, P.O. Box 7123, Berkeley, CA 94707.

Mitford, Jessica. "The Embalming of Mr. Jones" from *The American Way of Death Revisited* by Jessica Mitford. Copyright © 1998 by the Estate of Jessica Mitford. Used by permission of Alfred A. Knopf, a division of Random House, Inc.

Momaday, N. Scott. "Introduction" from *The Way to Rainy Mountain* by N. Scott Momaday. Copyright © 1969 by The University of New Mexico Press. First published in *The Reporter*, 26 January 1967.

Mukherjee, Bharati. "American Dreamer." Copyright © 1997 by Bharati Mukherjee. Originally published in *Mother Jones*. Reprinted by permission of the author.

Mumford, Lewis. "The Monastery and the Clock" from *Technics and Civilization* by Lewis Mumford. Copyright 1934 by Harcourt, Inc. and renewed 1961 by Lewis Mumford, reprinted by permission of the publisher.

Murray, Donald. "The Maker's Eye: Revising Your Own Manuscripts." *The Writer*, 1973. Copyright © 1973 by Donald M. Murray. Reprinted by permission of The Rosenberg Group.

Orwell, George. "Politics and the English Language." Copyright 1946 by Sonia Brownell Orwell and renewed 1974 by Sonia Orwell. Reprinted from his volume *Shooting an Elephant And Other Essays* by permission of Harcourt, Inc. and Bill Hamilton as the Literary Executor of the Estate of the late Sonia Brownell Orwell and Secker and Warburg Ltd.

Orwell, George. "Shooting an Elephant" from *Shooting an Elephant and Other Essays* by George Orwell. Copyright © 1950 by Sonia Brownell Orwell and renewed 1978 by Sonia Pitt-Rivers, reprinted by permission of Harcourt, Inc.

Oyama, Richard. "You Spoke Japanese." Copyright © 1989 by Richard Oyama. Reprinted by permission of the author. Richard Oyama teaches at the California College of Arts and Crafts.

Perrin, Noel. "The Greenest Campuses: An Idiosyncratic Guide" by Noel Perrin. Copyright © 2001 by Noel Perrin. Originally appeared in *Chronicle of Higher Education*. Reprinted by permission of the author.

Pogrebin, Letty Cottin. "Superstitious Minds" by Letty Cottin Pogrebin. Reprinted by permission of *Ms.* Magazine, © 1988.

Quindlen, Anna. "Men at Work" from *Thinking Out Loud* by Anna Quindlen. Copyright © 1993 by Anna Quindlen. Used by permission of Random House, Inc.

Quindlen, Anna. "Sex-Ed" from *Living Out Loud* by Anna Quindlen. Copyright © 1987 by Anna Quindlen. Copyright © 1987 by Anna Quindlen. Reprinted by permission of Random House, Inc.

Rau, Santha Rama. "By Any Other Name" from *Gifts of Passage* by Santha Rama Rau. Copyright © 1951 by Santha Rama Rau. Copyright © renewed 1979 by Santha Rama Rau. Reprinted by permission of HarperCollins Publishers, Inc. "By Any Other Name" originally appeared in *The New Yorker*.

Reed, Ishmael. "America: The Multinational Society" from *Writin' Is Fightin': Forty-Three Years of Boxing on Paper* by Ishmael Reed. Copyright © Ishmael Reed. Reprinted by permission of Lowenstein Associates.

Reich, Robert. "Why the Rich Are Getting Richer and the Poor, Poorer" from *The Work of Nations* by Robert Reich, copyright © 1991 by Robert Reich. Used by permission of Alfred A. Knopf, a division of Random House, Inc.

Rifkin, Jeremy. "The Age of Simulation" from *Biosphere Politics* by Jeremy Rifkin. Copyright © 1991 by Jeremy Rifkin. Reprinted by permission of the author.

Rodriguez, Richard. "Family Values." Copyright © 1992 by Richard Rodriguez. Originally appeared in *The Los Angeles Times*. Reprinted by permission of Georges Borchardt, Inc., for the author.

Rodriguez, Richard. "The Lonely, Good Company of Books" by Richard Rodriguez. Copyright © 1981 by Richard Rodriguez. Reprinted by permission of Georges Borchardt, Inc. for the author.

Rodriquez, Richard. "Los Pobres" by Richard Rodriguez. Copyright © 1981 by Richard Rodriguez. Originally appeared in *New West*. Reprinted by permission of Georges Borchardt, Inc. for the author.

Sagan, Carl. "Can We Know the Universe?" from *Broca's Brain* by Carl Sagan. Copyright © 1979 by Carl Sagan, © 2001 by the Estate of Carl Sagan.

Schlesinger, Arthur M. Jr. "The Cult of Ethnicity." *Time*, 7/8/81. Copyright © 1981 by Arthur M. Schlesinger, Jr. Reprinted by permission of the author.

Selzer, Richard. "Sarcophagus" from *Confessions of a Knife* by Richard Selzer. Copyright © 1979 by David Goldman and Janet Selzer, Trustees. Reprinted by permission of Georges Borchardt, Inc.

Steinbeck, John. "Americans and the Land" from *America and Americans* by John Steinbeck. Copyright © 1966 by John Steinbeck, text. Copyright © 1966 by Viking Penguin, photographs. Used by permission of Viking Penguin, a division of Penguin Putnam, Inc.

Steinem, Gloria. "The Good News Is: These Are Not the Best Years of Your Life." *Ms.* Magazine, 1979. Reprinted by permission of the author.

Takaki, Ronald. From *Strangers from a Distant Shore* by Ronald Takaki. Copyright © 1989 Ronald Takaki. By permission of Little, Brown and Company, Inc.

Tan, Amy. "The Language of Discretion" by Amy Tan. Copyright © 1990 by Amy Tan. Reprinted by permission of the author and Sandra Dijkstra Literary Agency.

Tannen, Deborah. "Sex, Lies, and Conversation: Why Is It So Hard for Men and Women to Talk to Each Other?" by Deborah Tannen. Permission granted by International Creative Management, Inc. Copyright © by Deborah Tannen.

Theroux, Paul. "Being a Man" from *Sunrise with Seamonsters* by Paul Theroux. Copyright © 1985 by Cape Cod Scriveners Co. Reprinted by permission of Houghton Mifflin Co. All rights reserved.

Thomas, Lewis. "The Technology of Medicine." Copyright © 1971 by The Massachusetts Medical Society, from *The Lives of a Cell* by Lewis Thomas. Used by permission of Viking Penguin, a division of Penguin Putnam, Inc.

Tuchman, Barbara. "This Is the End of the World: The Black Death" from *A Distant Mirror* by Barbara Tuchman. Copyright © 1978 by Barbara W. Tuchman. Used by permission of Alfred A. Knopf, a division of Random House, Inc.

Walker, Alice. "Am I Blue?" from *Living by the Word: Selected Writings 1973–1987*. Copyright © 1986 by Alice Walker. Reprinted by permission of Harcourt, Inc.

Index